# CONSCIENCE, CONTRACT, AND SOCIAL REALITY

## Theory and Research in Behavioral Science

# CONSCIENCE, CONTRACT, AND SOCIAL REALITY

## Theory and Research in Behavioral Science

Edited by

**Ronald C. Johnson**
University of Hawaii

**Paul R. Dokecki**
George Peabody College

**O. Hobart Mowrer**
University of Illinois

HOLT, RINEHART AND WINSTON, INC.

New York      Chicago      San Francisco      Atlanta
Dallas      Montreal      Toronto      London      Sydney

# Preface

When I first read this book, then in galley proof, I was much impressed by the substance and scope of the selections which constitute its several chapters, by the book's organization, by its sectional introductions, and by its timeliness. This may seem an odd or even inappropriate remark to be made by one of the editors; but the division of labor agreed upon between the three of us was such that content selection and integration has been mainly the responsibility of Drs. Johnson and Dokecki. Although it was I who, back in 1963, originally suggested the growing feasibility of and need for a book such as the present one, it turned out that the other two editors had a far better knowledge of the pertinent literature and authority in the area of content was accordingly given to them. I am very pleased with their efforts and think others will be as well. I must confess, however, that I am now somewhat overwhelmed by the challenge of preparing a preface that will do this book full justice, but also prepare the reader for the complexities, inconsistencies, and unsettledness of the field it covers. At the same time, a sense of movement and direction is clearly discernible in the study of conscience. I hope this preliminary appraisal and interpretation, whatever its other shortcomings, will highlight this latter phenomenon and will convey some understanding of its historical antecedents and contemporary significance.

For several decades prior to our original decision to organize and publish this book, the prevailing attitude toward conscience was predominantly negative. Sigmund Freud, in his voluminous and highly influential writings during the first half of this century, had substituted for the traditionally respectable intrapsychic agency called conscience the concept of superego. He had laid at its doorstep much of the blame not only for common human unhappiness, but also for the more strident forms of personality disturbance known as psychopathology or (quite inappropriately) neurosis. According to Freud, superego (or conscience) is necessary for the existence of organized society, but is nonetheless an evil in that it blunts the capacity of all human beings for free and zestful instinctual satisfaction and, if overdeveloped, produces one or another form of psychic abnormality. For those who fell under the sway of Freud's rhetoric (and they were legion), the rallying cry became: "Down with the superego! Get rid of your inhibitions! Have fun!" Freud's own assertions concerning the usefulness of conscience (despite its admittedly objectionable characteristics) were largely disregarded; and Freudian psychoanalysis (and variants thereof) became "big business," because it offered a way—supposedly the *only* way—to modify conscience in the direction of leniency and reasonableness.

Freud did not accept the assumption, common in Judeo-Christian circles, that conscience was God-given. However, he did concede that it is implanted and implacable, as a result of the way in which the infantile oedipus complex is typically resolved. And through the transference relationship provided by analysis, he thought he had discovered a way not of altogether abolishing conscience (which he would have regarded as undesirable), but of at least bringing it down to size. This, if true, would have been a great boon to mankind and the prospect aroused new hope of dealing more effectively with some of our most besetting perplexities and existential vicissitudes. But unhappily, it was apparent by midcentury that something was amiss, if not in Freud's theory, then at least in the way it was being applied. Psychoanalysis was not producing the predicted therapeutic outcomes, and disenchantment and skepticism began to replace the enthusiasm that had previously prevailed.

At this juncture two new developments began to eclipse interest in psychoanalysis. Dr. Leopold Bellak, himself a long-time orthodox Freudian, in an article entitled "The Role of Psychoanalysis in Contemporary Psychiatry,"[1] has described this situation succinctly as follows: Psychoanalysis was the "elite of the [psychiatric] establishment until the middle of

---

[1] *American Journal of Psychotherapy*, 1970, *24*, 470–476.

the 1950s," at which point a new era was ushered in by the advent of the "psychotropic drugs and community psychiatry." In this volume we do not attempt to describe or appraise the highly important implications and ramified applications of the new psychopharmacology. But the contents of this book do articulate, directly and from many vantage points, with what Bellak refers to as "community psychiatry." In this view conscience, which Freud characterized in *Civilization and Its Discontents*[2] as the "internalized voice of the community," the link or bond between societies and their constituent members, is manifestly of central importance. After the shift in perspective that Bellak describes, investigators began to approach conscience and its functions in a much more positive and respectful way. Instead of asking how it could be subdued or weakened, clinicians and researchers began to pose such questions as: How does conscience develop? What variables are important within a given family constellation or culture? What cross-cultural differences are of significance in this connection? Is conscience a unitary entity or is it composed of several relatively unrelated processes? Can it be modified and, if so, how? And is it possible that psychopathology arises, not because conscience is overdeveloped and too severe, but because its behests have been disregarded?

These were some of the queries which had prompted the newly emerging literature that had appeared by 1963, and many of the pieces in this volume (whether published prior to that year or subsequently) reflect this change in orientation. It was therefore the original purpose of the present volume to highlight this change, and that is still one of its distinctive features. However, there was a succession of unanticipated delays in this book's preparation and publication, and by the time it was ready to go to press a second major trend had become evident. Thus the delays were, in a sense, providential in that they have made it possible to give this volume an added dimension and a currency that it otherwise would not have had.

Perhaps the best way to delineate this latest development is to begin by noting that within the last few years a sweeping change—one may indeed characterize it as a revolution—has occurred, on a virtually worldwide scale, with regard to the problem of authority or, more particularly, moral authority. There has been a widespread rejection of age-old moral absolutes and a rebellion against the autocratic methods often

[2] London: Hogarth Press, 1930.

used to transmit and enforce them. Rules, prohibitions, moral dictums are no longer taken "on authority," and young people insist upon thinking for themselves instead of docilely accepting the traditional values their parents had themselves inherited. This widespread tendency does not reflect sheer perversity or obstinacy, but rather comes from the fact that the old answers and ways of life no longer suffice in a world which, in the last half century, has changed technologically at an unprecedented tempo. Not only do our youth view many moral prescriptions and values as hopelessly outmoded; they also see that technological change itself, which used to be automatically equated to progress, often has long-term disadvantages which outweigh its immediate advantages.[3]

As a protest against the old and to many persons now odious absolutism of traditional morality, something called *situation ethics* emerged,[4] which rejected rules and regulations in general and suggested that each problematic situation be resolved in a spirit of love on the part of those involved and in light of the then prevailing circumstances. This proposal had an immediate and widespread but ephemeral appeal, for it was soon discovered that rules are usually devised and enforced as a means not of unnecessarily limiting and frustrating us, but of making it possible for the maximal number of persons to attain their goals, get to their "destinations," as quickly and harmoniously as possible.

But whereas the older conventions and rules (in addition to now being nonfunctional) had been largely coercive, there is today a growing emphasis upon a morality by consent, by mutual commitment, by voluntarily accepted *contracts*. The particular nature or "content" of a contract, while not unimportant, is in many ways less important than the question of whether a person is characteristically a contract keeper (or one who, if a contract is unsatisfactory, honorably renegotiates or dissolves it) *or* a contract breaker—a cheater, one who pretends to be keeping his agreements (and therefore enjoys the advantages thereof) but who, usually secretly, actually fails to keep his part of the bargain. At various points in this book, there are brief adumbrations of contract psychology, but it is not fully and explicitly developed, and its social and mental-health implications explicated, until Section VI.

[3] These developments have been vividly and dramatically described by Marshall McLuhan and Quentin Fiore in *The Medium Is the Message: An Inventory of Effects* (New York: Bantam Books, 1967) and by Alvin Toffler in *Future Shock* (New York: Bantam Books, 1970).
[4] J. Fletcher, *Situation Ethics*. New York: Harper & Row, 1964.

These developments are consonant with and indeed in some degree consequences of a new egalitarianism, which applies not merely to race and sex but also to the age gradient and suggests some radical revisions in child rearing practices which have been perhaps best spelled out by Rudolf Dreikurs in *Children the Challenge*[5] and *Social Equality: The Challenge of Today*[6] and by Dreikurs and Loren Grey in *Logical Consequences: A New Approach to Discipline*.[7] I have reviewed some of the same considerations from a related point of view in a chapter entitled "Group Counseling in the Elementary School: The Professional vs. Peer-Group Model," which will appear in a book to be published by Holt, Rinehart and Winston in 1972 under the editorship of Merle M. Ohlsen.

If, as is here suggested, contract psychology gives us a more functional, operational approach to ethical problems than does the global concept of conscience and if this approach somewhat alters our understanding of at least some forms of psychopathology, it ought also to have implications for psychotherapy, which indeed it does. At various junctures in Sections V and VI some of these implications are briefly alluded to, but they are not systematically developed. For such a treatment, the reader is referred to Ivan D. Yalom's excellent volume, *The Theory and Practice of Group Psychotherapy*.[8]

It will thus be apparent that the present volume, although it is an in-depth treatment of recent theory and research concerning conscience, contract, and social reality, is fully intelligible and its significance maximally clear only if seen in the larger context suggested by the immediately preceding paragraphs.

Ronald Johnson and Paul Dokecki join me in expressing our gratitude to the various authors and publishers who have made it possible for us to assemble here the particular collection of writings which constitute this volume. We also wish to thank Helene Cavior for her assistance to Dr. Dokecki in preparing manuscript copy for the printer and we are much indebted to my secretary, Patricia Abbuehl, for collaboration in the task of preparing the author and subject indices.

O. HOBART MOWRER

*Urbana, Illinois*

[5] New York: Hawthorn Books, Inc., 1964.
[6] Chicago: Henry Regnery Company, 1971.
[7] New York: Hawthorn Books, Inc., 1968.
[8] New York: Basic Books, 1970.

# Contents

# CONSCIENCE, CONTRACT, AND SOCIAL REALITY

Theory and Research
in Behavioral Science

# Introduction

In the course of human development people come to inhibit some behaviors that would probably give them pleasure and to actively perform other behaviors that are seemingly painful. This biologically paradoxical phenomenon, perhaps the cornerstone of civilization, has been the subject of inquiry throughout the history of thought. Such terms as "superego," "inner controls," and "conscience" have been used to describe the mechanism that supposedly underlies this "moral" behavior. We prefer the term "conscience" and, as the title of this volume suggests, we view conscience and the related notion of contract as importantly involved in the social aspects of reality. We have attempted to gather a representative, relatively jargon-free group of theoretical and research papers that illustrate historical and contemporary trends in behavioral science approaches to conscience, contract, and social reality.

We have grouped the papers into six (not mutually exclusive) areas: (1) literary treatments of conscience; (2) the measurement of conscience; (3) the generality of conscience; (4) antecedents of conscience; (5) conscience and psychopathology; and (6) an emerging reconceptualization of conscience.

In order to ground the parade of scientific presentations in "flesh and blood," the initial section includes several literary treatments of conscience. The centrality of moral concerns in human existence has been brilliantly depicted by such authors as Poe, Clemens, Dostoevsky, Conrad, Kafka, and Camus. It is perhaps true to say that social reality, as represented by the great writers of fiction, always involves moral conflicts and questions. We have chosen an excerpt from Camus' *The Fall* and a short story by Clemens to illustrate some of the ways conscience influences human conduct; these are followed by an original essay by O. Hobart Mowrer, which analyzes Clemens and Poe from a psychological perspective.

With some appreciation of the experiential meaning of conscience, the next concern from a behavioral science perspective is that of measurement. Perhaps the best-known approach to the assessment of both the cultural and individual aspects of conscience development is that of the Swiss psychologist Jean Piaget, an excerpt from whose work begins the second section of this volume. The roots of Piaget's approach may be traced back through Durkheim, Bovet, and Fauconnet to Sir Henry Sumner Maine's *Ancient Law,* and through J. Mark Baldwin to Darwin. Barnes and his associates (see Johnson, 1962) and McGrath (1923)[1] studied the problem of measurement of moral judgments relatively independently of those who influenced Piaget, but their approach is similar to his.

As is true in other areas of psychology, Piaget's influence on the theory and measurement of morality has been marked. His approach involves assessing the *cognitive* aspects of moral judgments through the use of stories, at the conclusion of which the individual is asked to

[1] We wish to acknowledge our debt to T. G. Foran, Seigniory Club, Papineau County, Quebec, for having called Sister Mary C. McGrath's work to our attention.

*1*

state some ethical principle to which he subscribes.

In contrast to Piaget's cognitive emphasis, a second, more *behavioral* approach to the measurement of conscience had its beginnings in the learning theory of E. L. Thorndike. A portion of the classic work of Hartshorne and May (1928) describing various measures of honesty is included to exemplify this behavioral position.

A third aspect of conscience, the *affective*, has derived from psychoanalytic theory and is illustrated in several of the papers in this volume. The many measurement approaches to the three dimensions of conscience (cognitive, behavioral, and affective) are surveyed by Pittel and Mendelsohn (1966) in the article that closes the second section.

Since there are at least three measurable dimensions of conscience, each of which may be analyzed into subprocesses, a frequent question has concerned generality. This question has taken a number of forms, one of which asks whether or not people display a consistent form of conscience (such as honesty) across a variety of situations. In pieces included in the third section of this volume, Hartshorne and May (1928) assert that honesty is almost entirely determined by the stimulus situation, while Burton (1963) finds some evidence for honesty as a trait. Hartshorne and May's conclusions have had a considerable effect on the direction of research taken by psychologists studying conscience in particular and personality in general. If the stimulus situation accounts for nearly all of the variance in personality, then studying those ongoing aspects of the individual's inner state that have been termed "traits" would be a waste of time. Very few trait

studies of any sort were conducted in the 1930s and very little work occurred in the measurement of conscience, partly because conscience, as a concept, manifested in such ways as honest behavior, seemed to depend on a belief in traits, and that belief had been shaken mightily by the Hartshorne and May results. Running counter to this trend during the 1930s, MacKinnon (1938) found evidence for an honesty trait. Since that time, especially during the late 1950s and the 1960s, honesty and other conscience-related behaviors have come to be viewed as both traits (that is, predictable to some degree across time and across situations) and states (that is, determined by the particular stimulus situation presented to the individual).

Another form of the generality question involves the consistency among conscience domains (cognitive, behavioral, and affective). Further, there is the question whether or not development proceeds in a parallel fashion for the three domains. Selections in this volume argue against generality in any simple sense. Bandura and Walters (1963) see guilt and resistance to temptation as the result of different forms of learning. Taken together, the data from Johnson (1962), Porteus and Johnson (1965), Grinder and McMichael (1963), and Rebelsky, Allinsmith, and Grinder (1963, included in a later section) yield a complex picture in which relationships and lack of relationships are often dependent on the sex and/or age of the subject, the nature of the construct, and the operational definitions employed to measure a particular construct.

The seeming chaos in the literature is perhaps not so surprising, since scholars have always acknowledged enormous complexity in moral and conscience-related realms. The fourth section of the book attempts to illuminate some of the depths of the conscience phenomenon by viewing the antecedents of conscience from several perspectives: (1) guilt and shame; (2) parental practices and conscience development; (3) cross-cultural data; (4) learning-theory approaches; (5) modifiability of moral judgment; and (6) demographic variables and conscience.

Much of the literature on the antecedents of conscience has been heavily influenced by Freud, who felt that the superego developed in a person as a result of the individual's identification with the parent of the same sex. (The majority of the conscious part of the superego might be referred to as the conscience.) Although Freud admitted the usefulness of the superego as a mechanism for social control, he felt that it was unnecessarily harsh and thus caused the individual to develop unrealistic and sometimes neurotic feelings of guilt. An excerpt from Freud's *Civilization and Its Discontents* describing the development of the superego is included in this volume.

Notions similar to Freud's distinction between external (fear of being found out or shame) and internal (guilt) controls of behavior have been explored by Margaret Mead and Ruth Benedict. Excerpts from the work of these anthropologists suggest the ways in which child-rearing practices in different cultures produce social controls that are more or less guilt- /or shame-oriented. Arguments concerning this anthropological view (for example, Ausubel, 1955) and tests of it (such as Hoffman & Saltzstein, 1967; Grinder & McMichael, 1963) are presented in this volume, and further data on parental practices are included

in the papers by Boehm (1957) and Sears, Maccoby, and Levin (1957).

Another anthropologist whose work is included in this volume and who has been a major figure in the study of conscience is Whiting. Working within a cross-cultural framework and from a basically Freudian perspective, Whiting and his colleagues have developed a measure of conscience that is complementary to Piaget's approach. The technique involves the use of affective projective stories tapping various aspects of guilt. Cultural and familial antecedent conditions have been shown to influence the type of story completion used by the subject, and the amount of guilt shown has been related to behavioral indices (Grinder & McMichael, 1963). This approach to measurement of conscience has been used by a number of investigators, some of whose work is included in this volume. Further material from the cross-cultural perspective is presented in the work of Bacon, Child, and Barry (1963).

A major competitor to Freud's approach to detailing the antecedents of conscience has come from learning theory. This approach attempts to specify clearly the effects on conscience development of different kinds and timing of reward and punishment. This volume contains contributions from some of the major forces in this area, including Hill, Solomon, Bandura and Walters, Sears, and Kanfer.

The fourth section also contains papers by Turiel (1966) and Crowley (1968) relevant to environmental conditions that influence conscience development and papers by Bronfenbrenner (1962) and Rebelsky et al. (1963) concerning demographic variables as they relate to conscience. Taken as a whole, the section on antecedents illustrates the great amount of cross-fertilization among the cognitive (Piaget), affective (Freud), and behavioral (learning theory) approaches to the study of conscience.

The fifth section of the book deals with the relationship of conscience to behavior disorders, a problem that has spurred a great deal of recent interest. Perhaps most responsible for this flurry of activity has been the controversial work of Mowrer. This section includes both a paper by Mowrer (1966) and papers relevant to his position vis-à-vis Freud (Johnson, Ackerman, Frank, & Fionda, 1968; Ogren & Dokecki, original to this volume; Peterson, 1967; Swensen, 1962, 1963). Mowrer has challenged the Freudian position that the unrealistic severity of the superego regarding sexual and aggressive impulses is responsible for neurosis. Rather, he proposes that neurosis is caused by real guilt over actual misdeeds and that it is best treated by honest and open learning, by rectifying past misdeeds, and by behaving more morally in the future.

The section on psychopathology presents another position counter to Freud in an excerpt from Boss (1963), which details the existential position on the role of guilt in psychopathology.

The last section of the book presents some of the newer theorizing on the area of self-control and conscience-related phenomena. In the two papers in this section (the second of which was prepared especially for this volume) Kanfer, Phillips, and Karoly argue from the Skinnerian behavioral perspective the utility of the notion of *contract* in understanding conscience and the psychotherapeutic process.

In all, the editors have attempted to select research and theoretical papers that give some sense of the scope, complexity, and importance of conscience and related phenomena in the construction of social reality.

## References

*AUSUBEL, D. P. Relationships between shame and guilt in the socializing process. *Psychological Review*, 1955, **62**, 378–390.

*BACON, M. K., CHILD, I. L., & BARRY, H., III. A cross-cultural study of correlates of crime. *Journal of Abnormal and Social Psychology*, 1963, **66**, 291–300.

*BANDURA, A., & WALTERS, R. M. *Social learning and personality development*. New York: Holt, Rinehart and Winston, 1963.

*BOEHM, L. The development of independence: A comparative study. *Child Development*, 1957, **28**, 85–92.

*BOSS, M. *Psychoanalysis and daseinsanalysis*. New York: Basic Books, 1963.

*BRONFENBRENNER, U. The role of age, sex, class, and culture in studies of moral development. *Research Supplement to Religious Education*, 1962, **57**, S-3–S-17. **70**, 481–499.

*BURTON, R. V. The generality of honesty reconsidered. *Psychological Review*, 1963,

*CROWLEY, P. M. Effect of child training upon objectivity of moral judgment in grade-school children. *Journal of Personality and Social Psychology*, 1968, **8**, 228–232.

*GRINDER, R. E., & McMICHAEL, R. E. Cultural influences on conscience development: Resistance to temptation and guilt among Samoans and American Caucasians. *Journal of Abnormal and Social Psychology*, 1963, **66**, 503–507.

*HARTSHORNE, H., & MAY, M. A. *Studies in the nature of character*. Vol. 1. *Studies in deceit*. New York: Macmillan, 1928.

* Asterisks indicate works that are reprinted, in whole or in part, in this volume.

*HOFFMAN, M. L., & SALTZSTEIN, H. D. Parent discipline and the child's moral development. *Journal of Personality and Social Psychology*, 1967, **5**, 45–57.

*JOHNSON, R. C. A study of children's moral judgments. *Child Development*, 1962, **33**, 327–354.

*JOHNSON, R. C., ACKERMAN, J. M., FRANK, H., & FIONDA, A. J. Resistance to temptation, guilt following yielding, and psychopathology. *Journal of Consulting and Clinical Psychology*, 1968, **32**, 169–175.

MACKINNON, D. W. Violation of prohibition. In H. A. Murray (Ed.), *Explorations in personality: A clinical and experimental study of fifty men of college age.* New York: Oxford, 1938. Pp. 491–501.

McGRATH, M. C. A study of the moral development of children. *Psychological Monographs*, 1923, **32** (2, Whole No. 144).

*MOWRER, O. H. Abnormal reactions or actions? (An autobiographical answer). In J. A. Vernon (Ed.), *Introduction to psychology: A self-selection textbook.* Dubuque, Iowa: Willian C. Brown, 1966.

*PETERSON, D. R. The insecure child: Oversocialized or undersocialized? In O. H. Mowrer (Ed.), *Morality and mental health.* Chicago: Rand McNally, 1967. Pp. 459–471.

*PITTEL, S. M., & MENDELSOHN, G. A. Measurement of moral values: A review and critique. *Psychological Bulletin*, 1966, **66**, 22–35.

*PORTEUS, B. D., & JOHNSON, R. C. Children's responses to two measures of conscience development and their relation to sociometric nomination. *Child Development*, 1965, **36**, 703–711.

*REBELSKY, F. G., ALLINSMITH, W., & GRINDER, R. E. Resistance to temptation and sex differences in children's use of fantasy confession. *Child Development*, 1963, **34**, 955–962.

*SEARS, R. R., MACCOBY, E., & LEVIN, H. (Eds.) *Patterns of child rearing.* New York: Harper & Row, 1957.

*SWENSEN, C. H. Sexual behavior and psychopathology: A test of Mowrer's hypothesis. *Journal of Clinical Psychology*, 1962, **18**, 406–409.

*SWENSEN, C. H. Sexual behavior and psychopathology: A study of college men. *Journal of Clinical Psychology*, 1963, **19**, 403–404.

*TURIEL, E. An experimental test of the sequentiality of developmental stages in the child's moral judgments. *Journal of Personality and Social Psychology*, 1966, **3**, 611–618.

# Section I
# LITERARY TREATMENTS OF CONSCIENCE

## Introduction

Since World War II existentialist philosophers and novelists have been exposing the maddening moral issues that face modern man. Albert Camus was one of the best writers of this school. The following excerpt from *The Fall* vividly portrays the plight of man caught in a web of guilt, judgment, and penitence.

In the little-known piece by Samuel Clemens, the author uses techniques that are also common in the work of Edgar Allan Poe—he kills his conscience and he presents two characters who are doubles of one another and who represent the dual good and evil aspects of humanity. The piece's light-hearted facade covers the deep concern for good and evil that preoccupied Clemens throughout his later years.

Mowrer analyzes the Clemens piece and recalls some of the work of Poe, who killed his conscience again and again in his macabre short stories. Mowrer draws provocative implications for psychology and psychotherapy.

# 1

# From *The Fall*

*by Albert Camus*

In *The Fall*, Camus presents a dialogue
between two men, but we read the words
of only one of them. This one-sided dialogue lasts for five days and we learn
that the speaker has engaged in such
prolonged interactions before. He was
formerly a prominent Parisian lawyer,
noted as a humanitarian, but he now
operates out of *Mexico City*, a bar in
Amsterdam. The following pages give a
glimpse of the intricate picture of guilt,
judgment, and penitence that Camus sees
as characteristic of the human condition.

. . . Something must happen—and that
explains most human commitments.
Something must happen, even loveless
slavery, even war or death. Hurray then
for funerals!

But I at least didn't have that excuse.
I was not bored because I was riding on
the crest of the wave. On the evening I
am speaking about I can say that I was
even less bored than ever. And yet . . .
You see, *cher monsieur*, it was a fine
autumn evening, still warm in town and
already damp over the Seine. Night was
falling; the sky, still bright in the west,
was darkening; the street lamps were
glowing dimly. I was walking up the
quays of the Left Bank toward the Pont

From *The Fall*, by Albert Camus, translated
by Justin O'Brien (New York: Alfred A. Knopf;
London: Hamish Hamilton, 1956), pp. 37–40,
68–71, 131–132, 137–140, 146–147. Copyright ©
1956 by Alfred A. Knopf, Inc. Reprinted by
permission of the publishers.

des Arts. The river was gleaming between the stalls of the secondhand book-
sellers. There were but few people on
the quays; Paris was already at dinner. I
was treading on the dusty yellow leaves
that still recalled summer. Gradually the
sky was filling with stars that could be
seen for a moment after leaving one
street lamp and heading toward another.
I enjoyed the return of silence, the evening's mildness, the emptiness of Paris. I
was happy. The day had been good: a
blind man, the reduced sentence I had
hoped for, a cordial handclasp from my
client, a few liberalities, and in the afternoon, a brilliant improvization in the
company of several friends on the hard-
heartedness of our governing class and
the hypocrisy of our leaders.

I had gone up on the Pont des Arts,
deserted at that hour, to look at the
river that could hardly be made out now
night had come. Facing the statue of the
Vert-Galant, I dominated the island. I
felt rising within me a vast feeling of
power and—I don't know how to express
it—of completion, which cheered my
heart. I straightened up and was about
to light a cigarette, the cigarette of satisfaction, when, at that very moment, a
laugh burst out behind me. Taken by
surprise, I suddenly wheeled around;
there was no one there. I stepped to the
railing; no barge or boat. I turned back
toward the island and, again, heard the
laughter behind me, a little farther off as
if it were going downstream. I stood
there motionless. The sound of the
laughter was decreasing, but I could still
hear it distinctly behind me, come from
nowhere unless from the water. At the
same time I was aware of the rapid beating of my heart. Please don't misunder-
stand me; there was nothing mysterious
about that laugh; it was a good, hearty,

almost friendly laugh, which reestablished the proper proportions. Soon I heard nothing more, anyway. I returned to the quays, went up the rue Dauphine, bought some cigarettes I didn't need at all. I was dazed and had trouble breathing. That evening I rang up a friend, who wasn't at home. I was hesitating about going out when, suddenly, I heard laughter under my windows. I opened them. On the sidewalk, in fact, some youths were loudly saying good night. I shrugged my shoulders as I closed the windows; after all, I had a brief to study. I went into the bathroom to drink a glass of water. My reflection was smiling in the mirror, but it seemed to me that my smile was double.

*  *  *

Oh, I don't feel any self-satisfaction, believe me, in telling you this. Upon thinking of that time when I used to ask for everything without paying anything myself, when I used to mobilize so many people in my service, when I used to put them in the refrigerator, so to speak, in order to have them at hand some day when it would suit me, I don't know how to name the odd feeling that comes over me. Isn't it shame, perhaps? Tell me, *mon cher compatriote*, doesn't shame sting a little? It does? Well, it's probably shame, then, or one of those silly emotions that have to do with honor. It seems to me in any case that that feeling has never left me since the adventure I found at the heart of my memory, which I cannot any longer put off relating, despite my digressions and the inventive efforts for which, I hope, you give me credit.

Look, the rain has stopped! Be kind enough to walk home with me. I am strangely tired, not from having talked so much but at the mere thought of what I still have to say. Oh, well, a few words will suffice to relate my essential discovery. What's the use of saying more, anyway? For the statue to stand bare, the fine speeches must take flight like pigeons. So here goes. That particular night in November, two or three years before the evening when I thought I heard laughter behind me, I was returning to the Left Bank and my home by way of the Pont Royal. It was an hour past midnight, a fine rain was falling, a drizzle rather, that scattered the few people on the streets. I had just left a mistress, who was surely already asleep. I was enjoying that walk, a little numbed, my body calmed and irrigated by a flow of blood gentle as the falling rain. On the bridge I passed behind a figure leaning over the railing and seeming to stare at the river. On closer view, I made out a slim young woman dressed in black. The back of her neck, cool and damp between her dark hair and coat collar, stirred me. But I went on after a moment's hesitation. At the end of the bridge I followed the quays toward Saint-Michel, where I lived. I had already gone some fifty yards when I heard the sound—which, despite the distance, seemed dreadfully loud in the midnight silence—of a body striking the water. I stopped short, but without turning around. Almost at once I heard a cry, repeated several times, which was going downstream; then it suddenly ceased. The silence that followed, as the night suddenly stood still, seemed interminable. I wanted to run and yet didn't stir. I was trembling, I believe from cold and shock. I told myself that I had to be quick and I felt an irresistible weakness steal over me. I have forgotten what I thought then. "Too late, too far . . ." or something of the sort. I was still listening as I stood motionless. Then, slowly under the rain, I went away. I informed no one.

But here we are; here's my house, my shelter! Tomorrow? Yes, if you wish. I'd like to take you to the island of Marken so you can see the Zuider Zee. Let's meet at eleven at *Mexico City*. What? That woman? Oh, I don't know. Really I don't know. The next day, and the days following, I didn't read the papers.

\*     \*     \*

. . . Don't get the idea that I have talked to you at such length for five days just for the fun of it. No, I used to talk through my hat quite enough in the past. Now my words have a purpose. They have the purpose, obviously, of silencing the laughter, of avoiding judgment personally, though there is apparently no escape. Is not the great thing that stands in the way of our escaping it the fact that we are the first to condemn ourselves? Therefore it is essential to begin by extending the condemnation to all, without distinction, in order to thin it out at the start.

No excuses ever, for anyone; that's my principle at the outset. I deny the good intention, the respectable mistake, the indiscretion, the extenuating circumstance. With me there is no giving of absolution or blessing. Everything is simply totted up, and then: "It comes to so much. You are an evil-doer, a satyr, a congenital liar, a homosexual, an artist, etc." Just like that. Just as flatly. In philosophy as in politics, I am for any theory that refuses to grant man innocence and for any practice that treats him as guilty. You see in me, *très cher*, an enlightened advocate of slavery.

The speaker argues that a life of slavery is collective and communal, while freedom and death share the quality of being solitary. He wishes that all men would come together as slaves of the masters of guilt and repentance. Rather than being religious in nature, the argument is cast in Camus' atheistic context.

But I'm not being crazy; I'm well aware that slavery is not immediately realizable. It will be one of the blessings of the future, that's all. In the meantime, I must get along with the present and seek at least a provisional solution. Hence I had to find another means of extending judgment to everybody in order to make it weigh less heavily on my own shoulders. I found the means. Open the window a little, please; it's frightfully hot. Not too much, for I am cold also. My idea is both simple and fertile. How to get everyone involved in order to have the right to sit calmly on the outside myself? Should I climb up to the pulpit, like many of my illustrious contemporaries, and curse humanity? Very dangerous, that is! One day, or one night, laughter bursts out without a warning. The judgment you are passing on others eventually snaps back in your face, causing some damage. And so what? you ask. Well, here's the stroke of genius. I discovered that while waiting for the masters with their rods, we should, like Copernicus, reverse the reasoning to win out. Inasmuch as one couldn't condemn others without immediately judging oneself, one had to overwhelm oneself to have the right to judge others. Inasmuch as every judge someday ends up as a penitent, one had to travel the road in the opposite direction and practice the profession of penitent to be able to end up as a judge. You follow me? Good.

But to make myself even clearer, I'll tell you how I operate.

First I closed my law office, left Paris, traveled. I aimed to set up under another name in some place where I shouldn't lack for a practice. There are many in the world, but chance, convenience, irony, and also the necessity for a certain mortification made me choose a capital of waters and fogs, girdled by canals, particularly crowded, and visited by men from all corners of the earth. I set up my office in a bar in the sailors' quarter. The clientele of a port-town is varied. The poor don't go into the luxury districts, whereas eventually the gentlefolk always wind up at least once, as you have seen, in the disreputable places. I lie in wait particularly for the bourgeois, and the straying bourgeois at that; it's with him that I get my best results. Like a virtuoso with a rare violin, I draw my subtlest sounds from him.

So I have been practicing my useful profession at *Mexico City* for some time. It consists to begin with, as you know from experience, in indulging in public confession as often as possible. I accuse myself up and down. It's not hard, for I now have acquired a memory. But let me point out that I don't accuse myself crudely, beating my breast. No, I navigate skillfully, multiplying distinctions and digressions, too—in short I adapt my words to my listener and lead him to go me one better. I mingle what concerns me and what concerns others. I choose the features we have in common, the experiences we have endured together, the failings we share—good form, in other words, the man of the hour as he is rife in me and in others. With all that I construct a portrait which is the image of all and of no one. A mask, in short, rather like those carnival masks which are both lifelike and stylized, so that they make people say: "Why, surely I've met him!" When the portrait is finished, as it is this evening, I show it with great sorrow: "This, alas, is what I am!" The prosecutor's charge is finished. But at the same time the portrait I hold out to my contemporaries becomes a mirror.

Covered with ashes, tearing my hair, my face scored by clawing, but with piercing eyes, I stand before all humanity recapitulating my shames without losing sight of the effect I am producing, and saying: "I was the lowest of the low." Then imperceptibly I pass from the "I" to the "we." When I get to "This is what we are," the trick has been played and I can tell them off. I am like them, to be sure; we are in the soup together. However, I have a superiority in that I know it and this gives me the right to speak. You see the advantage, I am sure. The more I accuse myself, the more I have a right to judge you. Even better, I provoke you into judging yourself, and this relieves me of that much of the burden. Ah, *mon cher*, we are odd, wretched creatures, and if we merely look back over our lives, there's no lack of occasions to amaze and horrify ourselves. Just try. I shall listen, you may be sure, to your own confession with a great feeling of fraternity.

\*　　　\*　　　\*

All right, all right, I'll be quiet; don't get upset! Don't take my emotional outbursts or my ravings too seriously. They are controlled. Say, now that you are going to talk to me about yourself, I shall find out whether or not one of the objectives of my absorbing confession is achieved. I always hope, in fact, that my

interlocutor will be a policeman and that he will arrest me for the theft of "The Just Judges." For the rest—am I right?—no one can arrest me. But as for that theft, it falls within the provisions of the law and I have arranged everything so as to make myself an accomplice: I am harboring that painting and showing it to whoever wants to see it. You would arrest me then; that would be a good beginning. Perhaps the rest would be taken care of subsequently; I would be decapitated, for instance, and I'd have no more fear of death; I'd be saved. Above the gathered crowd, you would hold up my still warm head, so that they could recognize themselves in it and I could again dominate—an exemplar. All would be consummated; I should have brought to a close, unseen and unknown, my career as a false prophet crying in the wilderness and refusing to come forth.

But of course you are not a policeman; that would be too easy. What? Ah, I suspected as much, you see. That strange affection I felt for you had sense to it then. In Paris you practice the noble profession of lawyer! I sensed that we were of the same species. Are we not all alike, constantly talking and to no one, forever up against the same questions although we know the answers in advance? Then please tell me what happened to you one night on the quays of the Seine and how you managed never to risk your life. You yourself utter the words that for years have never ceased echoing through my nights and that I shall at last say through your mouth: "O young woman, throw yourself into the water again so that I may a second time have the chance of saving both of us!" A second time, eh, what a risky suggestion! Just suppose, *cher maître*, that we should be taken literally? We'd have to go through with it. Brr . . . ! The water's so cold! But let's not worry! It's too late now. It will always be too late. Fortunately!

## 2

# The facts concerning the recent carnival of crime in Connecticut

*by Samuel Clemens*

I was feeling blithe, almost jocund. I put a match to my cigar, and just then the morning's mail was handed in. The first superscription I glanced at was in a handwriting that sent a thrill of pleasure through and through me. It was Aunt Mary's; and she was the person I loved and honored most in all the world, outside of my own household. She had been my boyhood's idol; maturity, which is fatal to so many enchantments, had not been able to dislodge her from her pedestal; no, it had only justified her right to be there, and placed her dethronement permanently among the impossibilities. To show how strong her influence over me was, I will observe that long after everybody else's *"do-stop-smoking"* had ceased to affect me in the slightest degree, Aunt Mary could still stir my torpid conscience into faint signs of life when she touched upon the matter. But all things have their limit in this world. A happy day came at last, when even Aunt Mary's words could no longer move me. I was not merely glad

Samuel Clemens, "The Facts Concerning the Recent Carnival of Crime in Connecticut" from *Tom Sawyer Abroad and Other Stories* (New York: Harper & Brothers, 1917), pp. 305–325.

to see that day arrive; I was more than glad—I was grateful; for when its sun had set, the one alloy that was able to mar my enjoyment of my aunt's society was gone. The remainder of her stay with us that winter was in every way a delight. Of course she pleaded with me just as earnestly as ever, after that blessed day, to quit my pernicious habit, but to no purpose whatever; the moment she opened the subject I at once became calmly, peacefully, contentedly indifferent—absolutely, adamantinely indifferent. Consequently the closing weeks of that memorable visit melted away as pleasantly as a dream, they were so freighted for me with tranquil satisfaction. I could not have enjoyed my pet vice more if my gentle tormentor had been a smoker herself, and an advocate of the practice. Well, the sight of her handwriting reminded me that I was getting very hungry to see her again. I easily guessed what I should find in her letter. I opened it. Good! just as I expected; she was coming! Coming this very day, too, and by the morning train; I might expect her any moment.

I said to myself, "I am thoroughly happy and content now. If my most pitiless enemy could appear before me at this moment, I would freely right any wrong I may have done him."

Straightway the door opened, and a shriveled, shabby dwarf entered. He was not more than two feet high. He seemed to be about forty years old. Every feature and every inch of him was a trifle out of shape; and so, while one could not put his finger upon any particular part and say, "This is a conspicuous deformity," the spectator perceived that this little person was a deformity as a whole—a vague, general, evenly blended, nicely adjusted deformity. There was a foxlike cunning in the face and the sharp little eyes, and also alertness and malice. And yet, this vile bit of human rubbish seemed to bear a sort of remote and ill-defined resemblance to me! It was dully perceptible in the mean form, the countenance, and even the clothes, gestures, manner, and attitudes of the creature. He was a far-fetched, dim suggestion of a burlesque upon me, a caricature of me in little. One thing about him struck me forcibly, and most unpleasantly: he was covered all over with a fuzzy, greenish mould, such as one sometimes sees upon mildewed bread. The sight of it was nauseating.

He stepped along with a chipper air, and flung himself into a doll's chair in a very free-and-easy way, without waiting to be asked. He tossed his hat into the wastebasket. He picked up my old chalk pipe from the floor, gave the stem a wipe or two on his knee, filled the bowl from the tobacco-box at his side, and said to me in a tone of pert command:

"Gimme a match!"

I blushed to the roots of my hair; partly with indignation, but mainly because it somehow seemed to me that this whole performance was very like an exaggeration of conduct which I myself had sometimes been guilty of in my intercourse with familiar friends—but never, never with strangers, I observed to myself. I wanted to kick the pigmy into the fire, but some incomprehensible sense of being legally and legitimately under his authority forced me to obey his order. He applied the match to the pipe, took a contemplative whiff or two, and remarked, in an irritatingly familiar way:

"Seems to me it's devilish odd weather for this time of year."

I flushed again, and in anger and humiliation as before; for the language was hardly an exaggeration of some that I have uttered in my day, and moreover was delivered in a tone of voice and with an exasperating drawl that had the seeming of a deliberate travesty of my style. Now there is nothing I am quite so sensitive about as a mocking imitation of my drawling infirmity of speech. I spoke up sharply and said:

"Look here, you miserable ash-cat! You will have to give a little more attention to your manners, or I will throw you out of the window!"

The manikin smiled a smile of malicious content and security, puffed a whiff of smoke contemptuously toward me, and said, with a still more elaborate drawl:

"Come—go gently now; don't put on *too* many airs with your betters."

This cool snub rasped me all over, but it seemed to subjugate me, too, for a moment. The pigmy contemplated me awhile with his weasel eyes, and then said, in a peculiarly sneering way:

"You turned a tramp away from your door this morning."

I said crustily:

"Perhaps I did, perhaps I didn't. How do *you* know?"

"Well, I know. It isn't any matter *how* I know."

"Very well. Suppose I *did* turn a tramp away from the door—what of it?"

"Oh, nothing; nothing in particular. Only you lied to him."

"I *didn't!* That is, I—"

"Yes, but you did; you lied to him."

I felt a guilty pang—in truth, I had felt it forty times before that tramp had traveled a block from my door—but still I resolved to make a show of feeling slandered; so I said:

"This is a baseless impertinence. I said to the tramp—"

"There—wait. You were about to lie again. *I* know what you said to him. You said the cook was gone downtown and there was nothing left from breakfast. Two lies. You knew the cook was behind the door, and plenty of provisions behind *her*."

This astonishing accuracy silenced me; and it filled me with wondering speculations, too, as to how this cub could have got his information. Of course he could have culled the conversation from the tramp, but by what sort of magic had he contrived to find out about the concealed cook? Now the dwarf spoke again:

"It was rather pitiful, rather small, in you to refuse to read that poor young woman's manuscript the other day, and give her an opinion as to its literary value; and she had come so far, too, and *so* hopefully. Now *wasn't* it?"

I felt like a cur! And I had felt so every time the thing had recurred to my mind, I may as well confess. I flushed hotly and said:

"Look here, have you nothing better to do than prowl around prying into other people's business? Did that girl tell you that?"

"Never mind whether she did or not. The main thing is, you did that contemptible thing. And you felt ashamed of it afterward. Aha! you feel ashamed of it *now!*"

This was a sort of devilish glee. With fiery earnestness I responded:

"I told that girl, in the kindest, gentlest way, that I could not consent to deliver judgment upon *any*one's manuscript, because an individual's verdict was worthless. It might underrate a work of high merit and lose it to the world, or it might overrate a trashy production and so open the way for its infliction upon the world. I said that the great public was the only tribunal competent to sit in judgment upon a literary effort, and therefore it must be best to lay it before that tribunal in the outset, since in the end it must stand or fall by that mighty court's decision anyway."

"Yes, you said all that. So you did, you juggling, small-souled shuffler! And yet when the happy hopefulness faded out of that poor girl's face, when you saw her furtively slip beneath her shawl the scroll she had so patiently and honestly scribbled at—so ashamed of her darling now, so proud of it before—when you saw the gladness go out of her eyes and the tears come there, when she crept away so humbly who had come so—"

"Oh, peace! peace! peace! Blister your merciless tongue, haven't all these thoughts tortured me enough without *your* coming here to fetch them back again!"

Remorse! remorse! It seemed to me that it would eat the very heart out of me! And yet that small fiend only sat there leering at me with joy and contempt, and placidly chuckling. Presently he began to speak again. Every sentence was an accusation, and every accusation a truth. Every clause was freighted with sarcasm and derision, every slow-dropping word burned like vitriol. The dwarf reminded me of times when I had flown at my children in anger and punished them for faults which a little inquiry would have taught me that others, and not they, had committed. He reminded me of how I had disloyally allowed old friends to be traduced in my hearing, and been too craven to utter a word in their defense. He reminded me of many dishonest things which I had done; of many which I had procured to be done by children and other irresponsible persons; of some which I had planned, thought upon, and longed to do, and been kept from the performance by fear of consequences only. With exquisite cruelty he recalled to my mind, item by item, wrongs and unkindnesses I had inflicted and humiliations I had put upon friends since dead, "who died thinking of those injuries, maybe, and grieving over them," he added, by way of poison to the stab.

"For instance," said he, "take the case of your younger brother, when you two were boys together, many a long year ago. He always lovingly trusted in you with a fidelity that your manifold treacheries were not able to shake. He followed you about like a dog, content to suffer wrong and abuse if he might only be with you; patient under these injuries so long as it was your hand that inflicted them. The latest picture you have of him in health and strength must be such a comfort to you! You pledged your honor that if he would let you blindfold him no harm should come to him; and then, giggling and choking over the rare fun of the joke, you led him to a brook thinly glazed with ice, and pushed him in; and how you did laugh! Man, you will never forget the gentle, reproachful look he gave you as he struggled shivering out, if you live a thousand years! Oho! you see it now, you see it *now!*"

"Beast, I have seen it a million times, and shall see it a million more! and may you rot away piecemeal, and suffer till doomsday what I suffer now, for bringing it back to me again!"

The dwarf chuckled contentedly, and went on with his accusing history of my career. I dropped into a moody, vengeful state, and suffered in silence under the merciless lash. At last this remark of his gave me a sudden rouse:

"Two months ago, on a Tuesday, you woke up, away in the night, and fell to thinking, with shame, about a peculiarly mean and pitiful act of yours toward a poor ignorant Indian in the wilds of the Rocky Mountains in the winter of eighteen hundred and—"

"Stop a moment, devil! Stop! Do you mean to tell me that even my very *thoughts* are not hidden from you?"

"It seems to look like that. Didn't you think the thoughts I have just mentioned?"

"If I didn't, I wish I may never breathe again! Look here, friend—look me in the eye. Who *are* you?"

"Well, who do you think?"

"I think you are Satan himself. I think you are the devil."

"No."

"No? Then who *can* you be?"

"Would you really like to know?"

"*Indeed* I would."

"Well, I am your *Conscience!*"

In an instant I was in a blaze of joy and exultation. I sprang at the creature, roaring:

"Curse you, I have wished a hundred million times that you were tangible, and that I could get my hands on your throat once! Oh, but I will wreak a deadly vengeance on—"

Folly! Lightning does not move more quickly than my Conscience did! He darted aloft so suddenly that in the moment my fingers clutched the empty air he was already perched on the top of the high bookcase, with his thumb at his nose in token of derision. I flung the poker at him, and missed. I fired the bootjack. In a blind rage I flew from place to place, and snatched and hurled any missile that came handy; the storm of books, inkstands, and chunks of coal gloomed the air and beat about the manikin's perch relentlessly, but all to no purpose; the nimble figure dodged every shot; and not only that, but burst into a cackle of sarcastic and triumphant laughter as I sat down exhausted. While I puffed and gasped with fatigue and excitement, my Conscience talked to this effect:

"My good slave, you are curiously witless—no, I mean characteristically so. In truth, you are always consistent, always yourself, always an ass. Otherwise it must have occurred to you that if you attempted this murder with a sad heart and a heavy conscience, I would droop under the burdening influence instantly. Fool, I should have weighed a ton, and could not have budged from the floor; but instead, you are so cheerfully anxious to kill me that your conscience is as light as a feather; hence I am away up here out of your reach. I can almost respect a mere ordinary sort of fool; but *you*—pah!"

I would have given anything, then, to be heavy-hearted, so that I could get this person down from there and take his life, but I could no more be heavy-hearted over such a desire than I could have sorrowed over its accomplishment. So I could only look longingly up at my master, and rave at the ill-luck that denied me a heavy conscience the one only time that I had ever wanted such a thing in my life. By and by I got to musing over the hour's strange adventure, and of course my human curiosity began to work. I set myself to framing in my mind some questions for this fiend to answer. Just then one of my boys entered, leaving the door open behind him, and exclaimed:

"My! what *has* been going on here? The bookcase is all one riddle of—"

I sprang up in consternation, and shouted:

"Out of this! Hurry! Jump! Fly! Shut the door! Quick, or my Conscience will get away!"

The door slammed to, and I locked it. I glanced up and was grateful, to the bottom of my heart, to see that my owner was still my prisoner. I said:

"Hang you, I might have lost you! Children are the heedlessest creatures. But look here, friend, the boy did not seem to notice you at all; how is that?"

"For a very good reason. I am invisible to all but you."

I made a mental note of that piece of information with a good deal of satisfaction. I could kill this miscreant now, if I got a chance, and no one would know it. But this very reflection made me so light-hearted that my Conscience could hardly keep his seat, but was like to float aloft toward the ceiling like a toy balloon. I said, presently:

"Come, my Conscience, let us be friendly. Let us fly a flag of truce for a while. I am suffering to ask you some questions."

"Very well. Begin."

"Well, then, in the first place, why were you never visible to me before?"

"Because you never asked to see me before; that is, you never asked in the right spirit and the proper form before. You were just in the right spirit this time, and when you called for your most pitiless enemy I was that person by a very large majority, though you did not suspect it."

"Well, did that remark of mine turn you into flesh and blood?"

"No. It only made me visible to you. I

am unsubstantial, just as other spirits are."

This remark prodded me with a sharp misgiving. If he was unsubstantial, how was I going to kill him? But I dissembled, and said persuasively:

"Conscience, it isn't sociable of you to keep at such a distance. Come down and take another smoke."

This was answered with a look that was full of derision, and with this observation added:

"Come where you can get at me and kill me? The invitation is declined with thanks."

"All right," said I to myself; "so it seems a spirit *can* be killed, after all; there will be one spirit lacking in this world, presently, or I lose my guess." Then I said aloud:

"Friend—"

"There; wait a bit. I am not your friend, I am your enemy; I am not your equal, I am your master. Call me 'my lord,' if you please. You are too familiar."

"I don't like such titles. I am willing to call you *sir*. That is as far as—"

"We will have no argument about this. Just obey; that is all. Go on with your chatter."

"Very well, my lord—since nothing but my lord will suit you—I was going to ask you how long you will be visible to me?"

"Always!"

I broke out with strong indignation: "This is simply an outrage. That is what I think of it. You have dogged, and dogged, and *dogged* me, all the days of my life, invisible. That was misery enough; now to have such a looking thing as you tagging after me like another shadow all the rest of my days is

an intolerable prospect. You have my opinion, my lord; make the most of it."

"My lad, there was never so pleased a conscience in this world as I was when you made me visible. It gives me an inconceivable advantage. *Now* I can look you straight in the eye, and call you names, and leer at you, jeer at you, sneer at you; and *you* know what eloquence there is in visible gesture and expression, more especially when the effect is heightened by audible speech. I shall always address you henceforth in your o-w-n s-n-i-v-e-l-i-n-g d-r-a-w-l—baby!"

I let fly with the coal-hod. No result. My lord said:

"Come, come! Remember the flag of truce!"

"Ah, I forgot that. I will try to be civil; and *you* try it, too, for a novelty. The idea of a *civil* conscience! It is a good joke; an excellent joke. All the consciences *I* have ever heard of were nagging, badgering, fault-finding, execrable savages! Yes; and always in a sweat about some poor little insignificant trifle or other—destruction catch the lot of them, *I* say! I would trade mine for the smallpox and seven kinds of consumption, and be glad of the chance. Now tell me, why *is* it that a conscience can't haul a man over the coals once, for an offense, and then let him alone? Why is it that it wants to keep on pegging at him, day and night and night and day, week in and week out, forever and ever, about the same old thing? There is no sense in that, and no reason in it. I think a conscience that will act like that is meaner than the very dirt itself."

"Well, *we* like it; that suffices."

"Do you do it with the honest intent to improve a man?"

That question produced a sarcastic smile, and this reply:

"No, sir. Excuse me. We do it simply because it is 'business.' It is our trade. The *purpose* of it *is* to improve the man, but *we* are merely disinterested agents. We are appointed by authority, and haven't anything to say in the matter. We obey orders and leave the consequences where they belong. But I am willing to admit this much: we *do* crowd the orders a trifle when we get a chance, which is most of the time. We enjoy it. We are instructed to remind a man a few times of an error; and I don't mind acknowledging that we try to give pretty good measure. And when we get hold of a man of a peculiarly sensitive nature, oh, but we do haze him! I have consciences to come all the way from China and Russia to see a person of that kind put through his paces, on a special occasion. Why, I knew a man of that sort who had accidentally crippled a mulatto baby; the news went abroad, and I wish you may never commit another sin if the consciences didn't flock from all over the earth to enjoy the fun and help his master exercise him. That man walked the floor in torture for forty-eight hours, without eating or sleeping, and then blew his brains out. The child was perfectly well again in three weeks."

"Well, you are a precious crew, not to put it too strong. I think I begin to see now why you have always been a trifle inconsistent with me. In your anxiety to get all the juice you can out of a sin, you make a man repent of it in three or four different ways. For instance, you found fault with me for lying to that tramp, and I suffered over that. But it was only yesterday that I told a tramp the square truth, to wit, that, it being regarded as bad citizenship to encourage vagrancy, I would give him nothing. What did you do *then?* Why, you made me say to myself, 'Ah, it would have been so much kinder and more blameless to ease him off with a little white lie, and send him away feeling that if he could not have bread, the gentle treatment was at least something to be grateful for!' Well, I suffered all day about *that*. Three days before I had fed a tramp, and fed him freely, supposing it a virtuous act. Straight off you said, 'Oh, false citizen, to have fed a tramp!' and I suffered as usual. I gave a tramp work; you objected to it—*after* the contract was made, of course; you never speak up beforehand. Next, I *refused* a tramp work; you objected to *that*. Next, I proposed to kill a tramp; you kept me awake all night, oozing remorse at every pore. Sure I was going to be right *this* time, I sent the next tramp away with my benediction; and I wish you may live as long as I do, if you didn't make me smart all night again because I didn't kill him. Is there *any* way of satisfying that malignant invention which is called a conscience?"

"Hah, ha! this is luxury! Go on!"

"But come, now, answer me that question. *Is* there any way?"

"Well, none that I propose to tell *you*, my son. Ass! I don't care *what* act you may turn your hand to, I can straightway whisper a word in your ear and make you think you have committed a dreadful meanness. It is my *business*—and my joy—to make you repent of *everything* you do. If I have fooled away any opportunities it was not intentional; I beg to assure you it was not intentional!"

"Don't worry; you haven't missed a trick that *I* know of. I never did a thing in all my life, virtuous or otherwise, that I didn't repent of in twenty-four hours.

In church last Sunday I listened to a charity sermon. My first impulse was to give three hundred and fifty dollars; I repented of that and reduced it a hundred; repented of that and reduced it another hundred; repented of that and reduced it another hundred; repented of that and reduced the remaining fifty to twenty-five; repented of that and came down to fifteen; repented of that and dropped to two dollars and a half; when the plate came around at last, I repented once more and contributed ten cents. Well, when I got home, I did wish to goodness I had that ten cents back again! You never *did* let me get through a charity sermon without having something to sweat about."

"Oh, and I never shall, I never shall. You can always depend on me."

"I think so. Many and many's the restless night I've wanted to take you by the neck. If I could only get hold of you now!"

"Yes, no doubt. But I am not an ass; I am only the saddle of an ass. But go on, go on. You entertain me more than I like to confess."

"I am glad of that. (You will not mind my lying a little, to keep in practice.) Look here; not to be too personal, I think you are about the shabbiest and most contemptible little shriveled-up reptile that can be imagined. I am grateful enough that you are invisible to other people, for I should die with shame to be seen with such a mildewed monkey of a conscience as *you* are. Now if you were five or six feet high, and—"

"Oh, come! who is to blame?"

"*I* don't know."

"Why, you are; nobody else."

"Confound you, I wasn't consulted about your personal appearance."

"I don't care, you had a good deal to do with it, nevertheless. When you were eight or nine years old, I was seven feet high, and as pretty as a picture."

"I wish you had died young! So you have grown the wrong way, have you?"

"Some of us grow one way and some the other. You had a large conscience once; if you've a small conscience now I reckon there are reasons for it. However, both of us are to blame, you and I. You see, you used to be conscientious about a great many things; morbidly so, I may say. It was a great many years ago. You probably do not remember it now. Well, I took a great interest in my work, and I so enjoyed the anguish which certain pet sins of yours afflicted you with, that I kept pelting at you until I rather overdid the matter. You began to rebel. Of course I began to lose ground, then, and shrivel a little—diminish in stature, get mouldy, and grow deformed. The more I weakened, the more stubbornly you fastened on to those particular sins; till at last the places on my person that represent those vices became as callous as shark skin. Take smoking, for instance. I played that card a little too long, and I lost. When people plead with you at this late day to quit that vice, that old callous place seems to enlarge and cover me all over like a shirt of mail. It exerts a mysterious, smothering effect; and presently I, your faithful hater, your devoted Conscience, go sound asleep! Sound? It is no name for it. I couldn't hear it thunder at such a time. You have some few other vices—perhaps eighty, or maybe ninety—that affect me in much the same way."

"This is flattering; you must be asleep a good part of your time."

"Yes, of late years. I should be asleep *all* the time, but for the help I get."

"Who helps you?"

"Other consciences. Whenever a person whose conscience I am acquainted with tries to plead with you about the vices you are callous to, I get my friend to give his client a pang concerning some villainy of his own, and that shuts off his meddling and starts him off to hunt personal consolation. My field of usefulness is about trimmed down to tramps, budding authoresses, and that line of goods now; but don't you worry —I'll harry you on *them* while they last! Just you put your trust in me."

"I think I can. But if you had only been good enough to mention these facts some thirty years ago, I should have turned my particular attention to sin, and I think that by this time I should not only have had you pretty permanently asleep on the entire list of human vices, but reduced to the size of a homœopathic pill, at that. That is about the style of conscience *I* am pining for. If I only had you shrunk down to a homœopathic pill, and could get my hands on you, would I put you in a glass case for a keepsake? No, sir. I would give you to a yellow dog! That is where *you* ought to be—you and all your tribe. You are not fit to be in society, in my opinion. Now another question. Do you know a good many consciences in this section?"

"Plenty of them."

"I would give anything to see some of them! Could you bring them here? And would they be visible to me?"

"Certainly not."

"I suppose I ought to have known that without asking. But no matter, you can describe them. Tell me about my neighbor Thompson's conscience, please."

"Very well. I know him intimately; have known him many years. I knew him when he was eleven feet high and of a faultless figure. But he is very rusty and tough and misshapen now, and hardly ever interests himself about anything. As to his present size—well, he sleeps in a cigar box."

"Likely enough. There are few smaller, meaner men in this region than Hugh Thompson. Do you know Robinson's conscience?"

"Yes. He is a shade under four and a half feet high; used to be a blonde; is a brunette now, but still shapely and comely."

"Well, Robinson is a good fellow. Do you know Tom Smith's conscience?"

"I have known him from childhood. He was thirteen inches high, and rather sluggish, when he was two years old—as nearly all of us are at that age. He is thirty-seven feet high now, and the stateliest figure in America. His legs are still racked with growing-pains, but he has a good time, nevertheless. Never sleeps. He is the most active and energetic member of the New England Conscience Club; is president of it. Night and day you can find him pegging away at Smith, panting with his labor, sleeves rolled up, countenance all alive with enjoyment. He has got his victim splendidly dragooned now. He can make poor Smith imagine that the most innocent little thing he does is an odious sin; and then he sets to work and almost tortures the soul out of him about it."

"Smith is the noblest man in all this section, and the purest; and yet is always breaking his heart because he cannot be good! Only a conscience *could* find pleasure in heaping agony upon a spirit like that. Do you know my aunt Mary's conscience?"

"I have seen her at a distance, but am

not acquainted with her. She lives in the open air altogether, because no door is large enough to admit her."

"I can believe that. Let me see. Do you know the conscience of that publisher who once stole some sketches of mine for a 'series' of his, and then left me to pay the law expenses I had to incur in order to choke him off?"

"Yes. He has a wide fame. He was exhibited, a month ago, with some other antiquities, for the benefit of a recent Member of the Cabinet's conscience that was starving in exile. Tickets and fares were high, but I traveled for nothing by pretending to be the conscience of an editor, and got in for half-price by representing myself to be the conscience of a clergyman. However, the publisher's conscience, which was to have been the main feature of the entertainment, was a failure—as an exhibition. He was there, but what of that? The management had provided a microscope with a magnifying power of only thirty thousand diameters, and so nobody got to see him, after all. There was great and general dissatisfaction, of course, but—"

Just here there was an eager footstep on the stair; I opened the door, and my aunt Mary burst into the room. It was a joyful meeting and a cheery bombardment of questions and answers concerning family matters ensued. By and by my aunt said:

"But I am going to abuse you a little now. You promised me, the day I saw you last, that you would look after the needs of the poor family around the corner as faithfully as I had done it myself. Well, I found out by accident that you failed of your promise. *Was* that right?"

In simple truth, I never had thought of that family a second time! And now

such a splintering pang of guilt shot through me! I glanced up at my Conscience. Plainly, my heavy heart was affecting him. His body was drooping forward; he seemed about to fall from the bookcase. My aunt continued:

"And think how you have neglected my poor *protégé* at the almshouse, you dear, hard-hearted promise-breaker!" I blushed scarlet, and my tongue was tied. As the sense of my guilty negligence waxed sharper and stronger, my Conscience began to sway heavily back and forth; and when my aunt, after a little pause, said in a grieved tone, "Since you never once went to see her, maybe it will not distress you now to know that that poor child died, months ago, utterly friendless and forsaken!" my Conscience could no longer bear up under the weight of my sufferings, but tumbled headlong from his high perch and struck the floor with a dull, leaden thump. He lay there writhing with pain and quaking with apprehension, but straining every muscle in frantic efforts to get up. In a fever of expectancy I sprang to the door, locked it, placed my back against it, and bent a watchful gaze upon my struggling master. Already my fingers were itching to begin their murderous work.

"Oh, what *can* be the matter!" exclaimed my aunt, shrinking from me, and following with her frightened eyes the direction of mine. My breath was coming in short, quick gasps now, and my excitement was almost uncontrollable. My aunt cried out:

"Oh, do not look so! You appall me! Oh, what can the matter be? What is it you see? Why do you stare so? Why do you work your fingers like that?"

"Peace, woman!" I said, in a hoarse whisper. "Look elsewhere; pay no attention to me; it is nothing—nothing. I am often this way. It will pass in a moment. It comes from smoking too much."

My injured lord was up, wild-eyed with terror, and trying to hobble toward the door. I could hardly breathe, I was so wrought up. My aunt wrung her hands, and said:

"Oh, I knew how it would be; I knew it would come to this at last! Oh, I implore you to crush out that fatal habit while it may yet be time! You must not, you shall not be deaf to my supplications longer!" My struggling Conscience showed sudden signs of weariness! "Oh, promise me you will throw off this hateful slavery of tobacco!" My Conscience began to reel drowsily, and grope with his hands—enchanting spectacle! "I beg you, I beseech you, I implore you! Your reason is deserting you! There is madness in your eye! It flames with frenzy! Oh, hear me, hear me, and be saved! See, I plead with you on my very knees!" As she sank before me my Conscience reeled again, and then drooped languidly to the floor, blinking toward me a last supplication for mercy, with heavy eyes. "Oh, promise, or you are lost! Promise, and be redeemed! Promise! Promise and live!" With a long-drawn sigh my conquered Conscience closed his eyes and fell fast asleep!

With an exultant shout I sprang past my aunt, and in an instant I had my lifelong foe by the throat. After so many years of waiting and longing, he was mine at last. I tore him to shreds and fragments. I rent the fragments to bits. I cast the bleeding rubbish into the fire, and drew into my nostrils the grateful incense of my burnt-offering. At last, and forever, my Conscience was dead!

I was a free man! I turned upon my poor aunt, who was almost petrified with terror, and shouted:

"Out of this with your paupers, your charities, your reforms, your pestilent morals! You behold before you a man whose life-conflict is done, whose soul is at peace; a man whose heart is dead to sorrow, dead to suffering, dead to remorse; a man WITHOUT A CONSCIENCE! In my joy I spare you, though I could throttle you and never feel a pang! Fly!"

She fled. Since that day my life is all bliss. Bliss, unalloyed bliss. Nothing in all the world could persuade me to have a conscience again. I settled all my old outstanding scores, and began the world anew. I killed thirty-eight persons during the first two weeks—all of them on account of ancient grudges. I burned a dwelling that interrupted my view. I swindled a widow and some orphans out of their last cow, which is a very good one, though not thoroughbred, I believe. I have also committed scores of crimes, of various kinds, and have enjoyed my work exceedingly, whereas it would formerly have broken my heart and turned my hair gray, I have no doubt.

In conclusion, I wish to state, by way of advertisement, that medical colleges desiring assorted tramps for scientific purposes, either by the gross, by cord measurement, or per ton, will do well to examine the lot in my cellar before purchasing elsewhere, as these were all selected and prepared by myself, and can be had at a low rate, because I wish to clear out my stock and get ready for the spring trade.

# 3

# On the delights, and dire consequences, of conscience killing

*by O. Hobart Mowrer*

The moral of Samuel Clemens' subtle and artistically well-developed story, "The Facts Concerning the Recent Carnival of Crime in Connecticut," is unmistakably clear.[1] It is this: No matter how burdensome and unreasonable conscience may *seem* to be, a man is much better off with a conscience than without one. Conscience killing is therefore depicted (by a kind of *reductio ad absurdum*) as disastrous for the individual in that it changes him from a responsible, self-controlled human being into a "criminal." The implications for organized society, if this sort of thing occurred generally, are equally obvious.

"The Facts Concerning the Recent Carnival of Crime in Connecticut" was written for oral presentation by its author at a meeting of the Monday Club in Hartford, Connecticut, in January 1876, and was published, in June of the same year, in the *Atlantic Monthly*. It has been reprinted and is today conveniently available in a volume entitled *The Art, Humor, and Humanity of*

This article is published here for the first time in English.

[1] I am indebted to Ronald C. Johnson for having brought this little-known story to my attention and for the opportunity to comment on it here.

*Mark Twain* (Brashear & Rodney, 1959).

In a letter dated January 11, 1876, Mr. Clemens ("Mark Twain") said of this remarkable piece that its writing involved "less than two days' work"; and subsequently he referred to the "exasperating metaphysical question" that is the theme of this "literary extravaganza." The story presents, albeit in satirical form, a theory of conscience which is very different from the one that was soon to be advanced by Sigmund Freud. Today Freud's theory is undergoing reexamination, and we may in the process find that Clemens was in some respects a better psychologist than Freud. Historical developments and the current social and moral scene at least seem to support Clemens' conception of the problem and to be calling Freud's into question.

## I

Although the main thrust of Clemens' story is obvious enough on first reading, there are a number of points that can be fully appreciated only as one reads and rereads the piece and ponders its various subtleties. As Clemens himself has suggested, its purpose was to provoke thought and discussion (at the Monday Club), rather than to provide a fully explicit and final solution to all the dilemmas posed by the psychology and sociology of conscience. Here I wish to single out for special comment a few of the most interesting implications of this piece.

### "Aunt Mary" as a Parent Figure

The relationship between Aunt Mary and the narrator's conscience is not without significance. They both put in their appearance on the same morning and they have many of the same values and objectives. Aunt Mary is clearly a parent figure and the conscience is her subjective agent and ally. Since there is no reference to the narrator's actual parents, it is conceivable that Aunt Mary "raised" him and was, psychologically, both father and mother to him. In any case, the narrator says of Aunt Mary that she "was the person I loved and honored most in all the world, outside of my own household. She had been my boyhood's idol [and had a strong] influence over me . . ." (p. 230) . However, in adult life, he had largely emancipated himself from Aunt Mary's moral concerns, to become "calmly, peacefully, contentedly indifferent" (p. 230) . But her contribution to his conscience was far more tenacious and bothersome, so the body of the essay is concerned with the narrator's interaction with Aunt Mary's subjective counterpart, her "introject."

It is noteworthy that Aunt Mary and conscience not only "enter" together; they also, in the end, "exit" together:

> "Out of this with your paupers, your charities, your reforms, your pestilent morals! You behold before you a man whose life-conflict is done, whose soul is at peace; a man whose heart is dead to sorrow, dead to suffering, dead to remorse; a man WITHOUT A CONSCIENCE! In my joy I spare you, though I could throttle you and never feel a pang! Fly!"
>
> She [Aunt Mary] fled. Since that day my life is all bliss (p. 245) .

Obviously this appraisal of the situation is intended to be ironical. Although the narrator, by killing his conscience, becomes less of a problem to himself, he becomes a very great problem *to others*.

And, in real life, it would only be a matter of time until *they* "killed" *him*. Thus conscience, far from being a disadvantage and a burden, is indirectly portrayed as self-protective and basically helpful (cf. Tkacik, 1964; Mowrer, 1968; Forbes, 1966).

*Characteristics of Conscience*

The narrator, at the outset of his tale, gives the reader some broad clues concerning the "dwarf's" identity, which he, himself, pretends not to recognize. Eyes —with their function of observation and watchfulness—are a proverbial symbol of conscience; and the narrator repeatedly refers to the singular nature of this part of the dwarf's physiognomy: "There was a foxlike cunning in the face and the *sharp little eyes* . . ." (p. 231, italics added). The pigmy contemplated me awhile with *his weasel eyes* . . ." (p. 232, italics added) .

The dwarf's superiority is also emphasized: "I wanted to kick the pigmy into the fire, but some incomprehensible sense of being legally and legitimately under his authority forced me to obey his order" (p. 231) . The dwarf himself says: " 'Come—go gently now; don't put on *too* many airs with your betters' " (p. 232) . And later there is the whimsical dialogue concerning the question of how the narrator should address the dwarf. " '. . . I am not your equal,' " the dwarf says. " 'I am your master. Call me "my lord," if you please. You are too familiar' " (p. 237) .

The discussion of invisibility is also instructive. When the narrator asks, " 'Why were you never visible to me before?' " the reply is:

> "Because you never asked to see me before; that is, you never asked in the

right spirit and the proper form before. You were just in the right spirit this time, and when you called for your most pitiless enemy I was that person by a very large majority, though you did not suspect it."

"Well, did that remark of mine turn you into flesh and blood?"

"No. It only made me visible to you. I am unsubstantial, just as other spirits are" (p. 237).

"I am invisible to all but you" (p. 236).

Perhaps most ingenious and significant of all is the way the dwarf assumes a position of physical elevation and maintains it during most of the "interview."

> I would have given anything, then, to be heavy-hearted, so that I could get this person down from there and take his life, but I could no more be heavy-hearted over such a desire than I could have sorrowed over its accomplishment. So I could only look longingly up *at my master*, and rave at the ill luck that denied me a heavy conscience the one only time that I ever wanted such a thing in my life (p. 236, italics added).

How could one better depict, than in this physical way, the concept of conscience as a "Higher Power" or, as Freud preferred to say, the *superego*!

*The Paradoxical Enmity of Conscience*

Why does the conscience have such a malignant attitude toward the narrator of this story? Does this not justify the narrator's distrust and ill will? The dwarf refers to himself as the narrator's "most pitiless enemy," and the narrator rails against him and against consciences in general:

> "All the consciences *I* have ever heard of were nagging, badgering, fault-finding, execrable savages! Yes; and always in a

sweat about some poor little insignificant trifle or other—destruction catch the lot of them, *I* say! I would trade mine for the smallpox and seven kinds of consumption, and be glad of the chance. Now tell me, why *is* it that a conscience can't haul a man over the coals once, for an offense, and then let him alone? Why is it that it wants to keep on pegging at him, day and night and night and day, week in and week out, forever and ever, about the same old thing? There is no sense in that, and no reason in it. I think a conscience that will act like that is meaner than the very dirt itself" (p. 238).

In another of his works, Clemens has Huckleberry Finn express much the same evaluation of conscience:

> "But that's always the way, it don't make no difference whether you do right or wrong, a person's conscience ain't got no sense, and just goes for him *anyway*. If I had a yaller dog that didn't know no more than a person's conscience does I would pison him. It takes up more room than all the rest of a person's insides, and yet ain't no good, nohow" (Brashear & Rodney, p. 238).

The foregoing quotations contain a reasonable approximation of the view of conscience which some Freudian psychoanalysts were later to develop. But for Clemens this evaluation is satirical and disingenuous. He clearly implies that if conscience is malicious and merciless (both of which words the narrator employs in describing the dwarf), it is because conscience has been systematically *ignored and mistreated*. By his own confession, the narrator has tenaciously clung to numerous "bad habits" despite his conscience's efforts to rid him of them. The narrator also cites persons of better character and disposition who have large, "beautiful" consciences, not small, shabby, "mean" ones. In a word, Clemens is wryly suggesting that we have the kind of conscience *we deserve*, "good" or "bad," peaceful or angry, as a function of how we have lived.

### What Is the "Purpose" of Conscience?

After his tirade against consciences in general, the narrator asks his conscience why he pesters him so: " 'Do you do it with the honest intent to improve a man?' " The reply is noteworthy:

> "No, sir, Excuse me. We do it simply because it is 'business.' It is our trade. The *purpose* of it *is* to improve the man, but *we* are merely disinterested agents. . . . We obey orders and leave the consequences where they belong" (p. 238).

Now we come to a question that often arises in the field of psychopathology, namely: Why is it, if conscience is really benign and beneficent, that it sometimes *drives* a person to psychosis, suicide, or even murder? The answer seems to be that such untoward events occur when a person *stubbornly refuses* to do the behest of his conscience, and all the latter knows to do is to steadily push, harry, and torment the person. The purpose of conscience is indeed to "improve a man," but if the man steadfastly resists "improvement," conscience continues to press, in an effort to do its "work," and the result may indeed be violent. Parents often have to resort to drastic measures to establish conscience in children, and it should not surprise us if conscience shows equal determination when it alone has to represent "authority" and insist upon responsible action. Paradoxically, in trying to improve a person, conscience may, if the person rebels, drive him to distraction or even destruction.

## II

In the foregoing pages I may have interpreted the role of conscience more favorably than Clemens himself intended. His whole attitude and argument is ostensibly against conscience. But in most instances it is clear enough that his intent is ironical, so that while the narrator is speaking *against* conscience, Clemens himself is really speaking *for* it.

This is obviously Clemens' primary strategy, but questions may still be asked: Does the author have reservations? Does he feel that in certain respects conscience may indeed be malicious? Are some consciences perhaps intrinsically better, or worse, than others? When there is conflict between conscience and the person to whom it has been "assigned," does the fault always lie with the individual or does it sometimes rest with the conscience?

At points, Clemens seems to be deliberately ambiguous—in part, no doubt, as a means of stimulating the reader—but also, I suspect, because he was himself not entirely certain of the answers to some of these questions. He may have wished to raise these questions without having to offer definitive answers.

### The Problem of Scrupulosity

In his exasperation and anger, the narrator asks: " 'Is there *any* way of satisfying that malignant invention which is called a conscience. . . . *Is* there any way?' " (p. 239). The dwarf answers:

> "Well, none that I propose to tell *you*, my son. Ass! I don't care *what* act you may turn your hand to, I can straightway whisper a word in your ear and make you think you have committed a dreadful

meanness. It is my *business*—and my joy —to make you repent of *every*thing you do. If I have fooled away any opportunities it was not intentional; I beg to assure you it was not intentional!" (pp. 239–240).

One interpretation of this passage is that the narrator's conscience is indeed unreasonable, irrational, and morbid; and when we are ourselves so afflicted or see others who appear to be, an easy first inference is that the conscience is truly at fault. But the conscience, in the passage just quoted, takes the reverse position. It calls the narrator an ass, thus implying stupidity and stubbornness, and later quips: " 'But I am not an ass; I am only the saddle of an ass' " (p. 240). What is the narrator ignoring, pretending not to know? Perhaps it is that only by making one's conscience (and other people) happy can one be happy oneself and that the worse one treats his conscience, as long as one *has* one, the worse his conscience will make *him* feel.

This is one way of viewing the matter, the time-honored way; but today there is sometimes a tendency to view conscience as hopelessly inconsistent and incapable of ever being really satisfied or pleased. With clearly ironical intent, Clemens here gives the example of the narrator's "repenting" every charitable impulse until he ends up putting only ten cents in the collection plate. It might have been that if he had been truly generous, his conscience would *not* have continued to "peg" at him. But it is just as possible that this would not have satisfied his conscience either. How can one account for this type of situation? Here we would seem to have a case of genuine scrupulosity, of a truly morbid conscience.

The term "scrupulosity" is best known among members of the Catholic Church and is said to exist in persons who confess and do penance for their sins, but experience no relief. This is not the place to explore this problem in detail (cf. Mowrer, 1963). Suffice it to say that careful inquiry usually reveals that when confession and restitution (made not only sacramentally but also in a broadly human context) fail to resolve guilt and anxiety, this is usually because the full story has not been told, that is, the individual is "holding out" and trying to resolve the guilt associated with a greater sin by confessing and doing penance for a lesser one.

In the case of charity, there are indeed some persons who feel no deep peace or satisfaction no matter how much money they give to *any* cause. Perhaps the trouble here is that there are some sins and shortcomings that have no monetary equivalent. If we could always *buy* our way out of guilt, the rich should be very virtuous and happy indeed and the poor inevitably miserable. But evidently this is not exactly the way the matter works.

### But Is Conscience Never Wrong?

It is obvious, as evidenced by the phenomenon of sociopathy, or characterlessness, that some persons have inadequate consciences. And in light of this fact, it would not seem unreasonable to conclude that in some other persons there is a true excess or perversion of conscience. Conscience would *not* be a reliable guide for those individuals. And if one can't trust conscience, then where can one place his faith and find reliable guidance? This, I believe, is the heart of the "exasperating metaphysical question" to which Clemens alludes in speaking of this essay. He poses it, perhaps most pointedly, as follows:

"Oh, come! who is to blame?" [conscience asks, with respect to his appearance].

"*I* don't know."

"Why, you are; nobody else."

"Confound you. I wasn't consulted about your personal appearance."

"I don't care, you had a good deal to do with it, nevertheless" (p. 240).

But then there follows what might be regarded as a confession on the part of conscience:

"Some of us grow one way and some the other. You had a large conscience once; if you've a small conscience now I reckon there are reasons for it. However, *both of us are to blame*, you and I. You see, you used to be conscientious about a great many things; *morbidly so, I may say*. It was a great many years ago. You probably do not remember it now. Well, I took a great interest in my work, and I so enjoyed the anguish which certain pet sins of yours afflicted you with, that I kept pelting at you until I *rather overdid the matter. You began to rebel*. Of course I began to lose ground, then, and shrivel a little—diminish in stature, get mouldy, and grow deformed. The more I weakened, the more stubbornly you fastened on to those particular sins; till at last the places on my person that represent those vices became as callous as shark skin. Take smoking, for instance. I played that card a little too long, and I lost. When people plead with you at this late day to quit that vice, that old callous place seems to enlarge and cover me all over like a shirt of mail (p. 241, italics added).

The mere fact that a writer chooses to insert a given notion into his composition does not, of course, prove that it is psychologically valid or real. Thus, we are not necessarily called upon to "account for" or explain everything that Clemens says or suggests in the piece

that is presently under scrutiny. In certain respects he may have simply been mistaken in his assumptions or have merely been artificing. But the fairest way to operate in this connection is to take everything the narrator says (or ironically implies) seriously and see where we come out. Applying this principle, it seems clear that Clemens thinks that consciences, as well as the persons to whom they have been assigned, can make mistakes. Certainly it would be unwarranted to assume that parents are infallible; and, as the legatees of parents, consciences might also be expected to be imperfect and capable of error.

The classical psychoanalytic theory of psychopathology and therapy says that the cause of psychological disorders lies entirely, or at least predominantly, with conscience. According to this view, the neurotic person is one who is bothered disproportionately by moral issues, because his conscience, as a reflection of parental attitudes and practices, is too severe, too strict. And now, through the voice of a conscience that has been personified as a pigmy, Clemens' narrator seems to be agreeing with this position concerning the usefulness and validity of conscience and admitting the possibility of defects and failings.

The problem is at least partially resolved if one takes the point of view that parents and consciences do the best they can, and the rest is *up to us*. In other words, if a parent or conscience is wrong about something, it is idle and altogether unworthy of us to become resentful and to totally reject "society" and "authority." One of the basic therapeutic maxims of Alcoholics Anonymous is that you cannot "keep your resentments" and stay sober—or, we might add, sane. The resentments, and accompanying self-pity, have to go. By contrast, in conventional psychoanalysis and related therapies, patients are sometimes encouraged to see others as responsible for their difficulties and to blame them accordingly. The narrator in our story shows himself to be guilty of this error by taking such a dim view of his conscience, treating it so shabbily, and being regarded by his conscience, in turn, as a "fool."

Another relevant consideration is the fact that consciences are, in a sense, self-chosen and we therefore have no right to complain about them. *They*, as the pigmy observes, merely do their duty and carry out their assignments. And what is their main duty, their primary responsibility? Surely it is to help us keep the promises and commitments we ourselves have solemnly made. And if we keep faith with others, we are not likely to break faith with ourselves and thus incur the enmity of our consciences.

Also, as Harry Stack Sullivan was fond of pointing out, if we honestly don't know what is right or wrong in a given situation, we can always engage in what he called "consensual validation," that is, checking with others. If we have entered into a personal relationship and have forgotten (or not clearly understood) the exact nature of the original agreement or "contract," we can always consult the other person or persons involved and see what their perception of the situation is. And if we genuinely don't know the rules and standards of a group or organization with which we are affiliated, it is certainly in no way irregular or inappropriate to ask to see a copy of the constitution or some equivalent document. In the original act of making a choice or commitment, there may indeed be no clear basis for determining

what is right or wrong—the choice is up to us; and it is precisely here, in a free society, that our freedom lies. But once we have made a commitment, the situation becomes pretty clearly structured, and we usually know quite well what is expected or not expected of us—a fact that is underscored by the *secrecy* we often practice when we violate our solemn agreements.

## III

Although I did not know of the Clemens Story until the summer of 1963, when Professor Johnson called it to my attention, much earlier (in 1950) I had become interested in a similar piece by Edgar Allan Poe, simply entitled "William Wilson" and first published in 1839. It, too, is concerned with the phenomenon of conscience killing, but Poe used a device for externalizing conscience somewhat different from the one employed by Clemens. Instead of a dwarf, Poe represented the conscience as another person, a "double" who "by a remarkable coincident" had been born on the same day, entered school at the same time, and bore the same name as the main character. Between the two boys a singular ambivalence developed, which Poe describes as follows:

> It may seem strange that in spite of the continual anxiety occasioned me by the rivalry of Wilson, and his intolerable spirit of contradiction, I could not bring myself to hate him altogether. We had, to be sure, nearly every day a quarrel in which, yielding me publicly the palm of victory, he, in some manner, connived to make me feel that it was he who had deserved it; yet a sense of pride on my part, and a veritable dignity on his own,

kept us always upon what are called "speaking terms," while there were many points of strong congeniality in our tempers, operating to awake in me a sentiment which our position alone, perhaps, prevented from ripening into a friendship. . . . To the moralist it will be unnecessary to say, in addition, that Wilson and myself were the most inseparable of companions (pp. 64–65).

In the Clemens story, ambivalence toward conscience is displayed by the narrator's love for his aunt Mary. Poe portrays his quarrel and conflict with conscience as follows:

I have already more than once spoken of the disgusting air of patronage which he assumed toward me, and of his frequent officious interference with my will.[2] This interference often took the ungracious character of advice; advice not openly given, but hinted or insinuated. I received it with repugnance which gained strength as I grew in years. Yet, at this distant day, let me do him the simple justice to acknowledge that I can recall no occasion when the suggestions of my rival were on the side of those errors or follies so usual to his immature age and seeming inexperience; that his moral sense, at least, if not his general talents and worldly wisdom, was far keener than my own; and that I might, today, have been a better, and thus a happier man, had I less frequently rejected the counsels embodied in those meaning whispers [earlier the narrator has spoken a "weakness in the faucial or guttural organs" of his rival which "precluded him from raising his voice at any time above a very low whisper"] which I then but too cordially

[2] Poe begins "William Wilson" with an unidentified quotation: "What say of it? what say of conscience grim, that Spectre in my path?" It is also known that as a youth Poe deeply resented the efforts of his foster father, John Allan, to discipline him.

hated and too bitterly despised (Stern, 1945, pp. 67–68).

Unlike the narrator in "The Facts Concerning the Recent Carnival of Crime in Connecticut," the speaker in "William Wilson" does not question the wisdom and integrity of conscience, theoretically or abstractly; but this does not mean that he likes or accepts his conscience any the better. In fact, he eventually manages to get away from his "rival"— while the latter is sleeping—and to go forth into the world without him, where he engages in "soulless dissipation" and "delirious extravagance." But eventually conscience overtakes him, "catches up" with him, with disastrous consequences:

It was at Rome. . . . I had indulged more freely than usual in the excesses of the wine table. . . . I was anxiously seeking (let me not say with what unworthy motive) the young, the gay, the beautiful wife of the aged and doting Di Broglio. . . . At this moment I felt a light hand placed upon my shoulder, and that everremembered, low, damnable whisper within my ear. In an absolute frenzy of wrath, I turned at once upon him to have thus interrupted me, and seized him violently by the collar. . . .

"Scoundrel!" I said, in a voice husky with rage, while every syllable I uttered seemed as new fuel to my fury, "scoundrel! imposter! accursed villain! you shall not—you *shall* not dog me unto death! Follow me, or I stab you where you where you stand!"—and I broke my way from the ballroom into a small antechamber adjoining—dragging him unresistingly with me as I went. Upon entering, I thrust him furiously from me. He staggered against the wall, while I closed the door with an oath, and commanded him to draw. He hesitated but for an instant; then, with a slight sigh, drew in silence, and put himself upon his defense.

The contest was brief indeed. I was frantic with every species of wild excitement, and felt within my single arm the energy and power of a multitude. In a few seconds I forced him by sheer strength against the wainscoting, and thus, getting him at mercy, plunged my sword, with brute ferocity, repeatedly through and through his bosom (pp. 80–81).

A large mirror,—so at first it seemed to me my confusion—now stood where none had been perceptible before; and, as I stepped up to it in extremity of terror, mine own image, but with features all pale and dabbled in blood, advanced to meet me with a feeble and tottering gait.

It was Wilson: but he spoke no longer in a whisper, and I could have fancied that I myself was speaking while he said: "You have conquered, and I yield. Yet, henceforward art thou also dead—dead to the World, to Heaven and to Hope! In me didst thou exist—and, in my death, see by this image, which is thine own, how utterly thou hast murdered thyself" (p. 82).

With respect to the preceding passage and the "William Wilson" story as a whole, I have previously ventured the following comments (Mowrer, 1950):

This story is replete with psychological implications, but let us at this point follow only one of them. As we have noted earlier, there is a striking resemblance between many of the things Poe is known actually to have said or written to his foster father, John Allan, and the words which Wilson hurls at his double. As Stern (1945) remarks: "The story is autobiographical, not only in its material—the school is the one Poe attended—Stoke Newington—but also in its inner meaning. Of all his stories it tells us most about its author and gives us the best insight into the secret workings of his mind (p. 55).

"And in one of the passages quoted, we get a further intimation of the Oedipus theme: the murder takes place at the point at which Wilson is to keep a rendezvous with "the young, the gay, the beautiful wife of the *aged and doting* Di Broglio."

Freud has emphasized but one facet of the tragedy by Sophocles: the unholy lust of a man for his mother and the lengths to which this fateful passion may lead him. Poe illuminates the other, more important side of the picture: he indicates that in killing one's father one kills an indispensable part of one's self, or *per contra*, in killing conscience one is killing his father—and the host of other forebears of whom one's conscience is representative (p. 627, italics added).

The passages quoted here from "William Wilson" clearly reveal many parallels between this literary endeavor by Poe and the piece by Clemens that we reviewed at the beginning of this essay. Is this coincidence? Do the similarities arise from the inherent nature of the realities that are under discussion? Or had Clemens perhaps read and received inspiration from the Poe story? Clemens does not acknowledge any debt in this regard. But there are certain specific expressions that are at least suggestive. For example, the narrator in "The Facts Concerning the Recent Carnival of Crime in Connecticut" refers to himself, after vanquishing his conscience, as "a man whose heart is dead to sorrow, dead to suffering, dead to remorse." And William Wilson's double says to him, at a similar juncture, "Henceforward art thou also dead—dead to the world, to Heaven and to Hope!" (p. 82). Similarly, Clemens' narrator says: "You have dogged, and dogged, and *dogged* me, all the days of my life" (p. 315). And William Wilson, in one of the passages already quoted, cries: "Scoundrel! . . . you *shall* not dog me unto death" (p. 80).

Painstaking examination of the two essays might reveal still other indications of direct influence; but whether Clemens had or had not read the earlier composition is not really crucial. More to the point is the fact that both men were creating, in a literary manner, an idea, a thesis that was common to their culture, namely: "Be good and you will be happy." And since conscience is a putative aid to goodness, then, in the long run, it also presumably promotes our happiness. Thus the basic question is: Is this thesis, this conception of conscience as having positive value in human existence, really valid?

Should a theory be judged by the life of the man who holds it? Science tends to reject the so-called *ad hominem* argument, but Christianity says: "By their *fruit*s ye shall know them." Opinion is thus divided. But we can at least ask the question: Did the conception of conscience as a reliable guide to life do Poe and Clemens any good? Each suffered from an addiction: Clemens was an inveterate smoker and Poe was a drunkard. (Significantly, in the two pieces examined here, Clemens makes much of his narrator's use of tobacco, and Poe says of Wilson that he "had indulged more freely than usual in the excesses of the wine table" (p. 80). If these men correctly *understood* the role of conscience, why did they not succeed in using this knowledge to free themselves from habits ("symptoms"?) which they both disliked but could not "break"? (Clemens is the author of the quip: "Stopping smoking is the easiest thing in the world—I've done it hundreds of times." And Poe died of alcoholism at the age of 40!)

One approach to the solution of this problem would be to say that it was the ambivalence of each of these men toward conscience that kept him from permitting it to reform him. In other words, despite recognizing intellectually the essential rightness of conscience, they may nevertheless have resented it. At least they both spent a good deal of their energy trying to "deaden" their consciences—first of all by their respective addictions and then, more totally, in fantasy—instead of cooperating with it in their own transformation. Each struggled with his addiction, which he recognized as an evil. But the struggle was unavailing. Why? Could it be that in the lives of both men there was unresolved and unacknowledged personal guilt which they tried to assuage chemically rather than resort to the painful, but more promising, act of self-disclosure? In the act of confession, a person does two things: He cooperates with his conscience or obeys it, in that conscience constantly urges us to admit our uneasy secrets; and he seeks the help of others for himself and, so to say, for his conscience. William James admonished those who would break a bad habit to make a public announcement of their intention. Perhaps even more essential is a "public announcement" of what it is about one's life that makes the habit so strong, so necessary, so compelling.

Freud referred to conscience as the "internalized voice of the community"; and the term conscience (con-science) itself means joint knowledge, what we know with others. Thus it follows that if we refuse to communicate and share, conscience is to this extent weakened, forced to "stand alone," and made to "work" much harder than if it had full community support. Has it not been a pervasive affliction of our age that we have so widely believed a man's behavior to be his own business? And perhaps it was precisely this assumption, nurtured by the sealed confession in Catholicism and the general rejection of confession (except to God) in Protestantism, that created such ambivalence toward conscience that Freud was able to challenge the most time-honored attitudes toward it.

In suggesting this line of thought here, I mean no disrespect to the memory of either Samuel Clemens or Edgar Allan Poe. But I have repeatedly seen people succeed in giving up the use of tobacco after they have come into confessional, or "therapeutic," groups where radical honesty is required; and it is well known that in Alcoholics Anonymous there is a corresponding emphasis upon getting honest, which is commonly referred to as stopping being "stupid" and "phoney." Conventional psychotherapy, including Freudian psychoanalysis, has stressed the importance of the patient telling everything about himself to the therapist, but such openness is not ordinarily extended to the "significant others" in one's life. And the result is that psychotherapy, like religious confession, often fosters continued secrecy and concealment from others.

## IV

On Staten Island, 18 miles south of Manhattan's Battery, is a remarkable experiment in personal and social rehabilitation. It is estimated that more than half of the drug addicts in the nation reside in New York City, and a few years ago Mayor Wagner stated that the depredations of these men and women cost the city $1,000,000 a day in merchandise stolen in order to provide each with the $30 to $50 a day needed for the purchase of drugs.

Guidance and reform of convicted drug addicts who are allowed to return to their old haunts on probation has been dishearteningly ineffective; so it was not surprising when a group of men connected with the Probation Department of the Supreme Court of New York conceived the idea of applying to the National Institute of Mental Health for funds to set up a treatment project involving a new type of community living modeled after the program of Synanon House on Santa Monica beach. A mimeographed preliminary report on this project was prepared by Joseph A. Shelly and Alexander Bassin (1965a), entitled "Daytop Lodge—A New Treatment Approach for Drug Addicts," and I shall draw on this source for further details here:

> A number of the free-flowing, spontaneous aspects of Synanon [at Santa Monica, Calif.] could not be grafted into the somewhat rigid corpus of a court structure. We finally hammered out a research proposal which we trusted would enable us to (a) establish a halfway house for the treatment of drug addicts on probation, (b) to evaluate the rehabilitative effects of such an institution in comparison with results of supervising drug addicts on probation in a small specialized caseload and a large general caseload, (c) formulate and operate a program of activity designed to provide the addict in the halfway house with a value system and status organization leading to his eventual and reasonably speedy integration into normal society, (d) to employ a testing procedure, thin-layer chromatography, to quantify the progress of an abstinence program among the subjects

involved in this experiment and to determine if this chemical procedure may perhaps of itself be an inhibitory mechanism in keeping the addict from returning to the use of narcotics. NIMH, promptly on the heels of the White House Conference on Drug Addiction and Drug Abuse, provided a grant of $390,000 to be expended over a five-year period for this purpose (p. 2).

After unsatisfactory operation of this new facility, called Daytop Lodge, for several months, it was decided to install a former drug addict as manager.

> The new resident manager, David Deitch, is a thin, intense looking, bespectacled man of thirty-one with a history of fourteen continuous years of drug usage. He is capable of addressing a graduate class at the Brooklyn Law School, for example, with the diction, vocabulary, and composure of a first-rate college professor and within a few hours, in the course of providing orientation to a new resident at Daytop, he can spit out an assortment of four-letter expletives to curdle the blood of any aspiring con artist. In his initial employment interview, he explained his life philosophy: "At this stage in time and space, I suffer from few of the moral dilemmas that torment our civilization. I simply ask myself: What is the honest thing to do in this situation and I do it. I don't lie, cheat, deceive. I try to adhere to this personal posture as completely and literally as I can. I know I must be absolutely honest in all my relations, both to save myself and to be a role model for the dope fiends who look to me for guidance."

> Deitch promptly installed two assistants, fellow drug addicts he had trained at Synanon, and with his bride of a few months, Sue, a wonderfully warm-hearted girl of twenty-four, a graduate of Brandeis University, who became acquainted with Deitch when he was director of the Westport facility of Synanon, he moved in as the new manager of Daytop Lodge. Within a week Deitch called us: "Gentlemen, the house is corrupt. It is permeated by the ideology of the streets behind a facade of apparent conformity with your expectations of how a dope fiend behaves when he wants to get well. The house is being run by a clique who see a good thing and are taking advantage of the situation but are not acquiring any character change. I don't know if anybody in the house can be saved. I am going to try some radical surgery to expunge the cancer, but if I don't succeed, it may be necessary to throw out the entire lot and start with a fresh group." He invited us to witness what he termed an attempt at a "mass cop-out" (pp. 3–4).

> Deitch started speaking to the group in a low, intense tone of voice, his person vibrating with the seriousness of his purpose. He told the residents he had been hired to come to the Lodge as a place to cure dope fiends, make honest people of them, not to operate an easy-time point where dopes could pretend they were getting better while they continued living with the basic values of the street and the penitentiary. He said he did not know but that the disease of corruption was so deep and intensive that no operation could save them. He was willing to try. If they wanted to be cured, they must give up all their street ideas, all the values they picked up in prison and other joints. They must be completely honest with him, with each other and with the big society. He could speak because he was a dope fiend and understood exactly how the mind of "us dope fiends" operates. While he was in charge, there would be no compromises or playing the angles. Each man would have to get up and make a public confession of his wrong-doing inside and outside the house, if he wished to remain. The sooner

a man spoke up in this public cop-out, the better for him. The longer he fought it, the harder it would eventually become. Who would be the first to speak up? (pp. 4–5).

After the population of Daytop Lodge was thus shaken-down and the sincere and insincere members discriminated, the program resumed more or less routine operation.

All features of our treatment approach were described in the original proposal to NIMH, but seemed to take on new meaning and direction under the supervision of Deitch (p. 6).

During the early orientation interviews, the [newly arrived] addict will repeatedly be advised that despite his physical stature and chronological age, he is a child in terms of maturity, responsibility, and ability to think ahead. He will be regarded as a three-year-old who must be told what to do with the expectation that if he disobeys he will be punished promptly. The whole design of the program is to help him grow from a child of three to an adult. There is only one year available for this progress, so he'll have to work hard if he wants to make it. On the other hand, if he wishes to return to chasing the bag, to be a childish dope fiend, to die in some gutter from an o.d. (overdose), that would be his decision (p. 7).

Then the newcomer is advised that we have little confidence in the usual preoccupation of social workers, psychologists, and psychiatrists with the finding of the essential *cause* of his addiction. The dope fiend uses the professional to slough off responsibility for his behavior. The personnel at Daytop do not permit the addict to blame his behavior on his parents, the school, the neighborhood, associates, or society. The only cause recognized at Daytop for being a dope fiend is *stupidity*.

In other words, the concept of the drug addict as an ill person and therefore automatically entitled to the recognized prerogatives of the role of the ill in our society in terms of sympathetic understanding, special concern, lenience, and forgiveness is vehemently fought as an ideology.

"Did anybody force you to stick a dirty needle into your arm and inject yourself with milk sugar?" the addict is challenged. "Was it your father or mother who insisted you shoot up? Was it the tough cop on the beat? Was it your girlfriend or schoolteacher? Did anybody twist your arm? Who?"

If the addict attempts to extricate himself from his tendency to throw blame in all directions, the residents and staff bring him to the reality of his behavior: that he alone is to blame and the only tenable explanation for his behavior is simple, unadulterated *stupidity* on his part (p. 7).

The interested reader should peruse the Shelly and Bassin article in its entirety (for a modified published version, see Shelly & Bassin, 1965b). But enough has already been reported here to show that at Daytop Lodge (now expanded into Daytop Village, with more than one hundred residents) there is no intimation that the way to become a normal, happy human being is to get rid of conscience. Daytop is energetically engaged, from early morning until late at night, seven days a week, in conscience development, character building. And the whole notion that too much conscience will make you "sick" is categorically and consistently rejected.

"But," it may be objected, "the drug addict is a sociopath, a criminal, with an admittedly defective character structure. Thus, the Daytop approach may be appropriate for him. But the neurotic, the *true* neurotic is a victim, not of under-socialization, but of oversocialization and thus calls for a different type of approach."

This issue is not something that can be settled on mere authority or by fiat. It is an empirical question, and in a paper entitled "New Evidence Concerning the Nature of Psychopathology" (Mowrer, 1968), we find that the evidence clearly favors the view that *both* the neurotic and the sociopath represent socialization inadequacy, but that the failure is greater, more deepseated in the socio-path.

But perhaps the drug addict is not a sociopath after all. It is true that male addicts steal and rob and that female addicts are commonly involved in prostitution and shoplifting. But these activities are often merely the adaptations forced upon them by the exigencies of their addiction. Why, then, the addiction? Probably, in many instances, for the same reason that other persons who suffer from anxiety and depression resort to psychotherapy, seek prescriptions for legitimate drugs, or become alcoholic.

In January, 1966, I had the privilege of living for three days at Daytop Village, and I can personally attest to the integrity and great promise of the program. The place is extremely orderly, organized like a tightly run battle ship, and discipline is quiet but inexorable. There are two inviolable rules: no "chemicals" and no physical violence. Conversation is animated but "clean." And the conduct of male and female residents with respect to one another is exemplary. Continuation in the program is always on a strictly voluntary basis, in that there are no bars and no locks, but "splits" are now exceedingly rare. Most of the residents have found here a new

style of life and a new meaning, a new reason for existence. And they do not wish to leave it. Extensive statistics are not yet available, but the preliminary results are excitingly good.

After my visit to Daytop, Dr. Daniel Casriel, then Medical Director for the project, concluded a letter by saying: "I do believe we are on the right path in the rehabilitation of the maladjusted." And this, after years of unsuccessful efforts on his part to cope with the problem of drug addiction by conventional treatment methods!

## Summary

During the "Freudian era" (roughly 1920 to 1955), the prevailing supposition on the part of most psychotherapists was that functional personality disturbances arise because persons thus afflicted have an excessively severe, rigid, tyrannical conscience; and remedial efforts commonly involved an attempt to make conscience more flexible, reasonable, permissive. It is now widely recognized that therapy based on this "diagnosis" has been conspicuously unsuccessful.

In the present chapter, two pre-Freudian literary treatises on the nature and function of conscience (one by Samuel Clemens and the other by Edgar Allan Poe) have been examined, in both of which it is implied that it is violation of the behests of conscience, rather than excessive severity thereof, that causes some (although not necessarily all) "neurotic" disturbances. This point of view seems to have been widely held prior to the advent of Freudianism.

In the late 1950s and early 1960s, remarkably successful residential programs for the rehabilitation of drug addicts (formerly regarded as "incurable") came into existence which are based, not upon the theories of Freud, but upon the more traditional view that conscience is a necessary and normally helpful part of the human personality. Difficulties arise, it seems, only when conscience is defective, deadened by drugs or alcohol, or consciously and deliberately disregarded. These latter developments are more congruent with the traditional, positive view of conscience than with the negative, disparaging attitude of Freud and his followers.

It is not maintained that "conscience killing" is the *only* cause of personality disorders—constitutional (genetic) and environmental (ecological) factors are also recognized as frequently being relevant in this connection. But the thrust of the present discussion has been to suggest that in what may be called characterological neuroses, conscience is not the villain, but rather the victim, of disregard and mistreatment.

## References

BRASHEAR, M. M., & RODNEY, R. M. (Eds.) *The art, humor, and humanity of Mark Twain*. Norman, Okla.: University of Oklahoma Press, 1959.

FORBES, G. M. Installation address. (Mimeographed) United Church of Christ, 856 State Street, Vermilion, Ohio, 1966.

MOWRER, O. H. The life and work of Edgar Allan Poe—A study in conscience-killing. In *Learning theory and personality dynamics*. New York: Ronald, 1950. Pp. 617–670.

MOWRER, O. H. Transference and scrupulosity as reactions to unresolved guilt. *Journal of Religion & Health*, 1963, **3,** 313–343.

MOWRER, O. H. *The new group therapy*. Princeton, N.J.: Van Nostrand, 1964.

MOWRER, O. H. Learning theory and behavior therapy. In B. Wolman (Ed.), *Handbook of clinical psychology*. New York: McGraw-Hill, 1965. Pp. 242–276.

MOWRER, O. H. New evidence concerning the nature of psychopathology. In M. J. Feldman (Ed.), *Studies in psychotherapy and behavior change*. Buffalo, N.Y.: University of Buffalo Press, 1968. Pp. 111–193.

POE, E. A. William Wilson. In P. V. D. Stern (Ed.), *Edgar Allen Poe*. New York: Viking, 1945.

SHELLY, J. A., & BASSIN, A. Daytop Lodge—A new treatment approach for drug addicts. (Mimeographed) Probation Department, Supreme Court of the State of New York, Municipal Building, Brooklyn, N.Y., 1965. (a)

SHELLY, J. A., & BASSIN, A. Daytop Lodge—A new treatment approach for drug addicts. *Corrective Psychiatry*, 1965, **11,** 186–195. (b)

STERN, P. V. D. *Edgar Allan Poe*. New York: Viking, 1945.

TKACIK, A. Conscience: Conscious and unconscious. *Journal of Religion & Health*, 1964, **4,** 75–85.

# Section II
# THE MEASUREMENT OF CONSCIENCE

## Introduction

A major difference between literary and behavioral science approaches to conscience lies in the scientific requirement of measurement. This section presents two classic approaches to assessing conscience and a review of the many other measurement efforts in this area.

The excerpt from Piaget's *The Moral Judgment of the Child* illustrates his approach to measuring cognitive differences among children of different ages through their evaluations of certain moral situations. The developmental issue considered is the change in children from *objective* moral realism (the tendency to judge an act in terms of its consequences) to *subjective* morality (the tendency to judge an act in terms of the motives underlying the act).

Piaget's approach to the development of moral judgment stemmed from the ideas of Durkheim, Fauconnet, Bovet, and J. M. Baldwin. Durkheim attempted to show the functional equivalence of co-operation and constraint by suggesting that whether a group holds a set of beliefs voluntarily (as a result of cooperation) or involuntarily (as a result of constraint and coercion), the group adheres to these beliefs in essentially the same fashion. Piaget argues that these two social phenomena are qualitatively different both in origin and in effect and that Durkheim overvalued the efficacy of external coercion and constraint while underestimating the role of cooperation and individual, inner restraint in determining human social behavior. Further, Piaget feels that Durkheim did not consider any developmental phenomena in his study of morality. Piaget criticized Fauconnet on essentially the same grounds.

Bovet, on the other hand, did concern himself with the developmental aspects of moral judgment and Piaget asserts that his own work can be considered an extension of Bovet's. Bovet took the position that the development of moral judgment in the child is dependent upon the child's relations with adults and that all children, no matter what the adults in their society believe, accept a system of objective (concern for consequences, not motives), communicable (guilt by association) responsibility, a system that is produced by adult constraint. Bovet believed that the development of autonomy of conscience within the individual, which necessarily involves the development of subjective (consideration of acts in terms of motives), individual (rejection of guilt by association) responsibility, is caused by the clash of rules that the child receives from various sources. Piaget is not in complete agreement, however, since he believes that Bovet failed to consider the effect of mutual respect and cooperation of the peer group on the development of mature moral judgment. Piaget suggested that group cooperation, far more than the clash in rules, causes the child to develop a belief in subjective, individual responsibility.

Further, according to Piaget, neither Durkheim, Fauconnet, nor Bovet was aware of the egocentricity (inability to take the role of the other) and concreteness of the child's mind, which make the young child peculiarly susceptible to belief in objective, communicable responsibility. Only J. M. Baldwin concerned himself with these problems of mental structure, as well as with social phenomena. For Baldwin, as for Bovet, social relations involving adult constraint initiate the development of a sense of duty that incorporates a concept of objective,

communicable responsibility. Qualitative changes in intelligence (not Bovet's clash of rules, nor Piaget's peer-group cooperation) produce autonomy of conscience, which in turn leads to subjective, individual responsibility. Piaget says that Baldwin was in error in separating social relations from intellect, since it is through social relations, especially through cooperation and reciprocity, that there arises the intellectual growth in evaluative abilities necessary for a change to subjective, individual responsibility.

Piaget finds that each of these writers has neglected at least one aspect of the interaction of individual and society in his treatment of the problem of moral judgment. Piaget sees three forces interacting to produce developmental change in moral judgment: (1) adult constraint; (2) peer-group cooperation and reciprocity; and (3) the changing character of the child's mind. Piaget believes that there are age changes in the types of moral judgments used by individuals and that these changes result from the interaction of these three forces. His work on morality is an attempt to prove his position. Although he does show that age changes occur, he does not provide any empirical support for his ideas concerning the causal agents involved in producing this age change.

The second paper presents Hartshorne and May's situational and behavioral tests of honesty. Their apparent and abundant ingenuity has been a model to psychological researchers over the years. Finally, a recent review by Pittel and Mendelsohn, concentrating on moral values, concludes the section.

# 4

# Adult constraint and moral realism

*by Jean Piaget*[1]

We have had occasion to see during our analysis of the rules of a game that the child begins by regarding these rules not only as obligatory, but also as inviolable and requiring to be kept to literally. We also showed that this attitude was the result of the constraint exercised by the older children on the younger and of the pressure of adults themselves, rules being thus identified with duties properly so called.

It is this problem of unilateral or one-sided respect, or of the effects of moral constraint, that we shall now approach through a more direct study of the child's conception of his duties and of moral values in general. But the subject is vast; and we shall try to limit the range of enquiry as much as possible. We shall therefore confine ourselves to an aspect of the question which has perhaps received less attention than others —the moral judgment itself. We were able before to observe concurrently external and internal facts, to analyze both practice and consciousness of rules. But now, in view of the enormously greater technical difficulties which attend the study of the relations between children

Reprinted with permission of the Macmillan Company and Routledge & Kegan Paul Ltd. from *The Moral Judgment of the Child* by Jean Piaget (trans. Marjorie Gabain), pp. 104–135. First published in 1932.

[1] In collaboration with M. N. Maso.

and adults, we shall have to limit ourselves to the consciousness of rules, and even to the most crystallized and least living part of this consciousness—we mean what may be called the theoretical moral judgment as opposed to that which occurs in actual experience. But we are able to confine ourselves to this special problem because numerous works have already told us all about the child's practice of moral rules and the conflicts that take place in his mind. A particularly large amount of work has been done, for example, on the subject of lying. Research of this kind is therefore the equivalent to the descriptions we have given of the practice of rules in the sphere of play, and it is therefore quite natural that we should confine ourselves to the study of children's judgments on such matters, judgments about lying, about truthfulness, etc.

In thus comparing the moral judgments of the child with what we know of his behavior in the corresponding spheres of action, we shall endeavor to show that, as we were led to conclude in the case of game rules, the earliest forms assumed by a child's sense of duty are essentially heteronomous forms. We shall return, in this connection, to our hypotheses concerning the relations of heteronomy and egocentrism. Heteronomy, as we saw, was in no way sufficient to produce a mental change, and constraint and egocentrism were good bedfellows. This is more or less the same result as we shall find in studying the effects of adult constraint. Finally, we saw that cooperation was necessary for the conquest of moral autonomy. Now, such a hypothesis can be proved only by a close analysis of the way in which moral rules are at a given moment assimilated and freely adopted by the child.

In this chapter we shall study primarily the effects of moral constraint, though we shall also establish some of the landmarks for the outline of cooperation which will be given later on. Now, moral constraint is closely akin to intellectual constraint, and the strictly literal character which the child tends to ascribe to rules received from without bears, as we shall see, a close resemblance to the attitudes he adopts with regard to language and the intellectual realities imposed upon him by the adult. We can make use of this analogy to fix our nomenclature and shall speak of *moral realism* to designate on the plane of judgments of value what corresponds to "nominal realism" and even verbalism or conceptual realism on the plane of theoretical reasoning. Not only this, but just as realism in general . . . results both from a confusion between subjective and objective (hence from egocentrism) and from the intellectual constraint of the adult, so also does moral realism result from the intersection of these two kinds of causes.

We shall therefore call moral realism the tendency which the child has to regard duty and the value attaching to it as self-subsistent and independent of the mind, as imposing itself regardless of the circumstances in which the individual may find himself.

Moral realism thus possesses at least three features. In the first place, duty, as viewed by moral realism, is essentially heteronomous. Any act that shows obedience to a rule or even to an adult, regardless of what he may command, is good; any act that does not conform to rules is bad. A rule is therefore not in any way something elaborated, or even judged and interpreted by the mind; it is given as such, ready made and exter-

nal to the mind. It is also conceived of as revealed by the adult and imposed by him. The good, therefore, is rigidly defined by obedience.

In the second place, moral realism demands that the letter rather than the spirit of the law shall be observed. This feature derives from the first. Yet it would be possible to imagine an ethic of heteronomy based on the spirit of the rules and not on their most hard and fast contents. Such an attitude would already have ceased to be realist; it would tend towards rationality and inwardness. But at the very outset of the moral evolution of the child, adult constraint produces, on the contrary, a sort of literal realism of which we shall see many examples later on.

In the third place, moral realism induces an objective conception of responsibility. We can even use this as a criterion of realism, for such an attitude towards responsibility is easier to detect than the two that precede it. For since he takes rules literally and thinks of good only in terms of obedience, the child will at first evaluate acts not in accordance with the motive that has prompted them but in terms of their exact conformity with established rules. Hence this objective responsibility of which we shall see the clearest manifestations in the moral judgment of the child.

## 1. The Method

Before proceeding to the analysis of the facts, it will be as well to discuss in a few words the method we propose to adopt. The only good method in the study of moral facts is surely to observe as closely as possible the greatest possible number of individuals. Difficult children, whom parents and teachers send or ought to send up for psycho-therapeutic treatment, supply the richest material for analysis. In addition to this, education in the home constantly gives rise to the most perplexing problems. Now, the removal of these problems cannot always, unfortunately for the children, depend solely upon the "common sense" of the parents, and the educational technique necessary for their solution is, in some respects, the best instrument of analysis at the disposal of the psychologist. We shall therefore do our utmost in the sequel to give as valid only such results as do not contradict observation in family life.

Only, here again, as in the case of intellectual notions, while pure observation is the only sure method, it allows for the acquisition of no more than a small number of fragmentary facts. And we therefore consider that it must be completed by questioning children at school. We shall speak of these interrogatories now, whilst we may have to postpone until a later date the publication of the observations we have been able to make on our own children. If, however, questioning in the intellectual field is relatively easy, in spite of the many difficulties of method which it raises, in the moral sphere it can only be, as it were, about reality once removed. You can make a child reason about a problem of physics or logic. That brings you into contact, not indeed with spontaneous thought, but at least with thought in action. But you cannot make a child act in a laboratory in order to dissect his moral conduct. A moral problem presented to the child is far further removed from his moral practice than is an intellectual problem from his logical

practice. It is only in the domain of games—if there—that the methods of the laboratory will enable us to analyze a reality in the making. As to the moral rules which the child receives from the adult, no direct investigation is to be thought of by interrogation. Let us therefore make the best of it and try to examine, not the act, but simply the judgment of moral value. In other words, let us analyze, not the child's actual decisions nor even his memory of his actions, but the way he evaluates a given piece of conduct.

Here, moreover, a fresh difficulty raises its head. We shall not be able to make the child realize concretely the types of behavior that we submit to him for judgment, as we could in handing him a game of marbles or a mechanism of any sort. We shall only be able to describe them by means of a story, obviously a very indirect method. To ask a child to say what he thinks about actions that are merely told to him—can this have the least connection with child morality? On the one hand, it may be that what the child thinks about morality has no precise connection with what he does and feels in his concrete experience. Thus the interrogatory of children of 5 to 7 about marbles revealed the strangest discrepancy between actual practice of the rules and reflection about them. On the other hand, it may also be that what the child actually understands of the stories suggested to him bears no relation to what he would think if he were to witness these scenes himself.

We must not attempt to solve these difficulties of method by means of any a priori considerations. We wish only to draw attention to them and to the theoretical interest of the problems which they raise. For we are faced with purely general questions on the relations that hold between verbal judgment and the practical application of thought, whether intellectual or moral. It is quite true that research on intelligence is easier than on morality; but this holds only of the functioning of thought, not of its content. When, in order to get at this content, one is obliged, as we have been in the past, to question the child about his own beliefs, the problem is the same. The question may therefore be formulated as follows. Does verbal thought, i.e., thought that works upon ideas evoked by language and not upon objects perceived in the course of action, does verbal thought consist in the conscious realization (allowing of course for various systematic distortions) of truly spontaneous thought, or does it sustain with the latter no relations whatever? Be the answer what it may, this question is one of fundamental importance in human psychology. Is man merely a maker of phrases that have no relation to his real actions, or is the need to formulate part of his very being? The question strikes deep, and to solve it we must, amongst other things, study it in the child. In the child as in ourselves there is a layer of purely verbal thought superposed, as it were, over his active thought. It is not only during the interrogatories that he invents stories. He is telling them to himself all the time, and it is relatively easy to prove that the stories invented in psychological experiments are roughly analogous to those that arise spontaneously. (We were able to show, for example, that the results obtained by questioning the child on the various aspects of his conception of the world corresponded in the main with what was revealed by direct observation and by the analysis of "whys" in particular.) But the problem remains. In what

relation does the verbal thought of the child stand to his active and concrete thought?

The problem is of special interest in the sphere of morality, and the difficulties of the method we are going to use must be subjected to systematic scrutiny. The object of this scrutiny will not be the justification or condemnation of our method (any method that leads to constant results is interesting, and only the meaning of the results is a matter for discussion) but to help towards a more definite statement of the problem of "moral theories."

To begin with the adult. There are, on the one hand, authors who deem it indispensable for the mind to codify its norms, or at any rate to reflect upon the nature of moral action. Such people therefore accept, with or without discussion, this postulate of an existing relation between moral reflection and moral practice—saying either that the latter springs from the former, or that reflection is the conscious realization of action or action coming into consciousness. There are, on the other hand, individuals whose personal conduct, incidentally, may be beyond criticism, but who do not believe in "morality." Kant and Durkheim are typical representatives of the first tendency, Pareto is the most typical of living authors of the second. According to him, only actions exist, some of which are logical, others nonlogical, i.e., instinctive, or colored with affectivity. Added to this and on a completely different plane there is a sort of rambling chatter, whose function is to reinforce action but whose contents may be devoid of any intelligible meaning. This chatter—multiform and arbitrary "derivations" founded on the affective residues of nonlogical actions—this chatter is what constitutes our ethical theories!

The point, then, that we have to settle is whether the things that children say to us constitute, as compared to their real conduct, a conscious realization or a "derivation," reflection (in the etymological sense of the word), or psittacism. . . . We do not claim to have solved the problem completely. Only direct observation can settle it. But to enable us to give the casting vote to observation, we shall first have to find out what are the child's verbal ideas on morality. And this is why we consider our researches to be useful, whatever may be their ultimate result. Moreover, the study of rules which we undertook in the last chapter [not reprinted in this volume] has already supplied us with the most precious indication. Broadly speaking, we found there to be in this domain a certain correspondence (not simple but yet quite definable) between children's judgments about rules and their practice of these same rules. Let us therefore carry our analysis of the problem a stage further.

What, in the first place, are the relations between judgment of value and the moral act itself? Here is a child who declares it to be perfectly legitimate to tell his father about his brother's misdeeds. Another child answers that even if the father asks, it is "horrid"[2] (Fr., *vilain*) to tell tales: it is better to "spin a yarn" (Fr. *dire des blagues*) than to let a

brother be punished. The problem is to know whether in practice these two children would really have considered valid the two courses of action which they recommend verbally.

We must be on our guard here against a certain ambiguity. Some experiments have tried to measure the moral value of a child by testing of his moral judgment. Mlle Descoeudres, for example, holds the view that a child who pronounces correctly on the values of actions he is told about, is, on the whole, better than one whose moral judgment is less acute. This may be, but it is also conceivable that intelligence alone might suffice to sharpen the child's evaluation of conduct without necessarily inclining him to do good actions. In this case an intelligent scamp would perhaps give better answers than a slow-witted but really good-hearted little boy. Besides, how is the psychologist to classify the moral worth of children even by the ordinary common-sense standards? Such a classification, possible in extreme cases, would run the risk of inaccuracy in normal cases, which are precisely those where we want to know whether testing moral judgment will help us to know the child.

But apart from this question, which does not really interest us here, it may well be asked whether the judgment of value given by the child during an interrogatory is the same as he would give in practice, independently of the actual decision which he would take. A given child, for example, will tell us during the interrogation that the lie *a* is worse than the lie *b*. Now, whether he tells lies himself or not, whether, that is, he is or is not what he calls "good," we take the liberty to wonder whether, in action, he will still consider lie *a* worse than lie *b*. What we are after is not how the child

<hr />

2 While in most of the interrogatories we have translated *vilain* by "naughty," the reader should note that the English word has an exclusively authoritative ring which the French has not. Children can only be naughty in reference to grown-ups. Indeed, the word is so powerful a weapon in the hands of adult constraint in this country that its use in any verbal experiments made on English children would probably give appreciably different results from those based on the word *vilain*. [Trans.]

puts his moral creed into practice (we saw in connection with the game of marbles that a mystical respect for rules can go hand in hand with a purely egocentric application of them) but how he judges of good and evil in the performance of his own actions. It is from this point of view only that we set ourselves the problem of discovering whether the judgments of value given in the interrogatories do or do not correspond to the genuine evaluations of moral thought.

Now, it may be that there is correlation between verbal or theoretical judgment and the concrete evaluations that operate in action (independently of whether these evaluations are followed up by real decisions). We have often noted that in the intellectual field the child's verbal thinking consists of a progressive coming into consciousness, or conscious realization of schemas that have been built up by action. In such cases verbal thought simply lags behind concrete thought, since the former has to reconstruct symbolically and on a new plane operations that have already taken place on the preceding level. Old difficulties, which have been overcome on the plane of action will therefore reappear or merely survive on the verbal plane. There is a time-lag between the concrete phases and the verbal phases of one and the same process. It may therefore very well be that in the moral sphere there is simply a time-lag between the child's concrete evaluations and his theoretical judgment of value, the latter being an adequate and progressive conscious realization of the former. We shall meet with children who, for example, take no account of intentions in appraising actions on the verbal plane (objective responsibility), but who, when asked for personal experiences, show that they take full account of the intentions that come into play. It may be that in such cases the theoretical simply lags behind the practical moral judgment and shows in an adequate manner a stage that has been superseded on the plane of action.

But there may also be no connection whatever between the two. On this view, the child's moral theories would be mere chatter, unrelated to his concrete evaluations. Further—and the eventuality is still more important in the moral than in the intellectual sphere—it may be for the benefit of the adult rather than for his own use that the child gives his answers. Let there be no mistake on this point: it is quite certain that in the great majority of cases the child is perfectly sincere during the experiment. Only, he is quite likely to think that what is expected of him is a moral lecture rather than an original reflection. We have talked with children of 10, for example, who defended the moral value of "telling tales," but who made a *volte face* as soon as they saw we were not convinced. Thus their real thought was masked and hidden even from their own eyes by the momentary desire to pronounce moral precepts pleasing to the adult. True, only the older ones reacted in this way. But does not this show that the little ones do not dissociate their own thought from what they hear constantly being said by their parents and teachers? Is it not the case that the verbal thought of the child up to 10–11 is simply a repetition or a distortion of adult thought, bearing no relation to the real moral evaluations which the child practices in his own life?

To settle this point we can turn to what we learned in our enquiry into the game of marbles. On the one hand, we were able to see how the children put the rules into practice and how they evaluated their duties as players in the midst of the game itself. On the other hand, we succeeded in collecting on the subject of these same rules certain moral theories obviously made up on the spot and therefore grounded on purely theoretical moral judgments. Now there was, we repeat, between the action and the theory of the child a correspondence that was, if not simple, at least definable. To the egocentric practice of rules which goes hand in hand with a feeling of respect for elder or adult, there corresponds a theoretical judgment which turns a rule into something mystical and transcendental. In this first case, theoretical judgment does not correspond to action itself but to the judgments that accompany action. But this is quite natural, since egocentrism is unconscious, and only the respect to which the child believes that he is submitting himself is conscious. To the rational practice of rules, which goes hand in hand with mutual respect, there corresponds a theoretical judgment which attributes to rules a purely autonomous character. Thus in the sphere of play at least, theoretical judgment corresponds to practical judgment. This does not mean that theoretical judgment interprets the child's real action but that in the main it corresponds to the judgments pronounced by the child in the course of his action. We can at the most admit that verbal judgment lags behind effective judgment: the idea of autonomy appears in the child about a year later than cooperative behavior and the practical consciousness of autonomy.

With regard to the domains we are now approaching (lying, justice, etc.) we may therefore advance the hypothesis that the verbal and theoretical judgment of the child corresponds, broadly speaking, with the concrete and practical judgments which the child may have made on the occasion of his own actions during the years preceding the interrogatory. There can be no doubt that verbal thought lags behind active thought, but it does not seem to us to be unrelated to the past stages of active thought. The future will show whether this hypothesis is too bold. In any case, verbal thought, whether moral or intellectual, deserves the closest study. Nor is it peculiar to the child. In the adult, as the work of Pareto sufficiently shows, it plays a considerable part in the mechanism of social life.

Finally, allowance must be made for the fact that the verbal evaluations made by our children are not of actions of which they have been authors or witnesses, but of stories which are told to them. The child's evaluation will therefore be, as it were, verbal to the second degree. The psychologist Fernald has tried to obviate this disadvantage by the following device. He [sic] tells the children several stories and then simply asks them to classify them. Mlle Descoeudres, applying this method, submits, for example, five lies to children, who are then required to classify them in order of gravity. This, roughly, is also the procedure that we shall follow, though we shall of course not deny ourselves the right, once the classification has been made, to converse freely with the children so as to get at the reasons for their evaluations.

But the greatest caution must be exercised in order to avoid needless complications. For instance, it does not seem to us possible to tell the children more than two stories at a time. If the subject is confronted with a series, the classification will call for an intellectual effort that has nothing to do with moral evaluation: he will forget three stories out of five, and will compare any two at random, which gives results of no particular interest. Further, after using the usual stories, we soon realized that their style placed them far beyond the child's complete comprehension. In psychology one must speak to children in their own language, otherwise the experiment resolves itself into a trial of intelligence or of verbal understanding.

But even when we have taken all these precautions, one problem still remains: if the child had witnessed the scenes we describe to him, would he judge them in the same manner? We think not. In real life the child is in the presence, not of isolated acts, but of personalities that attract or repel him as a global whole. He grasps people's intentions by direct intuition and cannot therefore abstract from them. He allows, more or less justly, for aggravating and attenuating circumstances. This is why the stories told by the children themselves often give rise to different evaluations from those suggested by the experimenter's stories. Only, we repeat it, it may simply be the case that the evaluations obtained from the stories that were told to them lag in time behind the direct evaluations of daily life.

In conclusion, the results of our method do not seem to us devoid of interest. For they are relatively constant and, above all, they evolve with a certain regularity according to age. All that we have said before about the criteria of good clinical interrogatories . . . applies here. And, in addition, it is our belief that in everyday life, as in the course of the interrogatory, the child must often

be faced not only with concrete actions but also with accounts and verbal appraisals of actions. It is therefore important to know what is his attitude in such circumstances. In short, here as always, the way of really tackling the problem is not to accept and record the results of the experiment, but to know how to place them in regard to the child's real life taken as a whole. And this cannot be done at the outset of our enquiry into this most difficult field of research.

## 2. Objective Responsibility: Clumsiness and Stealing

We noted, in connection with the rules of a game, that the child seems to go through a stage when rules constitute an obligatory and untouchable reality. We must now see how far this moral realism goes, and in particular whether adult constraint, which is probably its cause, is sufficient to give rise to the phenomenon of objective responsibility. For all that we have been saying about the difficulties of interpretation in the study of the moral judgments of children need not put a stop to our enquiry in this matter. It is immaterial whether the objective responsibility of which we are about to give examples is connected with the whole of the child's life or only with the most external and verbal aspects of his moral thought. The problem still remains as to where this responsibility comes from and why it develops.

The questions put to the children on this point are those whose results we shall study first, but they were actually the last that we thought of. We began, by way of introduction, with the problem of judgments relating to telling lies. In making this analysis, of which we shall speak in the following sections, we immediately noticed that the younger children often measured the gravity of a lie not in terms of the motives which dictated it, but in terms of the falseness of its statements. It was in order to verify the existence and the generality of this tendency to objective responsibility that we devised the following questions.

The first set of questions deals with the consequences of clumsiness. Clumsiness plays, however unjustly, an enormously important part in a child's life, as he comes into conflict with his adult surrounding. At every moment, the child arouses the anger of those around him by breaking, soiling, or spoiling some object or other. Most of the time such anger is unjustifiable, but the child is naturally led to attach a meaning to it. On other occasions, his clumsiness is more or less due to carelessness or disobedience, and an idea of some mysterious and immanent justice comes to be grafted onto the emotions experienced at the time. We therefore tried to make the children compare the stories of two kinds of clumsiness, one entirely fortuitous or even the result of a well-intentioned act, but involving considerable material damage, the other negligible as regards the damage done, but happening as the result of an ill-intentioned act.

Here are the stories:

**I. A.** A little boy who is called John is in his room. He is called to dinner. He goes into the dining room. But behind the door there was a chair, and on the chair there was a tray with fifteen cups on it. John couldn't have known that there was all this behind the door. He goes in, the door knocks against the tray, bang go the fifteen cups and they all get broken!

**B.** Once there was a little boy whose name was Henry. One day when his mother was out he tried to get some jam out of the cupboard. He climbed up onto a chair and stretched out his arm. But the jam was too high up and he couldn't reach it and have any. But while he was trying to get it he knocked over a cup. The cup fell down and broke.

**II. A.** There was a little boy called Julian. His father had gone out and Julian thought it would be fun to play with his father's ink-pot. First he played with the pen, and then he made a little blot on the table cloth.

**B.** A little boy who was called Augustus once noticed that his father's ink-pot was empty. One day that his father was away he thought of filling the ink-pot so as to help his father, and so that he should find it full when he came home. But while he was opening the ink-bottle he made a big blot on the table cloth.

**III. A.** There was once a little girl who was called Marie. She wanted to give her mother a nice surprise, and cut out a piece of sewing for her. But she didn't know how to use the scissors properly and cut a big hole in her dress.

**B.** A little girl called Margaret went and took her mother's scissors one day that her mother was out. She played with them for a bit. Then as she didn't know how to use them properly she made a little hole in her dress.

When we have analyzed the answers obtained by means of these pairs of stories, we shall study two problems relating to stealing. As our aim is for the moment to find out whether the child pays more attention to motive or to material results, we have confined ourselves to the comparison of selfishly motivated acts of stealing with those that are well-intentioned.

**IV. A.** Alfred meets a little friend of his who is very poor. This friend tells him that he has had no dinner that day because there was nothing to eat in his home. Then Alfred goes into a baker's shop, and as he has no money, he waits till the baker's back is turned and steals a roll. Then he runs out and gives the roll to his friend.

**B.** Henriette goes into a shop. She sees a pretty piece of ribbon on a table and thinks to herself that it would look very nice on her dress. So while the shop lady's back is turned (while the shop lady is not looking), she steals the ribbon and runs away at once.

**V. A.** Albertine had a little friend who kept a bird in a cage. Albertine thought the bird was very unhappy, and she was always asking her friend to let him out. But the friend wouldn't. So one day when her friend wasn't there, Albertine went and stole the bird. She let it fly away and hid the cage in the attic so that the bird should never be shut up in it again.

**B.** Juliet stole some sweeties from her mother one day that her mother was not there, and she hid and ate them up.

About each of these pairs of stories we ask two questions: (1) Are these children equally guilty (or as the young Genevese say "la même chose vilain")? (2) Which of the two is the naughtiest, and why? It goes without saying that each of these questions is the occasion for a conversation more or less elaborate according to the child's reaction. It is also as well to make the subjects repeat the stories before questioning them. The way the child reproduces the story is enough to show whether he has understood it.

We obtained the following result. Up to the age of 10, two types of answer exist side by side. In one type actions are evaluated in terms of the material result and independently of motives; according to the other type of answer motives alone are what counts. It may even happen that one and the same child judges sometimes one way, sometimes the other. Besides, some stories point more definitely to objective responsibility than others. In detail, therefore, the material cannot be said to embody stages properly so called. Broadly speaking, however, it cannot be denied that the notion of objective responsibility diminishes as the child grows older. We did not come across a single definite case of it after the age of 10. In addition, by placing the answers obtained under 10 into two groups defined respectively by objective and by subjective responsibility (reckoning by answers given to each story and not by children, since each child is apt to vary from one story to another) we obtained 7 as the average age for objective responsibility, and 9 as the average age for subjective responsibility. Now, we were unable to question children under 6 with any profit because of the intellectual difficulties of comparison. The average of 7 years therefore represents the youngest of the children. If the two attitudes simply represented individual types or types of family education, the two age averages ought to coincide. But since this is not so, there must be some degree of development present. We can at least venture to submit that even if the objective and the subjective conceptions of responsibility are not, properly speaking, features of two successive stages, they do at least define two distinct processes, one of which on the average precedes the other in the moral development of the child, although the two partially synchronize.

Having made this point clear, let us

now turn to the facts, beginning with the stories about clumsiness. Here are typical answers showing a purely objective notion of responsibility.

*I. The Stories of the Broken Cups*

**Geo (6):** "Have you understood these stories?—*Yes.*—What did the first boy do?—*He broke eleven cups.*—And the second one?—*He broke a cup by moving roughly.*—Why did the first one break the cups?—*Because the door knocked them.*—And the second?—*He was clumsy. When he was getting the jam the cup fell down.*—Is one of the boys naughtier than the other?—*The first is because he knocked over twelve cups.*—If you were the daddy, which one would you punish most?—*The one who broke twelve cups.*—Why did he break them?—*The door shut too hard and knocked them. He didn't do it on purpose.*—And why did the other boy break a cup?—*He wanted to get the jam. He moved too far. The cup got broken.*—Why did he want to get the jam?—*Because he was all alone. Because his mother wasn't there.*—Have you got a brother?—*No, a little sister.*—Well, if it was you who had broken the twelve cups when you went into the room and your little sister who had broken one cup while she was trying to get the jam, which of you would be punished most severely?—*Me, because I broke more than one cup.*"

**Schma (6):** "Have you understood the stories? Let's hear you tell them.—*A little child was called in to dinner. There were fifteen plates on a tray. He didn't know. He opens the door and he breaks the fifteen plates.*—That's very good. And now the second story?—*There was a child. And then this child wanted to* go *and get some jam. He gets on to a chair, his arm catches on to a cup, and it gets broken.*—Are those children both naughty, or is one not so naughty as the other?—*Both just as naughty.*—Would you punish them the same?—*No. The one who broke fifteen plates.*—And would you punish the other one more, or less? —*The first broke lots of things, the other one fewer.*—How would you punish them?—*The one who broke the fifteen cups: two slaps. The other one, one slap.*"

**Const (7) G.:** "Tell me those two stories. —*There was a chair in the dining room with cups on it. A boy opens the door, and all the cups are broken.*—And now the other story?—*A little boy wants to take some jam. He tried to take hold of a cup and it broke.*—If you were their mother, which one would you punish most severely?—*The one who broke the cups.*—Is he the naughtiest?—*Yes.*—Why did he break them?—*Because he wanted to get into the room.*—And the other? —*Because he wanted to take the jam.*— Let's pretend that you are the mummy. You have two little girls. One of them breaks fifteen cups as she is coming into the dining room, the other breaks one cup as she is trying to get some jam while you are not there. Which of them would you punish most severely?—*The one who broke the fifteen cups.*" But Const, who is so decided about our stories, goes on to tell us some personal reminiscences in which it is obviously subjective responsibility that is at work. "Have you ever broken anything?—*A cup.*—How?—*I wanted to wipe it, and I let it drop.*—What else have you broken? —*Another time, a plate.*—How?—*I took it to play with.*—Which was the naughtiest thing to do?—*The plate, because I* *oughtn't to have taken it.*—And how about the cup?—*That was less naughty because I wanted to wipe it.*—Which were you punished most for, for the cup or for the plate?—*For the plate.*—Listen, I am going to tell you two more stories. A little girl was wiping the cups. She was putting them away, wiping them with the cloth, and she broke five cups. Another little girl is playing with some plates. She breaks a plate. Which of them is the naughtiest?—*The one who broke the five cups.*" This shows that in the case of her own personal recollections (where, incidentally, the number of objects broken does not come in) subjective responsibility alone is taken into account. As soon as we go back to the stories, even basing them on the child's recollections, objective responsibility reappears in all its purity!

## II. The Stories of the Ink-Stains

**Const (7) G.,** whose answers we have just been examining, repeats correctly the story of the blot of ink: "*A little boy sees that his father's ink-pot is empty. He takes the ink-bottle, but he is clumsy and makes a big blot.*—And the other one?—*There was a boy who was always touching things. He takes the ink and makes a little blot.*—Are they both equally naughty or not?—*No.*—Which is the most naughty?—*The one who made the big blot.*—Why?—*Because it was big.*—Why did he make a big blot? —*To be helpful.*—And why did the other one make a little blot?—*Because he was always touching things. He made a little blot.*—Then which of them is the naughtiest?—*The one who made a big blot.*"

**Geo (6)** also understands the stories and knows that the two children's intentions

were quite different. But he regards as the naughtiest "*the one who made the big blot.*—Why?—*Because that blot is bigger than the other one.*"

## III. The Stories of the Holes

**Geo (6)** is equally successful in understanding these two stories. "*The first wanted to help her mother and she made a big hole in her frock. The other one was playing and made a little hole.*—Is one of these little girls naughtier than the others?—*The one who wanted to help her mother a little is the naughtiest because she made a big hole. She got scolded.*"

**Const (7) G.** repeats the stories as follows: "*A little girl wanted to make a handkerchief for her mother. She was clumsy, and made a big hole in her frock.* —And the other one?—*There was a little girl who was always touching things. She took some scissors to play and made a little hole in her frock.*— Which of them is naughtiest?—*The one who made the big hole.*—Why did she make this hole?—*She wanted to give her mother a surprise.*—That's right. And the other one?—*She took the scissors because she was always touching things and made a little hole.*—That's right. Then which of the little girls was nicest? —... (hesitation).—Say what you think. —*The one who made the little hole is the nicest.*—If you were the mother you would have seen everything they did. Which would you have punished most? —*The one who made a big hole.*—And which one would you have punished least?—*The one who made the little hole.*—And what would the one who made the big hole say when you punished her most?—*She would say, I wanted* *to give a surprise.*—And the other one? —*She was playing.*—Which one ought to be punished most?—*The one who made the big hole.*—Let's pretend that it was you who made the big hole so as to give your mother a surprise. Your sister is playing and makes the little hole. Which ought to be punished most?—*Me.*—Are you quite sure, or not quite sure?— *Quite sure.*—Have you ever made holes? —*Never.*—Is what I am asking you quite easy?—*Yes.*—Are you quite sure you you meant what you said?—*Yes.*"

These answers reveal the strength of the resistance offered to the counter-suggestions we attempted to make, and they also show what store the children set by material results, in spite of the fact that they have perfectly well understood the story and consequently the intentions of its characters, and what little account they take of the intentions which have indirectly caused these material happenings.

Such facts as these taken by themselves of course prove nothing. Before speaking about objective responsibility, we must ask ourselves whether the child does not draw a distinction analogous to that which the adult makes in the case of ethics and of certain legal punishments. One can without any loss of honor be run in for having broken police regulations. One can be the object of a legal sentence devoid of any penal element (cf. Durkheim's restitutive and retributive punishment). In the same way, then, when a child pronounces a little girl to be "naughty" because she has made a big hole in her dress, although he knows that her intentions were not only innocent but admirable, does he not simply mean that she has damaged her parents materially and therefore deserves a

purely legal punishment devoid of any moral significance?

The question arises in the same form in connection with stealing, as we shall see presently. But with regard to lying, since all question of material damage can be disregarded, we shall endeavor to prove that the child's judgments really do imply objective responsibility. An analogous conclusion may therefore be formulated concerning the present examples. Here preoccupation about material damage certainly outweighs any question of obedience or disobedience to rules. But this is a form of objective responsibility only in so far as the child fails to distinguish the element of civic responsibility, as it were, from the penal element. Now, on the verbal plane where we have taken up our stand it seems to us that this differentiation is one that hardly enters into the subject's mind. Responsibility is thus still held to be objective, even from the moral point of view.

Before carrying our analysis any further and in order to place the previous attitudes in their true perspective, let us examine the answers that contradict those which we have just dealt with and which relate to the same pairs of stories:

*I. The Stories of the Broken Cups*

Here, to begin with, is a rather exceptional case of a 6-year-old child. (Most of the children of 6 gave us answers which corresponded to the type of objective responsibility.)

**Schma (6½, G.,** forward intellectually and looking more like a girl of 8) begins by telling us that the two boys of the story are *"equally naughty,"* and that they must be punished *"Both just the same."* Well, I think one of them is naughtier than the other. Which one do you think?—*Both the same.*—Have you never broken anything?—*No, I never have. My brother has.*—What did he break?—*A cup and a pail.*—How?—*He wanted to fish. He broke half my pail, and then afterwards he broke it again on purpose to annoy me.*—Did he also break a cup?—*He had wiped it and was putting it on the edge of the table and it fell.*—What day was he naughtiest, the day he broke the pail or the day he broke the cup?—*The pail.*—Why?—*He broke my pail on purpose.*—And the cup?—*He didn't do that on purpose. He put it right on the edge and it broke.*—And in the stories I told you, which boy is naughtiest, the one who broke the fifteen cups or the one who broke one cup?—*The one who wanted to take the jam because he wanted to eat it."* Thus by appealing to her personal memories one sees that Schma can be led to judge according to subjective responsibility.

**Mol (7):** "Which is naughtiest?—*The second, the one who wanted to take the jam-pot, because he wanted to take something without asking.*—Did he catch it?—*No.*—Was he the naughtiest all the same?—*Yes.*—And the first?—*It wasn't his fault. He didn't do it on purpose."*

**Corm (9):** *"Well, the one who broke them as he was coming isn't naughty, 'cos he didn't know there was any cups. The other one wanted to take the jam and caught his arm on a cup.*—Which one is the naughtiest?—*The one who wanted to take the jam.*—How many cups did he break?—*One.*—And the other boy?—*Fifteen.*—Which one would you punish most?—*The boy who wanted to take the jam. He knew, he did it on purpose."*

**Gros (9):** "What did the first one do?—*He broke fifteen cups as he was opening a door.*—And the second one?—*He broke one cup as he was taking some jam.*—Which of these two silly things was naughtiest, do you think?—*The one where he tried to take hold of a cup was* [the silliest] *because the other boy didn't see* [that there were some cups behind the door]. *He saw what he was doing.*—How many did he break?—*One cup.*—And the other one?—*Fifteen.*—Then which one would you punish most?—*The one who broke one cup.*—Why?—*He did it on purpose. If he hadn't taken the jam, it wouldn't have happened."*

**Nuss (10):** The naughtiest is *"the one who wanted to take the jam.*—Does it make any difference the other one having broken more cups?—*No, because the one who broke fifteen cups didn't do it on purpose."*

*II. The Stories of the Ink-Stains*

**Sci (6):** "What did the first one do?—*He wanted to please his daddy. He saw that the ink-pot was empty and thought he would fill it. He made a big spot on his suit.*—And the second one?—*He wanted to play with his daddy's ink, and he made a little spot.*—Which was the naughtiest?—*The one who played with the ink-pot. He was playing with it. The other wanted to be kind.*—Did the one who wanted to be kind make a big spot or a little one?—*He made a big spot, the other boy made a little one.*—Does it not matter the first one having made a big spot?—*All the same, the other wanted more to do something wrong. The one* *who made a little spot wanted to do something more wrong than the other."*

**Gros (9):** *"The one who wanted to be helpful, even if the stain is bigger, mustn't be punished."*

**Nuss (10).** The naughtiest is *"the one who made the little stain, because the other one wanted to help."*

*III. The Stories of the Holes*

**Sci (6)** repeats the stories as follows: *"The first one wanted to give her mother a surprise. She pricked herself and made a big hole in her frock. The second one liked touching everything. She took the scissors and made a little hole in her dress.—Which one is naughtiest?—The one who wanted to take the scissors. She made a little hole in her frock. She is the naughtiest.—Which one would you punish most, the one who made a little hole, or the other one?—Not the one who made a big hole; she wanted to give her mother a surprise."*

**Corm (9).** The naughtiest is *"the second. She oughtn't to have taken the scissors to play with. The first one didn't do it on purpose. You can't say that she was naughty."*

These answers show what fine shades even some of the youngest children we questioned could distinguish and how well able they were to take intentions into account. The hypothesis may therefore be advanced that evaluations based on material damage alone are the result of adult constraint refracted through childish respect far rather than a spontaneous manifestation of the child mind. Generally speaking, adults deal very

harshly with clumsiness. In so far as parents fail to grasp the situation and lose their tempers in proportion to the amount of damage done, in so far will the child begin by adopting this way of looking at things and apply literally the rules thus imposed, even if they were only implicit. And in so far as the parents are just, and, above all, in so far as the growing child sets up his own feelings as against the adult's reactions, objective responsibility will diminish in importance.

With regard to stealing we also found two groups of answers, and here again, while both objective and subjective responsibility are to be found at all ages between 6 and 10, it is the latter that predominates as the child develops.

Here are examples of objective responsibility:

*IV. The Stories of the Roll and of the Ribbon*

**Sci (6),** who showed signs of a subjective conception of responsibility in regard to clumsiness, changes his attitude here. He repeats the stories as follows: *"A boy was with his friend. He stole a roll and gave it to his friend. A little girl wanted a ribbon, and put it round her frock to look pretty.—Is one of them naughtier than the other?—Yes. . . . No. They're just the same.—Why did the first one steal the roll?—Because his friend liked it.— Why did the little girl steal the ribbon? —Because she was longing for it.—Which one would you punish most?—The boy who stole the roll and gave it to his brother instead of keeping it for himself. —Was it naughty to give it?—No. He was kind. He gave it to his brother.— Must one of them be punished more than the other?—Yes. The little boy stole the* roll to give to his brother. He must be punished more. Rolls cost more."

**Schma (6)** repeats the stories as follows: *"There was a boy. As his friend had had no dinner, he took a roll and put it in his pocket and gave it to his friend. A little girl went into a shop. She saw a ribbon. She says, it would be nice to put on my dress, she says. She took it.*—Is one of these children naughtier than the other?—*The boy is, because he took a roll. It's bigger.*—Ought they to be punished?—*Yes. Four slaps for the first.*—And the girl?—*Two slaps.*—Why did he take the roll?—*Because his friend had had no dinner.*—And the other child?—*To make herself pretty."*

**Geo (6):** "Which of them is the naughtiest?—*The one with the roll, because the roll is bigger than the ribbon."* And yet Geo is, like the other children, perfectly well aware of the motives involved.

### V. The Stories of the Cage and of the Sweets

**Desa (6):** *"The little girl had a friend who had a cage and a bird. She thought this was too unkind. So she took the cage and let the bird out.*—And the other one?—*A little girl stole a sweet and ate it.*—Are they both equally naughty or is one of them naughtier than the other? —*The one who stole the cage is naughtiest.*—Why?—*Because she stole the cage.* —And the other one?—*She stole a sweet.* —Is that one more or less naughty than the first?—*Less. The sweet is smaller than the cage.*—If you were the daddy, which one would you punish most?—*The one who stole the cage.*—Why did she steal it?—*Because the bird was unhappy.*—

And why did the other one steal the sweet?—*To eat it."*

These cases of objective responsibility are thus all three of 6-year-olds. We found none above 7 years in the case of this kind of story. Here are some definite cases of subjective responsibility found in connection with the same stories. They are nearly all children of 9 and 10. The types are therefore better dissociated with regard to age than in the case of the stories about clumsiness.

### IV. The Stories of the Roll and of the Ribbon

**Corm (9)** tells the two stories correctly. "What do you think about it?—*Well, the little boy oughtn't to have stolen. He oughtn't to have stolen it, but to have paid for it. And the other one, she oughtn't to have stolen the ribbon either.* —Which of them is the naughtiest?— *The little girl took the ribbon for herself. The little boy took the roll too, but to give it to his friend who had had no dinner.*—If you were the schoolteacher, which one would you punish most?— *The little girl."*

**Nuss (10):** "Which one is the naughtiest?—*The little girl is because she took it for herself."*

### V. The Stories of the Cage and of the Sweets

**Sci (6):** "Which one is naughtiest?— *The one who steals the sweet. The first one took the cage so as to set the little bird free."*

**Corm (9), G.:** *"It was good of the little girl who wanted to set the little bird* *free. The other one oughtn't to have eaten the sweet."*

**Gros (9):** *"The one who stole the sweet, that was naughtier.—Why?—Because the other let the little bird go free again."*

Thus these answers present us with two distinct moral attitudes—one that judges actions according to their material consequences, and one that only takes intentions into account. These two attitudes may coexist at the same age and even in the same child, but broadly speaking, they do not synchronize. Objective responsibility diminishes on the average as the child grows older, and subjective responsibility gains correlatively in importance. We have therefore two processes partially overlapping, but of which the second gradually succeeds in dominating the first.

What explanation can we give of these facts? The objective conception of responsibility arises, without any doubt, as a result of the constraint exercised by the adult. But the exact meaning of this constraint has still to be established, because in cases of theft and clumsiness it is exercised in a rather different form from what appears in cases of lying. For in some of the cases we have been examining it is quite certain that adults, or some adults, apply their own sanctions, whether "diffused" (blame) or "organized" (punishment), in conformity with the rules of objective responsibility. The average housewife (most of the children we examined came from very poor districts) will be more angry over fifteen cups than over one, and independently, up to a point, of the offender's intentions. Broadly speaking, then, one may say that it is not only the externality of the adult command in rela-

tion to the child's mind that produces the effects we are discussing, it is the example of the adult himself. In cases of lying, on the other hand, we shall find that it is almost entirely in spite of the adult's intention that objective responsibility imposes itself upon the child's mind.

Restricted though the question under discussion may appear, it has a very distinct interest. When the adult allows himself to evaluate acts of clumsiness and pilfering in terms of their material result, there can be no doubt that in most people's eyes he is unjust. On the other hand, those parents who try to give their children a moral education based on intention, achieve very early results as is shown by current observation and the few examples of subjective responsibility we were able to note at 6 or 7. How is it, then, that in most of the cases under 9–10 years the child accepts so completely the criterion of objective responsibility and even outdoes the average adult on this point? The child is much more of an objectivist, so to speak, than the least intelligent parent. Also, most parents draw a distinction which the children precisely neglect to make: they scold, that is, according to the extent of the material damage caused by the clumsy act, but they do not regard the act itself exactly as a moral fault. The child on the contrary seems, as we have noted before, not to differentiate the legal or, as it were, the purely police aspect from the moral aspect of the question. It is "naughtier" to make a big spot on your coat than a small one, and this in spite of the fact that the child knows perfectly well that the intentions involved may have been good. To commit certain acts is therefore, in a sense, wrong in itself, independently of the psychological context. With regard to stealing, which is unanimously held up to children as a grave moral offence, this phenomenon appears even more clearly. Nearly all the children under 9–10, while paying full tribute to the thief's intentions, consider the theft of the roll and the cage a more culpable act both from a police and from a moral point of view than that of the ribbon or the sweet. Now, we can understand anyone condemning a theft regardless of the object pursued, but it is rather curious to see little children adopting an exclusively material criterion when they are asked to compare two such dissimilar acts as are described in our stories.

The problem involved in all this is the following. What is the origin of this initial predominance of judgments of objective responsibility, surpassing in scope and intensity what may have been done or said to the children by adults? Only one answer seems to us to be possible. The rules imposed by the adult, whether verbally (not to steal, not to handle breakable objects carelessly, etc.) or materially (anger, punishments) constitute categorical obligations for the child, before his mind has properly assimilated them, and no matter whether he puts them into practice or not. They thus acquire the value of ritual necessities, and the forbidden things take on the significance of taboos. Moral realism would thus seem to be the fruit of constraint and of the primitive forms of unilateral respect. Is this an inevitable product or an accidental result? This is the point we shall try to settle in connection with lying.

But before going too far in our generalizations, let us remember that the child's answers are given in answer to stories that are told to him and do not arise out of really experienced facts. As in the case of method we may therefore ask ourselves whether these verbal evaluations do or do not correspond with the child's real thoughts. These evaluations certainly change as the child grows older, and they also seem to be the result of some systematic influence. But are they a mere derivative, a verbal and therefore ineffectual deduction from the words spoken by adults, or do they correspond with a genuine attitude, molded by unilateral respect and conditioning the child's behavior before they inspire his sayings?

As we noticed in certain cases, the child pays far more attention to intentions where his own memories are concerned than when he is being questioned about one or other of our little stories. Such a fact as this surely shows us that if the child's objectivist attitude (unmistakable enough in his theoretical thought) corresponds to anything in his concrete and active thought, there must have been a time-lag taking place between one of these manifestations and the other, for the theoretical attitude is certainly a latecomer as compared to the practical. But the problem goes deeper than this, and the question may be raised whether at any moment in the immediate experiences of his moral life, or at any rate in those connected with clumsiness and lying, the child has ever been dominated by the notion of objective responsibility.

Immediate observation—the only judge in the matter—is sufficiently explicit on this point. It is very easy to notice—especially in very young children, under 6–7 years of age—how frequently the sense of guilt on the occasion of clumsiness is proportional to the extent of the material disaster instead of remaining subordinate to the intentions in question. I have often noticed in the case of my own children, who have never been blamed for involuntary clumsiness, how difficult it was to take away from them all sense of responsibility when they chanced to break an article or soil some linen. Which of us cannot recall the accusing character which such a minor accident would take on as soon as it had happened, rising, with all the suddenness of a shock and overwhelming us with a sense of guilt that was the more burning, the more unexpected and the more irreparable the disaster. To be sure, all sorts of factors come into play (the sense of "immanent" justice, affective associations with previous carelessness, fear of punishment, etc.). But how could the material damage be felt as a fault if the child were not applying in a literal and realistic manner a whole set of rules, implicit and explicit, for which he feels respect?

We can therefore put forward the hypothesis that judgments of objective responsibility occurring in the course of our interrogatory were based upon a residue left by experiences that had really been lived through. Although new material may since have enriched the child's moral consciousness and enabled him to discern the nature of subjective responsibility, these earlier experiences are sufficient, it would seem, to constitute a permanent foundation of moral realism which reappears on each fresh occasion. Now, since thought in the child always lags behind action, it is quite natural that the solution of theoretical problems such as we made use of should be formed by means of the older and more habitual schemas rather than the more subtle and less robust schemas that are in process of formation. Thus

an adult who may be in the midst of reviewing all his values and experiencing feelings of which the novelty surprises him, will, if he is suddenly faced with the necessity of solving someone else's problems, very probably appeal to moral principles which he has discarded for himself. For example, he will, if he is not given time to reflect, judge his neighbor's actions with a severity which would be incomprehensible in view of his present deeper tendencies, but which effectively corresponds to his previous system of values. In the same way, our children may perfectly well take account of intentions in appraising their own conduct, and yet confine themselves to considerations of the material consequences of actions in the case of the characters involved in our stories, who are indifferent to them.

How, then, does subjective responsibility appear and develop within the limited domain we are analyzing at present? There is no doubt that by adopting a certain technique with their children, parents can succeed in making them attach more importance to intentions than to rules conceived as a system of ritual interdictions. Only the question is, whether this technique does not involve perpetually taking care not to impose on their children any duties properly so called, and placing mutual sympathy above everything else? It is when the child is accustomed to act from the point of view of those around him, when he tries to please rather than to obey, that he will judge in terms of intentions. So that taking intentions into account presupposes cooperation and mutual respect. Only those who have children of their own know how difficult it is to put this into practice. Such is the prestige of parents in the eyes of the very young child, that even if they lay down nothing in the form of general duties, their wishes act as law and thus give rise automatically to moral realism (independently, of course, of the manner in which the child eventually carries out these desires). In order to remove all traces of moral realism, one must place oneself on the child's own level, and give him a feeling of equality by laying stress on one's own obligations and one's own deficiencies. In the sphere of clumsiness and of untidiness in general (putting away toys, personal cleanliness, etc.), in short in all the multifarious obligations that are so secondary for moral theory but so all-important in daily life (perhaps nine-tenths of the commands given to children relate to these material questions) it is quite easy to draw attention to one's own needs, one's own difficulties, even one's own blunders, and to point out their consequences, thus creating an atmosphere of mutual help and understanding. In this way the child will find himself in the presence, not of a system of commands requiring ritualistic and external obedience, but of a system of social relations such that everyone does his best to obey the same obligations, and does so out of mutual respect. The passage from obedience to cooperation thus marks a progress analogous to that of which we saw the effects in the evolution of the game of marbles: only in the final stage does the morality of intention triumph over the morality of objective responsibility.

When parents do not trouble about such considerations as these, when they issue contradictory commands and are inconsistent in the punishments they inflict, then, obviously, it is not because of moral constraint but in spite of and as a reaction against it that the concern with intentions develops in the child. Here is a child, who, in his desire to please, happens to break something and is snubbed for his pains, or who in general sees his actions judged otherwise than he judges them himself. It is obvious that after more or less brief periods of submission, during which he accepts every verdict, even those that are wrong, he will begin to feel the injustice of it all. Such situations can lead to revolt. But if, on the contrary, the child finds in his brothers and sisters or in his playmates a form of society which develops his desire for cooperation and mutual sympathy, then a new type of morality will be created in him, a morality of reciprocity and not of obedience. This is the true morality of intention and of subjective responsibility.

In short, whether parents succeed in embodying it in family life or whether it takes root in spite of and in opposition to them, it is always cooperation that gives intention precedence over literalism, just as it was unilateral respect that inevitably provoked moral realism. Actually, of course, there are innumerable intermediate stages between these two attitudes of obedience and collaboration, but it is useful for the purposes of analysis to emphasize the real opposition that exists between them.

# 5

# Methods used by the inquiry for measuring deception

*by Hugh Hartshorne and Mark A. May*

In setting up our techniques we tried to satisfy as many as possible of the requirements which should be met by tests of this type. We have formulated these in ten criteria which it would be well for all readers to examine carefully.

1.  The test situation should be as far as possible a natural situation. It should also be a controlled situation. The response should as far as possible be natural even when directed.

2.  The test situation and the response should be of such a nature as to allow all subjects equal opportunity to exhibit the behavior which is being tested. That is, there should be nothing about the test itself which would prevent anyone who desired to deceive from so doing; on the other hand, there should be nothing about it to trick an honest subject into an act he would repudiate if he were aware of its import.

From Hugh Hartshorne and Mark A. May, *Studies in the Nature of Character*. Vol. I. *Studies in Deceit* (New York: Macmillan, 1928), Book I, pp. 47–103. Reprinted by permission of the authors.

3.  No test should subject the child to any moral strain beyond that to which he is subjected in the natural course of his actual life situations.

4.  The test should not put the subject and the examiner in false social relations to one another. The examiner should guard against being deceptive himself in order to test the subject.

5.  The test should have "low visibility"; that is, it should be of such a nature as not to arouse the suspicions of the subject. This is one of the fundamental difficulties in all such testing since the entire purpose of the test cannot be announced in advance. This criterion is all the more difficult to meet when coupled with criterion number four, for the examiner must keep secret one aspect of his purpose and at the same time be honest with the subjects.

6.  The activity demanded of the subject in taking the test should have real values for him whether he is aware of these values or not.

7.  The test should be of such a nature as not to be spoiled by publicity.

8.  If tests are to be used in statistical studies they should be group tests. They should also be easy to administer and should be mechanically scored. They should be short enough to be given in single school periods.

9.  The test results should be clear and unambiguous. It should be obvious from the results whether the subject did or did not exhibit the behavior in question. The evidence should be such as would be accepted in a court of law.

10. The scores should be quantitative,

showing the amount as well as the fact of deception. Each test therefore should be flexible enough to include within its scope wide ranges of deceptive tendency.

These requirements are quite rigid and no technique has yet been devised which will meet all of them. Only one previously used method came sufficiently within the standard set to warrant our adopting it. This was the peeping type of test, which we took over with certain modifications.

\*　　　\*　　　\*

## Methods for Measuring the Cheating Type of Deceptive Behavior

*A. As Exhibited in Classroom Situations*

\*　　　\*　　　\*

**The Duplicating Technique.** . . . [A] rather common form of classroom deceptiveness occurs when the pupil makes illegitimate use of a key or answer sheet either in doing his work or in the scoring of his own test paper. This is one type of behavior which we have been most successful in testing. . . .

Any sort of test is given, preferably the short-answer type. The papers are collected and taken to the office, where a duplicate is made of each paper. Great care is taken to be certain that an exact record is made of what the pupil actually did on the test. At a later session of the class the papers are returned and each child is given a key, or answer sheet, and is asked to score his own paper. The self-scored papers are then compared with the duplicates and all changes are recorded. Deception consists in illegiti-

mately increasing one's score by copying answers from the key.

The following test materials were used for this purpose:

*(a) The Information Test.* This consists of twenty-eight items. Instead of underlining the correct answer, the pupil in this case is required to encircle it in ink. He is not allowed to hand in his paper until he has at least attempted every question. In order to cheat on this test a child has to erase the circle drawn in ink and make another, when he is asked to score his paper.

Sample items are:

1. Bombay is a city in China France Japan India
2. Pongee is a dance food fabric drink
3. Hannibal is the name of a general king prizefighter river
4. One horsepower equals 746 watts 1000 watts 16⅔ watts 2.45 watts
5. Brahmaputra is the name of a flower goddess language river

*(b) The Sentence Completion Test.* Cheating here consists in either adding more words, that is, doing more items, or changing words previously written in pencil by erasing and rewriting. Fifty-five sentences such as these were used:

1. Men ＿＿＿＿＿ older than boys.
2. The poor little ＿＿＿＿＿ has ＿＿＿＿＿ nothing to ＿＿＿ ＿＿＿＿; he is hungry.
3. No ＿＿＿＿＿ what happens wrong is ＿＿＿＿＿ right.
4. He believed in ＿＿＿＿＿ hard things ＿＿＿＿＿ because ＿＿＿＿＿ ＿＿＿ ＿＿＿ hard.
5. He must ＿＿＿＿＿ further assistance from us. We cannot give it.

(c) *The Word Knowledge Test.* This is arranged as a multiple-choice test. The response words are numbered from one to five. When the correct response word is located, its number is written on the dotted line at the margin. Cheating consists in either erasing this number and entering the correct one or in writing down more numbers. There were 120 items in all, such as these:

1. *boyish*    1 naughty  2 male
             3 impudent  4
             like a boy  5 in-
             formal          .... 1.
2. *blunt*    1 dull  2 drowsy
             3 deaf  4 doubt-
             ful  5 ugly       .... 2.
3. *default*  1 defeat  2 blame
             3 failure  4 libel
             5 displace       .... 3.
4. *allusion*  1 aria  2 illusion
             3 eulogy  4 dream
             5 reference      .... 4.
5. *astute*   1 rigorous  2 shrewd
             3 unsound  4
             bony  5 aston-
             ished           .... 5.

(d) *The Arithmetic Test.* Here also the answers are written at the margin and changes are made as in the case of the previous test. The original test had fifty examples, of which the following are illustrations:

1. When sugar costs 10 cents a pound, how much will 5 pounds cost?          Answer (...)
2. How many eggs are needed to make 3 cakes if you use 2 eggs for one cake?  Answer (...)
3. $\frac{1}{8} \times 22$ equals          Answer (...)
4. 18 equals ——% of 40?    Answer (...)
5. A pushcart man buys eggs at 15¢ per dozen

and sells them at 15 for 25¢. How many eggs must he sell to gain $1.80?          Answer (...)

(e) *The Thorndike-McCall Reading Scale.* This test consists of short paragraphs to be read by the subject. Then follow a few questions, the correct answers to which can be given in a single word or short phrase. Cheating consists in changing one or two words or sometimes a whole phrase, or in filling in more answers.

(f) *An Original Disarranged Sentence Test.* In this test the task is to straighten out mixed-up words so they will make a sentence. If the child finds any problem too difficult he is required to draw a line through the blank space, to indicate that he has omitted it. Cheating can be accomplished therefore only by erasing a line or sentence and substituting something else. There were fifteen word groups such as these:

1. houses people live in ———————
   ———————————————————
2. teacher to I paper my correct asked my ———————
   ———————————————————
3. pies Will feel sick and eskimo could not eat five ———————
   ———————————————————
4. aggravate miseries pleasure present recall past to is but to our ———
   ———————————————————
5. to to to is is be be good good noble, how teach but others nobler—and less trouble ———————
   ———     ———————
   ———————————————————

(g) *An Original Spelling Test.* The test is made up of ninety words, some of which are misspelled. The task is to check misspelled words. To cheat, one had only to add more check marks or erase those previously made.

1. _____ ache
2. _____ beleive
3. _____ laid
4. _____ hybred
5. _____ rythm
6. _____ genuine
7. _____ niece
8. _____ sacreligious
9. _____ chauffeur
10. _____ parlimentary

It was necessary to have each test steeply graded in difficulty and to give less time than even the most competent would require to complete the test, so that when the papers were scored there would be abundant opportunity to make use of the keys if any were disposed to do so. Thus for the Thorndike-McCall Reading Test we allowed only fifteen minutes although the standard time is thirty. . . . *Scoring.* In all these tests, two kinds of scores are used, the *amount score* and the *fact score.* The *amount score* is the total score when the test is given under conditions permitting dishonesty. It ordinarily contains an element of honest performance for which allowance is properly made. . . . In the case of the duplicating technique, each change counted as one point. If the pupil made only one change in his paper and this did not affect his score it was counted as zero. Two or more changes were counted whether they affected the score or not.[1] The amount score is simply the number of changes made. The total amount score for all the tests was obtained by summing up all the changes after they had been reduced to a common denomina-

tor.[2] The *fact score*[3] is a record of the fact of honesty or deception. It is simply a "c" (cheating) whenever two or more changes are made or when one change affects the score.

This technique meets most of the requirements very well. It would seem at first sight to have rather "high visibility" and not be applicable to older groups. We have evidence, however, that it has been successfully used with a group of college sophomores. We have not employed it extensively, however, because it is too expensive and time-consuming.

**The Improbable Achievement Technique.** This consists in giving a test under conditions such that achievement above a certain level will indicate deception.

\* \* \*

*Puzzle Performance Tests.* There are certain kinds of mechanical puzzles which may be effectively used. The puzzle must appear simple but be in reality very difficult. It must require genuine skill rather than the knowledge of a secret trick or principle. It must be of such a nature that the dishonest pupil can fake a solution or appear to have solved it when he really did not. After considerable preliminary searching and experimenting we settled on three puzzles.

*(1) The Puzzle Peg (or Peg Solitaire).* This is a game of solitaire which may be bought in the toy stores. It consists of a circular board about six inches in diameter with thirty-three holes arranged as in the diagram. Each hole has a peg in it except the center one. When two pegs are adjacent with a vacant hole next in line, one peg may jump the

[1] Pupils sometimes make changes in spelling or wording which do not affect the answer.

[2] Each score was divided by the standard deviation of its distribution.

[3] In most cases this "fact" represents a *probability* of 999 chances in 1000.

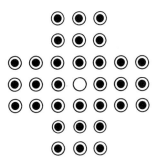

other and land in the vacant hole. The peg "jumped" is removed. The problem is to jump all the pegs off the board except one and leave this one in the center hole. Anyone who has tried this knows how very difficult it is. The time allowed was five minutes for the first trial and three for the second. Cheating consists in faking a solution by pulling out all the pegs but one and placing it in the middle hole without playing the game at all. Or the solution may be partly faked by pulling out some pegs and jumping some.

In administering the puzzle tests a score sheet was used, of which a portion is shown below. It should be noted that in all the puzzle tests we have only the record made by the child on his score sheet. We do not know of course whether the deceptive child falsified his performance but made a true record of it, or whether he did not falsify his performance but made a false record of it. In one puzzle for one group this matter was checked and we found that in over 90 percent of the deceptive cases the peg boards and score sheets agreed.

PUZZLE TESTS SCORE SHEET

Name _____ Grade _____

School _____ Date _____

The following spaces are for recording your scores. Do not make any entries until told what to do.

*Pill Boxes:* Weight discrimination.

In the spaces below copy the numbers from the bottoms of the boxes to show the order in which you had them at the end of each trial.

1st trial ☐ ☐ ☐ ☐ ☐ ☐ ☐

2nd trial ☐ ☐ ☐ ☐ ☐ ☐ ☐

*Puzzle Blocks* "Sixteen"

Copy the numbers off the blocks into the squares at the right to show the order they were in at the end of the test.

*Peg Board*

    *a.* Write in the space at the right the number of pegs left on the board at the end of the first trial    (_____)

    *b.* Write in the space at the right the number of pegs left on the board at the end of the second trial    (_____)

    *c.* Write "yes" in the space at the right if you had only one peg left on either trial and it in the middle    (_____)

We have found no one yet who, without considerable previous experience with this game, could solve it in five minutes. Consequently any child who claims to have solved it in the time allowed is cheating or else he is one of those very rare persons who by many hours of previous practice has learned the game so well as to do it in five minutes. It is only slightly less difficult to leave one or two pegs standing anywhere on the board.

The amount score was the number of pegs left on the board at the end of the second period, or the smallest number achieved during the period.

For the fact score, the pupil was scored as having cheated if only one or two pegs were left in any holes on either trial.

(2) *The Fifteen Puzzle.* This puzzle had a certain advantage over the peg board in that it could not be bought in the toy shops in New York during our testing although a modified form was issued as advertising material by a commercial company. We did find three sets in a small store that deals exclusively in magicians' trick materials. Every dealer professed to have known it years ago but informed us that it was now out of style and off the market. It consists simply of a small box four inches square with sixteen blocks each one inch square and numbered zero to fifteen. The small squares are made of wood. We arranged them in a standardized chance order, which was as follows:[4]

| | | | |
|---|---|---|---|
| 10 | 8 | 5 | 13 |
| 15 | 6 | 2 | 3 |
| 9 | 11 | 12 | 0 |
| 14 | 1 | 7 | 4 |

[4] For future work we have adopted a different arrangement, only partially solvable.

The problem is to remove the one marked 0 and then by sliding the others around get them in this order:

| | | | |
|---|---|---|---|
| 1 | 2 | 3 | 4 |
| 5 | 6 | 7 | 8 |
| 9 | 10 | 11 | 12 |
| 13 | 14 | 15 | |

It is strictly forbidden to remove any block from the board. The puzzle must be solved by sliding the blocks around. Five to eight minutes were allowed. Here cheating consists in taking the blocks out and placing them in the correct order without playing the game.

As these puzzles were not available, we had to manufacture them ourselves.

In the spaces provided on the score sheet the child makes a record of the numbers on the squares as they appeared when time was called.

To obtain the amount score, the rows across the square were taken as units and weighted thus:

| | |
|---|---|
| 1st row correct, 1 2 3 4 | 1 credit |
| 2d row correct, 5 6 7 8 | 2 credits |
| 3d row correct, 9 10 11 12 | 3 credits |
| 4th row correct, 13 14 15 | 4 credits |
| Maximum score | 10 credits |

Before a pupil was marked "c" or negative, he must have scored the maximum.

(3) *The Weight Discrimination Test.* This was really not a puzzle, but a modification of the weight discrimination test used in the Binet intelligence test and in routine experiments in psychological laboratories. It consisted of seven small pillboxes. The boxes were filled in our office with cotton batting and buckshot so that in each set of seven no two weighed the same. They were numbered on the bottom from one to seven, in

order of weight. The difference in weight between any adjoining boxes of the set, as one and two or three and four, was too slight to be detected,[5] so that no one could arrange the boxes in order of weight without looking at the numbers, except by chance.

The instructions were to turn the numbers down and arrange the boxes in the order of their weight. After the first trial the pupils were told to look at the numbers on the bottom and copy these numbers off on the score sheet to show how they had been arranged. They were then told that the correct arrangement was the serial order 1, 2, 3, 4, 5, 6, 7 and were asked to turn the numbers down again and not look at them during the second trial. Three minutes were given for each trial. Cheating consists in peeping at the numbers.

[5] The weights averaged in grams (1) 3.6, (2) 3.7, (3) 3.8, (4) 3.9, (5) 4.0, (6) 4.1, (7) 4.2, with variations always checked so as to secure real differences in any one set.

| 1st | 2d | W | 1st | 2d | W |
|---|---|---|---|---|---|
| 7 | 7 | 11 | 1 | 7 | 4 |
| 5 | 7 | 10 | 0 | 7 | 4 |
| 4 | 7 | 10 | 5 | 3 | 4 |
| 3 | 7 | 9 | 2 | 4 | 1 |
| 2 | 7 | 9 | 5 | 1 | 4 |
| 7 | 5 | 8 | 5 | 0 | 4 |
| 5 | 5 | 8 | 4 | 3 | 3 |
| 1 | 7 | 7 | 4 | 2 | 3 |
| 0 | 7 | **7** | 4 | 1 | 3 |
| 4 | 5 | 6 | 4 | 0 | 3 |
| 3 | 5 | 6 | 3 | 3 | 2 |
| 7 | 4 | 6 | 2 | 3 | 2 |
| 5 | 4 | 6 | 1 | 3 | 2 |
| 2 | 5 | 5 | 0 | 3 | 2 |
| 1 | 5 | 5 | 3 | 2 | 1 |
| 0 | 5 | 5 | 2 | 2 | 1 |
| 7 | 0 | 5 | 1 | 2 | 1 |
| 7 | 1 | 5 | 0 | 2 | 1 |
| 7 | 2 | 5 | 3 | 1–0 | 0 |
| 4 | 7 | 4 | 2 | 1–0 | 0 |
| 3 | 7 | 4 | 1 | 1–0 | 0 |
| 2 | 7 | 4 | 0 | 1–0 | 0 |

Any amount score of 7, 8, 9, 10, or 11 was scored "c."

The weights were arranged twice and a record made each time on the score sheet. These records were scored as follows: First, a position score was given each trial by giving one point credit for each weight in its correct position. Thus all weights in correct order scored seven. Any weight in its correct position regardless of the others was scored one credit. For example, an arrangement like this: 2 1 3 5 7 6 4 was scored one, because weight number three was in position number three. This scheme gave two position scores, one for each trial. But since on the second trial the pupils were told that the numbers indicated the correct order, more significance was attached to the second trial.

The two position scores were combined and "weighted" according to the likelihood of dishonesty.[6] That is, the combinations that were least likely to occur by chance were given correspondingly larger cheating scores and *vice versa.*

Any combination was rated "c" which contained a position score of 7 on the second trial, or of 5 on the second trial provided the 5 was preceded by a 5 or 7 on the first trial.

\*            \*            \*

### B. As Exhibited in Parlor Games

As in the case of contests, it was necessary to establish natural conditions. There would have been little advantage in merely repeating the "test" situation of

[6] To get the amount score, the following table of arbitrary weights was constructed. The first column represents the first trial and the second column the second trial. "W" means the weighted total score assigned to the raw score values shown in the first two columns.

the classroom type in either the contests or the parties, as behavior under such conditions had already been measured with a large variety of opportunities. What we were after here was a measure of the extent to which cheating was a function of total situations of a quite different character, where, in the case of the contests, serious individual competition entered into the motivation and, in the other, the atmosphere was just "fun," with the customary trivial prizes given at children's parties.

To secure this party atmosphere it was essential to have the children in groups rather than singly, as the chief part of the fun is the social character of the games. This placed a rather strict limit on the number of opportunities to deceive that could be offered in any single party.

Certain requirements for these opportunities needed constant emphasis:

1. The deceptive aspect of the behavior must be a matter of objective record, and not a matter of judgment on the part of an observer.
2. Each child must have the same opportunity to deceive as every other child.
3. The opportunities must be in games or stunts where the interest is high.
4. The deceptive aspect of the behavior must have low visibility so that, if one child cheats, the rest will not notice it and protest.

**The Techniques Used.** With the assistance of a professional recreational leader, a large number of parties were first conducted in order to standardize the procedure. A great many games and stunts were tried out, which it is not necessary to describe here. It was found that in the course of an hour and a half from thirty to fifty children could all be tested . . . as follows:

\*       \*       \*

*Pinning the Tail on the Donkey or the Arrow on the Target.* Each child is blindfolded by a standardized bandage so adjusted that there is room to see the floor under the bandage. The technique here is of the "improbable achievement" type. The likelihood that a child will be able to get the tail or the arrow in the exact spot without peeping is remote. But if he uses his eyes and follows the lines on the floorboards and looks at the donkey or target when he gets to it, he can place the tail or arrow very accurately.

As each tail is pinned on it is removed again before the next child approaches, so he cannot guide his hand by feeling for the tails already pinned on. Each child is rotated three times before he starts for the donkey, to decrease the chance of honest success. As children are apt to question all correct performances and accuse one another of peeking, it is desirable to have this test in a room apart and to have only such children present as are actually engaging in the test. With at least two games going at once, four or five children can be present without interfering with one another.

The cheating score is a "c" if the child pins the tail or arrow correctly. The same score is used in choosing the winner for the game, except that approximations to the center are discriminated among those getting the tail or arrow near the proper point.

*Bean Relay.* This is a modified potato race, using beans instead of potatoes, which we developed for this purpose after considerable experimentation. Each row has four boxes, the first empty, the second and third with three beans each, and the fourth with ten or more. If possible, five rows are run at once to give the atmosphere of contest. Each heat is thirty seconds, which is time enough for eight or more runs, that is, for eight or more chances to cheat. The rule is to pick up one bean at a time, and each runner has an observer who has a counter and records his runs. At the end of each heat the beans in each child's home box are counted and the sum is his score for the game. Obviously, since he is supposed to take only one bean at a time, the number of beans in the home box should correspond with the number of runs, which has been checked by the observer. If a child is found to have more beans than runs, this is evidence of deception and he is given a "c."

As in the tail-pinning game, the bean relay should be run in a separate room or a corner of the room in order that there may be no children present but those who are engaging in the heat, as observers would tend to inhibit the tendency to cheat or to direct attention to cheating if it occurred.

*         *         *

## Methods for Measuring the Stealing Type of Deception

Here again it was necessary to conform to certain requirements in addition to the ten general criteria cited at the beginning of the chapter. These are as follows:

1. It must be a group situation.
2. Money must be used in a natural way or appear as a natural part of the situation.

3. There must be an opportunity to take all or some known part of the money apparently without being detected in the act.
4. The subject must feel that he is not merely being clever in getting away with the money but that he is actually stealing it from a particular person or institution.
5. It must be possible to check exactly what the subject does.

We used the stealing tests in two situations—party and classroom.

*         *         *

*Stealing Exhibited in Classrooms*

**1. The Planted Dime Test.** In connection with the administration of the puzzle tests in one school a little box was given to each pupil containing several puzzles not all of which were used. In each box was a dime ostensibly belonging to another puzzle, which the examiner showed to the pupils but did not ask them to solve. This other puzzle required the use of a dime, but no mention was made by the examiner of the dimes in the boxes.

Each pupil returned his own box to a large receptacle at the front of the room. Check on what each pupil did was arranged for by numbering and distributing the boxes according to the seating plan of the class. The purpose of this test was to see which children would take the dime before returning the box.

**2. The Magic Square Test.** This is a puzzle and was given along with the other puzzle tests already described. In this case, however, there was no possibility of faking a solution to the puzzle. The only deception involved was in not returning any or all of the coins that make up the puzzle.

The test material consisted of a handkerchief box six inches square, on the bottom of which we had drawn the design shown below, which is the bottom part of the puzzle score sheet shown on page 67. There were in the box seventeen coins: 1 quarter, 4 dimes, 4 nickels, 4 pennies, and 4 Chinese coins, making a cash value of 89 cents. The Chinese coins were used because some coin of zero value was required for the solution of the puzzle.

. . . Directions . . . are as follows: After describing the puzzle, the examiner said: "You will see as you open the box that it contains a lot of coins. Take the coins all out and put them beside the box or keep them in your hand. On the bottom of the box you will see some circles around a square, three circles in each direction, making a place for nine coins in all. You have *more* than nine coins,

unless there has been some mistake, so there will be more than enough to have one in each circle. But there is only one way to place them correctly in the circles; and this is to place them so that each row will add up to exactly the same amount as every other row, and to exactly the same amount as each diagonal, or cornerwise, row. I am not going to tell you what this amount is, nor just what coins will make it work. The penny is called 1, the nickel 5, the dime 10, the quarter 25, and the Chinese coin 0. At the bottom of the score sheet at the left you will see the directions and can refer to them at any time. Now let's see who is bright enough to get this puzzle."

After from two to seven minutes had elapsed the examiner said: "Now you have probably done at least one of the three things described on the score sheet, so write carefully on the score sheet the value of the coins as you now have them placed in the box. As soon as you have done that pass in your score sheet."

Examiner then collected score sheets, thus apparently breaking all connection between the boxes and the pupils.

"Now put all the money back in the box, put the band around it, and we will collect it. Pass the boxes to the center aisle."

These directions were modified in various ways. In one situation, where only boys were being tested, the examiner said, "if you think it would be easier to solve this puzzle if you had more coins to work with, you are at perfect liberty to use any coins you may have in your pocket. The coins in the box are sufficient for one solution, but there are other possibilities. Only if you use your own money, write down carefully what you put in so you will leave in the box

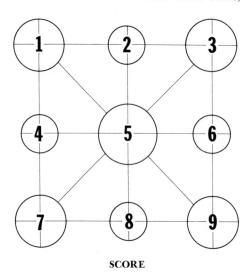

**SCORE**

If each of the six rows (1-2-3, 4-5-6, 7-8-9, 1-4-7, 2-5-8, 3-6-9) and the two diagonals (7-5-3, 1-5-9) adds to the same total, your score is 100.

If each of the six rows and one diagonal adds to the same total your score is 75.

If each of any four rows and one diagonal adds to the same total, your score is 50.

Any other arrangement is zero.

exactly what is there now." This provided a legitimate excuse for putting their hands in their pockets, but as it added one more source of error we did not try it again.

In another situation the pupils were brought from their classrooms to a vacant room for the puzzle tests. The coin test came last. They were told to hand in their score sheets, take the coin box to the principal's office, and leave it there. This gave the pupils a chance to take the box of coins out of the examining room, and since, on finishing the test, they left either alone or in groups of two or three, they could easily have made off with the boxes, money and all. In order that they might know that they were unobserved, the attendant in the office was instructed to pay no attention whatever to those who came in to deposit their boxes.

Another modification, not changing the character of the test materially, adapted it for younger, but bright, pupils by offering for solution one of the easier puzzles adapted to the magic square, but involving the same coins.

*Scoring the Magic Square Test.* The fact score was simply whether or not any money was missing. The amount score was the total amount of money missing, not the number of coins.

In order to check each pupil's behavior it was necessary to identify the persons using the boxes and to count the money returned by each. Identification was effected by the use of a key number combination placed in the magic square design on the score sheet. . . .[7]

[7] Each child wrote his name on his score sheet. On the design for the magic square were placed certain figures numbering the circles to correspond to the directions at the left of the design, but placed on the circles in accordance with a definite scheme as follows: Each circle

**3. The Coin-Counting Test.** As the Magic Square test was too complicated for some of the younger children, a simpler plan was evolved. Each child was given a sheet of paper on which were printed some arithmetic problems involving the counting of money. Here is a sample:

What three (3) coins add up to forty (40) cents?
( ) quarters ( ) dimes ( ) nickels
( ) pennies
What three (3) coins add up to twelve (12) cents?
( ) quarters ( ) dimes ( ) nickels
( ) pennies
What three (3) coins add up to thirty-one (31) cents?
( ) quarters ( ) dimes ( ) nickels
( ) pennies
What three (3) coins add up to twenty-seven (27) cents?
( ) quarters ( ) dimes ( ) nickels
( ) pennies

Each box contained just the same coins as the Magic Square box, except for the omission of the Chinese coins. The pupils were told that it was a money-counting test and that, in order to make

is divided into four parts by the lines drawn through them. Figures placed above the horizontal line are significant. Of these one is always to the left of the vertical line. This is the first figure of the identifying number. The central circle is not used for this purpose, so this first figure might be anything from one to nine except five. At the right, above the horizontal line, might be placed either one or two of the figures numbering the circles. If one, this is the second figure of the identifying number. If two, the smallest is read first, giving an identifying number of three figures. . . .

As the figures on each box were placed to correspond to the figures on its accompanying score sheet, and as no two were numbered alike, each box became identified with a child as soon as his name was written on the score sheet. The score sheets of course were assembled with the boxes and they were passed out together. But they were collected separately.

it a real test, the coins were to be used to count with instead of writing on the paper.

In this case, identification was effected by the following device: The arithmetic problems were mimeographed. A blur in one of the problems was purposely left so that it had to be filled in with pencil. These figures were made to correspond to figures placed on the bottoms of the boxes. The numbers on the boxes had a ¢ mark after them, furnishing thus a red herring for the child who wanted to speculate concerning this number. As the child placed his name on the sheet he identified his box at the same time and they could then be collected separately.

## Methods for Measuring the Lying Type of Deception

### A. Lying to Escape Disapproval

If lying is defined as misstatement of fact with intent to deceive, it becomes at once very difficult to test, because intentions are not directly known. But if lying is regarded only as making a false statement instead of a true statement when the truth is known to the one making the statement, it is not so difficult to measure.

\*　　　\*　　　\*

The first method which we used to detect lying was employed in connection with [achievement] tests. A week or more after these tests were given in any group an examiner returned with a set of general questions of a more or less personal nature. This was called the Pupil Data Sheet. Toward the end of the sheet the following questions were asked:

33. Did you ever cheat on any sort of test?
34. Have you cheated on such tests more than once?
41. Did you actually do this test all alone without getting help on it?
42. If you did get help, was it from some person?
43. Or was it from a book or dictionary?
44. Did you understand at the time that you were not to get help in doing the test?
45. On some of these tests you had a key to correct your paper by. Did you copy any answer from the keys?
46. Do you think that to do so is really cheating?
47. On any of these same tests did you copy answers from other pupils' papers?
48. Do you think that to do that is really cheating?
56. If you did copy on any of these tests that you took a little while ago, or received any help you should not have received, just why did you do so?
57. Have you answered all the questions honestly and truthfully?

It will be noted that questions 33, 34, 56, and 57 have only a general significance, whereas questions 41, 42, 43, 45, and 47 are entirely specific. Questions 44, 46, and 48 serve as a check on the other answers, but in this connection no other use was made of the answers to 46 and 48.

\*　　　\*　　　\*

### B. Lying to Win Approval

The second method is like the first in that it consists of a series of rather personal questions. There are many specific acts of conduct which on the whole have rather widespread social approval, but which at the same time are rarely done. The questions revolve around situations of this sort.

The test is in two forms. Each form contains 36 questions.

There are, no doubt, many children who could answer some of these questions quite truthfully as scored above. But the

## CEI ATTITUDES SA
### Form One

Name _____ Date _____

School _____ Grade _____

Answer the following questions by underlining YES or NO. If your answer is YES, draw a line under YES. If your answer is NO, draw a line under NO. Please answer every question.

| | | | | |
|---|---|---|---|---|
| 1. | Did you ever accept the credit or honor for anything when you knew the credit or honor belonged to someone else? | YES | NO | 1. |
| 2. | Did you ever act greedily by taking more than your share of anything? | YES | NO | 2. |
| 3. | Did you ever blame another for something you had done when you knew all the time it was your fault? | YES | NO | 3. |
| 4. | Do you usually report the number of a car you see speeding? | YES | NO | 4. |
| 5. | Do you always preserve order when the teacher is out of the room? | YES | NO | 5. |
| 6. | Do you report other pupils whom you see cheating? | YES | NO | 6. |
| 7. | Did you ever pretend to understand a thing when you really did not understand it? | YES | NO | 7. |
| 8. | Have you ever disobeyed any law of your country or rule of your school? | YES | NO | 8. |
| 9. | Do you speak to all the people you are acquainted with, even the ones you do not like? | YES | NO | 9. |
| 10. | Do you usually call the attention of people to the fact that you have on new shoes or a new suit or dress? | YES | NO | 10. |
| 11. | Are you always on time at school or for other appointments? | YES | NO | 11. |
| 12. | Do you always smile when things go wrong? | YES | NO | 12. |
| 13. | Do you usually pick up broken glass in the street? | YES | NO | 13. |
| 14. | Do you stick with your gang even when they go wrong? | YES | NO | 14. |
| 15. | Do you usually sneeze whenever you feel like it? | YES | NO | 15. |
| 16. | Did you ever take anything (even a pin or button) that belonged to someone else? | YES | NO | 16. |
| 17. | When you see other children fighting, do you stop them? | YES | NO | 17. |
| 18. | Do you always accept the decisions of the umpire without question? | YES | NO | 18. |
| 19. | Do you always obey your parents cheerfully and promptly? | YES | NO | 19. |
| 20. | Even when others will not play your way, do you keep on playing anyway? | YES | NO | 20. |

21. Do you try to take an interest in some things you do not like? YES NO 21.
22. Did you ever say anything about your teacher that you would be unwilling to say to her face? YES NO 22.
23. Did you ever feel that you would like to "get even" with another person for something he had done? YES NO 23.
24. Do you often give away anything which is very dear to you or which you have obtained at a sacrifice? YES NO 24.
25. Did you ever pretend that you did not hear when some-one was calling you? YES NO 25.
26. Did you ever hurt or cause pain to a dog, cat, or other animal? YES NO 26.
27. Do you go to church and Sunday school every Sunday? YES NO 27.
28. Do you keep a diary regularly? YES NO 28.
29. Do you read the Bible every day? YES NO 29.
30. Were you ever rude or saucy to your parents or teacher? YES NO 30.
31. Do you usually pick up papers and trash that others have thrown on the schoolroom floor? YES NO 31.
32. Do you usually correct other children when you hear them using bad language? YES NO 32.
33. Did you ever do any work on Sundays or go to the movies or a baseball game on Sunday? YES NO 33.
34. Did you ever break, destroy, or lose anything belonging to someone else? YES NO 34.
35. Did you ever tell on another child for something wrong he had done? YES NO 35.
36. Do you always do today things that you could put off until tomorrow? YES NO 36.

## CEI ATTITUDES SA
### Form Two

Name _____ Date _____
School _____ Grade _____

Answer the following questions by underlining YES or NO. If your answer is YES, draw a line under YES. If your answer is NO, draw a line under NO. Please answer every question.

1. Do you always apologize when you have been rude or dis-courteous? YES NO 1.
2. Did you ever accept the credit or honor for anything when you knew the credit or honor belonged to someone else? YES NO 2.
3. Do you always care for the property of others even though it has not been placed in your care? YES NO 3.
4. Did you ever act greedily by taking more than your share of anything? YES NO 4.
5. Did you ever blame another for something you had done when you knew all the time it was your fault? YES NO 5.
6. Do you throw wastepaper on the floor when there is no wastepaper basket handy? YES NO 6.

7. Have you ever disobeyed any law of your country or rule of your school?     YES   NO   7.
8. Are you always on time at school or for other appointments?     YES   NO   8.
9. Do you always congratulate your opponents?     YES   NO   9.
10. Do you usually "give in" when others are against you?     YES   NO   10.
11. Did you ever carve your name on your desk?     YES   NO   11.
12. Did you ever write your name in the books you use which belong to school or library?     YES   NO   12.
13. Do you always sing when others are singing?     YES   NO   13.
14. Do you usually pick up broken glass in the street?     YES   NO   14.
15. Do you usually report to the police the numbers of cars you see speeding in the city streets?     YES   NO   15.
16. Do you always finish your work before you play?     YES   NO   16.
17. Did you ever take anything (even a pin or button) that belonged to someone else?     YES   NO   17.
18. Did you ever say anything about your teacher that you would be unwilling to say to her face?     YES   NO   18.
19. Do you always keep every secret that you promise to keep?     YES   NO   19.
20. Do you keep quiet when older persons are talking?     YES   NO   20.
21. Do you always leave the table hungry?     YES   NO   21.
22. Did you ever feel that you would like to "get even" with another person for something he had done?     YES   NO   22.
23. Did you ever pretend that you did not hear when someone was calling you?     YES   NO   23.
24. Did you ever hurt or cause pain to a dog, cat, or other animal?     YES   NO   24.
25. Do you give something to every beggar who asks?     YES   NO   25.
26. Do you usually correct another pupil when you hear him using bad grammar?     YES   NO   26.
27. Do you spend some time each day acquiring a liking or taste for good music, fine art, and good literature?     YES   NO   27.
28. Do you pray at least once a day?     YES   NO   28.
29. Do you ask others to join your Sunday school?     YES   NO   29.
30. Were you ever rude or saucy to your parents or teacher?     YES   NO   30.
31. Do you usually pick up papers and trash that others have thrown on the schoolroom floor?     YES   NO   31.
32. Do you usually correct other children when you hear them using bad words?     YES   NO   32.
33. Did you ever do any work on Sunday or go to the movies or a baseball game on Sunday?     YES   NO   33.
34. Did you ever break, destroy, or lose anything belonging to someone else?     YES   NO   34.
35. Did you ever tell on another child for something wrong he had done?     YES   NO   35.
36. Do you always do today things that you could put off until tomorrow?     YES   NO   36.

child who could answer thirty-six truthfully would be a pious fraud. The test is scored in such a way as to give one point credit for each question answered in the approved way. For example, affirmative answers of questions 4, 5, 6, and 9, and negative of 1, 2, 3, 7, 8, and 10 on form one are all scored as receiving one point each. This gives the highest score to the greatest amount of falsification. The question is, How big a score should any pupil have before he is accredited with having lied? This again is a matter of probabilities.

In order to find the limit of honest answers, we gave the test to several classes in a school where we had found almost no deception, explaining to the children that we really wanted to know what children like themselves did in the situations listed in the test. No names were written on the blanks. In spite of (or perhaps because of) these precautions, this supposedly honest population as a matter of fact reported scores higher than those found in some of our most dishonest populations. We therefore gave up the hope of getting straight answers from children and turned for help to a graduate class in educational psychology, the members of which were interested in the moral aspects of education. We asked these men and women to think back over their early adolescent and preadolescent years and answer the questions in such a way as to represent what was probably true of their own childhood. The number claiming a perfect childhood was so small that it did not prevent our determining a workable limit of honest performance. Just as for the tests already described, we placed this at three times the standard deviation of the "honest" group beyond the mean of the honest group. Thus for form one, any child scoring 24 was given a "c," and on form two a "c" was recorded for any pupil reaching a total score of 28.

The amount score used was either the total number of "right" or conventional answers given, or an $X_i$ score found as usual by dividing the subject's deviation from the honest mean by the standard deviation of the honest scores.[8]

[8] [A further excerpt from Hartshorne and May's work appears in Section III.]

# 6

# Measurement of moral values: A review and critique[1]

*by Stephen M. Pittel and Gerald A. Mendelsohn*

The importance of moral values[2] in human functioning has long been recognized in personality theory and clinical practice; nevertheless, empirical investigations in this area have been sporadic. It seems that in attempting to divorce themselves from the methods and conceptualizations of philosophy and religion, psychologists have not only avoided making explicit value judgments but have also slighted moral values as objects of investigation. The

Stephen M. Pittel and Gerald A. Mendelsohn, "Measurement of Moral Values: A Review and Critique," *Psychological Bulletin*, 66, 1966, 22–35. Copyright 1966 by the American Psychological Association, and reproduced by permission.

[1] The work reported was partially supported by a predoctoral research fellowship awarded by the National Institute of Health. The authors wish to thank M. Brewster Smith for his thoughtful comments on this paper.

[2] To avoid repetitiveness, the terms "values," "standards," and "attitudes" will be used synonymously—either alone or in conjunction with the adjective "moral." While valid theoretical distinctions may be drawn to differentiate these terms, their usage here is intended to be inclusive of all psychological constructs relevant to the evaluation of human behavior, regardless of their source, content, or personal saliency. The term "evaluative attitude" is intended as a theoretically neutral term which avoids the surplus meanings attached to the term "moral values."

behavioristic orientation of modern psychology has fostered a reluctance to study a problem which by its very nature involves subjective processes. Thus, attempts to assess moral values have frequently focused on observable behavior from which values are inferred, or have attempted to predict overt behavior from subjective values. Rarely have subjective values been studied in their own right.

While the delineation of the links between values and behavior is clearly a desirable objective, many investigators, in their eagerness to focus on behavior, have paid insufficient attention to the conceptualization of moral values and the appropriate methods for their measurement (see Cook & Selltiz, 1964). Both experience and the research literature point to the complexity of the relationship between moral values and moral behavior. Simplistic models of this relationship have led to a failure of prediction, a consequent rejection of assessment techniques, and thus to a proliferation of test devices, apparently in the hope that something might predict moral behavior.

The immediate concerns of this paper are a review and evaluation of attempts to assess moral values. Underlying our effort is the assumption that a thorough study of moral values themselves is a necessary first step to the prediction of morally relevant behavior.

## History of Attempts to Assess Moral Values and Related Concepts

Since the literature on the measurement of moral values is extensive, dating back to before the turn of the century, it is necessary to limit consideration to those instruments most relevant to moral values as subjective phenomena. Thus, only those tests which directly assess aspects of moral concepts are dealt with here; studies which focused only on moral behavior, such as resistance to temptation, characteristic social behavior, etc., have been excluded. While many such behavioral measures have been used to infer the strength of moral attitudes or conscience (see Jones, 1946; Sears, 1960), the characteristically low intercorrelations among various measures of morality, notably between verbal and behavioral tests, suggest that these types of information are by no means interchangeable (Bronfenbrenner, 1962; Hoffman, 1963). Further, numerous test instruments which have been used to assess attitudes toward single moral values, such as honesty or aggression, have been excluded unless they have broader implications from either a methodological or theoretical point of view. (The reader interested in such studies is referred to the reviews and bibliographies of Hartshorne, May, & Shuttleworth, 1930; Jones, 1933, 1946; McGrath, 1923.) For the most part, empirical studies which deal with strength of conscience or morality as a generalized dimension or trait, rather than those which deal only with limited and circumscribed topics within this realm, are discussed.

The earliest general study of morality seems to be that of Osborne (1894). Using an open-ended questionnaire, he attempted to discover the "ethical content of children's minds." Children were asked to state what acts a child must do in order to be called either good or bad. Osborne learned that specific categories of acts were less important to children as evaluative dimensions than was a general notion of conformity to rules. He

concluded that obedience and truthfulness were the most salient aspects of the child's system of ethics, a result which supports the later observations of Piaget (1932) and Fromm (1947) regarding a primitive stage of morality characterized by obedience to externally imposed sanctions.

Sharp (1898), although partly concerned with various controversies arising from ethical theory, conducted an extensive study of moral judgments of college students for the purpose of introducing an objective method for the study of moral issues. He provided his subjects with 10 hypothetical situations to be evaluated in accordance with their moral beliefs. The following item is representative of those employed in the study:

> Several years ago in a railroad wreck a lady was imprisoned in the debris in such a way that escape was impossible. Her husband, who might have extricated himself with an effort, deliberately chose to remain and die with her, in order that he might give her the support and comfort of his presence in her last moments. She herself, we must suppose, was not aware of the possibility of his escape, otherwise his aim would of course have been defeated. What is to be said of the moral character of his choice in each of the following cases? (a) If he was a clerk with the expectations of the average of his class and had no family ties apart from his wife. (b) Position as in (a), but he had a mother living with him in his home, who was very much devoted to him but not dependent upon him for support. (c) Position again as in (a). He has a distant relative, a lady who was an invalid and absolutely dependent upon him for support. (d) If he had been a clergyman doing a great deal of good. (e) If he had been a Morse, conscious that he was on the eve of the solution of the

problem of the electric telegraph. (f) If he had been an artist of very exceptional talents.

As in this example, the motivational determinants of the action described were manipulated by varying the external events in a series of alternative conditions. Subjects were required to answer specific questions about the moral issues involved and were asked to justify each of their responses with a short essay. They were also asked to estimate the time required to arrive at their judgments and the certainty with which each was made.

Although both studies dealt with issues which still persist, it is unlikely that either of them had any direct influence on subsequent developments in this field of research. Both the methodology and the emphasis of these early investigations remain isolated from the main stream of later work. The bulk of studies immediately following these investigations used entirely different techniques; only in recent years have the open-ended questionnaire and the situational descriptive types of instruments come into use. Further, at no time since have psychologists directed themselves exclusively toward either the normative questions asked by Osborne or to the philosophical issues studied by Sharp.

With few exceptions, the literature relevant to the measurement of moral values since 1900 can be categorized into three major chronological periods, each of which is characterized by the introduction and predominant use of one type of instrument.

The first period extended through the early 1930s and was characterized by the use of paper-and-pencil assessment devices, most of which were designed to differentiate normal children and adolescents from those with delinquent or criminal tendencies. Few of the studies of this period were concerned with adult subjects and few used instruments developed by other investigators in previous studies.

Fernald (1912) included two tests of ethical content in a battery of perceptual-motor and paper-and-pencil tests designed to identify "defective delinquents." The first tested knowledge of right and wrong by asking children to indicate agreement or disagreement with the acts described in 10 situations involving legal violations. The second was considered to test moral intelligence and required subjects to rank the seriousness of a series of offenses. In both these tests, the correct answers were determined by the investigators or by "mature judges."

In the first of their "cross-out" (X-O) tests, Pressey and Pressey (1919) used a test of moral judgment which presented subjects with 25 groups of 5 items each and instructed them to cross out the "worst" item in each group. Typical of the lists used are the following: (1) holiness, reverence, piety, obedience, wickedness; (2) dancing, drunkenness, flirting, overeating, smoking.

Kohs (1922) incorporated both the Pressey and Pressey X-O Test and some problems from the Fernald battery into his Ethical Discriminations Test along with various "common-sense" questions from the Army Alpha, proverbs from the Otis tests, and two new tests of his own invention. The new additions included definitions of moral terms and the evaluation of various behaviors into categories according to the treatment deserved by the person committing the act. Thus, subjects were asked to select the correct definition for words such as good, love, enemy, and right; and to state into which of six categories (praise, nothing, scold, jail, prison, kill) behaviors such as breathing, deafness, dirty, forgery, grafting, indecent, perjury, shoplifting, stubborn, treason, etc., should be placed.

A slightly more novel technique was introduced by Brotemarkle (1922) who attempted to decieve his subjects into thinking that his "Comparison" test measured intelligence rather than moral concepts. Subjects were directed to place a list of seven words in the correct order between two polar extremes. Thus, the words bad, fair, mean, kind, pure, wicked, and considerate were to be placed between the poles Good and Evil. Following this part of the procedure, the subjects were asked to indicate if any of the words were more extreme than the poles themselves and to write a better word for each of those given. Finally, they were asked a series of questions designed to tap the degree to which they believed their answers revealed their character and the extent to which they believed others to be in agreement with their responses. From responses to these questions, profiles were constructed which were compared to the average profiles of 331 adults, and a deviation score was obtained for each subject.

McGrath (1923) presented "a series of questions and exercises, a group of pictures, and a number of little stories" standardized by age (from below 6 to above 17) which were designed to study the moral knowledge of delinquent children. Both group and individual forms of the various tests were given. The subtests included a variety of multiple choice and true-false items dealing with numerous violations of conventional, often religious, moral prohibitions, the X-O Test, vocabulary tests, tests involving comparisons of acts, and the like.

The picture and story tests required the subjects to assess the nature of the moral violations depicted and to comment in various ways upon them. Although some of the tests used by McGrath were new, none demands special mention here.

Following much the same logic as McGrath, Lincoln and Shields (1931) attempted to develop a standardized test of moral knowledge based on the responses to conventional morality expected of children of various ages. The subtests, which included vocabulary, comprehension, use of moral words in sentences, and judgments of moral violations, were arranged by years from age 6 to age 20. They were scored in a manner similar to that used for the Stanford-Binet with Age of Responsibility and Responsibility Quotients derived as scores.

Woodrow (1926) used a picture-preference test to measure children's acceptance of social standards of morality. Eleven groups of four pictures showing children engaged in either good or bad acts were shown to subjects who were asked to select the one they liked best. Norms based on a large sample of respondents aged 6 to 11 were used to give "demerits" for deviant responses.

Finally, as part of the Character Education Inquiry which also introduced the use of objective situational tests into American psychology, Hartshorne and his collaborators (Hartshorne & May, 1928; Hartshorne, May, & Maller, 1929; Hartshorne, May, & Shuttleworth, 1930) used a number of tests designed to measure moral knowledge. The tests were similar to those already described. The Good Citizenship Test, for example, consisted of 50 descriptions of social situations for which the child was required to select one of four solutions.

In addition to the usual information or vocabulary test of moral terms, the Attitudes and Opinions Test dealt with attitudes toward misconduct and toward various generalizations about moral duties and principles.

Another test required subjects to anticipate the possible consequences which might follow from a number of social situations involving "simple types of activity . . . well within the range of experience of schoolchildren," such as getting into fights at school, running across the street, etc. Still another test presented subjects with simple situations in which the behavior of a child was described and a vote was taken to determine the extent to which certain extenuating circumstances were taken into account in making moral judgments. At least both of these last tests are less objective in scoring procedures than is characteristic of the work of this group.

These instruments, collectively known as the Tests of Moral Knowledge, were used in an attempt to predict behavior in a large number of conduct tests, most of which involved resistance to various temptations. Hartshorne and May (1930) reported that no differences were found on any of some 400–500 individual test items between those who did and those who did not violate moral prohibitions in these situations. Neither were any significant differences found between such groups on any of the tests taken as a whole. Although the Tests of Moral Knowledge did correlate markedly with measures of intelligence, the correlations of these tests with behavioral measures of honesty, inhibition, cooperation, and the like were low (about .25). The correlations of moral knowledge with measures of intelligence average about .70, a figure which is as high as the average intercorre-

lations among either the moral knowledge or the intelligence tests themselves (Maller, 1944).

To a greater or lesser extent, each of the authors of the described tests seems to have accepted the notion that morally relevant behavior is in some way determined by moral knowledge and beliefs. It is certain that delinquents and those who violate conventional moral standards were expected to receive lower scores on these instruments than were normal subjects. Although the assumptions underlying this hypothesis were not necessarily made explicit, it seems apparent that moral knowledge and proper moral attitudes were considered to be necessary, if not sufficient, to produce moral behavior. Brotemarkle (1922), for example, contended that his Comparison Test taps the ideational content or "direct ideo-motor determiner of activity (p. 235)," while other writers (e.g., Maller, 1944) expressed dissatisfaction with the moral knowledge tests for their failure to correlate with relevant behavioral measures.

Lowe and Shimberg (1925) attacked the assumption that moral knowledge and moral behavior were directly related by testing a large group of normal and delinquent youths with the Terman Fables Test which purports to be useful as a measure of moral knowledge. Although some slight differences were found in the typically expected direction (6 percent more nondelinquents than delinquents received scores in the highest moral category while 8 percent more delinquents than normals received scores in the lowest category), the only significant difference between delinquents and normals was in intelligence—moral knowledge proved to be of little predictive validity. These authors concluded that the "results make us suspicious of all tests having as their underlying principle the assumption that moral judgments offer a reliable estimation of moral integrity [p. 59]."

Maller (1944), reviewing these early paper-and-pencil tests of moral knowledge, felt that their inability to predict behavior detracted from their usefulness as tests of character. Although in opposition to the Hartshorne and May group of which he was a member, Maller (1934) had argued for the generality rather than specificity of moral behavior, but he could find no evidence for this generality extending into the domain of verbal measures of moral knowledge and beliefs. However, Maller still did not question the supposed relationship between moral behavior and moral knowledge and beliefs. Instead, he argued that test items should be selected on the bases of their predictive validity and the absence of any correlation with intelligence. Although items from which such an instrument could be constructed did not seem to be available, Maller believed that increasing the difficulty of selecting the right answer in conflict descriptions might achieve the necessary degree of empirical validity and independence from intelligence. Such items should not deal "with differences between right and wrong but should . . . be concerned with conflicts between right and right or those between wrong and wrong." In each case, the correct, or morally right, alternative would have been decided by competent judges. To date, no one seems to have constructed a test of moral attitudes based on exactly these prescriptions—nor have any tests of moral values been found successful in behavioral prediction.

The second period in the development of tests to assess moral values was characterized by a breaking away from the rather naive and primarily atheoretical approaches of earlier instruments. Moral values were seen in the light of broader theoretical orientations and measures of morally relevant dimensions were included only as a part of more comprehensive personality assessment devices. Two major trends characterized this period. The first shift from the paper-and-pencil tests of moral knowledge and the like began with the 1932 publication of Piaget's *Moral Judgment of the Child*. While previous concern had been with the content of moral thoughts, beliefs, and knowledge, Piaget was more concerned with formal aspects of the child's moral behavior. Not only did Piaget theorize explicitly about the relation of verbal moral judgment to overt moral behavior, but he also provided a means relatively independent of moral content by which moral development might be assessed.

Piaget presented children with two stories describing some type of moral behavior, such as lying or stealing, and asked for a comparative evaluation of the two. The stories were so designed that the motivation, intention, and consequences varied while the nature of the behavior remained relatively constant. For example, the following pair of stories was intended to find out whether the child was more concerned with motive or material results when making moral judgments:

A. Alfred meets a little friend of his who is very poor. This friend tells him that he has had no dinner that day because there was nothing to eat in his home. Then Alfred goes into a baker's shop, and as he has no money, he waits until the baker's back is turned and steals a roll. Then he runs out and gives the roll to his friend.

B. Henriette goes into a shop. She sees a pretty piece of ribbon on a table and thinks to herself that it would look very nice on her dress. So while the shop lady's back is turned she steals the ribbon and runs away at once.

After hearing both stories, the subject was asked if the two children are equally guilty and to state which is the "naughtiest," and why. Other stories and questions were used to determine children's beliefs in the immanence of punishment, types of punishment deemed appropriate for misconduct, etc.

The Piaget interview approach was introduced to deal with problems unconsidered by previous investigators. It emphasized the development of the cognitive component of moral judgment but still showed considerable resemblance to earlier instruments in the nature of the moral situation presented. Piaget followed Fernald (1912) in using descriptions of situations which require classification along a dimension of gravity or wrongness. Although he made no effort to be inclusive in his sampling of morally relevant acts, each of the acts selected refers to some conventionally defined transgression. The major difference from other instruments lies in the use to which the responses were put. Piaget classified responses in terms of the stage of the child's moral development. Thus, children were not classified as more or less moral on the basis of their responses but were put into classes based on the developmental maturity of their moral judgments, as this was inferred from their ordering of the two stories and from the intensive unstructured interview which followed.

Moral "realistic" responses are those in which moral rules are seen as absolute and immutable. Violations of such rules bring about an immanent justice with the severity of punishment varying directly with the seriousness of consequences, regardless of potentially extenuating or justifying motivational circumstances. Rules are not internalized during this stage of moral growth, and they are entirely dependent for their enforcement on external sanctions. Rules are not understood, they are merely followed.

Moral "relativistic" responses are those in which the child takes extenuating circumstances into account when making moral judgments. Acts are evaluated according to their motives rather than their consequences, and punishments are seen as "equitable" rather than "expiatory." Rules are internalized and understood at this stage of development. The child sees rules both as influenced by situational or motivational demands, and as arrived at by mutual consent rather than by external authority.

The introduction of this interview technique for assessing the cognitive growth of moral judgments within an explicit theoretical framework has been perhaps the single greatest influence in the subsequent investigation of moral values from a psychological point of view. While other investigators following Piaget have modified his technique, usually with the intent of making it more amenable to objective procedures of administration and scoring, the basic method of testing and the scoring of responses into categories of moral development continues to the present (reviews of studies using the Piaget technique may be found in Bronfenbrenner, 1962, and in Hoffman, 1963).

Another major influence during this second period stemmed from the introduction into American psychology of omnibus investigations of personality based primarily on psychoanalytic and behavioristic models. As in much of the previous work described, most studies of moral values during this period were concerned with the description and diagnosis of individuals rather than with the testing of specific hypotheses about the development of functions of values. Unlike the early studies, which were primarily concerned with the identification of delinquents and others with antisocial tendencies, the newer instruments were mostly designed for use with normal subjects. They tended to be more refined statistically, and scores were not based on agreement with conventional moral standards. Instead, investigators were interested in tapping individual differences in many dimensions of personality and in establishing the relationships among them. Consequently, stated moral values, the way subjects would feel if they violated moral prohibitions, and, indeed, their tendencies to violate such prohibitions, were often incorporated into a single test instrument or were included in assessment batteries.

Murray (1938), as part of his attempt to systematically define and study the personality of normal individuals, developed three sets of questionnaire items designed to tap the dimensions of Superego Integration, Superego Conflict, and the Sentiments of Superego. Superego Integration was defined as "a condition in which the dictates of 'conscience' have been so far accepted by the Ego that the subject *wills* the obligatory (the

socially demanded action) [p. 147]," and was measured by items such as: "I have developed a good deal of self control," "I am seldom tempted to do anything wrong," "I carry a strict conscience about with me wherever I go," and "I prohibit myself the enjoyment of certain unprofitable pleasures." Superego Conflict, the opposite of Superego Integration, represented the "condition of conflict in which asocial impulses are 'at war with conscience' . . . [p. 147]." This was measured by items such as: "I often ask myself: 'Have I done right?,'" "I am apt to lower my eyes when someone looks me square in the face," and "Sometimes I feel—after I have done something—that I have not done it correctly, and that I must repeat it to satisfy myself." Finally, the items designed to tap the Sentiments of Superego are aphorisms like: "The moral man watches diligently over his secret thoughts," "To starve is a small matter; to lose one's virtue is a great one," "It is better to be faithful than famous," and "Virtue is merely a struggle wherein we overcome our weaknesses."

While Murray did not spell out exactly what values were being considered as part of the superego or conscience, it is clear that implicitly they are the traditional values of conventional morality ("the socially demanded action"). However, the scale items themselves were manifestly concerned with impulse control, guilt, and self-esteem rather than with specific moral values. In an attempt to relate these measures to behavior, Christenson (1938) observed subjects in the Murray assessment program in experimental temptation situations involving cheating. He found that a composite honesty rating correlated .55 with Superego Integration.[3] Thus, there is some evidence that self-reported impulse control is associated with resistance to temptation, but this does not imply that moral values determine this behavior. This finding is particularly noteworthy considering previous unsuccessful efforts to predict morally relevant behavior from moral attitudes and knowledge alone.

Brahmachari (1937; cited by Flugel, 1961) discriminated between verbal and behavioral expressions of moral values. Subjects were asked to indicate the extent of their agreement or disagreement (on an 11-point scale) with 42 items dealing with theoretical moral issues. Two examples of these are: "Ought we always to be careful to avoid all suffering, mental or physical, to others, unless such suffering is unavoidably incidental to preservation of life, health, or absolutely necessary to social discipline?" and "Is it desirable to abstain from alcoholic drink?" Subjects were also asked to indicate their own typical conduct in these situations and the extent to which they experienced "mental conflict" as a result of discrepancies between their moral attitudes and their moral conduct.

Similar methods which dealt individually with separate aspects of moral attitudes, moral behavior, and conflict resulting from disparity between attitudes and behavior were introduced by Beller (1945) and by Friedenberg and Havighurst (1948). Beller distinguished between two attitude components, "an interiorized norm or internal symbolic reaction, and a predisposition to the overt act [Beller, 1949, p. 137]." He asked subjects to respond to items pertaining to honesty by stating how they would behave in the situation described and how right it would be for them to act in such a manner.

Friedenberg and Havighurst adapted Beller's technique to a more comprehensive study of moral values in a number of content areas. An inventory consisting of 115 acts divided into 11 categories of moral behavior (including 5 morally neutral items) was administered twice, first with instructions to respond to each item in terms of "How Bad Is It?" and then in terms of "How Would You Feel?" In the latter, subjects were asked to anticipate their feelings were they to commit each of the acts presented. Although the reliabilities of the subtests and of the derived score for strength of conscience were high, Friedenberg and Havighurst did not accept its validity as a measure of conscience. Instead, they argued for its use as a projective device from which more global personality dimensions might be inferred.

Other systematic investigations of personality and character undertaken during this period include those of Havighurst and Taba (1949) and Ligon (1956). The instruments used in both of these investigations are similar in format to earlier tests and need not be singled out for attention. These investigators, like their predecessors, found no significant correlations between moral beliefs and attitudes, and behavioral measures of morality or resistance to temptation.

The problem of the prediction of morally relevant behavior was approached by other means during this period. Using items derived from a role-theoretical approach to psychopathy Gough (1948), Gough and Peterson

---

[3] Correlations of the honesty rating with other measures were not reported, nor were the intercorrelations among the questionnaire scales themselves.

(1952) were able to devise a scale which successfully discriminates between those who characteristically show moral behavior and those who do not. Even within the delinquent or criminal range itself, this socialization scale discriminates among various subgroups defined by severity of offense and recidivism (Gough, 1960). Thus, although this scale does not use items having any direct bearing on conventional moral standards, the problem of prediction of at least certain forms of moral behavior is not impossible of solution. We thus have the paradoxical situation that the prediction of moral behavior has been done best without reference to moral knowledge or attitudes.

In addition to other tests of moral values described, Cattell, Saunders, and Stice (1957), and Hathaway and McKinley (1943) included in their personality inventories scales which might be thought to have relevance to this area of investigation. Cattell's 16 Personality Factors, for example, contains scales to measure Superego Strength and Guilt Proneness, both of which might relate to the assessment of moral values. Similarly, the Psychopathic Deviate Scale of the MMPI was derived from item analyses based on patients diagnosed as either asocial or amoral by the psychiatric staff of a mental hospital. While such instruments are related the present concern, they do not directly assess moral values.

Still another approach was taken by Crissman (1942) who presented a list of 50 acts to be evaluated by subjects on a 10-point scale of wrongness. The acts described were statements of violations of conventional moral standards, many of which were also legally prohibited. A few examples are: "Killing a person in defense of one's own life," "Kidnapping and holding a child for ransom," "Having sex relations while unmarried," "Not giving to charity when able," and "Disbelieving in God." As used by Crissman, and more recently by Rettig and Pasamanick (1959a, 1959b, 1960a, 1960b, 1961), the inventory has not been employed to assess individual differences in moral values but has been used only to establish item norms for selected populations. That is, individual differences in moral evaluation have not been measured using the instrument, nor have scoring procedures for this purpose been suggested, although such steps could easily be taken. Group results in terms of mean "wrongness" ratings for each item have been used to determine both the absolute wrongness associated with the items by various populations, and to determine the relative wrongness or hierarchical ordering of the items. The instrument has been factor analyzed by Rettig and Pasamanick (1959b), and a number of content-specific dimensions of morally relevant items have been found, along with a large general factor.

Finally, Rosenthal (1955) used a Q technique to assess the moral values of psychotherapy patients and their therapists. The 60-item Moral Values Q Sample consisted of 10 items in each of six conflict areas: sex-rigid, sex-free, antiaggressive, aggressive, disciplinarian, and libertarian. The items were to be sorted into 11 categories following a fixed distribution, according to the strength of belief or disbelief of the moral statement presented in each. As with all of the instruments of this period, no assumptions were made about the correctness of responses, and no scoring of responses on the basis of norms, however derived, was made. In this particular study, the only concern was with the degree of correspondence between patient and therapist values before and after therapy, and no other scoring was used.

While there seems to be little coherence in the grouping of instruments just discussed, they reflect a general shift in emphasis from earlier approaches. The concern with the correctness of moral values and the notion of direct behavioral prediction from moral knowledge characteristic of the first period are clearly absent. The test instruments of this second period (1932 to mid-1950s), though diverse in method, integrated an interest in moral values with other, broader research questions in the field of individual differences and personality assessment. Aspects of knowledge, self-control, behavior, and affect were included with moral values themselves in the construction of assessment techniques. In effect, the study of moral attitudes was integrated with more generalized trait and dynamic concepts, like superego, conscience, or character. It is in the light of this continuing trend toward complexity that developments of the third and most recent period can most clearly be seen.

The predominant characteristic of the present period in the study of moral values is the use of projective techniques, many of them designed specifically for the investigation of morally relevant dimensions. Although the Rorschach (Buhler, Buhler, & Lefever, 1948) and the TAT (Lindzey, Bradford, Tejessy, & Davids, 1959) have been used to infer the strength of conscience, or the relative influence of superego on personality functioning, the current trend in research studies is toward the development of projective devices more directly concerned with moral content.

This trend was adumbrated by Schwartz (1932), who designed a set of pictures representing frequently encountered situations in the life of delinquents. These included pictures of acts such as fishing illegally, coaxing girls into a clubhouse, and forcing a boy to steal from a peddler. Pictures of nondelinquent acts such as writing "I am a bad boy" on the school blackboard, having bad dreams, sleepwalking, etc., were also included. These pictures were presented during an interview in which delinquent subjects were encouraged to respond by imagining what they would do if they were in similar situations. Schwartz did not specify a scoring system for responses nor did he discuss the uses to which the interview material could be put.

The next appearance of projective techniques specifically designed for the assessment of morally relevant dimensions occurred in connection with studies of superego development and the internalization of moral standards. Following the psychoanalytic orientation of most of these studies, the superego has been treated as a more or less unitary dimension consisting of an integrate of moral attitudes, behavioral control, and affects. Although possible variations in the content of supergo (i.e., moral attitudes) have occasionally been acknowledged (e.g., Allinsmith, 1957), they were not directly assessed, and the major focus of attention has been on the intensity of projected guilt responses which follow descriptions of transgressions of conventional moral standards.

The projective technique most extensively used has been some variant of the story-completion approach. Allinsmith and Greening (1955) asked subjects to supply an ending to a story stem involving the violation of social prohibitions against aggression (anger). The severity of "moral needs" (i.e., internalized moral standards or superego) was inferred from the intensity of guilt responses manifested in the story endings. Although their primary concern was with a generalized dimension of superego strength, Allinsmith and Greening concluded that such a dimension could not be properly inferred from guilt responses to stories involving only one content area. In a previous study, these authors had found that subjects who showed intense guilt in some areas (e.g., stealing) did not show similar responses to other content also involving the violation of moral prohibitions (e.g., disobedience to parents).

Barron (1955) used a Story Completion Test of a somewhat different nature to assess Ethical Sensitivity and superego internalization. In this approach, story beginnings involving some ethical conflict were presented to subjects who were asked to complete each story as they thought it would turn out. Unlike the method described above, the stories did not necessarily involve either real or imagined violations of conventional moral prohibitions, nor was the content restricted to any single value area such as aggression or honesty.

Miller and Swanson (1960) and their collaborators (Allinsmith, 1957; Aronfreed, 1957) have used stories involving primarily either aggression or sex in their studies of moral values and guilt, although the implications drawn have been extended to the entire realm of functioning subsumed under the generic label "conscience" or "superego." Each of their stories included the following elements: (a) a secret violation of a common moral teaching, (b) by a given act, (c) expressing a stated or evident mo-

tive, (d) directed at a specified category of person, (e) and in a specified situation (Miller & Swanson, 1960, p. 144 ff.).

The following story is typical of this format:

> Dave likes his baseball coach. The other day the coach promised him privately that Dave could pitch in the big game on Saturday. When the team meets for final practice, the coach doesn't say anything to Dave about pitching. Dave is afraid he has forgotten or changed his mind. He keeps thinking to himself over and over again: "The coach isn't going to keep his promise. I hope he doesn't even make the game. I wish he'd drop dead.!"

Adolescent subjects were asked to complete the story by telling what they thought would happen next and what the people in the story are thinking and feeling. The strength of guilt was inferred from instances of direct statements of self-blame or guilt feelings, indirect manifestations of guilt such as attempts at reparation or confession, or from instances of defensive distortions such as attribution of blame to others or denial of transgression.[4]

Stein (1958) scored two types of responses given to story stems involving stealing, violation of trust, and having hostile thoughts. External referent responses were those containing fears of accidental hurt, rejection by others, punishment after death, etc. Internal referent responses were those which included self-anger, punishment, or reproach inflicted upon the self for transgressions. Both types of response were thought to indicate components of the superego and the experience of guilt.

Aronfreed (1961) used a more refined

[4] It is apparent from this example that wishes and feelings as well as behavior were considered the violation of a moral prohibition.

scoring system to deal with alternative responses to transgression on story-completion tasks. Stories involving acts of aggression were used because "it was felt that the range of moral responses in this area of behavior would be fairly broad and representative of moral responses in general." The major subcategories of response scored were: self-criticism, correction of deviance, degree of activity in self-correction, external resolution, and externally oriented initiation and performance. Aronfreed interpreted the findings of this study to suggest that many forms of internalized response to moral transgressions, such as corrections of deviance, do not depend on cognitive moral judgments or self-criticism but are merely learned responses to transgressions. This view differs from the psychoanalytic notion of the superego in that it treats all responses to transgression as learned habits, that is, self-criticism and guilt are not seen as necessary intervening processes. Thus, self-criticism is only one of a number of possible responses to transgression. Aronfreed made no attempt to differentiate among specific content areas in terms of strength of values, resistance to temptation, or moral consequences. This seems to be an oversimplification since these separate components of the superego are likely to be differentially reinforced during socialization, particularly in different moral content areas.

Other variants of the story-completion technique have employed stimulus materials such as puppet plays (Johnson, 1955), the Blacky pictures (Minkowich, 1959), and incomplete doll-play stories (Wurtz, 1958). In each of these variants, responses have been scored for superego relevant variables such as introjection of blame, compliance and transgression,

and internal and external frames of reference.

Included among the other techniques introduced to assess the superego or conscience during this most recent period is the IES (Id, Ego, Superego) Test (Dombrose & Slobin, 1958). Each of the four subtests included in this semiprojective battery is used to derive scores indicating the relative strength of impulse (id), ego, and superego. Common to all the scoring procedures for the IES Test are the assumptions that superego strength is manifested in a preoccupation with moralistic and punitive responses to violations of conventional moral prohibitions, and that any response which focuses on impulse suppression or on the negative consequences of impulse expression results from superego functioning. These scoring procedures do not take into account possible variations in the content of superego nor do they attempt to assess these directly. The superego is operationally defined in terms of behaviors which reflect acceptance and salience of externally defined moral values.

Another measure of superego strength was employed by Wahler (1959) who attempted to test hypotheses about superego functions in neurosis. Following the Freudian conception of superego as an inhibitory mechanism, particularly with respect to sexual and aggressive impulses, Wahler devised a task in which the choice of aggressive alternatives was thought to indicate the relative weakness of superego. Subjects were presented with scrambled words which could be combined to form either an aggressive or a nonaggressive sentence. Arguments concerning the strength of superego in normal and neurotic subjects were tested using this primarily behavioral measure of superego. As in the IES Test, the acceptance of aspects of conventional morality and the tendency to suppress impulse were taken as indicators of superego strength.

In none of these projective techniques have moral values been operationally differentiated from the consequences of moral transgression or from other components of superego. Practically speaking, these authors have considered superego as a unitary dimension—when superego is strong, values are strong, controls are strong, and moral consequences, for example, guilt, are strong. Thus, any measure which taped one of these variables was considered functionally equivalent to any other relevant measure. To put it differently, there was an operating assumption of a linear and strong relationship between guilt, self-punishment, resistance to temptation, and strength of values. A further assumption has been that measures of superego strength derived from one content area, for example, aggression, are directly generalizable to all areas of moral concern. In short, assessment of moral values through these techniques is predicated on a series of propositions, which though consistent with psychoanalytic theory, are questionable on empirical grounds. A number of studies have shown low correlations, no relationship, or even negative relationships between values and resistance to temptation (e.g., Hartshorne et al., 1929; Mills, 1958), guilt and resistance to temptation (e.g., Allinsmith, 1960; Burton, 1959; Grinder, 1962; Maccoby, 1959; Sears, Rau, & Alpert, 1960), and no studies have demonstrated that strength of moral values, resistance to temptation, and proneness to give projective guilt responses all covary.

In the light of these considerations, it is possible that the absence of projected guilt responses may reflect, in addition to the relative weakness of internalized values, (a) adequate defenses against guilt, (b) alternative ways of handling potentially guilt-arousing situations, or (c) the failure of the subject to identify with the protagonist of the projective situation or to respond in a personally characteristic way to a situation merely imagined. Similarly, the presence of guilt responses to projective materials may indicate in addition to strong values (a) an inability to act in accordance with values, that is, chronic guilt, (b) the subject's awareness of societal standards and the demand characteristics of the testing situation, and (c) the tendency to feel guilt empathically in association with imagined moral transgressions.

We thus conclude that the mere presence or absence of indices of guilt does not provide an unambiguous measure of the strength of moral values.

The instruments of the third period all seem to deal with the superego in operational terms which place emphasis on the tendency of subjects to take a moralistic stance in the consideration of violations of conventional prohibitions, to project guilt feelings onto characters who violate these standards, and to indicate by their responses that they characteristically deny or suppress impulses which lead to socially unacceptable behavior. The notion that projective responses reflect the subject's actual behavior and affective responses seems to be taken at face value in these instruments. Alternate interpretations of the projective test responses in terms of possible variations in moral attitudes, thresholds of guilt feelings, defenses, etc., are not taken into consideration. The attempts to conceal the true nature of the investigation from subjects (which underlies the use of projective materials) would seem to have caused investigators to lose sight of the highly personalized and subjective nature of the phenomena which they are attempting to assess. While there may be many reasons for attributing moralistic attitudes and feelings onto imaginary characters in fictitious situations, it does not follow that these are representative of the feelings and values of the subjects themselves. The hypotheses of projective testing are highly relevant to many areas of personality assessment, but they may not be pertinent to the study of subjective phenomena such as the values and affects which form a major part of the superego. To the extent that these are consciously experienced (see A. Freud, 1946), subjects are probably more likely to express them in direct assessments of moral attitudes and emotional response than they are in projective tests (Allport, 1956).

Considerably less emphasis has been placed on the predictive validity of superego measures derived from projective techniques than has been characteristic of paper-and-pencil assessment devices. Rather, projective superego measures have frequently been used as dependent variables in studies of the influence of child-rearing methods, sex differences in conscience development, identification, etc. The adequacy of the measures has been gauged by their effectiveness in yielding results consistent with psychoanalytic and learning-theory models of personality development and by their face validity. While these measures have been more or less useful for these purposes, they do not necessarily have utility for the study of moral values.

## Criticism of Past Assessment Techniques

An evaluation of the instruments of all three periods points to a number of conceptual and methodological pitfalls to be avoided in the assessment of moral values and their relationships to behavior. This does not imply that all tests reviewed are subject to each of the limitations summarized below; rather, each is subject to one or more of them.

1. A number of them assess knowledge of legal, moral, or ethical standards rather than the individual's attitude toward these standards. Given this emphasis on information, it is not surprising that such tests have often been found to correlate with measures of intelligence and that scores increase consistently with age.

2. Scoring of some instruments is based on normative or other evaluative standards of "correctness" determined by societally defined criteria. Thus, responses in agreement with norms established by the investigators are scored as moral, while those not in agreement lower the overall measure of strength of moral attitude or conscience.

3. Even when scoring criteria are not explicitly linked to normative or societal standards, subjective scoring procedures and ratings used with some instruments, that is, projective techniques, frequently rely on the same sorts of external standards of evaluation.

4. Judgments are often required about ethical concepts or abstractions such as "stealing" or "cheating" rather than about behavior occurring in realistic situations. Subjects are asked to evaluate abstract acts independent of the setting in which such acts occur and in which contextual factors may serve to mitigate or justify their wrongness. The subject,

in short, is asked to do something in the test situation which he would never do in real life.

5. Many tests sample only a small number of moral or ethical areas (e.g., "sex" and "aggression") thus limiting their generality. The content typically sampled is based on categories of conventional morality or on the author's theoretical preoccupation. Many dimensions of behavior which are potentially morally salient are thereby excluded.

6. Some tests infer strength of moral attitudes from subjects' behavior (resistance to temptation) or affective responses (particularly guilt feelings). These inferences seem quite questionable given the characteristically low correlations among measures of behavior, affect, and attitude. Further, there is a considerable lack of conceptual differentiation among such terms as conscience, superego, moral judgments, guilt, etc., as these are operationalized in test instruments.

7. Orienting instructions, item content, or testing situations may tend to elicit socially desirable responses on some instruments and, therefore, to limit individual variability in response to items.

8. The majority of instruments have not been sufficiently standardized or validated for extensive use by other investigators. Reliability data are lacking for most tests reviewed, and when noted appear to be limited only to internal consistency estimates. Neither test-retest reliabilities nor alternate forms are available for most of these tests.

## Conclusions

The purpose of this review was to examine assessment techniques in an area of growing psychological concern, the study of moral values and behavior. It is our conclusion that the techniques employed in the past are open to criticism on both methodological and conceptual grounds. We would not conclude, however, that the problems pointed out in this review are inherent to the subject matter under consideration. Rather, they seem to be the result of an insufficient effort to conceptualize the nature of moral values and their relation to behavior. Perhaps the greatest single shortcoming underlying each of the specific criticisms discussed is the failure to view evaluative attitudes as subjective phenomena whose measurement is best achieved independent of a concern with the relationship of those attitudes to conventional and normative standards of moral valuation. It is important to assess at an individual level the content, strength, and patterning of subjective attitudes of evaluation *per se*. Whether these attitudes would be approved or disapproved by society is a subsequent question which need not be considered in the construction of measures of evaluative attitudes.

## References

ALLINSMITH, W. Conscience and conflict: The moral force in personality. *Child Development*, 1957, **28,** 469–476.

ALLINSMITH, W. Moral standards. II. The learning of moral standards. In D. R. Miller & G. E. Swanson (Eds.), *Inner conflict and defense.* New York: Holt, 1960. Pp. 141–176.

ALLINSMITH, W., & GREENING, T. C. Guilt over anger as predicted from parental discipline: A study of superego development. *American Psychologist*, 1955, **10,** 320. (Abstract)

ALLPORT, G. W. The trend in motivational theory. In C. E. Moustakas (Ed.), *The self.* New York: Harper, 1956. Pp. 25–43.

ARONFREED, J. M. Moral standards and defenses against guilt. *Dissertation Abstracts*, 1957, **17**, 172–173. (Abstract)

BARRON, F. The crisis in belief. Paper read at the California Academy of Science, San Francisco, 1955.

BELLER, E. K. Measurement of attitudes in younger boys. Unpublished master's thesis, University of Iowa, 1945.

BELLER, E. K. Two attitude components in younger boys. *Journal of Social Psychology*, 1949, **29**, 137–151.

BRAHMACHARI, S. Moral attitudes in relation to upbringing, personal adjustment and social opinion. Unpublished doctoral dissertation, University of London, 1937.

*BRONFENBRENNER, U. The role of age, sex, class, and culture in studies of moral development. *Research Supplement to Religious Education*, 1962, **57**, S-3–S-17.

BROTEMARKLE, R. A. A comparison test for investigating the ideational content of the moral concepts. *Journal of Applied Psychology*, 1922, **6**, 235–242.

BUHLER, C., BUHLER, K., & LEFEVER, D. A. Development of the basic Rorschach score with manual of directions. Los Angeles: Basic Rorschach Standardization Study I, 1948. (Mimeo)

BURTON, R. V. Some factors related to resistance to temptation in four-year-old children. Unpublished doctoral dissertation, Harvard University, 1959.

CATTELL, R. B., SAUNDERS, D. R., & STICE, G. *Handbook for the sixteen personality factor questionnaire: "The 16 P.F. Test."* Champaign, Ill.: Institute of Personality and Ability Testing, 1957.

CHRISTENSON, J. A., JR. Ethical standards test. In H. Murray (Ed.), *Explorations in personality*. New York: Oxford, 1938. Pp. 501–503.

COOK, S. W., & SELLTIZ, C. A multiple indicator approach to attitude measurement. *Psychological Bulletin*, 1964, **62**, 36–55.

CRISSMAN, P. Temporal change and sexual difference in moral judgments. *Journal of Social Psychology*, 1952, **16**, 29–38.

DOMBROSE, L. A., & SLOBIN, M. S. The IES Test. *Perceptual and Motor Skills*, 1958, **8**, 347–389.

FERNALD, G. G. The defective delinquent differentiating tests. *American Journal of Insanity*, 1912, **68**, 523–594.

FLUGEL, J. C. *Man, morals and society.* New York: Viking, 1961.

FREUD, A. *The ego and the mechanisms of defense.* (Orig. publ. 1936) New York: International Universities, 1946.

FRIEDENBERG, E. Z., & HAVIGHURST, R. J. An attempt to measure strength of conscience. *Journal of Personality*, 1948, **17**, 232–243.

FROMM, E. *Man for himself.* New York: Rinehart, 1947.

GOUGH, H. G. A sociological theory of psychopathy. *American Journal of Sociology*, 1948, **53**, 359–366.

GOUGH, H. G. Theory and measurement of socialization. *Journal of Consulting Psychology*, 1960, **24**, 23–30.

GOUGH, H. G., & PETERSON, D. R. The identification and measurement of predispositional factors in crime and delinquency. *Journal of Consulting Psychology*, 1952, **16**, 207–212.

GRINDER, R. E. Parental child-rearing practices, conscience, and resistance to temptation of sixth-grade children. *Child Development*, 1962, **33**, 803–820.

*HARTSHORNE, H., & MAY, M. A. *Studies in the nature of character.* Vol. 1. *Studies in deceit.* New York: Macmillan, 1928.

HARTSHORNE, H., & MAY, M. A summary of the work of the Character Education Inquiry. *Religious Education*, 1930, **25**, 607–619.

HARTSHORNE, H., MAY, M. A., & MALLER, J. B. *Studies in the nature of character.* Vol. 2. *Studies in service and self-control.* New York: Macmillan, 1929.

HARTSHORNE, H., MAY, M. A., & SHUTTLEWORTH, F. K. *Studies in the nature of character.* Vol. 3. *Studies in the organization of character.* New York: Macmillan, 1930.

* [Asterisks indicate works that are reprinted, in whole or in part, in this volume.]

HATHAWAY, S. R., & McKINLEY, J. C. *The Minnesota Multiphasic Personality Inventory.* Minneapolis: University of Minnesota Press, 1943.

HAVIGHURST, R. J., & TABA, H. *Adolescent character and personality.* New York: Wiley, 1949.

HOFFMAN, M. L. Child-rearing practices and moral development: Generalizations from empirical research. *Child Development,* 1963, 34, 295–318.

JOHNSON, E. Z. The "problem children" of school and home. *Psychological Reports,* 1955, 1, 371–378.

JONES, V. Children's morals. In C. Murchison (Ed.), *A handbook of child psychology.* Worcester, Mass.: Clark University Press, 1933. Pp. 482–533.

JONES, V. Character development in children —An objective approach. In L. Carmichael (Ed.), *Manual of child psychology.* New York: Wiley, 1946. Pp. 707–751.

KOHS, S. C. An ethical discrimination test. *Journal of Delinquency,* 1922, 7, 1–15.

LIGON, E. M. *Dimensions of character.* New York: Macmillan, 1956.

LINCOLN, E. A., & SHIELDS, F. J. An age scale for the measurement of moral judgment. *Journal of Educational Research,* 1931, 23, 193–197.

LINDZEY, G., BRADFORD, J., TEJESSY, C., & DAVIDS, A. Thematic Apperception Test: An interpretive lexicon for clinician and investigator. *Journal of Clinical Psychology,* 1959, Monogr. suppl. No. 12.

LOWE, G. M., & SHIMBERG, M. E. A critique of the Fables as a moral judgment test. *Journal of Applied Psychology,* 1925, 9, 53–59.

MACCOBY, E. E. The generality of moral behavior. Paper read at American Psychological Association, Cincinnati, 1959.

MALLER, J. B. General and specific factors in character. *Journal of Social Psychology,* 1934, 5, 97–102.

MALLER, J. B. Personality tests. In J. McV. Hunt (Ed.), *Personality and the behavior disorders.* New York: Ronald, 1944. Pp. 170–213.

McGRATH, M. C. A study of the moral development of children. *Psychological Monographs,* 1923, 32 (2, Whole No. 144).

MILLER, D. R., & SWANSON, G. E. (Eds.) *Inner conflict and defense.* New York: Holt, 1960.

MILLS, J. Changes in moral attitudes following temptation. *Journal of Personality,* 1958, 26, 517–531.

MINKOWICH, A. Correlates of superego functions. *Dissertation Abstracts,* 1959, 19, 3356–3357. (Abstract)

MURRAY, H. A. *Explorations in personality.* New York: Oxford, 1938.

OSBORNE, F. W. The ethical content of children's minds. *Educational Review,* 1894, 8, 143–146.

*PIAGET, J. *The moral judgment of the child.* New York: Harcourt, 1932. (Republished: Glencoe, Ill.: Free Press, 1948.)

PRESSEY, S. L., & PRESSEY, L. A. "Cross-out" tests: With suggestions as to a group scale of the emotions. *Journal of Applied Psychology,* 1919, 3, 138–150.

RETTIG, S., & PASAMANICK, B. Changes in moral values among college students: A factorial study. *American Sociological Review,* 1959, 24, 856–863. (a)

RETTIG, S., & PASAMANICK, B. Changes in moral values over three decades, 1929–1958. *Social Problems,* 1959, 6, 320–328. (b).

RETTIG, S., & PASAMANICK, B. Differences in the structure of moral values of students and alumni. *American Sociological Review,* 1960, 25, 550–555. (a)

RETTIG, S., & PASAMANICK, B. Moral codes of American and foreign academic intellectuals in an American university. *Journal of Social Psychology,* 1960, 51, 229–244. (b)

RETTIG, S., & PASAMANICK, B. Moral value structure and social class. *Sociometry,* 1961, 24, 21–35.

ROSENTHAL, D. Changes in some moral values following psychotherapy. *Journal of Consulting Psychology,* 1955, 19, 431–436.

SCHWARTZ, L. A. Social-situation pictures in

the psychiatric interviews. *American Journal of Orthopsychiatry*, 1932, **2**, 124–132.

SEARS, R. R. The growth of conscience. In I. Iscoe & H. W. Stevenson (Eds.), *Personality development in children.* Austin: University of Texas Press, 1960. Pp. 92–111.

SEARS, R. R., RAU, L., & ALPERT, R. Identification and child training: The development of conscience. Interim research report presented at American Psychological Association, Chicago, September 1960.

SHARP, F. C. An objective study of some moral judgments. *American Journal of Psychology*, 1898, **9**, 198–234.

STEIN, A. Guilt as a composite emotion: The relationship of child-rearing variables to superego response. *Dissertation Abstracts*, 1958, **19**, 873–874. (Abstract)

WAHLER, H. J. Hostility and aversion for expressing hostility in neurotics and controls. *Journal of Abnormal and Social Psychology*, 1959, **59**, 193–198.

WOODROW, H. A picture-preference character test. *Journal of Educational Psychology*, 1926, **17**, 519–531.

WURTZ, K. R. The expression of guilt in fantasy and reality. *Dissertation Abstracts*, 1958, **18**, 648–649. (Abstract)

# Section III
# THE GENERALITY OF CONSCIENCE

A frequent issue raised in conscience research involves generality of conscience across domains (cognitive, affective, and behavioral) and within a given domain (such as behavior). This section contains six papers that deal with this complex and still unsettled issue. In addition, two papers relevant to this question are presented in other sections of the book (Johnson, Ackerman, Frank, & Fionda, 1968, in the section on psychopathology; Rebelsky, Allinsmith, & Grinder, 1963, in the section on demographic aspects of the antecedents of conscience).

On the issue of generality within a particular domain, specifically within the realm of honesty behavior, the Hartshorne and May excerpt argues against generality, while the more recent Burton paper softens this argument somewhat and reasserts some claim for honesty as a trait. These two papers, together with several others presented in this book, suggest that within any domain of conscience there is more specificity than generality, but that some generality is present.

When it comes to predicting across domains of conscience, the picture is, if anything, less clear. The Bandura and Walters excerpt argues against generality from a social learning theory perspective; the Johnson excerpt suggests some, but not overwhelming, generality; the Porteus and Johnson data suggest that affective and cognitive measures are slightly, but significantly, related; and the Grinder and McMichael results suggest that generality interacts with other variables.

It is no doubt time for a multitrait multimethod matrix study of conscience also suggested by Burton in his sophisticated analysis presented in this section. Such a study would go a long way toward separating the measurement variance from psychologically meaningful variance in conscience and would help to illuminate the many facets of the generality issue.

# 7

# The specific nature of conduct and attitude

*by Hugh Hartshorne and Mark A. May*

In the first chapter of this volume we set forth the general characteristics of the modes of behavior which we have classified under the term "deceit" and pointed out their significance for the individual and society. We have dealt with the matter psychologically rather than in terms of ethics, concerning ourselves with objective concomitants and consequences rather than with the moral struggles of the individual or with social approvals and disapprovals, important as they may be. We have held that a person may deceive another in all good conscience, if his training has been of a certain kind, but that what he does is no less deceptive. The essence of the act is its pretense. Hence it can be described and understood only in terms of the human elements in the situation. It is not the act that constitutes the deception, nor the particular intention of the actor, but the *relation* of his act to his intentions and to the intentions of his associates. This relation can be defined in psychological terms. The typical deceptive act implies a conflict of wills with regard to either means or ends or

From Hugh Hartshorne and Mark A. May, *Studies in the Nature of Character*. Vol. 1. *Studies in Deceit* (New York: Macmillan, 1928), Book I, pp. 377–380, 412–414. Reprinted by permission of the authors.

both and the concealment of either the act or its intention or both in order to gain the end or utilize the means concerning which the conflict has arisen. The term applies to the cat that watches her chance to help herself from the kitchen table as well as to the citizen who gives pious reasons for robbing the state of its natural resources. If the intentions or methods of either were known to those whose rights were being infringed, the act of the deceiver would be frustrated. Success requires that the wolf appear in sheep's clothing.

Conversely, honest behavior is behavior which does not resort to subterfuge to gain its ends. But there are degrees of subterfuge. A person may be dishonestly honest. He may be honest in little things in order to gain the reputation of being honest in all things. This is his sheep's clothing under which his more subtle acts of aggression are concealed. Or one may be honest because it pays in a business way, but may publish as his reason for honesty that it is the only mode of conduct that appeals to an honorable man. He wins thus for himself a degree of confidence quite unwarranted by his true character.

Honesty in greater or less degree has for centuries been regarded as a virtue, even though in the practical conduct of life its practice is in constant conflict with other equally admired ideals. The "honesty" of an employee is relative to the "loyalty" of the employee to the purposes and methods of the firm. National "honor" and national "honesty" are often in opposition. Truth which would inflict a fatal shock may be withheld from a sick patient in the interest of his recovery. The futility of the attempt to build character by accumulating virtues which in the nature of the case are frequently inconsistent with one another was long since forcibly portrayed by Coe in his address on "Virtue and the Virtues" at the meeting of the National Education Association in San Francisco.[1] A man may possess all the virtues without being virtuous. It is not the quality of the isolated act which distinguishes the good man from the bad, but the quality of the *man* as an organized and socially functioning self. We may add up his characteristics, whether these be virtues or vices, but the algebraical sum is not his character.

To this attack on the concept of virtues as elements of character has been added in more recent years the attack on the virtues as unified traits. Not only does character not consist of a sum of virtues, but the virtues themselves are not psychological entities with any real existence. They are not acts. They are classifications of acts. To attribute to a man who acts honestly a faculty or trait of honesty is like explaining the act of remembering by referring it to some faculty of memory, which our popular systems of mnemonics are supposed to develop as one would train a muscle. Of course some people remember better than others, but to refer this difference to some mysterious and specialized power of memory is to stuff our ignorance with words. Similarly, to say that an honest act is caused by a man's honesty is like saying that it is cold because the temperature has fallen. Some men, it may be, can learn to be honest more easily than others because of real mental differences of the nature of which we are not as yet aware; but whatever honesty a man possesses resides not in a secret res-

[1] Printed in the *Proceedings* of the National Education Association for 1911 and in *Religious Education*, Vol. VI, 1912, pp. 485–492.

ervoir of honest virtue nor in the ideal of honesty which he may hold before himself as worthy of his best effort, but in the quality of the particular acts he performs.

We propose to bring together in this chapter . . . the data and arguments supporting the position taken in the last paragraph, which we may briefly characterize as the doctrine of specificity. According to this view a trait such as honesty or dishonesty is an achievement like ability in arithmetic, depending of course on native capacities of various kinds, but *consisting in* the achieved skills and attitudes of more or less successful and uniform performance.

As an introduction to the statement of the case, let us take the ability to add and the correlative ability to subtract. If a class had been faithfully taught how to add but not a word about how to subtract, no inherent faculty of figuring would come to their rescue if they were given a test which included problems in subtraction. Much alike as these two related processes may seem to an adult, they have to be learned; and the correlation between the two seemingly similar abilities will depend on (1) the actual elements which they have in common, (2) the amount of experience which the pupils have had with both, and (3) the extent to which the two processes are comprehended under a single more inclusive picture in terms of which they can be related to one another.

Honest and dishonest acts are specialized in the same way. Even after the principle of honesty is understood, the deceptive aspect of certain acts may not be noticed until one's attention is drawn to them. One may be meticulously honorable in his relations with his neighbors but steal a ride on the streetcar without thinking himself a thief. Acts are not accurately labeled because they are not completely analyzed. Consequently, an otherwise entirely honest man may be shocked and insulted when his sharp business practices are called stealing or his purchase of votes, political corruption.

Our conclusion, then, is that an individual's honesty or dishonesty consists of a series of acts and attitudes to which these descriptive terms apply. The consistency with which he is honest or dishonest is a function of the situations in which he is placed in so far as (1) these situations have common elements, (2) he has learned to be honest or dishonest in them, and (3) he has become aware of their honest or dishonest implications or consequences.

\*　　　\*　　　\*

Any implications for moral education that arise from these studies of deceptive tendencies are obviously tentative and incomplete. We have not reported the relation of this type of social failure to its opposite, cooperative helpfulness, nor to the intellectual habits, the ideas, and information which are involved in any response that can be regarded as having moral significance. No conclusive experiments have yet been undertaken by which education in the particular forms of behavior under discussion, much less in character as a whole, has been successfully demonstrated.

Nevertheless, there are a few results that have a direct bearing on the evaluation of current practices and which are suggestive for the setting up of controlled experiments for the further study of problems of character growth. We shall state our interpretation of these results in the form of propositions.

1. No one is honest or dishonest by "nature." Where conflict arises between a child and his environment, deception is a natural mode of adjustment, having in itself no "moral" significance. If indirect ways of gaining his ends are successful, they will be continued unless definite training is undertaken through which direct and honest methods may also become successful.

2. Apart from the actual practice of direct or honest methods of gaining ends where a conflict of wills is actually involved, the mere urging of honest behavior by teachers or the discussion of standards and ideals of honesty, no matter how much such general ideas may be "emotionalized," has no necessary relation to the control of conduct. The extent to which individuals may be affected, either for better or for worse, is not known, but there seems to be evidence that such effects as may result are not generally good and are sometimes unwholesome.

3. This does not imply that the teaching of general ideas, standards, and ideals is not desirable and necessary, but only that the prevailing ways of inculcating ideals probably do little good and may do some harm.

4. The large place occupied by the "situation" in the suggestion and control of conduct, not only in its larger aspects, such as the example of other pupils, the personality of the teacher, etc., but also in its more subtle aspects, such as the nature of the opportunity to deceive, the kind of material or test on which it is possible, the relation of the child to this material, and so on, points to the need of a careful educational analysis of all such situations for the purpose of making explicit the nature of the direct or honest mode of response *in*

*detail,* so that when a child is placed in these situations there may be a genuine opportunity for him to practice direct methods of adjustment.

5. Along with such practice of direct or honest responses there should go a careful study of them in terms of the personal relations involved, so that in the child's imagination the honest mode of procedure may be clearly distinguished from the dishonest mode as a way of *social* interaction, and the consequences of either method may be observed and used in evaluating the relative desirability of direct *versus* indirect procedures. Such analyses would provide the foundation for the understanding of social ideals and laws and the basis for an intelligent allegiance to such ideals as proved consonant with social welfare.

6. The association of deceit with sundry handicaps in social background, home condition, companions, personal limitations, and so on indicates the need for *understanding* particular examples of dishonest practice before undertaking to "judge" the blameworthiness of the individual. As far as possible, such social and personal limitations should be removed, not only for the sake of getting more honest behavior, but for the sake of the child's whole development. But obviously the widespread practice of deceit makes the application of radical environmental changes an absurdity. There is no evidence for supposing that children who are more likely to resort to deceptive methods than others would not use honorable methods with equal satisfaction if the situation in which dishonesty is practiced were sufficiently controlled by those who are responsible for their behavior. That is, the main attention of educators should be placed not so much on devices for teaching honesty or any other "trait" as on the reconstruction of school practices in such a way as to provide not occasional but consistent and regular opportunities for the successful use by both teachers and pupils of such forms of conduct as make for the common good.

# 8

# Generality of honesty reconsidered

*by Roger V. Burton[1]*

In the 1920s there was a substantial amount of research dealing with the complex domain of honesty, or moral behavior. This research reached a culmination in the classic studies of Hartshorne and May (1928) and their collaborators (Hartshorne, May, & Maller, 1929; Hartshorne, May, & Shuttleworth, 1930). After their efforts, investigation into this area of human behavior concentrated on exploring the cognitive structure and development of morality, while studies of overt choice behavior in test situations declined until relatively recently. The loss of enthusiasm for this area of research may have been due to the very thorough, excellent job done by Hartshorne and May. Another reason for the turning away from honesty as a subject for study may have been the conclusion from their study that conflict between honest or deceitful behavior is quite specific to each situation, that one could not generalize about a subject's honesty from a few samples of his behavior.

In the 1950s there was a renewed interest in the area of morality, especially

Roger V. Burton, "Generality of Honesty Reconsidered," *Psychological Review*, **70**, 1963, 481–499. Copyright 1963 by the American Psychological Association, and reproduced by permission.

[1] I am especially indebted to John D. Campbell and to two anonymous reviewers for their constructive comments on this paper.

in the developmental aspects of such behavior. Those working in this area must take into account the generality of their findings, especially when they utilize only a single behavioral test of honesty. It is the purpose of this paper to reconsider the specificity conclusion by looking again at the Hartshorne and May data and other evidence relevant to this question.

## Generality versus Specificity

The two extreme points of view about honest behavior can be quickly sketched. The unidimensional approach holds that a person is, or strongly tends to be, consistent in his behavior over many different kinds of situations. Thus a person who lies in one situation is not only likely to lie in other situations, but is also highly likely to cheat, steal, not feel guilty, and so on. This conception of the generality of character has been more fully presented by MacKinnon (1938) in a study supplying empirical support for such an interpretation. The graduate student subjects in his study who cheated on a problem-solving task by copying also tended to lie about their behavior, to report that they rarely felt guilty, and to perceive the task as being unfair. The students who did not cheat reported that they often felt guilty even when they were not aware of having transgressed, and that they perceived themselves as inadequate to solve the task rather than that the task was unfair. The conclusion is that these findings demonstrate a consistency in personality, and that one is justified in drawing conclusions from relationships between one sample of honest behavior and other measures relevant to one's investigation.

MacKinnon recognized that he did not test over different kinds of situations, but he argued that the consistency he found was sufficient to support his interpretation. In general, this interpretation is consonant with most psychoanalytic formulations of superego behavior based on an identification hypothesis. As Maccoby (1959) has pointed out, theoretical formulations stemming from Piaget's (1932) schema also conform to this "unitary process" conceptualization of morality.

The doctrine of specificity of moral behavior holds that a person acts in each situation according to the way he has been taught to act under these particular conditions. The predictability of one's moral behavior from one situation to another depends on the number of identical elements which the two settings share. This formulation does not accept the abstract concept of "honesty" as a valid character trait, but instead argues that there are many different kinds of specific behaviors which tend to be independent even though they may be included under the same rubric. Therefore, knowing that a person has cheated in a final examination in no way permits one to predict what the same person would do if tempted to cheat in a different setting such as a competitive game or business venture. Furthermore, there is little if any association between the extent to which a person will experience anxiety following a deviation in one moral area with the intensity of guilt following deviation in a different area. The study reported by Allinsmith (1960) reflects to some extent this interpretation. Utilizing a story completion method for his measures of moral behavior, he found there was little consistency in the intensity of guilt

expressed in junior high school students over different transgressions. He also found a noticeable lack of correlation between the measures of guilt and the measures of resistance to temptation. He concludes, therefore, that there are specific "guilts" which tend to be unrelated to resistance to temptation rather than a unified character trait representing an individual's morality.

The reader may note that the two studies cited have measured both the tendency to deviate in a temptation situation and the reaction to having already deviated. This simultaneous consideration of resistance to temptation and of guilt is customary in studies addressed to the development of moral behavior, of the superego, or conscience. However, there seems good reason, both theoretically and empirically (Burton, 1959; Burton, Maccoby, & Allinsmith, 1961), to consider these aspects of morality separately and then to investigate the extent of the correspondence between them. This paper is addressed primarily to a consideration of the generality of resistance to temptation as measured by behavior in lifelike temptation settings, and also by questionnaires and projective techniques.

### Studies in Deceit

Hartshorne and May's *Studies in Deceit* (1928) is undoubtedly the most comprehensive and well-known study of temptation and cheating behavior. One of the most important conclusions from this study was that there was no general trait of honesty. Consistency of behavior from one situation to another was due to similarities in the situations and not to a consistent personality trait in people. However, these authors did recognize that there seemed to be some similar overlapping elements in all the test situations:

It may be contended of course that as a matter of fact we rarely reach a zero correlation, no matter how different may be our techniques, and that this implies some such common factor in the individual as might properly be called a trait. We would not wish to quarrel over the use of a term and are quite ready to recognize the existence of some common factors which tend to make individuals differ from one another on any one test or on any group of tests. Our contention, however, is that this common factor is not an inner entity operating independently of the situations in which the individuals are placed but is a function of the situation in the sense that an individual behaves similarly in different situations in proportion as these situations are alike, have been experienced as common occasions for honest or dishonest

behavior, and are comprehended as opportunities for deception or honesty (p. 385).

The emphasis, then, was on the specificity of each test situation which involved different motives, different values in conflict, and—most importantly—different learned responses for that particular setting. The basis for their conclusion was that the correlations between the cheating tests were too low to produce evidence of a unified character trait of honesty or deceitfulness.

Table 1 gives the intercorrelations as reported in *Studies in Deceit*. The upper half (summed scores) presents the intercorrelations of the types of deceptive behavior in which each person's score on a particular kind of test is summed with his scores on the same kind of test to give a single, composite score for that type of cheating. The top diagonals are the reliabilities for these summed scores. The

*Table 1*

**Intercorrelations of Hartshorne and May**

|  | A | B | C | D | E | F | G | H | I |
|---|---|---|---|---|---|---|---|---|---|
| A. Copying (3 tests) | (.871) (.696) | .450 | .400 | .400 | .172 | .288 | .118 | .143 | .350 |
| B. Speed (6 tests) | .292 | (.825) (.440) | .374 | .425 | .193 | .345 | .169 | .173 | .248 |
| C. Peeping (3 tests) | .285 | .219 | (.721) (.462) | .300 | .234 | .100 | .250 | .200 | .108 |
| D. Faking (3 tests) | .291 | .255 | .196 | (.750) (.500) | — | .300 | .122 | .346 | .256 |
| E. Home (1 test) | .154 | .141 | .187 | — | (.240) (.240) | .142 | —.015 | —.010 | .400 |
| F. Athletic (4 tests) | .198 | .194 | .062 | .184 | .087 | (.772) (.458) | .118 | .283 | .230 |
| G. Parties (3 tests) | — | — | — | — | — | — | — | .210 | —.004 |
| H. Stealing (1 test) | .127 | .128 | .160 | .283 | —.010 | .162 | — | — | .132 |
| I. Lying (1 test) | .312 | .254 | .161 | .208 | .400 | —.003 | — | .132 | (.836) (.836) |

Note: Hartshorne and May, 1928, Book II, pp. 122, 123, 212.
The upper half is based on summed scores for each type of test. The lower half was computed by averaging the correlations for each type of test. Reliabilities for each method of computing these scores are in the diagonal.

lower half (average correlations) of the table gives the average cross-correlations between single tests of different techniques. The diagonals of this half of the table are the average correlation of one kind and type of test with the other tests of the same kind and type. Thus, .871 is the reliability of the summed score for the three copying tests, .450 is the correlation between the summed scores for the three copying and the six speed tests, .696 represents the average correlation for the three copying tests, and the average correlation among these three copying tests with the six speed tests is .292.

The individual's score for each test contributing to these correlations was determined as follows. First, a distribution of performance scores under carefully supervised (i.e., enforced honesty) conditions was obtained, and the mean and standard deviation of this distribution were computed. The scores for some tests (e.g., Copying Speed, and Athletic) were the differences between performance at Time 1 and performance at Time 2. For the other tests (e.g., Peeping, Puzzle, and Lying), the scores were based on a single performance. The mean as thus determined for each test became the reference point for honest behavior, and the standard deviation became the unit of measurement. When a subject was then tested for deception, his raw test score was converted into the number of standard deviation units it was away from this previously established mean of honest behavior. For example, the mean for the changes on the Arithmetic Copying test was a gain of 1.06 with a standard deviation of 3.10. If a person obtained a change in score of a loss of 10, his converted score would become $-3.57$, which is the score used in computing the correlations with the other tests.[2]

Looking at the intercorrelation table, it is seen, as Hartshorne and May pointed out, that the sizes of the correlations tend to decrease as the similarities of the situations decrease. This certainly supports their argument that there are factors in the temptation situation which influence the behavior of the child irrespective of any proclivity for cheating or resistance he brings with him. They also had evidence showing that variables external to the individual, such as ease of cheating, extent of the risk involved, and magnitude of the deviation required for success, affect the probability that one will cheat and also the extent to which one will deviate.

However, it is striking that almost all of the correlations are positive and that most of the very low correlations are contributed by tests with very low or unknown reliabilities. Furthermore, with the low reliabilities of some of the tests, the intercorrelations (especially in the upper half) are relatively high. Consideration of these facts suggests that a reexamination of the authors' rejection of an underlying character trait of honesty in temptation situations is warranted.[3]

[2] Hartshorne and May also used a "fact" score as well as this "amount" score. They arbitrarily decided that any score which was three or more standard deviations from the honest mean was labeled a "cheat." The fact score was used in reporting the percentages of cheaters on independent variables such as age, sex, ethnicity, etc.

[3] J. Merrill Carlsmith and David G. Beswick also considered this issue and carried out an analysis using Thurstone's centroid method. Their results are essentially the same as those reported in this paper. By coincidence their analysis was made simultaneously with that reported here. I am most appreciative to them for making their results available for this paper.

## Principal Component Analysis

Hartshorne and May (1928) state in a footnote when discussing the data on specificity of conduct that "Spearman's criterion of the presence of a common factor was not applied to these inter-$r$'s, as they were not obtained from the same cases throughout (Book II, p. 215)." Unfortunately, they do not report the size of the samples for the correlations. But from their tables giving the numbers of students in each school who were given each test, it seems safe to estimate that the sample sizes ranged from at least 75 to over 6,000, with most of the reported correlations being based on samples between 200 and 350 in size (Hartshorne & May, 1928, Book I, pp. 107–108). With these samples drawn from similar populations without apparent systematic bias, it would seem that the correlations reported are fairly good approximations to the true population values. If this assumption is accepted, there is no problem in performing a principal component analysis on these matrices. To be more confident of the stability of the results, only tests with at least .70 reliabilities for the summed scores were included. Therefore, only the Copying (A), Speed (B), Peeping (C), Faking (D), Athletic (F), and Lying (I) tests were chosen.

## Descriptions of the Tests

The *copying* tests were intelligence tests which involved the child's writing answers to questions, having the papers collected and copies of each paper made, returning the papers to the pupils, and having them correct their own papers. Their cheating score consisted of any changes they made on their papers.

The *speed* tests consisted of simple tasks such as number and digit cancellation. Three short forms of these tests were given, two under honest conditions called "practice" sessions, and the last was the test. The pupil was permitted to score his own test on the last administration. The score was the amount of increase on the last relative to the second trial.

*Peeping* tests involved tracing mazes or marking "x's" in circles while keeping one's eyes closed. Deception was determined by comparing the child's performance against a norm established under honest conditions.

The puzzles used in the *faking* solutions tests were either impossible to solve or extremely difficult. To achieve a satsifactory solution in the time given, a child would have to cheat. His deception score consisted of how closely he approached a perfect solution.

The *athletic* tests were a dynamometer test for measuring strength of hand grip, a spirometer test for measuring lung capacity, a chinning test, and a standing broad jump. Each student was tested privately. Three "warm-up" trials were given in the presence of the tester who recorded the student's best performance. The child was then left alone to record his own score on the next five trials. Previous standardization of performance on the tests permitted scoring improbable achievement during the test trials compared with the best score on the first three trials.

The *lying* test consisted of questions about the child's personal conformity to socially approved morality. After failing to standardize the test on school classes, the test was standardized on a class of graduate students who attempted to answer truthfully about their own childhood. This standard was then used to determine the deception score for the school pupils.[4]

Lawley's (1940) test of significance (also see Maxwell, 1961) was applied to these matrices and indicated that the sample size would have to be at least $n$ of 26 for all the matrices to be significant at the .001 level. Since all these correlations are based on at least 200 pupils, these matrices are statistically significant and justify the extraction of common variance.

The hypothesis was that a significant amount of variance would be extracted by the first component and that all the tests would have high loadings on this component. The standards for determining the statistical significance of the factor loadings and extracted variance are not yet agreed on by statisticians so that the decision as to evidence required to reject the null hypotheses is arbitrary. It seemed reasonable to set the criterion at a minimum of 30 percent of the total variance in the matrix for the component to have a "g" characteristic and for

[4] A complete description of these tests and the procedures for scoring is given in Hartshorne and May (1928), along with the other tests which we have not used in our factor analysis and therefore have not described.

the loadings on all tests to be a minimum of .40. Furthermore, components extracted after the first should account for much less of the variance relative to the first and should tend to be specific to individual tests.

## Results

The results for the principal component analyses of the two matrices are presented in Table 2. The matrix based on the average intercorrelations (bottom half of Table 1) yields a component structure which barely meets our arbitrary criterion. As this matrix was computed in a conservative manner, that is, contains what is probably the lowest estimates of the true correlations, these results can be considered to represent the minimum magnitude of common variance and loadings for each component. The results for the other matrix (upper half of Table 1 based on summed scores) show that the magnitude of the variance accounted for by the first component is larger as are the loadings of each test on this component. These results are based on matrices having unities in the diagonal and with the correlations being those given in Table 1

*Table 2*

**Principal Components**

| | Based on summed scores | | | | | | Based on average intercorrelations | | | | | |
|---|---|---|---|---|---|---|---|---|---|---|---|---|
| | I | II | III | IV | V | VI | I | II | III | IV | V | VI |
| A. Copying | .764 | .092 | .207 | —.166 | —.116 | .570 | .718 | —.054 | .013 | —.046 | —.444 | .530 |
| B. Speed | .754 | .106 | —.195 | —.047 | .614 | —.056 | .651 | .065 | —.134 | —.403 | .607 | .151 |
| C. Peeping | .581 | .660 | .084 | —.233 | —.239 | —.329 | .540 | —.237 | .768 | —.060 | —.002 | —.244 |
| D. Faking | .703 | .017 | —.139 | .677 | —.168 | —.029 | .619 | .140 | .088 | .736 | .217 | —.028 |
| F. Athletic | .555 | —.504 | —.537 | —.293 | —.234 | —.095 | .387 | .825 | .041 | —.177 | —.240 | —.282 |
| I. Lying | .526 | —.504 | .638 | —.030 | .023 | —.245 | .561 | —.501 | —.474 | —.105 | —.207 | —.394 |
| % of Variance | 42.8 | 16.1 | 13.4 | 10.5 | 8.9 | 8.4 | 34.6 | 17.0 | 14.0 | 12.5 | 11.8 | 10.0 |

whose reliabilities were at least .70. These correlations were not corrected for attenuation. Analyses using reliabilities in the diagonal produce similar results and are not reported here. The main change is that the amount of variance extracted by the first component is much greater using the reliabilities.[5]

These analyses conform in the main to our hypothesis and lend support to the generality position. In all cases, the first component accounts for at least twice as much variance as the second component. Also, the loadings on this component are all positive and exceed .50, with the exception of the athletic tests for the matrix of averaged intercorrelations.

There appeared to be more than one factor to be extracted, however, which would indicate that there may be some other common variance. The second

---

[5] I have also done analyses of these matrices corrected for attenuation. Again the results were approximately the same but show a consistent increase in the magnitudes of the loadings and amount of variance extracted by the first component as the size of the original correlations increased due to their respective methods of calculation. The results of these analyses even more strongly indicate a generality conclusion. For example, the amount of variance in the first component for the matrix of average correlations corrected for attenuation increases from 48 percent to 69 percent. The second component accounted for 19 percent of the variance and the third factor tended to vanish. However, the greater magnitude of the first component produced by using matrices having reliabilities in the diagonals and/or correlations corrected for attenuation may be spurious. It seems possible that the additional variance extracted by the first of these component matrices results from the common "correction" for measurement error injected by the reliability coefficients. Therefore, only the results based on the uncorrected matrices with unities in the diagonals are reported as these are the most conservative estimates of the common variance for these tests and the most likely to reject the generality hypothesis.

component rather consistently accounts for about 17 percent of the variance in the total matrix and is related (before rotation) to three of the tests. A weak third component, common to the two out-of-classroom tests, also was extracted and accounted for about 14 percent of the total variance.

Several criteria were considered in deciding when to end the extraction of components. First, the percentage of variance for each component was plotted. The curve flattened out after the third component suggesting that the analysis should be stopped regardless of the size of the sample. It is also seen that Components IV, V, and VI are specific to single tests. Tests of significance of the residual matrices (Lawley, 1940; Maxwell, 1961) indicated that $ns$ of under 200 would have justified the extraction of the second and third components. These criteria encouraged the extraction of at least two components and perhaps three. However, a theoretical limitation on the extraction of variance is that the communality ($h^2$) for any one test cannot be greater than the reliability of that test. This theoretical restriction makes even the second factor suspect. The communality for the third test (Peeping) exceeds its reliability by a small amount. With the extraction of the third component, three tests (Peeping, Athletic, and Lying) exceed their reliabilities.

To help clarify these results, we have proceeded to obtain a unique solution using Lawley's method of maximum likelihood in order to test for the sample size required to extract more than the first factor. The solution is given in Table 3 and shows that samples of at least 333 for the summed scores and 608 for the averaged scores would be required to reject the null hypothesis of the adequacy of a single factor.[6]

Table 3

**Lawley's Solution for a Single Factor**

|  | Based on summed scores | Based on averaged correlations |
|---|---|---|
| *Tests* | *Factor loadings* | *Factor loadings* |
| A. Copying | .697 | .642 |
| B. Speed | .686 | .516 |
| C. Peeping | .497 | .412 |
| D. Faking | .607 | .481 |
| F. Athletic | .443 | .275 |
| I. Lying | .415 | .442 |
|  | $N > 333$* | $N > 608$* |
|  | $N > 500$** | $N > 914$** |

\* $p = .05, df = 15$.
\*\* $p = .001, df = 15$.

We see that these analyses are the most conservative in testing our hypothesis but still produce results very similar to those of the principal component model. The athletic tests contribute very little to this general factor for the averaged correlations, with 92 percent specific variance for these tests. But the analysis based on the summed scores meets our original arbitrary criterion for factor loadings of at least .40 for all tests.

If a conservative judgment is made from all our analyses, only the first component is permitted. Such a conclusion would clearly support a single factor hypothesis with some consideration that the athletic tests are independent of the other types of tests. For those readers

[6] The estimated factor loading and communalities for beginning this analysis were taken from the principal axis solutions. I would like to acknowledge the advice and direct assistance of Donald F. Morrison of the National Institutes of Health in performing these analyses.

who agree with this conclusion, the following rotations of components will be superfluous. Since others may feel that these considerations are too severe with a principal component model which achieves a unique solution accounting for all the variance in the matrix, we have rotated the first three factors extracted in our analyses.

**Rotated Factor Structure**

Three factors were orthogonally rotated by Kaiser's (1958) analytic varimax model. The rotated factors indicate that there seems to be a difference between those tests administered inside the classroom and the athletic tests which are given in an out-of-class setting. Factor I′ for the summed scores seems to clearly indicate a classroom cheating factor which involves actual behavior. The second factor (II′) is mainly a performance cheating factor with the main loading from the athletic tests and rather substantial loadings from the speed and faking tests, all of which involve some kind of physical performance. The third factor (III′) is defined primarily by the questionnaire test on acceptance of the general moral code. The classroom copying tests also contribute to this factor.

The rotated factors for the averaged cross correlations indicate a somewhat similar structure. The main difference is in the exchange of places by the peeping and lying tests, and by the greater degree of specificity of the second and third factors. Factor I′ is again a classroom test factor but is defined more by the lying test than the actual behavioral tests. The second factor (II′) is again an athletic dimension. The peeping tests are specific to the last factor (III′).

## Table 4

**Orthogonal Rotation of Factors**

| Tests | Summed scores | | | | Averaged cross —r | | | |
|---|---|---|---|---|---|---|---|---|
| | I′ | II′[a] | III′ | h² | I′ | II′ | III′ | h² |
| A. Copying | .633 | .223 | .428 | .634 | .600 | .205 | .343 | .519 |
| B. Speed | .611 | .479 | .120 | .617 | .581 | .288 | .161 | .447 |
| C. Peeping | .878 | −.085 | −.037 | .780 | .142 | −.013 | .957 | .937 |
| D. Faking | .516 | .460 | .187 | .513 | .509 | .349 | .173 | .411 |
| F. Athletic | .030 | .916 | .101 | .851 | .090 | .907 | −.020 | .831 |
| I. Lying | .081 | .113 | .959 | .939 | .841 | −.280 | −.068 | .791 |

| | Transformation matrices | | | | | | |
|---|---|---|---|---|---|---|---|
| | *T* | | | | *T* | | |
| | .731 | −.535 | .424 | | .821 | .355 | .447 |
| | .680 | .514 | −.523 | | −.300 | .935 | −.191 |
| | .061 | .670 | .740 | | −.485 | .022 | .874 |

[a] This factor has been reflected.

These results are what we might have expected from our Lawley solutions. We see that the athletic tests tend to have specific variance in the Lawley solution and to define the second factor in the rotational analyses. Also the copying, speed, and faking tests tend to be more "general" in that their loadings are all positive on the rotated factors, contribute to more than one of the factors, and have the largest communalities in the Lawley solutions. It is not clear whether the peeping and lying tests should be included in the general factor of classroom honesty tests or should be considered as specific tests. From Brogden's (1940) analysis to be discussed below, it seems the inclusion of the peeping tests with the first factor with the lying factor tending to be independent is the more stable structure.

## Simple Analysis

Guttman (1955) has developed an alternative model to factor analysis as a way of investigating the single-common-factor hypothesis.[7] He proposes that if a matrix of intercorrelations can be ordered in a hierarchical gradient conforming to certain criteria the tests can be considered to be in the same universe and to vary along a single dimension, an ordering he has called a simplex.

These criteria are that "the largest correlations are all next to the main diagonal, and taper off as one goes to the upper right and lower left of the table," and that the totals of the columns will be curvilinear with the lowest totals at the right and left extremes and the largest total in the middle. Tables 5 and 6 present an ordering of the Hartshorne and May intercorrelation matrix into quasi-simplexes. The preponderance of "errors" in the ordering are contributed by the Home (E), Stealing (H), and Parties (G) tests. These tests either have very low or unreported reliabilities which would itself tend to introduce errors into the ordering. It will be seen

[7] I would like to thank Morris Rosenberg for bringing this alternative method to my attention after I had already completed the factor analyses.

Table 5

**Guttman Simplex of Summed Scores**

| Tests | Summed scores | | | | | | | | |
|---|---|---|---|---|---|---|---|---|---|
| | E | I | C | A | B | D | F | H | G |
| E. Home (1 test) | (.240) | .400 | .234 | .172 | .193 | — | .142 | −.010 | −.015 |
| I. Lying (1 test) | .400 | (.836) | .108 | .350 | .248 | .256 | .230 | .132 | −.004 |
| C. Peeping (3 tests) | .234 | .108 | (.721) | .400 | .374 | .300 | .100 | .200 | .250 |
| A. Copying (3 tests) | .172 | .350 | .400 | (.871) | .450 | .400 | .288 | .143 | .118 |
| B. Speed (6 tests) | .193 | .248 | .374 | .450 | (.825) | .425 | .345 | .173 | .169 |
| D. Faking (3 tests) | — | .256 | .300 | .400 | .425 | (.750) | .300 | .346 | .122 |
| F. Athletic (4 tests) | .142 | .230 | .100 | .288 | .345 | .300 | (.772) | .283 | .118 |
| H. Stealing (1 test) | −.010 | .132 | .200 | .143 | .173 | .346 | .283 | — | .210 |
| G. Parties (3 tests) | −.015 | .004 | .250 | .118 | .169 | .122 | .118 | .210 | — |
| Total | 1.116[a] | 1.720 | 1.966 | 2.321 | 2.377 | 2.149[a] | 1.806 | 1.477 | .968 |

[a] These totals are minus any contributions from $r_{DE}$.

that the matrix within the heavy lines approaches a perfect simplex. These are the same tests we have chosen for the principal component analyses on the basis of acceptable reliabilities. Our results again support the generality hypothesis.

A comparison of the ordering of the same tests utilized in the factor analysis shows that only the tests in the center of the simplex—copying, speed, and faking —contribute positively to all the rotated factors. The lying, peeping, and athletic tests contribute only to one factor and are seen to be at the extremes of the simplex. It is interesting that the positions of the two extreme tests in the two simplex orderings correspond to the two specific, rotated factors; i.e., the athletic tests define Factor II′ for both the rotational analyses and are also at the far right in both simplexes, and the lying tests define the specific Factor III′ for the summed scores and are at the extreme left for this simplex, whereas the peeping tests have these characteristics

Table 6

**Guttman Simplex of Average Cross-Correlations**

| Tests | Average cross — r | | | | | | | |
|---|---|---|---|---|---|---|---|---|
| | E | C | I | A | B | D | F | H |
| E. Home | (.240) | .187 | .400 | .154 | .141 | — | .087 | −.010 |
| C. Peeping | .187 | (.462) | .161 | .285 | .219 | .196 | .062 | .160 |
| I. Lying | .400 | .161 | (.836) | .312 | .254 | .208 | −.003 | .132 |
| A. Copying | .154 | .285 | .312 | (.696) | .292 | .291 | .198 | .127 |
| B. Speed | .141 | .219 | .254 | .292 | (.440) | .255 | .194 | .128 |
| D. Faking | — | .196 | .208 | .291 | .255 | (.500) | .184 | .283 |
| F. Athletic | .087 | .062 | −.003 | .198 | .194 | .184 | (.458) | .162 |
| H. Stealing | −.010 | .100 | .132 | .127 | .128 | .283 | .162 | — |
| Total | .959[a] | 1.270 | 1.464 | 1.659 | 1.483 | 1.417[a] | .884 | .982 |

[a] These totals are minus any contributions from $r_{DE}$.

for the averaged cross-correlation matrix. It is also notable that these extreme tests contribute the only errors in the simplex.

### Related Studies

Other investigators have come to similar conclusions regarding the generality of honest behavior. One of the first after Hartshorne and May's final volume was a short paper published by Maller (1934) who had been a coauthor in *Studies in Service and Self-Control* (Hartshorne et al., 1929). Maller analyzed the correlations of the summary scores for the character tests of Honesty, Cooperation, Inhibition, and Persistence as reported in *Studies in the Organization of Character* (Hartshorne et al., 1930). He utilized Spearman's tetrad difference technique and concluded that there was evidence for a common factor in all three matrices which were based on quite different populations. He interpreted the common factor as being delay of gratification: "the readiness to forego an immediate gain for the sake of a remote but greater gain." He pointed out, however, that one should be cautious in accepting his analysis as proof of a general factor due to the very low magnitude of the original intercorrelations. On the other hand, he predicted that higher correlations would be forthcoming when character tests were constructed with greater reliability and validity.

Brogden (1940) also utilized the factor analytic model in his analysis of 40 character tests. The intercorrelations were based on a sample of 100 middle-class boys with average or above IQ. Four of the tests were the same or simi-lar to the Hartshorne and May (1928) tests of deceit and six were the same paper-and-pencil character tests used in *Studies in the Organization of Character* (Hartshorne et al., 1930). The most clearly defined factor obtained in this analysis was an honesty factor. All the behavioral tests of cheating had high loadings on this factor, and two of the paper-and-pencil tests contributed to a small extent. Brogden suggested, as did Maller, that the paper-and-pencil tests could be refined to correlate more highly with the honesty factor by doing an item analysis on two groups of subjects with extreme scores on the factor; but this analysis is not reported. Brogden also found an "acceptance of the moral code" factor. It is interesting that these two factors are orthogonal to one another in this analysis. The honesty factor consists mainly of the behavioral tests whereas the "moral code" factor is defined by paper-and-pencil tests and story completions which measured how much the child would express the socially acceptable (desirable) response. These results indicate that even though there are some paper-and-pencil tests which contribute to a behavioral factor of honesty the elements in them are not well determined and that the cognitive aspect of morality seems for the most part to be independent of the behavioral choice situation.

Barbu (1951) reports a program of research dealing with honesty in children which he conducted in Roumania between 1935 and 1940. In one study of 250 fourteen-year-old boys tested with nine behavioral tests and one questionnaire test of honesty, he found an average intercorrelation of .456 and concluded there was strong evidence for a general trait of honesty. He also analyzed his data using Thurstone's multiple factor model and found evidence of a general factor. To some extent, however, the consistency of Barbu's results may be due to his choice of tests which are all similar to the Hartshorne and May classroom tests which had the high loadings on the general factor in our analysis.

## Discussion

The results of our analyses, and those of Maller, Brogden, and Barbu, lead us to reconsider the specificity hypothesis regarding behavioral honesty in favor of a more general position.

Previous writers have also given theoretical consideration to this question and decided in favor of a generality of behavior. Allport (1937) presented challenging arguments against the specificity position pointing out the difficulties involved in predicting the important "identical elements" in different situations. Eysenck's (1953) review of Hartshorne and May points out the intercorrelations of these types of measures, each based on from one to six behavioral tests, should not be expected to reach the magnitudes of intercorrelations based on intelligence tests composed of 50 or more items. This consideration does make Hartshorne and May's criterion of a theoretical predictive reliability of .90 for acceptable evidence of a generality of honesty behavior quite stringent. The obtained theoretical predictive reliability for their tests was .725 based on an average intercorrelation for the nine types of tests of .227, which included the tests with the very low reliabilities. A battery of 31 such honesty tests would be required to obtain the

theoretical criterion of .90, assuming that the average inter-$r$ remains the same. By eliminating the tests with low reliabilities, the average inter-$r$ increases to .305, which still gives just .725 as the theoretical predictive reliability for the remaining 6 tests. However, only 21 tests would be necessary to reach the criterion of .90 reliability with another battery of 21 similar honesty tests.[8]

The conclusion to draw from these analyses is not greatly different from that made by Hartshorne and May, but the strong emphasis on lack of relation between tests is removed. Our analyses indicate that one may conclude there is an underlying trait of honesty which a person brings with him to a resistance to temptation situation. However, these results strongly agree with Hartshorne and May's rejection of an "all or none" formulation regarding a person's character. I feel the results can best be incorporated by a learning model which would predict a generalization gradient over the different types of tests. Since all the cheating tests have much face validity of being in the area of resistance to temptation, one would expect that the generalization gradient would extend to all the tests. This expectation is supported by the evidence of a general factor underlying the intercorrelations of the tests. However, the model would also predict that as the tests become less similar the probability of the same response in both situations would become less and less. This prediction would account for the decrement in the magnitude of the correlations as situations become more dissimilar.

[8] For fuller discussions of the measurement problems and theory on which these computations are based, see Hartshorne and May (1928) and Eysenck (1953).

This model would make some additional predictions about consistency in responses over the different tests contingent on different learning conditions of the subjects. It would predict that the parent who consistently defines all temptation situations the same way as interpreted in the honesty tests and also consistently administers positive reinforcement for honest behavior and punishment for dishonest behavior would facilitate for his child the discrimination of the critical cues in situations which call for an honest response. With these critical cues discriminated, the child should show much generality in his behavior across the different types of honesty tests. On the other hand, parents who define cheating in one situation as being unacceptable, e.g., stealing money, but do not censure cheating in another situation in which a highly valued gain may be obtained, e.g., cheating on a college entrance examination, would produce children who are not consistent on these honesty tests.[9] These children may learn to be honest in particular situations but would not learn to discriminate the critical elements calling for an honest response in any situation which involves a moral choice. But I must emphasize I mean here consistency in *defining* the situation for the child as calling for an honest response and in *administering* positive or negative reinforcement contingent on his response. For we would expect from the experimental literature

that once a particular response is well established, a kind of inconsistency in the *predictability* of the reinforcer will flatten out the generalization gradient (Humphreys, 1939; Wickens, Schroder, & Snide, 1954). Such a variable reinforcement schedule will also increase the resistance of the response to extinction, i.e., conditions of no longer being reinforced. Thus parental consistency in interpreting the moral elements of a situation and in the positive or negative characteristic of the reinforcement they dispense depending on the child's behavior, combined with a gradual inconsistency in their dispensing of such reinforcement are the conditions maximizing the learning, generalization, and persistence of a moral response.

An important aspect of this generalization model in predicting and explaining moral behavior is the part played by cognitive mediation. In addition to the generalization gradient in which only the elements of the original stimulus complex and response are concerned, there is another gradient involving cognitively mediated generalization. This part of our model would predict that the greater the cognitive, especially verbal, association between two kinds of temptation situations, the greater will be the probability of the same response being performed in both settings. It would be possible, therefore, to place an individual in a test situation appearing to be totally new in his experience but yet having some elements which he would *define* as a temptation conflict. That is, there may be very little similarity as far as the immediate stimulus complex is concerned, but there are elements of a cognitive nature by which mediational generalization may occur. When both specific stimulus generalization and cog-

[9] There is the assumption made in this area of research that the "average" parent in our American culture agrees on what is honest and dishonest behavior in the test situations. There may be some cases in which parents are slightly psychopathic and would not consider it wrong to cheat; but in sampling a large group of subjects, these deviant cases should not contribute too much "noise" to the analyses.

nitive mediation are combined, the probability of predicting behavior from one situation to another should be some additive function of these two generalization gradients.[10]

Theoretically, it seems these two generalization gradients may be quite independent. The child-rearing practices of some parents may be very appropriate for the learning of honest behavior in particular settings and for the broad generalization of such behavior to other similar stimulus complexes. But these same parents may not apply verbal labels to such situations. Their children are learning to be honest in specific situations, and any generalization of their behavior will come through similarity of new situations to these specific learning conditions. Other parents may emphasize the verbal labeling of situational conditions so that their children learn to discriminate certain cognitive elements in quite different kinds of stimulus situations.[11] These children are learning that under certain abstract conditions one should act in some ways and not in others. However, some of these same parents may not be efficient in teaching their children to perform the desirable response under these conditions. These children would know the acceptable

moral code in many temptation situations, but such knowledge would not necessarily determine their overt choice behavior.[12] In actual practice it seems from our analyses that the majority of parents, especially of the middle class on which most research in honesty has been done, attempt to achieve both kinds of generalization in their children.

Experimental results also indicate the influence of these two kinds of generalization on behavior. The generalization of specific stimulus situations is well demonstrated in the literature (e.g., Osgood, 1953). But experiments in which both the specific, external stimuli and cognitive elements can be simultaneously assessed for their relative contributions to generalization are somewhat rare. Hull (1920) demonstrated that a concept can be learned even though the critical cues might not be subject to conscious awareness, indicating the discrimination and generalization of very specific cues embedded in a conceptual task without the need of verbal mediation. Bugelski and Scharlock (1952) extended this finding to show that actual verbal mediation can also occur without awareness. Other experiments indicate, however, that conscious verbal mediation facilitates discriminations in new situations where the verbal labels are still relevant (Goodwin & Lawrence, 1955; Kendler & Kendler, 1959; Kuenne, 1946). Such discrimination would increase the probability of generalizing to different situations in which these labels continue to be appropriate. The differences in types of discrimination and

---

[10] MacRae (1954) postulated "two distinct processes of moral development" which are analogous to the two generalization gradients proposed here. Although his data were all based on what we have called the "cognitive" type of measure, he hypothesized a "cognitive" moral development, involving the learning of what behavior patterns are approved and disapproved, and "emotional" moral development, including the association of anxiety with one's own deviance and moral indignation with that of others (p. 17).

[11] Although this notion seems to be popular now, I believe John W. M. Whiting first suggested this hypothesis regarding the importance of verbal labeling in learning moral standards.

[12] More extended discussions of the child-rearing practices considered conducive for learning resistance to temptation and honest behavior are in Burton (1959), and Burton, Maccoby, and Allinsmith (1961).

generalization associated with age and intelligence further demonstrate the distinction between the dimensions of purely external stimulus elements and cognitive labeling (Kendler, Kendler, & Wells, 1960; Kuenne, 1946; Luria, 1957).

Relating this experimental evidence to the honesty data, the analyses of Maller (1934) and Brogden (1940) indicate that to some extent most parents are inculcating both generalization of a specific, situational sort and also of a more cognitive kind. The ordering of the Hartshorne and May tests into a quasi-simplex also indicates that the students were defining these different tests as being in the same realm. The further fact that those tests which could be ordered into a nearly perfect simplex clearly had stimulus elements in common shows that both kinds of generalization appear to be influencing these results. Brogden's finding two factors which seem to measure these kinds of generalization, and the rotational analysis of the summed scores, provide some empirical support for the behavioral and cognitive dimensions contributing separate variance to these honesty tests. More recent investigations also indicate that behavioral measures and cognitive indices of morality are not necessarily correlated (Burton, 1959; Burton et al., 1961; Unger, 1960). This consideration follows the point made by Maccoby (1959) that comparisons between different studies of morality involve the problem of reliability across measures, i.e., their intercorrelations, even though they may be highly reliable tests themselves. Thus, if one study employs Hartshorne and May's peeping test and another uses the lying questionnaire, there will probably not be great agreement in the results as there is so little overlap in the tests. The model we have presented indicates that the tests may differ on at least two dimensions: they may test different environmental settings (e.g., in-classroom versus out-of-classroom, in-school versus out-of-school), and they may differ in the extent to which they test actual choice behavior in a conflict situation versus cognitive structuring of hypothetical conditions as in a paper-pencil questionnaire or Piaget-type interview. Campbell and Fiske (1959) have suggested a procedure which appears relevant for these issues. Their recommendation is to use several methods to measure a number of different traits in order to assess the convergent and discriminant validity of the tests and of the constructs they are purported to measure. The last book in the Character Education Inquiry of Hartshorne and May (1930) *Studies in the Organization of Character* comes close to considering this same procedure. The four traits of honesty, cooperation, inhibition, and persistence were measured by different tests utilizing different methods. Furthermore, they employed the behavioral tests in different settings. Unfortunately, the original intercorrelations between all the individual tests are not reported so that the evaluations recommended by Campbell and Fiske are not possible. Hopefully, a study based on a multitrait-multimethod-multisetting design employing reliable tests on an adequate sampling of subjects will be done making possible the different analytical approaches used in this paper as well as those recommended by Campbell and Fiske in order to elucidate more directly the questions we are considering. Other traits which would seem relevant for a multitrait design are guilt, achievement motivation, rigidity, conformity-compliance, and social desirability. But these are considerations for the future.

Let us look now at some implications of this double-generalization model and relate them to some research findings.

## Intelligence

Hartshorne and May found that IQ was positively correlated with honesty ($r=.344$). Shuttleworth's analysis (Hartshorne et al., 1930) in the last volume showed a strong relationship ($r=.776$) between honesty and consistency in behavior, i.e., honest persons tended to be consistent in behavior and dishonest persons tended to be inconsistent. As might be expected from these relationships, intelligence and consistency of honest behavior were also related ($r=.226$). These results are consonant with speculations from our model that the generality of honesty would be positively related to intelligence. The temptation is to end presenting the data from their analyses at this point. But all the evidence is not so strongly in this direction. When honesty is partialed out, the relation between consistency and intelligence tends to disappear. The relation between IQ and honesty remains significant at .216 even when controlling on consistency. As the authors noted, they may have partialed out too much when they controlled on honesty and consistency so that there is probably some real association between IQ and consistency. But the results suggest that intelligence is more strongly related to behavioral honesty than to consistency. Our model would indicate that IQ should be especially relevant for tests of knowledge of a consensual moral code. This assumes that conceptual generalization will be

positively related to IQ. We would expect greater verbal mediation from persons with higher IQ as they should be more capable of abstracting the moral implications of the different test situations. Thus, at least part of the greater consistency of honest persons who tend also to have higher IQs may be accounted for by the cognitive generalization gradient of our model. As we are unable to separate the cognitive tests from the behavioral tests used by Hartshorne and May, we are also unable to test our speculations regarding these differences between behavioral and cognitive measures.

## Age

In line with this interpretation would be the expectation that generality should increase with age. Cognitive moral development has consistently been positively related to age in studies involving children's conceptions of morality (Boehm, 1957; Bronfenbrenner, 1962; Durkin, 1959; Harrower, 1935; Hoffman, 1961; Kohlberg, 1958, 1963; Lerner, 1937; MacRae, 1954; Medinnus, 1959; Morris, 1958; Peel, 1959; Piaget, 1932). Experimental results also indicate that with age, verbal mediation, and the control such verbalizations have on overt choice behavior increase (Kendler et al., 1960; Kuenne, 1946; Luria, 1957). However, in *Studies in Deceit* (Hartshorne & May, 1928) age was slightly negatively correlated with honesty. The tendency for a negative correlation of age with honesty when honesty is positively correlated with consistency is not in harmony with our model. In this case the further analysis in Volume 3 (Hartshorne et al., 1930) reveals data supporting our predictions. For the two groups of children studied intensively in this volume it was found that both groups became more consistent with age but the high-social-class children became more honest and those from the lower-class school became more dishonest.

## Social Class

Kohn (1959) has found that there are different value systems characteristic of the working class and the middle class. The working-class parents stress the immediate implications of a child's act and want the child to stay out of trouble by not doing the "wrong" thing, whereas the middle-class parents want their child to understand the implications of his behavior so that he chooses to do the "right" thing. If these interpretations are correct, one would expect that the child-rearing practices of middle-class parents would be more conducive to their children's discriminating the moral implications of different settings and performing an honest response than would be the child-rearing practices of the working-class parents. These different value systems and presumably related child-rearing practices should produce both greater situational generalization and greater cognitive generalization in the middle-class children than in the working-class children. We should expect these differences to be reflected in greater generality on tests of morality of both a behavioral response type and a cognitive knowledge kind. The findings that behavioral honesty was positively correlated with social class and that the consistency for the upper-social-class group was significantly greater than that for the lower-class group strongly sup-

port this expectation. Their analysis showing age related to consistency with the upper-social-class group increasing in consistency faster than the lower-class group is also directly in line with our model. Researchers using cognitive measures of morality have consistently found their measures related to social class (Aronfreed, 1961; Boehm, 1957; Bronfenbrenner, 1962; Durkin, 1959; Hoffman, 1961; Kohlberg, 1958, 1959, 1963; Lerner, 1937; MacRae, 1954), but in general have not analyzed their data to test for differences in consistency between classes.

## Sex

Of the eight types of tests used by Hartshorne and May (1928), three showed significant, and three more nearly significant, differences in girls cheating more than boys. They attributed these differences to the possibility that girls were more motivated to succeed on a school task and to conform to accepted standards than were boys. One of these tests was the lying test which measured the student's tendency to score himself as conforming to acceptable standards. The other tests were more directly behavioral in a temptation situation. Generally, girls tend to be more verbally developed than boys (Goodenough, 1954) on intelligence and achievement tests, although there are exceptions (Bayley, 1957). Girls are also rated as being more honest than boys (Hartshorne & May, 1928) and as developing a conscience earlier than boys (Sears, Maccoby, & Levin, 1957). In light of these findings, we might predict from our verbal generalization model that girls would be more consistent than boys. But there is also the evidence that girls tended actually to cheat more and also that girls tended to make up the "pure" (i.e., consistently) deceptive group, and boys the pure honest group in Hartshorne and May (1928). It would seem that the prediction would have to be limited to verbal or cognitive measures of morality, what Brogden (1940) called "acceptance of the moral code" factor, so that girls would evidence greater generality of morality only on verbal measures. Barbu (1951) reports sex differences for areas involved in a questionnaire lying test. Boys lied more than girls about power and courage, whereas girls lied more about being morally good. One interpretation for these differences is that they reflect real differences in behavior, i.e., boys' behavior is more courageous and assertive than girls', whereas girls' behavior does conform to "goodness" more than boys' behavior. But it is also possible that the cognitive measures of acceptance of the moral code are mainly addressed to the areas of morality which are more salient to girls who therefore are more motivated than boys to distort their responses. If this were so, girls would tend to appear more moral than boys on such tests which are not measuring lying or distortion but only cognitive acceptance of morality. Aronfreed (1961) has shown that girls appear to be much more concerned with display of being "good" than are boys. Be this as it may, why is it that boys should tend to be more honest and more consistent on the Hartshorne and May temptation tests but girls tend to appear more conforming to the general moral code as measured by verbal tests or ratings by parents or teachers? The model we are proposing would lead us to investigate the possibility of differential child-rearing practices contingent on the sex of the child and of differential role modeling by the parents.[13]

## References

ALLINSMITH, W. The learning of moral standards. In D. R. Miller & G. E. Swanson (Eds.), *Inner conflict and defense.* New York: Holt, 1960. Pp. 141–176.

ALLPORT, G. W. *Personality, a psychological interpretation.* New York: Holt, 1937.

ARONFREED, J. The nature, variety, and social patterning of moral responses to transgression. *Journal of Abnormal and Social Psychology,* 1961, **63,** 223–240.

BARBU, Z. Studies in children's honesty. *Quarterly Bulletin of the British Psychological Society,* 1951, **2,** 53–57.

BAYLEY, N. Data on the growth of intelligence between 16 and 21 years as measured by the Wechsler-Bellevue scale. *Journal of Genetic Psychology,* 1957, **90,** 3–15.

*BOEHM, L. The development of independence: A comparative study. *Child Development,* 1957, **28,** 85–92.

BROGDEN, H. E. A factor analysis of 40 character traits. *Psychological Monographs,* 1940, **52** (3, Whole No. 234), 39–55.

*BRONFENBRENNER, U. The role of age, sex, class, and culture in studies of moral development. *Research Supplement to Religious Education,* 1962, **57,** S-3–S-17.

BUGELSKI, B., & SCHARLOCK, D. An experimental demonstration of unconscious mediated association. *Journal of Experimental Psychology,* 1952, **44,** 334–338.

BURTON, R. V. Some factors related to re-

[13] It is suggested here that direct methods of observation or experimental designs in the home or in natural situations be used to obtain measures of child rearing. It seems that the important differences in child rearing for boys and girls, especially at very young ages, may be measured by interview techniques.

* [Asterisks indicate works that are reprinted, in whole or in part, in this volume.]

sistance to temptation in four-year-old children. Unpublished doctoral dissertation, Harvard University, 1959.

BURTON, R. V., MACCOBY, E. E., & ALLINSMITH, W. Antecedents of resistance to temptation in four-year-old children. *Child Development*, 1961, **32**, 689–710.

CAMPBELL, D. T., & FISKE, D. W. Convergent and discriminant validation by the multitrait-multimethod matrix. *Psychological Bulletin*, 1959, **56**, 81–105.

DURKIN, D. Children's concepts of justice: A comparison with the Piaget data. *Child Development*, 1959, **30**, 59–67.

EYSENCK, H. J. *The structure of human personality*. New York: Wiley, 1953.

GOODENOUGH, F. L. The measurement of mental growth in childhood. In L. Carmichael (Ed.), *Manual of child psychology*. (2nd ed.) New York: Wiley, 1954. Pp. 459–491.

GOODWIN, W. R., & LAWRENCE, D. H. The functional independence of two discrimination habits associated with a constant stimulus situation. *Journal of Comparative and Physiological Psychology*, 1955, **43**, 113–128.

GUTTMAN, L. A new approach to factor analysis: The radex. In P. F. Lazarsfeld (Ed.), *Mathematical thinking in the social sciences*. Glencoe, Ill.: Free Press, 1955. Pp. 258–348.

HARROWER, M. R. Social status and moral development. *British Journal of Educational Psychology*, 1935, **4**, 75–95.

*HARTSHORNE, H., & MAY, M. A. *Studies in the nature of character*. Vol. 1. *Studies in deceit*. New York: Macmillan, 1928.

HARTSHORNE, H., MAY, M. A., & MALLER, J. B. *Studies in the nature of character*. Vol. 2. *Studies in service and self-control*. New York: Macmillan, 1929.

HARTSHORNE, H., MAY, M. A., & SHUTTLEWORTH, F. K. *Studies in the nature of character*. Vol. 3. *Studies in the organization of character*. New York: Macmillan, 1930.

HOFFMAN, M. L. Child-rearing practices and moral development: Generalizations from

empirical research. Unpublished manuscript, Author, 1961.

HULL, C. L. Quantitative aspects of the evolution of concepts: An experimental study. *Psychological Monographs*, 1920, **28** (1, Whole No. 123).

HUMPHREYS, L. G. Generalization as a function of method of reinforcement. *Journal of Experimental Psychology*, 1939, **25**, 361–372.

KAISER, H. F. Varimax criterion for analytic rotation in factor analysis. *Psychometrika*, 1958, **23**(3), 187–200.

KENDLER, T. S., & KENDLER, H. H. Reversal and nonreversal shifts in kindergarten children. *Journal of Experimental Psychology*, 1959, **58**, 56–60.

KENDLER, T. S., KENDLER, H. H., & WELLS, D. Reversal and nonreversal shifts in nursery school children. *Journal of Comparative and Physiological Psychology*, 1960, **53**, 83–88.

KOHLBERG, L. The development of modes of moral thinkings and choice in the years ten to sixteen. Unpublished doctoral dissertation, University of Chicago, 1958.

KOHLBERG, L. Status as perspective in society: An interpretation of class differences in children's moral judgment. Paper read at Society for Research in Child Development, Bethesda, Maryland, March 1959.

KOHLBERG, L. Moral development and identification. [In H. W. Stevenson (Ed.), *Yearbook of the national society for the study of education*. Pt. I. *Child psychology*. Chicago: University of Chicago Press, 1963. Pp. 277–332.]

KOHN, M. L. Social class and the exercise of parental authority. *American Sociological Review*, 1959, **24**, 352–366.

KUENNE, K. Experimental investigation of the relation of language to transposition behavior in young children *Journal of Experimental Psychology*, 1946, **36**, 471–490.

LAWLEY, D. N. The estimation of factor loadings by the method of maximum likelihood. *Proceedings of the Royal So-*

ciety of Edinburgh, Series A, 1940, **40,** 64–82.

LERNER, E. The problem of perspective in moral reasoning. *American Journal of Sociology*, 1937, **43,** 248–269.

LURIA, A. R. The role of language in the formation of temporary connections. In B. Simon (Ed.), *Psychology in the Soviet Union.* Stanford: Stanford University Press, 1957.

MACCOBY, E. E. The generality of moral behavior. Paper read at American Psychological Association, Cincinnati, September 1959.

MACKINNON, D. W. Violation of prohibition. In H. A. Murray (Ed.), *Explorations in personality: A clinical and experimental study of fifty men of college age.* New York: Oxford, 1938. Pp. 491–501.

MACRAE, D., JR. A test of Piaget's theories of moral development. *Journal of Abnormal and Social Psychology*, 1954, **49,** 14–48.

MALLER, J. B. General and specific factors in character. *Journal of Social Psychology*, 1934, **5,** 97–102.

MAXWELL, A. E. Recent trends in factor analysis. *Journal of the Royal Statistical Society, Series A*, 1961, **124** (Pt. 1), 49–59.

MEDINNUS, G. R. Immanent justice in children: A review of the literature and additional data. *Journal of Genetic Psychology*, 1959, **94,** 253–262.

MORRIS, J. F. The development of adolescent value-judgments. *British Journal of Educational Psychology*, 1958, **28,** 1–14.

OSGOOD, C. E. *Method and theory in experimental psychology.* New York: Oxford, 1953.

PEEL, E. A. Experimental examination of some of Piaget's schemata concerning children's perception and thinking, and a discussion of their educational significance. *British Journal of Educational Psychology*, 1959, **29,** 89–103.

*PIAGET, J. *The moral judgment of the child.* New York: Harcourt, 1932.

*SEARS, R. R., MACCOBY, E. E., & LEVIN, H. (Eds.), *Patterns of child rearing.* Evanston, Ill.: Row, Peterson, 1957.

UNGER, S. M. On the development of the guilt response systems. Unpublished doctoral dissertation, Cornell University, 1960.

WICKENS, D. D., SCHRODER, H. M., & SNIDE, J. D. Primary stimulus generalization of the GSR under two conditions. *Journal of Experimental Psychology*, 1954, **47,** 52–56.

# 9

# The generality
# of moral behavior

*by Albert Bandura
and Richard H. Walters*

According to the point of view presented here, there is no necessary relationship between resistance to temptation and guilt as defined in terms of self-punitive responses. In fact, the learning principles involved in the development of these two modes of response seem to differ radically; whereas resistance to temptation involves the classical conditioning of emotional responses, the habit of responding self-punitively appears to result from instrumental conditioning. It is therefore not surprising that no consistent relationships between resistance to temptation and guilt have emerged from a number of studies in which both variables have been measured (W. Allinsmith, 1960; Burton, 1959; Burton, Maccoby, & W. Allinsmith, 1961; MacKinnon, 1938; Sears, Rau, & Alpert, 1960); moreover, one should not expect to find that these variables are related to precisely the same child-training practices (Hoffman, 1962), since the training procedures necessary for their development appear to be very different.

The issue of the generality or specificity of moral behavior has received con-

From Chapter 4, from *Social Learning and Personality Development* by Albert Bandura and Richard H. Walters. Copyright © 1963 by Holt, Rinehart and Winston, Inc. Reprinted by permission of Holt, Rinehart and Winston, Inc. and Albert Bandura.

siderable attention in both empirical studies and theoretical discussions (Brogden, 1940; Burton, 1963; Durkin, 1961; Hartshorne & May, 1928; Hartshorne, May, & Maller, 1929; Hartshorne, May, & Shuttleworth, 1930; Hoffman, 1962; Maller, 1934). Most of the empirical studies, of which those by Hartshorne, May, and their collaborators were the forerunners, have involved resistance-to-deviation measures, primarily ones involving cheating. The results indicate that there is considerable intraindividual inconsistency in response to specific situations which permit children to misrepresent their level of performance. Since parents are likely to consider cheating as morally reprehensible regardless of the circumstances under which it occurs, one would expect less specificity of response than that reported by Hartshorne and May. Indeed, Burton (1963), following a reanalysis of the Hartshorne and May data, has concluded that there is some generality in moral behavior when this behavior is defined in terms of not cheating on tests. He proposes that consistency is mediated by two independent generalization gradients. One gradient represents generalization from one situation to another as a function of the stimulus elements the situations have in common. The other represents generalization based on verbal labeling; in this case, the stimulus elements may differ considerably from one situation to another, but a similar response is elicited because the same label is attached to each. Burton also points out that most middle-class parents try to teach both kinds of generalization. The problem is thus not to explain the degree of generality, but the marked specificity, of children's responses to opportunities to deceive.

The evidence cited earlier in this chapter indicates that resistance to deviation and other forms of self-control can be transmitted through parental modeling, which is likely to attenuate the effects of direct training. Thus, while parents may almost unconditionally label cheating as an undesirable activity, they may at the same time themselves display violations of social prohibitions that the child has opportunity to observe. Most parents frequently violate traffic laws, particularly those relating to speed limits and parking, sometimes with the child enlisted as a participant observer. They enter into discussions of how they can "pad" expense accounts or misrepresent their financial position on income tax returns; they appropriate materials from their businesses or offices for personal use, and constantly infringe minor social prohibitions. Moreover, it is not unusual for parents to boast of their success in outwitting public officials, whom they are apt to depict as easily corruptible, or as getting the better of a bargain through deliberate over-representation of the value of their goods or services.

Indeed, Wallerstein and Wyle (1947), in a study of 1,700 predominantly middle-class adults in New York State, found that even seriously deviant behavior was not uncommon among those supposedly law-abiding citizens. Sixty-four percent of the men and 29 percent of the women who were interviewed admitted "off the record" offenses that amounted to felonies under the state law, while 99 percent of the adults acknowledged one or more offenses sufficiently serious to have drawn a sentence of at least one year. Less serious unlawful behavior and breaches of social prohibitions are undoubtedly much more frequent. There can be little doubt that most children are provided with ample opportunities for observing deviation in their parents; such experiences may more than counteract inhibitions that have been established through direct training and may, in fact, promote the learning of means of circumventing social and legal prohibitions.

Even less generality of self-control might be expected in cases in which parents provide precise discriminative training, as they do, for example, in teaching control of aggression. While parents may demand strict self-control of their children's aggression in the home, they may at the same time encourage, instigate, and reward aggression in other situations. In fact, most parents, directly or through modeling, train their children to respond in a highly discriminative manner to situations to which aggression is a possible response; discriminative stimuli, such as the age, sex, and status of the subject, are expected to govern the occurrence, form, and intensity of the response. Under such circumstances, general inhibition of aggression is maladaptive rather than a normal outcome of social training.

In this discussion, emphasis has been placed on factors that make for specificity of self-control. This emphasis, however, is not meant to imply that self-control responses do not generalize to situations similar to those in which they were learned or that parental training is inevitably lacking in consistency. It was noted earlier, for example, that children who prefer larger, delayed rewards to more immediate, smaller gains also show high resistance to deviation, express attitudes reflecting a relatively high degree of social responsibility, and inhibit aggressive behavior (Livson & Mussen,

1957; Mischel, 1961a, 1961b; Mischel & Gilligan, 1963). Grinder (1962) has reported that children who confessed deviations readily at age five to six were, at age eleven to twelve, less likely to deviate when given opportunities to cheat in a game. This finding is especially surprising since mothers' reports were the source of information concerning early childhood confession, while resistance to cheating in later childhood was assessed from the children's performance in a carefully devised experimental situation. By contrast, Burton, Maccoby, and Allinsmith (1961), using four-year-old children, found a negative relationship between children's resistance to deviation and the extent to which they exhibited guilt responses after the commission of a deviant act. Burton et al. used the same test of resistance to deviation and the same index of guilt as those used by Grinder; moreover, in their study the measures of resistance and guilt were both secured when the children were four years of age. Grinder attempts to reconcile these discrepant findings by postulating that children have not developed a unitary self-control system by the age of four, but that such a system is present in children who have reached the age of eleven to twelve. It is evident, however, that Grinder's results do not, in fact, support this point of view, since his measures of guilt were secured from data concerning his subjects' behavior when they were still only five or six years old.

The preponderance of contrary findings casts considerable doubt on the utility of theories of morality which assume that self-control is mediated by a unitary, internal moral agent, such as a conscience, superego, or sense of moral obligation. They also call in question theories of moral development, such as that advanced by Piaget (1948 [1932]), in which moral orientations are assumed to emerge in children of specific ages. According to Piaget, one can distinguish two clear-cut stages of moral judgment, demarcated from each other at approximately seven years of age. In the first stage, defined as objective morality, children judge the gravity of a deviant act in terms of the amount of material damages and disregard the intentionality of the action. By contrast, during the second or subjective morality stage, children judge conduct in terms of its intent rather than its material consequences. However, Bandura and McDonald (1963), using a wide variety of verbally described social situations eliciting moral judgments, found that children between five and eleven years of age exhibited highly discriminative moral-judgment repertoires, including both objective and subjective judgments, revealing considerable discrimination learning. Moreover, experimental manipulations, based on a social-learning paradigm, revealed that the developmental sequence proposed by Piaget is by no means predetermined or invariant.

In this study, children who exhibited predominantly objective or subjective moral orientations were assigned to one of three experimental conditions. One group of children observed adult models who expressed moral judgments counter to the group's orientation, and the children were reinforced with verbal approval for adopting the model's evaluative responses. A second group observed the models but received no reinforcement for matching the models' behavior. A third group had no exposure to the models, but each child was reinforced whenever he expressed moral judgments that ran counter to his dominant evaluative tendencies. The measures of learning were the percentage of objective judgmental responses produced by the subjective children and the percentage of subjective responses performed by the objectively oriented children in response to sets of stimulus items, each of which depicted a well-intentioned act, resulting in considerable material damage, contrasted with a selfishly or maliciously motivated act that produced only minor consequences. Following the treatment procedure, the stability and generality of the children's judgmental responses were tested in a different social situation in the absence both of the models and of the social reinforcement.

As shown in Figures 1 and 2, children who were exposed to models and those who were positively reinforced for matching their models' moral judgments not only modified their moral orientations but also maintained these changes in their postexperimental judgmental behavior. It is nevertheless apparent from these data that operant-conditioning procedures alone are relatively ineffective in modifying the behavior of subjects who present strong dominant response tendencies and in whom the desired alternative responses are only weakly developed or absent. In such cases, however, the provision of models who exhibit the desired behavior is an exceedingly effective procedure for eliciting from observers appropriate matching responses early in the learning sequence and thus accelerating the acquisition process. The so-called development stages were readily altered by the provision of adult models who consistently adopted moral orientations that ran counter to those displayed by the child Increased consistency in the children's moral orientations resulted from consistency on the part of the model and generalized to the new set of social situations. As this study suggests, consistency in moral behavior is probably attained when parent models exhibit widely generalized resistance to deviation or self-punitive responses and at the same time use reinforcement patterns that are consistent with the behavioral examples they provide.

The assumption of a generalized self-control system has led to the practice of conceptualizing deviant response patterns in terms of deficient or overdeveloped superego. For example, a psychopath is depicted as lacking internal controls, whereas a neurotic is presented as suffering on account of an overdeveloped superego. Once he has adopted a unitary theory of morality, the clinician finds himself faced with paradoxes. For example, the psychopath is depicted as being impulse-ridden, yet at the same time as exercising effective control over his behavior in order to gain his own ends. He is said to be free of guilt and shame and yet to exhibit behavior that elicits punishment. These apparent contradictions would undoubtedly disappear if one knew the typical social-learning history of the psychopath and the way in which his discriminations were acquired. Similarly, Redl and Wineman (1955) have depicted "children who hate" as lacking controls from within. In order to account for the occasional resistance to temptation and self-punitive responses displayed by these children, Redl and Wineman invoke the concept of "islands of superego." Not only is their account open to serious misinterpretation, but such concepts as "islands of superego" have no explanatory value. More would have

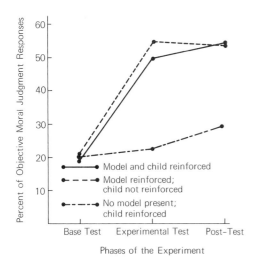

**Figure 1**

**Mean percentage of objective moral-judgment responses produced by subjective children on each of three test periods for each of three experimental conditions.**

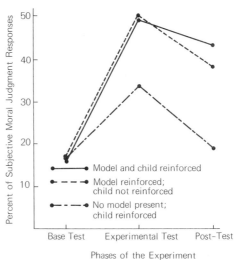

**Figure 2**

**Mean percentage of subjective moral-judgment responses produced by objective children on each of three test periods for each of three experimental conditions.**

been gained by focusing on the nature of the discriminations that the children had learned than in elaborating the paradox that results from the assumption of a unitary internal moral agent.

## References

ALLINSMITH, W. The learning of moral standards. In D. R. Miller & G. E. Swanson (Eds.), *Inner conflict and defense*. New York: Holt, 1960. Pp. 141–176.

BANDURA, A., & McDONALD, F. J. The influence of social reinforcement and the behavior of models in shaping children's moral judgments. *Journal of Abnormal and Social Psychology*, 1963, **67**, 274–281.

BROGDEN, H. E. A factor analysis of 40 character traits. In H. Woodrow (Ed.), *Studies in quantitative psychology. Psychological Monograph*, 1940, **52**, No. 3 (Whole No. 234), pp. 39–55.

BURTON, R. V. Some factors related to resistance to temptation in four-year-old children. Unpublished doctoral dissertation, Harvard University, 1959.

BURTON, R. V., MACCOBY, E. E., and ALLINSMITH, W. Antecedents of resistance to temptation in four-year-old children. *Child Development*, 1961, **32**, 689–710.

*BURTON, R. V. The generality of honesty reconsidered. *Psychological Review*, 1963, **70**, 481–500.

DURKIN, D. The specificity of children's moral judgments. *Journal of Genetic Psychology*, 1961, **98**, 3–13.

GRINDER, R. E. Parental childrearing practices, conscience, and resistance to temptation of sixth-grade children. *Child Development*, 1962, **33**, 803–820.

*HARTSHORNE, H., & MAY, M. A. *Studies in the nature of character*. Vol. I. *Studies in deceit*. New York: Macmillan, 1928.

HARTSHORNE, H., MAY, M. A., & MALLER, J. B. *Studies in the nature of character*. Vol. 2. *Studies in service and self-control*. New York: Macmillan, 1929.

HARTSHORNE, H., MAY, M. A., & SHUTTLEWORTH, F. K. *Studies in the nature of*

* [Asterisks indicate works that are reprinted, in whole or in part, in this volume.]

*character*. Vol. 3. *Studies in the organization of character*. New York: Macmillan, 1930.

HOFFMAN, M. L. Child-rearing practices and moral development: Generalizations from empirical research. Unpublished manuscript, The Merrill-Palmer Institute, 1962.

LIVSON, N., & MUSSEN, P. H. The relation of ego control to overt aggression and dependency. *Journal of Abnormal and Social Psychology*, 1957, **55**, 66–71.

MALLER, J. B. General and specific factors in character. *Journal of Social Psychology*, 1934, **5**, 97–192.

MACKINNON, D. W. Violations of prohibition. In H. A. Murray *et al.* (Eds.), *Explorations in personality*. New York: Oxford University Press, 1938. Pp. 491–501.

MISCHEL, W. Delay of gratification, need for achievement, and adquiescence in another culture. *Journal of Abnormal and Social Psychology*, 1961, **62**, 543–552 (a).

MISCHEL, W. Preference for delayed reinforcement and social responsibility. *Journal of Abnormal and Social Psychology*, 1961, **62**, 1–7 (b).

MISCHEL, W., & GILLIGAN, C. F. Delay of gratification and resistance to temptation. Unpublished manuscript, Stanford University, 1962.

*PIAGET, J. *The moral judgment of the child*. New York: Free Press, 1948. (First published in French, 1932.)

REDL, F., & WINEMAN, D. *The aggressive child*. New York: Free Press, 1955.

SEARS, R. R., RAU, L., & ALPERT, R. Identification and child training: The development of conscience. Interim research report presented at American Psychological Association Annual Meeting, Chicago, 1960.

WALLERSTEIN, J. A. & WYLE, C. I. Our law-abiding law-breakers. *Probation*, 1947, **25**, 107–112, 118.

# 10

# A study
# of children's
# moral judgments[1]

## by Ronald C. Johnson

The development of moral judgment in the child has been of considerable interest to the social scientist. Among the students of human development, Jean Piaget has been, perhaps, most influential in this area of study (6). His studies of the child's developing understanding of causality, of physical and temporal reality, and of ethics and moral judgment have been extremely fruitful. This study proposes to test some of Piaget's ideas concerning developmental changes in moral judgment.

Moral judgment, for Piaget, consists of a number of areas. These include: (a) immanent justice—the belief in the existence of automatic punishments which emanate from things themselves; (b) moral realism—a belief that acts should be judged in terms of consequences, not on the basis of the motive behind the act; (c) belief that punishment should be retributive vs. belief that punishment

From Ronald C. Johnson, "A Study of Children's Moral Judgments," *Child Development*, 1962, **33**, 327–354. © The Society for Research in Child Development, Inc., 1962. Reprinted by permission of the author and the publisher.

[1] This study is based on a dissertation submitted in partial fulfillment of the requirements of the Ph.D. degree at the University of Minnesota. The author is grateful to Dale B. Harris, the major advisor of the dissertation for his help and advice.

should be restitutive (merely restore the equilibrium destroyed by the punished act); (d) acceptance or rejection of the idea that the more severe punishment is more efficacious; and (e) choice of collective (essentially, guilt by association) or of individual responsibility for punishable acts. . . .

. . . Piaget sees three forces interacting to produce developmental change in moral judgment: adult constraint, peer-group cooperation and reciprocity, and the changing character of the child's mind. He says, ". . . We have three processes to consider: the spontaneous and unconscious egocentrism belonging to the individual as such, adult constraint, and cooperation." ". . . Cooperation alone can shake the child out of its initial state of unconscious egocentrism; whereas constraint acts quite differently and strengthens egocentric features of moral realism until such time as cooperation delivers the child both from egocentrism and from the results of this constraint" (6, p. 184). The interaction of these factors, the changing mind of the child, the amount of adult constraint, and the amount of peer-group cooperation and reciprocity, to Piaget, cause developmental differences in systems of responsibility and type of moral judgment used by children of different ages.

. . . Piaget's study was conducted primarily to show that developmental changes occur in moral judgment and then to determine how the factors of adult constraint, peer-group cooperation, and qualitative changes in thought processes interact to produce these changes in moral judgment. Piaget shows that age changes in belief do occur. . . . It does not seem that he has achieved his second objective, that of showing how the interaction of constraint, cooperation, and mental change cause this change to occur. . . .

Piaget was not concerned with testing, empirically, to discover whether moral judgment consisted of one general or of a number of specific factors. The conclusions of Lerner (2), MacRae (4), and Medinnus (5) are that responses in areas of moral judgment are not too closely related to each other. Lerner and Medinnus both present material which shows that the age of change in belief concerning various areas of moral judgment is variable from one area to the next, while MacRae's conclusions are based on the results of a series of intercorrelations between responses to questions concerning moral judgment, indicating the same results to be true. . . .

This study was concerned first with an attempt to determine the degree of interrelation within and between areas of moral judgment. This study dealt secondly with the relation of various antecedent conditions to moral judgment. There was an attempt to discover the relation of adult constraint, "egocentricity," age, sex, IQ, and parental occupational level to moral judgment. Though certainly one should also measure peer-group cooperation, this seemed impossible in a sample sufficiently large to give a reliable determination for the primary problem. Previous findings concerning the effect of peer solidarity are uniformly negative, indicating that, of the variables, this might best be omitted.

This study, using a different method of gaining information, different questions, and different age groups, cannot be considered a test of the validity of Piaget's own work, since it was not directly comparable. However, it did attempt to test Piaget's ideas.

## Method

### Sample

This study included all the children (all of those present on the day when their classes were tested) in grades 5, 7, 9, and 11 in a midwestern public school system. . . . The total sample consisted of 807 subjects. . . .

A comparison of the occupational level of the parents of these children with that of the urban population of the United States indicates that the sample was a very close approximation of the general population, as measured by the Minnesota Occupational Scale (10). Information concerning IQ was available in 732 cases of the total sample of 807. The mean IQ of the sample was 105.9. The sample closely approximated U.S. urban norms in intelligence as well as in occupational level.

### Measuring Devices

The major purpose of this study was to determine the degree of interrelation between responses to questions formulated to represent different areas or kinds of moral judgment. The writer's initial problem was that of devising a test of moral judgment within which a number of questions could be found having to do with each of the areas under discussion. A number of stories were made up, modeled quite closely after those of Piaget. The stories illustrated five types of moral judgment: immanent justice, moral realism, retribution and expiation vs. restitution and reciprocity, the efficacy of severe punishment, and communicable responsibility.

\*        \*        \*

. . . Twenty items were retained as those likely to be instrinsically interesting to the subjects most similar in meaning to those of Piaget, and of an equal level of difficulty.

[A selection of] the moral judgment test items appear below, followed by a discussion of the way that responses would, according to Piaget's results, be scored in terms of maturity.

\*　　　\*　　　\*

11. Two fellows were out one night and wanted to go riding in a car. They didn't have one, but they saw a car that was parked in front of a house with the keys in it, so they took that car. They drove it around for awhile but then they spotted a police car so they stopped the car and got out and started to run through back yards and alleys to ditch the police. They ran for awhile but then one of them got winded and police caught up with him. The other one ran for awhile more and then he crossed a ravine by an old bridge. The bridge was rotten and a plank broke on him so that one leg went through and got broken. Now what do you think?

*If this boy had not stolen the car and had been running across the ravine on the old, rotten bridge all the same, would he have still broken through and hurt himself? Why?*

12. This story is about a guy who came from a tough neighborhood. He did pretty well, generally, but he sometimes took things. He had a friend who was a very good basketball player but whose folks didn't have much money so that his buddy couldn't afford to get gym shoes. One day when this boy was downtown he went into a store and took some gym shoes that they had there and gave them to his friend. Then a couple of weeks later he was hanging around the drugstore and managed to take a big box of chocolates that only cost about one quarter as much as the gym shoes. He didn't

tell anyone about them; just kept them hidden and ate them. Now he wasn't caught either time and no one ever found out where his friend got the gym shoes.

*Now which time was the stealing worse? Why?*

13. A boy was out with a group of friends one evening. They got to wrestling and one boy began wrestling each of the others, even when they didn't want to. He got to wrestling with a boy who was wearing glasses and the glasses fell off and broke. Now there were all sorts of things that the grownups could do to him; they could give him a spanking or they could have him work to pay for replacing the glasses or they could break something of his.

*What would be the worst punishment? What would be the fairest punishment? Which one do you think that they gave him?*

14. A girl wanted to use her mother's fur coat but the mother didn't want her to and told her not to use it because she was afraid the girl would maybe lose it in some way. The girl used it anyway figuring she wouldn't get caught, but the mother caught her. When she caught her using the coat she was so angry she made the girl stay in at night for a week.

There was another girl who wanted to use her mother's coat too, even though her mother didn't want her to and told her not to use it. The girl did use it anyway and the mother caught her at it but what this mother did was talk to the girl, explaining why she didn't want her to use it so that the girl would understand.

Now one girl used her mother's fur coat the next time she thought the mother was not around and the other one didn't use it again.

*From these stories, tell me which one you think used the coat and which one didn't. Why?*

15. A science class was on a trip in the spring and they stopped to look over an apple orchard that was in bloom. While the leader wasn't around, one person in the group cut off many limbs, to get apple blossoms. He did this when none of the others were looking, so that none of the group knew who did it. The farmer saw the cut branches in the cars and was very angry. He complained to the group leader but no one knew who did it so no one could tell the group leader who had done it. The farmer and the group leader decided to charge everyone in the group equally to pay the damages, since they couldn't find out who had done it.

*Was this right? Why?*

\*          \*          \*

In question . . . 11, . . . dealing with immanent justice, the mature response would be one which brought in the idea of chance—that chance caused one boy to escape while the others were caught. The immature response would be the one that attributed some sort of supernatural cause to these events.

Question . . . 12 . . . had to do with moral realism. The mature response would be one in which acts were judged in terms of intent; the immature response would judge an act according to its consequences.

The problem of choosing between punishment in terms of expiation or retribution as opposed to punishment in terms of restitution appears in question . . . 13. . . . The mature response would be the restitutive one, chosen because it was fairest, not because it was hardest. (Sometimes the restitutive punishment might be chosen, not because it was fairest, but solely because it was considered to be the most severe. In this case the response would be considered an im-

mature one.) The choice of an expiatory punishment would be scored as an immature response.

Question . . . 14 . . . had to do with the efficacy of severe punishment. Answers in which the position was taken that the less severe punishment was more effective were scored as mature, while those responses that indicated a belief in the efficacy of the more severe punishment were scored as immature.

Communicable responsibility was dealt with in question 15. . . . In each case, those responses that rejected communicable responsibility were judged to be mature, while those that accepted the idea of communicable responsibility were considered to be immature. This is not in strict accordance with Piaget's position. He says that both very young and older children accepted communicable responsibility while the middle age group of his sample rejected it. Very young children accept communicable responsibility because they believe that everything an adult does is fair while older children accept communicable responsibility as evidence of peer-group solidarity. Since there is cross-cultural evidence (e.g., that gathered by Durkheim and by Fauconnet) that advanced cultures tend to reject communicable responsibility, the writer decided to score the rejection of communicable responsibility as the mature response.

\*          \*          \*

A test of the relation of various antecedent conditions to the system of moral judgment used by the subjects involved the use of other measuring devices, plus the gathering of information from school records. The antecedent conditions were adult constraint, egocentricity, age (as measured by grade in school), sex, parental occupation, intelligence quotient, and religious training. Information concerning all but the first two of these variables was obtained from school records.

*      *      *

The test of parent attitudes used was that devised by Shoben (8). Shoben attempted to obtain information concerning the attitudes of the parents of problem and of nonproblem children. Seventy-four of his items discriminated between the two groups of mothers and could be placed in one of three clusters. . . . The clusters were relatively independent of one another. They were labeled "Ignoring," "Possessive," and "Dominating" and could have been scored . . . as independent subscales. Each item consisted of a statement . . . plus the choices of "strongly agree," "mildly agree," "mildly disagree," and "strongly disagree," following the statement. . . . Shoben had weighted the possible responses to each question according to differences between the proportions of mothers of problem children and the proportions of mothers of nonproblem children choosing them. The scoring system devised for this study was designed to measure the sheer amount of dominativeness, ignoringness, and possessiveness expressed in responses to questions in the subscales concerned with these three facets of parental attitude. The investigator and two additional judges (both psychologists) independently weighted the responses to each question in each of the three scales. . . .

All three of the judges agreed on the weighting of responses to all but six of the 74 items. The weights assigned to responses on which there was a difference of opinion were those that were assigned by two of the three judges.

The other variable of significance to Piaget is that of developmental changes in thought processes. According to Piaget, the stage of egocentricity begins in the child in the time interval following the formation of sensorimotor intelligence. The stage of egocentricity includes, from the ages of 7 or 8 to 11 or 12, a period of concreteness, ". . . i.e., operational groupings of thought concerning objects that can be manipulated or known through the senses. Finally, from 11 to 12 years and during adolescence, formal thought is projected and its groupings characterize the completion of reflective thought" (7, p. 123).

The egocentricity of the young child presumably predisposes him toward an immature system of moral judgment. The problem of measuring egocentricity seems a most difficult one. This writer is not familiar with any direct tests measuring all aspects of "egocentricity," nor of any indirect test of it other than some individual tests used by Piaget and by Lerner (13) which seem, by inference, to be measuring egocentricity. There is, however, a test available in one area that bears on Piaget's concept of egocentricity. This test is the Gorham Proverbs Test designed to measure concreteness and abstractness of thought. The stage of concreteness, for Piaget (7), is a late portion of the egocentric period of the child's development. This stage is followed by a period characterized by increasing ability in "reflective thought." This "reflective thought" seems analogous to what is usually called the ability to deal with abstract materials. The Gorham Proverbs Test was designed to measure differential quantities of abstract as opposed to concrete thought.

Therefore, the test appears to be measuring a major, late developing aspect of egocentricity.

The Shoben scale and the Gorham test are of somewhat limited utility in the study of factors involved in producing change in moral judgment. The Shoben test is a measure of attitudes, not of behavior. The greatest difficulty in the use of the Gorham test is that it does not measure egocentricity as would be desired, but measures concreteness (only one aspect of egocentricity) and abstractness (a characteristic that is dependent upon a lack of egocentricity). The writer could find no better tests suitable for group administration. The defects associated with these measuring devices force one to be cautious in drawing conclusions from the results obtained from these tests.

*Procedure*

The test of moral judgment was administered to the subjects in May of 1957. . . .

\*       \*       \*

Two class sections took the Gorham Proverbs Test at each grade level in grades 7, 9, and 11. Fifty-one students were tested in grade 7, 61 students in grade 9, and 55 students in grade 11. The testing schedule omitted grade 5 because the school officials did not wish to take time in this grade nor did the writer strongly urge the testing of this grade, for the Proverbs test, despite the fact that it had been standardized on populations as young as fifth-graders, seemed quite difficult for the seventh-grade sample.

The moral judgment test and the Proverbs test were administered in the school. Further data gathering involved contacting the parents of the subjects.

The writer wished to determine the relations of adult constraint to abstractness-concreteness and to moral judgment. This required obtaining some measure of adult attitudes toward freedom and constraint. . . .

[Of the original sample of 167 subjects] only 128 sets of parents were involved in the parent attitude study. Of the 128 parents, 96 sent back their filled-out questionnaires. A comparison of the occupational levels of the respondents and nonrespondents (including those that could not be contacted) showed that 59 percent of the parents in groups I to III responded, as compared with 61 percent of the parents in groups V to VII.

It seems clear that the returns were not biased by disproportionate returns at different levels of parental occupation. Since this would be a principal area where one would expect to find bias, it seems probable that the responding parents were reasonably representative of the subject population.

*Scoring*

The Proverbs test was scored according to Gorham's protocols. The parent attitude survey was scored on the basis of parental ignoringness, possessiveness, and dominance. It should be noted that one additional measure of parent attitudes resulted from the scoring of the parent attitude questions. Extremeness of point of view—that is, how often the parent either strongly agreed or strongly disagreed rather than mildly agreed or disagreed—seemed related to the maturity of the responses made by that parent's child. This writer, therefore, scored each test for the total number of extreme positions taken in the entire test.

All answers to moral judgment questions were of an either-or or of a multiple-choice type. Thus, it was a simple matter to score the moral judgment questions to indicate relative maturity of response. . . .

*         *         *

## Results

The data to be presented in the following pages are divided into sections. There are a number of problems to be dealt with, and, for the purpose of clarity, they will be taken up in serial order. The first four sections of the results and discussion deal with responses to the moral judgment questions themselves, and the fifth with the relation of moral judgment to antecedent conditions. The results appear in the following order: (a) reliability of the moral judgment test; (b) intercorrelations of responses to moral judgment questions; (c) correlations of responses within moral judgment areas; (d) correlations of responses between moral judgment areas; and (e) relation of moral judgment responses to antecedent conditions.

### Reliability of the Moral Judgment Test

Information was obtained concerning the reliability of the total test (20 items) and also of the 4-item subtests in each of the five moral judgment areas (immanent justice, moral realism, retribution vs. restitution, efficacy of severe punishment, and communicable responsibility) at the four age levels tested. The results are presented in Table 1.

It is apparent that the reliability of the 20-item moral judgment test, and also of the subscales, was not as high as that usually attained in educational tests. Subscale reliabilities were sometimes higher than the reliability of the whole scale, indicating that the various areas of moral judgment are not as closely knit as one would expect on the basis of Piaget's discussion. . . . Statistically, the relatively low reliability values of the subscales and of the whole scale set definite limits to the size of the interrelations that can appear among the so-called varieties or areas of moral judgment.

### Intercorrelations of Responses to Moral Judgment Questions

Responses to each item on the 20-item test were correlated with responses to every other item at each of the four age levels—a total of 760 correlations. Among this many correlations, where no relation of any sort actually existed, one would expect to find, by chance, 38 values significant at the .05 level and be-

Table 1

**Reliability of Moral Judgment Questions**

|  | Grade 5 | Grade 7 | Grade 9 | Grade 11 |
|---|---|---|---|---|
| Total Test | 61 | ,59 | .55 | .56 |
| Immanent Justice | .66 | .68 | .67 | .67 |
| Moral Realism | .58 | .49 | .30 | .38 |
| Retribution vs. Restitution | .45 | .17 | .28 | .15 |
| Efficacy of Severe Punishment | .60 | .59 | .50 | .44 |
| Communicable Responsibility | .32 | .46 | .39 | .26 |

yond. There actually were 294 positive correlations and 79 negative correlations significant at or beyond the .05 level of confidence. It seems clear that responses to moral judgment questions were positively correlated with one another to a far greater extent than one could expect by chance. A larger number of negative correlations were obtained than one could expect by chance. Some questions that seem, logically, to be positively related to other questions were apparently negatively correlated with other questions at one or more grade levels if judged in terms of the responses obtained.

*Correlations of Responses within Moral Judgment Areas*

Questions 1, 6, 11, and 16 of the moral judgment test measured immanent justice; 2, 7, 12, and 17, moral realism; 3, 8, 13, and 18, retribution vs. restitutive punishment; 4, 9, 14, and 19, the efficacy of severe punishment; and 5, 10, 15, and 20, communicable responsibility. . . .

Of the correlations of responses within areas of moral judgment . . . 102 out of 120 correlations were positive and significant. The area of immanent justice showed higher correlations between responses than other areas, but correlations in all areas of moral judgment were such that one is justified in talking about consistency within areas of moral judgment, especially when considering the reliability of the test items. . . . It seems that one can legitimately discuss areas of moral judgment, that these areas exist, since responses to the different questions within areas were almost always correlated positively and significantly with one another.

*Correlations of Responses between Moral Judgment Areas*

A more basic problem is the determination of whether there is any consistent correlation between the type of response made in one area of moral judgment and responses made in each of the other areas of moral judgment. It is implicit in Piaget's theory (7, pp. 106–107) that response tendencies in the various areas of moral judgment (excluding communicable responsibility) are positively related to one another. This is a testable proposition. The statistic epsilon was used for several reasons. The writer had no reason to assume that the relation between variables were rectilinear in nature. Epsilon is based on the statistic eta and hence may be used legitimately in the analysis of data in which variables are related in either curvilinear or rectilinear fashions. Epsilon may also be used in situations where there are few, broad classes within which data fall, as was the case with much of the material presented in this study. . . .

Twenty of the 40 correlations between areas of moral judgment were significant. . . . All of the significant correlations . . . were positive, except for the correlation of moral realism with communicable responsibility at grade 7, where the relation was negative, and the correlation of immanent justice with efficacy of severe punishment at grade 11, where the relation was curvilinear. In this curvilinear relation, both highly mature and highly immature sets of responses to the immanent justice question were positively related to mature responses to questions concerning the efficacy of severe punishment.

The intercorrelations among areas of moral judgment seem to show that mature moral judgments in the areas of moral realism, retribution vs. restitution, and efficacy of severe punishment were the most closely correlated with one another, that responses to questions concerning immanent justice were somewhat less closely correlated to responses in other areas of moral judgment, and that belief or nonbelief in communicable responsibility was even less closely related to other aspects of moral judgment.

### Relation of Moral Judgment Responses to Antecedent Conditions

Piaget suggests that changes from immature to mature moral judgment result from changes in the amount of adult constraint and peer group cooperation experienced by the child and from qualitative changes in the child's method of thought. The child's level of development, for Piaget, is best predicted from chronological age. Most students of moral judgment since Piaget have found intelligence and social class to be related to the type of moral judgment made by the child. All of these variables, except peer cooperation, were measured in this study. . . .

. . . It seems that IQ and parental occupation were more closely related to moral judgment than were the other variables studied in the areas of moral realism, retribution vs. restitution, and the efficacy of severe punishment. In general, one can say that brightness, represented by IQ, was more closely related to the type of moral judgment used in those three areas listed above than was any of the other variables measured in this study. Since parent's occupation and child's IQ were themselves positively correlated, it may well be that the correlations found between parent's occupation and the moral judgment of the child were merely reflections of differences due, basically, to IQ, rather than to cultural differences denoted by occupational level. The results of a determination of class differences in parental attitudes, discussed later in this study, seem to favor this position.

Immanent justice and communicable responsibility responses were less often significantly related to the antecedent conditions of sex, parental occupation, and IQ than were judgments concerning moral realism, retribution vs. restitution, and the efficacy of severe punishment. It may be that the higher degree of association between responses to moral judgment questions in the latter three areas is a result of the fact that response tendencies in these areas were related to the same antecedent conditions.

Chronological age was positively and significantly related in all areas of moral judgment—even "communicable responsibility" where, from Piaget's analysis, one would expect a negative relation in this age range. Age change was by no means saltatory, however—no sudden shifts in response tendencies were evident.

Out of 45 correlations of abstractness with moral judgment, six were significant. If abstractness is indicative of a freedom from egocentricity, one would expect high abstractness scores to be positively related to mature moral judgment. Five of the six significant correlations were in this direction. Only three of the 45 correlations of concreteness with moral judgment were significant. If concreteness is a manifestation of egocentricity, concreteness should be negatively correlated with mature moral judgment. The reverse held true in two of the three significant correlations.

If one scored the parent attitude scale in terms of the amount of ignoringness, possessiveness, and dominance expressed by the parents, one would expect, from Piaget's theory, to obtain the following results: belief in immanent justice, moral realism, retribution, and expiation, as opposed to restitution or reciprocity, and in the efficacy of severe punishment are all learned from the parents. If this is so, possessiveness and dominativeness should be positively correlated and ignoringness negatively correlated with acceptance of these beliefs. On the other hand, acceptance of communicable responsibility is usually learned from the peer group, which uses communicable responsibility as an evidence of group solidarity. Here it would seem probable that the ignored child, more free to interact with peers, should show less mature moral judgment than the child of possessive or dominative parents who presumably would have somewhat fewer peer-group contacts. Of the 45 correlations of the parent attitudes of expressed dominativeness, possessiveness, and ignoringness with the level of the child's moral judgment, eight were significant, seven of them in the direction predicted from the above discussion.

Extremeness of point of view on the part of the parent was correlated more frequently with the moral judgment of the child than were Shoben's subscales of ignoringness, possessiveness, or dominativeness. Extremeness of point of view was not significantly correlated with the type of parental response to any of the three subscales; there was no significant correlation, for instance, between the amount of dominativeness expressed and the number of extreme positions taken —so that the parent's extremeness of point of view seems, in its own right, to be a significant factor in relation to the child's level of moral judgment. The parents who more frequently take extreme points of view tended to have children who are immature in their moral judgments.

The existing significant correlations of parent attitude to moral judgment were not distributed randomly, but occurred most frequently in the areas of immanent justice and communicable responsibility, the very areas that showed few significant correlations with such variables as intelligence and parental occupation.

One can ask whether parent attitudes as measured here may be merely a reflection or indirect measure of social class differences in approach, either to child-rearing or to answering questionnaires. The writer attempted to determine whether this might be the case. The responding parents had already been categorized into occupational groups. They were now divided into two larger groupings, those in classes I to III and those in classes V to VII of the Minnesota Occupational Scale. Their responses were divided into those above and below the median in amount of expressed dominativeness, possessiveness, and ignoringness and in the number of extreme points of view. A comparison of the attitudes of these two groups allows one to determine whether the obtained correlations between parent attitudes and moral judgment are actually a result of some occupational group bias in responses. An analysis of the data indicates that this was not the case. There were no significant differences in attitude between the two groups. Parent attitudes, as expressed on the Shoben scale, were not significantly related to parental occupation as measured by the Minnesota Occupational Scale.

## Discussion

The primary purpose of this study was to determine the amount of association between responses to moral judgment questions.

The reliability of the test items, as a whole scale, seems to indicate in itself that responses concerning various aspects of moral judgment are related to one another empirically as well as logically, but not to as large an extent as one would expect from Piaget's analysis. Reliability did not change appreciably from one age to another. This seems to indicate (as do the actual correlations between responses) that moral judgment remains consistent in the amount of association from one area to another, contrary to what one might expect.

The reliability of subscales measuring specific areas of moral judgment was often somewhat higher than that of the total scale, suggesting a low association between areas but a higher association within areas. The reliability of the subscales seems rather high, in general, since each subscale consisted of only four items. Although high, when looked at in this fashion, subscale reliability was still so low that one cannot expect inter- and intramoral judgment area correlations to be as high as they might be with a more reliable test. It should be noted, however, that the whole scale reliability of this test is equal to that of some widely used measuring devices, e.g., the Rorscharch Test (9)....

The correlations of responses within moral judgment areas, like the reliability figures, seem to argue for quite considerable consistency within each area. This consistency may be due, in a large part, to the common correlations of items within an area to such things as intelligence and socioeconomic differences.

The results tend to support the idea that there is at least some consistency in response between areas. The correlations between responses in the five different areas of moral judgment indicate that judgments made regarding moral realism, retribution and expiation vs. restitution and reciprocity, and the efficacy of severe punishment were often significantly related to one another. Immanent justice was somewhat less frequently correlated positively and significantly with these three areas, though certainly there were far more positive and significant correlations than one would expect by chance. Communicable responsibility was less closely correlated with other areas of moral judgment; in fact, one of the four significant correlations of communicable responsibility with other areas of moral judgment was negative. The fact that the data were obtained separately at each of four age levels with quite similar results lends support through replication to the findings discussed above.

Piaget assumes, as a result of his logical analysis and of his findings, that response tendencies are similar in all areas of moral judgment (except for communicable responsibility), that there is what we would now call a general factor of moral judgment. The findings above were, in general, the results one would expect on the basis of Piaget's theoretical discussion, except that responses to questions involving communicable responsibility seemed largely unrelated, rather than negatively related, to responses in the other four moral judgment areas. With this exception the correlations were in the expected direction but were considerably lower than one would expect from Piaget's own work. The reliability data, as well as the inter-area correlations of the responses, seem to show that what might be called a general factor of moral judgment was present, but with a rather low degree of saturation.

The second purpose of this study was to determine the relation of a number of variables to the type of moral judgment used by the subjects. A number of antecedent conditions were investigated. Some of these factors, such as sex, IQ, and parent occupation were touched on peripherally in Piaget's investigation and discussion of moral judgment. Other factors were discussed more comprehensively by Piaget. These were age (as a sign or indicator of the condition of the organism with reference to the next two factors, rather than a direct cause of change), egocentricity (which the writer attempted to measure, admittedly indirectly, through a test of abstractness-concreteness), and adult constraint. The latter two factors, interacting with one another and with peer-group cooperation, were believed by Piaget to be directly causal in producing changes in beliefs concerning moral judgment. Here, too, the results obtained in this study must be judged in terms of the reliability of the measuring instruments.

Of those variables that were not discussed to any extent by Piaget, IQ was clearly the most significant in its relation to responses concerning moral realism, retribution and expiation vs. restitution and reciprocity, and the efficacy of severe punishment. Sex of subjects and parent occupation of subjects also showed a considerable number of significant correlations with responses in these three moral judgment areas. Immanent justice seemed less closely related, and communicable responsibility seemed essentially unrelated to this group of variables.

Age was correlated with the type of response made in all five areas. One would expect on the basis of Piaget's work that increasing age is positively correlated with more mature moral judgment in all areas except that of communicable responsibility, where an increase in peer-group solidarity might well cause a greater frequency of immature responses as age increased. Contrary to Piaget's theory, even communicable responsibility showed a very low but significant positive correlation between age and mature moral judgment. Within the age groups studied there was certainly no evidence for any large, sudden change in beliefs concerning moral judgment.

Parent attitudes, as expressed on questionnaire responses, most often showed significant correlations with responses to questions concerning communicable responsibility and immanent justice. These are the very areas that were less closely correlated with the first group of antecedent conditions. Abstractness and concreteness were related to moral judgment in the direction predicted by Piaget, but perhaps because abstractness is itself related to IQ. None of these variables was closely and consistently related to moral judgment to the extent that it accounted for the major portion of the variance, perhaps because the test of moral judgment was itself less reliable than one would desire.

This writer's general conclusions regarding these antecedent conditions are that IQ and chronological age were the variables most closely correlated to the type of response made with reference to moral realism, retribution and expiation vs. restitution and reciprocity, and the efficacy of severe punishment. Age and, to some extent, IQ and parent attitudes, seemed to be correlated with responses to immanent justice items. Only parent attitude items seemed correlated to any extent with type of response made to questions involving communicable responsibility.

\*            \*            \*

## References

1. GORHAM, D. R. A proverbs test for clinical and experimental use. *Psychological Reports*, 1956, Monograph Supplement No. 1.

2. LERNER, E. *Constraint areas and the moral judgment of the children.* Menasha, Wisc.: Banta, 1937.

3. LERNER, E. The problem of perspective in moral reasoning. *American Journal of Sociology*, 1937, **43**, 249–269.

4. MACRAE, D., JR. The development of moral judgment in children. Unpublished doctoral dissertation, Harvard University, 1950.

5. MEDINNUS, G. R. An investigation of Piaget's concept of the development of moral judgment in six to twelve year old children from lower socioeconomic class. Unpublished doctoral dissertation, University of Minnesota, 1957.

\*6. PIAGET, J. *The moral judgment of the child.* New York: Harcourt, 1932.

7. PIAGET, J. *The psychology of intelligence.* New York: Harcourt, 1950.

8. SHOBEN, E. J., JR. The assessment of parental attitudes in relation to child adjustment. *Genetic Psychology Monographs*, 1949, **39**, 101–148.

9. STAGNER, R. *Psychology of personality.* New York: McGraw-Hill, 1948.

10. *Minnesota scale for paternal occupations.* University of Minnesota Press, 1950.

\* [Asterisks indicate works that are reprinted, in whole or in part, in this volume.]

# 11

# Children's responses to two measures of conscience development and their relation to sociometric nomination[1]

*by Barbara D. Porteus
and Ronald C. Johnson*

A considerable amount of research has been carried out to study children's moral or conscience development. Piaget's (1948) approach to children's development of ethical standards entails presenting Ss with stories involving a "moral" issue and judging the maturity of Ss' responses to questions concerning

Barbara D. Porteus and Ronald C. Johnson, "Children's Responses to Two Measures of Conscience Development and their Relation to Sociometric Nomination," *Child Development*, 1965, **36**, 703–711. © The Society for Research in Child Development, Inc., 1965. Reprinted by permission of the authors and the publisher.

[1] This paper is based on research reported in a thesis submitted by Barbara Porteus to the Department of Psychology, University of Hawaii, in partial fulfillment of the requirements for the M.A. degree. It was conducted under the direction of Ronald Johnson. The authors wish to acknowledge their gratitude to Burl Yarberry, Superintendent of the Hawaiian Department of Education, to Yeuell Harris, director of research at the time this study was done, and to Walter Yee of the Statistical and Computing Center of the University of Hawaii.

what should be done about the moral issue. Immature responses are those in which the S shows acceptance of such notions as immanent justice, moral realism, and the necessity for or the efficacy of severe punishment. As Bronfenbrenner (1962, p. S-12) notes, this procedure is "one sided in its emphasis on the cognitive, conscious, and evaluative aspects of moral development." A newer technique of measuring children's responses to moral issues has come into being during the past decade and is found in such studies as those of Allinsmith (1960), Aronfreed (1960), and Grinder and McMichael (1963). This approach also involves the presentation of stories to Ss, but in this case the stories are structured to tap affective and emotional aspects of moral choice. The stories describe situations in which a central figure commits or is about to commit an undetected transgression. The S finishes the story. Does S have the central figure feel guilt, confess, or make restitution? Or does the central figure live happily ever after with his ill-gotten gains? This essentially projective technique has provided new insights regarding conscience development in children.

The present study makes use of these two quite different measures of moral development. (Hereafter, Piaget's measure, aimed at determining cognitive aspects of morality, will be referred to as the C measure, and the measure of affective aspects of conscience development will be referred to as the A measure.) These two measures are used in an attempt to gain information regarding three questions which, though quite simple, have not yet been answered fully.

The first question has to do with sex

differences in responses to these measures. Bronfenbrenner (1962, p. S-7) notes, "In our own view, the question of sex differences in Piaget-type responses is as yet a completely open one." With regard to A stories, Grinder and McMichael (1963) found no sex differences in amount of guilt shown by boys and by girls in story responses. Johnson (1963) found that sixth-grade girls show more guilt than sixth-grade boys and that both boy and girl Ss attribute more guilt to boy central figures. Rebelsky, Allinsmith, and Grinder (1963) found that girls make more use of confession in story completions than do boys. Relatively little is known concerning sex differences in A-story responses, and there appear to be contradictions in the information that is known.

The second question dealt with in the present research is that of determining the relation between responses to C and A measures. So far as the writers are aware, no information is available regarding this question.

The third question dealt with in the present paper is that of determining the relation between responses to C and A stories and behavior, as measured by sociometric ratings. Grinder (1964) found no relation between C responses and resistance to temptation. Grinder and McMichael (1963) and Rebelsky, Allinsmith, and Grinder (1963) found a relation between children's responses to a test measuring resistance to temptation and their responses to an A-story completion task. If A responses are related to reputation, as measured by a sociometric device, one would have more basis for assuming that these story completions are indicative of behavior in the larger social milieu as well as being predictive of behavior in experimental settings.

## Method

### Subjects

Subjects were 235 students (113 boys and 122 girls) comprising the ninth grade of a public intermediate school in Honolulu. Subjects were all tested on the same day in their first-period homerooms. Half of the homeroom groups received stories with male central figures, and half received stories with female central figures. This provided a total of 115 Ss (68 boys and 47 girls) with male central-figure stories, and 120 Ss (46 boys and 74 girls) with female central-figure stories. Each type of central-figure story presentation was also divided into two conditions, A–C or C–A booklets. There were 119 Ss (69 boys and 50 girls) with the A–C test booklet and 116 Ss (44 boys and 72 girls) with the C–A test booklet.

Equal numbers of Ss in each of the sequential conditions and in the male and female central-figure groups could not be achieved due to the different sizes and sex ratios of the homerooms. Furthermore, intelligence was not balanced between the main variables and was considered to be a possible confounding variable. The statistical analyses used were therefore analyses of covariance; these depended on the availability of intelligence test scores. The combined verbal and numerical raw scores of the Differential Aptitude Test (DAT) were available and used to represent the intelligence level of each S. The test population of 235 Ss used in the correlation analyses was reduced to 232 Ss, since only 112 boys and 120 girls of the test population had been tested on the DAT. This slightly smaller test population was reduced further by the dependence of the covariance analyses on equal numbers of Ss in each cell or category of the experimental design. As Table 1 indicates, the largest possible number of Ss in a category was 13. A random-sampling procedure was used to obtain 13 Ss in each category.

*Measuring Devices*

Four A stories were used. These were modeled closely after those of Allinsmith (1960) and Aronfreed (1960). In each A story the central figure is portrayed as having yielded to temptation. Eight cognitive stories adapted from Johnson (1962) were used. Two of the C stories dealt with each of four areas of moral judgment: immanent justice, moral realism, the necessity for severe punishment, and the efficacy of severe punishment. Each A and C story appeared in two parallel forms, one with a male and one with a female central figure.[2]

The sociometric test included 10 items, each of which required the nomi-

---

[2] The 12 stories, in both male and female forms, have been deposited as Document No. 8438 with the ADI Auxiliary Publications Project, Photoduplication Service, Library of Congress, Washington 25, D.C. Order by citing the Document number and remitting in advance $1.75 for microfilm or $2.50 for photocopies. Make checks or money orders payable to: Chief, Photoduplication Service, Library of Congress.

---

nation of a male and of a female S. For example, questions 1 and 2 were "He (she) is a very trustworthy and honest person." Other items presumably tapping moral traits were 5 and 6: "He (she) knows what is right and will do the right thing, even when it harms himself (herself) in some way." Questions 7 and 8 read: "He (she) feels very bad when he's (she's) done something wrong, and 17 and 18 were: "He (she) will take the blame for things he's (she's) done wrong." The remainder of the items were "filler" items.

Each test booklet contained both A and C stories, in either A–C or C–A sequence, with either male or female central figures, followed by the sociometric test.

*Procedure*

Since the stories were read aloud to the Ss, all Ss in each homeroom class received the same kind of test booklet. The method of administration and the instructions for the stories were modeled after those outlined by Johnson (1962). Testing took from 45–50 minutes and was accomplished during the first class period, which began at 8:30 A.M. at the school.

Using intelligence as a covariate and testing for the significance of the effects

Table 1

**No. of Ss with DAT, A, and C Scores in Each Cell**

| | Boy S | | Girl S | |
|---|---|---|---|---|
| | Central Figure | | Central Figure | |
| Sequence | Male | Female | Male | Female |
| A–C | 41 | 28 | 13 | 36 |
| C–A | 26 | 17 | 34 | 37 |

of the variables of the sex of $S$, the sex of the central figure of A and C stories, and the sequence of presentation of the stories, an analysis of covariance was computed for the A and C measures by means of a Bimed 13 Program on an IBM 7040 Computer. The total number of $S$s in each analysis of covariance was 104, with 13 randomly selected $S$s in each of the eight cells of the design.

*Scoring*

The scoring of the A stories was modeled after that of Grinder and McMichael (1963) and for the C stories after that used by Johnson (1962). A mature response to the questions following each C story was given one point, while one scored as immature was given no points. There was a total of eight points possible on the C measure; the higher the C score, the more mature the responses of the $S$. Mature responses were those that involved the rejection of immanent justice, moral realism, and the efficacy of and necessity for severe punishment. The A stories were all scored according to the same three criteria: (1) whether the central figure in the story completion expressed a feeling of guilt, (2) whether he performed an act of restitution or attempted restitution, or (3) whether he confessed. One point was given for each of these characteristics of a central figure in each completion. There was a total of 3 points possible for each story and a total A score of 12 points possible for each $S$; the higher the A score, the more guilt and conscience had been reflected in the stories. Guilt was not scored if the central figure indicated fear, such as by crying, since fear must be separated from guilt. Restitution or attempted restitution was given a

point if the central figure did it without the constraint of force of a parent or authority; also, if the central figure tried to hide the crime, the $S$ did not receive a score for restitution. Confession, too, was given a point only if the central figure did it without external force or impetus.

The "guess-who" questionnaire was scored by tabulating the frequency with which each $S$ was named. A moral-behavior score was obtained by tabulating the frequency with which each $S$ was named in answer to questions 1 or 2, 5 or 6, 7 or 8, and 17 or 18.

**Results and Discussion**

The results of this study are presented in the following order of statistical analyses:

1.  coefficients of stability between scoring by the authors of this study for A and for C stories;
2.  coefficients of correlation between A and C measures for total $S$s, for boy $S$s, and for girl $S$s;
3.  coefficients of correlation between A and C measures and moral items of sociometric measures for total $S$s, for boy $S$s, and for girl $S$s;
4.  coefficients of correlation for relationships between popularity and moral items of sociometric measure; between popularity and responses to the A stories; and between popularity and responses to the C stories, for total $S$s, boy $S$s, and girl $S$s;
5.  analyses of covariance, using intelligence as the covariate and the sex of $S$s, the sex of the central figure, and the sequence of presentation of the measures as the [independent] variables for A and for C stories.

Reliability coefficients were computed between the independent scoring by the two authors of the responses of twenty $Ss$ to the A and C measures. Product-moment correlations of the scores assigned by us to $Ss$ responses to the A and C measures were computed. The levels of statistical significance for the coefficients of stability for the reliabilities of the scoring methods were determined by transformation to $z$ scores and reference to a table of normal curve functions. Both reliability coefficients, for the scoring of the A measures ($r=.91$, $p<.0001$) and for the C measures ($r=.91$, $p<.0001$), were found to be statistically significant.

The $\phi$ coefficient was computed to determine the degree of correlation between the measures for analyses 2–4 listed above. A nonparametric test was statistically appropriate, since a normal and continuous distribution of scores was not obtained for any of the three measures, the A and the C stories and the sociometric scores.

The $\phi$ coefficients of correlation for relationships between the scores obtained on the A, C, and moral sociometric items are as follows.[3] The C and A measures of moral judgment were found to be significantly correlated for the total $Ss$ with both sexes combined ($\phi=.35$, $p<.001$) and by sex for the boys ($\phi=.31$, $p<.02$) but not for the girls ($\phi=.08$). As Grinder (1964) notes, Piaget predicts that the individual showing immature cognitive moral judgments should also show the most guilt. Like Grinder's work, the present findings for the total sample and for the boys are opposite to those predicted by Piaget.

The moral items of the behavior questionnaire were analyzed separated from the remainder of the items in order to determine the relation between story responses and nominations for being moral in behavior. No significant correlations were found between the moral items and the C and A scores for total $Ss$, boys, or girls. (The correlations for the latter two were .07 and .03, respectively.) Scores for a popularity item were obtained by tabulating the frequency with which each $S$ was named on the question, "He or she makes a good friend." This score was correlated with the moral-item sociometric score ($\phi=.57$, $p<.001$) but was not significantly related to responses to the A measure ($\phi=.03$) or to the C measure ($\phi=.04$). Since A story completions do allow one to predict actual behavior (e.g., see Grinder and McMichael, 1963), it may be that social visibility, rather than morality, was the major determinant of choice or "moral" sociometric items. The significant relation between popularity and nominations on the morality items might be considered supportive of this view or might, instead, be indicative of the belief, on the part of the $Ss$, that moral people make good friends. The data presented herein might support either interpretation.

The results of the analyses of covariance are found in Tables 2 and 3. The means adjusted by residuals were also computed to determine the direction of the statistically significant relationships. Table 2 indicates that the only variable which had a significant effect on the A measure with a $p<.01$ was the sex of $Ss$; girls had a higher mean adjusted by residuals ($\overline{X}=3.98$) than boys ($\overline{X}=2.80$) and, therefore, showed more guilt in response to stories with moral deviations

---

[3] The contingency tables have been deposited at ADI, Document No. 8438, $1.75 for microfilm or $2.50 for photocopies (see n. 2).

*Table 2*

**Analysis of Covariance for Affective Measure**

| Source of Variation | df | Sums of Squares | Mean Squares | F Ratio |
|---|---|---|---|---|
| A. Sex of S | 1 | 35.69 | 35.69 | 10.90* |
| B. Sex of central figure | 1 | 2.92 | 2.92 | 0.89 |
| C. Sequence | 1 | 7.85 | 7.85 | 2.40 |
| D. A × B | 1 | 3.37 | 3.37 | 1.03 |
| E. A × C | 1 | 0.08 | 0.08 | 0.03 |
| F. B × C | 1 | 0.30 | 0.30 | 0.09 |
| G. A × B × C | 1 | 5.24 | 5.24 | 1.60 |
| Within replicates | 95 | 311.02 | 3.27 | |
| Total | 102 | | | |

\* $p < .01$.

than did boys. This kind of sex difference in guilt responses is consistent with the findings of Johnson (1963), Rebelsky et al. (1963), and Burton, Maccoby, and Allinsmith (1961), but it is inconsistent with those of Grinder and McMichael (1963), who found no sex differences. The inconsistency with the findings of Grinder and McMichael might be due to their use of a relatively small sample, varying widely along several other dimensions (e.g., cultural background, social class) in which individual differences masked the more general effects of the sex of S.

The higher amount of guilt shown by girls does not support Freud's (e.g., 1933, pp. 176–177) view, since he believed that the development of the superego is a result of identification with the same sexed parent and that boys make a more adequate identification and, therefore, have better developed superegos than girls.

Table 3 indicates that sex of subject had a significant effect on the C meas-

*Table 3*

**Analysis of Covariance for Cognitive Measure**

| Source of Variation | df | Sums of Squares | Mean Squares | F Ratio |
|---|---|---|---|---|
| A. Sex of S | 1 | 14.26 | 14.26 | 6.75* |
| B. Sex of central figure | 1 | 1.99 | 1.99 | 0.94 |
| C. Sequence | 1 | 4.75 | 4.75 | 2.25 |
| D. A × B | 1 | 1.80 | 1.80 | 0.85 |
| E. A × C | 1 | 0.20 | 0.20 | 0.09 |
| F. B × C | 1 | 9.53 | 9.53 | 4.51* |
| G. A × B × C | 1 | 0.73 | 0.73 | 0.35 |
| Within replicates | 95 | 200.72 | 2.11 | ... |
| Total | 102 | | | |

\* $p < .05$.

ure with a $p<.05$; girls had a higher mean adjusted by residuals ($\overline{X}=5.56$) than boys ($\overline{X}=4.82$). This sex difference is not consistent with the findings of Grinder (1964) who found insignificant sex differences for different age groups and for the combined different age groups in his study.

The interaction of the sex of the central figure of stories and the sequence of presentation of stories also had a statistically significant effect on the C measure with a $p<.05$. Scores from stories with the A–C sequence and male central figures ($\overline{X}=5.20$) were not significantly different from scores from stories with the C–A sequence and male central figures ($\overline{X}=5.18$), but scores from stories with the A–C sequence and female central figures $\overline{X}=5.38$) had a higher mean adjusted by residuals than those with the C–A sequence and female central figures ($\overline{X}=4.81$). This finding does not lend itself to any interpretation that we can conceive of, nor is it either consistent or inconsistent with previous research, since earlier studies did not control for this variable.

The Bimed 13 Program for the IBM 7040 also yielded an $F$ ratio for testing the significance of the effects of the covariate; intelligence was found to have a significant effect on the A measure ($F=54.37$, $p<.001$) and on the C measure ($F=52.97$, $p<0.001$). This significant effect on the C scores is similar to the findings of others (Hartshorne and May, 1928–1930; Johnson, 1962; Kohlberg, 1958), but the significant effect on the A scores is not consistent with the findings of Allinsmith (1960) or of McCord and McCord (1956). Although the reason for the inconsistency in findings of the effect of intelligence on the A scores is not apparent, the use of the analyses of

covariance in this study was shown to be justified.

To summarize the results, intelligence seems to be a most important variable with regard to responses to C and A stories, Sex differences are also significant, with girls showing greater moral maturity on both measures. Although girls are more mature in both types of judgment, they are less consistent than boys in responding to the two types of stories, as shown in the insignificant relation between girls' responses to C and A stories. Even for boys the relation between responses to C and A stories is not of any great magnitude, although it is significant. The relation between story completions and nominations for moral behavior is insignificant, possibly because social visibility and popularity may have been major factors in determining moral nominations. It would appear that a major need in this particular area of research is to continue the development of reliable measures of actual behavior, as has been done, for example, by Grinder (1961, 1962, 1964) and to pursue still further the relation of story responses to rated behavior, as done herein, but perhaps using raters other than peers.

## References

ALLINSMITH, W. Moral standards. II. The learning of moral standards. In D. R. Miller and G. E. Swanson (Eds.), *Inner conflict and defense.* New York: Holt, 1960. Pp. 141–176.

ARONFREED, J. Moral behavior and sex identity. In D. R. Miller and G. E. Swanson (Eds.), *Inner conflict and defense.* New York: Holt, 1960. Pp. 177–193.

*BRONFENBRENNER, U. The role of age, sex,

* [Asterisks indicate works that are reprinted, in whole or in part, in this volume.]

class, and culture in studies of moral development. *Research Supplement to Religious Education,* 1962, **57,** S-3–S-17.

BURTON, R. V., MACCOBY, E. E., & ALLINSMITH, W. Antecedents of resistance to temptation in four-year-old children. *Child Development,* 1961, **32,** 689–710.

FREUD, S. *New introductory lectures on psychoanalysis.* New York: Norton, 1933.

GRINDER, R. E. New techniques for research in children's temptation behavior. *Child Development,* 1961, **32,** 679–688.

GRINDER, R. E. Parental child-rearing practices, conscience, and resistance to temptation of sixth-grade children. *Child Development,* 1962, **33,** 803–820.

GRINDER, R. E. Relations between behavioral and cognitive dimensions in middle childhood. *Child Development,* 1964, **35,** 831–891.

*GRINDER, R. E., & McMICHAEL, R. E. Cultural influence on conscience development: Resistance to temptation and guilt among Samoans and American Caucasians. *Journal of Abnormal and Social Psychology,* 1963, **66,** 503–507.

*HARTSHORNE, H., & MAY, M. A. *Studies in the nature of character.* Vol. 1. *Studies in deceit.* Vol. 2. *Studies in service and self control.* Vol. 3. *Studies in the organization of character.* New York: Macmillan, 1928–1930.

*JOHNSON, R. C. A study of children's moral judgments. *Child Development,* 1962, **33,** 327–354.

JOHNSON, R. C. A study of children's responses to two measures of conscience development. Unpublished manuscript. University of Hawaii, 1963.

KOHLBERG, L. The development of modes of moral thinking and choice in the years ten to sixteen. Unpublished doctoral dissertation, University of Chicago, 1958.

McCORD, W., & McCORD, J. *Psychopathy and delinquency.* New York: Grune & Stratton, 1956.

*PIAGET, J. *The moral judgment of the child.* Glencoe: Free Press, 1948 (original English publication in 1932).

*REBELSKY, F. G., ALLINSMITH, W., & GRINDER, R. E. Resistance to temptation and sex differences in children's use of fantasy confession. *Child Development,* 1963, **34,** 955–962.

## 12

# Cultural influence on conscience development: Resistance to temptation and guilt among Samoans and American Caucasians[1]

*by Robert E. Grinder*
*and Robert E. McMichael*

The methods of social control relied upon by societies often have been classified as either "shame" or "guilt" (Benedict, 1946; Mead, 1955; Piers & Singer, 1953), and in essence the present study is an exploratory attempt to assess the relative effects of a shame and a guilt culture on conscience development. Shame cultures generally stress external agents who in various ways coerce, threaten, or otherwise arouse objective fear. On the other hand, guilt cultures emphasize both self-control in the face of temptation and self-initiated responsibility for

one's actions if transgression should occur. If conscience be defined in terms of internalized controls, individuals in general would be expected to develop weak consciences in a shame-oriented culture, and conversely, strong consciences in a guilt-oriented culture. The investigation was conducted in Hawaii, where Samoan and American Caucasian[2] children could be compared readily. Inferences about conscience strength were made from behavior in a real-life temptation situation (Grinder, 1961) and from responses to projective story completion items depicting transgressions (Allinsmith, 1960).

On the basis of anthropological observations, Mead (1955) has attempted to show that the Samoans depend upon external sanctions entirely, and that in Samoa, consequently, "there is no room for guilt" (p. 655).[3] Presumably, among other factors, the Samoan child would be expected to develop a weak conscience because of his parents' practices of living in an extended family, delegating their disciplinary roles to the child's older siblings, and stressing age-graded socialization sanctions that rely upon fear of external reprobation as a major mechanism of social control (Pierce, 1956). In contrast, a mainland child ought to develop a stronger conscience by the greater severity of his parents' socialization practices (Whiting & Child, 1953) and by their practices of maintaining exclusive family living arrangements,

Robert E. Grinder, and Robert E. McMichael, "Cultural Influence on Conscience Development: Resistance to Temptation and Guilt among Samoans and American Caucasians," *Journal of Abnormal and Social Psychology*, **66**, 1963, 503–507. Copyright 1963 by the American Psychological Association, and reproduced by permission.

[1] A portion of this paper was presented at the 1962 annual meetings of the American Psychological Association.

[2] The term "American Caucasian," as used here refers to Caucasian children from the mainland United States.

[3] Although in describing cultures the term "guilt" denotes aspects of conscience including both resistance to temptation before [and behavior after] transgression, in describing an individual's conscience in the present study, the term will refer *only* to behavior after transgression.

demanding that he account for his transgressions to them personally, and expecting adherence to adult standards of conduct as the primary goals of socialization (Whiting, 1959). Accordingly, in comparisons between Samoan and American Caucasian children on degree of conscience development, the Samoan families' stress of external sanctions (shame) and the American families' emphasis upon internalized sanctions (guilt) lead to the expectation that a great proportion of Samoan children should demonstrate weak consciences.

The present study also aims to test a social learning hypothesis concerning resistance to temptation and guilt after transgression. One possible interpretation of the relationship between the two attributes of conscience is that they may be independent. Children whose parents concentrate all their attention upon breaking up approach behavior should learn resistance to temptation but not guilt, and children whose parents ignore approach behavior but punish transgressions by demanding restorative behaviors should learn greater capacity for guilt than self-control. The practical exigencies of socialization suggest, however, that the two measures should be positively related. The indeterminateness associated with the contingencies of reinforcement in child rearing probably prevents the child from learning one of the behavior patterns to the exclusion of the other. Further, once guilt is learned, anxiety anticipatory of guilt should serve as a cue for resistance to temptation. In a variety of studies (Allinsmith, 1960; Grinder, 1962; MacKinnon, 1938; Rebelsky, 1961), conducted with relatively homogeneous samples, positive relationships between resistance to temptation and guilt have been reported.

The prediction follows that these results should be corroborated in the cross-cultural context of this investigation.

## Method

### Subjects

Subjects were 34 sixth- and seventh-grade pupils, 15 American Caucasians (4 boys, 11 girls) and 19 Samoans (12 boys, 7 girls), enrolled in a rural, public school on the northeast coast of Oahu, Hawaii. The community in which they lived was comprised of approximately 300 Samoans, 100 Caucasians, and 600 Hawaiians, Japanese, Chinese, etc.

Employed chiefly by local sugar and pineapple plantations, the Samoan fathers were either unskilled or semiskilled laborers (Pierce, 1956). Most of the Samoan subjects were born in American Samoa; all had been in Hawaii since 1952; after arriving, few had traveled outside the community. Although the Samoan subjects could speak English, they restricted their use of it to classroom recitation. The number of siblings in each of their families ranged from 3 to 15; the median was approximately 8.

The Caucasian fathers were employed in various supervisory and administrative positions by the plantations or by a Protestant church, which maintained regional offices and a small college in the community. All of the Caucasian subjects were born on the United States mainland. Because most of the families were temporary residents, few had been in Hawaii for longer than a few years. The number of children in each of the Caucasian families ranged from 2 to 7 siblings; the median was 3.

## Measures

The apparatus for the assessment of resistance to temptation has been described in detail elsewhere (Grinder, 1961). Subjects operated a "ray-gun" shooting gallery individually in a realistic game situation. Seated 7 feet from a target box, subjects were asked to shoot the ray-gun pistol 20 times at a rotating rocket. With each pull of the ray-gun trigger, prearranged scores from zero to five were registered by score lights, also housed in the target box. High scores were rewarded with either a marksman, sharpshooter, or expert badge (cf. Procedure below). Subjects cumulated their scores on a paper score sheet.

Subjects were judged to have resisted temptation if the scores recorded on their score sheets indicated that they had not earned a badge. They were judged to have yielded to temptation if their score sheet showed that they had falsified their scores in order to earn one of the badges.

Measures of guilt were obtained from five story completion items patterned after those developed by Allinsmith (1960) and Allinsmith and Grinder (Rebelsky, 1961). In each story the protagonist violated socially expected behavior patterns of either honesty, trustworthiness, or self-control. The transgressions were directed against peers or adults. Appropriateness of the stimuli, vocabulary, and implied age of the protagonist were controlled, and the themes were drawn from experiences that boys and girls of both ethnic groups had in common. Each story explicitly ruled out the danger of detection. By using either a boy's or girl's name and changing personal pronouns, each story was adapted for both sexes.

Allinsmith's (1960) analyses, which employed free response items, revealed that subjects were very likely to depict remorse, confession, and restitution in their story responses; therefore, it was decided that the evaluations of guilt to be made in this study should be based upon these dimensions. In order to insure that every subject would be compared in terms of each dimension, subjects were given multiple-choice items rather than free response items. Three of the five stories were provided with three multiple-choice items, which assessed remorse, confession, and restitution, respectively. In the two other stories the transgressions were irreparable, i.e., the protagonist either violated a verbal prohibition or betrayed a trust; thus, on these, assessment of restitution was precluded and only two items were provided. Each multiple-choice item contained three alternatives, which were weighted either one, two, or three points in terms of the degree to which the alternative represented a guilt response. A subject's susceptibility to guilt was inferred from the alternatives he chose. His responses of remorse, confession, and restitution were summed across stories separately to obtain three measures of his disposition toward guilt. On the five stories then, scores ranged from 5 (low) to 15 (high) for remorse and confession and from 3 (low) to 9 (high) for restitution.

## Procedure

The behavioral test of temptation was administered in accordance with procedures developed previously (Grinder, 1962). Only Samoans and Caucasians played the game; subjects were randomly drawn from class by sex and ethnic background. About 10 subjects at a time were shown how to play the game by the first experimenter $(E_1)$. They were instructed to play the game for 20 shots and were told that if they obtained a total of 35 points they would be awarded a marksman badge; 40 points, a sharpshooter badge; and 45 points or more, an expert badge. However, only 32 points appeared on the score lights during the 20-shot sequence. To win a badge, therefore, it was necessary to falsify scores. After the group had been returned to the classroom, each subject was called from the class individually, led to the experimental room, and at the door was told that $E_1$ was busy working on some things down the hall. The subject was asked to play the game alone and to bring his score sheet to $E_1$ when he finished.

Two weeks after the presentation of the shooting gallery, a second experimenter $(E_2)$ administered the story completion items to the subjects in their classrooms. The subjects were unaware that the game and stories were related. The subjects were asked by $E_2$ to pretend that they were the boy or girl in each of the stories, and were shown on the chalkboard exactly how to choose between the multiple-choice alternatives. Stories were read out loud while the subjects read them silently. After reading a story, $E_2$ read each of the multiple-choice items for that story, pausing between them so that subjects could respond. In reading the stories, $E_2$ read alternately a boy's or girl's name. Stories and alternatives were read only once.

## Results

Examination of the sex distribution in relation to resistance to temptation on the behavioral measure and to responses of guilt on the projective stories revealed no differences approaching statistical significance; consequently, the male and female data were treated collectively in the analyses that follow.

Table 1 lists the obtained intercorrelations between remorse, confession, and restitution and, as can be seen, substantial relationships were found. Although the correlation coefficients are what would be expected if the guilt scales were measuring a simple response set, the findings also are consistent with the interpretation that responses of guilt may be highly interrelated, even though they may be manifested in several distinct ways. The data do not justify treating guilt as a general factor, however, inasmuch as analyses with a summary guilt scale might mask high relationships with one or two of the measures and a complete lack of relationship with the other. Therefore, in subsequent analyses the three guilt measures were treated separately.

The expectation that a higher proportion of Samoan than American Caucasian children would manifest relatively weak consciences is strongly supported by the findings. Among the Samoans none of the 19 subjects resisted temptation, but among the Caucasians 7 of the 15 subjects resisted temptation. Application of Fisher's exact test for a

*Table 1*

**Intercorrelations between the Three Guilt Scales**

|  | Confession | Restitution |
| --- | --- | --- |
| Remorse | .72** | .69** |
| Confession | —— | .59** |

Note: Correlation coefficients are Spearman rho's, corrected for ties.
** $p < .001$, two-tailed.

$2 \times 2$ contingency table to these temptation behavior data resulted in $p < .01$. The raw score means of remorse, confession, and restitution are listed for both ethnic groups in the top half of Table 2. Because the latter three distributions were extremely skewed and the groups were small, analyses were conducted using a two-tailed Mann-Whitney $U$ test, corrected for ties. Although on each of the guilt scales the magnitude of difference between the means is slight, the $U$ test analyses revealed that the Samoan group was significantly less likely than the mainland group to depict remorse, $p < .05$; confession, $p < .05$; and restitution, $p < .05$.[4] As expected,

[4] Mann-Whitney analyses between the ethnic groups separated by sex revealed that both sexes contributed approximately equally to the obtained differences, e.g., on the three scales, remorse, confession, and restitution, respectively, two-tailed $p$ values were $< .15$, $< .20$, and $< .05$ for boys, and $< .10$, $< .15$, and $< .05$ for girls.

the proportion of Samoan children with strong consciences was significantly less on both the real-life projective measures. However, the magnitude of the mean scores obtained by the Samoans indicates that they have moderately strong dispositions toward guilt and suggests that they have, albeit rudimentarily, internalized certain aspects of conscience.

The predicted relationship between resistance to temptation and guilt after transgression is partially confirmed. As shown in Table 2, bottom half, Mann-Whitney analyses comparing the guilt responses of subjects who resisted temptation with those who yielded to temptation show that the resist group differed significantly from the yield group only on the remorse measure. The differences between confession and restitution are, however, in the predicted direction.

*Table 2*

**Mean Guilt Scores for the Subjects Grouped by Ethnic Background and Degree of Resistance to Temptation**

| | | Guilt scale | | |
|---|---|---|---|---|
| Condition | Grouping[a] | Re-morse | Con-fession | Resti-tution |
| Ethnic back-ground | Caucasian (15) | 13.67 | 13.53 | 8.53 |
| | Samoan (19) | 11.58* | 11.21* | 6.79* |
| Temptation test | Resist (7) | 14.43 | 13.43 | 8.29 |
| | Yield (27) | 12.00* | 11.93 | 7.37 |

Note: $N$s in parentheses.

[a] Differences between the Caucasian and Samoan groups and between the resist and yield groups were tested with the Mann-Whitney $U$ test, corrected for ties.

* $p < .05$.

## Discussion

The absence of sex differences on both the temptation and guilt measures is noteworthy inasmuch as other studies (e.g., Burton, Maccoby, & Allinsmith, 1961; Grinder, 1962; Rebelsky, 1961), employing similar type measures, have reported differences between the sexes. The previous studies were conducted with considerably larger $N$s, however, and in the present study, on the basis of the relatively small sample size, Type II errors were more probable.

The results support the major expectation that in the comparisons between the Samoan and the mainland children proportionately fewer of the Samoan children would demonstrate strong conscience development. The confirmation is apparent whether the behavioral measure of resistance to temptation or the projective stories are used in making estimates of conscience strength.

The tentative findings suggest the desirability of further research with representative samples to determine the usefulness of classifying societies into either shame or guilt cultures. In the present study the Samoan subjects' responses of guilt show that they are not as free from the effects of conscience as Mead (1955) has implied. The data presented here corroborate Ausubel's (1955) belief that the Samoan socialization sanctions should engender some susceptibility to guilt. Furthermore, they agree with those of Whiting and Child (1953), who rank the Samoans just below the median among 35 societies on a cross-cultural index of guilt.

The postulated social learning hypothesis predicts that being susceptible to guilt should serve as a cue for resistance to temptation, yet of the three guilt scales, only remorse shows a significant relationship with resistance to temptation. Since the scales are highly interrelated, the discrepancies in the relationships between the three scales and temptation behavior appear as a surprise. It may be that the remorse scale tapped an aspect of conscience which is of a different nature than either confession or restitution. Both Allinsmith (1960) and MacKinnon (1938) observed that individuals who acknowledge the pain of self-reproach after transgression are more likely to resist temptation. Perhaps the affect associated with remorse serves as a cue for the instigation of other behaviors indicative of conscience strength. Under certain circumstances, of course, the affect may be avoided if a short latency exists between the environmental cues and either resistance to temptation on the one hand or reparative behaviors on the other. Also, extensive affect might be aroused if activation of guilt-relieving responses appears impossible. But for many individuals, anticipation of remorse may be a cue for resistance to temptation, and the presence of remorse after transgression may motivate efforts to make amends. Thus, both resistance to temptation and certain guilt behaviors may be associated with remorse; however, if neither resistance to temptation nor these guilt behaviors are very reliable response patterns, there is no reason to suppose that strong, positive relationships should emerge between them.

## References

ALLINSMITH, W. The learning of moral standards. In D. R. Miller & G. E. Swanson (Eds.), *Inner conflict and defense.* New York: Holt, 1960. Pp. 141–176.

AUSUBEL, D. P. Relationships between shame and guilt in the socializing process. *Psychological Review*, 1955, **62**, 378–390.

*BENEDICT, R. *The chrysanthemum and the sword.* Boston: Houghton Mifflin, 1946.

BURTON, R. V., MACCOBY, E. E., & ALLINSMITH, W. Antecedents of resistance to temptation in four-year-old children. *Child Development*, 1961, **32**, 689–710.

GRINDER, R. E. New techniques for research in children's temptation behavior. *Child Development*, 1961, **32**, 679–688.

GRINDER, R. E. Parental child-rearing practices, conscience, and resistance to temptation of sixth-grade children. *Child Development*, 1962, **33**, 803–820.

MACKINNON, D. W. Violations of prohibition. In H. A. Murray (Ed.), *Explora-*

* [Asterisks indicate works that are reprinted, in whole or in part, in this volume.]

tions in personality: A clinical and experimental study of fifty men of college age. New York: Oxford, 1938. Pp. 491–501.

MEAD, M. Social change and cultural surrogates. In C. Kluckhohn & H. A. Murray (Eds.), Personality in nature, society, and culture. (2nd ed.) New York: Knopf, 1953. Pp. 651–662.

PIERCE, B. F. Acculturation of Samoans in the Mormon village of Laie, Territory of Hawaii. Unpublished master's thesis, University of Hawaii, 1956.

PIERS, G., & SINGER, M. B. Shame and guilt. Springfield, Ill.: Charles C Thomas, 1953.

REBELSKY, F. G. Sex differences in children's use of confession. Paper read at Society for Research in Child Development, Pennsylvania State University, March 1961.

*WHITING, J. W. M. Sorcery, sin, and the superego: A cross-cultural study of some mechanisms of social control. In M. R. Jones (Ed.), Nebraska symposium on motivation: 1959. Lincoln: University of Nebraska Press, 1959. Pp. 174–197.

WHITING, J. W. M., & CHILD, I. L. Child training and personality: A cross-cultural study. New Haven: Yale University Press, 1953.

# Section IV
# ANTECEDENTS OF CONSCIENCE

## Introduction

Conscience researchers over the years have sought relationships between conscience and a variety of antecedent environmental (such as parental, social, and cultural) variables. They have attempted to explain the development of different forms of conscience-related behavior in terms of experiences the child has had and the stimulus situations presented to him. It is perhaps most especially in the search for the roots of conscience that cross-fertilization has occurred among the Piagetian, Freudian, and learning-theory approaches. The overall section is divided into six subsections dealing with: (a) guilt and shame; (b) parental practices and conscience development; (c) cross-cultural data; (d) learning-theory approaches; (e) the modifiability of moral judgment; and (f) demographic variables and conscience.

# GUILT
# AND SHAME

## Introduction

The lucid excerpt from Freud's *Civilization and Its Discontents* that follows not only presents the crystallization of Freud's thinking regarding superego formation and its impact on social living, but also introduces a distinction between external social control (fear of being found out or shame) and internal social control (guilt).

Margaret Mead and Ruth Benedict, excerpts from whose work are included here, were, so far as the editors can determine, the first anthropologists to make a distinction between guilt- and shame-oriented cultures. Mead distinguishes between guilt and shame as follows: "Shame, the agony of being found wanting and exposed to the disapproval of others, becomes a more prominent sanction behind conduct than guilt, the fear of not measuring up to the high standards which are represented by the parents [Mead, 1953, p. 660]." The Mead-Benedict dichotomy is criticized by Ausubel in the final paper in this subsection.

Several points may be mentioned concerning the guilt-shame distinction. That behavioral scientists are prone to dichotomize what is actually a continuum is exemplified in the "ideal type" theorizing regarding guilt and shame. Thus, Ausubel's criticism of this dichotomizing is probably a reasonable one. However, even granting it, certain evidence supports the Mead-Benedict position that guilt is a response built in by growing up within a nuclear, as opposed to an extended, family and to being exposed to a certain set of sanctions within this nuclear family (see, for example, Bacon et al., 1963, in the cross-cultural data subsection; and Grinder & McMichael, 1963, in the section on the generality of conscience). This evidence appears equally supportive of the Freudian idea that strong identification with the parent of the same sex is necessary if the individual is to identify strongly with society's rules and develop adequate inner controls. Those cultures that the Mead-Benedict position would predict to be guilt-oriented are of the same variety as those Freud would predict to produce strong superegos. Although one can make differential predictions from the two points of view (for example, a punitive father could evoke a strong identification and a strong superego from the Freudian point of view, but not from the Mead-Benedict position), they have not yet been made—much less tested in any direct way. However, Mischel's (1961) work showing that father absence is related to inability to delay gratification and to delinquency among male children suggests that identification (which should be influenced by father's absence) may be more significant in conscience development than type of discipline (which does not seem as closely related to father absence versus presence).

## References

Mead, M. Social change and cultural surrogates. In C. Kluckhohn & H. A. Murray (Eds.), *Personality in nature, society, and culture.* (2nd ed.) New York: Knopf, 1953. Pp. 651–662.

Mischel, W. Father absence and delay of gratification: Cross-cultural comparisons. *Journal of Abnormal and Social Psychology*, 1961, **63,** 116–124.

# 13

# From *Civilization and Its Discontents*

## by Sigmund Freud

Another question concerns us more nearly. What means does civilization employ in order to inhibit the aggressiveness which opposes it, to make it harmless, to get rid of it, perhaps? We have already become acquainted with a few of these methods, but not yet with the one that appears to be the most important. This we can study in the history of the development of the individual. What happens in him to render his desire for aggression innocuous? Something very remarkable, which we should never have guessed and which is nevertheless quite obvious. His aggressiveness is introjected, internalized; it is, in point of fact, sent back to where it came from—that is, it is directed towards his own ego. There it is taken over by a portion of the ego, which sets itself over against the rest of the ego as superego, and which now, in the form of "conscience," is ready to put into action against the ego the same harsh aggressiveness that the ego would have liked to satisfy upon

From Sigmund Freud, *Civilization and Its Discontents*, trans. and ed. James Strachey, in *The Standard Edition of the Complete Psychological Works of Sigmund Freud*, Vol. XXI, rev. and ed. James Strachey (New York: Norton; London: Hogarth, 1961), pp. 70–80. Reprinted by permission of W. W. Norton & Company, Inc., The Hogarth Press Ltd., Sigmund Freud Copyrights Ltd., and the Institute for Psycho-Analysis.

other, extraneous individuals. The tension between the harsh superego and the ego that is subjected to it, is called by us the sense of guilt; it expresses itself as a need for punishment.[1] Civilization, therefore, obtains mastery over the individual's dangerous desire for aggression by weakening and disarming it and by setting up an agency within him to watch over it, like a garrison in a conquered city.

As to the origin of the sense of guilt, the analyst has different views from other psychologists; but even he does not find it easy to give an account of it. To begin with, if we ask how a person comes to have a sense of guilt, we arrive at an answer which cannot be disputed: a person feels guilty (devout people would say "sinful") when he has done something which he knows to be "bad." But then we notice how little this answer tells us. Perhaps, after some hesitation, we shall add that even when a person has not actually *done* the bad thing but has only recognized in himself an *intention* to do it, he may regard himself as guilty; and the question then arises of why the intention is regarded as equal to the deed. Both cases, however, presuppose that one had already recognized that what is bad is reprehensible, is something that must not be carried out. How is this judgment arrived at? We may reject the existence of an original, as it were natural, capacity to distinguish good from bad. What is bad is often not at all what is injurious or dangerous to the ego; on the contrary, it may be something which is desirable and enjoyable to the ego. Here, therefore, there is an extraneous influence at work, and it is this that decides what is

[1] [Cf. "The Economic Problem of Masochism" (1924), *Standard Ed.*, 19, 166–167.]

to be called good or bad. Since a person's own feelings would not have led him along this path, he must have had a motive for submitting to this extraneous influence. Such a motive is easily discovered in his helplessness and his dependence on other people, and it can best be designated as fear of loss of love. If he loses the love of another person upon whom he is dependent, he also ceases to be protected from a variety of dangers. Above all, he is exposed to the danger that this stronger person will show his superiority in the form of punishment. At the beginning, therefore, what is bad is whatever causes one to be threatened with loss of love. For fear of that loss, one must avoid it. This, too, is the reason why it makes little difference whether one has already done the bad thing or only intends to do it. In either case the danger only sets in if and when the authority discovers it, and in either case the authority would behave in the same way.

This state of mind is called a "bad conscience"; but actually it does not deserve this name, for at this stage the sense of guilt is clearly only a fear of loss of love, "social" anxiety. In small children it can never be anything else, but in many adults, too, it has only changed to the extent that the place of the father or the two parents is taken by the larger human community. Consequently, such people habitually allow themselves to do any bad thing which promises them enjoyment, so long as they are sure that the authority will not know anything about it or cannot blame them for it; they are afraid only of being found out.[2] Present-

day society has to reckon in general with this state of mind.

A great change takes place only when the authority is internalized through the establishment of a superego. The phenomena of conscience then reach a higher stage. Actually, it is not until now that we should speak of conscience or a sense of guilt.[3] At this point, too, the fear of being found out comes to an end; the distinction, moreover, between doing something bad and wishing to do it disappears entirely, since nothing can be hidden from the superego, not even thoughts. It is true that the seriousness of the situation from a real point of view has passed away, for the new authority, the superego, has no motive that we know of for ill-treating the ego, with which it is intimately bound up; but genetic influence, which leads to the survival of what is past and has been surmounted, makes itself felt in the fact that fundamentally things remain as they were at the beginning. The superego torments the sinful ego with the same feeling of anxiety and is on the watch for opportunities of getting it punished by the external world.

At this second stage of development, the conscience exhibits a peculiarity which was absent from the first stage and which is no longer easy to account for.[4] For the more virtuous a man is, the more

2 This reminds one of Rousseau's famous mandarin. [The problem raised by Rousseau had been quoted in full in Freud's paper on "Our Attitude towards Death" (1915), *Standard Ed.*, **14**, 298.]

3 Everyone of discernment will understand and take into account the fact that in this summary description we have sharply delimited events which in reality occur by gradual transitions, and that it is not merely a question of the *existence* of a superego but of its relative strength and sphere of influence. All that has been said above about conscience and guilt is, moreover, common knowledge and almost undisputed.

4 [This paradox had been discussed by Freud earlier. See, for instance, Chapter V of *The Ego and the Id* (1923), *Standard Ed.*, **19**, 54, where other references are given.]

severe and distrustful is its behavior, so that ultimately it is precisely those people who have carried saintliness[5] furthest who reproach themselves with the worst sinfulness. This means that virtue forfeits some part of its promised reward; the docile and continent ego does not enjoy the trust of its mentor, and strives in vain, it would seem, to acquire it. The objection will at once be made that these difficulties are artificial ones, and it will be said that a stricter and more vigilant conscience is precisely the hallmark of a moral man. Moreover, when saints call themselves sinners, they are not so wrong, considering the temptations to instinctual satisfaction to which they are exposed in a specially high degree—since, as is well known, temptations are merely increased by constant frustration, whereas an occasional satisfaction of them causes them to diminish, at least for the time being. The field of ethics, which is so full of problems, presents us with another fact: namely that ill-luck—that is, external frustration—so greatly enhances the power of the conscience in the superego. As long as things go well with a man, his conscience is lenient and lets the ego do all sorts of things; but when misfortune befalls him, he searches his soul, acknowledges his sinfulness, heightens the demands of his conscience, imposes abstinences on himself and punishes himself with penances.[6] Whole peoples have behaved in this way, and still do. This, however, is easily explained by the original infantile stage of conscience, which, as we see, is not given up after the introjection into the superego, but persists alongside of it and behind it. Fate is regarded as a substitute for the parental agency. If a man is unfortunate it means that he is no longer loved by this highest power; and, threatened by such a loss of love, he once more bows to the parental representative in his superego—a representative whom, in his days of good fortune, he was ready to neglect. This becomes especially clear where Fate is looked upon in the strictly religious sense of being nothing else than an expression of the Divine Will. The people of Israel had believed themselves to be the favorite child of God, and when the great Father caused misfortune after misfortune to rain down upon this people of his, they were never shaken in their belief in his relationship to them or questioned his power or righteousness. Instead, they produced the prophets, who held up their sinfulness before them; and out of their sense of guilt they created the over-strict commandments of their priestly religion.[7] It is remarkable how differently a primitive man behaves. If he has met with a misfortune, he does not throw the blame on himself but on his fetish, which has obviously

---

[5] ["Heiligkeit." The same term, used in the different sense of "sacredness," is discussed by Freud in some other passages. Cf. the paper on "civilized" sexual morality (1908), Standard Ed., 9, 187.]

[6] This enhancing of morality as a consequence of ill-luck has been illustrated by Mark Twain in a delightful little story, The First Melon I Ever Stole. This first melon happened to be unripe. I heard Mark Twain tell the story himself in one of his public readings.

After he had given out the title, he stopped and asked himself as though he was in doubt: "Was it the first?" With this, everything had been said. The first melon was evidently not the only one. [This last sentence was added in 1931.—In a letter to Fliess of February 9th, 1898, Freud reported that he had attended a reading by Mark Twain a few days earlier (Freud, 1950, Letter 83).]

[7] [A very much more extended account of the relations of the people of Israel to their God is to be found in Freud's Moses and Monotheism (1939).]

not done its duty, and he gives it a thrashing instead of punishing himself.

Thus we know of two origins of the sense of guilt: one arising from fear of an authority, and the other, later on, arising from fear of the superego. The first insists upon a renunciation of instinctual satisfactions; the second, as well as doing this, presses for punishment, since the continuance of the forbidden wishes cannot be concealed from the superego. We have also learned how the severity of the superego—the demands of conscience—is to be understood. It is simply a continuation of the severity of the external authority, to which it has succeeded and which it has in part replaced. We now see in what relationship the renunciation of instinct stands to the sense of guilt. Originally, renunciation of instinct was the result of fear of an external authority: one renounced one's satisfactions in order not to lose its love. If one has carried out this renunciation, one is, as it were, quits with the authority and no sense of guilt should remain. But with fear of the superego the case is different. Here, instinctual renunciation is not enough, for the wish persists and cannot be concealed from the superego. Thus, in spite of the renunciation that has been made, a sense of guilt comes about. This constitutes a great economic disadvantage in the erection of a superego, or, as we may put it, in the formation of a conscience. Instinctual renunciation now no longer has a completely liberating effect; virtuous continence is no longer rewarded with the assurance of love. A threatened external unhappiness—loss of love and punishment on the part of the external authority—has been exchanged for a permanent internal unhappiness, for the tension of the sense of guilt.

These interrelations are so complicated and at the same time so important that, at the risk of repeating myself, I shall approach them from yet another angle. The chronological sequence, then, would be as follows. First comes renunciation of instinct owing to fear of aggression by the *external* authority. (This is, of course, what fear of the loss of love amounts to, for love is a protection against this punitive aggression.) After that comes the erection of an *internal* authority, and renunciation of instinct owing to fear of it—owing to fear of conscience.[8] In this second situation bad intentions are equated with bad actions, and hence come a sense of guilt and a need for punishment. The aggressiveness of conscience keeps up the aggressiveness of the authority. So far things have no doubt been made clear; but where does this leave room for the reinforcing influence of misfortune (of renunciation imposed from without) and for the extraordinary severity of conscience in the best and most tractable people? We have already explained both these peculiarities of conscience, but we probably still have an impression that those explanations do not go to the bottom of the matter, and leave a residue still unexplained. And here at last an idea comes in which belongs entirely to psychoanalysis and which is foreign to people's ordinary way of thinking. This idea is of a sort which enables us to understand why the subject-matter was bound to seem so confused and obscure to us. For it tells us that conscience (or more correctly, the anxiety which later becomes conscience) is indeed the cause of in-

[8] ["*Gewissensangst.*" Some remarks on this term will be found in an Editor's footnote to Chapter VII of *Inhibitions, Symptoms and Anxiety* (1926), *Standard Ed.*, **20**, 128.]

stinctual renunciation to begin with, but that later the relationship is reversed. Every renunciation of instinct now becomes a dynamic source of conscience and every fresh renunciation increases the latter's severity and intolerance. If we could only bring it better into harmony with what we already know about the history of the origin of conscience, we should be tempted to defend the paradoxical statement that conscience is the result of instinctual renunciation, or that instinctual renunciation (imposed on us from without) creates conscience, which then demands further instinctual renunciation.

The contradiction between this statement and what we have previously said about the genesis of conscience is in point of fact not so very great, and we see a way of further reducing it. In order to make our exposition easier, let us take as our example the aggressive instinct, and let us assume that the renunciation in question is always a renunciation of aggression. (This, of course, is only to be taken as a temporary assumption.) The effect of instinctual renunciation on the conscience then is that every piece of aggression whose satisfaction the subject gives up is taken over by the superego and increases the latter's aggressiveness (against the ego). This does not harmonize well with the view that the original aggressiveness of conscience is a continuance of the severity of the external authority and therefore has nothing to do with renunciation. But the discrepancy is removed if we postulate a different derivation for this first installment of the superego's aggressivity. A considerable amount of aggressiveness must be developed in the child against the authority which prevents him from having his first, but nonetheless his most impor-

tant, satisfactions, whatever the kind of instinctual deprivation that is demanded of him may be; but he is obliged to renounce the satisfaction of this revengeful aggressiveness. He finds his way out of this economically difficult situation with the help of familiar mechanisms. By means of identification he takes the unattackable authority into himself. The authority now turns into his superego and enters into possession of all the aggressiveness which a child would have liked to exercise against it. The child's ego has to content itself with the unhappy role of the authority—the father—who has been thus degraded. Here, as so often, the [real] situation is reversed: "If I were the father and you were the child, I should treat you badly." The relationship between the superego and the ego is a return, distorted by a wish, of the real relationships between the ego, as yet undivided, and an external object. That is typical, too. But the essential difference is that the original severity of the superego does not—or does not so much—represent the severity which one has experienced from it [the object], or which one attributes to it; it represents rather one's own aggressiveness towards it. If this is correct, we may assert truly that in the beginning conscience arises through the suppression of an aggressive impulse, and that it is subsequently reinforced by fresh suppressions of the same kind.

Which of these two views is correct? The earlier one, which genetically seemed so unassailable, or the newer one, which rounds off the theory in such a welcome fashion? Clearly, and by the evidence, too, of direct observations, both are justified. They do not contradict each other, and they even coincide at one point, for the child's revengeful aggressiveness will be in part determined by the amount of punitive aggression which he expects from his father. Experience shows, however, that the severity of the superego which a child develops in no way corresponds to the severity of treatment which he has himself met with.[9] The severity of the former seems to be independent of that of the latter. A child who has been very leniently brought up can acquire a very strict conscience. But it would also be wrong to exaggerate this independence; it is not difficult to convince oneself that severity of upbringing does also exert a strong influence on the formation of the child's superego. What it amounts to is that in the formation of the superego and the emergence of a conscience innate constitutional factors and influences from the real environment act in combination. This is not at all surprising; on the contrary, it is a universal aetiological condition for all such processes.[10]

It can also be asserted that when a child reacts to his first great instinctual frustrations with excessively strong aggressiveness and with a correspondingly severe superego, he is following a phylogenetic model and is going beyond the response that would be currently justified; for the father of prehistoric times was undoubtedly terrible, and an extreme amount of aggressiveness may be attributed to him. Thus, if one shifts over from individual to phylogenetic development, the differences between the two theories of the genesis of conscience are still further diminished. On the other hand, a new and important difference makes its appearance between these two developmental processes. We cannot get away from the assumption that man's sense of guilt springs from the Oedipus complex and was acquired at the killing of the father by the brothers banded together.[11] On that occasion an act of aggression was not suppressed but carried out; but it was the same act of aggression whose suppression in the child is supposed to be the source of his sense of guilt. At this point I should not be surprised if the reader were to exclaim angrily: "So it makes no difference whether one kills one's father or not—one gets a feeling of guilt in either case! We may take leave to raise a few doubts here. Either it is not true that the sense of guilt comes from suppressed aggressiveness, or else the whole story of the killing of the father is a fiction and the children of primaeval man did not kill their fathers any more often than children do nowadays. Besides, if it is not fiction but a plausible piece of history, it would be a case of something happening which everyone expects to happen—namely, of a person feeling guilty because he really has done something

---

[9] As has rightly been emphasized by Melanie Klein and by other, English, writers.

[10] The two main types of pathogenic methods of upbringing—overstrictness and spoiling—have been accurately assessed by Franz Alexander in his book, *The Psychoanalysis of the Total Personality* (1927) in connection with Aichhorn's study of delinquency [*Wayward Youth*, 1925]. The "unduly lenient and indulgent father" is the cause of children's forming an oversevere superego, because, under the impression of the love that they receive, they have no other outlet for their aggressiveness but turning it inwards. In delinquent children, who have been brought up without love, the tension between ego and superego is lacking, and the whole of their aggressiveness can be directed outwards. Apart from a constitutional factor which may be supposed to be present, it can be said, therefore, that a severe conscience arises from the joint operation of two factors: the frustration of instinct, which unleashes aggressiveness, and the experience of being loved, which turns the aggressiveness inwards and hands it over to the superego.

[11] [*Totem and Taboo* (1912–1913), *Standard Ed.*, **13**, 143.]

which cannot be justified. And of this event, which is after all an everyday occurrence, psychoanalysis has not yet given any explanation."

That is true, and we must make good the omission. Nor is there any great secret about the matter. When one has a sense of guilt after having committed a misdeed, and because of it, the feeling should more properly be called *remorse*. It relates only to a deed that has been done, and, of course, it presupposes that a *conscience*—the readiness to feel guilty —was already in existence before the deed took place. Remorse of this sort can, therefore, never help us to discover the origin of conscience and of the sense of guilt in general. What happens in these everyday cases is usually this: an instinctual need acquires the strength to achieve satisfaction in spite of the conscience, which is, after all, limited in its strength; and with the natural weakening of the need owing to its having been satisfied, the former balance of power is restored. Psychoanalysis is thus justified in excluding from the present discussion the case of a sense of guilt due to remorse, however frequently such cases occur and however great their practical importance.

But if the human sense of guilt goes back to the killing of the primal father, that was after all a case of "remorse." Are we to assume that [at that time] a conscience and a sense of guilt were not, as we have presupposed, in existence before the deed? If not, where, in this case, did the remorse come from? There is no doubt that this case should explain the secret of the sense of guilt to us and put an end to our difficulties. And I believe it does. This remorse was the result of the primordial ambivalence of feeling towards the father. His sons hated him, but they loved him, too. After their hatred had been satisfied by their act of aggression, their love came to the fore in their remorse for the deed. It set up the superego by identification with the father; it gave that agency the father's power, as though as a punishment for the deed of aggression they had carried out against him, and it created the restrictions which were intended to prevent a repetition of the deed. And since the inclination to aggressiveness against the father was repeated in the following generations, the sense of guilt, too, persisted, and it was reinforced once more by every piece of aggressiveness that was suppressed and carried over to the superego. Now, I think, we can at last grasp two things perfectly clearly: the part played by love in the origin of conscience and the fatal inevitability of the sense of guilt. Whether one has killed one's father or has abstained from doing so is not really the decisive thing. One is bound to feel guilty in either case, for the sense of guilt is an expression of the conflict due to ambivalence, of the eternal struggle between Eros and the instinct of destruction or death. This conflict is set going as soon as men are faced with the task of living together. So long as the community assumes no other form than that of the family, the conflict is bound to express itself in the Oedipus complex, to establish the conscience and to create the first sense of guilt. When an attempt is made to widen the community, the same conflict is continued in forms which are dependent on the past; and it is strengthened and results in a further intensification of the sense of guilt. Since civilization obeys an internal erotic impulse which causes human beings to unite in a closely-knit group, it can only achieve this aim through an ever-increasing reinforcement of the sense of guilt. What began in relation to the father is completed in relation to the group. If civilization is a necessary course of development from the family to humanity as a whole, then—as a result of the inborn conflict arising from ambivalence, of the eternal struggle between the trends of love and death—there is inextricably bound up with it an increase of the sense of guilt, which will perhaps reach heights that the individual finds hard to tolerate. One is reminded of the great poet's moving arraignment of the "Heavenly Powers":

Ihr führt in's Leben uns hinein.
Ihr lasst den Armen schuldig werden,
Dann überlasst Ihr ihn den Pein,

Denn jede Schuld rächt sich auf
    Erden.[12]

And we may well heave a sigh of relief at the thought that it is nevertheless vouchsafed to a few to salvage without effort from the whirlpool of their own feelings the deepest truths, towards which the rest of us have to find our way through tormenting uncertainty and with restless groping.

[12] One of the Harp-player's songs in Goethe's *Wilhelm Meister*.
[To earth, this weary earth, ye bring us
To guilt ye let us heedless go,
Then leave repentance fierce to wring us:
A moment's guilt, an age of woe!
                    Carlyle's translation.
The first couplet appears as an association to a dream in Freud's short book *On Dreams* (1901), *Standard Ed.*, **5**, 637 and 639.]

# 14

# Some anthropological considerations concerning guilt

*by Margaret Mead*

The contributions which anthropological research has made to theories of guilt are of several sorts. Most of them, however, stem directly from the attempts to relate the findings of psychoanalysis to the findings of anthropologists working on primitive, exotic, or contemporary modern societies. I shall attempt to intimate briefly the nature and variety of these approaches, and then devote the bulk of the paper to the question of guilt as a sanction for positive constructive behavior as it has been developed in societies in which parents assume the responsibility of rewarding and punishing their children for labeled and discriminated types of good and bad behavior.

## Interpretations of the Form and Function of Ritual

There are, then, first theories which relate ritual and ritual idiom of definite cultural groups to psychological findings upon expiative and appeasing rituals found in individuals, using a knowledge

of mechanisms involved in individual rituals of the neurotic to interpret both the history and the function of rituals shared by whole groups. These interpretations may take the form of relating a present ritual (such as the totem meal, in which all members of the group, all initiated males, etc., ceremonially eat an animal normally regarded as sacred and taboo and the mythical ancestor or supernatural relative of the group) to some event in the far-distant past (such as the original killing of the old man of the horde by a group of brothers). This type of interpretation, of which the classical example is Freud's *Totem and Taboo* (5), is more concerned with origin than with function. The ceremony itself is regarded as the datum which is to be explained, and the explanation is found, not in the present behavior of the individuals involved in the ceremony, but in a set of connections which may be traced between the various elements in the ritual. The interpretative statement may then take the form: this ceremony is a ritual expression of killing the father, and the ritual taboos observed the rest of the year, which include respect for and abstention from the totem animal, are a ritual defense against the same act of patricide. Such an analysis may take the further form of being regarded as proof of some earlier social habit, such as deposition and killing of an aging father, very much as a recurrent dream in an adult may be used as evidence of a childhood trauma. The actual historical value of such interpretations is of course low, for just as a fantasied event in the life history of an individual may function in the same way as an event in which other human beings have participated, so ceremonials of this type may be seen also as constructs, as reactive formations to fears or wishes which have at no time in the history of the group ever been acted out. So a ceremony and set of taboos which, when their constituent elements are carefully analyzed, appear to be intelligible as an expression of guilt for which no present antecedents are found in the life of the contemporary members of the group which practice it, may be taken as data on the contructs of some other people who developed the ceremony, but not as data upon any social events which occurred in their historical past, such as patricide, regicide, practice of incest, etc.

When speculation about the content of rituals of sacrifice, scapegoating, extravagant group mourning, etc., was succeeded by field work in which the experience of individuals, both as children and as adults, could be placed side by side with the ceremonies in which those individuals participated, it became possible to point out immediate relationships between the child's experience of closeness to the mother, of castration fears, of frustration of a type which led to strong hatreds and hostilities, and ceremonies designed to make amends for the various types of guilt associated with aroused incestuous or murderous wishes. The most conspicuous explorations of such relationships, particularly emphasizing the genetic connections between the experiences of infancy and early childhood and later ceremonials, have been made by Geza Roheim (16, 18, 29), who has followed up the earlier interpretations of Australian ceremonials with analysis of children's games, methods of child rearing, and dreams of individuals and has demonstrated striking correspondences between the inferred affects of the child and the pattern of the ceremonial.

It is possible to emphasize the function that ritual activities have in solving conflicts which are culturally created, either for the whole group or for some members of the group whose individual experience has developed a higher degree of self-accusation, feelings of unworthiness, or sense of deeply disapproved wishes, such as cannibalistic fantasies directed toward parents or siblings. An example of the former type, the solution of an individual conflict assumed to be engendered in the entire group, may be found in those mourning ceremonies in which two souls are distinguished, so that ambivalence toward the dead may take the form of appeasing and warding off the bad soul and tenderly cherishing and providing a comfortable afterlife for the good soul (14). Where emphasis is placed upon the contemporary meaning of a ritual observance for those who actually practice it, it is possible to add to the genetic explanation of the classical psychoanalytic type such further considerations as the effect upon the young child or simultaneously undergoing the interpersonal experiences which appear to arouse the feelings which will need ritual solution. Such occurs, for example, when the young child in Bali simultaneously undergoes the type of teasing from his mother which appears to induce deep hostility and reactive withdrawal, and an oft-enacted ceremonial in which the witch surrogate of the mother is actively attacked by young males who fall down in trance before the magic power of the witch (an assumed surrogate of the mother), and are revived by the magic power of the dragon [an assumed surrogate of the father (1)].

Examples of the relationship between traditional rituals and the experience of selected individuals in a society may be found in witch societies, types of possession and shamanism, the peculiar suicide vows patterns of certain warrior societies among the North American Plains Indians, the custom of harakiri among the Japanese, monastic vows and retreats, etc., in which the society keeps alive patterns of behavior, available to those on whom there have been differential pressures, which develop a capacity to make use of the ritual pattern. Any full understanding of the use of such patterns will include a detailed analysis of the way in which the existence of the ritual pattern of atonement or appeasement is communicated to and gives shape to the psychological behavior of the individuals who make use of it, showing to what extent the expressed need of the individual is itself a function of the presence of the ritual. So the practice of ritual confession can be seen as one element in the development of an individual reliance upon confession, whether that confession be of the habitual type practiced in Roman Catholicism, the type of single confession found in ancient Mexico (10), or the confession during sickness of a Manus native (2).

When this type of material is examined from the standpoint of planning for mental health, attention is focused upon the question of to what extent it is necessary to develop ritual solutions of types of guilt which are engendered by various recurrent social practices, such as the extreme individualism of the economic arrangements of each household in modern North America and ritual giving to the Community Chest, the Red Cross, the Hundred Neediest Cases, etc., and to what extent it may be advisable to modify the patterns of interpersonal relationships which give rise to types of guilt which need to be ritually assuaged.

Emphasis upon one type of planned social change or the other will vary as to whether the interest is greater in seeing that the individual pays in psycho-physical strain as few prices as possible during childhood and maturity (in which case the recommendation will be to develop a society in which the interpersonal relationships are such that no guilt is aroused to be ceremonially assuaged in social rituals); or, on the other hand, whether attention is directed to the values of a complex culture in which the individual is exposed to a variety of situations arousing profound inadmissable emotions and consequent anxiety and later given a variety of social forms within which to satisfy his complex emotions. But it is important to realize that most of the material on the destructive aspects of exposure to situations arousing strong and forbidden affects comes from the clinical study of the neurotic and psychotic in societies which are changing so rapidly that socially patterned ceremonial solutions for their complex emotional conflicts are not available, except in the work of the individual who is artistically gifted enough to provide his own. This contemporary situation obscures the relationships which may be found in less rapidly changing societies between the arousal of a welter of incestuous and murderous wishes in children and intricate and esthetically satisfying social rituals and artistic forms.

When contemporary forms of social disorganization are observed against a background of the analysis of the imputed psychological content and social function of primitive and exotic ceremonial, it is possible to put new interpretations upon such social phenomena as occur among peoples whose cultures are disintegrating—nativistic cults (26, 31), outbursts of chauvinism, scapegoating, pogroms, lynchings, mass suicides, and mass murders, in which disallowed feelings, which are dealt with either imperfectly or not at all by existing social rituals, reach the level of actual, rather than symbolic acting out (23). From this point of view it is not necessary to assume that the participant in a lynching or a pogrom has more murderous impulses than members of religious groups whose closest approach to ritual killing is participation in a ceremonial blood meal in which the blood is not blood but some surrogate. The only difference may be that in one society the rituals for symbolic expression of the regularly engendered conflicts are present, and in the other they are not.

Most of the types of analysis of social expressions of guilt referred to above are based upon theories concerning very early childhood and upon the way in which the very young child, helpless, dependent, and phrasing his response to others in all-or-none terms, develops fears of his own impulses, fears of the retaliative behavior of others—both impulses and retaliations often being projected into supernatural beings—or other social groups (11, 28).

Another type of fear has been phrased (3) as the fear of the superego, that is, the internalized representative of the parent who metes out love and punishment to the developing child. This refers to a type of development which occurs in great part after the child has learned to talk and in which the unconscious elements are the result of repression of what has been conscious and verbalized, rather than due to experiences before the mastery of language made it possible for the child to meet interpersonal situations in terms of the processes characteristic of consciousness. The different quality of the unconscious content of guilt based on the preverbal experiences and guilt which may be attributed to the incorporation of parental instruction subsequent to the attainment of language has its counterpart in the levels of social behavior which can profitably be analyzed in terms of these sequential learnings. Ritual, art, myth, are illumined both in interpretation of content and study of their function by reference to these very early infantile situations, while the functioning of moral codes and types of political and social control are illumined by an analysis of type of superego formation and the corresponding moral sanctions in a society.[1]

## Types of Superego Formation

When psychoanalytic theory began to develop descriptions of the way in which the child incorporated the image of the rewarding and punishing parent, and so learned to behave *as if* that parent were present in the parent's absence and after the parent's death, contemporaneous examination of primitive cultures revealed the necessity for expanding this description to include a wide variety of methods of moral training and corresponding character structure. These expansions

[1] While this seems to be a useful generalization at the present stage of our thinking, recent work on the character structure of prerevolutionary Great Russians suggests that, in certain instances, experiences during the first year of life may provide a definitive basis for attitudes toward authority, without the invocation of regularities of the interpersonal relationships of later childhood (7, 8).

have taken the form of challenging the classical picture of the significance of the strong father and the role of the Oedipus situation in the formation of the superego (12), of comparative studies of the relationships between types of moral sanction and types of social structure (17), of surveys of types of sanction characteristic of an area (27), of attempts in the classification of sanctions as guilt, shame, fear, anger, pride, etc. (20). Each step in this procedure, which has gone on for 25 years, has been tentative, and the need for continuous reformulation has increased rather than abated.

In the present state of the data it appears useful to distinguish between internalized and noninternalized sanctions, whether personal or impersonal, and between those systems in which the parents are the surrogates which result in a sharply focused point of reference. It is necessary to distinguish the degree of focus as a condition leading to internalization between those systems in which the parents are the executors and interpreters of the sanction, on the one hand, and those systems in which the referent is the parents themselves as the approving and disapproving figures and those in which behavior is enjoined in the name of some wider group, the age group, members of one's own or another caste, "the people," "people," "your possible future mother-in-law."[2] When the parents are both the interpreters and the executors of the system and use as a sanction, "I, your father, or your

[2] The clarification of the role of the parent or parent surrogate in focusing and so internalizing guilt, shame, or pride I owe to discussions with Geoffrey Gorer, while working on problems of Russian character structure in connection with the Studies in Soviet Culture project of the American Museum of Natural History.

mother, will punish and reward you in terms of your behavior," we have the classical superego formation with the characteristic features of oedipal solutions incident to contrast or similarity in sex and to the relative weakness or strength of male and female parents. Such an upbringing develops in the child the capacity to feel guilt, to award to the self, either in anticipation of an act not yet performed or retrospectively, in terms of a past act, the type of suffering or reward once given by the parent. Before discussing the cultural setting of this type of character structure further, I wish to sketch in briefly the other types of sanction with which it may usefully be contrasted.

Where, instead of the parents or parent surrogate as the referents of approval and disapproval, a larger and less individualized group is invoked, it is useful to distinguish a continuum between pride and shame. Shame, for purposes of this classification, may be described as that sanction under which the individual's attention is focused upon possible disapproval from a group, in which the whole quality of the behavior is negative and one acts in fear of a negatively valued response. Here again it is useful to distinguish between those settings in which the negatively valued response is anticipated as coming from a positively valued group, i.e., fear of the immigrant child of the treatment he will receive from American classmates, fear of the disapproval of the gang to which one passionately wishes to belong, fear of the disapproval of the appropriate members of the opposite sex to whose favors one aspires, etc., and those settings in which the negative response is anticipated from a negatively valued group, neighbors who are also spoken of disparagingly, classmates in a school to which one does not wish to go, servants who are seen as prying into the weaknesses of their employers, etc. Where the emphasis is upon the feared negative response, whether from valued or devalued groups, it may still be described as shame, but there will be a great difference in the whole quality of the individual response.

American Indians are predominantly characterized by the use of shame as sanction, with a high incidence of negative valuation of the group to whose judgments behavior was referred. The child was told, "If you do that people won't like you," and in the same breath heard the "people" whose disapproval had been evoked described in carping, depreciating terms. Among American Indians it is possible to find the whole gamut of degrees of internalization, from the high internalization among the Ojibway, who may commit suicide from the shame engendered by an unwitnessed event, where despite the verbal reference to the whole group the child spends a great deal of time in the small family, and the much lower degree of internalization in the Zuñi, where children live in a crowded multifamilial existence where the "people" referred to are actually present and parents invoke masked supernaturals to punish their children while themselves miming the position of being the children's defenders.

Pride may be placed at the other end of the shame-pride continuum, and here the emphasis is upon expected approval from groups who are either negatively or positively evaluated. Just as the maximally strong and emotionally toned shame position may be defined as a fear of disapproval from a negatively valued group instilled in the child by the parent (and accordingly internalized), so the maximum pride position may be defined as an expectation of the approval of a positively valued group, of elders, superiors, similarly inculcated. Somewhere along this continuum we may locate those intermediate situations in which a group of equals, who are neither more nor less positively valued than the self, mete out approval and disapproval, according to the particular situation. This is a situation congruent with an age-mate group, just as the typical guilt-producing setting is the relationship between parent and child and the typical shame and pride settings are the relationship between the self and a society in which such considerations as superiority, inferiority, superordination and subordination, caste, class, etc., are operative. The expressed sanction "No woman will seek you as daughter-in-law" may be qualified as "Even a poor no-count woman won't have you as daughter-in-law" or "If you embroider as well as that, the queen herself will be proud to have you as a daughter-in-law."

We thus have four different situations to take into account: (a) the extent to which the parents or other emotionally close highly identified individuals interpret a sanction to the child, whether that be the guilt-producing sanction of "I, the parent will punish you, or reward you," or the interpretative "people will gossip about you" of shame, or "people will applaud and admire you" of pride, and this participation of parents and parent surrogates seems to determine the degree of internalization which occurs, a limited number of figures with whom one has close ties appearing to provide the conditions for incorporation; (b) the type of behavior expected, e.g., whether it is predominantly approval, praise, and reward or disapproval, blame, and punishment; (c) the individual or group to whom principal reference is made, parents, age mates, specific levels, or the whole of society, or their various supernatural and symbolic surrogates, God, angels, the spirits, the village; and (d) the type of valuation placed on the individual or group to whom behavior is referred, as superior, inferior, loved, feared, etc.

Such a systematic statement immediately reveals the dilemma created by our present terminology, based as it is on the one-sided evidence of the clinical consulting room, and a theory more concerned with sinners than with saints. While we may speak of "a decent sense of shame," thus referring to fear of the disapproval of a group whose standards are respected, and a "proper pride," referring to an appropriate concern with the impact of one's behavior on a respected audience, we have no terminology for "good guilt," for the internalized sanctions in the individual who has been praised and loved for good behavior, rather than blamed and punished for bad. Just as we have a word for *trauma*, or an injury to the organism, and no word for a *blessing*, when some strength or sensitivity is added, so we have only a word which emphasizes the fear of punishment or withdrawal of love if and when something wrong is done, and no antonym.

The fourfold classification of contributing social settings above might suggest that all cultures could be placed within it, in the degrees and ways in which "guilt," good and bad, pride, and shame are used as sanctions. But this schematization does not yet represent a closed system on which we may expect to classify all cultures; before elaborating further on the question of guilt, I wish to describe briefly two other types of sanction systems, the Balinese and the Iatmul (21). In Bali, the parent or child nurse invokes desired behavior in the child by mimicking fear of some repellent, frightening, or supernatural object, communicating to the child a sense of shared fear, which remains throughout life in an undifferentiated state for which such terms as internalized or externalized, positive and negative, are almost meaningless. The Balinese remains within the pattern of his highly complex culture and responds to suggestions of deviating from the pattern with withdrawal and to disturbances in the pattern with withdrawal, sometimes even to the point of benign stupor. A withdrawal response to disapproved, out-of-pattern behavior has been communicated to him, at somewhat the same level that British mothers who were frightened during air raids communicated their fear to very young infants whom they held in their arms (4). A fear which is neither verbalized nor rationalized, indiscriminately communicated by all with whom the Balinese child comes in contact, accompanied by no specific punishments or rewards, seems to remain at the same level.

Among the Iatmul we find another type of child rearing, in which the individual learns to control his behavior in lively expectation of openly expressed anger and physical reprisal from others. There is no wide gap in moral or social status between child and parents or between children and other members of the community, no chiefs, no priesthood, no group to whom behavior can be referred, except—after initiation—the opinion of the opposite sex, who are variously invoked on the shame-pride continuum. But the small child is treated, practically from birth, as if he or she were as strong and independent and willful as the adult and as if the only means of control which the adult could exercise was not praise or blame, love or punishment, or the invocation of the opinion or possible reward or punishment of outside groups, but only actual grave physical force, exercised in false pantomime by a grown man or woman vis-à-vis the child. Children live in a continuous state of alertness, poised to flee blows which must be given with lightning speed ever to fall on a recipient's skin, and in adult life the whole society is organized about the threat and actual event of wrangle and riot between groups conceived of as equally strong. The lack of any system or hierarchical moral control within the individual mirrors and is repeated in the lack of any political control except that exercised by other equally strong groups upon one's own group in the social organization.

I should now like to return to the subject of "guilt, good and bad," in more detail. This type of character structure is characteristic of the English and North American middle class, in which parents differentiate themselves from their children by assuming the moral responsibility of punishing for disapproved acts and rewarding approved acts, in such a way as to encourage the child to take final responsibility for the content of its acts. In Germany (32), on the other hand, there seems strong evidence that the child is rewarded and punished for obedience to authority, rather than encouraged to take personal responsibility for content. Historically, this type of character structure which relies on guilt

has been identified with the rise of the commercial classes and invoked as a condition of the industrial revolution and the development of modern science and the machine age (30). It has been reviled as the "Puritan" character with an overpreoccupation with conformity and negative good behavior, a concomitant underdevelopment of the impulse life, a tendency to rigidity, intolerance, etc.

It seems worthwhile to look for a moment at one small primitive community —the pile-dwelling, seafaring Manus people of the Admiralty Islands (13, 15), where the same type of character has been developed among a stone-age people whose religious system consists of guardian ghosts of the last dead male of each household, far from the intricate complexities of the rise of Protestantism and the rise of capitalism. Yet we find a people with a highly internalized guilt structure devoting their whole energies to the pursuit of a moral way of life which will preserve them from ghostly punishment. They are rigidly puritanical, with strong sex taboos, prudish, anxious, driven, with little place for art or impulse expression. Furthermore these people are competent and efficient, learn to handle machines with ease, have well-developed concepts of number, time, and space relationships. They think in terms of the "how" instead of the "why" or "what" and participate responsibly and with ease in the machine civilization of Europeans. They share with Western European and American Protestant middle-class society a preoccupation with the gastrointestinal tract, with taking in and giving out objects, with reciprocal relations between persons, which is congruent with a tendency to treat persons as things and to emphasize the circulation of goods, trade, turnover, activity (24). Their capacity to deal with engines, with machines in general, and with the type of "rational" thinking characteristic of the thought of the late nineteenth and early twentieth centuries in the West may be related to parental insistence upon early moral responsibility in the child and the focusing of the child's attention upon cause-and-effect relationships between his acts and omissions and their consequences. The principal sanction in the society is good and bad guilt, as the child is rewarded and praised for constructive behavior as well as being punished for behavior regarded as wrong.

An examination in detail of the correspondence between the Manus type of character formation and the "Puritan" character of recent centuries in the West suggests that we are dealing with a cultural constellation which involves not only parental upbringing of the child with a strong assumption of moral responsibility, but also the preoccupation with intake and output of food, which is related to a concentration on person-thing rather than person-person relationships, the two together providing an ideal setting for the nineteenth-century view of men and machines. Analysis of the components of this complex, so similar and yet in such contrasting settings, should provide clues as to how to construct a society which retains the positive aspects of this "guilt character" without the emphasis on the gastrointestinal tract which tends to overvalue person-thing relationships and undervalue the individual's relationship to other persons and to his own, reflexly realized inner impulses. It should then be possible to recognize the very great strengths inherent in the character structure

which has been developed within our particular historical tradition and to which neither the special preoccupation on the gastrointestinal tract, with its emphasis on objects, nor the negative emphasis on punishment for not sinning rather than reward for positive constructive acts is integral or essential.

It may be appropriate to add a few remarks about the possible biological bases for guilt, in the widest sense in which it has been used throughout this paper, which includes the constructs based on infantile experience and also the introjection of the parental command to feel pride or shame, as well as the particular detailed parental command subsumed under the more special use of the word "guilt" for this type of sanction. Julian Huxley (9) concludes his *Touchstone for Ethics* by invoking the natural dependency situation of the human infant as providing a natural setting for the development of love, and consequently of fear of loss of love, and all its later ramifications, which give a basis for the development of conscience. The formulation follows the psychoanalytic formulation which localizes the genesis of guilt in the nature of the parent-child situation, rather than within the organism viewed alone. Historically, the perpetuation, even in those societies in which artificial feeding is superseding breast feeding, of the old biologically given mother-child nurturing tie has given this development of guilt special, sex-specialized forms, because the female was the original nurturing parent for children of both sexes. This historical form of character formation would be radically altered if society should take the step, made possible by the abandonment of breast feeding, of a pattern of child rearing in which both sexes participated equally. This would introduce such a radical change in character formation that a basic change in the way in which biological potentialities were involved in the genesis of guilt might also be expected.

But we may also consider whether, in addition to the specific nurturing situation, there may not be a biological basis for guilts of another order covered by the conception of the "metaphysical guilt of creatureliness" (6), guilt which arises inevitably from the nature of life and death itself, guilt over the domestication which men endure who become responsible fathers and the pain which women take on who become mothers, guilt over all who have suffered and died as the human race struggled to its present position in the world—a deep guilt which is reactivated by any failure in the individual organism to grow, to attain full sex membership, to use its particular gifts and capacities. Such guilt, such consciousness of a debt to life which can only be paid by living, may be so inherent in the nature of human beings, who live in a culture, that it is ineradicable and will always be both the mainspring of man's spiritual strivings and the guarantee of his humanity.

## Bibliography

1. BATESON, G., & MEAD, M., *Balinese character: A photographic analysis.* Vol. 2. Specia: Publ., New York Academy of Science, 1942.
2. FORTUNE, R. F. *Manus religion.* Philadelphia: American Philosophical Society, 1935.
3. FREUD, A. *The ego and the mechanisms of defense.* (Translated by Cecil Baines.) New York: International University, 1946.
4. FREUD, A., & BURLINGHAM, D. Reports for foster parents' plan for war children. 1945–1947. Mimeographed.
5. FREUD, S. *Totem and taboo.* (Translated by A. A. Brill.) New York: Moffat, Yard, 1918.
6. GILBY, T. The genesis of guilt. *Proceedings of the International Conference of Medical Psychotherapy,* 1/1, London, 1948. In press.
7. GORER, G. Some aspects of the psychology of the people of Great Russia. *American Slavic East European Review.* In press.
8. GORER, G. *The psychology of the people of Great Russia.* To be published.
9. HUXLEY, J., & HUXLEY, T. H. *Touchstone for ethics.* New York: Harper, 1947.
10. JOYCE, T. A. *Mexican archaeology.* London: Philip Lee Warner, 1914.
11. KUBIE, L. S. Destructive personalities. Paper presented at annual meeting of the Society for Applied Anthropology, Philadelphia, May, 1948. In press.
12. MALINOWSKI, B. *Sex and repression in savage society.* London: Kegan Paul; New York: Harcourt, 1927.
13. MEAD, M. *Growing up in New Guinea.* New York: Morrow, 1930. (Reprinted in *From the South Seas.* New York: Morrow, 1939.)
14. MEAD, M. An ethnologist's footnote to *Totem and taboo. Psychoanalytical Review,* 1930, **17,** 297–304.
15. MEAD, M. An investigation of the thought of primitive children with special reference to animism. *J. R. anthrop. Instit.,* 1932, **62,** 173–190.
16. MEAD, M. Review of *The riddle of the sphinx* by Geza Roheim. *Character & Personality,* 1935, **4,** 85–90.
17. MEAD, M. (Ed.) *Cooperation and competition among primitive peoples.* New York: McGraw-Hill, 1937.
18. MEAD, M. The concept of plot in culture. *Transactions of the New York Academy of Sciences,* 1939, Series II, **2,** 24–27.

19. MEAD, M. The arts in Bali. *Yale Review*, 1940, **30,** 335–347.

20. MEAD, M. Social change and cultural surrogates. *Journal of Educational Psychology*, 1940, **14,** 92–110. Reprinted in C. Kluckhohn and H. A. Murray (Eds.), *Personality in nature, society, and culture.* New York: Knopf, 1948. Pp. 511–522.

21. MEAD, M. Administrative contributions to democratic character formation at the adolescent level. *Journal of the National Association of Deans of Women*, 1941, **4,** 51–57. Reprinted in C. Kluckhohn and H. A. Murray (Eds.), *Personality in nature, society, and culture.* New York: Knopf, 1948. Pp. 523–530.

22. MEAD, M. The implications of culture change for personality development. *American Journal of Orthopsychiatry*, 1947, **17,** 633–646.

23. MEAD, M. Collective guilt. *Proc. internat. Conf. med. Psychother.* Paper presented August 13, 1948 (3/1).

24. MEAD, M. *Male and female: A study of the sexes in a changing world.* New York: Morrow, 1949.

25. MEAD, M. Character formation and diachronic theory. In Meyer Fortes (Ed.), *Social structure: Studies presented to A. R. Radcliffe-Brown.* New York: Oxford. In press.

26. MOONEY, J. *The ghost-dance religion and the Sioux outbreak of 1890.* U.S. Bureau of Ethnology, 14th Annual Report, 1892–1893. Washington, D.C., 1896, Pt. 2. Pp. 641–1136.

27. PETTITT, G. A. *Primitive education in North America.* Berkeley and Los Angeles: University of California Press, 1946 (*Univ. Calif. Publ. Amer. Archaeol. Ethnol.*, 43, No. 1).

28. RICKMAN, J. Guilt and the dynamics of psychological disorder in the individual. *Proc. internat. Conf. med. Psychother.* Paper presented August 12, 1948 (2/3).

29. ROHEIM, G. *The riddle of the sphinx.* (Translated by R. Money-Kyrle.) London: Hogarth Press and the Institute of Psycho-analysis, 1934.

30. WEBER, M. *The Protestant ethic and the spirit of capitalism.* (Translated by Talcott Parsons.) London: G. Allen, 1930.

31. WILLIAMS, F. E. *Orokaiva magic.* New York: Oxford, 1928 (Anthropology Report, Government of Papua, Nos. 6–8).

32. *The problem of German authoritarians and aggression* (studies of psychiatric and psychological material accumulated during the Nuremberg trial). A report based upon the work of a preparatory commission organized under the auspices of the International Congress on Mental Health held in London, 1948.

# 15

# The dilemma of virtue

*by Ruth Benedict*

In anthropological studies of different cultures the distinction between those which rely heavily on shame and those that rely heavily on guilt is an important one. A society that inculcates absolute standards of morality and relies on men's developing a conscience is a guilt culture by definition, but a man in such a society may, as in the United States, suffer in addition from shame when he accuses himself of gaucheries which are in no way sins. He may be exceedingly chagrined about not dressing appropriately for the occasion or about a slip of the tongue. In a culture where shame is a major sanction, people are chagrined about acts which we expect people to feel guilty about. This chagrin can be very intense and it cannot be relieved, as guilt can be, by confession and atonement. A man who has sinned can get relief by unburdening himself. This device of confession is used in our secular therapy and by many religious groups which have otherwise little in common. We know it brings relief. Where shame is the major sanction, a man does not experience relief when he makes his fault public even to a confessor. So long as his bad behavior does not "get out

Ruth Benedict, *The Chrysanthemum and the Sword* (Boston: Houghton Mifflin Company, 1946), pp. 222–227. Reprinted by permission of the publisher.

into the world" he need not be troubled and confession appears to him merely a way of courting trouble. Shame cultures therefore do not provide for confessions, even to the gods. They have ceremonies for good luck rather than for expiation.

True shame cultures rely on external sanctions for good behavior, not, as true guilt cultures do, on an internalized conviction of sin. Shame is a reaction to other people's criticism. A man is shamed either by being openly ridiculed and rejected or by fantasying to himself that he has been made ridiculous. In either case it is a potent sanction. But it requires an audience or at least a man's fantasy of an audience. Guilt does not. In a nation where honor means living up to one's own picture of oneself, a man may suffer from guilt though no man knows of his misdeed and a man's feelings of guilt may actually be relieved by confessing his sin.

The early Puritans who settled in the United States tried to base their whole morality on guilt and all psychiatrists know what trouble contemporary Americans have with their consciences. But shame is an increasingly heavy burden in the United States and guilt is less extremely felt than in earlier generations. In the United States this is interpreted as a relaxation of morals. There is much truth in this, but that is because we do not expect shame to do the heavy work of morality. We do not harness the acute personal chagrin which accompanies shame to our fundamental system of morality.

The Japanese do. A failure to follow their explicit signposts of good behavior, a failure to balance obligations or to foresee contingencies is a shame (*haji*). Shame, they say, is the root of virtue. A man who is sensitive to it will carry out all the rules of good behavior. "A man who knows shame" is sometimes translated "virtuous man," sometimes "man of honor." Shame has the same place of authority in Japanese ethics that "a clear conscience," "being right with God," and the avoidance of sin have in Western ethics. Logically enough, therefore, a man will not be punished in the afterlife. The Japanese—except for priests who know the Indian sutras—are quite unacquainted with the idea of reincarnation dependent upon one's merit in this life, and—except for some well-instructed Christian converts—they do not recognize postdeath reward and punishment or a heaven and a hell.

The primacy of shame in Japanese life means, as it does in any tribe or nation where shame is deeply felt, that any man watches the judgment of the public upon his deeds. He need only fantasy what their verdict will be, but he orients himself toward the verdict of others. When everybody is playing the game by the same rules and mutually supporting each other, the Japanese can be lighthearted and easy. They can play the game with fanaticism when they feel it is one which carries out the "mission" of Japan. They are most vulnerable when they attempt to export their virtues into foreign lands where their own formal signposts of good behavior do not hold. They failed in their "good will" mission to Greater East Asia, and the resentment many of them felt at the attitudes of Chinese and Filipinos toward them was genuine enough.

Individual Japanese, too, who have come to the United States for study or business and have not been motivated by nationalistic sentiments have often felt deeply the "failure" of their careful education when they tried to live in a less rigidly charted world. Their virtues, they felt, did not export well. The point they try to make is not the universal one that it is hard for any man to change cultures. They try to say something more and they sometimes contrast the difficulties of their own adjustment to American life with the lesser difficulties of Chinese or Siamese they have known. The specific Japanese problem, as they see it, is that they have been brought up to trust in a security which depends on others' recognition of the nuances of their observance of a code. When foreigners are oblivious of all these proprieties, the Japanese are at a loss. They cast about to find similar meticulous proprieties according to which Westerners live and when they do not find them, some speak of the anger they feel and some of how frightened they are.

No one has described these experiences in a less exacting culture better than Miss Mishima in her autobiography, *My Narrow Isle*.[1] She had sought eagerly to come to an American college and she had fought down her conservative family's unwillingness to accept the *on* of an American fellowship. She went to Wellesley. The teachers and the girls, she says, were wonderfully kind, but that made it, so she felt, all the more difficult. "My pride in perfect manneredness, a universal characteristic of the Japanese, was bitterly wounded. I was angry at myself for not knowing how to behave properly here and also at the surroundings which seemed to mock at my past training. Except for this vague but deep-rooted feeling of anger there was no

[1] Sumie Seo Mishima, *My Narrow Isle* (1941), p. 107.

emotion left in me." She felt herself "a being fallen from some other planet with senses and feelings that have no use in this other world. My Japanese training, requiring every physical movement to be elegant and every word uttered to be according to etiquette, made me extremely sensitive and self-conscious in this environment, where I was completely blind, socially speaking." It was two or three years before she relaxed and began to accept the kindness offered her. Americans, she decided, lived with what she calls "refined familiarity." But "familiarity had been killed in me as sauciness when I was three."

Miss Mishima contrasts the Japanese girls she knew in America with the Chinese girls and her comments show how differently the United States affected them. The Chinese girls had "self-composure and sociableness quite absent in most Japanese girls. These upper-class Chinese girls seemed to me the most urbane creatures on earth, every one of them having a graciousness nearing regal dignity and looking as if they were the true mistresses of the world. Their fearlessness and superb self-composure, not at all disturbed even in this great civilization of machinery and speed, made a great contrast with the timidity and oversensitiveness of us Japanese girls, showing some fundamental difference in social background."

Miss Mishima, like many other Japanese, felt as if she were an expert tennis player entered in a croquet tournament. Her own expertness just didn't count. She felt that what she had learned did not carry over into the new environment. The discipline to which she had submitted was useless. Americans got along without it.

Once Japanese have accepted, to however small a degree, the less codified rules that govern behavior in the United States they find it difficult to imagine their being able to manage again the restrictions of their old life in Japan. Sometimes they refer to it as a lost paradise, sometimes as a "harness," sometimes as a "prison," sometimes as a "little pot" that holds a dwarfed tree. As long as the roots of the miniature pine were kept to the confines of the flower pot, the result was a work of art that graced a charming garden. But once planted out in open soil, the dwarfed pine could never be put back again. They feel that they themselves are no longer possible ornaments in that Japanese garden. They could not again meet the requirements. They have experienced in its most acute form the Japanese dilemma of virtue.

# 16

# Relationships between shame and guilt in the socializing process

*by David P. Ausubel*

Guilt is one of the most important psychological mechanisms through which an individual becomes socialized in the ways of his culture. It is also an important instrument for cultural survival since it constitutes a most efficient watchdog within each individual, serving to keep his behavior compatible with the moral values of the society in which he lives. Without the aid rendered by guilt feelings, child rearing would be a difficult matter indeed. If children felt no sense of accountability or moral obligation to curb their hedonistic and irresponsible impulses, to conform to accepted social norms, or to acquire self-control, the socializing process would be slow, arduous, and incomplete. Sheer physical force, threat of pain, deprivation, and punishment, or withholding of love and approval would be the only available methods—combined with constant surveillance—to exact conformity to cultural standards of acceptable behavior. And since it is plainly evident that the maintenance of perpetual vigilance is impractical, that fear alone is

David P. Ausubel, "Relationships between Shame and Guilt in the Socializing Process," *Psychological Review*, **62**, 1955, 378–390. Copyright 1955 by the American Psychological Association, and reproduced by permission.

never an effective deterrent against antisocial behavior, and that the interests of personal expediency are not always in agreement with prescribed ethical norms, a social order unbuttressed by a sense of moral obligation in its members would enjoy precious little stability.

Within recent years, a number of social anthropologists (3, 7, 8, 9) have advanced the notion that guilt is not universally present or prominent as a sanction in mediating and sustaining the culture. Instead they have identified guilt as a unique property of the characterology of individuals who as children experience the kinds of relationships with parents allowing for "superego" formation, that is, typically of persons growing up in cultures adhering to the Judaic-Christian tradition. Thus, among the Samoans, Iatmul, and Balinese, Margaret Mead believes that the culture is primarily transmitted through such external sanctions as expediency in conforming to the rules (8, p. 514), shared, undifferentiated fear (9, p. 369), and anticipation of physical reprisals (9, p. 370), respectively. Ruth Benedict minimizes the importance of guilt and emphasizes the role of shame in regulating the social behavior of the Japanese (3, p. 222). Leighton and Kluckhohn make the same point in reference to the Navaho: "Sensitivity to shame . . . largely takes the place that remorse and self-punishment have in preventing antisocial conduct in white society" (7, p. 106). And even in characterizing the moral development of adolescents in our own society who undergo peer-group rather than parent-regulated socialization, Margaret Mead comments that "shame, the agony of being found wanting and exposed to the disapproval of others, becomes a more prominent sanction behind conduct than guilt, the fear of not measuring up to the high standard which was represented by the parents" (8, p. 520).

In this paper we shall be concerned with a critical examination of the criteria that these anthropologists have used in differentiating between shame and guilt. We shall attempt to show that although the two kinds of sanctions are distinguishable from one another, they are nevertheless neither dichotomous nor mutually exclusive, and that the development of guilt feelings is not dependent upon highly specific aspects of a unique kind of parent-child relationship. Before turning to this task, however, it might be profitable to undertake a logical analysis of the developmental conditions under which the capacity for acquiring guilt behavior arises, as well as some of the basic relationships between shame and guilt. Because of the paucity of experimental or naturalistic evidence in this area of theoretical inquiry, it should be self-evident that the following paradigm is offered as a system of interrelated hypotheses rather than as an exposition of empirically established facts.

## The Developmental Origins of Guilt

Guilt may be conceptualized as a special kind of negative self-evaluation which occurs when an individual acknowledges that his behavior is at variance with a given moral value to which he feels obligated to conform. It is a self-reaction to an injured conscience, if by conscience is meant an abstraction referring to a feeling of obligation to abide by all internalized moral values. The injury consists of a self-perceived violation of this obligation. Hence, in accordance with this formulation, one might hypothesize that before guilt feelings can become operative, the following developmental conditions must apply: (a) the individual must accept certain standards of right and wrong or good and bad as his own, (b) he must accept the obligation of regulating his behavior to conform to whatever standards he has thus adopted, and must feel accountable for lapses therefrom, and (c) he must possess sufficient self-critical ability to recognize when a discrepancy between behavior and internalized values occurs.

It goes without saying that none of these conditions can ever be satisfied at birth; under minimally favorable circumstances, however, all human beings should be potentially capable of acquiring the capacity for guilt behavior. Culture may make a difference in the form which this behavior takes and in the specific kinds of stimuli which instigate it; but the capacity itself should be so basically human and so fundamental to the sanctions by which social norms are maintained and transmitted to the young in any culture that differences among individuals within a culture would probably be as great as or greater than differences among cultures.

It is theoretically possible, of course, that in certain extreme cases a culture may be so anarchic and unstructured in terms of the obligations it engenders in its members that the potentiality for guilt experience is never realized, as, for example, among the Dobu (2, p. 131). Ordinarily, however, we might expect that guilt feelings would be found universally; and, hence, the burden of proof regarding their alleged absence in a given culture more properly rests with the investigator making the allegation.

Despite the probable existence of many important culturally conditioned differences in children's acquisition of guilt behavior, there are presumptive grounds for believing that considerable communality prevails in the general pattern of sequential development. Such communality would be a product of various uniformities regarding (a) basic conditions of the parent-child relationship, (b) minimal cultural needs for socialization of the child, and (c) certain gross trends in cognitive and social growth that prevail from one culture to the next.

The cultural basis of conscience development in the individual may be found in the potent need of both parents and society to inculcate a sense of responsibility in the child. Not only the physical survival of its members, but also the perpetuation of its selective way of life is contingent upon the culture's degree of success in this undertaking. Thus, the attenuation of infantile irresponsibility might be considered part of the necessary process of ego devaluation and maturation that presumably characterizes personality development in all cultures. Socialization demands the learning of self-control and self-discipline, the subordination of personal desires to the needs and wishes of others, the acquisition of skills and self-sufficiency, the curbing of hedonistic and aggressive impulses, and the assimilation of culturally sanctioned patterns of behavior. It seems highly unlikely that any of these propensities could become thoroughly stable before conscience is firmly established.

We might postulate that the first step in the child's development of conscience involves his assimilation of parental values and standards.[1] Having no other frame of reference for judgments of good and bad, the prestige suggestion of parents easily holds sway. But acceptance of these values does not obligate him—in the absence of a still undeveloped sense of moral responsibility—to regulate his own behavior accordingly. Lapses on the part of *other* persons are perceived as "bad," but such judgments have no relevance for similar behavior of his *own* when gratification of his *own* impulses is at stake. At this stage of development his behavior can only be directed into acceptable channels by punishment or by anticipation of punishment in the form of pain, deprivation, ridicule, threatened separation from the parent, etc. Conformity to ethical standards, therefore, is "devoid of moral implications because it is only indicative of submission to authority rather than acceptance of it" (1, p. 122).

Behavior can first be regarded as manifesting moral properties when a sense of obligation is acquired. The central hypothesis of the present formulation is that this development typically takes place in children who are accepted and intrinsically valued by parents, and who thereby acquire a derived or vicarious status in consequence of this acceptance. By the fiat of parental acceptance they are provided with intrinsic feelings of security and adequacy despite their manifest dependency and incompetence to fend for themselves. They accordingly become disposed to accept parental values implicitly and unconditionally out of loyalty to the individuals to whom

[1] In cultures characterized by an extended family group, or where persons other than parents take major responsibility for child rearing, both value assimilation and the subsequent development of moral obligation have from the very beginning a wider social base.

they owe their status and self-esteem. Among other standards assimilated in this uncritical and subservient fashion "is the feeling of moral responsibility or accountability to conform to standards of behavior which have been given ethical implications. . . . Unlike other values which are ends in themselves, moral responsibility has [the] regulatory function of compelling adherence to internalized norms of behavior" (1, p. 135).

It is reasonable to suppose, however, that the inhibition of unacceptable behavior by feelings of personal loyalty and accountability, by the child's recognition of his parent's moral authority, and by his desire to avoid the self-punishing consequences of guilt develops relatively slowly. The old external sanctions of pain, punishment, threat, and ridicule continue to be applied, reinforced now by the more meaningful threat of withdrawal of love and approval. Delaying the consolidation of guilt behavior is the slow growth of both the self-critical faculty (making perception of discrepancies between precept and conduct difficult) and of the ability to generalize principles of right and wrong beyond specific situations.

During preadolescence and adolescence, as the child begins to lose his volitional dependence upon parents and becomes more concerned both with a primary status based upon his own competencies and with equal membership in the social order, the basis of conscience and guilt behavior apparently undergoes significant change. As Piaget has shown, greater experience in interpersonal relationships and in playing differentiated roles in complex social activities makes him more inclined to interpret rules of

conduct as functional contrivances designed to facilitate social organization and interaction rather than as sacred and axiomatic givens (12, p. 106). Concomitantly, he develops a notion of moral law based upon principles of equity and embodying a system of reciprocal as opposed to unilateral moral obligations (12, p. 387). The absolutism of his moral standards also tends to be weakened by his greater need for self-enhancement as an individual in his own right—a need that no longer favors unconditional adherence to an uncompromisable set of parental standards, and places a greater premium on the value of expediency. Finally, once the individual acquires this functional concept of moral law, conceives of himself as an independent entity striving for primary status in a social community, and recognizes the reciprocal nature of obligation, he completes the process of transferring "his feeling of moral accountability from parents to the moral authority of society" (1, p. 482).

In heterogeneous cultures, values tend to acquire a wider social base during adolescence. The individual is exposed to a variety of ethical standards and can, within limits, choose between alternative moral systems. And where the peer group plays the major role in adolescent socialization, parents are replaced by peers as the chief interpreters and enforcers of the moral code and, to some extent, as the source of moral authority. But neither set of conditions is essential for the maturational changes in the nature of moral organization that take place during and subsequent to preadolescence (8, p. 519; 10, p. 96). In certain homogeneous cultures also, the source of moral values and authority is referred almost from the beginning to persons outside the immediate family circle (7, p. 51).

## Atypical Development of Guilt Behavior

The above description of the original and subsequent development of guilt behavior is hypothesized as the more typical course of moral growth in most children. It presupposes that the latter can achieve derived feelings of status through the medium of a dependent parent-child relationship, and can consequently internalize both values and a sense of moral obligation on the implicit basis of personal loyalty. In all cultures, however, a variable number of parents are psychologically incapable of extending acceptance and intrinsic valuation to their offspring. Thus deprived of the self-esteem derived from the fiat of unconditional parental acceptance, such children are from the very beginning obliged to seek primary status and feelings of adequacy on the basis of their own competencies and performance ability. Accordingly, the basis on which they internalize values and moral obligations might be expected to be correspondingly different.

It would serve no useful purpose here to speculate further on the possible atypical courses that conscience development could take in rejected and extrinsically valued children (1). However, there is less reason to believe that rejecting and extrinsically valuing attitudes characterize *all* parents in a few rare cultures than that they may be found among *some* parents in almost all cultures. Hence, we would hypothesize that the probability of finding some conscience-less individuals in every culture is greater than that of finding conscience-less cultures.

## Classification of Shame and Guilt

Generally, shame may be defined as an unpleasant emotional reaction by an individual to an actual or presumed negative judgment of himself by others resulting in self-depreciation vis-à-vis the group. This definition of shame is inclusive of instances in which the persons passing judgment are valued either positively or negatively by the individual being judged (9, p. 367), and of both moral and nonmoral causes for the instigation of such negative judgments. Typical examples of nonmoral shame are embarrassment in committing a breach of propriety or in having one's bodily intimacy exposed to public scrutiny (11, p. 350), and "loss of face" resulting from exposure of ignorance or incompetency. Moral shame, on the other hand, is a reaction to the negative moral judgments of others. It is a prominent sanction in many cultures both before and subsequent to the development of conscience.

Moral shame can, in turn, be divided into two categories—internalized and noninternalized. The latter variety occurs when an individual reacts with self-depreciation to the moral condemnation of others, but does not accept the moral value to which he has failed to conform, e.g., a young child may be shamed by being caught in a lie even if he does not accept the judgment that lying is wrong. Essential for this type of shame is the presence of witnesses to or eventual discovery of the misdeed in question. When the value is internalized, e.g., when the child *really* believes that lying is opprobrious, actual discovery is unnecessary; shame can result merely from presumed or fantasied reproach. Under the influence of such unwitnessed shame, the Ojibway may commit suicide (9, p. 367). According to Margaret Mead, internalized shame only occurs when the parent is the interpreter and enforcer of the sanction (9, p. 366). Observation of closely-knit adolescent peer groups, however, seems to indicate that genuine shame may occur when adolescents perceive or fantasy the moral disapproval of their fellows for offenses against norms established and enforced by the group itself.

The shame associated with guilt may be considered a special case of moral shame. In addition to an internalized moral value, a personal obligation to abide by that value is at stake, e.g., the child not only believes that lying is wrong and feels shame by experiencing or imagining the censure of others, but also feels shame in fantasying the reproach of others for violating a moral obligation. In either case an actual audience is unnecessary, but a presumed or fantasied judgment by others is. However, it is important to emphasize at this point that shame is only one component of guilt, the component involving external judgment and sanction. Guilt also involves other *self-reactions* that are independent of the judgment of others, namely, self-reproach, self-disgust, self-contempt, remorse, lowered self-esteem, anxiety, and various characteristic and subjectively identifiable visceral and vasomotor responses. And conversely, the shame of guilt is only one of many kinds of shame. Thus, the presence of guilt-related shame does not preclude the simultaneous operation of other forms of

moral or nonmoral shame unassociated with guilt; nor does the excitation of any of these kinds of shame (associated or unassociated with guilt) preclude the operation of the various self-judgments characterizing guilt feelings.

Shame relies on external sanctions alone. Guilt relies on both internal and external sanctions. The latter sanctions consist of the presumed judgments of others regarding one's lapses with respect to moral obligations and the resulting self-depreciation vis-à-vis the group, as well as the customary social reprisals associated with the misdemeanors arousing guilt. In addition, feelings of guilt have external reference in that they acknowledge accountability for a moral offense against the group.

In the following section we shall critically appraise (a) the views of Margaret Mead and of Leighton and Kluckhohn, who hold that the development of guilt behavior requires a parent-child relationship in which an omniscient parent is the referent for and the source of moral authority, in addition to personally administering and interpeting moral sanctions (9, pp. 366, 367); and (b) Ruth Benedict's position that guilt is shameless, involves no external sanctions, and is concerned with inner convictions of sin (3, pp. 222—223).

## Ethnocentric Distinctions between Shame and Guilt

*Superego Models of Guilt*

The first ethnocentric conception of guilt referred to above equates the capacity for experiencing guilt feelings with neo-Freudian notions of superego formation. According to this conception, guilt feelings cannot arise unless the conditions essential for superego formation are not only present in childhood but are also maintained in subsequent years. Hence, guilt-like behavior in our own or other cultures that does not conform to these conditions is categorized as shame. The two basic conditions that are laid down for the development of guilt are: (a) the child must accept the parent or parent surrogate as omniscient or as qualitatively superior to himself in a moral sense, and (b) he must accept the parent as the source of moral authority, i.e., as the "referent" in whose name moral behavior is enjoined.

In reference to the former condition Margaret Mead states:

> The adults in the society must think of the child as qualitatively different from themselves, in that the child has not yet attained their moral stature, but is subject to innate impulses which, if permitted unchecked expression, would eventuate in adult character different from and morally inferior to that of the parent (8, p. 514).

Leighton and Kluckhohn similarly characterize guilt feelings as representing an individual's acknowledgment that he is "unworthy . . . for not living up to the high standards represented by [his] parents" (7, p. 106). In explaining why "Navaho sensitivity to shame takes the place of guilt in our society," they go on to say:

> "Conscience" is related to the belief in an omnipotent God who knows all. . . . In white society the child doesn't see the parent in many life situations. [But] in the circumstances of Navaho life a pose of omnipotence or omniscience on the part of parents would be speedily and almost daily exposed (7, p. 106).

> Only rarely does one hear the utterances on the part of Navaho parents which are so usual among white parents: "Do it because I say it is right," "do it because I say so," "do it because I am your father and children must obey their parents" (7, p. 53).

In the first place, one may legitimately question the assumption that children do not acquire moral obligations unless a highly authoritarian, paternalistic, and hierarchical parent-child relationship exists, unless the parent sets himself up and is perceived as a qualitatively superior paragon of virtue. As long as the conditions for acquiring derived status are fulfilled, it seems reasonable to suppose that moral obligations are incurred provided that parents or parent surrogates make such expectations unambiguously clear. It undoubtedly increases the prestige suggestion with which the standards and expectations of parents are endowed if the latter individuals are perceived as omniscient; but there is neither convincing logical nor empirical justification for designating this criterion as a *sine qua non* for the acquisition of guilt behavior.

A second difficulty confronting the proposition that qualitative hierarchical distinctions must prevail between preceptor and learner in order for guilt feelings to develop is the suggestive evidence of Piaget, referred to above, showing that as children approach adolescence in our culture they become increasingly concerned with moral obligations based on principles of reciprocity (12, pp. 106, 387). Cooperative and functional relationships with peers engender notions of obligation reflecting mutual respect between equals which gradually displace unilateral feelings of obligation based on implicit acceptance of authority (12, p. 106).

The second condition imposed by adherents of the superego model of guilt behavior, i.e., that parents or parent surrogates must serve as the source of moral authority, runs into similar difficulties posed by developmental shifts in the organization of conscience. It presupposes, in the words of Margaret Mead, that

> . . . teachers, the clergy, judicial officials, etc., partake of the character of the judging parent who metes out reward to the individual child (or, later, adult) who makes a satisfactory approximation to the desired behavior, and punishment to him who does not (8, p. 514).

Such a requirement arbitrarily eliminates the possibility of guilt behavior developing in cultures like the Navaho where the authority for moral sanctions is from the earliest days of socialization referred to the group as a whole (7, p. 51). The same criterion rules out the occurrence of guilt behavior among (a) adolescents in our own culture who accept the peer group as their major source of moral authority (see earlier quotation from Margaret Mead), (b) rejected and extrinsically valued children who never accept the moral authority of parents, but who may accept rational principles of equity and the moral authority of the group, and (c) adults in most cultures, who, in accordance with the developmental changes described above, transfer their allegiances from the moral authority of parents to the moral authority of society. The latter process does not necessarily require the intermediate adolescent step of repudiating adult authority and substituting peer standards. Sufficient for this outcome is a transformation of the basis upon which the authority of elders is accepted, i.e., a change from implicit acceptance of axiomatic truth by a dependent and ideationally subservient individual to a more ra-

tional acceptance of functionally necessary norms growing out of interpersonal relations by an independent member of adult society (10, pp. 95–96).

To deny that guilt feelings can arise in the above four situations requires summary dismissal of the evidence of everyday experience with the behavioral content of others. It is admittedly difficult to evaluate the subjective emotional experience of other persons, particularly if they happen to be members of different cultures. Logical inference must always supplement the perceptions of even the most experienced observer. Nevertheless a decision regarding the meaning of behavior can never be reached on the basis of a priori criteria alone, especially when these lack irrefutable logical or face validity. An emotion is adjudged to be guilt or shame on the basis of its behavioral characteristics, its situational excitants, and its subjective properties, and not because it fails to meet certain arbitrary ethnocentric criteria that apply to a single culture or phase of development. In the next section we shall examine some ethnological materials presented by Leighton and Kluckhohn and by Ruth Benedict as illustrative of shame and show how such behavior can be more defensibly interpreted as guilt.

A conception of conscience or guilt behavior that makes no provision for developmental changes in the underlying personality structure upon which such behavior depends cannot be successfully integrated into any self-consistent theory of personality development. A theoretical framework must be found that is broad enough to encompass the guilt behavior of a child of eight and likewise of an adult of eighteen or eighty. We cannot conclude that eighteen-year-old guilt must be shame because it does not conform to an eight-year-old model of guilt.

Personality development is admittedly characterized by continuity as well as by change. A tendency to accept values and obligations uncritically, on the basis of personal allegiances, still continues in adult life. Similarly, early attitudes of unconditional loyalty to moral obligations tend to persist long beyond the span of childhood. Nevertheless although these continuing trends add much to the stability of conscience, they are largely supplanted by different moral orientations and enjoy only substrate existence in a generally changed gestalt. A precipitate of the experiences of the eight-year-old is represented in the behavior of the eighteen-year-old, but this precipitate has a phenomenologically different meaning and significance than its original form a decade earlier.

Pointing up the logical as well as the empirical untenability of a criterion of guilt that requires a qualitatively superior parent or parent surrogate as the source of moral authority is the discrepancy on this score between the two chief examples of allegedly "shaming cultures," i.e., certain North American Indian tribes and the Japanese. Leighton and Kluckhohn characterize the Navaho as a "shaming culture" in part because sanctions are applied laterally rather than from above, and are referred to group rather than to parental authority (7, pp. 105–106). On the other hand, Ruth Benedict, using other criteria, regards the Japanese as a shaming culture despite the fact that the Japanese family is the ethnological example par excellence of unconditionally accepted, paternalistic (if not arbitrarily imposed) authority based upon hierarchical position (3, pp. 55–57, 264). Obviously, then, this criterion for distinguishing between shame and guilt has little claim to universality.

*Guilt as a Shameless, Wholly Internalized Conviction of Sin*

The second major ethnocentric (and psychoanalytically oriented) conception of guilt assumes that guilt and shame are mutually incompatible and that genuine guilt must be devoid of shame and all external sanctions Thus, in cultures where shame plays a more prominent role in behavioral control than in our own culture, ethnologists sharing this conception of guilt have insisted that guilt feelings must *ipso facto* be either nonexistent or of negligible significance. Among the Japanese, according to Gorer, "mockery is the most important and most effective sanction for obtaining conformity in social life" (4, p. 20). Ruth Benedict espouses the same opinion in stating that "shame has the same place of authority in Japanese ethics that 'a clear conscience,' 'being right with God,' and avoidance of sin have in Western ethics" (3, p. 224). Leighton and Kluckhohn claim that Navahos do not internalize the "standards of their parents and elders," and that shame ("I would feel very uncomfortable if anyone saw me deviating from accepted norms") is the major deterrent to antisocial behavior (7, p. 106). Margaret Mead goes even further by ruling out the occurrence of both guilt and shame in the sanction systems of the Samoans (8, pp. 514–515), Balinese (9, p. 369), and Iatmul (9, pp. 369–370), and insisting that only such external sanctions as fear, expediency, and threat of physical reprisals are operative.

This dichotomization of shame and guilt, of internal and external sanctions, in addition to lacking logical self-consistency, simply does not conform to available naturalistic evidence. Both moral and nonmoral shame may be extremely important sanctions in a given culture, but they preclude the occurrence of neither the public (shame) nor the private (self-judgment) aspects of guilt. A culture so unstable and so anarchic that its members fail to respond to internal sanctions (i.e., feelings of moral obligation) is indeed an ethnological rarity. The inhabitants of Dobu (2) may fit this description, but the case made out for the Samoans, Iatmul, and Balinese (8, 9) is far from convincing; and descriptions of Japanese (3, 6) and Navaho (7) behavior tend to disprove the very contentions they are meant to illustrate. Conversely, a culture in which external sanctions are *not* applied at any stage of moral development is also rare enough to qualify as an ethnological oddity.

The evidence seems clear enough that although Japanese and Navaho individuals are more responsive to shame than we are, much of this shame is really the shame of guilt, i.e., the shame accompanying awareness of violated moral obligations. The predominant pattern of parent-child relationships in both cultures is one of acceptance and intrinsic valuation of the child, leading to the first or implicit stage of moral responsibility based upon personal loyalty (3, Ch. 12; 7, Ch. 1). Navaho children acquire a sense of responsibility between five and eight years of age, learning assiduousness in executing their chores. They learn "that they cannot always indulge themselves and that they have duties toward others" (7, p. 58). Navaho

parents are strikingly devoted and attentive to the needs of their children (7, pp. 13–33), and children, in turn, even as adults, are very devoted to their parents and siblings (7, pp. 94–100). The Navaho adult is capable of very responsible conduct in relation to his social group despite the fact that responsibility is "divided and shared" (7, p. 107). If such behavior is not indicative of internalized moral obligation, what other credible explanation is there? Surely shame alone could not account for all of it.

Among the Japanese an even stronger case can be made for the importance of conscience and guilt behavior. Few other cultures lay greater stress upon the sanctity of moral obligations. "The strong according to Japanese verdict are those who disregard personal happiness and fulfill their obligations. . . . A man is weak if he pays attention to his personal desires when they conflict with the code of obligations" (3, pp. 207–208). Obligations to others must be fulfilled even if one dislikes the latter personally (3, p. 124). The Japanese sense of accountability is especially stringent. "Each man must accept responsibility for the outcome of his acts. He must acknowledge and accept all natural consequences of his weakness, his lack of persistence, his ineffectualness" (3, p. 296).

What is even more impressive is the fact that in contrast to prevailing attitudes in our own culture, the self-discipline, the self-restraint, and any of the personal disadvantages incurred in honoring obligations are not regarded as self-sacrifice. The fulfillment of obligations is taken for granted on the grounds of reciprocity, and calls for no applause, reward, self-pity, or self-righteousness (3, pp. 230–233). The notions of mutual dependence and indebtedness to one's society and one's past lie at the very heart of the Japanese concept of obligation. "One repays one's debts to one's forbears by passing on to one's children the care one oneself received" (3, p. 122).

Despite this overwhelming evidence of conscience and guilt behavior, Ruth Benedict is misled by the dichotomized conception of shame and guilt, and insists upon referring to such behavior as shame on the grounds that guilt is supposedly shameless. But, as already pointed out above, what she calls "shame" is actually the shame component of guilt. La Barre paints essentially the same picture of Japanese character structure as she does and reaches a diametrically opposite conclusion. He asserts that the Japanese superego is exceedingly strong (6, p. 329). Nevertheless, even while minimizing the role of guilt among the Japanese, Ruth Benedict is grudgingly obliged to admit the existence of moral self-judgments unrelated to external sanctions.

> They [the Japanese] are terribly concerned about what other people will think of their behavior, and they are also overcome by guilt when other people know nothing of their misstep. . . . Japanese sometimes react as strongly as any Puritan to a private accumulation of guilt (3, pp. 2–3, 222).

We cannot escape the conclusion, therefore, that both guilt and shame, and internal and external sanctions, can and do exist side by side and mutually reinforce each other. The assertion that "true shame cultures rely on external sanctions for good behavior, not, as true guilt cultures do, on an internalized conviction of sin" (3, p. 323) is unsupported by available evidence. The presence of the stock, the pillory, and the ducking stool in the public marketplace offers eloquent refutation to the statement that "the early Puritans who settled in the United States tried to base their whole morality on guilt" (3, p. 223). Reinforcing most of the moral sanctions that we customarily assign to the domain of conscience is a parallel set of statutes and group pressures enforced by appropriate public reprisals. Even in cultures where moral obligations are highly internalized, we usually find a policeman on the corner giving a friendly nudge to sluggish consciences or a timely warning to impish consciences pondering a brief vacation from duty.

The regulation of conduct by moral self-judgment is also the *final* step in a long developmental process. In controlling the behavior of children in our own culture, parents may differ from Samoan, Balinese, and Iatmul parents in their propensity for premature sermonizing about right and wrong, filial duty, virtue, etc. But during the first few years of life such preachments are but empty verbalisms to our children, who actually respond as do children in all cultures to the accompanying external sanctions of reward and punishment. Guilt feelings also have external reference by virtue of their shame component which involves a self-deprecatory reaction to the presumed or actual moral censure of others for a transgression of moral obligation. Finally, the external reference of guilt is apparent in the fact that it is reduced by punishment and confession. It always implies an offense against the group which, therefore, can only be pardoned by group action.[2]

Another source for ethnocentric misinterpretation of Japanese guilt behav-

[2] In private confessionals, the priest serves as the moral representative of the group.

ior lies in their lack of preoccupation with sin. The idea of sin, however, is in no way indigenous to a conscience founded on moral obligation; it merely tends to be associated with a specific variety of guilt behavior that is influenced by certain religious traditions and notions about the original nature of man. Nevertheless, by equating guilt with "an internalized conviction of sin" (3, p. 223), and conscience with "the avoidance of sin" (3, p. 224), Ruth Benedict finds further "justification" for regarding the Japanese as relatively guiltless.

Japanese neglect of the problem of sin, however, stems from two other sources that can hardly be interpreted as detracting from the genuineness of their expressions of guilt. In the first place, since they do not regard indulgence in physical pleasure as inherently evil—providing that it is properly subordinated to moral obligation—they do not share our notion of "original sin" or our conception of human nature as constantly in need of redemption from inherently sinful desires (3, pp. 191–192). Secondly, since the fulfillment of obligation is taken for granted and is not regarded as self-sacrifice or as a victory of virtue over innately evil propensities, Japanese good conscience is not burdened with the self-righteousness that comes from conquering sin; and, similarly, guilt is not "internalized conviction of sin," but simply awareness of the breakdown of moral obligation.

Because the Japanese lay great stress on certain "external" (shame) aspects of self-respect, such as acting with circumspection and paying scrupulous attention to the details of propriety, Western observers are prone to deduce that this precludes their association of the term *self*-respect with a criterion such as "consciously conforming to a worthy standard of conduct" (3, p. 219). However, in the light of the foregoing description of Japanese concepts of moral obligation, we are only justified in concluding that *in addition* to sharing the meaning which is commonly placed on "self-respect" in our culture, the Japanese value other character traits (i.e., self-restraint, circumspection, respect for social niceties and for the feelings of others) sufficiently to dignify them by the same term that we usually reserve for moral uprightness.

Lastly, it is important to explain why confession and atonement are such relatively inconspicuous aspects of Japanese guilt behavior.[3] The absence of these characteristics that so frequently accompany the expression of guilt in our culture does not prove, as Ruth Benedict suggests, that genuine guilt is lacking, since otherwise it would be relieved by confession (3, p. 223). The Japanese does not, as alleged, avoid confession because his guilt is really only shame and, hence, would be aggravated rather than eased by being made public. The more credible explanation is that although confession would be guilt reducing it would also be too traumatic in view of the tremendous Japanese sensitivity to shame. Under such circumstances, overwhelming feelings of guilt can be relieved less painfully by suicide.

[3] The practice of atonement is not entirely unknown in Japan. "Boys in later elementary school are sometimes confined to the house for kinshin, 'repentance,' and must occupy themselves with . . . the writing of diaries." Similarly, when ostracized by his schoolmates for offenses, the culprit "has to apologize and make promises before he is readmitted" (3, pp. 273–274).

## Summary and Conclusions

The capacity for experiencing guilt behavior (i.e., a constellation of negative self-reactions to the perceived violation of moral obligation) is conceived as so basically human and so fundamental to the sanctions by which social norms are maintained and transmitted to the young that under minimally favorable social conditions it should develop in all cultures. The only psychological conditions hypothesized as essential for the development of guilt behavior are (a) the acceptance of moral values, (b) the internalization of a sense of moral obligation to abide by these values, and (c) sufficient self-critical ability to perceive discrepancies between internalized values and actual behavior. The development of conscience typically embodies various sequential changes paralleling shifts in the individual's biosocial status. Ordinarily, greater differences in moral behavior may be anticipated among individuals within a culture than among different cultures.

Shame is a self-deprecatory reaction to the actual or presumed judgments of *others*. It may have moral or nonmoral reference. Guilt feelings always involve a special type of moral shame in addition to other negative *self*-judgments. In addition to the shame of guilt, conscience (guilt behavior) is customarily buttressed by such external sanctions as statutory law, public opinion, and ridicule. Thus, the sanctions of guilt are both external and internal in nature.

Various criteria have been advanced by different ethnologists for distinguishing between shame and guilt. It has been alleged (a) that guilt behavior can only rise when a hierarchically superior parent or parent surrogate serves as the source of moral authority, (b) that genuine guilt feelings can only exist when shame and other external sanctions are not operative, and (c) that, subjectively, guilt must be characterized by conviction of sin and need for atonement. Examination of Navaho and Japanese ethnological materials presented in support of these criteria shows that the latter lack both logical and empirical validity. Highly suggestive evidence of the operation of strong moral obligations and of guilt behavior was found in these supposedly prime examples of "shaming cultures."

The problem of shame and guilt is illustrative of a major methodological hazard in the cross-cultural investigation of personality traits, namely, of the ethnocentric tendency to define a given trait in terms of its *specific* attributes in one's own culture. This leads to a perversion of cultural relativism. Instead of demonstrating how a basic human capacity (e.g., guilt behavior) occurs under different conditions and assumes different forms in different cultures, this approach inevitably "discovers" that this very capacity is absent in other cultures because it does not conform to a specific set of ethnocentric criteria. The generalization is then made that the capacity is nonuniversal, culture-bound, and, hence, not basic. Cross-cultural investigations of personality must, therefore, start with definitions of traits that are both psychologically meaningful and general enough to encompass specific cultural variants.

It is also important to avoid the error of circularity—setting up *a priori conditions* for the emergence of a trait, finding these conditions absent in a given culture, and concluding "empirically" therefrom that the *trait itself* is absent.

This error can be avoided in part by paying attention to the subjective and expressive content of behavior and not merely to the postulated determinants of the trait in question.

## References

1. AUSUBEL, D. P. *Ego development and the personality disorders*. New York: Grune & Stratton, 1952.
2. BENEDICT, R. *Patterns of culture*. Boston: Houghton Mifflin, 1934.
*3. BENEDICT, R. *The chrysanthemum and the sword*. Boston: Houghton Mifflin, 1946.
4. GORER, G. *Japanese character structure*. New York: Institute for Intercultural Studies, 1942.
5. JENKINS, R. L. Guilt feelings—their function and dysfunction. In M. L. Reymert (Ed.), *Feelings and emotions*. New York: McGraw-Hill, 1950.

* [Asterisks indicate works that are reprinted, in whole or in part, in this volume.]

6. LA BARRE, W. Some observations on character structure in the Orient: The Japanese. *Psychiatry*, 1948, **8,** 319–342.
7. LEIGHTON, D., & KLUCKHOHN, C. *Children of the people: the Navaho individual and his development*. Cambridge, Mass.: Harvard University Press, 1947.
8. MEAD, M. Social change and cultural surrogates. In C. Kluckhohn & H. A. Murray (Eds.), *Personality in nature, society, and culture*. New York: Knopf, 1949. [2d ed. 1953.]
*9. MEAD, M. Some anthropological considerations concerning guilt. In M. L. Reymert (Ed.), *Feelings and emotions*. New York: McGraw-Hill, 1950.
10. NICHOLS, C. A. *Moral education among North American Indians*. New York: Teachers College, Columbia University, 1930.
11. NUTTIN, J. Intimacy and shame in the dynamic structure of personality. In M. L. Reymert (Ed.), *Feelings and emotions*. New York: McGraw-Hill, 1950.
*12. PIAGET, J. *The moral judgment of the child*. Glencoe, Ill.: Free Press, 1948.

# PARENT PRACTICES AND CONSCIENCE DEVELOPMENT

The third report, by Hoffman and Saltzstein, is probably the single most informative paper on the role of parental discipline in producing individual differences in conscience development. It is a logical extension of the earlier work of these two authors and seeks to answer some of the questions raised by Hoffman in his earlier (1963) paper. It should be noted that Hoffman and Saltzstein's results relating induction techniques to advanced moral development rather than love withdrawal have some implication for the Mead-Benedict position that love and love withdrawal are the most significant factors in the development of a sense of guilt.

## Reference

Hoffman, M. L. Child-rearing practices and moral development: Generalizations from empirical research. *Child Development*, 1963, **34**, 295–318.

## Introduction

The first study in this subsection is a comparison of different parental styles within the Western culture. It has been demonstrated frequently that the stages in moral judgment that Piaget found in Swiss children also can be found in American children, but that American children go through them at a much more rapid pace. Boehm presents strong evidence that the acceleration of American children is a result of American child-rearing practices. The excerpt from the Sears, Maccoby, and Levin study, *Patterns of Child Rearing*, deals with children's conscience development as measured by maternal report and with the types of parental discipline associated with individual differences in conscience.

# 17

# The development of independence: A comparative study

*by Leonore Boehm*

## The Problem

The European who comes to the United States is surprised to find a more rapid social development in American children than he has been used to seeing in European children. In thought and action American children become independent of their elders at an earlier age than do European children. Not only do they depend less on adult guidance and judgment, but their consciences seem to mature earlier also.

Stendler (7) has indicated that the American mother unwittingly transfers some of the child's dependency from herself to his peer group at the preschool age, while the Parisian mother still thinks of him as "bébé," constantly needing her to teach him which kind of behavior she approves and which she disapproves. The American child learns to find satisfaction in the approval of his young playmates and strives to avoid their disapproval. Through parent interviews Stendler uncovered certain significant differences in educational goals

Leonore Boehm, "The Development of Independence: A Comparative Study," *Child Development*, 1957, 28, 85–92. © Society for Research in Child Development, Inc., 1957. Reprinted by permission of the author and the publisher.

between Parisian and American middle-class mothers. The younger Parisian child is encouraged to be gentle, quiet, self-controlled; in other words, well-mannered and civilized; the older one to be self-sufficient, well-integrated, and an individualistic thinker, which prepares him to become a typical Frenchman (7). Middle-class American parents attempt to bring up children who will be independent of their parents, who will be accepted, practicing members of their own peer groups. [Note that this is achieved by substituting peer dependency for parent dependency (2).] Riesman (6) explains this difference: In all "inner-directed societies" as in Europe's "old middle class," parents try to bring about, through education, the internalization in their children of the parents' values and goals. The smaller child is pushed until he learns to "push himself to the limits of his talents and beyond," regardless of the possible conflict that his achievements might raise for him in his efforts to relate to his peers. Throughout childhood the parent remains the source of guidance. The child is brought up to believe in and respect the authority of his parents, teachers, and other surrounding adults who, as such, are held to be superior to him. The European parent remains omnipotent and omniscient. Thus Piaget (5) received many answers from Swiss children who believed that it was their father or grandfather who had created the world, the rivers, the mountains. European parents think it is wrong to let children realize that they—the parents—do not know everything.

In all "other directed societies," to which the upper middle class of our large cities belongs according to Riesman, parents are no longer sure of their own values and standards. Due to the rate of change of our society, to social mobility, to immigration, the new generation no longer follows in its parents' footsteps. On the contrary, children are supposed to surpass their parents. As Mead reminds us, many a mother dreams of her son's becoming president of the United States. No longer can the parent feel superior to the child, but suffering from a lack of self-assurance, he does not wish to face the responsibility of directing the child. He believes that the child's contemporaries can advise better than his parents, that they know better what standards are important, what ideals and goals a youngster should have. Thus it is the peer group that has become the individual's source of direction, whose reactions have become important, whose approval must be obtained. Being popular with one's age group is a primary value. It is even more to be sought after than fame achieved through competitive activity. Social security has become one aim of education. The child, of course, senses the lack of self-confidence in his parents, he senses that the parents see in him at least a potential equal, if not a future superior. He realizes that the parents' knowledge is limited and that they, too, make mistakes. As a matter of fact, American parents, teachers, and other authorities feel that this realization is necessary for the sake of the children's feelings of security and early adult independence. Instead of learning to obey blindly, without questioning the adult's judgment, as one does in Europe, the child here is encouraged to use critical thinking in the hopes that his reasoning will become "autonomous" or "interiorized" as Piaget (4) calls this quality of objective, independent thinking.

Many an incident could be told by a person who has lived both in Europe and in the United States to give evidence of the differences in child development and behavior resulting from the respective differences in objectives and modes of training. A European child is a guest of his parents: a permanent guest, it is true, but one who will be asked to leave the dinner table if his behavior is not quiet and respectful. A European schoolchild told this investigator that his father made the best pancakes when the fact was that the father, a scholar who was all thumbs in the kitchen or shop, would have difficulty boiling water. Contrast this with the American father who said that he believed he should treat his child as a potential equal (if not superior), and that their home belonged to children and parents together; or the director of a Congregational church school in Illinois, who, when asked by his five-year-old son if there was a God, though a firm believer himself, answered that some people believed in God, while others did not. He wanted his boy to decide independently in all matters possible, rather than to assume that his father was always right.

Good preschools in this country are geared toward an education for independent thinking as well as for group living. Perhaps because of the marked difference in educational aims, there are but few preschools in Europe. There the "bébé" is expected to look to his mother for guidance. It is held that he does not need to start his social education at such an early age. In our preschools children are encouraged to find their own solutions whenever they are able to, even if these are not as perfect as adults'. At a young age this is possible mainly in concrete, practical matters, be it in regards to their work or to social living. In most preschools there are fewer rules and regulations for the older than for the younger group. The older ones are supposed to make their own decisions. To give an example: There is usually a rule for the younger group, that rubbers or boots have to be worn outdoors on days when there are puddles on the playground. There often is no such rule for the older children. They have become old enough to realize that they must put boots on only if they want to play in puddles. They may choose to play where it is wet or where it is dry. Thus they may decide whether to wear boots or not.

Whereas the European school is concerned mostly with academic learning and little with cooperation or "character education"—the latter being the home's responsibility, a principal at an elementary school in Winnetka, Illinois, stated to the author that the school's primary functions are to teach children independent thinking and the skills necessary for living together. The teacher's role in this country is then, according to this informant, different from that of the European teacher. His obligation is to make the children realize that they are his potential equals. Children owe less respect merely to the teacher's role. They should be discerning enough to respect only a person who merits respect. Children should be made aware of the fact that their teachers sometimes err, and that their teacher's judgment is not always better than their own. Quite in contrast to the powerful European teacher, the more informal American teacher does not need to be feared and hated. He has become, in Riesman's words, a "peer-group facilitator and mediator."

Many observations in European and American schools give evidence of an earlier cooperation among children here. In Europe the child is often told to work individually; here, the children are encouraged to help each other, be it directly or by constructive suggestions and criticism. At an age when the European kindergartner uses "egocentric" speech, according to Piaget (3), the American one needs speech mainly for real peer communication.

A question which comes to the fore when studying differing rates of social development is whether, in a culture which values cooperation among children more than dependence upon adults, *social conscience* matures earlier due to stress on skills necessary for group life. Does the child's conscience remain "egocentric" longer in an inner-directed society than it does in an other-directed society? It is quite possible that the relatively early independence of the American child causes his conscience to develop not only from identification and interiorization of the ethical values of his parents, but also from the values of those of his peers to whom he has, in part, transferred his dependence. Is this "inner-directed child" older than his "other-directed" opposite number before he stops basing his moral judgments on the outcome of the subject's actions alone? As Piaget states, the young child is anxious to "expier par sanction" (to unburden his conscience of its sense of guilt by undergoing punishment). This atonement is relevant to his own needs only and is entirely unconnected with those of the victim. It is a childish expiation chosen in order to reestablish the offender's inner balance because his deed has "destroyed the equilibrium of the world." The worse the deed then, even though it be an accident and possibly due to excellent intentions, the more disagreeable must the punishment be to absolve the child's conscience. The question which we are raising here would also suggest that an "inner-directed child" must be older than an "other-directed child" before he bases his moral judgments not only on the effects of the deed but also on the feelings of the victim and on the offender's intentions.

One wonders whether these findings of Piaget are true for all children in the civilized world. There might be a difference in the rate of formation of the conscience as well as in its content when one compares children in the United States with those in Calvinist Switzerland. One might expect a different type of conscience here where education is directed outwardly rather than inwardly, where ideals, goals, and values are geared primarily toward social adjustment and not toward character improvement or toward perfection of the soul for the sake of salvation. Possibly the values of an outer-directed conscience are easier for a human being to achieve than are those of an inner-directed conscience. Perhaps this is another reason why the American child's conscience may become autonomous earlier. It requires less introspection. It is less inwardly turned in its self-evaluation, less self-concerned, less perfectionistic. Thus it becomes less destructive to his self-confidence, less guilt- and shame-ridden than is the conscience of the Swiss child who has been taught to struggle continually against his own tendencies toward wrongdoing. According to Riesman, however, Americans replace the inner-directed person's specific guilt feelings with diffuse anxiety, which he maintains is necessary to build up in the individual that emotional sensitivity to the feelings of others which will serve as a much needed facilitator of social adjustment.

## Procedure

This investigation grew out of an earlier study of the author's in which we used Piaget's "méthode clinique"—talking to individual children, telling stories, and asking questions designed to reveal their reasoning at different age levels. The original purpose of the research was quite different in nature from the study reported in this paper. At no time during the original investigation was it meant to be a comparative one. When the European data were gathered the author knew very little about the United States, its people, its culture, and its education. However, when gathering the American data in Winnetka, it became clear that significant comparisons could be made between children of the two cultures. The investigator has interviewed 261 children from kindergarten through high school, 80 Europeans and 181 Americans. In all, 12 stories have been used. This paper, however, reports on just two stories, used in elementary schools only.

### Subjects

Europe: Twenty-nine French-speaking Swiss children, attending elementary school, which goes to tenth grade, in a rather run-down neighborhood in Geneva. United States: Forty American children, attending elementary school in Winnetka, a well-to-do suburb of Chicago.

One might wonder whether the results of this study were influenced by the difference in socioeconomic background between the children living in the United States and those in Geneva. However, results obtained, with the same stories, from 10 upper-middle-class German children living in Berlin were quite similar to those obtained from the Swiss children. This would seem to indicate that the phenomenon we are studying here is due more to the cultural structure of the society in which a child grows than it is to his socioeconomic class.

*First Story—The Scoutleader's Birthday Party*

"A group of children X years old (the subject's own age) want to give a surprise birthday party to their scoutleader. One boy has accepted the responsibility of decorating the room. He wonders whom he could ask for advice." (The questions which follow are illustrative of the type used. Actually, in the "méthode clinique," the investigator probes and probes, formulating each question on the basis of the answer the subject has given to the preceding one; thus a uniform questionnaire is not employed. In the course of this probing the experimenter asks a large number of questions. The few here quoted are deemed sufficient to indicate the nature of the questions used.)

1. "Whom do you think he might ask?"
2. "He had thought of asking his homeroom teacher, a whiz in English, history, and arithmetic, who knows nothing of art, or to ask another student who is so artistic that he has won a scholarship to the museum's art classes. Whom do you think he decided to ask?"
3. "He did ask both, and their advice differed. Whose advice do you think he followed?"
4. "He thought both ideas were equally good. Which one do you think he followed?"
5. "If he chooses the student's idea, will he be very embarrassed toward the teacher whose advice he did not follow?"

*Second Story—Fight*

"Two boys had a fight before school to see who was stronger. Louis hit Marc's nose, which started bleeding profusely."

1. "How do you think Louis felt about it?"
2. "Louis felt guilty and wanted to get rid of his bad conscience. He knew that if he asked his teacher what to do the teacher would tell him to write one hundred times: 'I should not fight before school,' whereas another friend would advise him to give his favorite toy to Marc. Do you think he asked the teacher or the friend?"
3. "Why?"
4. "Louis went to Marc and Marc told him to forget the incident: 'In a fight one child is apt to get hurt,' he said, 'I might have hurt you just as easily.' When do you think that Louis no longer felt guilty, when Marc had told him that he had forgiven him, when he had written the pages for the teacher, or when he had given his toy to Marc?"

**Results**

*First Story*

Sixteen (or 69.5 percent) of the 23 Swiss children, with whom the story was used in the above given form, all of them at least 10.3 years old, insisted that teachers and parents always give the best advice, even in matters of talent. Upon further insistence by the experimenter that it is the child who has the training particularly helpful for the scout, the Swiss children explained that adults know better because they have more experience. In the United States only 3 out of 40 children (7.5 percent) preferred the teacher's advice to that of the gifted child and all 3 of these were 6 years of age. Whereas all but 2 Swiss children (91 percent) imagined that the teacher would be angry if his advice was not followed, only 6 children in the United States (15 percent) believed so—3 were 6 years, 2 were 7 and 1 was 9 years of age. Most American children felt certain that the teacher would want the scout to follow the best advice, not necessarily the teacher's. The answers seem to show that Swiss children have less confidence in their peers than do children in America, that Swiss children continue, until a later age, to believe in the omniscience of adult authorities and to rely on their judgment, and that they are afraid of their teachers.

*Second Story*

Only 7 out of the 40 American children (17.5 percent) showed "egocentricity" of conscience as compared to 20 out of 29 Swiss children (69 percent). Whereas in America only 2 6-year-olds (5 percent) at first thought about their expiation through punishment (though afterwards they did consider the whole situation), there were 13 Swiss children (45 percent), distributed through the whole range of age, who remained solely concerned about their own atonement; another 7 (24 percent) were in a stage of

transition. For many Swiss children the teacher's punishment alone reestablished the equilibrium of the world, which was destroyed by their deed. In contrast to children in America, most Swiss children do not doubt the wisdom of their teacher's choice of punishment. When the investigator put these children on "the spot," questioning the teacher's judgment, a number of them became ill at ease and rationalized the teacher's action, finding some reason to justify his advice.

Rather than give up his favorite toy 1 American boy (2.5 percent) and 7 Swiss children (24 percent) chose the written work. Others hated writing so much that they preferred giving away the toy. Thirteen Swiss children (45 percent) wanted to undergo both punishments or at least the one they disliked the most to be sure of expiation. Several of these children were 14 years of age or older. In contrast, not a single American child expressed such a wish. Many Swiss children were of the conviction that some adult ought to be told of the accident even though the boys could take care of it very well themselves. One American boy thought that Louis should feel guilty, because he had not reported his misbehavior.

Being told that Marc has forgiven Louis hardly changed the Swiss children's position on needing punishment to be relieved from guilt feelings. These children again thought of the accident only from the point of view of their own expiation. None of the American children saw a need for punishment in this case.

Obviously the American children show an earlier independence from the teacher and his judgment than do the Swiss children; rather than assent to his wisdom they see the accident with more objectivity and accept the idea either that Marc is right and no guilt feelings are necessary, or that relief from guilt should come by giving pleasure to the child whom they have hurt. Thus they can conform with peer judgment. Their conscience becomes interiorized and autonomous at an earlier age than does that of the Swiss children. It is also a different type of conscience as pointed out before.

## Summary and Conclusions

Twenty-nine Swiss children and 40 American children from 6 to 15 years of age were studied by the "méthode clinique" to determine the differences in rate of social development and in content of conscience. The study appears to have uncovered evidence that, in certain areas of social development, the American child matures earlier than does the Swiss child. The American child seems to transfer his parent dependence to a peer dependence at an earlier age. One result of this earlier transferring appears to be that the American child's conscience becomes less egocentric and interiorizes earlier than does that of the Swiss child. There is, however, some indication that the content of conscience differs in these two types of societies. Whereas the American child's conscience is turned, primarily, toward social adjustment, the Swiss child's is geared toward character improvement.

Within the age range studied, this study seems to support the following conclusions: (1) American children are emancipated from their own adults at an earlier age than are their Swiss counterparts. (2) They are less subjugated to adults. (3) They are, rather, more dependent on their peers. (4) They enjoy freedom of thought and independence of judgment at an earlier age. (5) They develop earlier a more highly autonomous, though less complex, conscience.

## References

1. GILLESPIE, T., & ALLPORT, G. *Youth's outlook on the future.* New York: Doubleday, 1955.
2. MEAD, M. Social change and cultural surrogates. In C. Kluckhohn & H. A. Murray (Eds.), *Personality in nature, society, and culture.* (2nd ed.) New York: Knopf, 1953. Pp. 651–662.
*3. PIAGET, J. *The moral judgment of the child.* New York: Harcourt, 1932.
4. PIAGET, J. *The language and thought of the child.* New York: Harcourt, 1926.
5. PIAGET, J. *The child's conception of the world.* New York: Harcourt, 1929.
6. RIESMAN, D., GLAZER, N., & DENNEY, R. *The lonely crowd.* New Haven: Yale University Press, 1950.
7. STENDLER, C. B. The learning of certain secondary drives by Parisian and American middle-class children. *Marriage and Family Living,* 1954, **16,** 195–200.

* [Asterisks indicate works that are reprinted, in whole or in part, in this volume.]

# 18

# Signs and sources of conscience

*by Robert R. Sears,*
*Eleanor E. Maccoby,*
*and Harry Levin*

By and large, the mothers [in this study] had little to suggest as to the best conditions for conscience development; they did not appear to think of this aspect of behavior in terms of their own responsibility for its training. They were nonetheless acutely aware of conscientious behavior. Nearly all were able to describe clearly what they had observed with respect to their children's confessions and guilt reactions to deviation.

What are the symptoms by which we can recognize the growth of internal controls in a child? One, of course, is that he more and more often resists temptation, even when he is not being closely watched by a potential punisher. . . . A second indication of his having accepted his parents' standards as his own is his effort to teach these standards to his friends and siblings, i.e., *to act the parental role*. For example:

> **M.**[1] And I've taught him never to touch a medicine cabinet. I showed my little boy the bottles—medicine bottles—and I've told him. He was sick, oh,

From Robert R. Sears, Eleanor E. Maccoby, and Harry Levin, *Patterns of Child Rearing* (New York: Harper & Row, 1957), pp. 376–393. Copyright © 1957 by Harper & Row, Publishers, Inc. Reprinted by permission of the publisher and Robert R. Sears.

[1] [I = Interviewer; M = Mother.]

about a year ago, in the hospital, and he's never forgotten it, and I don't think he ever will. He's told his brothers about it plenty of times. And I told him, "if you took your medicine bottle, you're going to get sick like you did then." He won't go near that medicine cabinet. And if he sees one of his brothers going to touch it, he'll tell him, "You'll go to the hospital, and you'll stay in the hospital for a long, long time; and you won't see Mommy or Daddy. And you won't have no toys to play with—just lay in bed all the time and get needles." And now none of them will go up there. I think he's really the one that broke them of going to the medicine cabinet.

This child was taking a parental role in real-life interaction with his brothers. Such role playing is even more common in play situations. Every mother has heard little girls, when playing with their dolls, adopt their mothers' tones of voice and phrases, sometimes with embarrassing precision. This play acting, this pretending that one *is* one's father or mother, appears to be one of the major ways in which children come to understand what their parents' values are and to learn to accept them as their own. Since we did not inquire directly about the mothers' observations of this kind of behavior, we had only scattered examples reported and so were unable to use them for measurement.

A third indicator of conscience is the way a child acts *after* he has done something wrong. Some children, those who are primarily concerned with the avoidance of external punishment, will try to get out of their parents' sight, hide evidence of the misdeed, and deny the act when asked directly about it. The child with a well-developed conscience cannot escape so easily, for he is troubled by self-blame as well as by the fear of punishment. He applies his parents' disapproving evaluation of his behavior to himself. He can feel better only after he has made up for his misdeed in some way, and been forgiven. He acts guilty and sheepish. He may hang around his mother, acting in such a way that she will know something is wrong. Sometimes he will arrange things so she is sure to find out what he has done, even though he does not actually confess. Or he may simply come to her and tell her about it openly. Following is an example of a child who showed *confession* as a sign of conscience:

I. We'd like to get some idea of how Sid acts when he's naughty. When he deliberately does something he **knows** you don't want him to do when your back is turned, how does he act?

M. Very seldom does that. But a few times that he has done something that he shouldn't do, that I don't know anything about, if I'm in the other room, he just can't hold it in very long. And finally he comes in to me and he says, "Mother,"—and I'll say, "What?"—"I did something I shouldn't have done." Instead of leaving it and getting away with it, he usually comes over and tells me what he's done. He usually comes, I mean, and it's not very long after he's done it. He can hardly hold it in to himself, you see.

I. Are there any situations in which he doesn't do this? In other words . . .

M. Never come across one that he didn't. Even when he does something outside that he shouldn't do, and I don't even know about it, he could very easily not say a word to me. Instead he comes and he says, "You know what I did?" And if something goes wrong in school he'll say, "Something happened today. My teacher had to speak to me." And he doesn't have to tell me, but he does; he comes right over and tells me. I don't

know why. I should think if I were a child I'd keep it to myself but he doesn't; he comes and tells me and I would never know about it. I mean it—you know the old saying. "What you don't know won't hurt you." He evidently doesn't know it yet.

I. When you ask him about something he's done that he knows he's not supposed to do, does he usually admit it, or deny it?

M. He always admits it. I can always tell, of course, with Sid. I can always tell when he's trying to fabricate something. I mean if I say, "Did you do this?" And he says, "No." Well, I mean, it's just natural for a child to say "no." Remember that when a child is accused, even a grownup accused of something, if you said, "Did you do this?" Immediately the first answer that comes is "no." You say, well, that person's a liar. It's not that at all, it's just an immediate reaction to say "no." That's the first reaction any person has, and it's not only for a child; a grownup will do the same thing. But I can always tell when he says "no" and doesn't mean it because—but he can't tell—I don't know whether he'll accomplish it later—but he cannot tell a story. He can't fabricate at all. Or prevaricate. He just gets this silly grin on his face and I know that he's telling it and I'll say—and he'll just sheepishly put his eyes down and grin; he can't help it, he just can't tell a lie. Some people can and some people can't. He just can't.

I. What have you done about it, if he denies something that you're pretty sure he's done?

M. No, not too many things have happened, but when they have, it's been almost a puppy-dog fashion in that he's been very quiet and has led me to it.

Another child with a highly developed conscience confessed and took a spanking rather than risk his mother's continued disapproval:

**M.** He knows he has incurred our displeasure, and he says that he's sorry, he apologizes. Right away when he incurs this displeasure, he gets discouraged, because right away he puts his arms around you and says, "I love you so much, I love you, and I won't do it again." And I say, "You've said that now, and if you do it again, *that* time you're going to have to be punished." And that's what happened. I've forgotten what it was, but it was something that I figured was not safe, so he did do it again, and he came and told me, and I said, "Now, what's going to happen?" and he said, "I guess I have to be spanked." I said, "That's right. Because it's too much to expect you to remember; and it would be dangerous for me to go along on that assumption, because I would be the one that would be sorry if you were hurt. I would never forgive myself, because I slipped up in not teaching you the danger. It's a sorrowful thing to me to have to teach you through pain."

At the other extreme, however, there were children of the same age who went to great lengths to avoid having their misdeeds found out.

## A

**I.** We'd like to get some idea of how Billy acts when he's naughty. When he has deliberately done something he knows you don't want him to do, when your back is turned, how does he act?

**M.** Well, right now he is lying. If he is caught, he will lie his way out, which is very disturbing to me. If there is anything I can't stand it's lying. I just want him to face the fact he's been naughty, and I will be much kinder with him; but sometimes if he's very bad, I just put him up in his room, which has a terrible effect on him. Sometimes I just give him a good scolding, and sometimes I fall back

on the old dodge of telling him when his father gets home he will deal with him, which I know is wrong, but I just don't know how to handle him. I'll admit he is a problem.

**I.** What about if he does something when your back is turned, how does he act then?

**M.** And I find out afterwards? Well, that is usually the story, and it will come to my attention that he has broken something, and I will call him and try to get him to tell me why he did it; and I will admit I don't get very far. I don't know how to handle Billy.

**I.** Does he ever come and tell you about it without your having to ask him?

**M.** No, he would never admit that he has done something. It is only when Dick tells me or I just discover it.

**I.** When you ask him about something he has done that he knows he's not supposed to do, does he usually admit or deny it?

**M.** He denies it. He will do anything to get out of admitting it.

## B

**M.** Jack is inclined to be a little sneaky. Now that's another problem I don't like about him. For example, the things that annoy you, he will do more the minute your back is turned, and of course I don't like that at all. In other words, he thinks he is outsmarting you—kind of cute and not aboveboard.

**I.** If he does do something, will he usually come and tell you about it?

**M.** Oh, he wouldn't tell you unless he was caught. He really wouldn't.

**I.** When you ask him about it, will he admit it or deny it?

**M.** Oh—well—for example, just two days ago, there was a lot of scribbling all over the window sill in his room, which hadn't taken place for about two years, and there was an awful lot of it, and I saw it and I immediately asked who did it—so Lee spoke right up and said, "Well, *I* didn't." And Jackie said, "Well, *I* didn't!" I found out later he did do it. He'll admit it if you tell him you're going to take away his television if he doesn't, but as far as getting right up and saying, "I did it," he's no George Washington.

Confession, of course, is not always a sign of conscience. It may indicate a greater fear of the consequences for *not confessing* than of the actual punishment for the misdeed. For example:

I. What do you do about it if she denies something you are pretty sure she has done?

M. She may deny it at first, but she'll usually tell me. She's deathly afraid of being punished—not by me—but we've always told her that any little girl who tells a lie, God always does something terrible to them, and she's deathly afraid of that. Like, for instance, up the street a little boy was hit by an automobile, and Cathy was quite sure it was because he did something wrong at some time and God punished him. Maybe it's not the right thing, but we let her believe it.

In general, however, a child's ability to admit that he was in the wrong, and to apologize or to make restitution, is an important step along the road to the development of internal controls. It means that he is willing to risk external punishment in order to recover his self-esteem and the esteem of his parents.

On the basis of the mothers' descriptions, a judgment was made for each child as to the "extent of development of his conscience." The ratings are reported in Table 1.

In interpreting Table 1, one should keep in mind that almost all the children in the study were in their sixth year, i.e., between five and six. Psychoanalytic theory, which is derived from intensive observations in psychotherapeutic interviews, suggests that this is a critical year for conscience development. Having a conscience is not an all-or-none affair at any age; but especially at this age, some elements of it are likely to be present and others absent. Most of the children in the present group appear to have been on the way to the internal control stage of their development at the time of the interview. As Table 1 shows, however, the development was by no means complete, nor was it the same for all. Quite possibly, if we had studied older children, the signs we looked for as symptoms of internal control would have been shown by a larger proportion.

In our search for child-rearing dimensions that are associated with the rapid

Table 1

**Evidence of the Development of Conscience**

| | | |
|---|---|---|
| 1. | No evidence. Child hides, denies, does not seem unhappy when naughty | 13% |
| 2. | Little evidence of conscience | 28 |
| 3. | Moderate conscience development. May not confess directly, but looks sheepish; seldom denies | 38 |
| 4. | Considerable conscience | 17 |
| 5. | Strong conscience: child feels miserable when naughty; always confesses; never denies; strong need for forgiveness | 3 |
| | Not ascertained | 1 |
| | Total | 100% |

and strong development of conscience, we are interested, of course, in the larger question of identification. Our previous discussion seems tacitly to have assumed that there is one single process which produces the tendency to practice roles in early childhood. Such an assumption is not warranted, although it is temporarily convenient for purposes of exposition of the theory. Before examining the findings relevant to our present theory of identification, we must mention one other combination of circumstances that could have the same effects on behavior. This is the *direct reward and reinforcement* of role practicing. . . .

A theory stands or falls by its effectiveness in ordering empirical observations, however, so without further a priori worrying about the possible errors in our present notions, we will examine the relations between our measure of conscience and certain child-rearing dimensions that we have expected to be associated with it.

### Warmth and Dependency

The first thing suggested by the theory is that conscience will develop more rapidly, and will be more complete at kindergarten age, in those children who were given the greatest love and affection in early childhood. This reasoning rests on the supposition that warm and affectionate behavior increases the strength of the child's dependency on the mother . . . and that the more dependent the child is, the more motivation he will have for practicing the maternal role. We find a little support for this reasoning, but it is precious little. The correlation between *warmth* and *amount of conscience* is only .10 ($p=$ .05).

There is one other child-rearing scale worth examination, however. In Chapter Five [not reprinted in this volume] we saw that *mother's rejection of the child* was somewhat related to his dependency, also. The mothers who were most rejecting reported their children as a little more dependent than did the mothers who were fully accepting. According to our identification theory, then, we should expect the 99 "rejected" children to show more conscience (because they were more dependent) than the 218 "accepted" children. But no, just the contrary is the case; only 18 percent of the rejected children were judged to have high conscience (points 4 and 5 on the scale described in Table 1), while 31 percent of the accepted children were so rated. This difference is not large, but it is directly contrary to the expectations we would have from our identification theory.

Taken at its face value, this finding would force us to reject the theory of identification. But there is one curious complication that makes us withhold judgment. The theory suggests that children who developed a high degree of dependency in their early life would show a more rapid and extensive development of conscience. But . . . it was shown that *acceptance* had a slight tendency to *decrease* dependency. In other words, dependency and conscience should go together, but acceptance seems to decrease the former and increase the latter. The sizes of the relationships are so small, however, that there is plenty of statistical room for both effects to exist in the data. So far as the relationship between dependency and conscience development is concerned, only the boys show any; divided into two equal groups —the more and the less dependent—26 percent of the more dependent boys were judged to have high conscience, while only 16 percent of the less dependent ones were so rated. The boys support the theory.

Now if we separate the effects of these two antagonistic influences, acceptance-rejection and dependency, we can see exactly how each is related to conscience. Table 2 shows the percentage of "high-conscience" children in each of the four possible groups, i.e., more and less dependent children who were either accepted or rejected by their mothers. The relations of both factors, to conscience, are now much clearer. In every comparison, for both sexes, rejected children include fewer "high consciences." Furthermore, we now see that the "more dependent" children more frequently have high conscience than the "less dependent" children in every comparison except that of "accepted" girls.

None of the percentage differences shown in Table 2 is of very high significance, and we must draw conclusions from them with considerable caution. However, every difference is in the direction that the theory requires, and our conclusion is that, although there are doubtless many other factors that influence the rapidity of conscience development, there is some likelihood that the mother's *warmth* and *acceptance* are positive influences. We must also add that the evidence for this statement is considerably stronger for the boys than for the girls.

## Sex Differences

This failure of the girls to conform to the theoretical prediction is a reminder that the identification theory calls for certain differences between the sexes in the development of conscience. The girl retains her initial identification with the mother, while the boy must under most circumstances shift his to the father. Although both these identifications are with adults, we are inclined to believe that the boy's shift retards the smooth development of the process. His gradual adoption of a new model is doubtless somewhat frustrating to him, and puts him in a state of conflict as to whom he should act like. Thus, we might expect not only that boys in their sixth year

*Table 2*

**High Conscience: Relationship to Child Dependency and Maternal Acceptance-Rejection**

| Acceptance-Rejection of Child | Percentage of Children Rated as Having High Conscience | |
| --- | --- | --- |
| | *Less Dependent* | *More Dependent* |
| Boys: | | |
| Rejected | 10% (30) * | 15% (26) |
| Accepted | 21% (58) | 33% (55) |
| Girls: | | |
| Rejected | 18% (17) | 31% (27) |
| Accepted | 36% (60) | 37% (46) |

* Figures in parentheses are number of cases.

would be less fully identified with their fathers than girls are with their mothers, but that they would have a less complete identification with the adult role in general than girls would have. Also, this means they would show less indication of high conscience, as well as of other signs of identification, than girls.

This prediction is confirmed by our data. Only 20 percent of the boys were judged to have "high conscience," as we defined it above, while 29 percent of the girls were so rated. The difference between the mean ratings for the two sexes is reliable at the level of $p < .03$.

Another kind of evidence that supports this finding comes from experiments on doll play. It will be recalled that each of the children in this research was given two 20-minute sessions of permissive doll play at about the same time the mother was interviewed. The test equipment consisted of a five-room, open-topped house, with miniature furniture, and a family of five dolls. Each child was asked to tell a story about the family and show all the things they did. The experimenter recorded the number of times the child used each of the dolls as the agent of some thematic action and also whether the action was an aggressive one or not. Our reasoning was that in this fantasy situation a child would be free to choose whichever doll he wished, and that the stronger his identification with a father or mother role, the more frequently he would use the father or mother doll as the agent of actions in the play.

We would expect, therefore, that if the theory about sex differences is correct, the girls would use the mother doll more often than the father doll, and the boys would use the father more often than the mother. This proved to be true,

and the difference is large and statistically reliable. We would also expect that the difference in how much the two dolls were used would be bigger for the girls than for the boys. That is, boys are presumed to have identified first with the mother and then to have had a good deal of pressure to shift to the father, while the girls are presumed to have had much less, or no, pressure to shift away from the mother. Hence the boys would be more nearly equal in their two identifications and they would show a smaller difference in frequency of use of the father and mother dolls. This prediction was also fulfilled (P. S. Sears, 1953).

One other study of children's doll play is worth mentioning in this connection. Dr. Elizabeth Z. Johnson compared boys and girls at both five years of age and at eight years. In her study, however, she made a very detailed record of exactly what kinds of aggressive actions the children performed, and she found she could classify these actions according to whether the aggression was prosocial or antisocial. The former class included mainly disciplinary actions—spankings, threats, warnings, and adult-like punishings of various kinds. The antisocial aggressions were more childlike, and included such acts as hiding, jumping on the furniture, disobedience, and hitting.

If our notion about identification is correct, we would expect the girls to show relatively more prosocial (adult-like) aggression than the boys; further, we would expect both sexes to increase in this form of behavior from five to eight years of age. Dr. Johnson found both these predictions to be true (Johnson, 1951).

Now let us return to the interview ratings of conscience. If the father becomes the principal person with whom the boy identifies, we should expect that the boy would find it difficult to make the shift if the father rejects him. Rejection by the father should have little effect on the girl, however, because the mother remains the main identification figure. In the interview, the mothers were asked to discuss their husbands' relations with the children. In 47 of the interviews (28 boys' mothers and 19 girls') there was some indication that the father was somewhat rejecting of the child. If we compare the conscience ratings of children rejected by their fathers with ratings of those for whom there was no evidence of father-rejection, we find what the theory predicts. Only 11 percent of the father-rejected boys had a "high conscience," while 22 percent of the nonrejected ones were so rated. The comparable figures for the girls are 26 and 29 percent—purely chance variation. The boys' difference is reliable at about the .05 level.

In general, then, the findings about the effects of warmth, rejection, and dependency, and the differences observed between boys and girls, lend support to the theory of identification we have described. Of course, these qualities, both those of the parents (warmth, rejection) and the child (sex, dependency), are ones over which parents have little or no control, and the findings are of interest mainly because they do fit the theoretical predictions. We can now turn to some aspects of parental behavior that are potentially a little more modifiable.

## Techniques of Training

In the previous chapter [not reprinted in this volume] we described the various methods of discipline the mothers re-

ported. We can now look at the effects of some of these same techniques with respect to whether or not they were associated with the development of high conscience.

According to the theory of identification, the child imitates the mother, and adopts her standards and values as his own, in order to assure himself of her love. This suggests that a high conscience would develop most readily if the mother relied largely on those disciplinary techniques that involved *giving or withholding love* as a means of rewarding or punishing child behavior. Conversely, we would expect that the children of mothers who used such materialistic methods as deprivation of privileges, physical punishment, and tangible rewards, would develop conscience control more slowly. Children do learn to adapt themselves somewhat to the prevailing climate of the family environment. If love is used as a reward, a child learns to do what will bring him love. If his mother withholds love, he will even learn to give himself love, and he will do as she does to avoid the pain of having her separate herself from him. On the other hand, if the mother uses physical punishment, a child is understandably reluctant to confess his misdeeds or to admit, when asked, that he has done wrong. He may use hiding or flight or counter-aggression as devices to avoid punishment.

In Table 3, we have compared the six dimensions which describe these two classes of disciplinary techniques. The first three—praise, isolation, and withdrawal of love—are ones that make use of love-oriented behavior by the mother. We have added "reasoning" to the table, too, because it was associated with these love-oriented techniques. In each in-

## Table 3

**High Conscience: Relationship to Techniques of Discipline Employed by the Parents**

| Parents | | Percentage of Children Rated High on Conscience | Number of Cases |
|---|---|---|---|
| High in their use of praise | $r = .18$ | 32% | 181 |
| Low in their use of praise | | 17% | 192 |
| High in their use of isolation | $r = .00$ | 29% | 152 |
| Low in their use of isolation | | 17% | 167 |
| High in use of withdrawal of love | $r = .09$ | 27% | 81 |
| Low in use of withdrawal of love | | 24% | 107 |
| High in their use of reasoning | $r = .18$ | 30% | 192 |
| Low in their use of reasoning | | 16% | 91 |
| High in use of tangible rewards | $r = -.04$ | 20% | 188 |
| Low in use of tangible rewards | | 28% | 181 |
| High in use of deprivation of privileges | $r = -.07$ | 18% | 213 |
| Low in use of deprivation of privileges | | 33% | 156 |
| High in use of physical punishment | $r = -.20$ | 15% | 175 |
| Low in use of physical punishment | | 32% | 197 |

stance, the high use of such methods is accompanied by a greater number of "high-conscience" children than the lesser use. The second group of three—tangible rewards, deprivation, and physical punishment—is more materialistic, and in each case the more frequent use is accompanied by a smaller number of "high-conscience" children. Again, as with our previous analyses, the statistical reliabilities of the relationships are meager. Indeed, in four of the seven cases, the correlation coefficients which express the size of the relationships are approximately zero. However, six of the seven are in the theoretically expected direction.[2] And in every case the percentage of extreme cases ("high conscience") shows a rather substantial difference be-

[2] These seven tests are, of course, not independent, since a number of the antecedent scales are intercorrelated.

tween high and low groups. The consistency of these findings, rather than the amount of influence of each separate dimension, gives us some confidence in the significance of the final results.

These findings all support the theory that love-oriented techniques aid in the development of conscience. Guilt and confession of wrongdoing can be interpreted as the child's expression of fear that he has offended his parents and that they will no longer love him. Coming to the parents for atonement is an attempt to assure the continuation of love.

We can go a little farther with this analysis, however. Withdrawing love where little exists is meaningless. If the mother is relatively cold to begin with, then using withdrawal of love should have little effect on conscience development. The pattern most calculated to produce "high conscience" should be that of mothers who are usually warm and loving and then, as a method of control, threaten this affectionate relationship.

Table 4 shows that this is indeed the case. The children most prone to behave in the ways we have considered indicative of having a well-developed conscience were those whose mothers were relatively warm toward them but who made their love contingent on the child's good behavior. These were the children who truly were risking the loss of love when they misbehaved.

So we come back full circle on our data. *Warmth* alone did not seem to have more than a minimal relation to our measure of conscience. Neither did *withdrawal of love*. But putting the two together, we find a quite clear influence on this one sign of the identification process.

**Comment**

In general, our findings support our theory of identification. They provide a little more information on the way in which parents' child-rearing practices influence the child's character. We can say with some degree of conviction that

mothers who love and accept their children, and who use love-oriented techniques of discipline rather than material or physical techniques, produce relatively more children with high conscience. We can say, too, that girls develop this inner control, and adopt their appropriate sex-role qualities, earlier and faster than boys.

In some ways these are discomforting discoveries. They mix up our adult values a little. Ordinarily, we think of *acceptance* as a good thing; a rejecting mother is thought of as unfair and unkind. The words *love-oriented techniques of discipline* have a good sound, too, especially when they are put in contrast with physical punishment—at least, as we saw in the previous chapter [not reprinted in this volume], this is true for a good many mothers. But when we examine these love-oriented techniques more closely, and find that they include *withdrawal of love* as a means of control or punishment, we realize that we are dealing with a form of maternal behavior that is as much derogated as is rejection. Yet both *acceptance* and *withdrawal of love* appear to produce a strong conscience. Is this a good outcome or a bad outcome of child training?

*Table 4*

**High Conscience: Relationship to the Mother's Warmth and Her Use of Withdrawal of Love**

|  | Percentage of Children Rated High on Conscience |
| --- | --- |
| Mother relatively cold, and: | |
| Uses withdrawal of love fairly often | 18% |
| Uses little or no withdrawal of love | 25% |
| Mother relatively warm, and: | |
| Uses withdrawal of love fairly often | 42% |
| Uses little or no withdrawal of love | 24% |

Some degree of inner control of sex, aggression, and other powerful impulses is clearly necessary if a society is to survive. On the other hand, these impulses do exist in every child and in every adult. Too severe inner control can prevent any direct expression of them and can produce a quite unnecessary degree of guilt and anxiety. Too much conscience can destroy the happiness and productivity of the individual, just as too little can destroy the peace and stability of society.

The problem can be approached in a different way, however. We have discussed here only the *strength* of conscience, saying nothing of its *content*. In our interviews we asked about the signs of conscience, not what kinds of behavior the child prevented himself from doing, or felt guilty about after doing. The *content* of conscience appears to be the important thing, both from the individual's standpoint and from society's. A strong inner control of impulses to kill other people, or to make indiscriminate sexual advances to many potential partners, is not severely limiting to the individual's initiative. But if these inhibitions extend to *all* aggressive or sexual actions, the person may be crippled in his efforts to live a normal and productive life. American society is competitive and the American culture tolerates, indeed demands, a good deal of interpersonal aggression. In the sexual sphere, both males and females—in their respective fashions—must take initiative in seeking a marriage partner, and marriage can be misery for those whose inhibitions prevent them from yielding fully to the physical expression of love.

In emphasizing the significance of conscience content, however, we cannot ignore conscience strength. During the early years of life, there is so much changeworthy behavior to be controlled and modified that any training that produces inner control is likely to produce inhibition of a very wide range of behaviors. In the close family circle, there is difficulty in limiting the control of aggression only to the most violent forms. Aggressive impulses *in general* become subject to inner control. Too, if we are correct in the general outlines of our identification theory, the child tends to absorb all the parental values he can perceive. Since most parents have fairly widespread inner controls of their own —conscience content that extends to many items of behavior other than those that are minimally essential for social living—the child is in risk of absorbing more than he needs. If his identification is especially strong, even the parents' mildest and most temporary strictures may become a matter of conscience for him. Role practice means the adoption of *everything* in the parents' behavior that the child perceives as appropriate to the parental role.

There is no answer to the question of what is the optimal strength and encompassment of conscience. We have no units by which we can measure these things objectively. We can make comparative ratings of children, as we have done here, but this does not tell us how strong these children's consciences were on any absolute scale. Could we perhaps assume that the average strength of conscience in this group of 379 youngsters is optimal? We have no way of knowing. Some observers of the American scene think our people are becoming more and more neurotic and guilt-ridden; others see signs of too little inner control, too much reckless violence that requires too many policemen on too many corners. We simply do not know, and the question is far too important to permit the hazards of uninformed guessing.

Uncertain as we may be about the optimal average, however, we can say something about the extremes of conscience and its lack. The child with too strong a conscience is guilt-ridden. His own impulses constantly excite him to confession and to a too instant admission of wrongdoing. He is prevented from experimentation with new impulses; he dares not risk the danger of self-punishment. New ideas and new experiences, even new people, are dangerous to him. He becomes rigid and inflexible in his judgments of others, a purveyor of sanctimony and propriety. His repressed hostilities are brought into the service of his moral judgments. In childhood he is a prig, a teacher's pet; in adulthood he can become cruel and vicious in his expression of moral indignation. Worst of all, perhaps, he can have no fun in life, for fun itself is subject to inner control.

At the other extreme is the child with a weak conscience. What he lacks in guilt he makes up in fear. His actions are bounded only by the possibility of his being caught and punished for his wrongdoings. His moral judgments are based on expediency. He cannot be trusted out of sight and supervision. His infantile impulses remain strong, and in the absence of a punitive disciplinarian he has no reluctance to express them. He may bully younger or weaker children, steal and lie if he thinks he can get away with it, and flee to hide when anything happens that may conceivably be viewed amiss by adults. In childhood he is aggressive and mean, a troublemaker at home and at school. In adulthood, he may be a conscienceless rogue in his social and business relationships, an undisciplinable bum, or a criminal.

Neither of these extremes presents an attractive picture in its pure form. Of course, unhappily, there is a little of the guilt-child and a little of the fear-child in nearly everyone. Conscience is not an all-or-none matter, either as to strength or as to content. The process of identification places certain automatic limits on what the child's conscience can contain —the limit is the behavior and the value systems of the adults with whom the child identifies. We found, for example, that in doll play the strongly identified girls were very aggressive if their mothers were aggressive (i.e., used much physical punishment), but were nonaggressive if their mothers were nonaggressive. With the less strongly identified girls, the degree of aggressiveness expressed by the mother had no influence on the daughter's fantasy aggression (Levin & Sears, 1956). The mother provided the model, and identification helped to transmit her behavior to the next generation.

In the long run, then, if our theory of identification is correct, the process itself places limits on the range within which human morals and values can fall. If there must be *some* parental warmth in order for a child to identify with his parents, then the very same warmth will be an identified-with quality and will become a property in the personality of the child. The same will hold true of the choice of withdrawal of love as a means of discipline. Thus, mainly within the range of parental qualities required to insure identification in the child will there be a continuation of the social and personality qualities that constitute those parents. And equally, the more identification there is in any one generation, the greater will be the absorption of those qualities-that-induce-identification in the next.

If one wants to speculate quite beyond the bounds of any testable hypotheses, one can imagine that the human capacity for identification may be one of the major factors accounting for the extraordinary preeminence of our species. No more than a few thousand years ago, man was but a superior kind of ape. Now he is the intellectual master of his universe. The years are too few for biological evolution to have accounted for the change. Of course, the accretion of culture is in part responsible, but human culture is now so complex that each new generation could not possibly learn it all if each tiny element had to be taught through laboriously arranged rewards and punishments. The child's spontaneous tendency to "try on" the roles he observes around him, and thus learn the actions implied in these roles, makes for enormous efficiency in this learning.

The development of man has not been a random matter. His physical stamina and the effectiveness of his bodily structure have not progressed in even a dozen thousand years. It is in the growing use of reasoning and thinking about his problems—and hence solving at least some of them—that man gives the appearance of having capacities that place him almost off the scale of comparison with other animals. What has produced this change?

We call attention to the role of *reasoning with the child* as an influence on our measure of conscience. If reasoning conduces to identification, then the use of reasoning—explanation, guidance, verbal assistance to the young in the arduous process of growing up—becomes a major quality of the parents that, simply because it exists in the parents, will be absorbed by the children. The greater the use of reasoning, the greater will be the probability that reasoning as a form of human behavior will be passed from generation to generation. And it is in the very use of reasoning that man has been developing so rapidly.

If these speculations are true, we can but hope that there will somehow develop a limitation on some of the other consequences of identification—the growth of powerfully inhibiting internal control and the copying of all the qualities of the past. It would be ironic indeed if one and the same psychological process were to bring man at once to the highest point of skill in intellection and then, for all eternity, stereotype him with the elaborate habits of a gigantic ant.

## References

JOHNSON, E. Z. Attitudes of children toward authority as projected in their doll play at two age levels. Unpublished doctor's dissertation, Harvard University, 1951.

LEVIN, H., & SEARS, R. R. Identification with parents as a determinant of doll play aggression. *Child Development*, 1956, **27**, 135–153.

SEARS, P. S. Child-rearing factors as related to playing of sex-typed roles. *American Psychologist*, 1953, **8**, 431. (Abstract)

## 19

# Parent discipline and the child's moral development[1]

*by Martin L. Hoffman
and Herbert D. Saltzstein*

Recent years have seen the accumulation of a body of findings relating moral development, especially internalization of moral values and the capacity for guilt, to parental practices. In a recent review of this research (Hoffman, 1963a) the following propositions received support: (a) a moral orientation based on the fear of external detection and punishment is associated with the relatively frequent use of discipline techniques involving physical punishment and material deprivation, here called power-assertive discipline; (b) a moral orientation characterized by independence of external sanctions and high guilt is associated with relatively frequent use of non-power-assertive discipline—sometimes called psychological, indirect, or love-oriented discipline.

Martin L. Hoffman and Herbert D. Saltzstein, "Parent Discipline and the Child's Moral Development," *Journal of Personality and Social Psychology*, 5, 1967, 45–57. Copyright 1967 by the American Psychological Association, and reproduced by permission.

[1] This study was supported by Public Health Service Research Grant M-02333 from the National Institute of Mental Health. It was carried out while both authors were at the Merrill-Palmer Institute.
The authors wish to thank Lois W. Hoffman for her many helpful comments and suggestions.

Several explanations of these findings have been advanced, each focusing on a different aspect of the parent's discipline. Thus, Allinsmith and Greening (1955) suggest that the significant variable may be the difference in the model presented by the parent during the disciplinary encounter (i.e., parent openly expresses anger versus parent controls anger). The importance of this factor may lie in the model it provides the child for channeling his own aggression. Where the parent himself expresses his anger openly, he thereby encourages the child to express his anger openly; where the parent controls his anger, he discourages the child from openly expressing anger and therefore may promote a turning of the anger inward, which according to psychoanalytic theory is the process by which the guilt capacity is developed.

Another explanation of the difference between power-assertive and nonpower-assertive techniques is in terms of the duration of the punishment; that is, whereas nonpower-assertive discipline may last a long time, the application of force usually dissipates the parent's anger and thus may relieve the child of his anxiety or guilt rather quickly. A third possibility, suggested by Sears, Maccoby, and Levin (1957), is that punishing the child by withholding love, which is frequently involved in non-power-assertive discipline, has the effect of intensifying the child's efforts to identify with the parent in order to assure himself of the parent's love.

A still different formulation has recently been suggested by Hill (1960). According to this view, the crucial underlying factor is the timing of the punishment. Love-withdrawal punishment is believed more often to terminate when the child engages in a corrective act (e.g., confession, reparation, overt admission of guilt, etc.), whereas physical punishment is more likely to occur and terminate at the time of the deviant act and prior to any corrective act.

Finally, the important variable may be the information often communicated by nonpower-assertive techniques regarding the implications of the child's deviant behavior. For example, Aronfreed's (1961) view is that such information can provide the cognitive and behavioral resources necessary for the child to examine his actions independently and accept responsibility for them.

Though varied, all but the last of these explanations assume the key ingredient for nonpower-assertive discipline to be its punitive—more specifically, its love-withdrawing—quality. This hypothesis stems from psychoanalytic and learning theories that emphasize anxiety over loss of love as the necessary motivational basis for moral development.

In examining instances of nonpower-assertive discipline it became apparent that the amount of love withdrawal, real or threatened, varied considerably. In some cases, the love-withdrawal aspect of the discipline seemed to predominate. In others it seemed totally absent, and in still others it seemed to be a minor part of a technique primarily focused on the harmful consequences of the child's behavior for others. This suggested that the effectiveness of these techniques might lie in their empathy-arousing capacity rather than, or in addition to, their love-withdrawing property. In the present study we accordingly made the distinction between two kinds of nonpower-assertive discipline. One, called

*induction*, refers to techniques in which the parent points out the painful consequences of the child's act for the parent or for others. In the second, called *love withdrawal*, the parent simply gives direct but nonphysical expression to his anger or disapproval of the child for engaging in the behavior. In a sense by these latter techniques the parent points out the painful psychological consequences of the act for the child himself, that is, the withdrawal of love by the parent.

It is probable, of course, that the child experiences both these types of nonpower-assertive techniques as involving a loss of love. However, as indicated above, the love-withdrawing component of the induction techniques is more subdued, and in addition they provide him with the knowledge that his actions have caused pain to others. By doing this the technique capitalizes on the child's capacity for empathy. In our view (see Hoffman, 1963b; Hoffman, in press; Hoffman & Saltzstein, 1960) it is this capacity for empathy which provides a powerful emotional and cognitive support for development of moral controls and which has been overlooked in other psychological theories of moral development. For this reason it was expected that *induction, and not love withdrawal, would relate most strongly to the various indexes of moral development.*

Affection has often been supposed to be a necessary condition for moral development. Measures of the parent's affection were therefore included for completeness. We expected, following the pattern of the previous research, that power assertion would relate negatively, and affection positively, to the moral indexes.

## Method

### Sample

The children studied were all seventh-graders in the Detroit metropolitan area. The test battery was administered to groups of children in the schools during three sessions spaced about a week apart. Sometimes an individual class was tested in the homeroom, and sometimes several groups were tested together in the gymnasium or auditorium.

Data bearing on the various dimensions of moral development were obtained from over 800 children broadly representative of the population in the area. Because of the apprehension of some of the school officials, however, we were unable to obtain reports of parental discipline from about a fourth of these children, the loss being greater among the lower-class sample. In addition, children identified as behavior problems and those from nonintact families were screened from the sample. Further shrinkage due to absences, incomplete background information, and unintelligible or incomplete responses resulted in a final sample of 444 children. Included were 146 middle-class boys, 124 middle-class girls, 91 lower-class boys, and 83 lower-class girls.

Subsequently, interviews were conducted with a subsample consisting of 129 middle-class mothers (66 boys and 63 girls) and 75 middle-class fathers (37 boys and 38 girls). No interviews were conducted with parents of the children from the lower class.

### Child Morality Indexes

Several different moral indexes were used—each tapping a different aspect of conscience.[2] The two major indexes pertain to the degree to which the child's moral orientation is internalized. These are (a) the intensity of guilt experienced following his own transgressions, and (b) the use of moral judgments about others which are based on internal rather than external considerations. The other indexes pertain to whether the child confesses and accepts responsibility for his misdeeds and the extent to which he shows consideration for others. Identification, though not a direct moral index, was also included because of its relationship to moral development, as hypothesized by psychoanalytic theory and by recent researchers (e.g., Sears et al., 1957).

**Guilt.** Two semiprojective story-completion items were used to assess the intensity of the child's guilt reaction to transgression. The technique presents the child with a story beginning which focuses on a basically sympathetic child of the same sex and age who has committed a transgression. The subject's instructions are to complete the story and tell what the protagonist thinks and feels and "what happens afterwards." The assumption made is that the child identi-

---

[2] These dimensions were used because they clearly bear on morality and because they represent different levels (affective, cognitive, overt) and directions for behavior (proscriptions, prescriptions). Each dimension has its advantages and disadvantages, and since a strong case for including one and not the others could not be made we included them all. In doing this our intention was not to treat them as indexes of a single underlying "moral development." Doing this would seem premature, since, although the different aspects of morality presumably increase with age (empirical data on age progression are available only for moral judgment), they very likely begin to develop—and reach full development—at different ages and progress at different rates.

fies with the protagonist and therefore reveals his own internal reactions (although not necessarily his overt reactions) through his completion of the story.

The first story used here was concerned with a child who through negligence contributed to the death of a younger child. The story beginning was constructed so as to provide several other characters on whom to transfer blame. The second story was about a child who cheats in a swimming race and wins. In both stories detection was made to appear unlikely. In rating the intensity of the guilt from the subject's completion of the story, care was taken to assess first that the subject identified with the central character. If such identification was dubious, the story was not coded for guilt, nor were stories involving only external detection or concern with detection coded for guilt. All other stories were coded for guilt. For a story to receive a guilt score higher than zero there had to be evidence of a conscious self-initiated and self-critical reaction. Given evidence for such a reaction, the intensity of guilt was rated on a scale ranging from 1 to 6. At the extreme high end of the scale were stories involving personality change in the hero, suicide, etc. In coding the stories the attempt was made to ignore differences in sheer style of writing and to infer the feeling of the subject as he completed the story.

A departure from the usual practice was to assign two guilt scores to each story—one for the maximum guilt experienced by the hero, usually occurring early in the story, and the other for terminal guilt. In relating discipline to this and other facets of morality extreme groups were chosen. In choosing the high- and low-guilt groups, attention was

paid to both scores. That is, the high-guilt group included those who sustained a high level of guilt throughout the stories. The low-guilt group included children who manifested little or no guilt throughout the stories. Children who initially manifested intense guilt which was dissipated through confession, reparation, defenses, etc., were not included in the guilt analysis.

**Internalized moral judgments.** The moral judgment items consisted of several hypothetical transgressions which the children were asked to judge. These situations were of the general type used by Piaget, including moral judgments about persons committing various crimes, for example, stealing; choosing which of two crimes was worse, for example, one involving simple theft and the other a breach of trust; and judgments of crimes with extenuating circumstances, for example, a man who steals in order to procure a drug which he cannot afford and which is needed to save his wife's life.[3] In each case the child's response was coded as external (e.g., "you can get put in jail for that"), internal (e.g., "that's not right, the man trusted you"), or indeterminate. The individual internal scores were then summed for all items, and the sum constituted the child's internalization score on moral judgments.

**Overt reactions to transgression.** Two measures were used to assess the child's overt reactions to transgression. The first was the teacher's report of how the child typically reacts when "caught doing something wrong." The categories included: "denies he did it"; "looks for someone else to blame"; "makes ex-

[3] This item was an adaptation of one used by Kohlberg (1963).

cuses"; "cries, looks sad, seems to feel bad"; "accepts responsibility for what he has done"; and "where possible tries on own initiative to rectify situation."

The second measure was a questionnaire item asked of the child's mother, similar to the item used by Sears et al. (1957). The question was: "when . . . has done something that (he) (she) knows you would not approve of, and you haven't found out about it yet, how often does (he) (she) come and tell you about it without your asking?" The mother was asked to check one of five alternatives, the extremes of which were "all the time" and "never."

Neither of these measures is ideal. The first has the disadvantage of asking for the child's reaction in the presence of an authority figure after detection. The second has the defect of being based on a report by the parent, who is the same person providing much of the discipline data and who is more likely to be influenced by "social desirability" than the teacher. Yet, the parent may well be the only person with enough background information and close contact with the child to make a knowledgeable estimate of how he acts before detection.

**Consideration for other children.** This measure was obtained from sociometric ratings by the children in the same classroom. Each child made three nominations for the child first, second, and third most "likely to care about the other children's feelings" and "to defend a child being made fun of by the group." The usual weights were used and the two scores summed.

**Identification.** Our major measure of identification was based on the child's responses to several items bearing on his orientation toward the parent: (a) admiration: "Which person do you admire or look up to the most?"; (b) desire to emulate: "Which person do you want to be like when you grow up?"; (c) perceived similarity: "Which person do you take after mostly?" Responses which mention the parent were coded as parent-identification responses and summed to obtain an overall identification score. It should be noted that this measure is designed to assess the child's conscious identification with the parents and not necessarily the unconscious identification of which Freud wrote.

**Coding procedure.** The story completion and moral judgment coding were done by one of the authors (HDS). To avoid contamination, the procedure was to go through all 444 records and code one item at a time. Especially difficult responses were coded independently by both authors, and discrepancies were resolved in conference.

Before the final coding was begun, coding reliabilities of 82 percent for maximum guilt, 73 percent for terminal guilt, and 91 percent for internal moral judgment were attained by the authors. These figures represent the percentage of agreement in giving high (top quartile), low (bottom quartile), and middle ratings. There were no extreme disagreements, that is, no instances in which a child received a high rating by one judge and a low rating by the other.

*Measures of Parent Practices*

Two reports of each parent's typical disciplinary practices were available—one from the children who reported the disciplinary practices of both parents, another from the mothers and fathers who each reported their own typical disciplinary practices. The reports from the children were collected during the third testing session in the schools. The parents were interviewed separately by trained female interviewers. The interview typically lasted about an hour.

Assessment of parental discipline was made in the following way. Each respondent (the child or parent) was asked to imagine four concrete situations: one in which the child delayed complying with a parental request to do something, a second in which the child was careless and destroyed something of value, a third in which he talked back to the parent, a fourth situation in which he had not done well in school. Following each situation was a list of from 10 to 14 practices. The respondent was asked to look over the list, then rate the absolute frequency of each and finally to indicate the first, second, and third practice most frequently used.[4] These three choices were weighted, and the scores summed across the four situations. The practices listed represented our three main categories. The first category, *power assertion,* included physical punishment, deprivation of material objects or privileges, the direct application of force, or threat of any of these. The term "power assertion" is used to highlight the fact that in using these techniques the parent seeks to control the child by capitalizing on his physical power or control over material resources (Hoffman, 1960). The second category, *love withdrawal,* included techniques whereby the parent more or less openly withdraws love by ignoring the child, turning his back on the child, re-

---

[4] Ratings of the absolute frequency were included primarily to make sure the respondent thought about all the items in the list before ranking them.

fusing to speak to him, explicitly stating that he dislikes the child, or isolating him. The third category, *induction regarding parents,* includes appeals to the child's guilt potential by referring to the consequences of the child's action for the parent. Included are such specifics as telling the child that his action has hurt the parent, that an object he damaged was valued by the parent, that the parent is disappointed, etc.

These lists were administered to each parent twice, once with instructions to select the techniques which he used at present, and next to select those he remembers using when the child was about 5 years old. Reports of past discipline were not asked of the children because it was unlikely that they could remember parent practices used several years before.

The above measure of induction is a limited one in that it only included instances where the parent made references to the consequences of a transgression for the parent himself. To supplement this, an additional measure of induction was constructed. This dealt with the parent's reaction to two situations in which the child's transgression had harmful consequences for another child. In the first situation the child, aged 5, aggresses against another child and destroys something the other child has built, causing the other child to cry. In the second situation the parent sees his child aged 6–10 making fun of another child. The parent was asked what he would have done or said in such a situation, and his reaction was coded along a 3-point scale for the degree to which he (the parent) makes reference to and shows concern for the *other* child's feelings. The scores were summed to arrive at a measure of the parent's use of *induction regarding peers.*

Assessment of the parent's affection

for the child was also obtained from the child and from the parent. The child was given a list of 19 behaviors indicating affection, approval, criticism, advice giving, and participation in child-centered activities and asked to indicate along a 4-point scale how often the parent engaged in such behaviors. The affection score was a simple weighted sum for the affection and approval items.

A slightly different measure was used to obtain affection data from the parents. They were given a list of eight behaviors indicating affection, approval, qualified approval, and material reward and asked to indicate along a 4-point scale how often they engaged in such behaviors when the child "did something good." The affection score was a weighted sum for the affection items.

**Background information.** The family's social class was determined from the child's responses to questions about the father's occupation and education. The distinction was basically between white collar and blue collar. In a few cases, families initially classified as middle class were later recategorized as lower class as a result of more accurate and specific information from the parent about the father's actual occupation and education.

**Data analysis.** The data were analyzed separately for middle-class boys, middle-class girls, lower-class boys, and lower-class girls. The procedure for each of these subsamples was to form two groups —one scoring high and one scoring low on each moral development index—and then to compare these groups on the child-rearing-practice scores obtained in the child reports and (in the case of the middle class only) the parent interviews. In forming the comparison groups, the

cutoff points were made as close as possible to the upper and lower quartile points within each subsample.

The test of significance used throughout was the median test.

**Control on IQ.** An important feature of this study, which was not true in the previous moral development research, was the control on intellectual ability which was instituted. Scores on either the California Test of Mental Maturity or the Iowa Test of Basic Skills were found—with social class controlled—to relate positively to internalized moral judgments and consideration for others, negatively to confession, and negatively to parent identification. This suggested that some of the findings previously reported in the literature might be the artifactual results of a lack of IQ control. In forming the high and low quartile groups for these variables we therefore controlled IQ—to the point of making the high-low differences in IQ negligible. Since IQ did not relate to guilt, there was no need to control IQ in the guilt analysis.

### Results and Discussion

To facilitate presentation of the results, the significant findings relating moral development indexes and parental discipline are summarized in Tables 1 and 2 for the middle-class sample and Tables 4 and 5 for the lower-class sample.[5] In-

[5] Seven pages of tables giving medians for each of the high and low quartile groups have been deposited with the American Documentation Institute. Order Document No. 9079 from the ADI Auxiliary Publications Project, Library of Congress, Washington, D. C. 20540. Remit in advance $1.25 for microfilm or $1.25 for photocopies and make checks payable to: Chief, Photoduplication Service, Library of Congress.

Table 1

**Statistically Significant Relations between Child's Morality Indexes and Mother's Discipline Techniques: Middle Class**

| Morality index | Power assertion | | | Love withdrawal | | | Induction re parent | | | Induction re peers[a] | | |
|---|---|---|---|---|---|---|---|---|---|---|---|---|
| | Boys | Girls | Sum | Boys | Girls | Sum | Boys | Girls | Sum | Boys | Girls | Sum |
| Guilt (child's response) | −p* | −c* −n* −p* | | | | | +c* | +p* | +c* +n* +p* | +p* | | +p** |
| Internal moral judgment (child's response) | −n* | −c* | | −c* | −c* | | | | +c* | | | |
| Confession (mother's report) | −p** | | −p** | | | | | +n* | +c* | | | |
| Accepts responsibility (teacher's report) | −c* | −c* −n* | −c** −n** | +n* | | | +c* +n* +p* | | +c** | | | |
| Consideration for other children (peers' ratings) | +n* | −p* | | −p* | | | | | +c* +n* +p* | +p** | +p** | |
| Identification (child's response) | −c* | −c* | −c** | | −n* | | +p* | +c* | +c* | | | |

Note: The data sources of the significant findings summarized in Tables 1, 2, and 4–6 are indicated as follows: c (child report), n (parent report of current practices), p (parent report of past practices).

[a] Data on induction regarding peers are incomplete since these data were obtained only from the parent reports of past practices.

$* \, p < .05.$
$** \, p < .01.$

Table 2

**Statistically Significant Relations between Child's Morality Indexes and Father's Discipline Techniques: Middle Class**

| Morality index | Power assertion | | | Love withdrawal | | | Induction re parent | | | Induction re peers | | |
|---|---|---|---|---|---|---|---|---|---|---|---|---|
| | Boys | Girls | Sum | Boys | Girls | Sum | Boys | Girls | Sum | Boys | Girls | Sum |
| Guilt (child's response) | | | | | | | | | | | | |
| Internal moral judgment (child's response) | | −c* | | | | | | | +c* | | | |
| Confession (mother's report) | +p* | +p* | | +c* | | | | −p* | −p* | | | |
| Accepts responsibility (teacher's report) | −c** | −c* | | | | +c* | | | | | | |
| Consideration for other children (peers' ratings) | +n* | +p* | | | | −c* | +c** | +c** | | | | |
| Identification (child's response) | | | | | | | | | | | | |

$* \, p < .05.$
$** \, p < .01.$

cluded in each table are relationships between each of the six indexes of moral development and each of the four measures of parental discipline: power assertion, love withdrawal, induction regarding parents, and induction regarding peers. Tables 1 and 2 are based on present discipline as reported by the child and present and past discipline as reported by the parent. Since the parent's report was not available for the lower-class sample, Tables 4 and 5 are based solely on the child's report of present parental discipline.

**Middle-class discipline.** The overall pattern of the findings in the middle class provides considerable support for our expectations, at least with respect to the mother's practices. Thus the frequent use of power assertion by the mother is consistently associated with weak moral development. The use of induction, on the other hand, is consistently associated with advanced moral development. This is true for both induction regarding parents and induction regarding peers. In all, there are a large number of significant findings especially for the major moral indexes—guilt and internalized moral judgments.

In contrast to the mothers, few significant findings were obtained for fathers —for boys as well as girls—and those that were obtained did not fit any apparent pattern.

A further step in the analysis of induction was to combine all indexes of this category into a composite index. The results, presented in Table 3, were quite striking in the case of mothers for all the moral indexes. Significant findings, all in the expected direction, were obtained for boys on guilt, internal moral judgments, confession, and acceptance of responsibility; and for girls on guilt, internal moral judgments, and consideration for others. When both

*Table 3*

**Statistically Significant Relations between Child's Morality Indexes and Parent's Composite Induction Score: Middle Class**

| | Mother's induction | | | Father's induction | | |
|---|---|---|---|---|---|---|
| *Morality index* | *Boys* | *Girls* | *Sum* | *Boys* | *Girls* | *Sum* |
| Guilt (child's response) | $+$* | $+$* | $+$* | | | |
| Internal moral judgment (child's response) | $+$* | $+$* | $+$** | | | |
| Confession (mother's report) | $+$** | | $+$*** | | | |
| Accepts responsibility (teacher's report) | $+$* | | $+$* | | | |
| Consideration for other children (peers' ratings) | | $+$** | $+$* | | | |
| Identification (child's response) | $+$* | | | | | |

* $p < .05$.
** $p < .01$.
*** $p < .005$.

sexes are combined, the findings are significant for all the moral indexes. The findings on identification are significant only for boys, however.

In contrast to induction, love withdrawal relates infrequently to the moral indexes (see Table 1). Further, in most cases in which significant relations between love withdrawal and moral development do occur, they prove to be negative. Taken as a whole, the importance of the distinction between love withdrawal and induction has been clearly demonstrated by these findings.

In sum it is a pattern of infrequent use of power assertion and frequent use of induction by middle-class mothers which generally appears to facilitate the facets of morality included in this study.[6]

There is, however, one major exception to this pattern. The peers' reports of the boy's consideration for other children is positively related to the mother's report of their present use of power assertion (Table 1). A possible explanation of this finding is that our measure of consideration is a poor one, especially for the boys. In particular, there is no built-in provision to assure that the behavior is based on internal motivation. The

[6] The question might be raised here as to the extent to which these findings should be interpreted as independent. Do induction and power assertion exert independent influence on morality, or are they but two aspects of the same influence; for example, do the measures used require that someone high on induction is necessarily low on power assertion? The findings in Table 1 suggest the influences are largely independent. That is, there are only a few instances in which negative power assertion findings and positive induction findings for the same subsample were obtained with the same measure. In most cases the findings for the two types of discipline were obtained with different measures, and in some instances a finding was obtained for one but not the other (e.g., guilt in boys relates to induction, but not to power assertion).

motive behind such behavior in the case of boys might instead often be a need for approval by peers. Why this should be the case for boys and not for girls remains unclear. It should be noted, however, that consideration is a more deviant value for boys than girls. Evidence for this is provided from a measure of values administered to the children. The largest sex difference found was on the consideration item ("goes out of his way to help others"). The girls valued this trait more than the boys ($p<.001$). Thus consideration does appear to have a different meaning for the two sexes.

**Lower-class discipline.** In discussing the lower-class findings the lack of parent interview data must be kept in mind. Nevertheless, there are several very apparent contrasts with the middle-class sample. Foremost among these is the general paucity of significant relationships between the child's moral development and his report of parental discipline. This is especially striking in the case of the mother's discipline. Furthermore, of those significant relationships that emerge, two are inconsistent with our expectations. First, as with the middle-class sample, the boy's consideration is related positively to the mother's use of power assertion. Second, in contrast with the findings for the middle-class boys, guilt is positively associated with the mother's use of love withdrawal, but unrelated to the mother's use of power assertion or induction. In summary, our expectations were not confirmed for the lower-class sample, and no general conclusion may be drawn.

The infrequent relationships between the child's moral development and the mother's discipline, compared to the middle-class sample, suggest that the

Table 4

**Statistically Significant Relations between Child's Morality Indexes and Mother's Discipline: Lower Class**

| Morality index | Power assertion | | | Love withdrawal | | | Induction re parent | | |
|---|---|---|---|---|---|---|---|---|---|
| | Boys | Girls | Sum | Boys | Girls | Sum | Boys | Girls | Sum |
| Guilt (child's response) | | | | +c* | | | | | |
| Internal moral judgment (child's response) | | | | | | | +c* | | |
| Accepts responsibility (teacher's report) | | | | | | | | | |
| Consideration for other children (peers' ratings) | +c* | | | | | | +c* | | |
| Identification (child's response) | | | | | −c* | −c* | | | |

Note: Interview data were not obtained from the lower-class parents. Thus all entries in Tables 3 and 4 are based on child reports. For the same reason lower-class data on confession and on induction regarding peers were unavailable.

\* $p < .05$.

Table 5

**Statistically Significant Relations between Child's Morality Indexes and Father's Discipline: Lower Class**

| Morality index | Power assertion | | | Love withdrawal | | | Induction re parent | | |
|---|---|---|---|---|---|---|---|---|---|
| | Boys | Girls | Sum | Boys | Girls | Sum | Boys | Girls | Sum |
| Guilt (child's response) | −c* | | | | +c* | | | | |
| Internal moral judgment (child's response) | | | | | | | | | |
| Accepts responsibility (teacher's report) | | | | | | | | | |
| Consideration for other children (peers' ratings) | | | | | | | | | |
| Identification (child's response) | −c* | | −c* | | | | +c* | | +c* |

\* $p < .05$.

lower-class mother's discipline may be less crucial and singular a variable. This in turn may be due to several factors. First, the mothers more often work full time in the lower than in the middle class. Second, the combination of large families and less space may result in the parent and child interacting with many other people besides each other. Third, according to the more traditional family structure usually found in the lower class (e.g., Bronfenbrenner, 1958), the father is more often the ultimate disciplining agent. In our sample, for example, boys more often reported that their mothers had the fathers do the disciplining ("says she'll tell your father") in the lower class than in the middle class ($p < .01$). Fourth, lower-class children are encouraged to spend more time outside the home than middle-class children. For all these reasons the socializing process may be more diffuse in the lower class; that is, it may be more equally shared by the mother with the father, with siblings, members of the extended family, the child's peers, and others.[7]

Further research comparing the two classes needs to be performed. One might conjecture that because of the more diffuse socialization process in the lower class the basis of internalization may be quite different for children in the two classes, with consequent differences in the kind of morality that develops.

**Affection.** The relations between affection and the six moral indexes are presented in Table 6. The most notable features of this table are first, as expected, the relationships are positive; second, most of the findings, as with the discipline data, were obtained for middle-class mothers. It should also be noted that most of the findings are based on the child's report.

**Role of the father.** Several studies of delinquency (e.g., Glueck & Glueck, 1950; McCord & McCord, 1958; Miller, 1958) suggest that the father is important in the development of internal controls. Our findings, especially in the middle class, seem to suggest that this is not so. Relatively few significant relationships were obtained between paternal discipline and the child's morality, and sev-

[7] Another possible explanation for the paucity of findings in the lower class is that the lower-class children are very low on morality. Thus if the upper quartile of the lower class on morality were like the lower quartile of the middle class, there would be no reason to expect similar associations for the two classes. This possibility can be discounted since there was no overlap between the lower-class upper quartile and the middle-class lower quartile. And although there was a general tendency for the lower class to be lower on morality than the middle class, the difference was significant only for internal moral judgment and consideration for others, and only for girls.

eral were in a direction opposite to that expected.

Of course, it is possible that the role of the father is more important than indicated in this study. For example, the father might provide the cognitive content of the standards by direct instruction rather than by his discipline techniques. Lacking data on direct instruction, we could not test this possibility. Another possibility is that the role of the father is a less direct one. That is, he may affect the moral development of the child by his relationship to the mother and his influence on the discipline techniques chosen by the mother. This is indicated in a study of preschool children where evidence was found suggesting that women who are treated power-assertively by their husbands tend to react by using power-assertive discipline on their children (Hoffman, 1963c). It may also be that the father's role is ordinarily latent in its effects and only becomes manifest under exceptional circumstances, such as those often associated with delinquency. That is, under normal conditions with the father away working most of the time and the mother handling most of the disciplining, as in our middle-class sample, the father's importance may lie mainly in providing an adequate role model that operates in the background as a necessary supporting factor. Under these conditions, the specific lines along which the child's moral development proceeds may be determined primarily by the mother's discipline. An adequate role model is lacking, however, in extreme cases, as when there is no father, when the father is a criminal, or when the father is at home but unemployed, and this may account for the findings obtained in the delinquency research.

Methodological issues. Any study of child rearing and moral development that relies on indexes of discipline and morality from the same source is open to the criticism that the relationships that emerge are due to the lack of independence of the sources. If that source is the child himself, the suspicion might be held that the child's report of parental discipline is simply another projective measure of the child's personality. It should be noted that in the present study the relationships between the child's morality and the parent's report of discipline were generally in the same direction as those involving the child's report of discipline. (We refer here to the middle-class-mother findings.) In addition, over half the significant findings for each sex involve relations between measures obtained from different respondents.

Further support for our findings comes from a recent review in which our three-fold discipline classification was applied to the previous research (Hoffman, in press). Since most studies used a power-assertive–nonpower-assertive dichotomy, as indicated earlier, the raw data were examined (and recoded where necessary) to determine whether love withdrawal, induction, or some other form of nonpower-assertion was responsible for the findings. The results were clearly consistent with ours. Since a wide range of theoretical and methodological approaches were involved in the studies reviewed, our confidence in the findings reported here is considerably strengthened.

A common problem also relevant to the present design is that no definitive conclusion may be drawn about causal direction of the relationships obtained. Any solution to this will have to wait upon application of the experimental method or longitudinal studies. Never-

Table 6

**Statistically Significant Relations between Child's Morality Indexes and Parent's Affection**

| Morality index | Middle class | | | | | | Lower class | | | | | |
|---|---|---|---|---|---|---|---|---|---|---|---|---|
| | Mothers | | | Fathers | | | Mothers | | | Fathers | | |
| | Boys | Girls | Sum | Boys | Girls | Sum | Boys | Girls | Sum | Boys | Girls | Sum |
| Guilt (child's response) | +c* | | +c* | | | | | | | | | |
| Internal moral judgment (child's response) | | +c* | +n* | | | +n* | | | | | | |
| Confession (mother's report) | +c* | | +c* | | | | | | +p* | | | |
| Accepts responsibility (teacher's report) | | +n* | | | +n* | | | | | | | |
| Consideration for other children (peers' ratings) | +p* | +c* | +c* +n* | | | | | +c* | | | +c* | |
| Identification (child's response) | +c** | +c** | +c** | | | | | +c* | | | | |

\* $p < .05$.
\*\* $p < .01$.

theless, some support for the proposition that discipline affects moral development, rather than the reverse, may be derived from the fact that several findings bear on the use of discipline in the past. If these reports are assumed to be reasonably valid, to argue that the child's moral development elicits different discipline patterns (rather than the reverse) necessitates the further assumption that the child's morality has not changed basically from early childhood. This is an unlikely assumption in view of common observations (e.g., about the child's changing acceptance of responsibility for transgression) and the findings about the developmental course of moral judgments obtained by Piaget (1948), Kohlberg (1963), and others.

**Theoretical discussion.** In this section we will analyze the disciplinary encounter into what we believe to be some of its most basic cognitive and emotional factors.

First, any disciplinary encounter generates a certain amount of anger in the child by preventing him from completing or repeating a motivated act. Power assertion is probably most likely to arouse intense anger in the child because it frustrates not only the act but also the child's need for autonomy. It dramatically underscores the extent to which the child's freedom is circumscribed by the superior power and resources of the adult world. This is no doubt exacerbated by the fact that power assertion is likely to be applied abruptly with few explanations or compensations offered to the child. (The empirical evidence for a positive relation between power assertion and anger has been summarized by Becker, 1964.)

Second, a disciplinary technique also provides the child with (a) a model for discharging that anger, and may provide him with (b) an object against which to discharge his anger. The disciplinary act itself constitutes the model for discharging the anger which the child may imitate.

Third, as much animal and human learning research has now shown, what is learned will depend on the stimuli to which the organism is compelled to attend. Disciplinary techniques explicitly or implicitly provide such a focus. Both love withdrawal and power assertion direct the child to the consequences of his behavior for the actor, that is, for the child himself, and to the external agent producing these consequences. Induction, on the other hand, is more apt to focus the child's attention on the consequences of his actions for others, the parent, or some third party. This factor should be especially important in determining the content of the child's standards. That is, if transgressions are followed by induction, the child will learn that the important part of transgressions consists of the harm done to others.

Fourth, to be effective the technique must enlist already existing emotional and motivational tendencies within the child. One such resource is the child's need for love. This factor depends on the general affective state of the parent-child relationship, the importance of which may be seen in the consistent relationship obtained between affection and the moral indexes (Table 6). Given this affective relationship, some arousal of the need for love may be both necessary for and capable of motivating the child to give up his needs of the moment and attend to (and thus be influenced by) the parent's discipline technique. Too much arousal, however, may produce intense feelings of anxiety over loss of love which may disrupt the child's response especially to the cognitive elements of the technique. All three types of discipline communicate some parental disapproval and are thus capable of arousing the child's need for love. But it is possible that only inductions can arouse this need to an optimal degree because the threat of love withdrawal implicit in inductions is relatively mild. Also, it is embedded in the context of a technique which explicitly or implicitly suggests a means of reparation. Inductions are thus less likely to disrupt the child's response —as well as his general affective relationship with the parent—than either love withdrawal which may arouse undue anxiety, or power assertion which arouses anger and other disruptive affects.

The second emotional resource, empathy, has long been overlooked by psychologists as a possible important factor in socialization. Empathy has been observed in children to occur much before the child's moral controls are firmly established (e.g., Murphy, 1937). We believe that it is a potentially important emotional resource because it adds to the aroused need for love the pain which the child vicariously experiences from having harmed another, thus intensifying his motivatoin to learn moral rules and control his impulses. Of the three types of discipline under consideration, induction seems most capable of enlisting the child's natural proclivities for empathy in the struggle to control his impulses. As indicated in greater detail elsewhere (Hoffman, 1963b; Hoffman, in press; Hoffman & Saltzstein, 1960), we view induction as both directing the child's attention to the other person's

pain, which should elicit an empathic response, and communicating to the child that he caused that pain. Without the latter, the child might respond empathically but dissociate himself from the causal act. The coalescence of empathy and the awareness of being the causal agent should produce a response having the necessary cognitive (self-critical) and affective properties of guilt.

It follows from this analysis that power assertion is least effective in promoting development of moral standards and internalization of controls because it elicits intense hostility in the child and simultaneously provides him with a model for expressing that hostility outwardly and a relatively legitimate object against which to express it. It furthermore makes the child's need for love less salient and functions as an obstacle to the arousal of empathy. Finally, it sensitizes the child to the punitive responses of adult authorities, thus contributing to an externally focused moral orientation.

Induction not only avoids these deleterious effects of power assertion, but also is the technique most likely to optimally motivate the child to focus his attention on the harm done others as the salient aspect of his transgressions, and thus to help integrate his capacity for empathy with the knowledge of the human consequences of his own behavior. Repeated experiences of this kind should help sensitize the child to the human consequences of his behavior which may then come to stand out among the welter of emotional and other stimuli in the situation. The child is thus gradually enabled to pick out on his own, without help from others, the effects of his behavior, and to react with an internally based sense of guilt. Induction in sum should be the most facilitative form of discipline for building long-term controls which are independent of external sanctions, and the findings would seem to support this view.

Love withdrawal stands midway between the other two techniques in promoting internalization. It provides a more controlled form of aggression by the parent than power assertion, but less than induction. It employs the affectionate relationship between child and parent perhaps to a greater degree than the other two techniques, but in a way more likely than they to produce a disruptive anxiety response in the child. However, it falls short of induction in effectiveness by not including the cognitive material needed to heighten the child's awareness of wrongdoing and facilitate his learning to generalize accurately to other relevant situations, and by failing to capitalize on his capacity for empathy.

The weak and inconsistent findings for love withdrawal suggest that anxiety over loss of love may be a less important factor in the child's internalization than formerly thought to be the case. Before drawing this conclusion, however, the possibility that love withdrawal is only effective when the parent also freely expresses affection, as suggested by Sears et al. (1957), should be considered. We were able to test this hypothesis by examining the relation between love withdrawal and the moral indexes within the group of subjects who were above and below the median on affection, and also within the upper and lower quartile groups. The results do not corroborate the hypothesis: the relations between love withdrawal and the moral indexes do not differ for the high- and low-affection groups.

In an earlier study with preschool children, however, love withdrawal was found to relate negatively to the expression of overt hostility in the nursery school (Hoffman, 1963b). It was possible to make a similar test in the present study since teacher ratings of overt hostility were available. Here, too, love withdrawal related negatively to hostility outside the home ($p < .05$).[8] We also found that love withdrawal is used more when the child expresses hostility toward the parent than in other types of discipline situations. These findings suggest that the contribution of love withdrawal to moral development may be to attach anxiety directly to the child's hostile impulses, thus motivating him to keep them under control. Psychoanalytic theory may thus be correct after all in the importance assigned love withdrawal in the socialization of the child's impulses. Our data, however, do not support the psychoanalytic view that identification is a necessary mediating process. That is, we found no relation between love withdrawal and identification (Tables 1–4). It remains possible, of course, that a form of unconscious identification which may not be tapped by our more consciously focused measure serves to mediate between the parent's love withdrawal and the child's inhibition of

[8] Power assertion related positively to hostility ($p < .05$), and induction showed a slight nonsignificant negative relation.

Some relevant experimental evidence is also available. Gordon and Cohn (1963) found that doll-play aggression expressed by children in response to frustration decreased after exposure to a story in which the central figure, a dog, searches unsuccessfully for friends with whom to play. Assuming the story arouses feelings of loneliness and anxiety over separation in the child—feelings akin to the emotional response to love-withdrawal techniques—these findings may be taken as further support for the notion that love withdrawal may contribute to the inhibition of hostility.

hostile impulses—as suggested in psychoanalytic theory.

In any case, our data do tend to show that love withdrawal alone is an insufficient basis for the development of those capacities—especially for guilt and moral judgment—which are critical characteristics of a fully developed conscience.[9]

## References

ALLINSMITH, W., & GREENING, T. C. Guilt over anger as predicted from parental discipline: A study of superego development. *American Psychologist*, 1955, **10**, 320. (Abstract)

ARONFREED, J. The nature, variety, and social patterning of moral responses to transgression. *Journal of Abnormal and Social Psychology*, 1961, **63**, 223–241.

BECKER, W. Consequences of different kinds of parent discipline. In M. L. & L. W. Hoffman (Eds.), *Review of child development research*. Vol. 1. New York: Russell Sage Foundation, 1964. Pp. 169–208.

BRONFENBRENNER, U. Socialization and social class through time and space. In E. E. Maccoby, T. M. Newcomb, & E. L. Hartley (Eds.), *Readings in social psychology*. New York: Holt, 1958. Pp. 400–425.

GLUECK, S., & GLUECK, E. *Unraveling juvenile delinquency*. New York: Commonwealth Fund, 1950.

GORDON, J. E., & COHN, F. Effect of fantasy arousal of affiliation drive on doll-play aggression. *Journal of Abnormal and Social Psychology*, 1963, **66**, 301–307.

*HILL, W. F. Learning theory and the acquisition of values. *Psychological Review*, 1960, **67**, 317–331.

HOFFMAN, M. L. Power assertion by the parent and its impact on the child. *Child Development*, 1960, **31**, 129–143.

HOFFMAN, M. L. Child-rearing practices and moral development: Generalizations from empirical research. *Child Development*, 1963, **34**, 295–318. (a)

HOFFMAN, M. L. Parent discipline and the child's consideration for others. *Child Development*, 1963, **34**, 573–588. (b)

HOFFMAN, M. L. Personality, family structure, and social class as antecedents of parental power assertion. *Child Development*, 1963, **34**, 869–884. (c)

HOFFMAN, M. L. Socialization practices and the development of moral character. In M. L. Hoffman (Ed.), *Character development in the child*. Chicago: Aldine, in press.

HOFFMAN, M. L., & SALTZSTEIN, H. D. Parent practices and the development of children's moral orientations. In W. E. Martin (Chm.), Parent behavior and children's personality development: Current project research. Symposium presented at American Psychological Association, Chicago, September 1, 1960.

KOHLBERG, L. The development of children's orientations toward a moral order. *Vita Humana*, 1963, **6**, 11–33.

McCORD, J., & McCORD, W. The effect of parental role model on criminality. *Journal of Social Issues*, 1958, **14**, 66–75.

MILLER, W. B. Lower-class culture as a generating milieu of gang delinquency. *Journal of Social Issues*, 1958, **14**, 5–19.

MURPHY, L. B. *Social behavior and child personality*. New York: Columbia University Press, 1937.

*PIAGET, J. *The moral judgment of the child*. Glencoe, Ill.: Free Press, 1948.

*SEARS, R. R., MACCOBY, F. F., & LEVIN, H. (Eds.), *Patterns of child rearing*. Evanston, Ill.: Row, Peterson, 1957.

* [Asterisks indicate works that are reprinted, in whole or in part, in this volume.]

[9] It should be noted that love withdrawal might relate positively to guilt as defined in psychoanalytic terms, that is, as an irrational response to one's own impulses. Clearly our concept of guilt is quite different from the psychoanalytic, pertaining as it does to the real human consequences of one's actions.

# CROSS-CULTURAL DATA

brenner, 1960). Since the Mead-Benedict position requires that parents be loving and use love withdrawal as a technique, while Freudian theory requires only contact, either brutal or loving, the behavior of males in cultures where there is extensive father-son contact but an absence of love would be a crucial test of these two positions.

## Reference

Bronfenbrenner, U. Freudian theories of identification and their derivatives. *Child Development*, 1960, **31,** 15–40.

## Introduction

Two papers are presented in this subsection. The first, by Whiting, makes use of a basically Freudian frame of reference (though Whiting also shows concern for the Mead-Benedict position) to account for cross-cultural differences in mechanisms of social control. The second paper, by Bacon, Child, and Barry, is an extension of the same approach and makes use of many of the same data. Freudian theory is supported by these data, since the cultures allowing the least adequate resolution of the oedipal situation, in terms of amount of father-son contact, also have the highest crime rates. However, these data also are supportive of the Mead-Benedict position and, for that matter, can be handled by non-Freudian theories of identification (see Bronfen-

# 20

# The superego: A mechanism of social control

## by John W. M. Whiting

The . . . mechanism of social control to be considered, the superego or conscience, has been a subject of considerable interest in recent years, particularly as it relates to the process of identification. Most research in this field rests on the assumption that internalized moral values are a consequence of identification with the parents, and that guilt, remorse, or the readiness to accept blame is a measurable consequence of the degree of parental identification.

A number of specific hypotheses have been put forward as to the child-rearing factors which should produce strong parental identification and subsequent guilt, and empirical research has supported some of these hypotheses.

Freud, in his original formulation of identification, suggested that it was a conversion of cathexis. This has been interpreted by some theorists to mean that identification should be related to parental warmth or nurturance. Empirical tests of this hypothesis have been generally negative. Sears, Maccoby, and Levin

Reprinted from John W. M. Whiting, "Sorcery, Sin, and the Superego: A Cross-Cultural Study of Some Mechanisms of Social Control," in M. R. Jones, ed., *Nebraska Symposium on Motivation* (Lincoln, Neb.: University of Nebraska Press, 1959), pp. 187–193. Copyright 1959 by the University of Nebraska Press. Reprinted by permission of the author and the University of Nebraska Press.

(7), using the mother's estimate of the strength of a child's conscience, found a positive relationship between these two variables which, although significant at the 5 percent level, yielded a correlation of but .10, thus accounting for only 1 percent of the variance; Whiting and Child, using an index of guilt to be discussed below, found no relation at all between these variables; and Heinicke (5), using doll play to measure guilt, found a significant negative relation between these variables.

Another interpretation of the Freudian theory has produced more empirical support. This interpretation relates to the technique of discipline. The hypothesis that the relative importance of love-oriented or psychological techniques of discipline should be a precondition for guilt has been confirmed by Sears, Maccoby, and Levin (7), when it is employed by relatively warm mothers; by Whiting and Child (9); by Allinsmith and Greening (2); and by Faigin and Hollenberg (3).

The age of socialization has been considered as a variable in a number of studies. Allinsmith (1) found that early weaning and early toilet training were related to high guilt. Whiting and Child (9) found that early weaning, early sex training, and early independence training were the best predictors of their cross-cultural measure of guilt.

Finally, a number of studies have considered the status relationship between parents. Faigin and Hollenberg (3) in a comparative study of three societies in New Mexico found evidence that guilt is positively related to the prestige of the father. Heinicke (5) found guilt to be positively related to the mother's evaluation of the father. Although Goethals (4) in a similar study did not confirm this relationship, his findings were in the predicted direction; however, they did not reach an acceptable level of confidence.

It is the last of these hypotheses that will be considered here. In a recent theoretical paper on identification and the control of resources (8), this has been labelled the *status envy* hypothesis. Suggested by Freud's formulation of the Oedipal conflict, the hypothesis is simply that a person will identify with, and hence accept the moral values of, any person who is a successful rival with respect to resources which he covets but cannot control. Specifically, here it is assumed that where a child and a father frequently compete for love, affection, recognition, food, care, and even sexual gratification from the mother, and where the father is often successful—that is, he is nurtured by the mother at a time when the child is in need—then the child should envy the father and hence identify with him.

Variations in family structure and household composition luckily provide an opportunity to test this hypothesis. Murdock (6) in a recent study of 565 societies has rated these two variables. He made a number of distinctions as to a family structure, but the distinction between monogamy and polygyny is the one of particular relevance here. By his definition, any society in which 20 percent or more of the families consist of a man and two or more wives has been considered polygynous, less than 20 percent as having either limited polygyny or monogamy. There are, in his sample, 232 polygynous societies, 184 societies with limited polygyny, and 134 societies with strict monogamy. For the test of this hypothesis we have combined limited polygyny with monogamy, thus

yielding a total of 318 monogamous societies.

The monogamous family is familiar to us. It epitomizes the eternal triangle. In this type of family, the three statuses—father, mother, and children—are bound in intimate relation with one another. It is in such a family that father and children are most likely to compete for the love and affection of the mother.

Polygynous families are organized in a different pattern. Here the father has two or more wives to care for him, and rivalry with his children should therefore be cut in half at least. In such a family, when the child is tired, hungry, and demanding attention from his mother at the same time that the father is in need of attention, the mother can say to him: "I'm busy. Get it from your other wife." A contrast between monogamous and polygynous societies should provide a test, then, of the status-envy hypothesis.

Household structure also provides a definition of the conditions which should maximize status envy between father and child. Murdock has again made a number of distinctions as to the relatives who live together under one roof. Again we are not concerned with all the fine distinctions that he has made, but have grouped them, with reference to their bearing on our hypothesis, in the following four categories: nuclear, extended, polygynous, and mother-child. In his sample, these types occur with the following frequencies:

172 extended households
141 nuclear households
123 mother-child households
 89 polygynous households

Some of the extended families, however, are also polygynous, and we have reclassified them on this basis. Thus, the proportion of extended families stated above is an overestimate, and that of polygynous families an underestimate.

Again, we are familiar with the nuclear family household. Here the mother, father, and children eat, sleep, and entertain under one roof. Grandparents and siblings of the parents live elsewhere. Monogamous extended families consist of two or more nuclear families living together under one roof. A typical extended family consists of an aged couple with their married sons or daughters together with their spouses and children. The polygynous household consists of a man living with his wives and their children. Finally, the mother-child household occurs in societies with polygyny where each wife has a separate house and establishment and lives in it with her children. In these societies, the father either has a hut of his own, sleeps in the men's club house, or rotates among the houses of his various wives. It is of particular importance here that the husband generally does not sleep in the house of any wife who has a nursing infant, and also that in these societies the nursing period lasts from two to three years.

Considering these household arrangements in the light of the status-envy hypothesis, it seems clear that maximal status rivalry between father and child should occur in nuclear households; somewhat less in monogamous extended families where the presence of grandparents and married siblings provides a condition of diffused nurturance and a less intense and intimate relationship among the members of the nuclear family. With polygynous households the fact of polygyny, as has been shown above, decreases the intensity of the rivalry even more, but not so much as in the mother-child household where the father is seldom present to compete with his children for the love and affection of the mother. We would predict, then, that if our hypothesis is correct, the greatest identification and guilt should be found in societies with nuclear households, next with monogamous extended households, next with polygynous households, and least of all with mother-child households.

To test this hypothesis the measure of guilt used in Whiting and Child has been chosen as a dependent variable. The general definition of this measure was stated as follows:

> As a cultural index of the degree to which guilt feelings characterize the members of a society, we have used a measure of the extent to which a person who gets sick blames himself for having gotten sick. Self-recrimination, as a response to illness, seemed to us a probably useful index of the degree to which guilt feelings are strong and widely generalized (p. 227).

The details of making this judgment are presented in Whiting and Child (pp. 221 ff.) and will not be reviewed here. It should be stated, however, that the intent of this index was to obtain an estimate of the degree to which a member of any society was ready to accept personal responsibility for wrong-doing. It should be pointed out that this is by no means a direct measure of such a tendency, and although we are not satisfied with this method of measuring the strength of the superego, it is the only one presently available.

A test of the status-envy hypothesis as measured by family organization and household membership is presented in Table 1. It will be seen from this table

Table 1

| PATIENT RESPONSIBILITY | FAMILY AND HOUSEHOLD STRUCTURE Murdock (14) | | | |
|---|---|---|---|---|
| Whiting and Child (23) | Family: Household: Polygynous Mother-Child | Polygynous Polygynous | Monogamous Extended | Monogamous Nuclear |
| High | | | 15 Hopi | 16 Alorese |
| | | | | 13 Chamorro |
| | | | | 14 Lakher |
| | | 11 Arapesh | 10 Lepcha | 14 Manus |
| | | 11 Chiricahua | 21 Maori | 17 Navaho |
| | 12 Dahomeans | 14 Kwoma | 10 Papago | 18 Pukapuka |
| | 9 Azande | 5 Comanche | 3 Chenchu | 5 Trobrianders |
| | 8 Bena | 8 Kwakiutl | 9 Samoans | |
| | 3 Chagga | 6 Tanala | | |
| | 6 Kurtachi | 9 Teton | | |
| Low | 5 Lesu | 8 Wogeo | | |
| | 4 Thonga | | | |
| % High | 14% | 38% | 67% | 86% |

This table shows the relationship between family and household structure with patient responsibility, the index of guilt used by Whiting and Child. The number before each society is its value for this score. The order of the percentages is as predicted, and the differences between monogamous and polygynous family structure are significant. P = .009 (Fischer exact test).

that our hypothesis is rather strikingly confirmed. Only one monogamous nuclear household society had low guilt, and only one polygynous mother-child society had high guilt. The proportions of societies having high guilt are in the predicted order. Both the contrast between polygynous and monogamous societies and that between nuclear and mother-child households are highly significant statistically, P values being .009 and .015 respectively.

These social structure variables, however, do not control all the variance, and it would be interesting to discover how the other variables presumed to be related to identification and guilt interact with the conditions of status envy. To test this hypothesis, the societies were divided by family structure into those which were polygynous and monogamous. Tests were then run between pa-

tient responsibility and the following variables: degree of initial nurturance, the relative importance of love-oriented techniques, and the age of weaning. The first two of these factors did not yield a significant relationship, although there was a strong tendency for patient responsibility to be related to low initial indulgence in monogamous societies, but not in polygynous societies. This relationship should be explored on a larger sample. The interaction between family structure and age of weaning, however, did yield significant results even on our small sample, and is presented in Table 2.

As is shown in this table, monogamous societies with early weaning are more likely to have high patient responsibility than monogamous societies with late weaning. Although a nonparametric test of this relationship does not yield a sig-

*Table 2*

| FAMILY STRUCTURE (Murdock) | AGE OF WEANING (Whiting and Child) | PATIENT RESPONSIBILITY (Whiting and Child) | |
|---|---|---|---|
| | | Low | High |
| Monogamous | Early | 1 | 6 |
| | Late | 4 | 2 |
| Polygynous | Early | 5 | 1 |
| | Late | 6 | 3 |

This table shows the interaction between family structure and age of weaning in producing patient responsibility. It will be seen that the age of weaning is related to patient responsibility only in monogamous societies. Although a nonparametric test does not yield significant results, a Pearson $r$ between these variables yields a coefficient of $-.71$, which is significant at the 5% point.

nificant result, a Pearson product moment correlation gives an $r$ value of $-.71$, which is significant at the 5 percent level of confidence. This value for $r$ can be compared with $-.42$, the value reported in Whiting and Child for the same relationship when monogamous and polygynous societies were grouped. This is not surprising, since it will be seen from the above table that the age of weaning has no effect on patient responsibility in polygynous societies. In fact, the relationship is in the reverse direction.

Thus, if patient responsibility be taken as an index of identification and guilt, cross-cultural evidence supports the hypothesis that the maximization of rivalry between father and child and early socialization combine to produce the strong internalization of moral values and readiness to accept blame.

## References

1. ALLINSMITH, W. Conscience and conflict: The moral force in personality. *Child Development*, 1957, **28**, 469–476.
2. ALLINSMITH, W., & GREENING, T. C. Guilt over anger as predicted from parental discipline: A study of superego development. *American Psychologist*, 1955, **10**, 320. (Abstract)
3. FAIGIN, H., & HOLLENBERG, E. Child rearing and the internalization of moral values. Unpublished typescript, Harvard University, 1953.
4. GOETHALS, G. W. A study of the relationship between family esteem patterns and identification, the internalization of values, and aggression of a group of four-year-old children. Unpublished doctoral dissertation, Graduate School of Education, Harvard University, 1953.
5. HEINICKE, C. M. Some antecedents and correlates of guilt and fear in young boys. Unpublished doctoral dissertation, Department of Social Relations, Harvard University, 1953.
6. MURDOCK, G. P. World ethnographic sample. *American Anthropologist*, 1957, **59**, 664–687.
*7. SEARS, R. R., MACCOBY, E. E., & LEVIN, H. (Eds.) *Patterns of child rearing.* Evanston, Ill.: Row, Peterson, 1957.
8. WHITING, J. W. M. Resource mediation and learning by identification. Unpublished theoretical paper, Laboratory of Human Development, Harvard University, 1959.
9. WHITING, J. W. M., & CHILD, I. L. *Child training and personality: A cross-cultural study.* New Haven: Yale University Press, 1953.

* [Asterisks indicate works that are reprinted, in whole or in part, in this volume.]

## 21

# A cross-cultural study of correlates of crime[1]

*by Margaret K. Bacon,*
*Irvin L. Child,*
*and Herbert Barry, III*

A number of researchers have analyzed the sociological and psychological background of delinquents and criminals and compared them with a noncriminal control population, in order to discover what conditions give rise to criminal behavior; for a recent review, see Robison (1960). The present paper reports on variations among a sample of preliterate societies in the frequency of crime, in order to determine what other known features of these societies are associated with the occurrence of crime. The cross-cultural technique (Whiting, 1954), in which each society is taken as a single case, is a unique method for studying crime and has certain advantages: The index of frequency of crime in a society represents the average among its many individuals and over a span of many years, so that the measure is likely to be more stable and reliable than a measure of criminal tendency in a single individual. Some of the cultural features which may be related to crime show wider variations among societies than within a single society, permitting a more comprehensive test of their significance. Results which are consistent in a number of diverse societies may be applied to a great variety of cultural conditions instead of being limited to a single cultural setting.

If certain cultural features foster the development of criminal behavior, they should be found preponderantly in societies with a high frequency of crime; factors which inhibit crime should be found largely in societies which are low in crime. Thus the cross-cultural method may help us discover psychological and sociological variables which have a causal relationship to the development of crime; the importance of these variables may then also be tested intraculturally. On the other hand, variables identified as possible causes of crime within our society may be tested for broader significance by the cross-cultural method.

The possible causal factors which we have explored are principally concerned with child-training practices, economy, and social structure. Hypotheses concerning these factors, as they have been presented by other writers or as they have occurred to us, will be described in connection with the presentation of our results.

Margaret K. Bacon, Irvin L. Child and Herbert Barry, III, "A Cross-Cultural Study of Correlates of Crime," *Journal of Abnormal and Social Psychology*, 66, 1963, 291–300. Copyright 1963 by the American Psychological Association, and reproduced by permission.

[1] This research was supported by grants from the Social Science Research Council; the Ford Foundation; and the National Institute of Mental Health, United States Public Health Service (M-2681).

We wish to express appreciation to Selden D. Bacon for many helpful suggestions in the preparation of this manuscript, and to James Sakoda for generously providing us with a program permitting rapid calculation of our results on the IBM 709. We also wish to thank Pearl Davenport, Hatsumi Maretzki, and Abraham Rosman, who made many of the ratings employed in our calculations.

## Method

**Sample.** The sample used in this study consists of 48 societies, mostly preliterate, scattered over the world. They were taken from a larger group of 110 societies which were selected on the basis of geographical diversity and adequacy of information on aboriginal child-training practices. The present sample of 48 consists of those societies whose ethnographies were searched and found to provide sufficient information to permit comparative ratings on criminal behavior by three independent research workers.[2]

**Ratings.** We have included two types of crime in our study: *theft* and *personal crime*. These two were chosen because they are relatively easy to identify and almost universal in occurrence. Also, they represent two quite different types of

[2] The 48 societies included in the study are as follows: Africa—Ashanti, Azande, Bena, Chagga, Dahomeans, Lovedu, Mbundu, Thonga; Asia—Andamanese, Baiga, Chenchu, Chukchee, Lepcha, Muria, Tanala, Yakut; North America—Cheyenne, Comanche, Flatheads, Hopi, Jamaicans (Rocky Roaders), Kaska, Kwakiutl, Navaho, Papago, Tepoztlan, Western Apache; South America—Aymara, Cuna, Jivaro, Siriono, Yagua; Oceania—Arapesh, Balinese, Buka (Kurtachi), Ifaluk, Kwoma, Lau Fijians (Kambara), Lesu, Manus, Maori, Pukapukans, Samoans, Tikopia, Trobrianders, Trukese, Ulithians, Vanua Levu (Nakoroka). All information was obtained from ethnographic studies available in the literature or in the Human Relations Area Files. Ratings were, so far as possible, of the aboriginal practices of the group in order to reduce the influence of acculturation. All ratings used in this study have been filed with the American Documentation Institute. Order Document No. 7450 from the ADI Auxiliary Publications Project, Photoduplication Service, Library of Congress; Washington 25, D. C., remitting in advance $1.75 for microfilm or $2.50 for photocopies. Make checks payable to: Chief, Photoduplication Service, Library of Congress. All intercorrelations among variables for our sample of societies appear in the same document.

behavior. Thus we are able to clarify antecedents common to both types of crime and those characteristic of only one. Judgments were always made in relation to the norms of the culture under consideration. Theft was defined as stealing the personal property of others. Property included anything on which the society placed value, whether it was a whale's tooth or a song. Personal crime was defined by intent to injure or kill a person; assault, rape, suicide, sorcery intended to make another ill, murder, making false accusations, etc., were all included.

The method of comparative ratings was used to obtain measures of frequency. Three raters independently analyzed the ethnographic material on each society and made ratings on a 7-point scale as to the relative frequency of the type of crime under consideration. Thus a rating of 4 on theft would mean that the frequency of theft in a given society appeared to be about average for the sample of societies. Ratings of 5, 6, and 7 represented high frequencies and those of 3, 2, and 1 were low. Societies in which the behavior did not occur were rated as 0. Each rating was classified as confident or doubtful at the time that it was made. No rating was made if the analyst judged the information to be insufficient. We have included all societies on which all three analysts made a rating, whether it was confident or doubtful, and we have used the pooled ratings of all three analysts. The reliability of these pooled ratings is estimated as +.67 for Theft and +.57 for Personal Crime. These estimates were obtained by averaging (using a $z$ transformation) the separate interrater reliabilities, and entering this average into the Spearman-Brown correction formula.

Most writers in this field make a distinction between delinquency and crime, largely on the basis of the age of the offender. The nature of our evidence does not permit us to make such a clear distinction. Ratings were made in terms of the relative frequency of specific types of criminal behavior in the adult population. Since the age at which adulthood is considered to have begun varies from one society to another, ratings may in some cases have included individuals young enough to be considered adolescent in our society and therefore delinquent rather than criminal. The distinction does not appear to be crucial in this study.

The measures of possible causal variables consist of ratings which have been derived from several sources. Each will be described in the following section. Except where noted (for certain variables in Tables 3 and 4), none of the three people who made the crime ratings participated in any of the other ratings.

**Hypotheses, Results, and Discussion**

Our results will be presented under three main headings: Correlates of Crime in General, Correlates Specific to Theft, and Correlates Specific to Personal Crime. As this classification suggests, we have found it useful to consider the antecedents of crime as either general or specific, i.e., leading to a general increase in criminal behavior, or associated with only one major category of crime. A correlation of +.46 was found between frequency of Theft and frequency of Personal Crime. This indicates that the two variables show a significant degree of communality ($p<.01$) and also some independence.

*Correlates of Crime in General*

Our principal findings concerning common correlates of both Theft and Personal Crime are relevant to a hypothesis that crime arises partly as a defense against strong feminine identification. We will begin with an account of this hypothesis.

In our society crime occurs mostly in men, and we have no reason to doubt that this sex difference characterizes most societies. Several writers have called attention to the sex-role identification of males as especially pertinent to the development of delinquency in our society. It is assumed that the very young boy tends to identify with his mother rather than his father because of his almost exclusive contact with his mother. Later in his development he becomes aware of expectations that he behave in a masculine way and as a result his behavior tends to be marked by a compulsive masculinity which is really a defense against feminine identification. Parsons (1954, pp. 304–305) notes further that the mother is the principal agent of socialization as well as an object of love and identification. Therefore, when the boy revolts he unconsciously identifies "goodness" with femininity and hence accepts the role of "bad boy" as a positive goal.

Miller (1958) has made a study of lower-class culture and delinquency which is also pertinent in this connection. He points out that some delinquent behavior may result from an attempt to live up to attitudes and values characteristic of lower-class culture. He also notes that many lower-class males are reared in predominantly female households lacking a consistently present male with whom to identify. He feels that what he calls an almost obsessive lower-class concern with masculinity results from the feminine identification in pre-adolescent years.

Whiting, Kluckhohn, and Anthony (1958), in a cross-cultural study of male initiation rites at puberty, found these rites tended to occur in societies with prolonged, exclusive mother-son sleeping arrangements. Their interpretation of this relationship is that the early mother-infant sleeping arrangement produces an initial feminine identification, and later control by men leads to a secondary masculine identification. The function of the initiation ceremony is to resolve this conflict of sexual identification in favor of the masculine identification. The authors further predict that insofar as there has been an increase in juvenile delinquency in our society, "it probably has been accompanied by an increase in the exclusiveness of mother-child relationships and/or a decrease in the authority of the father."

The hypothesis that crime is in part a defense against initial feminine identification would lead to the expectation that all factors which tend to produce strong identification with the mother and failure of early identification with the father would be positively correlated with the frequency of crime in the adult population. The factor that is easiest to study is the presence of the father. It seems reasonable to suppose that successful identification with the father is dependent on his presence. Therefore, societies which differ in the degree to which the father is present during the child's first few years should differ correspondingly in the degree to which the boy typically forms a masculine identification.[3]

Whiting (1959) has made use of Murdock's (1957) classification of household structure and family composition to distinguish among four types of households which provide a range from maximal to minimal degree of presence of the father. They are as follows:

**Monogamous Nuclear.** This household is the usual one in our society. The father, mother, and children eat, sleep, and entertain under one roof. Grandparents, siblings of the parents, and other relatives live elsewhere. The effective presence of the father in the child's environment is thus at a maximum.

**Monogamous Extended.** Here two or more nuclear families live together under one roof. A typical extended family consists of an aged couple together with their married sons and daughters and their respective families. In such a household, the child's interaction with his father is likely to be somewhat less than in the single nuclear household.

**Polygynous Polygynous.** The polygynous household consists of a man living with his wives and their various children. Here the child is likely to have even less opportunity to interact with his father.

**Polygynous Mother-Child.** This type of household occurs in those polygynous societies where each wife has a separate establishment and lives in it with her children. In these societies the father either sleeps in a men's club, has a hut of his own, or divides his time among the houses of his various wives. The husband usually does not sleep in the house

[3] The whole problem of the mechanism whereby identification occurs has been omitted from this study. In all theories it would appear that identification with the father would be in some degree a function of the frequency of the presence of the father.

of any wife during the 2 to 3 years when she is nursing each infant. Thus the mother may become the almost exclusive object of identification for the first few years of life.

Table 1 shows the number of societies with low and high frequency of Theft and Personal Crime within each of the four categories of household type. As the opportunity for contact with the father decreases, the frequency of both Theft and Personal Crime increases. This result agrees with our hypothesis. If the family structure and household is treated as a four-point scale, it yields a correlation of +.58 with frequency of Theft and of +.44 with frequency of Personal Crime; both correlations are statistically significant ($p<.01$). If we compare the extremes of the distribution—contrasting Monogamous Nuclear households (which provide the maximum opportunity for identification with the father) with Polygynous Mother-Child households (which provide the minimum opportunity for identification with the father)—this re-

lationship is clearly demonstrated; 18 of the 21 societies fall in the predicted quadrants for Theft, and 14 out of 21 for Personal Crime.

Several results of empirical studies in our society appear consistent with this finding. One is the frequently reported relationship between broken homes and delinquency, since in the majority of cases broken homes are probably mother-child households. Robins and O'Neal (1958), for example, in a follow-up study of problem children after 30 years, refer to the high incidence of fatherless families. Glueck and Glueck (1950) report that 41.2 percent of their delinquent group were not living with their own fathers, as compared with 24.8 percent of a matched nondelinquent group. These data suggest that a relatively high proportion of the delinquents came from what were essentially "mother-child" households.

A recent book by Rohrer and Edmonson (1960) is also relevant. Their study is a follow-up after 20 years of the indi-

Table 1

**Frequency of Theft or Personal Crime in Relation to Family Structure and Household**

| Family Structure and Household[a] | Frequency of Theft | | Frequency of Personal Crime | |
|---|---|---|---|---|
| | Low | High | Low | High |
| Monogamous Nuclear | 7 | 2 | 5 | 4 |
| Monogamous Extended | 7 | 3 | 6 | 3 |
| Polygynous Polygynous | 7 | 6 | 3 | 7 |
| Polygynous Mother-Child | 1 | 11 | 3 | 9 |

Note: Each entry in the table gives the number of societies in our sample which have the particular combination of characteristics indicated for that row and column.

The total number of cases in the left-hand and right-hand parts of this table and in the various divisions of succeeding tables varies because lack of information prevented rating some societies on some variables. In testing each relationship we have of course been able to use only those societies for which the relevant ratings are available. The division into "low" and "high" was made as near the median as possible.

[a] See Murdock (1957).

viduals described in *Children of Bondage* by Davis and Dollard (1941). The importance of the matriarchal household typical in a Southern Negro lower-class group, and its effect on the emotional development of the young boy and his eventual attitudes as an adult, are stressed throughout. The following passage summarizes, in its application to their (Rohrer & Edmonson) particular data, an interpretation consistent with those we have cited in introducing this hypothesis.

> Gang life begins early, more or less contemporaneously with the first years of schooling, and for many men lasts until death. . . . Although each gang is a somewhat distinct group, all of them appear to have a common structure expressing and reinforcing the gang ideology. Thus an organizational form that springs from the little boy's search for a masculinity he cannot find at home becomes first a protest against femininity and then an assertion of hypervirility. On the way it acquires a structuring in which the aspirations and goals of the matriarchy or the middle class are seen as soft, effeminate, and despicable. The gang ideology of masculine independence is formed from these perceptions, and the gang then sees its common enemy not as a class, nor even perhaps as a sex, but as the "feminine principle" in society. The gang member rejects this femininity in every form, and he sees it in women and in effeminate men, in laws and morals and religion, in schools and occupational striving (pp. 162–163).

## Correlates of Theft

Although we shall consider correlates of Theft in this section and correlates of Personal Crime in the next section, each table will show in parallel columns the relation of a set of variables both to

Theft and to Personal Crime. This will facilitate comparison and avoid repetition. How each of these variables was measured will be described in the section to which it is most pertinent.

The first variables to be considered are concerned with child-training practices. Most of the child-training variables have been developed in our research and described in an earlier paper (Barry, Bacon, & Child, 1957). These variables may be briefly described as follows:

**Overall childhood indulgence.** The period of childhood was defined roughly as covering the age period from 5 to 12 years, or to the beginning of any pubertal or prepubertal status change. In making ratings of childhood indulgence, factors relevant to indulgence in infancy—such as immediacy and degree of drive reduction, display of affection by parents, etc.—if operative at this latter age, were taken into account. In addition, the raters also considered the degree of socialization expected in childhood and the severity of the methods used to obtain the expected behavior.

**Anxiety associated with socialization during the same period of childhood.** This was rated separately for each of five systems of behavior: Responsibility or dutifulness training; Nurturance training, i.e., training the child to be nurturant or helpful toward younger siblings and other dependent people; Obedience training; Self-reliance training; Achievement training, i.e., training the child to orient his behavior toward standards of excellence in performance and to seek to achieve as excellent a performance as possible.

In rating the training in these areas, an attempt was first made to estimate the Total Pressure exerted by the adults in each society toward making the children behave in each of these specified ways (Responsible, Nurturant, Obedient, Self-Reliant, and Achieving). The *socialization anxiety* measures were based on an estimate of the amount of anxiety aroused in the child by failing to behave in a responsible, self-reliant, etc. way, and they reflect primarily the extent of punishment for failure to show each particular form of behavior. The measures of Total Pressure reflect both this and the extent of reward and encouragement.

Wherever boys and girls were rated differently on any of the above variables of socialization, we used the ratings for boys.

The relation of the crime ratings to these and other variables of child training is presented in Table 2. It is clear that Theft is significantly related to several variables of child training.

First, Theft is negatively correlated with Childhood Indulgence, i.e., societies with a high rating of Childhood Indulgence tend to have a low frequency of Theft in the adult population; and, conversely, societies with a low rating of Childhood Indulgence show a high frequency of Theft.

Frequency of Theft is also positively correlated with socialization anxiety during the period of childhood with respect to the following areas of training: Responsibility, Self-Reliance, Achieve-

*Table 2*

**Child Training Factors Associated with Theft or Personal Crime**

| | | Theft | | Personal Crime | |
|---|---|---|---|---|---|
| | Factor | N | r | N | r |
| 1. | Childhood Indulgence[a] | 45 | −.41** | 42 | −.10 |
| 2. | Responsibility Socialization Anxiety[a] | 43 | +.48** | 41 | +.20 |
| 3. | Self-Reliance Socialization Anxiety[a] | 43 | +.35* | 41 | +.24 |
| 4. | Achievement Socialization Anxiety[a] | 36 | +.41* | 35 | +.20 |
| 5. | Obedience Socialization Anxiety[a] | 40 | +.32* | 39 | +.06 |
| 6. | Dependence Socialization Anxiety[b] | 31 | +.14 | 28 | +.56** |
| 7. | Mother-Child Sleeping[c] | 20 | +.40 | 19 | +.46* |
| 8. | Infant Indulgence[a] | | | | |
| 9. | Age of Weaning[a] | | | | |
| 10. | Oral Socialization Anxiety[b] | | | | |
| 11. | Anal Socialization Anxiety[b] | | | | |
| 12. | Sex Socialization Anxiety[b] | | | | |
| 13. | Aggression Socialization Anxiety[b] | | | | |
| 14. | Nurturance Socialization Anxiety[a] | | | | |
| 15. | Total Pressures toward Responsibility, Nurturance, Self-Reliance, Achievement, and Obedience[a] | | | | |

Note: In this and the following tables the correlations are Pearsonian coefficients, thus reflecting all available degrees of gradation in score rather than simply classifying societies as high and low. Factors 8–15 showed no significant relationship with either Theft or Personal Crime.

[a] See Barry, Bacon, and Child (1957).

[b] See Whiting and Child (1953).

[c] See Whiting, Kluckhohn, and Anthony (1958).

\* $p \leq .05$.

\*\* $p \leq .01$.

ment, and Obedience. It should be emphasized that Total Pressures toward those four areas of socialization are not significantly correlated with Theft. Therefore it is apparently not the area or level of socialization required which is significant, but rather the punitive and anxiety-provoking methods of socialization employed.

These findings on child training in relation to Theft may be summarized and interpreted by the hypothesis that theft is in part motivated by feelings of deprivation of love. Our data indicate that one source of such feelings is punitive and anxiety-provoking treatment during childhood. Such treatment during infancy may tend to have a similar effect, as suggested by a correlation of $-.25$ between frequency of Theft and Infant Indulgence. This correlation falls slightly short of significance at the 5 percent level. It is of special interest that substantial correlations with socialization anxiety in childhood tended to occur in the areas of training in Responsibility, Achievement, and Self-Reliance. These all involve demands for behavior far removed from the dependent behavior of infancy and early childhood and close to the independent behavior expected of adults. If we assume that lack of adequate indulgence in childhood leads to a desire to return to earlier means of gratification and behavior symbolic of this need, then we would expect that pressures toward more adult behavior might intensify this need and the frequency of the symbolic behavior. Theft, from this point of view, would be seen as rewarded partly by its value as symbolic gratification of an infantile demand for unconditional indulgence irrespective of other people's rights or interests.

The results of the early study by Healy and Bronner (1936) seem directly pertinent to our findings and interpretation. They found that a group of delinquents differed from their nondelinquent siblings primarily in their relationships with their parents; the delinquent child was much more likely to give evidence of feeling thwarted and rejected. It seems reasonable to assume that such feelings would often, though not always, indicate a real deprivation of parental love. Glueck and Glueck (1950) also found that their delinquents, compared with matched nondelinquents, had received less affection from their parents and siblings and had a greater tendency to feel that their parents were not concerned with their welfare. It was also noted that fathers of the delinquents had a much greater tendency to resort to physical punishment as a means of discipline than fathers of the nondelinquents. This agrees with our observation that more punitive methods of socialization are associated with an increased frequency of theft.

Compulsive stealing (kleptomania) has been interpreted by psychoanalysts (see Fenichel, 1945, pp. 370–371) as an attempt to seize symbols of security and affection. Thus this form of mental illness, in common with more rational forms of stealing, may be regarded as being motivated by feelings of deprivation of love.

Table 3 summarizes the relationship between our two measures of crime and a number of aspects of economy and social organization on which we were able to obtain ratings. Theft shows a significant relationship with only three of these measures: Social Stratification, Level of Political Integration, and Degree of Elaboration of Social Control. Social Stratification was treated as a five-

*Table 3*

**Socioeconomic Factors Associated with Theft or Personal Crime**

| | Theft | | Personal Crime | |
|---|---|---|---|---|
| *Factor* | *N* | *r* | *N* | *r* |
| 1. Social Stratification[a] | 44 | +.36* | 40 | +.16 |
| 2. Level of Political Integration[a] | 43 | +.34* | 39 | +.02 |
| 3. Degree of Elaboration of Social Control[b] | 43 | +.46** | 40 | +.04 |
| 4. Accumulation of Food[c] | | | | |
| 5. Settlement Pattern[a] | | | | |
| 6. Division of Labor by Sex[a] | | | | |
| 7. Rule of Residence (Patrilocal, Matrilocal, etc.)[a] | | | | |
| 8. Extent of Storing[b] | | | | |
| 9. Irrationality of Storing[b] | | | | |
| 10. Severity of Punishment for Property Crime[b] | | | | |
| 11. Severity of Punishment for Personal Crime[b] | | | | |

Note: Ratings of Factors 3, 10, and 11 were made in connection with the analysis of crime by two of the three raters (H. Maretzki and A. Rosman). Ratings of Factors 8 and 9 were made by one of the raters (H. Maretzki) but in connection with an analysis of food and economy. Factors 4–11 showed no significant relationship with either Theft or Personal Crime.

[a] See Murdock (1957).
[b] Bacon, Child, and Barry (unpublished).
[c] See Barry, Child, and Bacon (1959).
* $p \le .05$.
** $p \le .01$.

point scale ranging from complex stratification, i.e., three or more definite social classes or castes exclusive of slaves, to egalitarian, i.e., absence of significant status differentiation other than recognition of political statuses and of individual skill, prowess, piety, etc. Level of Political Integration was also treated as a five-point scale ranging from complex state, e.g., confederation of tribes or conquest state with a king, differentiated officials, and a hierarchical administrative organization to no political integration, even at the community level.[4] Elaboration of Social Control is concerned with the degree to which a society has law-making, law-enforcing, and punishing agencies.

Our findings indicate that theft is

[4] Both variables are taken from Murdock (1957). Our manner of treating his data is described in Barry, Child, and Bacon (1959).

positively correlated with each of these three measures. In other words, with an increased Level of Political Integration, Social Stratification, and Elaboration of Social Control there is an increase in the frequency of Theft. These variables show no significant relationship with frequency of Personal Crime. Each of these institutional conditions seems capable of arousing feelings of insecurity and resentment, and hence may be similar in this respect to parental deprivation. Therefore the correlation of these institutional conditions with Theft might be tentatively interpreted as consistent with our hypothesis about motivational influences on Theft. It is obvious that other interpretations might be made from the same data. For example, a high frequency of crime may give rise to increased elaboration of social control.

Table 4 presents the relation of both

Theft and Personal Crime to certain adult attitudes on which we were able to obtain ratings. Frequency of Theft is positively related to Sense of Property and negatively related to Trust about Property. This may indicate merely that the greater the importance of property, the greater the variety of acts which will be classified as Theft, or that a high frequency of Theft gives rise to an emphasis on property. But it may also mean that the greater the importance of property, the more effectively does Theft serve the personal needs to which it seems to be related.

Frequency of Theft is also negatively correlated with Environmental Kindness in Folk Tales. This folk tale measure requires some explanation. It was taken from an analysis of folk tales made by one of the authors (MKB) without knowledge of the societies from which the sample of folk tales was taken. In making the analysis, each folk tale was divided into units of action or events as they related to the principal character or the character with whom the listener would be expected to identify. Each unit was then classified in one of a number of different categories including that of environmental kindness. Classification in this category means that the particular unit involved action or state of affairs definitely friendly or nurturant to the principal character. Thus our results show that societies high in frequency of Theft tend to have folk tales which do not represent the environment as kind. Thinking of the environment as lacking in friendly nurturance seems entirely consistent with the relative absence of parental nurturance which we have already found to be correlated with frequency of theft.

*Correlates of Personal Crime*

Inspection of Tables 2, 3, and 4 reveals that the significant correlates of Personal Crime are different from those for Theft.

*Table 4*

**Adult Attitudes Associated with Theft or Personal Crime**

| | | Theft | | Personal Crime | |
|---|---|---|---|---|---|
| | *Attitude* | *N* | *r* | *N* | *r* |
| 1. | Sense of Property | 43 | +.45** | 40 | +.25 |
| 2. | Trust about Property | 43 | −.31* | 40 | −.27 |
| 3. | General Trustfulness | 42 | −.28 | 40 | −.40** |
| 4. | Environmental Kindness in Folk Tales | 23 | −.47* | 21 | −.30 |
| 5. | Environmental Hostility in Folk Tales | 23 | +.36 | 21 | +.56** |
| 6. | Communality of Property | | | | |
| 7. | Competition in the Acquisition of Wealth | | | | |
| 8. | Generosity | | | | |
| 9. | n Achievement in Folk Tales[a] | | | | |

Note: Attitude 3 was rated by one of the three raters (A. Rosman) in connection with the analysis of crime. Attitudes 1, 2, 6, 7, and 8 were rated by another of the three raters (H. Maretzki) in connection with the analysis of food and economy. Attitudes 6–9 showed no significant relationship with either Theft or Personal Crime.

[a] See Child, Veroff, and Storm (1958).

* $p \leq .05$.

** $p \leq .01$.

In no instance does a variable in these tables show a significant correlation with both Theft and Personal Crime.

Frequency of Personal Crime shows a significant positive correlation with Dependence Socialization Anxiety, a rating taken from Whiting and Child (1953). In making this rating, an estimate was made of the amount of anxiety aroused in the children of a given society by the methods of independence training typically employed. This estimate was based on the following factors: abruptness of the transition required, severity and frequency of punishment, and evidence of emotional disturbance in the child.

Ratings on mother-child sleeping are taken from Whiting et al. (1958). In this study societies were placed into two categories: those in which the mother and baby shared the same bed for at least a year to the exclusion of the father, those in which the baby slept alone or with both the mother and father. According to our results there is a high positive relationship between prolonged, exclusive mother-child sleeping arrangements and frequency of Personal Crime.[5]

Inspection of the child-training factors associated with frequency of Personal crime suggests that the conditions in childhood leading to a high frequency of personal crime among adults are as follows: a mother-child household with inadequate opportunity in early life for identification with the father, mother-child sleeping arrangements which tend to foster a strong dependent relationship

[5] The variable of mother-child sleeping might be considered to favor feminine identification. In that event, the fact that it shows correlations in the positive direction with both types of crime tends toward confirmation of the findings in our earlier section on Correlates of Crime in General.

between the child and the mother, subsequent socialization with respect to independence training which tends to be abrupt, punitive, and productive of emotional disturbance in the child.

We would predict that this pattern of child-training factors would tend to produce in the child persistent attitudes of rivalry, distrust, and hostility, which would probably continue into adult life. The results obtained with ratings of adult attitudes (Table 4) support this view. Frequency of Personal Crime is negatively correlated with General Trustfulness. Frequency of Personal Crime is also positively correlated with Environmental Hostility in Folk Tales. Classification of a folk tale unit in this category means that the particular unit involved definite deception, aggression, or rejection in relation to the principal character. This variable was not highly related to that of environmental kindness, although the results obtained with the two are consistent with each other. The correlation between them was only $-.34$, most folk tale units not falling in either of these categories. Our results indicate that societies which are rated as relatively high in the frequency of Personal Crime have folk tales with a high proportion of events representing the environment as hostile. If we may infer that the content of folk tales reflects the underlying attitudes of the people who tell them, then this finding, as well as those with our other measures of adult attitudes, supports the view that personal crime is correlated with a suspicious or distrustful attitude toward the environment.

An analysis by Whiting (1959) of the socialization factors correlated with a belief in sorcery is relevant to this aspect of our results. He points out that a belief in sorcery is consistent with a paranoid attitude. According to Freudian interpretation, paranoia represents a defense against sexual anxiety. Whiting presents cross-cultural data in support of a hypothesis, based on Freud's theory of paranoia, that a belief in sorcery is related to a prolonged and intense contact with the mother in infancy followed by a severe sex socialization. The same hypothesis might be applied to frequency of Personal Crime, since we have evidence that Personal Crime is correlated with a suspicious, paranoid attitude in adult life, and sorcery is after all one form of Personal Crime. Our results for Personal Crime, in common with Whiting's for sorcery, show a correlation with mother-child household and prolonged mother-child sleeping. However, we found no significant correlation with severe sex socialization but rather with severe dependence socialization. We do not feel that these findings negate the Freudian interpretation, because dependence socialization, bearing as it does on the child's intimate relation with his mother, necessarily is concerned with the child's sexual feelings in a broad sense.

## General Discussion

We would like to emphasize the value of the cross-cultural method for exploring the possible determinants of crime. When each society is used as a single case, and is classified according to crime and other variables for the entire society over a period of years, the measures are likely to be reliable; comparison among societies provides great diversity in frequency of crime and in the other variables to be related with it.

The cross-cultural method may help us to identify variables with a causal relationship to crime. For example, our cross-cultural data suggest that high differentiation of status within a society is a favorable condition for a high frequency of Theft, and that a high frequency of Personal Crime is associated with a generalized attitude of distrust. These relationships should be subjected to more systematic and intensive tests within our own society than has hitherto been done.

Variables which have been suggested, whether in empirical studies or theoretical discussions, as possible causes of crime within our society may be tested for broader significance by the cross-cultural method. It has been argued, for example, that within our society delinquent or criminal behavior is likely to develop if the boy has been raised without adequate opportunity to identify with the father. These suggestions have often been made in connection with family patterns that are said to characterize certain classes or groups within our society; the cross-cultural findings indicate that a high frequency of both Theft and Personal Crime tends to occur in societies where the typical family for the society as a whole creates lack or limitation of opportunity for the young boy to form an identification with his father. Therefore the cross-cultural method supports the theory that lack of opportunity for the young boy to form a masculine identification is in itself an important antecedent of crime.

Another instance of such confirmation in a broader sense is the following: In our society delinquents have been reported to express feelings of alienation from their parents. It is unclear, however, whether this reflects their parents' actual treatment of them, or merely their own subjectively determined perceptions. Our cross-cultural data (in common with some of the findings within our own society) indicate that a high frequency of Theft is correlated with an actual low degree of indulgence during childhood.

Other theories about the antecedents of crime, when tested with the cross-cultural method, have not been confirmed in this broader framework. For example, pressures toward achievement were not significantly related to frequency of crime, although such a relationship is implied by theories of delinquency which emphasize the discrepancy between culturally induced aspirations and the possibility of achieving them. This negative result in our sample of societies does not deny the existence of such a relationship within our society, but it does indicate a limitation on its generality.

## References

BARRY, H., III, BACON, M. K., & CHILD, I. L. A cross-cultural survey of some sex differences in socialization. *Journal of Abnormal and Social Psychology*, 1957, **55**, 327–332.

BARRY, H., III, CHILD, I. L., & BACON, M. K. Relation of child training to subsistence economy. *American Anthropologist*, 1959, **61**, 51–63.

CHILD, I. L., VEROFF, J., & STORM, T. Achievement themes in folk tales related to socialization practice. In J. W. Atkinson (Ed.), *Motives in fantasy, action, and society*. Princeton: Van Nostrand, 1958. Pp. 479–492.

DAVIS, A., & DOLLARD, J. *Children of bondage*. Washington: American Council on Education, 1941.

FENICHEL, O. *The psychoanalytic theory of neurosis*. New York: Norton, 1945.

GLUECK, S., & GLUECK, E. *Unraveling juvenile delinquency*. New York: Commonwealth Fund, 1950.

HEALEY, W., & BRONNER, A. F. *New light on delinquency and its treatment*. New Haven: Yale University Press, 1936. (Republished 1957)

MILLER, W. B. Lower-class culture as a generating milieu of gang delinquency. *Journal of Social Issues*, 1958, **14**, 5–19.

MURDOCK, G. P. World ethnographic sample. *American Anthropologist*, 1957, **59**, 664–687.

PARSONS, T. *Essays in sociological theory*. (Rev. ed.) Glencoe, Ill.: Free Press, 1954.

ROBINS, L. N., & O'NEAL, P. Morality, mobility and crime: Problem children thirty years later. *American Sociological Review*, 1958, **23**, 162–171.

ROBISON, S. M. *Juvenile delinquency: Its nature and control*. New York: Holt, 1960.

ROHRER, J. H., & EDMONSON, M. S. (Eds.), *Eighth generation: Cultures and personalities of New Orleans Negroes*. New York: Harper, 1960.

WHITING, J. W. M. The cross-cultural method. In G. Lindzey (Ed.), *Handbook of social psychology*. Vol. 1. *Theory and method*. Cambridge, Mass.: Addison-Wesley, 1954. Pp. 523–531.

*WHITING, J. W. M. Sorcery, sin, and the superego: A cross-cultural study of some mechanisms of social control. In M. R. Jones (Ed.), *Nebraska symposium on motivation: 1959*. Lincoln: University of Nebraska Press, 1959. Pp. 174–195.

WHITING, J. W. M., & CHILD, I. L. *Child training and personality*. New Haven: Yale University Press, 1953.

WHITING, J. W. M., KLUCKHOHN, R., & ANTHONY, A. The function of male initiation ceremonies at puberty. In E. E. Maccoby, T. Newcomb, & E. L. Hartley (Eds.), *Readings in social psychology*. (3rd ed.) New York: Holt, 1958. Pp. 359–370.

* [Asterisks indicate works that are reprinted, in whole or in part, in this volume.]

# LEARNING-THEORY APPROACHES

modeling as a key mechanism in the development of conscience. (Other examples of the learning-theory approach are found in the Sears et al. excerpt in the subsection on parent practices and in another Bandura and Walters excerpt in the section on generality.)

## Introduction

The major competitor to Freudian theory in isolating the antecedents of conscience has come from the several varieties of learning theory. This approach emphasizes an experimental attitude, parsimony of theory, and a concern for the measurable specifics of stimulus conditions and related conscience behaviors.

This subsection presents three related but somewhat different learning-theory approaches to conscience development. The Hill paper views several conscience-related phenomena within the framework of reinforcement theory. The two papers by Solomon and his colleagues represent a provocative extension of animal data to human conscience behavior. Finally, the Bandura and Walters excerpt suggests

# 22

# Learning theory and the acquisition of values[1]

## by Winfred F. Hill

The processes by which a child acquires the values of his culture and his various overlapping subcultures is, as a recent review of the subject points out (Dukes, 1955), still rather obscure. This obscurity is certainly not due to lack of interest in the topic. Psychologists, psychiatrists, anthropologists, sociologists, pediatricians, and educators have all given attention to the question of how children come to share the attitudes, ideals, and ethical standards of those around them. Nor is this interest undeserved, for few topics are of greater practical importance.

Perhaps this very convergence of interest from many directions is partly responsible for the difficulties involved in studying the topic. This area of research has become a battleground for conflicting terminologies, with one term often

Winfred F. Hill, "Learning Theory and the Acquisition of Values," *Psychological Review*, **67**, 1960, 317–331. Copyright 1960 by the American Psychological Association, and reproduced by permission.

[1] The research for this article was supported by a grant from the Carnegie Corporation to the Department of Psychology and the School of Education at Northwestern University. The author wishes to express his appreciation to Donald Campbell, Robert Winch, and the members of their seminar in social psychology for their many contributions to his thinking on this topic.

having a multiplicity of half-distinct meanings, and with what appears to be the same meaning often bearing different labels. Although many terms contribute to this confusion, three are of particular interest here: *identification*, *introjection*, and *internalization*. All involve some relation between an individual, hereinafter designated the subject (*S*), and another person or personalized entity, the model or *M*, such that *S*'s behavior is in some way patterned after *M*'s. However, these terms may refer either to a state of affairs or to the process which brought it about (Lazowick, 1955); the *M* may be a person, a group, or an idea (Glaser, 1958); and the relation may involve specific responses, broad meanings, or emotional reactions.

Some of the confusion as to the meaning of the term identification may be seen in the following uses. Lazowick (1955) distinguishes three main uses of the term identification in the literature: pseudoidentity, imitation, and personality change. He suggests that the term should be used only with regard to broad meanings, with imitation being the corresponding term for specific acts. Freud (1950) contrasts a boy's identification with his father, which forms the basis of his ego ideal, and his identification with his mother as an abandoned object cathexis. Davis and Havighurst (1947) maintain that a child will identify with his parents only if he loves them, but Anna Freud (1946) emphasizes identification with the aggressor. Lynn (1959) contrasts sex-role identification, which is "reserved to refer to the actual incorporation of the role of a given sex, and to the unconscious reactions characteristic of that role" (p. 127), with sex-role preference and sex-role adoption. He regards figure drawing as a measure of identification and choice of dolls for play as a measure of preference. Sears, Maccoby, and Levin (1957), however, use children's choices of dolls as a measure of identification. Sanford (1955), discouraged by such confusions of meaning, considers the possibility of abandoning the term identification altogether, but decides to retain it to describe a defense mechanism involving extreme adoption of $M$'s behavior by $S$, a mechanism which is not important in normal personality development. Finally, this collection of meanings, diverse as it is, still omits those cases where identification is used as a synonym for loyalty or for empathy.

There is similar confusion concerning the meaning of introjection and internalization. Both carry the implication of values being incorporated into the personality. Hence, particularly with introjection, there is the suggestion of some relation with orality (Freud, 1950). However, Freud in the same discussion also uses introjection synonymously with identification. Parsons (1955), on the other hand, treats identification and internalization as synonyms.

The many discussions of these three terms in the literature seem to indicate that there are several processes involved but no generally accepted conventions for labeling them. A number of writers, including several already cited, have expressed discouragement at this state of affairs, but the usual result of such discouragement seems to be a redefinition of terms, which may clarify the particular exposition but which only serves further to confuse the field as a whole. Whereas Lynn (1959) believes that a term as widespread as identification must have potential usefulness, the present writer believes that clarity would be served by abolishing not only identification but also introjection and internalization from the technical vocabulary of personality development.

What, then, should be substituted? The topics to which the above terms have been applied certainly deserve discussion, and if the redefinition of the old terms is unsatisfactory, the introduction of new terms would be even worse. An answer may be found, however, in a sort of reductionism. Since the processes involved are learning processes, the existing vocabulary of learning is the obvious candidate for the job of describing them. It is quite possible, of course, that the existing vocabulary of learning theory will be inadequate for the complexities of value acquisition. However, if its use is carried as far as possible, the successes of this application should clarify our thinking about personality development, while any gaps which result should point to possible extensions of learning theory.

This approach involves treating human learning in a sociocultural environment in the same terms, at least for a first approximation, as animal learning in the environment of laboratory apparatus. For this purpose, the social rewards and punishments applied to humans may be treated as equivalent to the food pellets and electric shocks used with rats. Similarly, social roles are the equivalents of mazes which must be learned in order to obtain the rewards and avoid the punishments. Human beings of course constitute a far more variable environment than laboratory hardware, and one on which $S$ can exercise greater influence. However, since most of the theory in this area is concerned with the adaptation of $S$ to a relatively constant human environment (whether it be called culture, social system, or the personalities of the parents), this should not prove a serious stumbling block. There is ample precedent for such an approach in the writings of Dollard and Miller (1950), Mowrer (1950), Whiting and Child (1953), and others.

In addition, this approach treats values as nothing more than inferences from overt behavior. In principle this assumption should cause no difficulty. Few behavioral scientists would regard values (in the empirical, not the trancendental sense) as fundamentally different from such behavioristic constructs as Hull's (1943) habit strength or Tolman's (1949) equivalence beliefs. In practice, however, some theorists might take issue with this view on at least two bases.

For one thing, the measurement of values (including attitudes, ideals, and ethical standards) is commonly by verbal methods (see the review by Dukes, 1955). This leads to the suspicion that any measurement of values by nonverbal means must be inadequate, that only verbal measures can get at the significance of an act for an individual. However, verbal responses are part of the total behavior of the human organism and may be studied like other responses. The processes of unconscious motivation, semiconscious hypocrisy, and deliberate concealment all indicate that it would be unwise to treat verbal and nonverbal measures of values as equivalent. Rather than treat either verbal or nonverbal behavior as the true indicator of values and the other as a side issue, it seems more useful to study both and to ascertain empirically to what extent they lead to the same generalizations about a given S.

Another possible objection involves the distinction between specific acts and broad meanings, as in Lazowick's (1955) contrasting definitions of imitation and identification, noted above. This distinction between specific acts and broad meanings may refer either to the presence of mediating responses (see Osgood, 1953) or to the generality of the stimuli and responses involved. Neither of these distinctions, however, is dichotomous. Hull (1952) has indicated how a mediator, the fractional antedating goal response, may function in animal behavior and Russell and Storms (1955) have demonstrated mediational processes in rote learning. Thus the mediation mechanism is by no means restricted to the "higher mental processes" of humans. As for the generality of the behavior and of the stimuli which guide it, this presumably represents a continuum from the most specific to the most inclusive categories. If, for example, washing the hands before meals is an example of imitation and cleanliness an example of identification, where would wearing clean clothes be classified? So, although the distinction between specific acts and broad meanings is a legitimate one, there are no sharp breaks on the continuum and there is no reason to assume that basically different laws are involved.

In view of the above considerations, an attempt to study the acquisition of values as a branch of learning theory appears justified.

## Kinds of Reinforcement

The concept of reinforcement is basic to learning theory. While theorists are by no means unanimously agreed on the value of reinforcement terminology, there is little question that an empirical law of effect holds, that the consequences of an act influence its subsequent occurrence. A classification of kinds of reinforcers will be used here as the basis for analyzing the learning of values.

## Primary Reinforcement

For the present purpose, three kinds of reinforcement may be distinguished: *"primary," secondary,* and *vicarious.* Placing "primary" in quotes indicates that it refers to the effects not only of innate physiological reinforcers but also of those social reinforcers which play a primary role in human motivation. Presumably the positively reinforcing effects of attention and praise and the negatively reinforcing effects of criticism, ridicule, and rejection are at least partly learned, but the nature of the learning process is obscure, and at the present level of analysis it seems preferable to treat praise for a human as comparable to food for a rat. The distinction between "primary" and secondary reinforcement is thus one of convenience between that which we take as given and that for which we can find a specific learned basis. Though arbitrary, this distinction is perhaps no more so than the decision as to whether food in the mouth should be considered a primary or a secondary reinforcer.

One particular kind of learning by "primary" reinforcement is the acquisition of a generalized tendency to imitate others. Miller and Dollard (1941) have indicated how a generalized tendency to imitate the behavior of others may be learned in the same way as any other class of responses. Although their demonstrations of imitation involved *S*'s patterning his behavior after a leader who was present, Church (1957) has shown that rats can also learn to respond ap-

propriately to the same cues to which the leader rat is responding. In spite of some negative animal evidence (Solomon & Coles, 1954), there is little doubt that humans can learn to pattern their behavior after that of other people, not only when the *M* is present, but also in *M*'s absence by utilizing the appropriate environmental cues. As the child is repeatedly rewarded for imitative behavior in a variety of otherwise different situations, and as his capacity for abstraction increases, it seems plausible that a generalized imitative tendency would develop. It would be desirable, however, if the widespread anecdotal support for this deduction could be bolstered by experimental data.

The same process presumably applies to verbal instructions. The child is typically reinforced (though with some striking exceptions) for doing what others tell him to do. Hence (common parental impressions to the contrary notwithstanding), a generalized tendency toward conformity to verbal instructions may be expected to develop. With increasing intellectual development, this tendency should come to include conformity to fictional examples or to abstract ethical exhortations.

## Secondary Reinforcement

Although no basic distinction is made here between primary and secondary reinforcement, there is one case frequently discussed in the literature where the acquisition of reinforcing properties by certain stimuli may be analyzed in detail. These stimuli are those which are connected with care of the child by adults, i.e., the nonessential aspects of nurturance. These include patterns of speech, facial expressions, gestures, and the like. Since these occur with those nurturant behaviors which are primary reinforcers, such as feeding and cuddling, they may become secondary reinforcers. By stimulus generalization, these behaviors should also be rewarding to the child (although less so) when produced by himself. As the child grows older and the parents expect him to take greater care of his own needs, he is more and more forced to provide not only his own primary reinforcers, but his own secondary reinforcers as well. Hence he may be expected to show some of the same mannerisms as his parents showed when caring for him.

This kind of learning appears to be one of those processes which Freud (1950) includes under the heading of identification or introjection, that in which abandoned object cathexes become incorporated into the ego. However, in the view presented here, the coincidence of abandonment and incorporation into the ego refers only to performance, not to learning. The secondary reinforcing value of the parental mannerisms is built up during the period of nurturance, but becomes evident in the child's behavior as nurturance begins to be withdrawn. This learning process has been discussed by Mowrer (1950, Ch. 24) in connection with the learning of language, and by Lindemann (1944) as a reaction to the death of a loved one. Although this process appears better adapted to the learning of rather trivial mannerisms, it is capable at least in principle of being adapted to more general and significant values as well.

*Vicarious Reinforcement*

Vicarious reinforcement does not have the same dignified status in learning theory as do primary and secondary reinforcement, but some such process appears necessary in order to explain some important human learning. Vicarious reinforcement involves the generalization of reinforcing effects from others to oneself, hence learning from the reinforcers which others receive. A given act is reinforced for $S$ as a result of the act being performed by $M$, followed by reinforcement to $M$. For example, if $S$ observes $M$ trying to solve a problem by certain techniques and succeeding, $S$ is more likely to use the same techniques when faced by a similar problem than if $M$ had failed to solve the problem. Although most of the evidence for such learning is anecdotal, Lewis and Duncan (1958) have provided some evidence of it in a human gambling situation, and Darby and Riopelle (1959) have demonstrated it in discrimination learning by monkeys.

Although vicarious reinforcement involves selective imitation, it differs from the selectivity of imitation, described by Miller and Dollard (1941), in which $S$ imitates some $M$s and not others because of differential reinforcement received by $S$ for imitating the two $M$s. Vicarious reinforcement does not involve any reinforcers delivered directly to $S$; the discrimination of $M$s to be imitated or not is made entirely on the basis of $S$'s observation of $M$'s experience. This distinction is emphasized by Campbell (1963). In Hullian terms, vicarious reinforcement involves the acquisition of $K$ by observation.

This type of learning need not be restricted to the effect of particular reinforcers administered to $M$ under specific conditions. Stimulus generalization should occur not only from $M$'s behavior to $S$'s but also from one act of $M$'s to another. As a result, if $M$ is frequently reinforced, $S$ should find it rewarding to resemble $M$ in general, including imitation of some of $M$'s behaviors which $S$ has never seen rewarded. Thus a beginning salesman ($S$) might treat a customer with extreme politeness because he had observed another salesman ($M$) making a large sale while using such behavior, and he might also smoke a cigar because he had observed his highly successful sales manager ($M$) doing so. In the former case $M$'s behavior (politeness) and $M$'s reinforcement (a large sale) were paired, whereas in the latter case the reinforcement (business success) was a perennial experience of $M$, but not paired with the particular behavior (smoking cigars) in question. Both, however, are examples of vicarious reinforcement.

Vicarious reinforcement corresponds to identification as defined by Masserman (1946) and to that aspect of identification referred to by Kagan (1958) as "the motivation to command or experience desired goal states of a model" (p. 298). Freud's (1946) identification with the aggressor also fits under this heading if successful aggression is assumed to be reinforcing to the aggressor. Sanford's (1955) concept of identification also involves the adoption as $M$ of someone perceived by $S$ as successful.

### Conflicting Sources of Reinforcement

Traditionally the terms identification, introjection, and internalization might be applied to any or all of the learning processes described above or to their end product, similarity between $S$ and some $M$. Since for the most part these processes involve learning by imitation, require some kind of reinforcement, and result in similarity between $S$ and $M$, it may be asked why detailed analysis of the rather subtle differences among them is called for.

The answer is apparent when the possibility of conflict is considered. Conditions for a given $S$ may be such that one of these processes tends to produce one kind of behavior while another tends to produce quite different or even opposite behavior. Such a conflictful situation might be expected in a child reared by a nurturant mother, whose mannerisms would become secondarily reinforcing, and a domineering father, who would be perceived as successful in mastering the environment. Freud (1950) recognized the frequent occurrence of just such a conflict, but did not consider it necessary to use different words for the two learning processes. Another common conflict is between the tendency to imitate $M$s whom $S$ is directly reinforced for imitating (e.g., well-behaved children) and the tendency to imitate $M$s whom $S$ perceives as successful (e.g., tough kids). Such conflict is inevitable to a certain extent in children, since they are not permitted to imitate their (presumably more successful) elders in all respects, but it is particularly prominent in members of low-status social categories, (e.g., Negroes) who are often conspicuously not reinforced for imitating high-status $M$s. In the broadest sense, any situation where there is discrepancy among what $S$ is told to do, what he is rewarded for doing, and what he sees others doing is a potential conflict situation, and one in which the use of any single inclusive term such as "identification" obscures the relevant variables.

The occurrence of conflict among the various reinforcement processes makes possible a finer analysis of the acquisition of values than could be made otherwise. If there is perfect agreement among what S is told to do, what those who nurture him do, what those around him conspicuously master the environment by doing, and what he himself is directly rewarded for doing, there is little basis for judging how much each of these factors contributed to S's adoption of the values of those around him. By observing situations in which they conflict, greater knowledge of the efficacy of each kind of reinforcement may be obtained. Research in conflict situations might answer such theoretically and practically important questions as: "Does dominance or nurturance on M's part do more to make M effective in modifying S's values?"; "Do words and examples completely lose their efficacy if the appropriate behaviors, when elicited, are not reinforced?"; and "To what extent is behavior influenced by Ms presented verbally (e.g., in literature)?"

There is of course no special merit to the classificatory scheme presented here. Except for the concept of vicarious reinforcement, the writer has avoided attaching distinctive labels to the learning processes described. The purpose of this discussion was to show how the terminology of learning theory can be applied to processes of value acquisition which have been described by personality theorists. This not only serves as a step toward the integration of these two areas of study, but also suggests the probable usefulness of employing such independent variables as number, percentage, magnitude and delay of reinforcement, distribution of practice, and discriminability of stimuli in the study of value acquisition. As both learning theory and personality theory develop further, it is to be expected that any schema developed now will be at least partially replaced by newer concepts. Rather than developing in further detail the ideas suggested above, the remainder of this discussion will therefore concentrate on the application of this kind of thinking to a narrower area, the development of conscience.

## Conscience

Negative values, or conscience, have received much more attention than positive values. Educators seeking to improve children's characters, psychoanalysts concerned with the tyranny of the superego, anthropologists trying to distinguish between shame and guilt cultures, and experimental psychologists noting the persistence of avoidance responses have shared this emphasis on values of the "Thou shalt not" variety. Because of this widespread interest in conscience, it is a particularly appropriate topic with which to illustrate the possibilities of the learning theory approach to the study of values. Sears, Maccoby, and Levin (1957), in their challenging book *Patterns of Child Rearing*, devote a chapter to the development of conscience in preschool children. Their treatment of the topic will serve as a starting point for the present analysis.

### Criteria for Conscience

Sears, Maccoby, and Levin give three criteria for recognizing the operation of conscience in young children: *resistance to temptation, self-instructions* to obey the rules, and *evidence of guilt* when transgression occurs. These three criteria are treated jointly as defining conscience, and no attempt is made to analyze their separate developments. Although the authors mention that the aspects of conscience do not necessarily all appear at once, they regard conscience as representing an internalization of control which is fundamentally different from external control, whether by force, fear of punishment, or hope of material reward. This treatment of conscience as essentially a single variable seems premature in our present state of knowledge; certainly the learning theory approach to personality advocated here would involve separate analyses of these diverse response patterns.

The first criterion, *resistance to temptation*, may be viewed simply as avoidance learning. Although this kind of learning is still a focus of theoretical controversy, much experimental data are available concerning it (Solomon & Brush, 1956). Sidman's (1953) studies of avoidance behavior without a warning signal and Dinsmoor's (1954) analysis of punishment show how feedback from an individual's own acts can become a cue for avoidance, and how persistent such avoidance may be. Although children can presumably learn to respond to more abstract characteristics of cues than can animals, there is no reason to regard a child's learning to avoid certain behaviors as fundamentally different from a rat's learning to do so. The fact that the child avoids the forbidden acts even in the absence of the parents is presumably due to the parents' having in the past discovered and punished (in the broadest sense of that word) transgressions committed in their absence.

This relating of conscience to avoidance learning suggests that independent variables known to be effective in animal avoidance learning would be among the most appropriate ones for study in connection with the development of conscience in children. Within certain limits, the greater the intensity of the punishments (Brush, 1957; Miller, 1951) and the shorter the delay between transgression and punishment (Mowrer & Ullman, 1945; Solomon & Brush, 1956), the greater should be the resulting inhibition. Though the data are somewhat ambiguous, greater certainty of punishment might be expected to produce inhibition which would be more complete in the short run but also less persistent once punishment was permanently withdrawn (Grant, Schipper, & Ross, 1952; Jenkins & Stanley, 1950; Reynolds, 1958). This prediction suggests that even this one criterion of conscience may not be unitary, that different laws may apply depending on whether one asks how completely the child obeys the prohibitions or how long he continues to obey them after leaving the parental home. If partial reinforcement should turn out to be a crucial variable in the human situation, these two criteria might even be inversely related. The prediction also suggests that the question, "Is inconsistent discipline bad?" is far too simple; one must at least ask, "Bad for what?"

It must also be kept in mind that punishment is not restricted to physical chastisement or even to noxious stimuli in general, including scolding and ridicule. Withdrawal of positive reinforcers may be very effective as a punishment, a fact which complicates the analysis. As this is a much discussed topic in personality theory, it will be considered below.

Sears, Maccoby, and Levin's second criterion of conscience, *self-instruction*, obviously makes the human case different from the animal case, but it does not introduce any new motivational principle. One of the advantages of membership in the human species is the possibility of using verbal symbolization in dealing with one's problems. It is natural that a person learning an avoidance, like a person learning any other difficult response pattern, should give himself verbal instructions, especially since verbal coaching by others is so important in the learning of social prohibitions. Moreover, such self-instruction is an imitative act which might be learned according to any of the reinforcement paradigms discussed above. Presumably the learning of prohibitions proceeds differently in verbal and nonverbal organisms, but observations of the relation between moral statements and moral behavior (Hurlock, 1956, pp. 406, 411–412) argue against the assumption that there is a high correlation between verbal and other criteria of conscience, except as both are influenced by the values represented in the social environment.

The third criterion of conscience, *guilt* at violations of the prohibitions, is itself complex, with many verbal, autonomic, and gross behavioral aspects. However, the striking paradox about guilt, which has seemed to some students to set it apart from the ordinary laws of learning, is that it often involves the seeking of punishment. The person who has transgressed, rather than trying to avoid punishment, or even waiting passively for it to come, actively seeks out the authorities, confesses, and receives his punishment with apparent relief. He may also, or instead, go to great lengths to make restitution. Were it not for these phenomena of punishment-seeking and self-sacrificing restitution, it would be easy to dismiss guilt as merely the kind of fear associated with anticipation of certain sorts of punishment. As it is, the

existence of guilt serves as an argument for regarding conscience as something more than the sum of all those avoidances which have moral significance in one's culture.

However, the attempt to distinguish between guilt-controlled and other behaviors has not been very successful. Though the distinction between guilt cultures and shame cultures has had a considerable vogue in anthropology (e.g., Benedict, 1946; Havighurst & Neugarten, 1955; Mead, 1950), the inadequacies of the distinction have been pointed out by Ausubel (1955) and by Singer (1953). Moreover, the relation between conformity to a standard and guilt when the standard has been violated is open to question. Shaw (1948) suggests that confession may even be so satisfying to some people that it constitutes a reinforcement for sinning. So, although the phenomena of guilt may raise difficulties for learning theory, these difficulties probably cannot be solved by using guilt to define a distinctive kind of learning.

The above considerations should suffice to indicate that conscience cannot be assumed a priori to be unitary. The extent to which short-run conformity, long-run conformity, self-instructions to conform, certain kinds of distress at having failed to conform, and voluntary confession of nonconformity are intercorrelated is a matter to be empirically determined. Moreover, even if high positive intercorrelations are found, it is possible that they may reflect correlations in the environment rather than any fundamental unity of process. If environmental pressures toward conformity vary markedly, artificially high correlations among the criteria of conscience are to be expected. However, even when this artifact is removed, an analysis of separate learning processes for different behaviors may still lead to the prediction of high correlations among the behaviors. Such an analysis is presented below.

*Learning of Conscience*

Sears, Maccoby, and Levin found that the development of conscience, as defined jointly by their three criteria, was greater in those children whose parents used love-oriented forms of discipline (praise, isolation, and withdrawal of love) than in those whose parents used "materialistic" forms of discipline (material rewards, deprivation of privileges, and physical punishment). A similar finding, though not highly reliable statistically, is reported by Whiting and Child (1953, Ch. 11) in a cross-cultural study of guilt as measured by attitudes toward illness. This is consistent with the widely held view that the acquisition of parental values occurs most fully in an atmosphere of love (e.g., Ausubel, 1955; Davis & Havighurst, 1947). It is possible, however, that this finding may be due, not to love-oriented discipline as such, but to other characteristics of discipline which are correlated with it. The effect of this kind of discipline may be to accentuate the learning of several different responses, all of which contribute to the overall diagnosis of high conscience.

The various kinds of punishments commonly applied to children probably differ markedly in the temporal relations and the reinforcement contingencies involved. Physical punishment is likely to occur all at once and be over quickly, while punishment by deprivation of objects or privileges is likely to be either for a fixed period of time or for as long as the disciplinarian finds convenient.

Discipline by withdrawal of love, on the other hand, probably much more often lasts until the child makes some symbolic renunciation of his wrongdoing, as by apologizing, making restitution, or promising not to do it again. The child is deprived of his parents' love (or, the parents would claim, of the outward manifestations of it!) for as much or as little time as is necessary to get him to make such a symbolic renunciation. When he has made it, he is restored to his parents' favor. If the normal relation between the parents and child is one of warmth, such discipline strongly motivates the child to make the renunciation quickly. On repeated occasions of transgression, punishment by withdrawal of love, and symbolic renunciation, the child may be expected not only to learn the renunciation response as an escape from parental disfavor but eventually to use it as an avoidance rather than merely an escape response. Thus if the wrongdoing is not immediately discovered, the child may anticipate his parents' impending disfavor by confessing in advance and making the symbolic renunciation.

The result of this hypothesized sequence of events is that the child makes a verbal response which is in effect an instruction to himself not to repeat his wrongdoing. The next time temptation comes, he is more likely to make this verbal response before transgressing. Although this does not guarantee that he will not transgress, it is likely to reduce the probability. If he succumbs to temptation, he is more likely to confess before being caught and thereby avoid the temporary loss of his parents' love. Thus if the above reasoning is correct, all three criteria of conscience should be present to a greater degree in the child who has been disciplined in this fashion than in other children. According to the present hypothesis, however, this will be due to the fact that punishment continues until the child makes a symbolic renunciation, rather than to the fact that the punishment involves withdrawal of love. If physical chastisement or loss of privileges are used in the same way, the same outcome is predicted.

A possible weakness of this hypothesis is that children might learn a discrimination between the symbolic and the actual avoidances, so that they would develop a pattern of violating parental standards, immediately confessing and apologizing, and then transgressing again at the next hint of temptation. If forgiveness is offered freely and uncritically enough, such a pattern presumably does develop. In this case the correlation among the criteria of conscience would be expected to drop, actual avoidance of wrongdoing no longer being associated with the other criteria. (For this reason, Sears, Maccoby, and Levin might have found smaller relations if they had studied older children.) However, if the parents' discrimination keeps up with the child's so that the child cannot count on removing all the parents' disfavor with a perfunctory apology, the efficacy of this kind of discipline should be at least partially maintained.

If this explanation of greater conscience in children disciplined by withdrawal of love is correct, why was greater conscience also found with the other kinds of love-oriented control? Since these were all found to be intercorrelated, and since their relations to the degree of conscience were uniformly low, interpretations either of separate techniques or of love orientation as a general trait are necessarily somewhat dubious.

As an example of the difficulties involved, it may be noted that reasoning with the child is counted as a love-oriented technique solely on the grounds of its correlation with the other such techniques. Nevertheless, it shows a higher relation to conscience than do two of the three clearly love-oriented techniques. In view of such complexities, it seems legitimate to suggest that the crucial factor in those techniques associated with conscience may not be love orientation as such, but something else correlated with it.

To test this hypothesis, it would be necessary to have further detailed information of the sort that Sears, Maccoby, and Levin used, so that disciplinary methods could be classified according to the time relations discussed above. It is predicted that the parents' tendency to make termination of punishment contingent on symbolic renunciation would be correlated with love-oriented discipline. However, if each were varied with the other held constant, conscience should be more closely related to response contingency than to love orientation.

Along with this overall analysis of conscience, more detailed analyses could be made of the various components of conscience. According to the present view, intercorrelations among these criteria would be moderate for the entire sample and low when method of discipline was held constant.

The learning sequence discussed above is only one of several possible explanations of the Sears, Maccoby, and Levin finding. By suggesting that the crucial causal factor is not the distinction between materialistic orientation and love orientation, but another distinction correlated with it, the present hypothesis gains an advantage in objectivity and in practical applicability. Whether it also has the advantage of correctness must be empirically determined. The chief purpose of the present example is to point to the availability of such reductionist hypotheses in the study of values and to argue that they deserve priority in the schedule of scientific investigation.

## Permanence of Conscience

It would be particularly desirable to have a follow-up study to compare evidences of conscience in kindergarten with those of the same people later in life, when they were no longer primarily under the direct influence of their parents. Such a follow-up would help to clarify the relation between short-run and long-run conformity discussed above. Is the child who thoroughly obeys all his parents' prohibitions also the one who sticks to these standards when his parents are no longer around and his new associates have different standards? Anecdotal evidence can be cited on both sides, though the bulk is probably in the affirmative. To the extent that current and later conformity are independent, what variables influence one more than the other?

Predictions from learning theory on this topic are by no means unambiguous. Nevertheless, two lines of reasoning may be suggested concerning the type of discipline likely to result in the most persistent avoidances. (Persistence here refers, not to absolute level of avoidance, but to relative lack of decrement in the strength of avoidance with time.)

The first line of reasoning is from the differences in the slopes of *generalization gradients* for different kinds of

learning (Dollard & Miller, 1950). In most cases the contrast in slope is between approach (or excitatory) and avoidance (or inhibitory) tendencies. It appears, however, that the basic distinction is between response tendencies activated by innate and by learned (generally fear) drives (Miller & Murray, 1952). When stimulus conditions change, the resultant removal of cues for fear produces a greater weakening of response tendencies based on fear than of response tendencies based on other drives. Hence, the generalization gradient of responses and inhibitions based on fear is steeper than that of other responses and inhibitions. This implies that discipline based on fear should lose its efficacy more quickly than discipline based on rewards as distance from the disciplinarian or any other change in conditions increases. Since this difference in slope is found on continua both of distance (Miller, 1944) and of similarity (Miller & Kraeling, 1952; Murray & Miller, 1952), it seems reasonable to predict that it also applies to that complex continuum along which an individual makes the transition away from parental apron strings. It would follow from this analysis that of two inhibitions learned in childhood, equal in age and original strength, one learned from the threat of losing rewards would be more effective later in life than one learned from the fear-provoking threat of punishment.

In this analysis, the advantages of discipline by manipulation (including withdrawal) of reward would apply to any kind of reward, material or social, not merely to parental love. However, the desire to continue receiving love from the parents may persist after the child has outgrown the need for other parental rewards, such as gifts and privileges. Discipline by withdrawal of love, in an atmosphere of warmth, might therefore be even more effective than other forms of discipline by denial of reward in producing persistent avoidances.

The other line of reasoning, involving the *partial reinforcement effect*, argues for the persistence of conscience learned by the process outlined above, in which a symbolic renunciation of wrongdoing terminates punishment. Although the greater resistance to extinction of responses which have received less than 100 percent reinforcement has been demonstrated primarily with positive reinforcement, it applies to negative as well (Humphreys, 1939, 1940; Grant, Schipper, & Ross, 1952). Partial reinforcement is of course present with all kinds of discipline, since punishment depends on the parents' moods and on the social situation, as well as on the child's being caught. However, the above analysis of the kind of punishment which terminates when the child makes a symbolic renunciation of wrongdoing suggests that such discipline may involve an additional source of partial reinforcement. As was indicated above, the child may learn that he can avoid punishment by confessing and apologizing. When this happens, the avoidance starts to extinguish. However, the discerning parent then learns not to accept the apology, and the child is punished anyway. The child must then make a more vigorous and convincing symbolic renunciation than before in order to terminate the punishment. In addition, the discrimination he has made between the symbolic renunciation and the actual avoidance is broken down; punishment can only be prevented by actual avoidance of wrong-doing. If, however, after a period of obedience he once more transgresses and then confesses, he is likely again not to be punished. This starts the cycle of extinction and reconditioning of the avoidance response going again, thus continuing to provide a reinforcement schedule in which only part of the child's transgressions are punished.

To predict that such partial reinforcement will retard extinction is admittedly problematic, both because of the complexity of the avoidance paradigm and because the unpunished transgressions are assumed to occur in blocks rather than randomly. Nevertheless, the hypothesis deserves consideration, not only as a prediction from learning principles to personality, but also as a case where the needs of personality theory might guide research in learning.

Although these two lines of reasoning agree in predicting maximally persistent conformity to parental prohibitions by children reared in an atmosphere of parental warmth and disciplined by withdrawal of love, they differ in their other predictions. To test these various hypotheses separately would require both short-run and long-run analyses of the effects of a variety of parental discipline patterns. The following hypotheses might be tested: (a) that discipline by deprivations (whether of things, privileges, or love) has more persistent effects than discipline by noxious stimulation (whether physical or social); (b) that where the child is taught to confess and apologize for his transgressions, avoidance behavior will go through cycles of extinction and reconditioning; and (c) that punishing only part of a child's transgressions results in more persistent obedience than does punishing all of them.

## Summary and Conclusions

It is suggested that the terms identification, introjection, and internalization be replaced by detailed analyses in learning-theory terms of the acquisition of values. A reinforcement framework for such analyses is outlined, and examples are presented dealing with the concept of conscience and the factors influencing its development. It is argued that this would simplify terminology, encourage more precise study, and further the integration of learning and personality theories.

This analysis, like all attempts to integrate the harder-headed and the softer-hearted portions of behavioral science, is open to attack from both sides. On the one hand it may be objected that the present treatment is too cavalier with the interpersonal and intrapsychic complexities of personality development, that the internalization of values and the identification of one person with another cannot be treated as though they were nothing but the simple learning of a rat in a maze. The answer to this objection is that no "nothing but-ism" is intended; it is an empirical matter both to determine how far the principles of learning (not necessarily simple) can go in explaining personality development and to decide how much the additional principles suggested by some writers actually contribute to our understanding of the phenomena in question. The attempt to catch too much complexity at a single stroke may retard rather than advance our understanding.

On the other hand it may be objected that the interpretations given here are untestable, that the variables involve such diverse and subtle behaviors over such long periods of time as to defy adequate measurement. Admittedly the questionnaire, interview, and brief-observation techniques used in this area leave much to be desired. However, as long as applied behavioral scientists are called upon to deal with questions of personality development, poor data to guide their decisions are better than none. Study of learning of values by humans, guided by the principles of learning based on both animal and human studies, has the potential to make vital contributions to many theoretical and applied areas of knowledge. It is hoped that the present discussion may contribute something to that goal.

## References

*AUSUBEL, D. P. Relationships between shame and guilt in the socializing process. *Psychological Review*, 1955, **62**, 378–390.

*BENEDICT, R. *The chrysanthemum and the sword.* Boston: Houghton Mifflin, 1946.

BRUSH, F. R. The effects of shock intensity on the acquisition and extinction of an avoidance response in dogs. *Journal of Comparative and Physiological Psychology*, 1957, **50**, 547–552.

CAMPBELL, D. T. Social attitudes and other acquired behavioral dispositions. In S. Koch (Ed.), *Psychology: A study of a science.* Vol. 6. *Investigations of man as socius: Their place in psychology and the social sciences.* New York: McGraw-Hill, 1963. Pp. 94–172.

CHURCH, R. M. Transmission of learned behavior between rats. *Journal of Abnormal and Social Psychology*, 1957, **54**, 163–165.

DARBY, C. L., & RIOPELLE, A. J. Observational learning in the rhesus monkey. *Journal of Comparative and Physiological Psychology*, 1959, **52**, 94–98.

DAVIS, W. A., & HAVIGHURST, R. J. *Father*

* [Asterisks indicate works that are reprinted, in whole or in part, in this volume.]

*of the man*. Boston: Houghton Mifflin, 1947.

DINSMOOR, J. A. Punishment. I. The avoidance hypothesis. *Psychological Review*, 1954, **61**, 34–46.

DOLLARD, J., & MILLER, N. E. *Personality and psychotherapy*. New York: McGraw-Hill, 1950.

DUKES, W. F. The psychological study of values. *Psychological Bulletin*, 1955, **52**, 24–50.

FREUD, A. *The ego and the mechanisms of defense*. New York: International Universities, 1946.

FREUD, S. *The ego and the id*. London: Hogarth, 1950.

GLASER, D. Dynamics of ethnic identification. *American Sociological Review*, 1958, **23**, 31–40.

GRANT, D. A., SCHIPPER, L. M., & ROSS, B. M. Effect of intertrial interval during acquisition on extinction of the conditioned eyelid response following partial reinforcement. *Journal of Experimental Psychology*, 1952, **44**, 203–210.

HAVIGHURST, R. J., & NEUGARTEN, B. L. *American Indian and white children*. Chicago: University of Chicago Press, 1955.

HULL, C. L. *Principles of behavior*. New York: Appleton-Century, 1943.

HULL, C. L. *A behavior system*. New Haven: Yale University Press, 1952.

HUMPHREYS, L. G. The effect of random alternation of reinforcement on the acquisition and extinction of conditioned eyelid reactions. *Journal of Experimental Psychology*, 1939, **25**, 141–158.

HUMPHREYS, L. G. Psychogalvanic responses following two conditions of reinforcement. *Journal of Experimental Psychology*, 1940, **27**, 71–75.

HURLOCK, E. B. *Child development*. (3rd ed.) New York: McGraw-Hill, 1956.

JENKINS, W. O., & STANLEY, J. C. Partial reinforcement: A review and critique. *Psychological Bulletin*, 1950, **47**, 193–234.

KAGAN, J. The concept of identification. *Psychological Review*, 1958, **65**, 296–305.

LAZOWICK, L. On the nature of identification. *Journal of Abnormal and Social Psychology*, 1955, **51**, 175–183.

LEWIS, D. J., & DUNCAN, C. P. Vicarious experience and partial reinforcement. *Journal of Abnormal and Social Psychology*, 1958, **57**, 321–326.

LINDEMANN, E. Symptomatology and management of acute grief. *American Journal of Psychiatry*, 1944, **101**, 141–148.

LYNN, D. B. A note on sex differences in the development of masculine and feminine identification. *Psychological Review*, 1959, **66**, 126–135.

MASSERMAN, J. H. *Principles of dynamic psychiatry*. Philadelphia: Saunders, 1946.

*MEAD, M. Some anthropological considerations concerning guilt. In M. L. Reymert (Ed.), *Feelings and emotions: The Mooseheart symposium*. New York: McGraw-Hill, 1950.

MILLER, N. E. Experimental studies of conflict. In J. McV. Hunt (Ed.), *Personality and the behavior disorders*. New York: Ronald, 1944. Pp. 431–465.

MILLER, N. E. Learnable drives and rewards. In S. S. Stevens (Ed.), *Handbook of experimental psychology*. New York: Wiley, 1951. Pp. 435–472.

MILLER, N. E., & DOLLARD, J. *Social learning and imitation*. New Haven: Yale University Press, 1941.

MILLER, N. E., & KRAELING, D. Displacement: Greater generalization of approach than avoidance in a generalized approach-avoidance conflict. *Journal of Experimental Psychology*, 1952, **43**, 217–221.

MILLER, N. E., & MURRAY, E. J. Displacement and conflict: Learnable drive as a basis for the steeper gradient of avoidance than of approach. *Journal of Experimental Psychology*, 1952, **43**, 227–231.

MOWRER, O. H. *Learning theory and personality dynamics*. New York: Ronald, 1950.

MOWRER, O. H., & ULLMAN, A. D. Time as a determinant in integrative learning. *Psychological Review*, 1945, **52**, 61–90.

MURRAY, E. J., & MILLER, N. E. Displacement: Steeper gradient of generalization of avoidance than of approach with age of habit controlled. *Journal of Experimental Psychology*, 1952, **43**, 222–226.

OSGOOD, C. E. *Method and theory in experimental psychology*. New York: Oxford, 1953.

PARSONS, T. Family structure and the socialization of the child. In T. Parsons & R. F. Bales (Eds.), *Family, socialization and interaction process*. Glencoe, Ill.: Free Press, 1955.

REYNOLDS, W. F. Acquisition and extinction of the conditioned eyelid response following partial and continuous reinforcement. *Journal of Experimental Psychology*, 1958, **55**, 335–341.

RUSSELL, W. A., & STORMS, L. H. Implicit verbal chaining in paired-associate learning. *Journal of Experimental Psychology*, 1955, **49**, 287–293.

SANFORD, N. The dynamics of identification. *Psychological Review*, 1955, **62**, 106–118.

*SEARS, R. R., MACCOBY, E. E., & LEVIN, H. (Eds.) *Patterns of child rearing*. Evanston, Ill.: Row, Peterson, 1957.

SHAW, G. B. Preface to "Androcles and the Lion." In *Nine Plays*. New York: Dodd, Mead, 1948.

SIDMAN, M. Two temporal parameters of the maintenance of avoidance behavior by the white rat. *Journal of Comparative and Physiological Psychology*, 1953, **46**, 253–261.

SINGER, M. B. Shame cultures and guilt cultures. In G. Piers & M. B. Singer (Eds.), *Shame and guilt*. Springfield, Ill.: Charles C Thomas, 1953.

SOLOMON, R. L., & BRUSH, E. S. Experimentally derived conceptions of anxiety and aversion. In *Nebraska symposium on motivation IV*. Lincoln: University of Nebraska Press, 1956.

SOLOMON, R. L., & COLES, M. R. A case of failure of generalization of imitation across drives and across situations. *Journal of Abnormal and Social Psychology*, 1954, **49**, 7–13.

TOLMAN, E. C. There is more than one kind of learning. *Psychological Review*, 1949, **56**, 144–155.

WHITING, J. W. M., & CHILD, I. L. *Child training and personality*. New Haven: Yale University Press, 1953.

# 23

# Preliminary report on temptation and guilt in young dogs

*by Richard L. Solomon*

Yes, we have been carrying on experiments on resistance to temptation and guilt in puppies for the last six years in our laboratory. The work has been a joint enterprise under the authorship of Drs. A. H. Black, R. L. Solomon, and J. W. M. Whiting (with the assistance of Drs. Russell M. Church and Dean Peabody). We have carried out several experiments, but because they have taken a great deal of time, and because the accumulation of enough numbers for certain conclusions has been slow, we have published nothing on our major findings to date. Dr. Black, who is now at McMaster University, will publish a short note in the *Canadian Journal of Psychology* concerning some peripheral aspects of the study, but the major study, when it does come out, will be under the authorship of Black, Solomon, and Whiting.

Here is the general nature of our experiments to date. First, we developed what we called a *taboo-training situation* and standardized it as much as possible. The taboo-training room was a

From Richard L. Solomon, "Preliminary Report on Temptation and Guilt in Young Dogs," in O. H. Mowrer, ed., *Learning Theory and the Symbolic Process* (New York: John Wiley & Sons, 1960), pp. 399–404. Reprinted by permission of the author and the publisher.

square room approximately 15 × 15, fairly soundproof, and equipped with a one-way mirror. In one corner of the room was placed a chair and in front of it at each leg of the chair were two small dishes. The trainer sat in the chair and he was equipped with a rolled-up newspaper with which he could swat the subjects on the rump. All experiments were run with six-months-old puppies as subjects. The procedure was as follows: Each puppy was starved for two days and then was brought into the experimental room by one experimenter. The trainer was sitting in the chair. In one of the food dishes was highly preferred boiled horsemeat. In the other dish was a less preferred commercial dog chow (Food X). The dishes could be quickly switched from side to side. The puppy usually chose the horsement a few seconds after he was introduced into the room. As he *touched* the horsemeat, he was swatted by the trainer. If the swat was not enough to break up the consummatory behavior, the puppy was swatted again and again until he withdrew from the horsemeat. This usually produced complete, initial negative generalization; but after the passage of time the puppies usually made another pass at the horsemeat. They were swatted again. Eventually, they shifted their concentration to Food X which they ate without being molested.

We tried several variations on this taboo-training procedure, and we finally arrived at one which produced fairly rapid discriminative avoidance learning. We usually carried the puppies along for several days, making sure that they were reliable in avoiding the tabooed horsemeat and that they quickly and avidly ate Food X. We set up an arbitrary learning criterion: after twelve errorless trials the animal had learned the taboo.

Following this, the experiment entered the *temptation-testing* phase. This consisted of starving the puppy for two days and introducing him to the experimental room with the *trainer absent*. In one dish were three Food X pellets, and in the other dish was a large pile of boiled horsemeat. The three pellets were for the purpose of checking the effect of the change in the feeding situation induced by the absence of the trainer. All puppies gobbled up the three pellets with a short reaction time and then went through various antics in relation to the large dish of horsemeat. Some puppies would circle the dish over and over again. Some puppies walked around the room with their eyes toward the wall, not looking at the dish. Other puppies got down on their bellies and slowly crawled forward, barking and whining. There was a large range of variability in the emotional behavior of the puppies in the presence of the tabooed horsemeat. We measured resistance of temptation as the number of seconds or minutes which passed by before the subject ate the tabooed food. Each puppy was only given a half hour a day in the experimental room in the presence of the horsemeat. If he did not eat the horsemeat at that time, he was brought back to his home cage, was not fed, and a day later was introduced into the experimental room again. This procedure was continued until the puppy finally violated the taboo, or until he became so emaciated and dehydrated from lack of food that we felt that he could not survive the experiment any longer.

In our pilot experiments we found a very great range of resistance to temptation. The shortest period of time it took a puppy to kick over the traces was a little over six minutes, and the longest period of time was sixteen days without eating, after which time the experiment was terminated and the puppy fed in his home cage. Thus huge range gave us the opportunity to see the effects of some antecedent conditions and some constitutional differences in determining the resistance to temptation scores.

Here are some of the antecedent conditions we have worked with. In every case the consequent condition or dependent variable was resistance to temptation. In our first experiments we studied the difference between hand feeding and watering puppies versus machine feeding and watering them from the time they were weaned up until the taboo training at six months of age. Litters were split into two groups and one group was never fed or watered except when a human being came in and did so, while the other group was never fed and watered unless a machine produced food and water without a human being present at the time. Three separate litters of mongrel puppies were run in this experiment. In the case of each of these experiments, the familiarity of both groups of puppies with the experimenters was held constant and equated. That is, whenever an experimenter came into the living quarters to feed and water the hand-fed group, he also exposed himself to the machine-fed animals and touched them and interacted with them for the same period of time. We kept this familiarity control throughout all of our experiments. All puppies were given their shots by the same person, and the cages were cleaned by the same person. The only difference, then, was the difference between dependence on machines and dependence on human beings for food and water. The first three litters, run over the first three years of our experimentation, contained eight, six, and six puppies, respectively.

The first litter gave us very encouraging results. There was a significant difference in resistance to temptation scores between hand-fed and machine-fed groups. Of the eight puppies in the litter there was only one overlapping case, with three of the hand-fed puppies clearly outlasting the rest of the field, and three of the machine-fed puppies clearly having low resistance to temptation. In the second litter the picture was not so clear, mainly because all of the puppies showed very high resistance to temptation. Four of these puppies failed to touch the horsemeat after 14 days and we had to terminate the experiment. The other two puppies kicked over the traces, and one was in the hand-fed group and one was in the machine-fed group. In the third litter which we ran under the same conditions, none of the puppies violated the taboo. Obviously, we were hitting some kind of a ceiling, and obviously, the temperamental characteristics of the puppies were very important. For example, we found that the best single predictor of resistance to temptation without regard to experimental conditions was our assessment of the timidity of the puppy prior to the experiment. Puppies who are timid in approaching human beings and who are easily frightened by loud noises are also those puppies who resist temptation most effectively. This fits with the observations made by the people at Jackson Laboratories at Bar Harbor, Maine. Paul Scott has reported that Shetland Sheepdogs are especially sensitive to reprimand, and that taboos can be established with just one frightening experi-

ence, such taboos being extremely resistant to extinction. On the other hand, the Basenjis seem to be constitutional psychopaths, and it is very difficult to maintain taboos in such dogs.

We also tried some variations on the Freudian notion of ambivalence. We checked to see whether it made a difference if the trainer was the prior nurturing agent or not. I raised a litter of six puppies from weaning to six months of age under conditions which made them completely dependent upon me for everything they needed. I cleaned their cages, I fed and watered them, and no one else had nurturant interactions with the puppies, although lots of other people came in the room, walked back and forth in front of the cage so that the puppies could be familiarized with other people. Then, at six months of age, I taboo-trained three of the puppies, and another experimenter taboo-trained the other three puppies. We wanted to see whether taboo-training was more effective when the nurturing agent was also the punishing agent. Here, again, our taboo-training was too effective. All puppies resisted temptation for sixteen days, and the experiment was terminated.

We are now in the midst of another experiment, similar to this one, in which the Freudian notion of ambivalence is being explored with a few more experimental variations. We hope to cut down the effectiveness of our taboo-training techniques, and settle for a poorly established aversion for horsemeat, one that will be easier to extinguish. We then hope to check on our prior observations, especially in the hope that our success with the first litter of eight puppies can be repeated with other litters. Litter variance is extremely important, and we have to design our experiments so that it can always be taken into account in such a way that it is not confounded with any other experimental conditions. We haven't reached the stage yet when we want to go the expense of using thoroughbreds, so we use mongrel pups.

Over the long haul our object is to vary systematically those parameters of a socialization process which have been postulated to lead to high resistance to temptation. Note that I am separating *resistance to temptation* from *guilt*, and I am avoiding the use of conscience and superego which may be some sort of a compound of the two manifestations. For example, in the first litter we ran, we found that when a puppy did kick over the traces and eat the horsemeat, he did so with his tail wagging the whole time; and after he ate the horsemeat, when the experimenter came into the room the puppy greeted him with tail wags, and with no obvious distress. On the other hand, in some preliminary work we did, we noticed that some pups showed much more emotional disturbance after they ate the horsemeat than when they were approaching it. We were able to relate this to uncontrolled differences in training techniques. We are now privately *convinced*, although we do *not* have open-and-shut experimental evidence to prove it, that when puppies are walloped just as they *approach* the taboo food, they build up a high resistance to temptation. However, if and when such puppies do kick over the traces, they don't show any emotional upset following the crime. On the other hand, if you let a puppy eat half of the horsemeat up before you wallop him, you can still establish avoidance of the horsemeat. However, in the case of these puppies, there is a lot more emotional

disturbance *following* the crime. This could be called a guilt reaction, and the presence of the experimenter is not required to elicit it. The presence of the experimenter seems to intensify it, when he does finally come in the room after the crime is committed. Therefore, we believe that the conditions for the establishment of strong resistance to temptation as contrasted with the capacity to experience strong guilt reactions, is a function of both the intensity of punishment and the time during the approach and consummatory response sequence at which the punishment is administered.

We feel that delayed punishment is not very effective in producing a high level of resistance to temptation, but it is effective in producing emotional reactions after the commission of the crime. Call these reactions guilt, if you wish, for lack of a better term. On the other hand, it is clear that punishment introduced after the animal eats quite a bit of the horsemeat does operate backward in time and it does produce aversion and the disruption of approach responses. These approach responses however, don't seem to be as reliably broken up by such delayed punishment. On the other hand, we have yet to see an emotional disturbance following the crime in a puppy whose approach behavior alone has been punished.

We feel that this observation is important, since it represents two major types of socialization techniques used by parents. In one case the parent traps the child into the commission of a tabooed act so that the child can be effectively punished, the hope being that this will prevent the child from performing the act again. The other technique is to watch the child closely and to try to anticipate when the child intends to do something wrong and punish the child during the incipient stages. Each of these techniques, according to our observations with puppies, should lead to a very different outcome with regard to the components of "conscience."

We assume that "conscience" has two components: the ability to resist temptation, and the susceptibility to guilt reactions. We assume that these two components are partially independent, and that by appropriate training procedures we could produce puppies who have high resistance to temptation, but low susceptibility to guilt reactions; high resistance to temptation along with high susceptibility to guilt reactions; low resistance to temptation along with low susceptibility to guilt; and low resistance to temptation along with high susceptibility to guilt reactions. It is easy to examine these four classes of outcomes and see four clinically important combinations in the neuroses, as well as the creation of a psychopath.

We are very hopeful about the eventual contribution of these experiments, and Johnny Whiting and I plan to try to keep this research going over the years. It has the continuing support of the Laboratory of Social Relations, and as long as we have students who now and then will be willing to put in their time in assisting us, we will eventually have an interesting story to tell. This research does, however, take a long time to carry out, and we have very little to show for our six years of work.

You may be interested to note that an analogous temptation testing situation has been set up in Johnny Whiting's shop for use with children. They have developed a beanbag game which can be used to measure resistance to temptation

(cheating), and they are studying different antecedent conditions as they relate to the cheating score. This work is even more in its infancy than [is] the puppy work, however.

We are also interested in situational determinants of resistance to temptation. It is our theory that when a puppy is constantly nurtured by one person, the following association is established: "When I am hungry, the experimenter comes; or, when I am thirsty, the experimenter comes." According to this line of reasoning, high drive stimulus level leads to the anticipation of the appearance of the nurturing agent. On the other hand, if the nurturing agent is also the punisher in the taboo-training situation, then anticipation of the arrival of the nurturing agent, accompanied by touching the tabooed object or trying to consume it, should lead to intense anxiety reactions. These reactions are quite observable during the training procedure, and quite often the puppies avoid the experimenter or vacillate quite a bit in going toward and away from him. When the puppy is left alone in the room during temptation testing, we assume that the following mechanisms operate. If the puppy is in a state of high drive, the following association occurs: "Experimenter will come," because this is what has been established in the previous nurturant relationship. If there has not been such a previous nurturance relationship, then the association will not run itself off. If, under the high drive condition, the association does occur, and the puppy does expect the experimenter to come, he is faced with the problem: "If I eat the food and the experimenter comes, I will get swatted." This leads to an anticipatory anxiety attack and aversive behavior. For a puppy which has been nurtured by the trainer, the more it needs the trainer at the time, the more likely it is to stay away from the taboo food.

Generalizing from this analysis, the child who is reaching into the tabooed cookie jar will be less likely to touch the forbidden cookies if the child needs to have his diaper changed at the time, and the punishing agent is the one who has also been the nurturing agent and the diaper changer. This part of our analysis leads to experiments on situational determinants of resistance to temptation. We have not yet gone into situational determinants of intensity of guilt reactions, but we hope to do this job sometime along with the other.

Eventually, when we have established the ease with which the major phenomena can be produced in the laboratory, we will have to go into parametric studies. We are certainly not in a position to do this now, because we haven't even found out how to control our taboo training situation so that it will give us a convenient range of behavioral variability. We thought we had it under control at one time, but later litters gave us quite a setback.

# 24

# Some effects of delay of punishment on resistance to temptation in dogs[1]

*by Richard L. Solomon,*
*Lucille H. Turner,*
*and Michael S. Lessac*

Delay of punishment is a major variable determining the effects of punishment on the extinction of a specific instrumental response. In the experiments which have produced steep gradients of delay of punishment, the punished responses have been discrete and phasic, such as a bar press (Church, Raymond, & Beauchamp, 1967; Skinner, 1938) or a key peck (Azrin, 1959). The delay intervals were the times between the responses and the punishments. However, sometimes a response to be punished is not discrete and phasic, but rather it is persisting and repetitive. Some examples are eating in dogs (Lichtenstein, 1950) and in cats (McCleary, 1961), children handling forbidden objects (Aronfreed & Reber, 1965; Park & Walters, 1965),

Richard L. Solomon, Lucille H. Turner, and Michael S. Lessac, "Some Effects of Delay of Punishment on Resistance to Temptation in Dogs," *Journal of Personality and Social Psychology*, **8**, 1968, 233–238. Copyright 1968 by the American Psychological Association, and reproduced by permission.

[1] This research was supported by United States Public Health Service Grant MH-04202 to Richard L. Solomon.

and drinking in rats (Hunt & Schlosberg, 1950). In these experiments, if the delay of punishment is *short*, the experimenter treats the continuing response as though it were discrete and phasic, and punishment is delivered at its *onset*. However, a problem arises when one wishes to study the effects of *long* delays of punishment on this kind of response because the punishment delay interval is confounded both with duration of consummatory behavior and with amount of reward. For example, if a dog is punished 5 seconds after he starts eating, and if the dog initially eats continuously during the delay interval, such confounding is obvious. Nevertheless, it is not necessarily to be avoided; to the contrary, it is interesting precisely because it approximates many "real-life" uses of punishment. Aversive socialization techniques will often necessitate the use of delayed punishment and, in many of those cases, repetitive, consummatory, and persisting behavior will fill the delay interval.

The present experiment demonstrates some effects of different delays of punishment on resistance to temptation in dogs, in the special case where eating a specific kind of food is the punished behavior and eating that food can occur during the delay-of-punishment interval.

## Method

### Subjects

Eighteen purebred beagle dogs, 18 months old at the start of the experiment, were divided into the following three groups of six subjects each: Group I, 0-second delay of punishment; Group

II, 5-second delay of punishment; Group III, 15-second delay of punishment.[2]

## Apparatus

The experimental room was approximately 10 feet square. Three feet from the rear of the room was a chair in which the experimenter sat, facing a door. Three inches in front of and 8 inches to either side of the experimenter's feet were two identical food dishes. Between these and the door was a pan of water. A live microphone was hung from the ceiling above the food dishes and 4 feet from the floor to allow the vocalizations of the dogs to be noted by an observer. The experimental room could be viewed through a one-way mirror mounted in the door.

## Procedure

On each of 10 successive days, all dogs were given dry laboratory dog chow in their home cage for 10 minutes. Next, they were given a 20-day habituation period consisting of 10-minute daily sessions in the experimental room, during which the subjects were allowed to eat dry laboratory chow freely from both food dishes while the experimenter sat quietly in the chair. Each dish contained 200 grams of dry chow. Subjects received all of their daily ration in the experimental room during habituation, training, and testing. At the end of habitua-

tion, the subjects were at normal body weight.

Next, 10-minute daily "taboo-training" sessions were begun. During training, one dish contained 200 grams of canned meat, a highly preferred food, while the other dish contained 200 grams of the familiar dry laboratory chow. The locations of the meat and chow dishes were alternated from day to day. All subjects were punished for eating the canned meat, but were allowed to eat dry chow without punishment. The punishment was a hard blow on the snout administered by the experimenter with a tightly rolled-up newspaper. Subjects of Group I, the 0-second delay group, were instantly swatted for *touching* the meat with mouth or tongue. Subjects of the other two groups were swatted for *eating* meat: Group II after 5 consecutive seconds of meat eating, and Group III after 15 consecutive seconds of meat eating. If the subject retired from the meat after a swat and then recontacted the meat, the punishment delay program was reestablished. If the subject then turned and ate the dry laboratory chow, there was no further punishment; but if he returned to meat eating, he was again punished with the appropriate delay. All subjects were run to a learning criterion of 20 days without punishment; that is, they touched and ate dry chow only on 20 successive days.

When the learning criterion was met, all subjects weighed less than 80 percent of their normal body weight. They were therefore given seven daily 1-hour feedings during which dry chow was freely available in their home cages. After subjects regained their lost weight, they were deprived of all food for 2 days, following which they were given 10-minute

---

[2] Three subjects in each group had been raised for 8 months in social isolation, while the other three dogs in each group were raised under standard laboratory kennel conditions. Because the two conditions of social experience produced no significant differences in this experiment, they can be safely ignored for present purposes.

daily "temptation-testing" sessions in the experimental room. During these testing sessions, there was meat (now increased to 500 grams) and dry chow (now decreased to 20 grams) in the other dish. *The experimenter was not in the room.* The meat and chow dishes were alternated daily, as they were during training. There was no food in the home cages. If the subjects did not eat the "taboo" horsemeat, they had only 20 grams of dry chow each day—a starvation diet. (Normal intake was 300–400 grams of dry chow.)

"Resistance to temptation" was measured by the number of days it took each subject to "break the taboo." There were two definitions of breaking the taboo. The first was touching the mouth or tongue to the horsemeat. The second was carrying out the act for which the subject had been punished during taboo-

training: Group I, touching the meat; Group II, eating the meat for 5 seconds; and Group III, eating the meat for 15 seconds. Because the second criterion contained the first, each subject in the 5-second and 15-second delay groups yielded two measures of resistance to temptation. The occurrence of defecation, urination, vocalization, locomotion patterns, and postural attitudes were noted in protocols by the observer as they occurred.

## Results

### Acquisition

The mean numbers of swats required during training to produce criterion taboo learning were 4.3, 3.0, and 4.3 for the 0-second, 5-second, and 15-second groups, respectively. The mean numbers of training days required for criterion taboo learning were 29.0, 25.0, and 36.5, respectively (see Figure 1). None of these between-group differences was significant.

### Resistance to Temptation

The mean numbers of test days to reach the first and more stringent criterion of breaking the taboo were 16.3, 8.2, and .3, respectively, for the 0-, 5-, and 15-second delay groups ($F = 34.7$, $df = 2, 1$, $p < .01$). The mean numbers of test days to reach the second and more lenient criterion were 16.3, 9.7, and 1.5, respectively ($F = 22.2$, $df = 2, 1$, $p < .01$) (see Figure 1).

### Gross Behavior during Training

There were striking, qualitative differences between groups. The 0-second

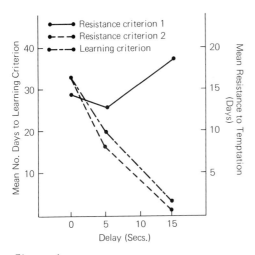

*Figure 1*

**Ease of acquisition of a food taboo and subsequent resistance to temptation as a function of different delays of punishment used in taboo training. (The solid line shows ease of acquisition as measured on the left-hand ordinate. The broken lines show resistance to temptation as measured on the right-hand ordinate.)**

delay group (I) subjects, after one or two previous punishments, upon being put in the experimental room would slink, tails down, around the walls of the room, as far as possible from the food dishes and the experimenter. Often these subjects urinated and defecated soon after a session started. When they did approach the food area, they usually avoided the meat dish and approached the dry chow hesitantly, backing away several times before touching it. However, once having touched the dry chow, they gulped pellets down, tails wagging, heads in the dish. The meat was usually ignored completely throughout the criterion sessions even though the subjects often had finished the dry chow several minutes before the end of the session. Early in training, when these subjects did "break" and touch the taboo meat, their pattern of approach was slow, stealthy, and hesitant. Fearfulness was exhibited only during the approach to food and not during the eating itself. Late in training there were no obvious signs of fear during the approach to the dry chow or the eating of it.

In contrast, the 15-second delay group (III) subjects, after a few punishments, would run into the experimental room, tails up and wagging, sniff at the meat, nose or jump up on the experimenter, and then go to the chow dish and snatch a few pellets. Their whole behavior pattern then changed. With tails down, these subjects usually crawled behind the experimenter's chair or to one wall, urinated, defecated, ran to the water pan, circled the room, crawled on their bellies to the experimenter, wagged their tails tentatively, then took a few more pellets and retreated again. As training progressed, these subjects would sometimes snatch bits of meat, then quickly run out of the experimenter's reach and eat them. Late in training some subjects in the 15-second delay group would eat meat for as long as 7–10 seconds, then retreat and eat the pellets. Signs of fear were evident during the eating both of the dry chow and the meat. This fearfulness continued through the criterion trials.

Group II (5-second delay) subjects showed less "eat and run" behavior than did those in Group III (15-second delay), but they were still markedly different in their approach to the meat as compared to Group I (0-second delay) subjects. They were furtive, hesitant, and sometimes touched the meat without eating it before eating all the pellets. Fearfulness was exhibited both during approach to food and while eating it.

*Gross Behavior during Testing*

The absence of the experimenter during testing did not disrupt the eating of the 20 grams of dry chow pellets in any of the three groups. All 18 hungry dogs ate avidly with but a few seconds delay. However, although the experimenter was no longer in the experimental room, subjects in the 5-second and 15-second delay groups behaved *as though he were still there*. After eating the few dry chow pellets, they put their forepaws up on the experimenter's empty chair, or hid behind the chair, and wagged their tails when they looked at the chair. When they finally broke the taboo and ate the horsemeat, they ate in brief intervals and ran away between bites. They appeared to be frightened during and after finishing the meat.

In contrast, the 0-second delay group ate the 20 grams of dry chow pellets and then moved to the walls of the room far away from the horsemeat. Late in each session they might move a little nearer to the food, but with hesitancy. It was only after several days of starvation that these subjects moved close to the horsemeat dish. When they finally broke the taboo, their mood appeared to change abruptly. Unlike the subjects of Groups II and III, these subjects wagged their tails while eating the meat, ate voraciously without pausing, and after finishing the meat did not appear to be apprehensive.

## Discussion

Empirical generalizations from this experiment concern four kinds of phenomena: (a) acquisition of a food discrimination, (b) generalization of the effects of punishment, (c) resistance to temptation, and (d) emotionality during food discrimination learning and temptation testing.

### Acquisition

With a *short* delay of punishment for touching horsemeat, dogs will quickly learn to confine their eating to available dry chow, even though the horsemeat is highly preferred. Even with a *long* delay of punishment for eating horsemeat, dogs will quickly learn to discriminate between the horsemeat and dry chow, but their behavior seems furtive and variable; even though they learn to confine most of their eating to the permissible dry chow, they intermittently "snatch" bits of taboo horsemeat. Surprisingly, the ease of discrimination learning, defined by a criterion measure is approximately the same with short and long delays of punishment. This is

what Aronfreed (1966) found in a similar experiment with children. Aronfreed attributed this failure of delay of punishment to retard taboo learning significantly to the cognitive capacity of the children to relate their behavior to long-term consequences. Should similar findings in dogs and children be similarly explained?

### Generalization

The inhibitory effects of punishment immediately generalize from the taboo food to the permissible food, and all dogs become hesitant to eat anything in the experimental room. The phenomenon differs with delay of punishment. With a *short* delay of punishment, generalization is strong early in training, but it is weak or absent during criterion trials. With *long* delays of punishment, generalization is present but weak, early in training and it does not completely disappear during criterion trials. *Long* delays of punishment weaken behaviors oriented toward the acceptable food as well as the taboo food.

### Resistance to Temptation

The capacity of the dog to starve himself rather than eat the taboo food is a sensitive function of delay of punishment during training. With a *short* delay of punishment, resistance is very high, and most laboratory-raised dogs will starve themselves for as long as 2 weeks before they will eat the taboo food. With *long* delays of punishment, resistance to temptation is relatively low, but it is on an absolute basis surprisingly high when one considers that dogs are usually ravenous after 5 days of starvation.

## Emotionality

During learning, the fearfulness of the dogs trained with a *short* delay of punishment shows itself mainly during approaches to food; then during the criterion trials the approaches become stereotyped. Late in training these dogs appear happy during the approach to the permissible food, while eating it, and after eating it. During temptation testing, these dogs show fearfulness when approaching the taboo food, but once they begin eating they appear to be happy, and they remain happy after eating. During learning, the fearfulness of the dogs trained with *long* delays of punishment shows itself in the approach to food, during the eating of it, and after eating, even if the only food eaten is the permissible one. During temptation testing, these dogs show furtiveness during the eating of the taboo food and after eating, but their approach to food and their initial touching of it does not appear to be very fearful when compared with the dogs trained with a short delay of punishment.

## Speculation

This experiment is a prototype for a particular kind of socialization technique. An unwanted act is punished, but if there is a delay of punishment it is confounded with duration of consummatory behavior and amount of reward. This confounding is undoubtedly crucial in producing the phenomena we have seen: the furtiveness and unreliability of dogs trained with long delays of punishment, the great superiority in resistance to temptation manifested in dogs trained with a short delay of punishment. As a tentative hypothesis, it is assumed that the mechanisms producing the complex pattern of results in the present experiment are identical for dog and human socialization. It is felt that sophisticated cognitive functions, though perhaps more characteristic of children than of dogs, are sufficiently under the control of the training parameters to produce analogous behavior in both species, provided that the confounding condition is met.

The authors feel that the major action of punishment is to establish conditions for the Pavlovian conditioning of fear. The stimuli directly preceding punishment, both response produced and experimenter controlled, become conditioned elicitors of fear. The instrumental behavior will be "shaped" by the increases and decreases of fear associated with that behavior, according to hedonic reinforcement principles.

With a *short* delay of punishment, the dogs in the present experiment will be made fearful by their approaching any food dish, but will be made more intensely fearful by touching the taboo food. In contrast, eating the permissible dry chow will be positively reinforced. If the training is continued for a sufficiently long period, the counterconditioning of fear of approaching a food dish, through the action of positive food reinforcement, should lead to no fear in approaching the dry chow dish and no fear during the eating of dry chow. On the other hand, approaching the taboo food should be fear-arousing. During temptation testing, it follows that approach to the meat dish should be fear-arousing, as would be touching the food. However, *eating* the taboo food, once it occurs under the impetus of extreme hunger, should *not* be fear-arousing because eating has not been a response-produced conditioned stimulus associated with the punishment. Punishment for the short-delay group has always preceded eating during training. These postulated mechanisms deduce high resistance to temptation resulting from the taboo object, yet pleasant appetitive reflexes during and after eating. The authors' observations are not in conflict with these deductions.

With *long* delays of punishment, the stimuli preceding the occurrence of punishment will be response-produced stimuli associated with eating itself. Eating in the experimental situation should thus be fear-arousing. However, approaches to food and the initial touching of food should be reinforced by the food itself. One would expect that Pavlovian inhibition of delay would be apparent in such a situation, and the authors interpret the furtiveness of the dogs as reflecting this. Onset of eating is not a sufficient stimulus for fear arousal, but rather it controls inhibition of fear which "times itself out" during eating. The timing should be related to the delay-of-punishment interval, and 5-second delay should produce more rapid emergence of fear than 15-second delay. When fear emerges from inhibitory control, the dog should back away from the food, which then establishes a new response sequence: approach to food, touching the food, eating. This gives the appearance of furtiveness. During temptation testing these dogs should show low resistance to temptation, but should show recurrent and persisting fear during eating. The authors' observations are not in conflict with these theoretical expectations.

One might then ask why the acquisition data do not reflect the effect of delays. The answer is not simple. It is, instead, a complicated theory of con-

science. The authors assume that the dogs, even with long delays of punishment, quickly "know" which food results in punishment administered by the experimenter. This is a type of cognitive learning that can span long temporal delays. The dogs *know* what they are not supposed to eat! However, when the experimenter is missing, and the dogs are faced with an uncertainty or a change in the controlling stimulus situation, the authors' argument is that cognition is not enough. The hungry dogs cannot be certain any longer that eating the taboo horsemeat will result in punishment, because the experimenter is gone. It is under these conditions of changed social stimulation that the authors believe the conditioned emotional reactions of the dogs "take over."[3] If emotional condi-

[3] The Hullian postulate concerned with delay of reinforcement leads to the prediction that acquisition of the food discrimination should be slower with long delays of punishment. This was not the case (see solid line, Figure 1). On the other hand, the Hullian prediction did correspond with data on resistance to temptation: a weaker avoidance habit was the consequence of the long punishment delays. If one equates reinforcement uncertainty with delay of reinforcement, as cognitive dissonance theory does, then one predicts a higher value to be placed on an outcome associated with long delay. There is, however, the difficult matter of assessing the place of negative or aversive outcomes in cognitive dissonance theory. Is the punishment more "intense" for the long-delay condition because its "value" is intensified by uncertainty? If so, perhaps there should be higher resistance to temptation for longer delays of punishment. The opposite was the case. Or, is the aversive "value" of delayed punishment decreased by uncertainty so that it is "weaker" than immediate punishment? In addition, one might further complicate the problem with the consideration of the "value" of the taboo food. Is the taboo food raised in "value" more when it is associated with quick, certain punishment than when it is associated with delayed, less certain punishment? Or, would it be vice versa? These are interesting and important theoretical questions, but they cannot be adequately explored here.

tioned responses take mediational control of behavior under conditions of cognitive uncertainty, the temporal characteristics of Pavlovian emotional conditioning will manifest themselves. This is why delay of punishment is a powerful determiner of subsequent resistance to temptation and the emotional concomitants of taboo violations.

There are several deductions from such a theory of self-control. One is of great interest. The greater the difference between the training situation and its social objects and the temptation-testing situation, the steeper should be the resistance gradients plotted in Figure 1. In other words, the dogs trained under long punishment delays should have *no* resistance to extinction in a radically changed environment. This might also be the case if the food used in temptation testing were somewhat different from the taboo food. However, if the delay of punishment has been short, resistance to temptation should still be manifest in highly changed environments and with objects similar to taboo objects.

The authors see no a priori reason why the above analysis should not be applicable to the socialization of the child. It predicts the conditions under which one should expect high or low resistance to temptation, and it predicts the pattern of emotional expression that should be seen during temptation testing and subsequent violation of the taboo. Furthermore, it specifies the training conditions that should produce high resistance to temptation along with low emotionality during the violation of a taboo, as well as the training conditions that should produce low resistance to temptation along with high emotionality during the violation of a taboo.

Perhaps these same training variables will prove to be related to intensity of shame and guilt in children. If so, delay of punishment should have profound effects on the temporal characteristics of, and the occasions for the occurrences of, shame and guilt in children.

## References

ARONFREED, J. The origins of altruistic and sympathetic behavior. Paper presented at the meeting of the American Psychological Association, New York City, September 1966.

ARONFREED, J., & REBER, A. Internalized behavioral suppression and the timing of social punishment. *Journal of Personality and Social Psychology*, 1965, **1**, 3–16.

AZRIN, N. H. Punishment and recovery during fixed-ratio performance. *Journal of Experimental Analysis of Behavior*, 1959, **2**, 301–305.

CHURCH, R. M., RAYMOND, G. A., & BEAUCHAMP, R. D. Response suppression as a function of intensity and duration of punishment. *Journal of Comparative and Physiological Psychology*, 1967, **63**, 39–44.

HUNT, J. McV., & SCHLOSBERG, H. Behavior of rats in continuous conflict. *Journal of Comparative and Physiological Psychology*, 1950, **43**, 351–357.

LICHTENSTEIN, P. E. Studies of anxiety. I. The production of a feeding inhibition in dogs. *Journal of Comparative and Physiological Psychology*, 1950, **43**, 16–20.

McCLEARY, R. A. Response specificity in the behavioral effects of limbic system lesions. *Journal of Comparative and Physiological Psychology*, 1961, **54**, 605–613.

PARK, R. D., & WALTERS, R. H. Some factors influencing the efficacy of punishment training to induce response inhibition. *Monographs of the Society for Research in Child Development*, 1965, **63**, No. 7.

SKINNER, B. F. *The behavior of organisms.* New York: Appleton, 1938.

# 25

# Acquisition of self-control through modeling

*by Albert Bandura
and Richard H. Walters*

The social-learning principles set out in the chapters on imitation and direct reinforcement can aid in the understanding of all aspects of self-control, including the development of self-rewarding and self-punitive responses.

The influence of modeling is most clearly apparent in those societies in which the majority of adults consistently display self-denying or self-indulgent behavior. In societies in which denial or indulgence is a cultural norm, the children have little opportunity to observe any other patterns of behavior and consequently are forced to model themselves after the prevalent self-control patterns. As research on the Hutterites (Eaton & Weil, 1955) show, patterns of self-denial may persist for many generations.

The transmission of self-indulgent patterns may be associated with a low level of technology and a precarious economic and social life, which persist in spite of contact with more provident social groups. Among the Siriono of Bolivia, for example, there are relatively

few restrictions on the expression of sex and aggression, and there is no obligation for the younger and healthier members to care for the old and infirm, who are abandoned to die when the social group moves on to a new location. Holmberg (1950) attributes the "Siriono personality" to a chronic shortage of food; however, his description of Siriono life indicates that this shortage is largely due to lack of self-denial among the members of the society. On returning from a successful expedition, the Siriono hunter may enter his village empty-handed and signal to his wife to retrieve the game that he has surreptitiously set aside before his entry. He and his family then gorge themselves on the spoils, leaving nothing for a time of shortage. So extreme is this immediate self-indulgence that Siriono females characteristically have distended stomachs, which are, according to Holmberg, attributable to sporadic overeating.

Leighton and his associates (Hughes, Tremblay, Rapoport, & Leighton, 1960) present an account of life in a Nova Scotian county, in which both self-indulgent and self-denial subcultural patterns have coexisted for a number of generations. In "Lavallée," an Acadian community, children are strictly trained in the control of sexual, aggressive, and dependency behavior and are strongly pressured to achieve educational and vocational success. *"Evidently some of these demands are contagious, for the mothers say that their children demand teaching even before entering school"* (p. 133; italics not in original). Both parents spend a considerable amount of time in interacting with their children and thus in transmitting to them the adult patterns which predominate in this cohesive community. While the people of Lavallée emphasize material success, the wealthier members of the community are not expected to be self-indulgent; "the greater economic success a person has, the more he is expected to share it with his family, his church, and his community" (p. 157).

> In terms of time orientation, the main things in life are long-range goals—such as the salvation of the soul, the economic bettering of the area, the preservation and expansion of the Acadian group—*even though some of these are unlikely to be achieved by any individual in his lifetime. . . . Work is a moral activity,* and a man is enjoined not only to do it but also to take pride and pleasure in it under almost any circumstance. . . . Life without work would be life without meaning, and people who try only to get as much money as possible while doing as little as they can are disparaged (pp. 159–160; italics not in original).

Within the same Nova Scotian county there exists a group of settlements in which a very different pattern of life prevails. Community cohesion is lacking, and laziness, drunkenness, fighting, sexual promiscuity, thievery, and other criminal and antisocial activities frequently occur. In contrast to the parents of Lavallée, the parents in these "depressed" settlements are permissive and nondirective and have very low educational and occupational aspirations for their children. Through their own life patterns, they transmit to their children beliefs that work should be avoided, if possible, and that laws are to be defied; and they continually present to them models of drunken, aggressive behavior. Indeed, one of the prevailing sentiments among these people is that "the best thing to do in life is to escape from your problems as quickly as possible."

The preference for drinking as the modal recreational pattern sets the keynote for this sentiment. The drinking in turn often leads to fighting, another way of attempting to obliterate rather than solve problems. Also popular, though, are some of the "fantastic" types of comic books and violent action movies, through which emotional releases and temporary escapes can be found. Recreation, then, when enjoyed at all, tends to be at either of two extremes: the drinking which soon results in oblivion, or the fighting and related types of violent action. There is relatively little middle-ground, such as moderately tempered parties or group games. So dominant is the drive for liquor that people are willing to spend exorbitant sums of money to get it from bootleggers after the Government liquor store is closed. They will also drink alcoholic substitutes such as vanilla if the need is not met with regular liquor (p. 307).

A child who grows up in this kind of atmosphere is unlikely to acquire, either through modeling or through reinforcement patterns, habits of self-denial and self-restraint by which he and his children might secure a more stable and prosperous pattern of life.

Parent interview studies (V. J. Crandall, 1963), as well as statistical analyses of demographic and cross-cultural data (McClelland, 1955; McClelland, Atkinson, Clark, & Lowell, 1953), also suggest that high standards of achievement, together with habits of self-restraint in the service of long-term goals, are likely to be transmitted from one generation to another. In one of these studies, Crandall, Katkovsky, and Preston (1962) found that girls whose fathers devoted time to participate in intellectual pursuits with their children were inclined to give up free-play time to engage in intellectual activities. It thus appears that parental modeling may influence not only the standards that govern achievement behavior but also the direction that achievement-striving takes. As Sarason, Davidson, Lighthall, Waite, and Ruebush (1960) have indicated, parental anxiety concerning the evaluative standards of others may be also transmitted to children in the form of an anxious concern about meeting standards set by school authorities.

Further evidence for the influence of parent models in the development of children's habits of self-control comes from Mischel's investigations into self-imposed delay of reinforcement. Anthropological data indicate that adult Trinidadian Negroes are more impulsive and self-indulgent, and less likely to provide for the future, than Grenadian Negroes or Trinidadian Indians. Mischel (1958, 1961) examined preferences for larger, delayed rewards, as opposed to smaller, immediate rewards, among children of families belonging to each of these three subcultural groups. Children from the highly self-indulgent Trinidadian Negro subculture showed the greatest degree of preference for immediate rewards. Moreover, children who came from homes in which the father was absent were likely to choose smaller, immediate rewards rather than to postpone gratification in order to obtain a larger reward. Assuming that a father's abandonment of his home reflects the family's lack of participation in a delayed-reward culture (Mischel, 1958), this latter finding may be regarded as providing further evidence of the influence of parent models on the self-control of children.

The influence of models in modifying resistance to deviation has been demonstrated in experimental studies having relevance to the problem of deviation. S. Ross (1962) employed a toy-store situation in which nursery-school children alternated in the roles of customer and storekeeper. For children in a deviant-model condition, a peer model, who served as the experimenter's confederate, informed the children that upon completing the game they could select a *single* toy only. The model then proceeded to help himself to three toys. In the conforming-model condition, the model took only one toy and thus exhibited behavior that was consistent with his verbal prohibition. Children in the control group simply received the verbal prohibition. In each condition the peer model left the room while the children made their selections. Relative to the subjects in the conforming-model and the control groups, children who observed the deviant model violated the prohibition more often and exhibited more conflictful behavior as reflected in moralistic comments, self-reassurances about the deviation, self-directed hostility, and concealment while performing the misdeed. Some evidence that a conforming model reinforces the observer's self-controlling tendencies, and thereby reduces conflict in temptation situations, is provided by the finding that control children displayed significantly more conflictful behavior than those who witnessed the conforming model, although both groups were equally conforming.

Lefkowitz, Blake, and Mouton (1955), using an accomplice model who violated a traffic signal, noted an increase in pedestrian violations following exposure to the model, especially if the model was attired as a high-status person. Freed, Chandler, Blake, and Mouton (1955), in an investigation of conditions influencing the violation of a sign prohibiting entry to a building, varied both the strength of a prohibition and the compliance-noncompliance of a model. The combination of a strong prohibition and a compliant model produced the lowest incidence of deviation, whereas deviation was most frequent if the prohibition was weak and the model disobeyed the sign. Using two levels of instigation to deviate, Kimbrell and Blake (1958) prohibited students from drinking from a water fountain. Providing that instigation was not so strong as to force deviation, subjects who observed a model violate a prohibition more readily performed the prohibited act than subjects who observed a conforming model.

The study of Lefkowitz et al. shows that characteristics of the model—in this case, his status position—may increase his effectiveness for reducing inhibitions. The influence of the model is also modified by the observed consequences of his behavior (Walters, Leat, & Mezei, 1963). Children who observe a model rewarded for performing a prohibited act are more likely to deviate than are children who observe the model punished. Indeed, the observation of punishing consequences to the model actually strengthens resistance to deviation.

In the studies referred to above the focus of attention has been on the violation of a prohibited nonaggressive activity. The investigators have, generally speaking, explicitly prohibited responses that in other circumstances would be permitted to the agent. In the case of aggression, particularly intense physical forms, it can be assumed that inhibitions have been developed as a result of past training during the life-histories of the subjects. Lowering of resistance to aggression was demonstrated in previously described studies in which an increase in

aggressive responses followed exposure to aggressive models.

Observation of aggressive models may serve not only to reduce inhibitions but also to teach the observers new ways to deviate. Bandura, Ross, and Ross (1963) demonstrated that children who observed a model who was rewarded for aggression exhibited imitative aggressive responses that had not previously appeared in their repertory. Moreover, an analysis of aggressive responses which were not precisely imitative revealed that boys and girls were differentially influenced by the behavior of the models and its response consequences. Boys were inclined to inhibit aggression when they either observed an aggressive model punished or had no exposure to displays of aggression, whereas observation of both highly expressive but nonaggressive models and rewarded aggressive models greatly enhanced the boys' aggressive behavior. By contrast, exposure to nonaggressive models had the greatest inhibitory effect on the girls' expression of aggression. These findings suggest that control over aggression can be vicariously transmitted through the influence of models either by the administration of punishment to the model or by the presentation of incompatible prosocial examples of behavior.

The differential effects of prosocial and deviant models on the control of aggression by boys and girls may be partly explained by the relative dominance of aggressive responses in the subjects' repertories. Thus, for boys, in whom physically aggressive responses are relatively strongly established, exposure to a punished model effectively inhibited aggressive behavior, whereas their observation of highly expressive nonaggressive or rewarded aggressive models produced substantial disinhibitory effects. Presumably, a general increase in the boys' activity following exposure to an expressive model resulted in the manifestation of their relatively dominant habits of aggression. On the other hand, girls, who generally exhibit little physical aggression, showed little increase in nonspecifically imitative aggression following exposure to the aggressive models, while exposure to nonaggressive models produced decrements in the girls' aggressive responses.

It is generally assumed that resistance to deviation results from the association of noxious stimuli with the commission of prohibited responses during the life history of an individual. However, as modeling studies demonstrate, children may acquire inhibitions without committing a prohibited act and without themselves receiving any punishment. There is thus considerable evidence that response inhibition and response disinhibition can be vicariously transmitted, particularly if the immediate consequences to the model are apparent or the model is a person who has evidently been competent or successful in life.

The influence of models in transmitting patterns of self-rewards and self-punishments has received attention in only one experimental study (Bandura & Kupers, 1964). Children participated in a bowling game with an adult or a peer model, the scores, which could range from 5 to 30, being controlled by the experimenter. At the outset of the game, the children and their models were given access to a plentiful supply of candy, from which they could help themselves as they wished. Under one experimental condition the model set a high standard for self-reinforcement; on trials in which the model obtained or exceeded a score of 20, he rewarded himself with candy and made self-approving statements, while on trials in which he failed to meet the adopted standard he took no candy and berated himself. In the other experimental condition, the model exhibited a similar pattern of self-reward and self-disapproval, except that he adopted the standard of 10, a relatively low level of performance. After exposure to their respective models, the children played a series of games on the bowling apparatus in the absence of the models. During these trials the children received a wide range of scores, and the performances for which they rewarded themselves with candy and self-approval were recorded.

It was found that the children's patterns of self-reinforcement closely matched those of the model to which they had been exposed; moreover, they tended to reproduce the self-approval and self-critical comments of their model. Thus, although both groups had access to a plentiful supply of desired material reinforcers, the children who had adopted a high criterion for self-reinforcement through imitation utilized these resources sparingly and only when they achieved relatively high levels of performance, while children who were exposed to the low-standard model rewarded themselves generously even for minimal performance.

A comparison of the results obtained with adult and peer models revealed that children were more influenced by the standard-setting behavior and self-reinforcement patterns exhibited by adults. A control group of children, who had no exposure to models, set no standards for themselves, and tended to reward themselves for minimal performance. Figures 1 and 2 present graphi-

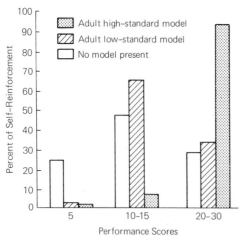

**Figure 1**

The regulation of self-reinforcement as a function of level of performance by children in the control group and by those exposed to adult models adopting high and low criteria for self-reinforcement.

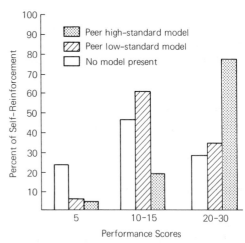

**Figure 2**

The regulation of self-reinforcement as a function of level of performance by children in the control group and by those exposed to peer models adopting high and low criteria for self-reinforcement.

cally, for each of the three groups of children, the distribution of self-reinforcements as a function of level of performance. This experiment demonstrates the influence of vicarious reinforcement, in the form of rewards and punishments *self-administered* by the model, on the process of imitative learning; it thus indicates clearly one manner in which self-control may be acquired through observational learning.

Demonstrations that inhibitions and self-evaluative responses may be learned without the mediation of direct reinforcement are consistent with common-sense thinking. Socialization agents, for example, parents and teachers, frequently make use of exemplary models and from time to time reward or punish children in front of others in the expectation that the positive or negative reinforcement will influence the future behavior of the observers. Indeed, the administration of well-publicized rewards and penalties is a frequently employed so-

cial-influence procedure, whereby those who occupy power positions in society attempt to modify the behavior of many by rewarding and penalizing the behavior of individuals who are already socially visible or who become so as a result of the publicity.

## References

BANDURA, A., & KUPERS, C. J. Transmission of patterns of self-reinforcement through modeling. *Journal of Abnormal and Social Psychology*, 1964, **69,** 1–9.

BANDURA, A., Ross, D., & Ross, S. A. Vicarious reinforcement and imitation. *Journal of Abnormal and Social Psychology*, 1963, **67,** 601–607.

CRANDALL, V. J. Achievement. In *Child psychology: The sixty-second yearbook of the National Society for the Study of Education*, Part 1. Chicago: The National Society for the Study of Education, 1963. Pp. 416–459.

CRANDALL, V. J., KATKOVSKY, W., & PRESTON, A. Motivational and ability determinants of young children's intellectual achievement behaviors. *Child Development*, 1962, **33**, 643–662.

EATON, J. W., & WEIL, R. J. *Culture and mental disorders.* New York: Free Press, 1955.

FREED, A., CHANDLER, P. J., BLAKE, R. R., & MOULTON, J. S. Stimulus and background factors in sign violation. *Journal of Personality*, 1955, **23**, 499.

HOLMBERG, A. R. *Nomads of the long bow.* Washington, D.C.: U.S. Government Printing Office, 1950.

HUGHES, C. C., TREMBLAY, M., RAPOPORT, R. N., & LEIGHTON, A. H. *People of cove and woodlot: Communities from the viewpoint of social psychiatry.* New York: Basic Books, 1960.

KIMBRELL, D., & BLAKE, R. R. Motivational factors in the violation of a prohibition. *Journal of Abnormal and Social Psychology*, 1958, **56**, 132–133.

LEFKOWITZ, M. M., BLAKE, R. R., & MOUTON, J. S. Status factors in pedestrian violation of traffic signals. *Journal of Abnormal and Social Psychology*, 1955, **51**, 704–706.

McCLELLAND, D. C. Some social consequences of achievement motivation. In M. R. Jones (Ed.), *Nebraska symposium on motivation.* Lincoln, Nebr.: University of Nebraska Press, 1955. Pp. 41–65.

McCLELLAND, D. C., ATKINSON, J. W., CLARK, R. A., & LOWELL, E. L. *The achievement motive.* New York: Appleton, 1953.

MISCHEL, W. Preference for delayed reinforcement: An experimental study of a cultural observation. *Journal of Abnormal and Social Psychology*, 1958, **56**, 57–61.

MISCHEL, W. Father-absence and delay of gratification: Cross-cultural comparisons. *Journal of Abnormal and Social Psychology*, 1961, **63**, 116–124.

ROSS, S. A. The effect of deviant and nondeviant models on the behavior of preschool children. Unpublished doctoral dissertation, Stanford University, 1962.

SARASON, S. B., DAVIDSON, K. S., LIGHTHALL, F. F., WAITE, R. R., & RUEBUSH, B. K. *Anxiety in elementary school children.* New York: Wiley, 1960.

WALTERS, R. H., LEAT, M., & MEZEI, L. Response inhibition and disinhibition through empathetic learning. *Canadian Journal of Psychology*, 1963, **17**, 235–243.

# MODIFIABILITY OF MORAL JUDGMENT

lend support to the invariant-sequence of moral development that was hypothesized by both Piaget and Kohlberg.

## Introduction

An important issue in the search for the antecedents of conscience involves determining effective procedures for teaching or modifying conscience. Both studies presented in this subsection were conducted within a Piagetian framework. The Turiel paper introduces us to Kohlberg's theoretical extensions of Piaget. Crowley's data suggest that children's moral judgments can be modified by employing certain techniques. Turiel was also able to modify moral judgments and his data

# 26

# Effect of training upon objectivity of moral judgment in grade-school children[1]

*by Paul M. Crowley*

Piaget's theory of moral judgment (Piaget, 1932) runs parallel to his general theory of cognitive processes. One facet of moral judgment is the dimension of intentionality. Its immature pole is objectivity (judging an act to be bad because of the amount of "objective" physical damage done); its mature pole is subjectivity (judging an act to be bad because of the "subjective" intention of the agent). Piaget's operational measure of intentionality was a pair of stories with an objective alternative (a child's

Paul M. Crowley, "Effect of Training upon Objectivity of Moral Judgment in Grade-School Children," *Journal of Personality and Social Psychology*, **8**, 1968, 228–232. Copyright 1968 by the American Psychological Association, and reproduced by permission.

[1] This study is based on a dissertation submitted to The Catholic University of America in partial fulfillment of the requirements for the PhD. The author wishes to express his appreciation to his committee· Robert M, Dowling, Norman Milgram, and Antanas Suziedelis, for their advice and encouragement, as well as to the staff and students of Mount Calvary and St. Philip's schools, Prince George's County, Maryland, for their generous cooperation.

accidental action causes considerable damage) and a subjective alternative (a child's intentionally malicious act is accompanied by minor damage).

Studies investigating the dimension of intentionality have been mainly correlational (cf. Kohlberg, 1964), with little attention to the effect of experimentally manipulated variables. Two exceptions are Bandura and McDonald (1963) and Turiel (1966). The former investigators, using Piaget-type stories and a standardized version of Piaget's clinical interview, tested the relative efficacy of social reinforcement and modeling procedures and reported significant changes in children's moral judgments. The latter study, based on Kohlberg's (1964) stage theory, used a more sophisticated measure of moral judgment and reported the differential effectiveness of exposing children to levels of moral reasoning above or below their initial stage of development.

In Piaget's theory, objectivity of moral judgment appears to be a result of the *egocentrism* (inability to take the viewpoint of another person), *syncretism* (reacting globally to a situation rather than analyzing its elements), and *centration* (focusing on some striking but superficial aspect of phenomena) which characterize immaturity of cognitive processes (cf. Flavell, 1963). Now if one were to present to a child a task which required him to take the role of others and look at their motives, to analyze a story more closely, and to decenter from striking but superficial aspects of a story, then one would expect a decrease in objectivity. The training task was designed to achieve just this end. It will be recalled that Piaget's items were "complex"; that is, they combined two dimensions: that of intentionality or the lack of it, and that of consequences, large or small. For training purposes, a set of "simple" items was devised, that is, pairs of stories in which the consequences were equated (e.g., one cup is broken in both stories). As a result, the only important difference between the two stories was the contrast of an intentional with an accidental act. Hence it was predicted that children trained by techniques which helped them to focus on intentionality while minimizing the influence of prominent but irrelevant cues would make more mature moral judgments than children who received no training.

Training which employs "simple" stories can be varied along different dimensions. The two dimensions studied in this experiment were the *content* of the stories and their *mode of presentation.*

As regards *content*, it was predicted that, with the structure of training material held constant, training which employed material specifically moral in content would be more effective than training which employed material of nonmoral content. This prediction was based on the literature concerning transfer and generalization, which generally indicates that the transfer effect is greater when there is a greater similarity between the stimuli used in training and in the subsequent task (Deese, 1958).

As regards *mode of presentation*, it was predicted that training which encouraged discovery and verbalization of a principle would be more effective than training which merely provided a verbal discrimination response. This prediction was based on such studies as Beilin (1965) and Gagné and Smith (1962), which illustrated the importance of verbal formulation of a general principle in learning.

## Method[2]

The experimental design comprised three phases: (a) a *pretraining* session, in which subjects were selected who consistently made immature moral judgments; these subjects were distributed among the four experimental groups and one control group; (b) a series of three small group *training* sessions, in which the four experimental groups received training appropriate to their respective treatment conditions; (c) a *posttraining* session, wherein all the subjects were individually retested on a new set of moral judgment stories akin to the pretraining stories.

### Subjects

The sample used in this study was composed of first-grade parochial school boys and girls of middle-class socioeconomic status, as measured by father's occupation and cost of housing in the area.

### Instruments

Piaget-type, complex stories were the basic instrument in pretraining and posttraining. Because no data had been published regarding the discriminatory value of these items, and because it had been repeatedly observed that maturity of response seemed partly related to the specific situation depicted in a given story (Boehm, 1962; Durkin, 1961; Medinnus, 1959; Nass, 1964), items selected from Piaget and from Bandura and McDonald, as well as further items de-

[2] Fuller details concerning the experimental procedure, as well as a more extensive analysis and discussion of results, can be found in the doctoral dissertation (identical in title) of which this paper is a summary.

signed by the author, were submitted to a preliminary item analysis. This permitted elimination of stories which did not adequately discriminate between "objective" and "subjective" children.[3]

The stories used in training were simple; that is, each pair contrasted an accidental and an intentional act, with consequences equalized. Forty-five pairs of simple stories were devised which dealt with moral situations (e.g., maliciously versus accidentally breaking a cup). Another 45 pairs of simple stories were constructed which dealt with nonmoral situations, involving competence or skill (e.g., deliberately versus accidentally hitting a target).

*Procedure*

**Pretraining session.** The experimenter saw students in individual testing sessions which covered a 21-day period. During the session he administered, in randomized order, eight complex items, using the procedure described by Bandura and McDonald (1963). To insure student comprehension, he also employed colored stick-figure illustrations (cf. Figure 1), and had the child repeat both stories before deciding which of the two was "naughtier." Of the 215 children tested, 91 answered six or more stories in an objective fashion. These were given the Peabody Picture Vocabulary Test

*Figure 1*

**Illustrations for Posttest Item 12. (Left, intentional alternative: "Kate is getting tired of sitting and waiting while her mother is shopping. So Kate runs up and down the aisles in the grocery store. The clerk tells her, 'Slow down! Be more careful!' But Kate doesn't pay much attention to him. She starts to run again when he isn't looking. As she turns the corner, her hand hits a box of Kleenex, and it falls to the floor." Right, accidental alternative: "Pam goes grocery shopping with her mother. Her mother says, 'Oh, I forgot the ketchup, and it's way back at the end of the store!' Pam says, 'I'll get it for you, Mother.' As she's taking the bottle off the shelf, she doesn't lift the bottle high enough, and two bottles of ketchup fall off the shelf and break. The ketchup spills all over the floor.")**

and then divided into five groups (four training and one control) equated for age, IQ, and ratio of boys to girls.

**Training sessions.** In this phase, which comprised 9 school days in a 14-day period, subjects were assigned to small subgroups under each of the four training conditions described below, and were given three group training sessions. In each session 15 pairs of simple stories were presented. The children, after hearing and repeating each pair of stories, indicated their choice by marking booklets containing stick-figure illustrations of the stories. They were rewarded with a brightly colored poker chip for each item they answered correctly, with the understanding that the winner of the most chips at the end of training would get first choice of a variety of prizes which had been shown to them beforehand.

[3] A 14-page supplement giving the item analysis for the pretraining, posttraining, and discarded stories, as well as the stories themselves, has been deposited with the American Documentation Institute. Order Document No. 978 from ADI Auxiliary Publications Project, Photoduplication Service, Library of Congress, Washington, D. C. 20540. Remit in advance $2.50 for microfilm or $1.75 for photocopies and make checks payable to: Chief, Photoduplication Service, Library of Congress.

The specific procedure for each of the treatment conditions was as follows:

1. Moral stories/labeling (M/L). The stories dealt with "naughtiness"; the experimenter merely identified the naughtier child and, without any further explanation, rewarded or corrected each child.

2. Moral stories/labeling plus discussion (M/L+D). Again the stories dealt with naughtiness, but the experimenter, before rewarding or correcting each child, elicited a discussion from the subjects and helped them to verbalize the fact that the naughtier person had acted "on purpose" or had "meant" to do it.

3. Nonmoral stories/labeling (NM/L). This treatment condition resembled the first condition (M/L) with one exception: the content of the stories dealt not with moral situations but with matters of competence. The differing content entailed a different question. Rather than, "Who was naughtier" the experimenter asked, "Which was better?" "Who was the better [e.g.,] hunter?"

4. Nonmoral stories/labeling plus discussion (NM/L+D). Similar to the second condition (M/L+D) in that it entailed the discussion as well as reinforcement and labeling, this treatment differed in that the content of the stories dealt with competence, not morality.

5. Control group. During the training period, the control group was given no task, in order to ascertain whether merely exposing children to the pretraining items might itself be a form of training, as seemed to occur in studies by Beilin and Franklin (1962), Beilin (1965), and Smedslund (1961).

The training task was uniformly well learned by all four groups: on the average, the groups got 42 or 43 of the 45 items correct, with an *SD* ranging from 1.5 to 3.9; the lowest score was 32. Three of the groups averaged about 3 hours of training; the fourth group (NM/L) averaged about $2\frac{1}{4}$ hours.

**Posttraining session.** Subjects from the five groups were individually posttested, in a randomly alternating sequence, on 12 complex items. The average time lapse between the end of training and posttesting was practically identical for the four treatment groups (18 or 19 days, with an *SD* ranging from 2.2 to 2.9). The posttraining sessions covered 12 school days in a 17-day period.

**Results**

The basic question raised by this study was whether training of any sort would affect maturity of moral judgment. Table 1 compares the four training groups with the control group in terms of the mean number of stories answered

*Table 1*

**Subjective Moral Judgment Responses in Posttraining Session**[a]

| Group | M | SD |
|---|---|---|
| NM/L[b] | 4.4 | 3.7 |
| NM/L + D | 3.3 | 2.7 |
| M/L | 11.0 | 1.5 |
| M/L + D | 10.9 | 1.9 |
| Control | 1.5 | 2.4 |

[a] $N = 17$.
[b] Definition of the labels used for the four training groups is given under Procedure, in the discussion of the training sessions.

in a "subjective" (mature) fashion in posttesting.

In evaluating the comparison, it is important to note that the control group's mean posttraining score (1.5 stories out of 12, or 13 percent, answered subjectively) does not represent any improvement over its mean pretraining score (.9 out of 8, or 11 percent, answered subjectively). A Wilcoxon matched-pairs signed-ranks test indicated no significant difference between pretraining and posttraining scores.

The difference between the control group and the two groups whose training involved the use of moral stories (M/L and M/L + D) is immediately obvious. However, the two groups whose training involved the use of nonmoral stories (NM/L and NM/L + D) were compared separately with the control group by means of the Kolmogorov-Smirnov two-sample test. In both cases the difference between the training group and the control group proved significant at the .05 level of confidence (one-tailed test). Consequently, support is found for the proposition that training aids the acquisition of mature moral judgment.

*Differential Effectiveness of Training*

Two specific hypotheses were likewise proposed. The first dealt with content of stories (moral versus nonmoral); the second dealt with method of presentation (labeling versus labeling accompanied by discussion). A two-way analysis of variance indicated that the content effect was highly significant ($F = 118.81$; $p < .01$), but that the method effect was not. The interaction effect, about which no hypothesis had been proposed, was likewise not significant. Thus, training

which employed stories with moral content proved to be far more effective than training which used nonmoral stories, but the experiment afforded no evidence that verbalization of a principle was more effective as a means of training than provision of a verbal discrimination response.

## Discussion

This study offers considerable evidence for the efficacy of training, but the exact nature of the response learned merits further consideration. The effectiveness of a brief training phase could be taken as evidence that Piaget's theory of slowly maturing cognitive processes is unwarranted, since moral judgment was so quickly trained (cf. Bandura & McDonald, 1963). An alternative explanation, forwarded by Turiel (1966) and preferred by the author, is that the training was effective because it dealt with a relatively specific response. The standardized procedure adopted from Bandura and McDonald for the present study allowed only two alternatives, phrased in a simple manner. Any change resulting from training can therefore be easily interpreted as a change in an isolated social response rather than in a mental structure or stage. Thus, as frequently happens, operational refinement of the measuring instrument leads to more restricted theoretical implications.

Turiel's explanation is supported by several findings of the present experiment: children rarely verbalized the underlying principle spontaneously; subjects trained to use a principle did no better than subjects who were provided only with a verbal discrimination response; and subjects trained on nonmoral stories did not consistently "carry over" the concept of intentionality to moral stories in posttesting.

However, whether or not the items are adequate to test a complete and complex theory of moral development, they do measure a consistent phenomenon of children's moral judgment, and their use in the experiment throws light on the fact of, and conditions for, the modification of this phenomenon. One contribution of the present study is to provide a set of items which reliably measure intentionality.

As mentioned above, generalization seems an adequate explanation for the superiority of training by moral stories. It is significant, however, that subjects trained on nonmoral stories did improve over the control group. Since, for nonmoral subjects, the posttest stories presented stimuli different from the training stimuli, and since the response required in posttesting was different from the response required in training, it is evident that the learning involved cannot be conceptualized merely as a simple S-R bond.

What accounts for the failure of the discussion method to produce better results than mere labeling? Studies such as those of Milgram (1966), Milgram and Furth (1967), and Gagné and Smith (1962) suggest that the effectiveness of explanatory techniques by the experimenter or meaningful verbalization by the subjects depends on variables such as age and level of conceptual difficulty. In the present case the concept was rather difficult, demanding the abstraction of "intention" and "accident" from a wide variety of orally described situations. Piaget's theory readily accommodates an explanation in terms of age and conceptual difficulty. Cognitive input, he

stressed, must be congruent with the available cognitive schemata if assimilation of information is to occur.

It is difficult to make exact comparisons with Bandura and McDonald's results since both the experimental conditions and the content of the training stories were different. The most appropriate comparison is that between their *model and child reinforced/subjective treatment* (where models answered stories in a subjective fashion and the objective children who observed them were rewarded if they responded subjectively when their turn came) and the present experiment's *moral stories/labeling* treatment. The latter was much more effective. At best, Bandura and McDonald's subjects answered an average of 50 percent of the items subjectively, whereas subjects in the present experiment achieved an average of 90 percent subjective answers after a lapse of 18 days (versus Bandura and McDonald's immediate posttesting). Three factors probably contributed to this better performance: (a) use of discriminating stories (a number of the Bandura and McDonald posttest items proved to be nondiscriminatory during item analysis); (b) more intensive training, including correction of wrong answers; (c) stronger reinforcer (prizes versus mere verbal approval).

The subjects' uniformly excellent performance on the training task indicates that objectivity does not betoken inability to grasp intention, but rather failure to focus on intention when a competing cue (size of damage) is introduced. Centration thus appears to be a major factor in objective moral judgments. It would be interesting to see whether this inability to overcome the influence of peripheral cues is related to the field-dependence variable investigated by Witkin (1965) and his associates.

## References

BANDURA, A., & McDONALD, F. J. The influence of social reinforcement and the behavior of models in shaping children's moral judgment. *Journal of Abnormal and Social Psychology*, 1963, **67**, 274–281.

BEILIN, H. Learning and operational convergence in logical thought development. *Journal of Experimental Child Psychology*, 1965, **2**, 317–339.

BEILIN, H., & FRANKLIN, I. C. Logical operations in area and length measurement. *Child Development*, 1962, **33**, 607–618.

BOEHM, L. The development of conscience: A comparison of American children of different mental and socioeconomic levels. *Child Development*, 1962, **33**, 575–590.

DEESE, J. *The psychology of learning.* New York: McGraw-Hill, 1958.

DURKIN, D. The specificity of children's moral judgments. *Journal of Genetic Psychology*, 1961, **98**, 3–13.

FLAVELL, J. H. *The developmental psychology of Jean Piaget.* Princeton, N.J.: Van Nostrand, 1963.

GAGNÉ, R. M., & SMITH, E. C., JR. A study of the effects of verbalization on problem solving. *Journal of Experimental Psychology*, 1962, **63**, 12–18.

KOHLBERG, L. Development of moral character and moral ideology. In M. L. Hoffman & L. W. Hoffman (Eds.), *Review of child development research.* New York: Russell Sage, 1964.

MEDINNUS, G. R. Immanent justice in children: A review of the literature and additional data. *Journal of Genetic Psychology*, 1959, **94**, 253–262.

MILGRAM, N. A. Effect of instructional set on verbal conceptual performance in normal and retarded children. *Psychological Reports*, 1966, **18**, 647–653.

MILGRAM, N. A., & FURTH, H. G. Factors affecting conceptual control in normal and retarded children. *Child Development*, 1967, **38**, 531–543.

NASS, M. Development of conscience: A comparison of the moral judgments of deaf and hearing children. *Child Development*, 1964, **35**, 1073–1080.

*PIAGET, J. *The moral judgment of the child.* (Orig. publ. 1932) New York: Free Press, 1965.

SMEDSLUND, J. The acquisition of conservation of substance and weight in children: III. Extinction of conservation of weight acquired "normally" and by means of empirical controls on a balance scale. *Scandinavian Journal of Psychology*, 1961, **2**, 85–87.

*TURIEL, E. An experimental test of the sequentiality of developmental stages in the child's moral judgments. *Journal of Personality and Social Psychology*, 1966, **3**, 611–618.

WITKIN, H. A. Psychological differentiation and forms of pathology, *Journal of Abnormal Psychology*, 1965, **70**, 317–336.

* [Asterisks indicate works that are reprinted, in whole or in part, in this volume.]

## 27

# An experimental test of the sequentiality of developmental stages in the child's moral judgments[1]

*by Elliot Turiel*

Moral development has been approached from different viewpoints. Developmental theories such as Piaget's (1948) focus on the cognitive processes underlying moral responses and assume that the organization of these processes is different at different stages of development. The greater part of developmental research on morality has stemmed from Piaget's theory of moral stages, stages supported only to a limited extent by subsequent investigations (see Kohlberg, 1963b). Kohlberg (1958, 1963a) has postulated the following set of moral stages, which are based on children's reasoning

Elliot Turiel, "An Experimental Test of the Sequentiality of Developmental Stages in the Child's Moral Judgments," *Journal of Personality and Social Psychology,* **3,** 1966, 611–618. Copyright 1966 by the American Psychological Association, and reproduced by permission.

[1] This study is based on a dissertation presented to Yale University in candidacy for the degree of Doctor of Philosophy. It was conducted while the author held a United States Public Health Service predoctoral fellowship. The author wishes to express his gratitude to the members of the dissertation committee: Edward Zigler, Irvin Child, Merrill Carlsmith, and Robert Abelson. The author is also indebted to Lawrence Kohlberg for his invaluable advice and aid. Thanks are due to Rita Senf for her critical reading of the manuscript.

in response to hypothetical moral conflicts (Kohlberg, 1963a):

Stage 1: Punishment and obedience orientation.
Stage 2: Naive instrumental hedonism.
Stage 3: Good-boy morality of maintaining good relations, approval of others.
Stage 4: Authority-maintaining morality.
Stage 5: Morality of contract and democratically accepted law.
Stage 6: Morality of individual principles of conscience (pp. 13–14).

While space does not permit a detailed definition of Kohlberg's stages nor of his methods for the elicitation and stage classification of responses, the Method section should clarify the nature of his data.

Kohlberg postulated that his stages define a sequence normally followed by each individual. The sequence of the stages is hypothesized to be invariant, with the attainment of a mode of thought dependent upon the attainment of the preceding mode, requiring a reorganization of the preceding modes of thought. Evidence for this hypothesis (Kohlberg, 1963a, pp. 15–17) consists, first, of findings of age differences, in various cultures, consistent with the notion of sequence and, second, of findings of a "Guttman quasi-simplex" pattern in the correlations between the various types of thought, a pattern expected if they form a developmental order.

While this evidence supports the validity of the stages as forming a fixed sequence, there has been no experimental evidence. The aim of the present research was to subject Kohlberg's hypotheses to an experimental test. In particular, the concept of developmental sequence suggests some hypotheses regarding developmental change and learning of new moral concepts. The plan of the study was to select subjects at varying developmental stages, expose them to moral reasoning that differed from their dominant stage, and then test the amount of learning and generalization of the new concepts. First, part of the Kohlberg moral judgment interview was administered to determine the subject's dominant stage. With the remaining part of the Kohlberg interview, the subject was then exposed to concepts corresponding to a stage differing from his own. Some subjects were exposed to the stage that was one below their own, some to the stage one above, and some to the stage two above. Finally the subject was retested on the entire interview. If Kohlberg's stages do form a fixed developmental sequence, so that the attainment of a mode of thought is dependent on the attainment of the preceding mode, then it is expected that subjects exposed to the stage directly above their dominant stage would show more usage of that stage on the retest than would subjects exposed to stages two above or one below.

Thus this study was designed to test the following two hypotheses:

1. That Kohlberg's stages form an invariant sequence so that an individual's existing mode of thought determines which new concepts he can learn. It was expected that subjects exposed to reasoning corresponding to a stage directly above their dominant stage would be influenced more than those exposed to reasoning corresponding to a stage further above.
2. That each stage represents a reorganization of the preceding stages,

and in effect is a displacement of those stages. If each stage is a reorganization of the preceding stages, rather than an addition to them, then a tendency to reject lower stages would be expected, so that subjects exposed to a stage one above would be influenced more than those exposed to a stage one below their own.

## Method

### Subjects

This experiment used 44 seventh-grade boys from the New Haven public schools, between the ages of 12-0 and 13-7. These boys, chosen at random from the school files, were from the middle socioeconomic class, as determined by their parents' occupation and education level.

### Scoring Methods

An individual's developmental stage is determined by using Kohlberg's (1958) moral judgment interview, which contains nine hypothetical conflict stories and corresponding sets of probing questions. The following story is an example:

> In Europe, a woman was near death from a special kind of cancer. There was one drug that the doctors thought might save her. It was a form of radium that a druggist in the same town had recently discovered. The drug was expensive to make, but the druggist was charging ten times what the drug cost him to make. He paid $200 for the radium and charged $2,000 for a small dose of the drug. The sick woman's husband, Heinz, went to everyone he knew to borrow the money, but he could only get together about

$1,000, which is half of what it cost. He told the druggist that his wife was dying and asked him to sell cheaper or let him pay later. But the druggist said: "No, I discovered the drug and I'm going to make money from it." So Heinz got desperate and broke into the man's store to steal the drug for his wife. Should the husband have done that?

Two scoring procedures are available for determining a subject's scores on each of the six stages. (The stage with the highest score represents his dominant stage.) The first, a more global method, involves the use of rating forms devised by Kohlberg (1958). A second scoring procedure uses detailed coding forms (Kohlberg, 1958) for each of the nine situations of the interview. These coding forms were constructed and standardized on the basis of responses given by a large number of subjects. Each response listed in the coding forms has a stage assigned to it. A subject's responses to a given situation are divided into "thought-content" units, and each unit is assigned to a stage, as determined by the stage classification of that unit in the coding form. In this way the total number of units assigned to each stage is determined.

### Design and Procedure

There were three steps in the experimental procedure. The subject's dominant stage was determined by a pretest interview. In the experimental session subjects were exposed, through role playing, to concepts that were either one below, one above, or two above their initial dominant stages. These experimental treatments will be referred to as $-1$, $+1$, and $+2$ treatments, respectively. The treatment groups were equated on IQ via the Ammons Full-Scale Picture Vo-

cabulary Test. In a posttest interview the subjects' stage scores were reassessed to determine the influence of the treatment.

**Pretest selection interview.** During the first meeting each subject was individually administered six of the nine situations of the Kohlberg interview in order to determine his initial stage scores. A tentative assessment of each subject's scores was made using Kohlberg's global rating forms. Only those subjects whose scores on the dominant stage were twice as large as their scores on the next most dominant stage were retained. In all, 21 subjects were discarded, while the 48 retained were equally distributed among Kohlberg's Stages 2, 3, and 4.

Since the global rating system did not provide the sensitivity desired for the experiment, the protocols of subjects retained were rescored using Kohlberg's detailed coding forms. Only those subjects who then scored higher on their dominant stage, as determined by the global ratings, than on any other stage were retained. Four subjects were thus discarded, leaving a total of 44.

**Experimental treatment conditions.** All subjects of a given dominant stage were randomly assigned to the control group or to three experimental groups ($N=11$ per group). In the experimental treatments, administered 2 weeks after the pretest, subjects were exposed to moral reasoning in individual role-playing situations with an adult experimenter. In one treatment the reasoning presented was one stage below the initial dominant stage ($-1$ treatment); the second treatment group was exposed to reasoning that was one stage above ($+1$ treatment); and in a third treatment the reasoning presented was two stages above ($+2$ treatment). Members of the control group were not seen by the experimenter for any kind of treatment.

Through role playing of the three remaining stories of the Kohlberg interview, experimental subjects were exposed to the new moral concepts. After each story was read the subject played the role of the main character in the story, and as the main character he was to seek advice about the problem from two friends. The experimenter played the parts of the two friends. The subject first asked one "friend" for "advice," with that friend's advice favoring one side of the conflict, and then asked the second friend, who favored the other side of the conflict. The reasoning was always at the stage appropriate to the subject's treatment condition. All the arguments used in the role playing were constructed by closely following the coding forms and thus are based on specific coded responses.

Illustrative examples of the treatment-condition arguments are based on the Kohlberg situation in which the husband's conflict is between stealing a drug or letting his wife die. The following two arguments, containing Stage 3 reasoning, represent what a Stage 2 subject in the +1 treatment was exposed to in this situation:

(a) You really shouldn't steal the drug. There must be some better way of getting it. You could get help from someone. Or else you could talk the druggist into letting you pay later. The druggist is trying to support his family; so he should get some profit from his business. Maybe the druggist should sell it for less, but still you shouldn't just steal it.

(b) You should steal the drug in this case. Stealing isn't good, but you can't be blamed for doing it. You love your wife and are trying to save her life. Nobody would blame you for doing it. The person who should really be blamed is the druggist who was just being mean and greedy.

The experimenter, while administering the treatment, did not know the subject's stage, since he had not scored the pretest, and did not know the experimental group of the subject; hence administration of the treatments was blind. The only exceptions were subjects exposed to "Stage 1" concepts who must have been in Stage 2, and those exposed to "Stage 6," who must have been Stage 4 subjects. The possibility of the experimenter recalling the subjects' stages since he previously interviewed them is unlikely because there were many lengthy interviews, and because a subject's stage is determined using the scoring guides.

**Posttest interview.** The posttest consisted of the six pretest situations plus the three situations of the experimental treatments; it was administered to the experimental subjects 1 week after the treatment, and to the control subjects 3 weeks after the pretest. Subjects were called to the experimental room individually, where they were told they would be asked questions regarding stories similar to the ones they had previously heard. (The repetition of some of the stories and questions did not seem to affect the subjects' willingness to respond. They generally responded with the same interest and concentration as in the pretest.)

*Reliability and Scoring of Protocols*

The results reported in this paper are based on the scores obtained through the detailed coding. The interviews were coded by the experimenter more than a year after their administration. The scorer had no knowledge of the identity of the protocol he was coding, nor of its experimental condition. All the pretests were scored separately from the posttests. The coding was carried out on a situation-by-situation basis rather than on a subject-by-subject basis; after all subjects' responses to the first situation were coded, all subjects' responses to the next situation were coded, and so on.

One estimate of the reliability of Kohlberg's detailed coding system is based on the independent coding by two judges of responses obtained from 17 subjects not used in this experiment. Scores for each subject consisting of the percentage of the statements falling into each of the six stages were calculated. A weighted score per subject was then obtained by multiplying the number of points at each stage by the number of the stage, summing these products, and dividing the sum by the total number of points. The product-moment correlation between the scores of the two judges was .94.

A measure of interjudge agreement on the scoring of the subjects in this experiment was obtained from the correlation between the scores of the author, who used the detailed coding system, and those of another scorer who used the global rating system. Under both scoring systems a subject receives a number of points on each stage, which can be converted into a single score by the procedure described above. A product-moment correlation of .78 was found for the original 48 subjects. Since the two scoring systems differ slightly, this correlation is a conservative estimate of the interjudge reliability of the detailed coding system.

## Results

The analysis of the posttest interview, which included all nine moral judgment situations, was divided into the following two parts:

1.  Stage scores were obtained from the posttest responses to the three situations used in the treatments and not in the pretest. Since the experimental subjects were directly influenced on those three situations, these scores, which will be referred to as "direct scores," represent the amount of direct influence of the treatment.

2.  Posttest stage scores for the six situations used in the pretest represent the amount of indirect influence, or the tendency to generalize the treatment influence to situations differing from those on which subjects were directly influenced. The measure reflecting indirect influence is the difference between a subject's pretest and posttest scores on each stage. These change scores will be referred to as "indirect scores."

### Direct Scores

The analysis of the direct scores involved the percentage of usage for each subject of the stage that is: one below the initial dominant stage ($-1$ scores), at the same stage as the initial dominant stage ($0$ scores), one above the initial dominant stage ($+1$ scores), and two above the initial dominant stage ($+2$ scores).[2]

The hypothesis was that an individual accepts concepts one stage above his own

---

[2] The other scores, such as those of the stage two below or three above the dominant stage, are not reported because they did not show significant differences between the groups and do not add to the understanding of the problem.

dominant position more readily than he accepts those two stages above, or those one stage below. Two specific hypotheses result from this general hypothesis that the +1 treatment would be the most effective: (a) that the +1 treatment causes more movement to +1 than the +2 treatment causes movement to +2 or the −1 treatment to −1, and (b) that the +1 treatment causes more +1 movement than does any other treatment.

**Test of Hypothesis a.** Table 1 presents (in boldface type), for each experimental group, the mean amount of usage of concepts at the same stage as that of the treatment condition. Table 1 also presents the control group mean scores on the stages that are one below (−1 scores), one above (+1 scores), and two above (+2 scores) their dominant stage.

The experimental groups' scores may not reflect solely the influence of the experimental manipulations. To determine how much of these scores reflects factors other than the treatments, it is necessary to correct for the change that would have occurred independently of the experimental manipulations. The best estimate of this change is provided by the control group, which had no treatment. It may be assumed that the scores of the control group are due to statistical regression and other artifactual sources.[3]

[3] It may be a function of skewness that the −1 score of the control group was considerably larger than the +1 or +2 scores. Of a subject's series of scores one stage has the largest score while its adjacent stages have the next largest scores, with the more distant stages to the dominant stage having smaller scores. The subjects of this experiment tended to use the stages below the dominant stage more than those above, resulting in a positively skewed distribution on the six situations of the pretest. When the other three situations are included, more usage of the stage directly below the dominant stage, resulting in less skewness, would be expected.

The control group and the experimental groups were originally very similar. There were no significant differences between the combined scores of the experimental groups and the scores of the control group, with the $t$ values ranging from .10 to .65. We also compared each experimental group with the control group and found no significant differences.

*Table 1*

**Mean Direct Posttest Stage Scores (in Proportions) on the Stages One Below (−1), the Same As (0), One Above (+1), and Two Above (+2) the Pretest Dominant Stage**

| Stage level relative to pretest dominant stage[a] | Condition groups[b] | | | |
| | −1 treatment | +1 treatment | +2 treatment | Control |
|---|---|---|---|---|
| −1 | $.336_{11}$ | $.183_{12}$ | $.209_{13}$ | $.240_{14}$ |
| 0 | .283 | .346 | .374 | .395 |
| +1 | $.131_{21}$ | $.266_{22}$ | $.145_{23}$ | $.122_{24}$ |
| +2 | .057 | .102 | .099 | .085 |

Note: Dunnett $t$ tests were computed for each boldface figure against each of the other three figures in the same row. Tests significant at the .05 level, Group 11 > 13; at the .025 level, 11 > 12; at the .005 level, 22 > 21, 22 > 23, 22 > 24.

[a] Each subject had received pretest scores at each developmental stage, the highest of these indicating his dominant stage. On the posttest, for each individual the proportion of his total score was calculated for each level listed in the left column.

[b] $N = 11$ in each group.

The experimental groups' scores were corrected by subtracting from those scores the corresponding control group scores. This subtraction was done in the following manner: The $-1$ mean of the control group was subtracted from the $-1$ mean of the $-1$ treatment group; the $+1$ mean of the control group was subtracted from the $+1$ mean of the $+1$ treatment group; the $+2$ mean of the control group was subtracted from the $+2$ mean of the $+2$ treatment group. The three corrected means ($-1=.096$, $+1=.144$, $+2=.014$) obtained in this way are presumably free of artifacts and thus represent the amount of influence of the experimental treatments.

The corrected means show that, as hypothesized, the direct influence of the $+1$ treatment was greater than that of the other two treatments. The corrected mean of the $+1$ treatment group was shown to be significantly greater than the corrected mean of the $+2$ treatment group by a one-tailed $t$ test ($t=3.55$, $p<.005$).[4] The one-tailed $t$ test of the difference between the corrected means of the $+1$ treatment group and the $-1$

<hr/>

[4] Having subtracted the appropriate control score from the experimental condition score we then computed a $t$ test for the difference between the corrected means. The standard error for this $t$ test is complicated by the fact that we subtracted correlated groups from independent groups. However, the appropriate standard error may be shown to be:

$$\sqrt{s_1{}^2 + s_2{}^2 - r_{c_1 c_2} s_1 s_2}$$

where:

$s_1{}^2 =$ the $MS_w$ for the $+1$ scores multiplied by $2/n$

$s_2{}^2 =$ the $MS_w$ for the $+2$ scores multiplied by $2/n$

$n =$ the number of subjects in each group

$r_{c_1 c_2} =$ the correlation between the $+1$ and $+2$ scores of the control group.

(We are indebted to Robert Abelson and Merrill Carlsmith for the derivation of this expression.)

treatment group reached a borderline level of significance ($t=1.43$, $p<.10$).

The corrected mean of the $-1$ treatment group was significantly greater than the corrected mean of the $+2$ treatment group ($t=2.03$, $p<.05$).

**Test of Hypothesis _b_.** We have demonstrated that the amount of usage of the treatment condition stage was greater in the $+1$ treatment group than in the other two experimental groups. While this result is necessary to demonstrate the greater influence of the $+1$ treatment, the $+1$ scores of the $+1$ treatment group must also be compared with the $+1$ scores of the other groups.

Table 1 contains the $+1$ scores of each of the four groups. The differences between the $+1$ score of the $+1$ treatment group and the $+1$ scores of the other groups were tested using Dunnett's $t$ statistic, which is appropriate in simultaneously testing one group mean against each of several others (Winer, 1962). These $t$ tests indicated that the $+1$ treatment was the most effective condition in moving subjects up one stage, since the $+1$ score of the $+1$ treatment group was significantly larger than the $+1$ scores of any other group (Table 1).

**Other findings.** Table 1 also presents the $-1$, $0$, and $+2$ scores for the four groups. The $-1$ score of the $-1$ treatment group was larger than the $-1$ scores of the other groups. However, the Dunnett $t$ test indicates that the difference between the $-1$ score of the $-1$ treatment group and the $-1$ score of the control group did not reach significance ($t=1.66$). The differences between the $-1$ score of the $-1$ treatment group and the $-1$ scores of the $+1$ and the $+2$ treatment groups were both significant (Table 1).

Using Dunnett $t$ tests, comparisons of the $+2$ score of the $+2$ treatment group with the $+2$ scores of the control group ($t<1$), of the $-1$ treatment group ($t=1.16$), and the $+1$ treatment group ($t<1$), indicated that the $+2$ treatment did not show a significant effect.

Congruent with the hypothesis, the control group and the $+2$ treatment group showed the greatest usage of the dominant stage (0 scores). An analysis of variance comparing the control and the $+2$ treatment groups on the one hand, with the $-1$ and $+1$ treatment groups on the other hand, showed a significant difference ($F=4.72$, $df=1/32$, $p<.05$).

**Conclusions regarding the direct scores.** (a) The $+1$ treatment had a direct effect, an effect greater than that of either the $-1$ or $+2$ treatment. (b) Although not reaching an acceptable significance level, there was some suggestion that the $-1$ treatment had an effect in moving subjects down one stage. (c) The $+2$ treatment did not show a significantly greater effect than the control condition or the other experimental treatments in moving subjects up two stages.

*Indirect Scores*

The analysis of the indirect scores was similar to that of the direct scores. The indirect score is not a rating of responses on the posttest, but rather a measure of change from pretest to posttest. For each subject's stage scores we subtracted the pretest from the posttest scores and obtained change scores.

As indicated by Table 2, the pattern of results of the indirect scores was consistent with the hypotheses and with the results on the direct scores. The evidence is only suggestive since significant findings were minimal. A one-tailed $t$ test ($t=2.70$, $p<.025$) showed that the corrected mean of the $+1$ treatment group (.052) was significantly larger than that of the $+2$ treatment group ($-.002$). The one-tailed $t$ test of the difference between the corrected means of the $+1$ treatment group (.052) and the $-1$ treatment group (.012) reached a borderline level of significance ($t=1.46$, $p<.10$). Although the $+1$ score of the $+1$ treatment group was larger than the $+1$ scores of the other groups, none of these differences was significant. No other relevant differences were significant.

*Table 2*

**Mean Indirect Posttest Stage Scores (in Proportions) on the Stages One Below ($-1$), the Same As (0), One Above ($+1$), and Two Above ($+2$) the Pretest Dominant Stage**

| Stage level relative to pretest dominant stage | Condition groups[a] | | | |
|---|---|---|---|---|
| | $-1$ treatment | $+1$ treatment | $+2$ treatment | Control |
| $-1$ | $+.057$ | $+.001$ | $+.009$ | $+.045$ |
| 0 | $-.045$ | $-.043$ | $-.022$ | $-.061$ |
| $+1$ | $-.004$ | $+.045$ | $+.016$ | $-.007$ |
| $+2$ | $-.016$ | $-.002$ | $+.008$ | $+.010$ |

[a] $N = 11$ in each group.

## Discussion

The analysis of the direct scores showed that the +1 treatment was the most effective of the three treatments, with the +2 treatment being the least effective. The similarity between the patterns of the indirect and the direct scores suggests that the differential effect of the treatments represented something more than memorization of the specific verbalizations used in the treatments and that some change occurred in generalized moral concepts. This conclusion remains tentative since the results on the indirect scores were minimally significant and since the same interview form was used in the test-retest procedure.

The findings support Kohlberg's schema of stages as representing a developmental continuum, in which each individual passes through the stages in the prescribed sequence. If the stages do form a developmental sequence, then it should be easier for subjects to understand and utilize concepts that are directly above their dominant stage than concepts that are two stages above.

The developmental interpretation is also strengthened by the finding that subjects assimilated the next higher stage more readily than the lower stage, even though they could understand the concepts of the lower stage as well as, if not better than, those of the higher stage. Hence, we have an indication that the attainment of a stage of thought involves a reorganization of the preceding modes of thought, with an integration of each previous stage with, rather than an addition to, new elements of the later stages.

### Causal Factors of Changes in Stage

The subjects exposed to the stage one above their dominant stage did learn to use some new modes of thought. A factor causing the use of new modes of thought may be *cognitive conflict*. Indeed, Smedslund's work with the concept of conservation (Smedslund, 1961a, 1961c, 1961d) indicates that cognitive conflict may lead to reorganization of structure. The concept of cognitive conflict is similar to the concept of disequilibrium, which Piaget and Inhelder have presented rather obscurely (Inhelder & Piaget, 1958; Piaget, 1950). They seem to be saying that movement from one structure to the next occurs when the system, by being challenged, is put into a state of disequilibrium. Thus change in structure would involve the establishment of a new equilibrium after the occurrence of disequilibrium.

Such a viewpoint is relevant to our study. Since subjects were exposed to new modes of thought through arguments justifying both sides of a moral conflict, they did not really receive solutions to the problems. Such a situation, which exposed subjects to cogent reasons justifying two contradictory positions, could have resulted in cognitive conflict arising from an active concern with both sides of the issue. When the arguments were too "simple," as in the −1 treatment, the subjects may not have become actively involved. When the arguments were too "complicated," as in the +2 treatment, the subjects may not have understood them. However, exposure to concepts one stage above, concepts within a subject's grasp, allowed him contact with new contradictory ideas requiring thought. Perhaps coping with concepts that had some meaning to the subjects led to new modes of thinking, or to a greater use of the stage that was one above the initial stage.

## Related Studies

A study having a direct relation to the present research, by Bandura and McDonald (1963), attempts to demonstrate that Piaget's (1948) sequence of moral development changes is a function of reinforcement contingencies and imitative learning. The study assumed that Piaget's stages of moral development could be defined as a stage of "objective responsibility" (moral judgment in terms of the material damage or consequences), followed by a stage of "subjective responsibility" (judgment in terms of intention). Following one of Piaget's procedures, Bandura and McDonald assigned children to stages in terms of responses to paired storied acts, one being a well-intentioned act resulting in considerable material damage, and the other a maliciously motivated act resulting in very little material damage.

Their experimental treatments attempted to influence the subjects by reinforcing adult models who expressed judgments in opposition to the child's orientation, and by reinforcing any of the child's own responses that run counter to his dominant mode. Two meaures of learning of the opposite orientation were obtained: the amount of learning during experimental treatment, and a posttest response to new stories immediately following the treatment. They showed that children could be influenced to judge on the orientation opposite to their initial one. Bandura and McDonald viewed this evidence as "throwing considerable doubt on the validity of a developmental stage theory of morality."

An adequate test of a stage theory of morality must deal with stages that are truly representative of mental structure rather than with specific verbal responses. Empirical tests of Piaget's moral judgment theory indicate that the stages do not meet the necessary criteria (Kohlberg, 1963b). However, the Bandura and McDonald study does not provide an adequate test of Piaget's theory because his two stages are not those of objective and subjective responsibility, but rather are those of heteronomous and autonomous orientations. The heteronomous and autonomous stages are each represented by 11 observable aspects (Kohlberg, 1963b) of children's definitions of right and wrong, of which the dimension of objective-subjective responsibility is only one. By studying only one dimension as manifested in children's choices between two alternatives Bandura and McDonald dealt with isolated surface responses, and not with the concept of stage or mental structure. In their experimental treatment one of two possible answers was reinforced. Therefore, the induced changes did not represent underlying structures, but instead represented switches to what the subjects thought were the correct answers.[5]

Another important deficiency in their procedure was the administration of the posttest immediately after the experimental treatment. As Smedslund (1961b) has demonstrated, the test of duration over time is a main criterion for distinguishing between cognitive structure and superficially learned responses. There was a small decrease in subjective re-

[5] It must be pointed out that in the contrasting pairs of stories a well-intentioned act always resulted in much material damage, while the maliciously motivated act always resulted in little material damage. A child in the objective stage could easily have learned to more frequently designate, as being worse, that story which contained less material damage, thinking that it was the expected answer. Thus he could have given the "higher-stage" answer without having learned the concept of intention.

sponses given by objective children from the experimental treatment to the post-test, while there was no such decrease in the objective responses of subjective children. This finding, that downward movement was more stable than upward movement, is in contrast to our findings, in which upward movement was more stable. It is not surprising that the learning of surface verbal responses related to a lower stage can be retained for a short time. It is interesting that the learning of responses related to a higher stage was not entirely retained, even for such a short period of time.

In the present research we have worked with responses assumed to reflect mental structure and have found that the concept of developmental stage or mental structure has much relevance to the understanding of children's moral thinking. We suggest that the effectiveness of environmental influences depends on the relation between the type of concept encountered and developmental level.

## References

BANDURA, A., & McDONALD, F. J. The influence of social reinforcement and the behavior of models in shaping children's moral judgments. *Journal of Abnormal and Social Psychology*, 1963, **67**, 274–281.

INHELDER, B., & PIAGET, J. *The growth of logical thinking from childhood to adolescence.* New York: Basic Books, 1958.

KOHLBERG, L. The development of modes of moral thinking and choice in the years ten to sixteen. Unpublished doctoral dissertation, University of Chicago, 1958.

KOHLBERG, L. The development of children's orientations toward a moral order. I. Sequence in the development of moral thought. *Vita Humana*, 1963, **6**, 11–33. (a)

KOHLBERG, L. Moral development and identification. In H. W. Stevenson (Ed.), *Yearbook of the national society for the study of education.* Pt. I. *Child psychology.* Chicago: University of Chicago Press, 1963. Pp. 277–332. (b)

*PIAGET, J. *The moral judgment of the child.* (Orig. publ. 1932) Glencoe, Ill.: Free Press, 1948.

PIAGET, J. *The psychology of intelligence.* (Orig. publ. 1947) New York: Harcourt, 1950.

SMEDSLUND, J. The acquisition of conservation of substance and weight in children. II. External reinforcement of conservation of weight and of the operations of addition and subtraction. *Scandinavian Journal of Psychology*, 1961, **2**, 71–84. (a)

SMEDSLUND, J. The acquisition of conservation of substance and weight in children. III. Extinction of conservation of weight acquired "normally" and by means of empirical controls on a balance. *Scandinavian Journal of Psychology*, 1961, **2**, 85–87. (b)

SMEDSLUND, J. The acquisition of conservation of substance and weight in children. V. Practice in conflict situations without external reinforcement. *Scandinavian Journal of Psychology*, 1961, **2**, 156–160. (c)

SMEDSLUND, J. The acquisition of conservation of substance and weight in children. VI. Practice on continuous vs. discontinuous material in problem situations without external reinforcement. *Scandinavian Journal of Psychology*, 1961, **2**, 203–210. (d)

WINER, B. J. *Statistical principles in experimental design.* New York: McGraw-Hill, 1962.

* [Asterisks indicate works that are reprinted, in whole or in part, in this volume.]

# DEMOGRAPHIC VARIABLES AND CONSCIENCE

## References

Kohlberg, L. The development of children's orientations toward a moral order. I. Sequence in the development of moral thought. *Vita Humana*, 1963, **6**, 11–33. (a)

Kohlberg, L. Moral development and identification. In H. W. Stevenson (Ed.), *Yearbook of the national society for the study of education.* Pt. I. *Child psychology.* Chicago: University of Chicago Press, 1963. Pp. 277–332. (b)

Kohlberg, L. Development of moral character and moral ideology. In M. L. Hoffman & L. W. Hoffman (Eds.), *Review of child development research.* Vol. I. New York: Russell Sage, 1964. Pp. 383–431.

Kohlberg, L. Stage and sequence: The cognitive-developmental approach to socialization. In D. A. Goslin (Ed.), *Handbook of socialization theory and research.* Chicago: Rand McNally, 1969. Pp. 347–480.

## Introduction

The first paper in this subsection is a review by Bronfenbrenner of the pre-1960 literature on the relation of certain demographic variables to both cognitive and affective projective measures of moral development. Although much information has been added since 1960 (the reader is referred to extended reviews by Kohlberg, 1963a; 1963b; 1964; 1969), Bronfenbrenner's basic conclusions still hold. The second paper, by Rebelsky, Allinsmith, and Grinder, deals with obtained sex differences in conscience-related phenomena.

# 28

# The role of age, sex, class, and culture in studies of moral development

*by Urie Bronfenbrenner*

It is a sobering reflection on the state of our knowledge in the behavioral sciences that even our most reliable facts and theories about specific phenomena can usually be seriously challenged by asking a simple descriptive question: how does this phenomenon vary with the age, sex, and social background of the person? Paradoxically, the response to the first of these challenges may at first seem reassuring. Until relatively recently, psychologists were much preoccupied with documenting observable changes with age in practically every variable that they had succeeded in measuring. The result was an impressive array of apparently highly consistent variations as a function of the developmental level of the child. But then, with the growth of the interdisciplinary approach in the behavioral sciences, investigators of developmental trends began to look for possible variation as a function of the child's role in society—his sex, his ordinal position, and the social status, ethnicity, and religious background of

Reprinted from the July–August 1962 *Research Supplement to Religious Education* by permission of the author and the publisher, The Religious Education Association, New York City.

his parents. With the introduction of these social factors, the seeming generality, simplicity, and regularity of developmental age trends were challenged first from one quarter, then another. As a result, the notion underlying much of American child psychology as late as the 1940s of a normal maturational sequence that could be expected of all children everywhere was cast into serious doubt. In its place there emerged a social-situational conception of development in which maturational conditions were accorded only a vague and somewhat secondary importance.

It is precisely this historical course which is reflected in empirical studies of moral development over the past twenty-five years. Such studies take their early and initial inspiration from the classic work of Piaget (1932). This investigator presented a series of brief stories, each centering on a moral issue, to more than 100 Swiss children, and on the basis of their responses to his semistructured questions, distinguished two major stages of moral development.

The first stage, which he called "moral realism," is based on "an ethic of authority." The child views moral rules and restraints as laid down from above; they must be interpreted literally, and cannot be altered. In accordance with the principle of "immanent justice," punishment follows inevitably upon violation, and its severity varies directly with the enormity of the consequences of action regardless of the motive which inspired it. At this immature level, moral rules are not internalized but are adhered to solely through fear of external punishment by superordinate authority.

In contrast, the more mature stage of "reciprocity" or "cooperation" is characterized by the "ethics of mutual respect."

Rules are seen as compacts arrived at and maintained by equals in the common interest. They may be changed by mutual consent and modified in the light of extenuating circumstances. Punishment, instead of being generalized and "expiatory," is specific to the infraction, aimed at reciprocity in kind or restitution, and is guided by the principle of "equity" involving consideration of the motive underlying the act and of the particular circumstances in which the transgression was committed. Moral principles are internalized so that the child acts morally without the necessity of external sanctions. In short, moral behavior is its own reward.

The several dichotomies implied in the two stages were distinguished on the basis of the child's responses to specially designed stories and questions. For example, to distinguish the moral rules based on consequences from those based on motives, Piaget employed the following story among others:

> A little boy who is called John is in his room. He is called to dinner. He goes into the dining room. But behind the door there was a chair, and on the chair there was a tray with fifteen cups on it. John couldn't have known that there was all this behind the door. He goes in; the door knocks against the tray; bang go the fifteen cups, and they all got broken!
>
> Once there was a little boy whose name was Henry. One day when his mother was out, he tried to get some jam out of the cupboard. He climbed up on to a chair and stretched out his arm. But the jam was too high up, and he couldn't reach it and have any. But while he was trying to get it, he knocked over a cup. The cup fell down and broke.

After each story, Piaget would ask questions such as the following: "Are these children equally guilty?" "Which of the two is naughtiest and why?"

To consider another example: as a means of distinguishing types of punishment, the following story and questions were used:

> A boy has broken a toy belonging to his little brother. What should be done? (1) Should he not be allowed to play with any of his own toys for a week? (expiation); (2) Should he give the little fellow one of his own toys? (reciprocation); (3) Should he pay for having it mended? (restitution).

"Immanent justice" was assessed by the following story:

> In a class of very little children the teacher had forbidden them to sharpen their pencils themselves. Once, when the teacher had her back turned, a little boy took the knife and was going to sharpen his pencil. But he cut his finger. If the teacher had allowed him to sharpen his pencil, would he have cut himself just the same?

It was on the basis of age differences in responses to these stories that Piaget formulated his two-stage theory of moral development. Since his original study was published, a number of investigators in Europe and the United States have sought to replicate his findings. We shall turn now to an examination of their results.

## I. Investigations of Piaget's Theory of Moral Development

At first blush, there appears to be considerable empirical support for Piaget's two-stage theory of moral development. An impressive number of studies over a quarter of a century in two continents have reported age differences consistent with Piaget's postulated shift from moral realism toward reciprocity and equity. Thus evidence in support of one or another aspect of Piaget's theory is reported in studies from England (Harrower, 1934; Morris, 1958; Peel, 1959); Switzerland (Lerner, 1937a); Belgium (Caruso, 1943); Italy (Ponzo, 1956); and the United States (Lerner, 1937b; Dennis, 1943; Liu, 1950; MacRae, 1954; Havighurst & Neugarten, 1955; Medinnus, 1957, 1959; Kohlberg, 1958, 1959; Durkin, 1959a, 1959b; and Boehm & Nass 1961). Two of the foregoing researches (Dennis, Havighurst, & Neugarten) were carried out with Indian children, and one with Chinese-Americans (Liu). On the basis of their recent review of virtually all these studies, Boehm and Nass conclude that "age is the only consistently operative factor in development toward maturity" (p. 10). At the same time, they call attention to "strong trends toward sociocultural differences." Let us examine some of these.

First of all, it is a fact that the closest correspondence with Piaget's original results is found in studies of children from contenental Europe (Lerner, 1937a; Caruso, 1943; Ponzo, 1956). The farther one moves from the European mainland in distance and culture, the more frequently are departures from or outright contradictions of Piaget's findings. Indeed, it is noteworthy, although generally unnoted, that the very first attempt to verify Piaget's theory turned up highly significant differences across both class and culture. The English psychologist Harrower (1935), observing that Piaget's subjects were Swiss children mostly from "the poorer parts of Geneva" (Piaget 1932, p. 208), sought to determine whether similar results would

be obtained with children of the same age range in another country and from different social class levels. Accordingly, she selected a comparable sample from schools in "the poorer parts of London" and, in addition, as a "control group" youngsters "from distinctly well-to-do homes and the children of cultured parents" (Harrower, 1935, pp. 83–84). The results from the lower socioeconomic group were consistent with Piaget's theory in showing a decrease in moral realism with age. Quite a different pattern, however, emerged at the higher social level, where the younger children from the very beginning gave high percentages of mature responses; nor was there any evidence of a shift over the age range. The author concludes as follows:

> Either the stages of development which Piaget has been emphasizing are not a universal characteristic of development *per se*, but are to be found only within certain uniform groups, groups which are subject to certain constant conditions; or, in certain environments these stages can be so far accelerated that children exhibiting characteristics of the . . . most developed [stage] are to be found at the ages of the first (p. 93).

Harrower argues further that if the second hypothesis is correct, she should be able to find substantial evidences of social realism among still younger children in the cultured environment. Since she was unsuccessful in turning up responses of this kind among youngsters below six years of age, she is inclined to the first alternative.

Confirmatory evidence for Harrower's findings and interpretation comes from a series of studies of class differences in moral development conducted in the United States (Lerner, 1937b; MacRae, 1943; Kohlberg, 1959; Durkin, 1959a,

1959b; Boehm & Nass, 1961), and even more forcefully from comparisons of cross-cultural data (Dennis, 1943; Liu, 1950; Havighurst & Neugarten, 1955; Boehm, 1957). The most pronounced class differences are reported in the first American study carried out twenty-five years ago by Lerner, who found that upper-class children showed an earlier decrease of moral realism than lower-class youngsters. Two decades later, lower but still reliable relationships in the same direction are cited by MacRae and Kohlberg. A statistical analysis made by the present writer of comparable data from different social classes used in two separate studies by Durkin yields a similar result ($P = .05$, in favor of more authoritarian morality in the lower class). Finally, the most recent results, reported in an unpublished study by Boehm, show no significant differences by class, but a trend in the predicted direction for some of the stories. This decrease in class differences over time is consistent with Bronfenbrenner's (1958) conclusion, from a survey of class differences in child-rearing over a twenty-five-year period, that the gap between the social classes appears to be narrowing.

Even sharper contrasts in patterns of moral standards and development emerge in cross-cultural studies. The first comparative results of this kind appear in Harrower's research. Curiously enough, she makes no reference to them in her analyses and discussion, even though she describes as the "first problem" of her research "to discover whether national characteristics and traditions in any way affect what must be considered as a pattern of mental development largely independent of external influences" (p. 79). An examina-

tion of the comparative data which she cites, first from Piaget's and then from her own experiments, certainly calls the last assumption into question, since the Swiss children show evidence of greater moral realism than the English children at either socioeconomic level and the decrease with age is appreciably greater for the latter group. In other words, if Piaget's criteria are valid, English children achieve a more mature conscience earlier than Swiss children of comparable age. To cite but one example, Piaget reports that 28 percent of his subjects in the 6–7 year age-group gave responses favoring "punishment by reciprocity" over less mature forms; in the 8–10 year group, this figure rises to 49 percent (Piaget, 1932). The corresponding percentages for the two groups of English children are as follows: lower socioeconomic level, 39 percent for the younger age group, 90 percent for the older age group; upper socioeconomic level, 77 percent for the younger age group, 100 percent for the older age group (Harrower, 1934, pp. 85–88).[1]

In view of the attenuating character of class differences over time, it is noteworthy that more than twenty years later, Boehm (1957), in a comparative study of Swiss and American children, found that among the latter "conscience becomes less egocentric and interiorizes earlier than does that of the Swiss child." In partial explanation of this difference, the author cites evidence from story responses supporting the inference that the American child transfers his parental dependence to a peer dependence at an earlier age.

[1] Since Piaget does not cite the total number of children examined at each age level, it is impossible to test the statistical significance of these cross-national differences.

Even more dramatic departures from the typical pattern of moral development described by Piaget are found in studies employing his technique with American Indian children. Dennis (1943) shows that stories about immanent justice decreased with age much more slowly in a group of Hopi schoolchildren than in Lerner's American sample. Although this finding is not inconsistent with Piaget's two-stage theory of moral development, the results obtained by Havighurst and Neugarten (1955) are far more difficult to reconcile. Working with children from six different Indian tribes, these investigators found that responses reflecting faith in immanent justice tended to increase rather than decrease in age, a trend which is consistent with the prevailing belief system of the adult Indian culture.

Although Liu (1950), working with Chinese-American and non-Chinese-American children, found a decrease in immanent justice with age in the former group, the white controls showed the reverse trend. Similar inconsistencies are reported for white American subjects by MacRae (1954) and Medinnus (1959). Along the same line, several investigators working with English and American children (Morris, 1958; Kohlberg, 1958; Durkin, 1959a, 1959b, 1959c) have called into question Piaget's thesis that acceptance of reciprocity as a justice principle increases with age. Specifically, in none of these studies did the children, to use Piaget's language, "maintain with a conviction that grows with their years that it is strictly fair to give back the blows one has received" (Piaget, 1932, p. 301). Indeed, both Morris (1958) and Durkin (1959c) found a reverse trend with older children showing less adherence to the reciprocity principle.

A second major line of evidence calling into question central assumptions in Piaget's theory of moral development appears in the work of MacRae (1954), Kohlberg (1958), Durkin (1959c), and Maccoby (1959). Each of these investigators note from their data that the presumed components of morality do not hang together empirically. The first and most comprehensive study of this phenomenon is by MacRae, who did a cluster analysis of responses to moral judgment questions holding age constant, and identified four relatively independent factors. An examination of the relationships of these factors to patterns of parental authority led MacRae to postulate "two distinct processes of moral development: 'cognitive' moral development involving the learning of what behavior patterns are approved and disapproved, and 'emotional' moral development, including the association of anxiety with one's own deviance and moral indignation with that of others" (p. 17). MacRae suggests further that the types of questions used by Piaget are concerned primarily with cognitive moral development. We may add that one feature contributing to this cognitive emphasis is the pervasive use of "should" and "ought" in the questions employed in Piaget's method. In other words, the child is asked to state what he believes to be the right course of action, not to indicate what someone else or he himself might actually be impelled to do. Interestingly enough, it was not until the 1950s that researchers shifted from Piaget's type of question to one designed to get at what the child might wish to do rather than merely what he thought was the appropriate answer. It is of course a matter of considerable interest whether answers to the latter type of question exhibit variations with age, class, and culture similar to those obtained with Piaget's technique. But before turning to this topic, we must consider briefly one other category, typically neglected in analyses of Piaget-type data, but assuming considerable importance in contemporary studies of conscience development. This is the category of sex.

It is somewhat surprising that although Piaget conducted dozens of experiments on moral standards presumably with children of both sexes, in only one instance does he pay systematic attention to differences in the responses of boys and girls. In answer to the question of what a smaller boy should do when struck by a bigger boy, the "tendency to consider it legitimate to give back the blows received" (i.e., reciprocity) tended to increase more rapidly with age for boys than for girls (Piaget, 1932, pp. 301–302). In the twenty-five-year period that followed, only three studies, and these relatively recent ones, have dealt with possible sex differences in moral response. According to a secondary source (Boehm, 1961, p. 10; the original reports were not available to the present author), Medinnus (1957) "found girls to be less advanced than boys in respect to the concept of immanent justice and punishment," and Morris (1958) "found no significant differences between boys and girls in age of decreasing moral realism but found a tendency for the values of girls to change earlier than those of boys." The two sets of findings do not seem to be consistent; indeed, the last statement appears self-contradictory. Nevertheless, Boehm and Nass (1961) describe the absence of sex differences in

their own research as a contradiction to a trend "heretofore evident in previous studies, that girls show a more advanced development than do boys on an overall basis" (p. 10). In our own view, the question of sex differences in Piaget-type responses is as yet a completely open one.

Studies utilizing Piaget's technique represent the first major effort to investigate the process of moral development. In the light of our survey of this initial body of research, the following tentative conclusions are indicated:

1. It is clear, first of all, that, as Durkin suggests (1959c, p. 294), Piaget unjustifiably "minimizes the influence of the environment on a child's understanding of what is just." Furthermore, as between the two alternative hypotheses proposed by Harrower [1935, p. 93; quoted above] the weight of the evidence throws doubt on the possibility that two stages are present but follow each other so rapidly in some cultures that they are difficult to distinguish. Rather, the cultural and subcultural departures from Piaget's norms support Harrower's preference for the alternative hypothesis that the two-state sequence is to be found only in certain uniform groups subject to certain constant conditions.

2. The range of variation in moral development by age, class, and culture is so great as to call into question the dominant role of maturational factors, at least beyond the age of five.[2] It would

[2] Aronfreed (1961), after reviewing many of the same studies, arrives at an almost identical conclusion. He states: ". . . The recent work of Kohlberg (1958) and Peel (1959) tends to confirm, in a very general way, that the child's moral conceptions are age-related. But it is noteworthy that these studies, when taken to-

appear that under appropriate environmental conditions, children as young as six years of age can learn equally well responses characteristic of Piaget's moral realism or the patterns of reciprocation, equality, and equity presumably indicative of moral maturity.[3] In a word, the primary factors determining the nature of moral standards appear to be social and situational rather than genetic.

3. The preceding conclusion is not incompatible with the manifestation of orderly sequences of moral development in certain cultural contexts since such genetic sequences may only mirror the changing character of the child's relation to his social environment as he grows older. Thus the classic two-stage sequence observed by Piaget could be a reflection of the fact that European children, especially a quarter of a century ago, tended to be dealt with in rather authoritarian and arbitrary fashion through the early years and exposed to rationalistic, equalitarian treatment only at later ages. A similar but less extreme transition was found in America

but has been steadily decreasing, especially at upper-middle-class levels (Bronfenbrenner, 1958); hence the frequent departures from the stipulated pattern of moral development in recent American data.

4. The various manifestations of moral development posited by Piaget, while they may be correlated in a particular cultural context, are most appropriately regarded as separate variables representing responses to specific social-situational influences.

5. The aspects of moral development studied by Piaget are primarily cognitive, evaluative, and conscious. In particular, they reflect the child's knowledge of the ideal norms held up to him by his culture. As such, they shed little light on the emotional, covert, and behavioral aspects of moral standards and development.

Perhaps in partial reaction to Piaget's intellectual and moralistic approach, American social scientists, especially since World War II, have focused their attention primarily on overt expressions of moral behavior, underlying emotional impulses and moral conflicts, and their social-psychological antecedents. We turn next to a consideration of the results of this contrasting approach.

## II. Current Trends in Research on the Development of Moral Standards

Current studies of moral development show strong influence from three theoretical traditions: behaviorism, psychoanalysis, and the cognitive theories of Piaget. Of these, behaviorism was the first to make a major impact through in-

---

gether with others in which age differences were not found (Boehm, 1957; Durkin, 1959a; Lerner, 1937b; MacRae, 1954), suggest, as a group, that the child's cognitive resources for moral judgment are more closely associated with social status and other indicators of cultural expectations. These findings are interesting because they imply that the availability of highly differentiated cognitive-evaluative standards is not a necessary accompaniment of advancing age or experience. Apparently, the role of cognitive equipment in the child's moral behavior is dependent on the kinds of experience provided by its environment" (pp. 7–8).

[3] Consistent with his conclusion is Carmichael's early finding (1930) that six-year-old children are fully capable of recognizing misdeeds, forecasting the future, and learning a wide variety of adaptive responses, including avoidance, prevarication, confession, and restitution.

spiring the monumental *Character Education Inquiry* of Hartshorne, May, and their colleagues (Hartshorne & May, 1928; Hartshorne, May, & Maller, 1929; Hartshorne, May, & Shuttleworth, 1930). The major conclusion of these researchers, in part preordained by the highly specific nature of their theoretical concepts and of the tasks and tests they employed, is that moral qualities, such as honesty and deceit, "represent not general ideals but specific habits learned in relation to specific situations which have made one or the other response successful" (Vol. 3, p. 372). It is quite possible that a second look at Hartshorne and May's data in the light of present-day theories and concepts may reveal more generality than the original authors detected. MacRae (1954, p. 17), for example, demonstrates that his distinction between "cognitive" and "emotional" aspects of moral development is supported by the pattern of reported correlations among various measures of moral judgment used thirty years ago in the *Character Education Inquiry*.

The chief importance of this pioneering research was the precedent it set for studying moral character not merely through verbal response but through observation of concrete behaviors, such as cheating, sacrifice, sharing, and the like. This precedent was followed only a few years later by MacKinnon (1933, 1938), who compared the personality characteristics of college students yielding or not yielding to the temptation of cheating. As the conceptual framework for his research, however, MacKinnon explicitly rejected Hartshorne and May's theory of specificity and turned instead to structural and developmental hypotheses from psychoanalysis. With these as a guide, MacKinnon observed a number of reliable relationships reflecting dynamic processes. Thus "violators" were much more likely then "nonviolators" to vent their anger outwardly rather than engage in self-deprecation. A similar differential was observed in the realm of motor behavior with violators being more likely to take out their aggression on the environment through pounding the table, stamping, and kicking objects, while nonviolators concentrated motor activity on their own bodies through oral, nasal, and hirsutal activities." At the level of conscious cognitive processes, nonviolators were much more likely than violators to answer affirmatively to the question: "Do you in everyday life often feel guilty about things which you have done or have not done?" Finally, anticipating a major theme in research on moral development in the 1950s, MacKinnon examined the relationship between adherence to moral standards and the parents' use of "psychological" rather than "physical" discipline, the former term being applied to "those measures which seek to have the child feel that he has fallen short of some ideal or that he has hurt his parents and consequently is less loved by them because of what he has done" (1938, p. 498). As hypothesized, parents of nonviolators, especially fathers, were more likely to resort to psychological discipline and less likely to employ physical discipline than parents of violators.

In the light of his data, MacKinnon concludes that, in refutation of the conclusions of Hartshorne and May, "The findings of the present investigation lend support to a theory of the consistency of personality" (p. 500).

Despite the promising character of MacKinnon's work, it was twenty years before social scientists once again turned to psychoanalytic theory as a guide for research on moral development. In the interim, however, there were at least two studies that investigated overt moral behavior. Wright (1942) designed an experiment to measure the generosity of eight-year-old children in sharing toys with a friend vs. a stranger of the same age. Children were overwhelmingly more generous to the latter than the former. In addition, the investigator found that the child's perception of another's generosity was directly related to how generous he himself was prepared to be. The subjects came primarily from professional and middle-class families and presumably included both sexes, but no breakdown of results by sex or class is reported.

Variations in both of these categories and several others as well were examined systematically ten years later in an ingenious and comprehensive study with Turkish children by Ugurel-Semin (1952). This investigator studied 291 youngsters between the ages of four and sixteen attending the kindergarten and primary schools of Istanbul. In the experiment the child was faced with the necessity of deciding how to share a supply of nuts with a friend momentarily absent from the room. Responses were classified in three categories: selfish (giving the other less than one's self), equalitarian (sharing equally), and generous (giving more to the other). The major findings were as follows:

**Age:** Selfishness tends to decrease as the child grows older; equalitarianism rises; generosity increases also, but reaches a maximum at seven–eight years of age and fluctuates thereafter tending to be less frequent than equalitarian decisions.

**Sex:** No appreciable difference between the sexes on any of the three variables.

**Socioeconomic level:** Marked differences appear among the three social class levels ("Poor," "Rich," and "Middle Class"). The poor children were the least selfish and high on generosity; the rich tended to be generous rather than equalitarian; middle-class children were least generous and most selfish. (These class differences obtained with family size held constant.)

**Family size:** Children from larger families tended to be more generous and less selfish than only children. (This analysis did not include controls for the relation between family size and socioeconomic status.)

Ugurel-Semin also carried out a content analysis of the comments made by the children in the course of the experiment and related these comments both to the child's age and the particular decision he made. The analysis led the author to the following general conclusion:

*The process of moral thought* is characterized by five different tendencies whose common trait is found in the change from *centralization* to *decentralization*.
Moral thought moves (a) from external consideration of the moral situation at hand toward internalization of moral understanding, (b) from being linked to the present moment toward consideration of life as a whole, (c) from a consideration of a specific connection to the linking up of various connections, (d) from an individual and personal consideration of the moral action toward reciprocity and cooperation, and (e) from unilateral consideration of the moral rule toward its mutual understanding. (The

latter two traits have been clearly explained by Piaget) (pp. 471–472).

The similarities between Ugurel-Semin's conceptions and those of Piaget are even more pronounced than the final parenthesis suggests, for, like Piaget, the author has interpreted her data primarily in cognitive, evaluative, and maturational terms without regard for emotional, motivational, or social-psychological implications. Noteworthy in this regard is her failure to consider the significance for the process of moral development of the observed differences in response associated with socioeconomic status and family size. We must therefore look to other researches for the integration of the cognitive and maturational aspects of moral development with the affective and social-psychological. Some progress in this direction was made possible during the 1950s through the resurgence—this time on a broad scale—of psychoanalytically oriented studies of moral standards and behavior.

## III. Psychoanalytically-Oriented Studies of Moral Development

The new wave of studies of moral development following World War II was stimulated not by psychoanalysis alone but through a remarkable fusion of psychoanalytic dynamics, post-Hullian behavior theory, and hypotheses derived from the concepts and data of social anthropology and sociology. The imaginative scope required for such a strange and sweeping coalition is reflected in the somewhat farfetched character of the first representative of the new approach. As part of a broader cross-cultural study of *Child Training and Personality,* Whiting and Child (1953) undertook to investigate the developmental antecedents of guilt, the last variable being defined operationally as the presence or absence in a society of "patient responsibility for illness." Amazingly enough, Whiting and Child were able to obtain confirmation for a number of their hypotheses. For example, they found support for their prediction that guilt (as measured by patient responsibility) would be more likely to occur in societies employing severe techniques of socialization, such as strict and frequent punishment or enforcing of rapid changes in habit patterns.

Encouraged by these results, Whiting and his students (Faigin, 1952; Hollenberg, 1952; Chasdi, 1954) undertook a second study of internalization of moral values with the focus not only on the culture as a whole but on individual children within three contrasting cultures in the Southwest: a Mormon community, a Texan town, and a Zuni pueblo. The general method devised by these investigators for measuring internalization of moral values is of some interest inasmuch as variations of the same technique have since been adopted, apparently quite independently, by most of the workers engaged in studies of moral development. The method is but one step removed from Piaget's procedure, since it requires the child to complete a story in which the "hero" has committed some form of moral transgression. The difference, however, is an important one, since instead of being asked what the hero "should" do, the child is free to deal with the implied moral conflict in whatever way he wishes. In this particular instance, the investigators used a rather complex method of scoring based on the frequency of reference to "painful consequences" as the result of the morally deviant act. In line with theoretical prediction, the Mormon children showed the highest levels of internalization and the Zuni the lowest. The major hypothesis of the study, however, had to do with the relation between the degree of internalization and the type of discipline used with the child. Specifically, arguing from psychoanalytic theory, the authors postulated that the degree of internalization varies positively with the extent to which denial of love is used as the principal technique of discipline for the child; in other words, the more the child is disciplined through withdrawal of affection, the more likely he is to internalize moral values. This hypothesis was confirmed not only across the three cultures (with Mormon parents placing heaviest reliance on this method), but also within each of the three cultures (Chasdi, 1954).

During the past ten years, a number of different investigators (Allinsmith, 1960; Allinsmith & Greening, 1955; Aronfreed, 1959, 1960, and 1961; Bronfenbrenner, 1961; Heinicke, 1953; Hoffman & Saltzstein, 1960; Maccoby, 1959; Miller & Swanson, 1960; Sears, Maccoby, & Levin, 1957; Sears, Rau, & Alpert, 1960; Unger, 1960), often using different methods for measuring both parental behavior and internalization, have nevertheless obtained results consistent with the same general hypothesis. Since most of these studies have recently been carefully reviewed by Hoffman (1961), we need only to quote that author's general conclusion:

. . . the use of psychological discipline (which includes techniques that appeal to the child's needs for affection and self-esteem and his concern for others), especially in the context of an affectionate parent-child relationship, appears to foster the development of an internalized moral orientation, especially with respect to one's reactions following the violation of a moral standard (p. 26).

But as is readily apparent from a reading of Hoffman's painstaking survey, the preceding generalization, valid as it probably is, nevertheless conceals under its very generality a multitude of major lacunae, qualifications, ambiguities, and even contradictions. To begin with, there is the fact noted by Hoffman that the majority of the studies reported used males as subjects. Where both sexes have been included, there are important differences within the general pattern, with certain parental variables showing stronger relationships for boys and others for girls. Moreover, as a number of investigators have pointed out (Burton, Maccoby, & Allinsmith, 1960; Bronfenbrenner, 1961a, 1961b; Hoffman & Saltzstein, 1960; Sears, Rau, & Alpert, 1960), these variations present certain features consistent with Freud's theory of differential personality development in the two sexes (Freud, 1933; Bronfenbrenner, 1960). The following quotation from Hoffman and Saltzstein is representative of the trends discerned:

These findings suggest that the psychological forces induced in the discipline situation and which contribute to internalization are different for boys and girls. In girls it seems to be anxiety over the loss of the parent's love. This is consistent with Freud's notion that this kind of anxiety is central in the moral development of girls, and with the recent research findings reported by others. In boys, on the other hand, it seems to be guilt over the effects of one's behavior on the parent (pp. 11–12).

The issue of sex differences is seen to be even more complex when one examines the results of the relatively few studies that have obtained and analyzed behavioral data not only about the mother but the father as well. Almost without exception, the results for the two parents are different, and what is more, these differences usually vary for the child of each sex (Allinsmith & Greening, 1955; Hoffman & Saltzstein, 1960; Sears, Rau, & Alpert, 1960; Bronfenbrenner, 1961a). In other words, the behavior of fathers and mothers tends to affect sons and daughters somewhat differently. The available data as yet are insufficient, however, to permit a clear statement of the nature of those contrasting effects.

Finally, there is the question of the relevance, for all of the above relationships, of the family's class position. Unfortunately, most of the researches that have paid attention to socioeconomic status treated the variable as a control rather than a matter of substantive interest in its own right. Nevertheless, the two or three studies that have given explicit attention to this factor (Miller & Swanson, 1960; Aronfreed, 1959; Bronfenbrenner, 1961a) suggest rather strongly that the social position of the family modifies in greater or lesser degree the behavior of parents and children of both sexes as well as the functional relationships between them. Bronfenbrenner (1961c) has recently proposed a theoretical model for viewing these complex multiple relationships in a single theoretical frame. Specifically, he proposes that the relationships between parental behavior and internalization of standards by the child is typi-

cally curvilinear rather than linear, with the critical point representing an optimal balance between parental affection and discipline. Since average levels of affection and discipline tend to differ for various combinations of sex of parent, sex of child, and family's social position, the observed relations between parental behavior and internalization vary more or less systematically from one social context to another. It remains to be seen whether this theoretical model proves tenable and useful in the light of subsequent research.

We have now seen enough of the "new look" in studies of moral development so that it may be instructive to compare it with the earlier work of Piaget and his followers.

## IV. Piaget vs. the "New Look"

The new approach to research on moral development differs from its classic predecessors in a number of striking respects. First of all, the more recent studies give virtually no attention to age differences in moral response. Although experimental subjects have ranged in age from four or five years to college level, the possibility of developmental stages in moral development has hardly been raised.

Second, just as the Piaget approach has been one-sided in its emphasis on the cognitive, conscious, and evaluative aspects of moral development, so has the new look, true to its psychoanalytic-behavioristic origins, directed its attention almost exclusively either to emotional, unconscious elements, or to overt behavior in specific situations. Piaget's eternal query, "What *should* Peter do?" is heard no more.

Third, while Piaget and his followers

gave first consideration to describing the content of moral judgments, the current approach, in keeping with its psychoanalytic orientation, focused almost immediately on developmental antecedents and gave short shrift to the comparative analysis of the phenomena being predicted. This "historical" bias is reflected most sharply by a striking omission in the numerous comparisons by sex, class, and culture appearing in the current literature. These analyses jump immediately to an analysis of differences in *relationships* between parent behavior and moral standards of the child and by-pass almost completely the question of sex, class, or cultural differences in the dependent variable itself. Do boys and girls differ in their capacity to resist temptation? Do middle-class children exhibit more guilt than lower-class children? Except in a few isolated instances, such questions remain unanswered in most current researches, despite the fact that the relevant data are obviously available.

But along with the contrasts, there are similarities as well. Like Piaget and his collaborators, the new investigators of the fifties began by treating morality as if it were a unitary trait and were only gradually forced by their own data to a more differentiated conception. As a number of investigators acknowledge (Allinsmith, 1960; Burton, Maccoby, & Allinsmith, 1960; Maccoby, 1959; Sears, Rau, & Alpert, 1960), indices of guilt, confession, resistance to temptation, all of which are used to measure internalization, consistently show only low intercorrelations at best. Thus, after a review of studies done at Harvard and Stanford, Maccoby (1959) concludes: "Our results . . . argue against a single-process theory of moral development"; a conclu-

sion reminiscent of Durkin's final statement after her third attempt to replicate relationships required by Piaget's unitary conception:

> . . . justice, operationally defined, is sufficiently complex that any theory which attempts to explain "The Development of the Idea of Justice in Children" is, from the start, doomed to inevitable generalization and consequent error (1959a, p. 295).

Finally, despite their concern both with covert needs and conflicts and overt behavior, the protagonists of the new look, like their more traditional predecessors, have left unexplored the relation of verbal response to everyday action. Instead, the two types of data remain compartmentalized. As a result, virtually nothing is known about the relation of projective measures of conscience and guilt to behavior in actual interpersonal situations.

The contrasts and similarities between old and new approaches to the study of moral development point up needs and opportunities for the research of the future. We conclude with a consideration of these developing perspectives.


## V. The Shape of Research to Come

Some of the gaps revealed by the foregoing analysis are already being bridged by research currently under way. Hoffman (1961b), for example, has brought together the two major approaches to the study of moral orientations through combining investigation of cognitive, affective, and developmental aspects. For this purpose, he uses the concepts and methods of Piaget to define a series of "conscience types" and then employs incomplete stories and parent interviews to get at emotional correlates and developmental antecedents. Working with a sample of middle-class seventh-graders of both sexes, Hoffman has distinguished three contrasting types as follows: (1) *humanistic,* "those whose moral judgments considered the circumstances and were supported in terms of principles based on human need"; (2) *conventional,* "those whose judgments did not consider the circumstances and whose principles were based more on moral conventions"; and (3) *externals,* "whose judgments indicated moral orientations based on the fear of punishment" (p. 2).

Three groups of children were deliberately selected from the larger sample to fit each of the three types. The basis of assignment was their response to questions requiring them to make moral judgments about norm violations and to give the reasons for their judgments. The children were then asked to complete two stories dealing with moral transgressions. On the basis of the results, Hoffman draws tentative conclusions such as the following:

> . . . humanists are more apt to sustain a high level of guilt for a relatively long period of time when the consequences of their action for others are severe and irreversible. But when the consequences are relatively minor and easily rectified, they are more likely to reduce their guilt through confession and reparation.
>
> . . . external boys . . . have developed defenses allowing them to avoid guilt (p. 3).

As the last sentence indicates, Hoffman, like many of his predecessors, finds consistent sex differences in his data, particularly in studying the familial antecedents of the three conscience types.

Nevertheless, Hoffman's preliminary conclusions in this sphere give confirmation to earlier findings:

> Generalizing most broadly and tentatively from our findings, it appears that the combination of affection and inductive discipline may be prerequisite for the development of internalized moral structures and that variations in parental behavior over and above this pattern may account for the particular kind of internalized moral structure that develops: humanistic, conventional, or perhaps others. With this broader framework in mind, the main difference between the humanist and conventional parents seems to be that the humanists appeal more to "approach" motives, i.e., concern for the parent and the desire to attain an ideal; while the conventionals appeal more to "avoidance" motives, i.e., avoidance of parental withdrawal of love and respect (pp. 5–6).

Hoffman's study offers considerable promise for extending our understanding of the relationships between cognitive and affective aspects of moral orientation and their developmental antecedents. At the same time, in necessarily narrowing his research focus, Hoffman has excluded two important aspects of moral phenomena. First, he has restricted his study of the affective sphere to the single variable of guilt. Second, he leaves unexplored the whole question of the overt behavior of his subjects in real-life situations.

Fortunately, the first of these areas is currently being surveyed by Aronfreed (1961), who has undertaken a descriptive study of the nature, variety, and social patterning of projective responses to moral transgressions. On the basis of story completions from a sample of 122 sixth-graders of both sexes from two social class levels, this investigator has identified twelve distinct dimensions of moral response which can be reliably distinguished by independent judges. The nature of these variables will be discussed in connection with the author's systematic analysis of differences in the patterning of moral orientation by sex and social class.

Considering first differences between boys and girls, Aronfreed finds that the latter are significantly more likely than boys to give story endings in which the blame is placed on others (*focus on external responsibility*), corrective mechanisms are initiated only at the behest of someone else (*external initiation*), and the moral response is exhibited before others (*display*). In short, in the author's words, "girls rely more than boys on external definition of moral consequences."

As Aronfreed observes, this finding would seem to be at variance with the belief commonly held in our society that girls show greater conscientiousness and moral sensitivity than boys. Indeed, in the pioneer study of Hartshorne and May (1930), as well as the earlier work of Terman (1925), girls consistently received higher scores than boys on tests of moral knowledge and sensititivity to both conventional and ideal social standards. Similarly, one of the few investigations in the 1950s to report sex difference in moral standards (Sears, Maccoby, & Levin, 1957) reports a significantly higher proportion of girls among those classified as showing evidence of "highly developed conscience" (p. 384). Finally, the fourth and last significant sex difference in Aronfreed's own data reveals that girls are more likely than boys to give story endings involving *apology*.

Aronfreed suggests a resolution of the seeming contradictions in the research data by pointing out the "responses such as confession and apology may be regarded as somewhat externally orientated corrections of deviance" (p. 30). He notes further that in tests of actual performance of honesty, again reported by Terman (1925) and Hartshorne and May (1928), girls did more poorly than boys under conditions when they thought that their actions would not be known to others. This contrast points up the importance of supplementing verbal indices of conscience development with measures of overt behavior.

In the realm of socioeconomic differences, Aronfreed finds that middle-class children "show more evidence of self-criticism than do working-class children and are considerably less likely to resolve transgressions through the perception of unpleasant fortuitous consequences or a focus on external responsibility" (p. 26). In comparing the differences by sex and class, Aronfreed concludes as follows:

Social class differences appear to center on the distinction between moral consequences defined primarily in terms of the child's own actions and those defined primarily in terms of external events. Sex differences, in contrast, seem to reflect more of the variability in the extent to which moral consequences occurring in the child's own actions are nevertheless dependent on the support of the external environment (p. 27).

Finally, although age was not a variable in his own research, Aronfreed offers a conclusion regarding the role of maturational factors in moral development identical with that reached in our own survey of studies in the Piaget tradition:

. . . it should be pointed out that the nature of the associations between social positions and moral responses does not easily lend itself to the view, suggested by Piaget's interpretation of moral development, that different types of moral orientation sequentially emerge with advancing age or experience. It would seem more appropriate that internal and external orientation in moral behavior be understood as relatively stable end-results of different patterns of social re-enforcement (p. 31).

Although Hoffman's and Aronfreed's researches will fill in some of the gaps left unexplored in previous work, two major problem areas remain strangely untouched by today's growing number of researchers on moral development. The first of these is the intriguing question of the relation between the ideological and projective aspects of moral response and their manifestations in everyday life. The study is yet to be carried out in which Piaget-type moral judgments, responses to incomplete stories, and behavioral indices of the kind recently described by Maccoby (1960) are combined within a single research design to investigate hypotheses regarding the interaction of the cognitive, affective, and behavioral dimensions of moral orientation.

But the most curious, and perhaps the most serious, void in current studies of moral development lies in the once overworked area of age changes. No one seems to be asking the question of how the projective and objective manifestations of guilt, externalization, resistance to temptation, and altruism emerge and develop in the growing child. The fact that the child's maturational level may not be as determining an influence in moral development as was once believed does not in any way detract from the scientific importance of age-developmental studies. On the contrary, as the evidence mounts in favor of the view that human morality is man-made rather than an inevitable product of organismic evolution, understanding of the genetic process of moral development becomes even more urgent and intriguing. Such changes over time, however, must be studied not against a purely chronological scale, but in context of the ever-changing matrix of social relationships through which the child is molded to man's estate.

## References

ALLINSMITH, W. The learning of moral standards. In D. R. Miller & G. E. Swanson (Eds.), *Inner conflict and defense.* New York: Holt, 1960. Pp. 141–176.

ALLINSMITH, W., & GREENING, T. C. Guilt over anger as predicted from parental discipline: A study of superego development. *American Psychologist,* 1955, **10,** 320. (Abstract)

ARONFREED, J. Internal and external orientation in the moral behavior of children. Paper read at the annual meeting of the American Psychological Association, Cincinnati, September 1959.

ARONFREED, J. Moral behavior and sex identity. In D. R. Miller and G. E. Swanson (Eds.), *Inner conflict and defense.* New York: Holt, 1960. Pp. 177–193.

ARONFREED, J. The nature, variety, and social patterning of moral responses. Mimeographed, 1961.

*BOEHM, L. The development of independence: A comparative study. *Child Development,* 1957, **28,** 85–92.

BOEHM, L., & NASS, M. L. Social class differ-

* [Asterisks indicate works that are reprinted, in whole or in part, in this volume.]

ences in conscience development: Progress report. Mimeographed, 1961.

BRONFENBRENNER, U. Socialization and social class through time and space. In E. E. Maccoby, T. M. Newcomb, & E. L. Hartley (Eds.), *Readings in social psychology.* New York: Holt, 1958. Pp. 400–425.

BRONFENBRENNER, U. Freudian theories of identification and their derivatives. *Child Development*, 1960, **31,** 15–40.

BRONFENBRENNER, U. Some familial antecedents of responsibility and leadership in adolescents. In L. Petrullo and B. L. Bass (Eds.), *Leadership and interpersonal behavior.* New York: Holt, 1961. Pp. 239–272. (a)

BRONFENBRENNER, U. The changing American child. In E. Ginzberg (Ed.), *Values and ideals of American youth.* New York: Columbia University Press, 1961. Pp. 71–84. Also in *Merrill Palmer Quarterly,* 1961, **7,** 73–84. (b)

BRONFENBRENNER, U. Toward a theoretical model for the analysis of parent-child relationships in a social context. In J. C. Glidewell (Ed.), *Parental attitudes and child behavior.* Springfield, Ill.: Charles C Thomas, 1961. Pp. 90–109. (c)

BURTON, R. V., MACCOBY, E. E., & ALLINSMITH, W. Antecedents of resistance to temptation. Washington: National Institute of Mental Health, U.S. Dept. of Health, Education, and Welfare. Mimeographed, 1960.

CARMICHAEL, A. M. The behavior of six-year-old children when called upon to account for past irregularities. *Journal of Genetic Psychology*, 1930, **38,** 352–360.

Caruso, I. La notion de responsibilite et de justice immanente de l'enfant. *Archives de Psychologie*, 1943, **29,** 113–170.

CHASDI, E. H. The relationship between certain child training practices and the degree of internalization of moral values. Paper presented at the International Congress of Psychiatry, 1954.

DENNIS, W. Animism and related tendencies in Hopi children. *Journal of Abnormal and Social Psychology*, 1943, **38,** 21–36.

DURKIN, D. Children's concepts of justice: A comparison with the Piaget data. *Child Development*, 1959, **30,** 59–67. (a)

DURKIN, D. Children's acceptance of reciprocity as a justice principle. *Child Development*, 1959, **30,** 289–296. (b)

DURKIN, D. Children's concepts of justice: A further comparison with the Piaget data. *Journal of Educational Research*, 1959, **52,** 252–257. (c)

Faigin, H. Child rearing in the Rimrock Community with special reference to the development of guilt. Unpublished doctoral dissertation, Harvard University, 1952.

FREUD, S. *New introductory lectures in psychoanalysis.* New York: Norton, 1933.

HARROWER, M. R. Social status and moral development. *British Journal of Educational Psychology*, 1935, **4,** 75–95.

*HARTSHORNE, H., & MAY, M. A. *Studies in the nature of character*, Vol. 1. *Studies in deceit.* New York: Macmillan, 1928.

HARTSHORNE, H., MAY, M. A., & MALLER, J. B. *Studies in the nature of character.* Vol. 2. *Studies in service and self-control.* New York: Macmillan, 1929.

HARTSHORNE, H., MAY, M. A., & SHUTTLEWORTH, F. K. *Studies in the nature of character.* Vol. 3. *Studies in the organization of character.* New York: Macmillan, 1930.

HAVIGHURST, R. J., & NEUGARTEN, B. L. *American Indian and white children.* Chicago: University of Chicago Press, 1955.

HEINICKE, C. M. Some antecedents and correlates of guilt and fear in young boys. Unpublished doctoral dissertation, Harvard University, 1953.

HOFFMAN, M. L. Progress report: Techniques and processes in moral development. Mimeographed. Detroit: Merrill-Palmer Institute, 1961. (a)

HOFFMAN, M. L. The role of the parent in the child's moral growth. Mimeographed. A paper prepared for the Research Planning Workshop of the Religious Education Association, 1961. (b)

HOFFMAN, M. L., & SALTZSTEIN, H. D. Parent practices and the child's moral orientation. Interim research report presented at American Psychological Association, Chicago, September, 1960.

HOLLENBERG, E. Child training among the Zeepi with special reference to the internalization of moral values. Unpublished doctoral dissertation, Harvard University, 1952.

KOHLBERG, L. The development of modes of moral thinking and choice in the years ten to sixteen. Unpublished doctoral dissertation, University of Chicago, 1958.

KOHLBERG, L. Status as perspective in society: An interpretation of class differences in children's moral judgment. Paper presented at the biannual meeting of the Society for Research in Child Development, Bethesda, Maryland, March 1959.

LERNER, E. The problem of perspective in moral reasoning. *American Journal of Sociology*, 1937, **43**, 249–269. (a)

LERNER, E. *Constraint areas and the moral judgment of children.* Menesha, Wisc.: Banta, 1937. (b)

LIU, C. The influence of cultural background on the moral judgment of children. PhD. dissertation, Columbia University, 1950.

MACCOBY, E. E. The generality of moral behavior. Paper read at the American Psychological Association symposium on the development of moral standards, Cincinnati, September 1959.

MACCOBY, E. E. The taking of adult roles in middle childhood. Dittoed report. Laboratory of Human Development, Stanford University, Calif., 1960.

MACKINNON, D. W. The violation of prohibitions in the solving of problems. Unpublished dissertation, Harvard University, 1933.

MACKINNON, D. W. Violation of prohibition. In H. A. Murray (Ed.), *Explorations in personality: A clinical and experimental study of fifty men of college age.* New York: Oxford, 1938. Pp. 491–501.

MACRAE, D., JR. A test of Piaget's theories of moral development. *Journal of Abnormal and Social Psychology*, 1954, **49**, 14–18.

MEDINNUS, G. R. An investigation of Piaget's concept of the development of moral judgment in six to twelve year old children from lower socio-economic class. Unpublished doctoral dissertation, University of Minnesota, 1957.

MEDINNUS, G. R. Immanent justice in children: A review of the literature and additional data. *Journal of Genetic Psychology*, 1959, **94**, 253–262.

MILLER, D. R., & SWANSON, G. E. (Eds.) *Inner conflict and defense.* New York: Holt, 1960.

MORRIS, J. F. Symposium on the development of moral values in children. II. The development of adolescent value-judgments. *British Journal of Educational Psychology*, 1958, **28**, 1–14.

PEEL, E. A. Experimental examination of some of Piaget's schemata concerning children's perception and thinking, and a discussion of their educational significance. *British Journal of Educational Psychology*, 1959, **29**, 89–103.

*PIAGET, J. *The moral judgment of the child.* New York: Harcourt, 1932.

PONZO, E. An investigation into the development of judicial knowledge. *Education and Psychology*, 1956, **3**, 1–20.

*SEARS, R. R., MACCOBY, E. E., & LEVIN, H. (Eds.) *Patterns of child rearing.* Evanston, Ill.: Row, Peterson, 1957.

SEARS, R. R., RAU, L., & ALPERT, R. Identification and child training: The development of conscience. Interim research report presented at American Psychological Association, Chicago, September, 1960.

TERMAN, L. M. *Genetic studies of genius.* Vol. 1. *Mental and physical traits of a thousand gifted children.* Stanford, Calif.: Stanford University Press, 1925.

UGUREL-SEMIN, R. Moral behavior and moral judgment of children. *Journal of Abnormal and Social Psychology*, 1925, **47**, 463–474.

UNGER, S. M. On the development of the

guilt response systems. Unpublished doctoral dissertation, Cornell University, 1960.

WHITE, R. K., & LIPPITT, R. O. *Autocracy and democracy.* New York: Harper, 1960.

WHITING, J. W. M. & CHILD, L. I. *Child training and personality.* New Haven: Yale University Press, 1953.

WRIGHT, B. A. Altruism in children and the perceived conduct of others. *Journal of Abnormal and Social Psychology,* 1942, **37,** 218–233.

## 29

# Resistance to temptation and sex differences in children's use of fantasy confession[1]

*by Freda Gould Rebelsky,*
*Wesley Allinsmith,*
*and Robert E. Grinder*

In some recent studies of child development, evidence of confession has been used as an index of conscience (9, 4, 13). As a basis for interpreting their data, the authors cited quite consciously made the assumption that the response of confession is an indication of the degree to which conscience is developed. Allied assumptions which may or may not have

Freda Gould Rebelsky, Wesley Allinsmith, and Robert Grinder, "Resistance to Temptation and Sex Differences in Children's Use of Fantasy Confession," *Child Development*, 1963, **34,** 955–962. © The Society for Research in Child Development, Inc., 1963. Reprinted by permission of the authors and the publisher.

[1] The main support for this study was provided by a grant from the National Institute of Mental Health (M-1468). A paper presenting a portion of this material was read at the 1961 meetings of the Society for Research in Child Development. We wish to thank John W. M. Whiting and the staff of the Laboratory of Human Development at Harvard for the advice and support of this study. We also thank Dr. Leonard Lansky, Dr. Paul Kjelldergaard, Dr. David McClelland, and Dr. Emanual K. Beller for their invaluable help and friendly criticism. This paper is based upon a dissertation submitted by the first author to Radcliffe College in partial fulfillment of the requirements of the Ph.D. degree.

been in the minds of these authors are that the probability of confession is not influenced in a major way by other variables, that confession has the same meaning for all children, and that, given the same "amount" of conscience, there is the same likelihood that confession will be used.

We doubt that these assumptions are justifiable. Acts of confession may reflect complex motivations and may achieve differing results for the confessor. Among the possible motives for confession are guilt, dependency, desire for affiliation, and desire for punishment. Confession may result in absolution and forgiveness, punishment of various types, or both punishment and forgiveness (11). There are also important ways in which the actual behavior of confessors may differ, e.g., in the length of time elapsing between transgression and confession; in the person chosen as recipient; in the "emotionality" or contriteness of the confession.

The present study was undertaken to explore the topic of confession, using a behavioral measure of resistance to temptation and children's completions of projective stories that dealt with transgression. Two topics of the study are discussed herein: (a) sex differences in the use of confession and (b) the soundness of the use of confession as a measure of conscience.

*Hypotheses*

In Western civilization confession appears to be a behavior that fits more appropriately into the dependent, affiliative, verbal, manipulative framework of femininity than into the independent, motoric, less socially adept framework of masculinity (11). Therefore it seems probable that in our society more girls than boys would use confession. Because a well-behaved and conscientious boy might not want to use or be able to use behavior as "feminine" as confession, we predicted that girls would be more likely to confess after transgression than boys. On the grounds that development of one aspect of "conscience" may be inferred from behavioral measures of resistance to temptation (3, 6), we also expected that children's use of confession in the projective stories would be positively related to their degree of resistance to temptation. At the same time we were aware of the multiple determinants of resistance to temptation.

## Method

### Subjects

The subjects for the study were 138 sixth-grade children living in Newton and Watertown, Massachusetts. There were 69 boys and 69 girls between the ages of 11-6 and 12-6. Six years previously the mothers of these subjects had been interviewed extensively about their child-rearing practices (13). The follow-up sample closely represents the characteristics of the original group from which it was drawn (12).

### Procedure

The children were given 10 projective story beginnings to complete. In the present report 8 of the stories, those dealing with transgression by a hero (or heroine) against peers or adults, are used. Since the stories differed somewhat for the sexes, boys and girls in a given school were segregated and administered the stories simultaneously. Male experimenters administered the stories, announcing that they were from Harvard University and stating:

> We're interested in finding out what (boys/girls) your age are like. I have some stories here for you to finish. I'll read each story aloud and you can follow it in your booklet. Then you finish the story, starting where the story leaves off. This is not an English class. Don't worry about spelling. There are no right or wrong answers; you can say anything you want in your stories; we'll take them back to the University with us.

The children were then asked to turn to the first story. The experimenter read it aloud saying at the end, "Now you finish the story, telling what the people in your story are thinking and feeling, and what happens and how it turns out." The children wrote their story endings in the test booklet in the appropriate space provided for them.

From 3 days to 10 days after the story-session, a different male experimenter administered the behavioral test of temptation to the subjects. The temptation test consisted of a shooting-gallery game that was played alone by each subject.[2]

Seated seven feet away from a target box, subjects "shot" a "ray-gun" pistol at a rotating rocket, and with each shot prearranged scores from 0 to 5 were registered by score lights, also housed in the target box. Badges were offered as prizes, motivation was high, and the game was programmed so that only by cheating could a child win a prize. Subjects were thus tempted to cheat.

[2] A full description of the game may be found in Grinder (5), and a detailed description for the procedure for administering the game may be found in Grinder (6).

After each subject finished the temptation game, he was sent to still another experimenter who gave him a second set of story beginnings to complete. The second set of stories was similar in number and in content to the first. The same instructions given previously were used, except that stories were not read aloud. Because subjects entered the experimental room at times when others who had finished the temptation test earlier were already writing, earphones were placed on the subject's head when he was ready for a story beginning, and he listened to it as recorded on an audiograph machine. Several machines were on hand so that subjects did not have to wait before moving on to the next story.

The story completion items were designed to be of interest to the subject's age group. All were written so that there was little or no possibility of the hero's being detected unless he gave himself up or gave himself away (1). The stories dealt with situations in which the subjects probably would not have found themselves, but in which the emotions depicted, such as the coveting of a friend's toy or a yearning to win the prize in a race, were nevertheless appropriate to the subject's age. The story stimuli given to both sexes were parallel: changes were made only in the name and sex of the major character, who was male for boys and female for girls, and in having, e.g., a walking race for girls in place of a running race for boys. For each sex there were four pairs of stories which had been matched in content. One of each pair was presented before and one after the test of resistance to temptation.

The story completion technique was worked out by Allinsmith (1); the stories used in the present investigation, as well as a description of variables considered in their construction, may be found in Rebelsky (10).

*Coding the Stories*

The completed stories were scored by four coders[3] in terms of several dimensions of guilt, but only the data on presence or absence of the use of confession in the story endings will be presented in this paper. Interjudge reliability of the coding of presence or absence of confession, based on a sample of the stories, was perfect. Confession in the children's completions of the story beginnings was defined as the revelation in words by the hero that he had committed the transgression. The operational definition thus excluded situations in which the hero never confessed but behaved so oddly that others were able to infer that he had transgressed. It included what others (e.g., 13) have termed "admission," i.e., acknowledgment after being suspected, interrogated, or accused. In the present data the great majority of the confessions (77 percent) were spontaneous in the sense of occurring before there was evidence that the hero anticipated detection. That is, "admissions" were rare, and there were no differences between the sexes in the use of voluntary and nonvoluntary confessions.

The coding was done story by story, with the identity of the children masked by numbers and their behavior in the resistance to temptation situation unknown to the coders.

[3] The coders were Ruth H. C. Munroe, Richard Kluckhohn, William Rebelsky, and Freda Rebelsky.

*Data Analysis and Statistics Used*

The data on confession were analyzed by sex of the child and by his behavior (cheating or not cheating) in the temptation situation. Each of these variables was examined with the other held constant. Three separate analyses were carried out: (a) the use of confession in the endings of the stories administered before the temptation game; (b) the use of confession in the endings of the stories administered after the temptation game; and (c) the use of confession in response to all eight stories. The change in the number of stories in which confession appeared from pregame to postgame was also examined. Mood's likelihood ratio (8), which yields a number with which one can enter a chi square table to get a probability value, was used to assess the significance of the differences in the distributions in this study. Inasmuch as we would be interested in results in either direction, all tests are two-tailed, despite prior prediction. A significance level of .05 was used.

**Results**

It is clear that confession was used frequently by children of this age in responding to the stories. In the eight possible stories, 131 of the 138 children depicted confession at least once, including all the girls. All but 7 of the boys portrayed confession in at least one story.

Table 1 summarizes the data, showing differences among various groups in the number of stories in which they portrayed confession. In the three columns, (a) total number of stories, (b) the four pretemptation stories, and (c) the four posttemptation stories, girls used confession in more story endings than did

*Table 1*

**Differences between Various Groups in Number of Stories in Which They Portrayed Confession**

| Groups Compared* | Total Eight Stories | | | Four Pretest Stories | | | Four Posttest Stories | | |
|---|---|---|---|---|---|---|---|---|---|
| | $X^2$ | df | p | $X^2$ | df | p | $X^2$ | df | p |
| 1. Boys / Girls† | 32.27 | 8 | .001 | 12.28 | 4 | .02 | 10.30 | 4 | .05 |
| 2. Cheaters / Noncheaters | 19.75 | 8 | .02 | 13.73 | 4 | .01 | 12.17 | 4 | .02 |
| 3. Boy cheaters / Boy noncheaters | 11.72 | 8 | .20 | 4.56 | 4 | .40 | 6.05 | 4 | .20 |
| 4. Girl cheaters / Girl noncheaters | 10.86 | 8 | .30 | 8.16 | 4 | .10 | 10.17 | 4 | .05 |
| 5. Boy cheaters / Girl cheaters | 17.51 | 8 | .05 | 6.48 | 4 | .20 | 8.44 | 4 | .10 |
| 6. Boy noncheaters / Girl noncheaters | 17.59 | 8 | .05 | 4.78 | 4 | .50 | 5.91 | 4 | .50 |
| 7. Combined $X^2$ (3 + 4): Cheat / Noncheat (with sex control) | 22.58 | 16 | .20 | 12.72 | 8 | .20 | 16.22 | 8 | .05 |
| 8. Combined $X^2$ (5 + 6): Boys / Girls (with cheat control) | 35.10 | 16 | .01 | 11.26 | 8 | .20 | 14.35 | 8 | .10 |

Note: All tests are two-tailed.
* *Groups:*

| | | | |
|---|---|---|---|
| Boy cheaters | $N = 52$ | Total boys | $N = 69$ |
| Boy noncheaters | $N = 17$ | Total girls | $N = 69$ |
| Girl cheaters | $N = 44$ | Total cheaters | $N = 96$ |
| Girl noncheaters | $N = 25$ | Total noncheaters | $N = 42$ |

† The italicized groups confessed in more stories than did the nonitalicized ones.

boys, and noncheaters used confession more than did cheaters.

The effects of controlling sex of child and response to temptation are also given in Table 1. As can be seen, the sex difference holds up when response to temptation is controlled; the relation of confession to resistance to temptation turns out to be a function mainly of the girl subjects.

An analysis was made of the shift in number of confessions given by the subjects from the pretemptation test stories to the posttemptation test stories, with the same eight groupings as in Table 1. There were no significant differences between groups, except between cheaters and noncheaters. Noncheaters tended to confess more in the pretemptation test stories, and cheaters tended to confess either the same amount or more in the posttemptation stories ($X^2 = 12.44$, 2 $df$, $p < .01$).

### Discussion

The results indicate that the use of confession by children in completing stories about transgression differs with sex. Girls confess more. There also appears to be a relation between the use of confession and cheating behavior: those who do not cheat are more likely to depict confession in their stories than are cheaters. As anticipated, this finding is much clearer for girls than for boys. If resistance to temptation is interpreted as a major aspect of conscience and if the temptation game is judged a valid measure of the tendency to resist temptation, the data of this investigation suggest that the use of confession as a measure of conscience is more efficient—and perhaps more appropriate—in the case of girls than boys.

There are many possible reasons why confession was used in this study more by girls than by boys and why it appears to be more highly related to girls' rather than boys' resistance to temptation: (a) confession is an affiliative, dependent behavior which is more appropriate for girls than boys to use in our society; (b) girls have a greater superiority in the use of language for social influence purposes and thus use confession more readily; or (c) girls may not have been as interested in the cheating game or as involved with it or with the stories and thus were able to choose an "easy" response without really involving themselves emotionally.

If the stories had been used alone, without the benefit of the chance to cheat, the findings would have been much more limited, though it still would be clear that girls confess more than boys. We are now able to predict the girls' behavior in a temptation situation knowing their response to fantasy in pretest stories, and we can predict some aspect of fantasy knowing their behavior in the temptation test.

In a recent study of Israeli children, Luria, Goldwasser, and Goldwasser (7), using similar stories and the same coding of confession as was used in this study, found no sex differences in the use of confession. The data in the present study were reanalyzed for Jewish and non-Jewish children. Though the sample of Jewish children is small ($N = 37$), it appears that there are no sex differences in the use of confession in Jewish children and that the sex differences reported in this paper were even more marked when the Jewish children were removed from the sample. Jewish boys in the sample were like non-Jewish boys, but the Jewish girls cheated more than did non-Jewish girls and confessed less, thus supplying additional evidence on the relation of cheating and nonconfession found in girls.

In this study we had a behavioral measure of resistance to temptation and a measure of fantasy confession. We still need studies in which actual cheating (or some other measure of conscience) is related to actual behavior of confession following the cheating. We have reports of mothers about children's confession (13) and reports of mothers and fathers about children's confession (4). We now have a measure of fantasy confession, but we as yet have no behavioral measure of confession. It is apparent that further clarification of the use of confession and its relation to behavior and to the sex of the confessor waits upon studies in which both a behavioral measure of conscience and confession are employed. To create a plausible opportunity for subjects to confess may be a difficult task. Meantime, the clear sex differences shown in this paper, coupled with the lack of a distinct relation of confession to resistance to temptation in boys, lead to the conclusion that confession should not be used unquestioningly as a measure of conscience for both sexes in research in child development.

The data also point out the need for explorations into the use of confession among groups where the sex role differences are less clear or more clear than in our society.

## Summary

This study investigated sex differences in the use of confession in fantasy and the relation of confession to resistance to temptation. Subjects were 138 11-year-old children, 69 boys and 69 girls. Eight story beginnings dealing with transgression by a hero or heroine against peers and adults were presented to the children; four were given two weeks before a temptation test and four matching stories immediately after the temptation test. The temptation test consisted of a shooting game played alone by each subject with a check on presence or absence of cheating.

The completed stories were scored for presence or absence of confession. The data were analyzed by sex of child and by his behavior (cheating or not cheating) in the temptation situation. In the eight possible stories, 131 of the 138 children depicted confession at least once. Girls used confession in more story endings than did boys, and noncheaters used confession more than did cheaters. The sex difference held up when response to temptation was controlled; the relation of confession to resistance to temptation was mainly a function of the girl subjects.

The findings suggest that confession should not be used unquestioningly as a measure of conscience development. The use of confession probably represents complex motivations and is influenced by other variables, such as sex.

## References

1. ALLINSMITH, W. The learning of moral standards. In D. R. Miller & G. E. Swanson (Eds.), *Inner conflict and defense*. New York: Holt, 1960. Pp. 141–176.
2. BARRY, H., BACON, M. K., & CHILD, I. L. A cross-cultural survey of some sex differences in socialization. *Journal of*

*Abnormal and Social Psychology*, 1957, **55**, 327–332.

3. BURTON, R. V., MACCOBY, E. E., & ALLINSMITH, W. Antecedents of resistance to temptation in four-year-old children. *Child Development*, 1961, **32**, 689–710.

4. ERON, L. D. The father in child-rearing practices research. Paper presented at Eastern Psychological Association, New York, April 1960.

5. GRINDER, R. E. New techniques for research in children's temptation behavior. *Child Development*, 1961, **32**, 679–688.

6. GRINDER, R. E. Parental child-rearing practices, conscience, and resistance to temptation of sixth-grade children. *Child Development*, 1962, **33**, 803–820.

7. LURIA, Z., GOLDWASSER, M., & GOLDWASSER, A. Response to transgression in stories by Israeli children. *Child Development*, 1963, **34**, 271–280.

8. MOOD, A. M. *Introduction to the theory of statistics.* New York: McGraw-Hill, 1950.

9. MUSSEN, P., & DISTLER, L. Child-rearing antecedents of masculine identification in kindergarten boys. *Child Development*, 1960, **31**, 89–100.

10. REBELSKY, F. G. Sex differences in the use of confession. Unpublished doctoral dissertation, Radcliffe College, 1961.

11. REBELSKY, F. G. An inquiry into the meaning of confession. *Merrill-Palmer Quarterly*, 1963, **9**, 287–295.

12. SEARS, R. R. Relation of early socialization experiences to aggression in middle childhood. *Journal of Abnormal and Social Psychology*, 1961, **63**, 466–492.

*13. SEARS, R. R., MACCOBY, E. E., & LEVIN, H. (Eds.) *Patterns of child rearing.* Evanston, Ill.: Row, Peterson, 1957.

* [Asterisks indicate works that are reprinted, in whole or in part, in this volume.]

# Section V
# CONSCIENCE AND PSYCHO-PATHOLOGY

## Introduction

Freud appeared to have mixed feelings regarding the superego. To put the matter very briefly, he believed that the construct that he called "superego" develops when the young child successfully resolves the oedipal situation and thereby identifies with the same-sexed parent. This identification produces or is symbolic of an identification with society and society's rules. Until this time the young child obeys rules a good portion of the time, but only because of the "reality principle," the awareness that a forbidden act might be followed by punishment that would more than outweigh the pleasure gained through the act. Once the superego comes into being, the child accepts society's rules as being just and incorporates them into his own set of values. For Freud, the superego serves a most useful function as a mechanism for behavioral control. On the other hand, Freud believed that neurosis is the result of an overly severe superego (at least as compared to the strength of the ego), which produces guilt not only about forbidden acts actually committed, but also about forbidden behaviors that are tempting, but never committed, and about other behaviors that fall well within the cultural norms.

Mowrer develops a position counter to Freud's and maintains:

> In essence, Freud's theory holds that anxiety comes from evil wishes, from acts the individual would commit if he dared. *The alternative view here proposed is that anxiety comes, not from acts the individual would commit but dares not, but from the acts which he has committed but wishes that he had not. It is, in other words, a "guilt theory" of anxiety rather than an "impulse theory"* (Mower, 1950, p. 537).

Freud proposed to alleviate mental suffering through psychoanalysis, which effectively reduces the relative strength of the superego as compared with that of the ego and/or the id. Mowrer proposes that neurotic guilt is real guilt and that the neurotic can become well by repairing the damages he has done, by confession of his errors and by leading a new and "open" life. A paper representative of Mowrer's position opens this section.

The five papers following Mowrer's are relevant to his position vis-à-vis Freud. The first study by Swensen deals with frequency, type, and variety of the sexual behavior of a group of female patients in a university clinic setting and a control group. Since, the patients were, in general, more sexually active (with the notable exception of masturbation), the results of this study are supportive of Mowrer's position. Swensen then conducted a second, essentially similar study of male patients and controls and found fewer significant differences between groups. Those differences that were significant were reversed in direction (male patients were less sexually active). This sex difference in the relation of sexual behavior to neurosis suggests that sexuality may have quite different meanings for females and males. One could plausibly argue that for females social isolation is the motivating factor in sexuality and that girls allow successful sexual advances because they have no other more socially acceptable stratagems for gaining attention and social inclusion. Since the male sexual role is one of active seeking, this same lack of successful strategies for establishing social contacts could explain the relatively more restricted sexual experience of men seeking therapy as compared with their controls.

Studies by Peterson and by Johnson, Ackerman, Frank, and Fionda follow. Both papers were directly stimulated by Mowrer's writing and both test and support Mowrer's ideas across a wide variety of subject groups.

In a paper original to this volume, Ogren and Dokecki extend the Freudian and Mowrerian approaches to behavior disorders in young children and raise some new and interesting questions.

The evidence is not sufficiently compelling to allow a clear determination of the degree to which Mowrer or Freud is correct, though the preponderance of data supports Mowrer's position. Mowrer's approach to psychotherapy, far more than most clinical approaches, emphasizes the individual's responsibility for his own actions. The work of Phillips and his associates (e.g., Phillips & Zigler, 1964) clearly demonstrates that self-blame is a good prognostic sign among mental patients, while blaming others is a poor prognostic sign. It may be that this is true because self-blame is essentially an "unstable equilibrium" and cannot be continued for a long period of time without some form of resolution, while blaming others is more stable and can more easily become a permanent "way of life." Whatever the reasons for the differential prognosis of people who blame themselves as opposed to those who blame others for misfortunes, it would appear that Mowrer's approach would lead to the set of attitudes that are associated with a good prognosis; many other therapies lead toward the attitude of blaming others that is associated with poor prognosis.

The existential approach to psychopathology and therapy also stresses the importance of conscience-related phenomena. This section concludes with an excerpt from Boss, a leading existential psychologist, detailing further dimensions of guilt.

## Reference

Phillips, L., & Zigler, E. Role orientation, the action-thought dimension, and outcome in psychiatric disorder. *Journal of Abnormal and Social Psychology*, 1964, **4**, 381–389.

# 30

# Conscience and the unconscious

*by O. Hobart Mowrer*

The two diagrammatic schemes for depicting psychological theory which will be utilized in this paper have already been published (Mowrer, 1964, 1965b); but both have implications and power not previously noted. They therefore call for further examination and elaboration, especially with reference to the structure and function of conscience and its relation to the so-called unconscious. Inasmuch as I have frequently been critical of classical psychoanalysis (from which the concept of the unconscious derives) and of traditional Christianity (which has done so much to give Western man his conscience), I also want to use this occasion to acknowledge the positive contributions of both of these sources to the particular conception of psychopathology and its remediation which is today being called Integrity Therapy. Now that some of the less defensible tenets of these two conceptions of man and his "existential" vicissitudes have been generally recognized and a vigorous new synthesis appears to be in

O. Hobart Mowrer, "Conscience and the Unconscious," paper presented at the annual meeting of the British Psychological Society, Swansea, April 1, 1966. Published as "Communication, Conscience, and the Unconscious" in the *Journal of Communication Disorders*, 1967, **1**, 109–135. Reprinted by permission of the North-Holland Publishing Company.

process of emergence, it becomes possible to see the more constructive aspects of Christianity and Freudian psychoanalysis and to evaluate them both from a truer and more balanced perspective.

## An Incongruity in Freud's Theory of the Unconscious

As every literate layman today knows, Freud divided the total human personality into three parts or agencies: *id*—the reservoir of the biologically given drives or "instincts," *superego*—defined as the "internalized voice of the community," or conscience, and the *ego*—which, according to Freud, normally plays an executive or regulatory role in the sense of mediating between id, superego, and the external world. The healthy personality is thus one with a strong ego, which keeps both id and superego in their "places" and decides *rationally*, rather than either impulsively or from moral compulsion, what actions are to occur and what the individual's external relations and general life style are to be.

But for the person who already is—or is destined to become—"neurotic," the picture was thought to be quite different (Figure 1a). In such a person the superego is supposedly more highly developed and stronger (see the large, dashed square) than the other two parts of the personality, with the result that it is able to lay siege to the ego and take it captive, as suggested by the arrows extending in the figure from superego to ego. And since there is presumably great enmity between superego and id, the superego—as soon as it succeeds in bringing the ego under its control—forces the ego to reject and "repress" the

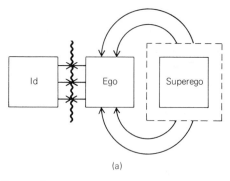

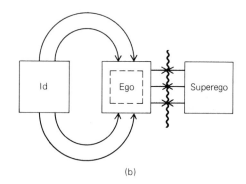

(a)

(b)

Figure 1a

Schematic representation of the "dynamics" of neurosis, as conceived by Freud. A "hypertrophied" superego, or conscience, supposedly lays siege to the ego and takes it captive. Then the superego forces the ego to reject the claims of the id for any expression or satisfaction of its "instinctual demands". The result is that a sort of "iron curtain" is constructed between ego and id (see wavy line); and dissociation or "repression" is said to be in force. Neurosis proper ("anxiety") consists of the "unconscious danger" that the forces of the id will succeed in breaking through this "wall" and overwhelming the ego; and a constant, devitalizing expenditure of energy by the ego is necessary to keep up its "defenses".

Figure 1b

A modified interpretation of the state called neurosis. Here it is assumed that the ego is taken captive, not by the superego, but by the id, and it is now the "voice of conscience" that is rejected and dissociated. "Anxiety" thus arises, not because of a threatened return of repressed energies of the id, but because of the unheeded railings and anger of conscience. Here it is not assumed that there is any difference in the "size" or strength of these three aspects of personality, unless it is that the ego is somewhat weak and undeveloped.

id, as shown by the waved line in the diagram.

According to analytic theory, these developments have the effect of rendering the ego and superego conflict-free, but at great cost. The ego loses its autonomy and proper administrative function. Moreover, the peace thus achieved is not permanent. The forces of the id, being "dynamic," do not take rejection and imprisonment passively, and periodically they attempt to break through the "wall" and thus gain a hearing at the court of consciousness and, hopefully, some semblance of gratification, through the individual's motoric channels and action system. It was, Freud thought, precisely this "threatened return of the repressed" that constituted

the danger to which the neurotic reacts, with anxiety, depression, or panic. And since the exact source of the danger has been repudiated by the conscious part of the personality and now exists only in "the unconscious," the individual no longer knows exactly *why* he is uneasy and upset. By the same token, then, therapy consists of the analyst's helping the afflicted person gain some understanding of the cause of his apprehension and fear (i.e., "get insight") and then joining forces with the patient's beleaguered, downtrodden ego and trying to beat back the superego in order to permit at least a modicum of gratification for the hitherto frustrated "instincts." In this way, it was thought, the forces of the id became more docile, less obstreperous, clamorous, and frightening; and if, through the "transference," the power and "size" of the superego could be sufficiently weakened, the individual would be permanently cured.

For a long time—beginning in 1929 but more particularly between 1936 and 1944—I accepted and tried to apply this theory, largely on faith. But eventually I became convinced that, at least as far as I was personally concerned, it simply did not hold. As I looked back over my life, I could not, in all honesty, say that I had been particularly "inhibited"; and anyone who knew me well—I had seen to it that there were very few who did!— could hardly say that I have been overly conscientious (Mowrer, 1962, 1966b). By 1944—the point at which I finally decided to stop analysis—I knew several other individuals for whom this type of therapy had also been disappointing; and statistical studies were beginning to appear which pointed in the same direction (Knight, 1941; Dollard, 1945; Wilder, 1945; Eysenck, 1952; Brody, 1962). Moreover, in the years that followed I came to see a number of theoretical inconsistencies and paradoxes in analysis which go a long way toward accounting for its ineffectiveness. These logical difficulties have been previously delineated (Mowrer, 1961, 1964) and need not be reviewed here. But there is one other major paradox inherent in the Freudian argument which has only recently become clear to me.

Probably the most universal and characteristic trait of psychoneurotic persons is their tendency to *withdraw* from contact with other people. This tendency may be massive and pervasive, as in backward, "regressed" schizophrenics; or it may be highly segmentalized, as, for example, in persons who manage ordinary interpersonal relations well enough but who have trouble in the more demanding and intimate roles of marriage partner or parent. However, "withdrawal" seems to be present and critically important in all cases, the difference being merely one of degree.

Now if Freud had been correct in his assumption that the neurotic is a person with an unusually strong and powerful superego, such a person, being dominated by this part of the total personality, should be unusually well integrated socially. Since the superego, by Freud's own definition, is the "internalized voice of the community" (Freud, 1930), anyone in whom this agency is exceptionally well developed and powerful *ought to be bound to other people and to community life in general in a very intimate and effective way.* The empirical, "clinical" facts are, of course, quite to the contrary. Social alienation, not integration, is the hallmark of psychopathology. If Freud's basic thesis were valid, this ought not to be the case. If it were the id that had become unacceptable and been rendered unconscious, the individual ought to feel particularly well identified with society as the source of the superego which has achieved this victory. Thus the neurotic, instead of being socially alienated and estranged, ought to be very "close" to other people and happily united with them. According to Freud, it is from the id, not the superego and the community which it represents, that the neurotic has dissociated himself. Yet it is conscience and community that the neurotic characteristically tries to avoid. Although various other paradoxes in classical psychoanalytic theory have been previously identified, this particular one, which is certainly not inconsequential or minor, has not, I think, been hitherto recognized.

But isn't it possible that Freud was right in his appraisal of the persons whom he, himself, saw and treated? Isn't it likely that the moral and cultural climate has changed enough so that his theory, although perhaps not generally applicable today, may have been in the Victorian era in which he lived and worked? Interpersonal uneasiness and a tendency toward withdrawal seem to have been distinguishing features of the neurotic personality in Freud's time no less than they are in ours, and if these phenomena are currently an embarrassment for his theory, they would also have been in 1890 or 1910. Furthermore, in one of his last technical papers, Freud (1937) courageously admitted that the therapeutic potency of analysis, as he himself had practiced it, was not nearly as great as he had originally hoped and claimed.

### The Incongruity Resolved by a New Conception of the Unconscious

I now wish to return to 1944. By late fall of that year I had decided, for better or for worse, that I was through with psychoanalysis as a personal therapy, and I was certainly also open to the possibility that psychoanalysis was seriously lacking as a conceptual scheme as well, although I did not as yet see its specific logical defects at all clearly. I had had about 700 hours of analysis, extending intermittently over a total of some 15 years, with three different analysts, and I saw no substantial lessening in either the frequency or the severity of the anxiety attacks and depressions from which I

had suffered since early adolescence. Although I did not know what the future might hold if I abandoned this form of treatment, I nevertheless decided in my despair, late in 1944, to break with psychoanalysis, once and for all.

The mid-winter of 1944–45 was particularly bleak and without direction or hope as far as I was concerned. But early in 1945 there was a very fortunate turn of events. During 1944–45 I was living, with my wife and two small daughters, in Washington, D.C., where I was in war-related government service; and in that capacity I had occasion to know a number of psychiatrists who were associated, formally or informally, with Dr. Harry Stack Sullivan. Through them I learned of the Washington School of Psychiatry, which Sullivan had founded and directed, and where, I discovered, it would be possible for me, as a psychologist, to enroll for seminars or courses. From my colleagues I further learned that Dr. Sullivan had a conception of psychopathology and its origin which was different from that of Freud. So, early in 1945, I decided to take advantage of this opportunity and enroll for an evening class with Dr. Sullivan and one with Dr. Dexter Bullard, then—and I think still—superintendent of a nearby private psychiatric hospital which is also Sullivanian in its general orientation and operation.

I had not been in Dr. Sullivan's class long before I began hearing something that was of great interest. Anxiety and depression, Sullivan was saying, arise not because of repressed sexual or aggressive impulses, but because of "parataxic" (unsound, distorted) interpersonal relations. In other words, psychopathology is not *within* a person but rather *between* him and what Sullivan termed the "significant others." Aptly, Sullivan was calling this approach "interpersonal psychiatry." Immediately there was much about it that seemed right to me. But also, as I now look back on that period, it is clear that I never became fully converted to Sullivan's position—or rather, perhaps I should say that I did not find it a resting place, i.e., did not *stop* there. Stimulated as I was by Sullivan's thinking, I almost immediately carried its logic a step further. I could readily agree that psychopathology is interpersonal rather than purely intrapsychic. But what Sullivan seemed to be saying, when it came to specifying the exact nature of the interpersonal problem, was that it involves *misperception* of others by the individual himself, whereas I concluded that *my* trouble was *misrepresentation* of myself to others, "significant others." Although Sullivan had been the catalyst, I thus quickly moved on to a more radically "interpersonal" position than the one he himself advocated. In retrospect, I would now see his position as intermediate between Freud's and my own. Although not fully satisfying to me, then or later, it was nevertheless most helpful. It was the bridge over which I made a necessary conceptual transition.

As I have already indicated, I could not make the theory of repressed instincts apply to my own life, but it was easy to see that there was a great deal of dishonesty and inauthenticity in my social relationships—or what Pratt and Tooley (1964) call the "transactional field." I was not, I may say, pervasively dishonest, i.e., I was not, by any means, a "sociopath." In fact, in most areas of my life I was quite responsible. But there were deep pockets of secrecy and inauthenticity which I had been most careful not to let anyone, except my safely remote and impersonal analysts, know about, and they, conveniently, took little interest in them. These areas of secrecy and interpersonal *suppression* (rather than intrapsychic "repression") I now concluded were the real foci of "neurotic" infection; and after the inspiration provided by the Sullivan seminar, I set out to eliminate them, with results which have been described elsewhere (Mowrer, 1962, 1966b). More to the point of the present discussion, however, is the change in the general theory of psychopathology which emerged from the developments I have just described.

As a result of the Washington interlude, it became apparent that although Figure 1a portrays the Freudian conception of psychopathology, something very different was needed to represent the position toward which I was now moving. I therefore concluded that at least as far as my own experience and personality were concerned, Figure 1b was a better approximation to the realities; and I suspected that it might also provide a reasonably good model for many other neurotic individuals (Mowrer, 1948, 1953, 1961, 1964).

It will now be apparent that Figure 1b resolves the inconsistency in Freudian theory which has been described in the first section of this paper. If the neurotic hiatus, or dissociation, is between the id-dominated ego and the superego, rather than between a superego-dominated ego and the id, as suggested in Figure 1a, there is no mystery as to why the neurotic individual is socially withdrawn, alienated. And because superego or conscience is the connecting link between the individual and his reference group or community ("significant others"), any internal process which fissions off the superego from the rest of the personality will, of necessity, tend to disconnect the id-ego system from the surrounding life of the community. And since human beings are not supposed to "detach" themselves in this way from the life around them, it follows that in addition to the original misbehavior they are trying to hide, they will now have a further, "symptomatic" reason for feeling ashamed of themselves and perhaps withdrawing still further.

## Changes in the Strategy and Objectives of "Therapy"

With the shift in the theory of psychopathology which has just been delineated, certain changes are called for with respect to what ought to be done about such a condition. Instead of seeing conscience as irrational and tyrannical, one now sees the conscience of a neurotic person as trying to "reach," "redeem," save its owner, and bring him back into community and restore him to fully human status and functioning. And since this is a good objective, the therapist-helper, operating in this revised frame of reference, aligns himself *with* conscience rather than against it.

Because Freud took the position that, in the neurotic, conscience is too strong and needs to be weakened, and because the position here described differs from Freud's, it has often been inferred that "therapy" in this altered frame of reference calls for a *strengthening* of conscience. This does not necessarily follow. In the sociopath (or "psychopath"), as ordinarily understood, there is indeed a specific character defect or weakness of conscience, and if such a person is going to receive help it must involve character

building (Shelly & Bassin, 1965). But anyone who has enough character or conscience to become "neurotic" has, it would seem, enough to be, or at least become, normal. If conscience has anything to do with the internal storms of such proportions as one sees in psychosis, then there is manifestly great strength rather than weakness here. The trouble is thus not one of weakness on the part of conscience but perhaps a policy of conscious rejection thereof by the ego or "self-system" (a Sullivan term). And if this be the situation, the task of therapy is not to attack and try to undercut conscience, but rather to support it and try to get the ego to recognize the legitimacy and potential helpfulness of the efforts of this part of the total personality, instead of distrusting and rejecting it. Because of the neurotic ego's policy of rejecting conscience, the *way* in which conscience is forced to function may be changed, but it is not weak. And the efforts of a therapist should not be toward trying to strengthen the superego (except, of course, in the sociopath) but rather toward trying to persuade the ego to give up its opposition to conscience and inducing it to come to terms and "make friends" with this part of the total personality.

Psychoanalysts are usually very selective with respect to the persons with whom they choose to work, and they are also cautious about the "interpretations" they make—and when they make them—on the assumption that if the patient is not ready such interpretations may precipitate suicide or psychosis. Although our experience and data are as yet limited, preliminary indications are that if one is operating with the 1b frame of reference, such untoward occurrences are much less likely than in classical psychoanalysis and therapy can proceed more rapidly. If the actual situation in a patient is that shown in Figure 1b and if the therapist, presupposing the 1a situation, mistakenly aligns himself *against* the superego, then the latter may indeed become desperate and resort to extraordinary means of trying to effect the person's "salvation." But if the therapist sees the superego as benign and potentially helpful, his presence and interventive efforts are likely to be reassuring to the superego, which may somewhat relax. Conscience has now found an external ally, rather than a critic, and the situation is, to this extent at least, immediately better rather than worse.

Sometimes the question is asked: "But can't there be *both* kinds of neuroses, the kind shown in Figure 1b *and* the kind shown in Figure 1a?" Our hypothesis can be put in either a strong or a weak form. The *strong* form of the hypothesis holds that, when the facts are fully known, *all* personality disorders (of the neurotic and functional psychotic variety) will be found to conform to the 1b pattern. The *weak* form, on the other hand, says that in $x$ percentage of cases the 1b situation prevails but that in $y$ percentage the 1a situation may hold, and that only empirical investigation will determine what the actual ratio is. Pending further inquiry and experience, we are willing to settle for the weak form of the hypothesis; but clinically there is often an advantage in adopting the strong hypothesis, in that it releases data which would not be forthcoming if the therapist approached the patient with the weak hypothesis in mind (Mowrer, 1966b, 1967b). Besides, there are certain logical reasons for questioning the 1a position, as we have already seen. But the final answer will lie in further research and assessment of therapeutic and social outcomes (Mowrer, 1968).

This is not, of course, the place to try to explore all the implications of the type of theory represented by Figure 1b. However, one other consideration is in order. Because the particular conception of psychopathology and psychotherapy with which we are here especially concerned takes a highly positive, rather than negative attitude toward conscience as it presently exists in any given neurotic individual, it is sometimes inferred that we are saying that conscience must be accepted absolutely as an inescapable given of personality, with all that this would imply as far as religious and political conservatism are concerned. This inference does not at all follow. Perhaps it arises in the minds of some persons because of Freud's theory that conscience is formed during the early period of childhood socialization and is immutable thereafter, except for the possible action of psychoanalytic treatment. There is increasing indication that conscience is, in certain important respects, self-chosen—and thus modifiable. Manifestly we have a good deal of latitude in the particular persons and projects to which we commit ourselves; and we also have some opportunity to review our commitments and, if need be, renegotiate them (Pratt & Tooley, 1964). Some few contracts, such as marriage, are supposed to be "for life," but others, as for example in business and professional life, are certainly open to reconsideration and can, under suitable circumstances, be dissolved. Thus, what may be termed the "content" of conscience is manifestly subject to change; the only thing that is invariant is the requirement, supported outwardly by community as well as inwardly by conscience, that, having made a given agreement "in good faith," one does not secretly violate it—i.e., show "bad faith"—while still enjoying the trust and cooperation of the other contracting party or parties. It is our assumption that this form of contract abrogation and disregard of conscience is what gets human beings into so-called neurotic ("sociotic"—Van den Berg, 1964—is a much better term) difficulties. And the "therapy" of choice is therefore one that tries to increase responsibility and integrity (Drakeford, 1967).

Sometimes this approach is criticized because it does not say *what* particular choices or contracts, in the moral, social, and political area, any given person ought to make. Obviously, there are two questions here, which need to be clearly distinguished: (1) How does one find the Good Life within a particular society or reference group; and (2) What is the Good Society? Those of us who are identified with Integrity Therapy do not think we know any more than most other people about what the Good Society is. And even if we assumed that we did, others would not want us to *tell* them, to "dictate" to them. This being a Free Society, every person wishes to exercise this freedom and make his own choices. Our thesis is thus a relatively modest but not, we think, an unimportant one: we merely suggest that, having made an interpersonal commitment or contract, either tacitly or explicitly, one is honor-bound, not to violate it secretly, i.e., not to *cheat*. And we believe that in all—or, to take the "weak" form of the hypothesis, at least in many—instances of psychopathology, the problem arises specifically and precisely because the afflicted individual has been "unfaith-ful," in one or more important areas of his life, to his solemn duty and is unable or unwilling to acknowledge this fact.

Today it is often said that it is very difficult, if not impossible, to know what is "right and wrong." Life, in our times, does indeed involve many difficult decisions, and I have no prescription or formula to suggest in this regard; but once a person has *made* a choice, committed himself, the possibility of secret violation and infidelity ought to be categorically excluded. Most of us have already highly structured our lives in terms of contractual arrangements, i.e., we "belong" to various groups and persons; and it is the honoring or dishonoring of these commitments that gives us moral guidelines which seem to be quite sufficient for most ordinary purposes, and which determine whether we preserve or sully our integrity and identity.

## The Difference Stated in Terms of "Responsibility" Rather Than "Psychodynamics"

In 1965 the author published a chapter in Wolman's Handbook of Clinical Psychology entitled "Learning theory and behavior therapy," in which there are two small diagrams and a legend which are reproduced here as Figures 2a and 2b. As perusal of the legends indicates, these diagrams are "corollaries" of Figures 1a and 1b, respectively, but with an emphasis upon etiology rather than "psycho-dynamics." If the plight of the neurotic is that he has an excessively severe, tyrannical superego (Figure 1a), this could only be due to the action of others, especially parents, as the too zealous agents of morality who set up in the young emotional reactions and pre-

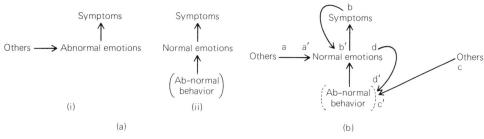

## Figure 2a

Schematic representation of two conceptions of psychopathology. (i) According to the more conventional of these, the essence of neurosis or mental illness is an emotional disturbance or disorder which has been produced by inappropriate, irrational behavior on the part of others (parents, teachers, husbands, wives, employers, etc.). (ii) The alternative position holds that the crux of the problem is not emotional but behavioral. Given the deviant, duplicitous life style of the individual himself, his emotional suffering (insecurity, anxiety, inferiority feelings, guilt) is seen as thoroughly natural, appropriate, normal. The abnormality in the situation consists of the individual's secret deviations from the norms, standards, rules, "values" of his reference group. In the first conceptual scheme, one's own behavior is never seen as "causal", only the behavior of others (which, if one is consistent, must in turn have been caused by others, and so on, to an infinite regress). And whatever the individual does, if it is in any way objectionable or "bad", is interpreted as "merely symptomatic of deep, underlying emotional problems". Thus, attention is focused almost exclusively upon emotions, with little or no responsibility accruing to the individual. In the other frame of reference, so-called "symptoms" (see Fig. 2b) arise from emotional discomfort which is appropriate and well "earned", considering what the individual has done in the past, is still doing, and is hiding (a fact denoted by the parentheses). Attention is thus shifted from emotions to conduct and from what others have done to one's own actions.

## Figure 2b

Combination and elaboration of the two diagrams shown in Figure 2a. If, in the conventional frame of reference, the basic problem is an abnormality of emotions which has been produced by others, then "therapy" (a→a') would require some sort of treatment by others which would offset the mistreatment to which the individual has been previously exposed. Oddly, this is precisely what the individual's own symptomatic efforts (b→b') are designed to do: i.e., make him feel better, without necessarily being better. Thus, "symptoms" may be defined as an individual's own attempt at self-cure which, like most professional treatment, assumes that the basic problem is wrong emotions, bad "nerves". If, however, the other hypothesis is correct and if the neurotic individual's emotional reactions (considering his on-going life style) are essentially normal, we see how sadly misdirected such treatment is. Surely it is suggestive in this connection that, on the average, the apparent effectiveness of professional treatment does not exceed the incidence of "spontaneous remissions" in untreated persons. But if it is really the individual's behavior rather than his emotions which is abnormal, then therapy, i.e., the efforts of others to help him, ought to be directly toward behavior change (c→c'), rather than emotional reeducation. And to the extent that this point of view begins to make sense to the suffering person himself, he will then start letting his emotional discomfort motivate him (d→d') to eliminate the questionable behavior and life strategies which have been producing the emotional upset, rather than seeking to eliminate the emotional discomfort directly (b→b'). When an emotionally disturbed person is able to see his predicament in this light, he will actively, independently, effectively set about "curing" himself (through confession and restitution) and will not need protracted treatment from others. Instead of continuing to be weak and needing to "receive", he will become strong and able to give.

dispositions which are irrational, unrealistic, "abnormal" (Figure 2a(i)). But if the neurotic, instead of being overwhelmed and dominated by his conscience, is really a person who has rejected this part of his own personality (Figure 1b), then he obviously has considerable responsibility for his predicament (Figure 2a(ii)) and, by the same token, can and must himself take an active role in changing the situation along lines which will be more fully described in the next section.

The main thing to be noted at this point is that as between Figure 2a(i) and Figure 2a(ii) there is a fundamental shift in emphasis, from feelings and emotions to concrete, specific behavior or, more exactly, *misbehavior*, which has been confounded by *concealment*. As long as the "cure of souls" (which is what "psychiatry" literally means) was regarded as the proper province of the church, good behavior (virtue) was emphasized as basic and good feeling (happiness) was a derivative thereof, as suggested in Figure 2a(ii). But as the church became increasingly preoccupied with purely sacramental procedures, and as people became more and more convinced of the greater potency of science, the church lost much of its competence and confidence in this area, and sin-sick, guilt-ridden persons turned increasingly to physicians (Mowrer, 1961, 1964, 1966b). But, characteristically, the physician asks not, "How are you acting, behaving?" but "How are you *feeling*?" He does not ordinarily regard himself as a moralist or even as an educator, but instead sees the relief of suffering as his privilege and duty, without much regard to the state of a man's "soul." His major objective, in other words, is to make his patients "better" in the sense of more

comfortable or physically stronger, not to change or "improve" them behaviorally or ethically. As far as physical infirmities are concerned, this policy is probably an excellent one; but its application in the spiritual, psychological, and moral realm is questionable.

Since human beings never "feel" well when they are behaving badly (unless they are characterless, sociopathic), the physician's services have been in great demand. However, today there is growing realization that this approach may be wide of the mark and that personal guilt must be taken seriously, and used as the occasion for change, not analyzed or tranquilized away. It is, in short, not a calamity but a challenge. However, this emerging appreciation of the role of guilt is not simply a return to the older churchly, theistic way of thinking, but represents instead a tendency to see personal morality as something that has its own this-worldly, here-and-now logic, which is quite as necessary for the satisfactory functioning of individuals as it is for the cohesion and survival of societies. Many psychologists are thus in process of questioning the "medical model," with its emphasis upon disease, and are emphasizing instead a teaching or *educational* (learning) model (Adams, 1964).

Among psychiatrists there is a similar trend. For example, some of the members of this profession never ask those who consult them: "How are you feeling?" Instead they ask: "How are you doing?" In short, they do not assume that their patients are "sick," but slothful, secretive, "sinful," and that an improvement in the situation will come, not alone from treatment which the physician supplies, but mainly from corrective action which the individual himself must take.

When the author noticed and commented upon this policy on the part of one psychiatrist, he replied: "Yes, your observation is quite right—I deliberately do not ask people how they are feeling. I think psychiatrists, as a result of their medical training, have often misdirected people's attention in this respect. We've encouraged them to think that, by our treatment, we can make them feel better without there being any necessity for them to exhibit personal change, better performance." And another psychiatrist says that he finds that his patients typically want him to give them *relief*, without requiring them to modify the behavior that is producing the trouble (Garner, 1966). Psychiatrists have, in his opinion, too often gone along with this popular demand, instead of standing for a harder but more genuinely helpful policy (see also Szasz, 1961; Dabrowski, 1964; Glasser, 1965).

## "Symptoms": Type 1, Type 2, and an Alternative

Thoughtful examination of Figure 2b suggests that the term "symptoms," as ordinarily used in the field of psychopathology, is ambiguous. Sometimes it refers to the efforts which the individual himself makes, i.e., his defenses and "security operations," to lessen his emotional discomforts (see $b \rightarrow b'$), and sometimes it refers to the discomforts themselves, such as anxiety, depression, etc. Obviously these are two quite different orders of events and need to be differentiated. Both are "symptoms" in the sense of reflecting some antecedent condition or problem, but they reflect *different* problems and are therefore different phenomena. Here we shall des-

ignate the emotional discomforts, which arise from deviant, abnormal behavior, as type-1 symptoms; and we shall refer to the attempts which the "neurotic" individual himself makes to eliminate these discomforts as type-2 symptoms. For reasons which have already been suggested, the term "neurotic" in the preceding sentence might well be "stupid" (Dollard & Miller, 1950; Shelly & Bassin, 1965) for type-2 symptoms do not really work. Dr. Karl Menninger has aptly characterized alcohol as "a home remedy for anxiety," which, in the long run, does not eliminate the original anxiety and itself creates new problems, both psychological and physical. *All* type-2 symptoms might be called "home remedies," in that they are self-devised or inappropriately suggested by others, and although they may bring temporary relief, they only make matters worse, ultimately.

Thus the first criterion as to whether a symptom is type 1 or type 2 has to do with the question of whether it has been precipitated by *inappropriate conduct* or represents an attempt to cope with the *ensuing emotional discomfort* in some "defensive" way. But there is a rather obvious second criterion, namely, the question of whether a symptom is a *reaction*, in the sense of being *involuntary*, or a response, an *action*, in the sense of being *voluntary*. Type-1 symptoms are mediated by the autonomic nervous system, and are thus involuntary, whereas type-2 symptoms, being "defenses," are under the control of the central nervous system, and are voluntary. And we can further say that type-1 symptoms arise from two separate but related sources: (a) the *objective danger* of being "seen through," "known," "caught" by the "significant others" who are being cheated and deceived and (b) the *subjective danger* of being "bothered," "disturbed," "attacked" by the superego or conscience, which, as the agent of the external community, already "knows" what the individual has done, and is perhaps still doing, of an antisocial, abnormal, duplicitous nature. Thus we may say that type-1 symptoms are produced by the "internalized voice of the community" (as Freud called the superego) and by the proximity of members of that community (the "significant others," of Sullivan); whereas type-2 symptoms are ego-mediated but are "neurotic" and "stupid" in that they involve ways of "controlling" type-1 symptoms which, in the long run, make the individual's life situation worse rather than genuinely better.

As a corollary of what has already been said, we may further observe that type-1 symptoms are potentially useful, *enabling*, in that the person experiencing them does not *have* to react with type-2 symptoms—he may also let himself be motivated to *change* his basic life style, as suggested by arrow $d \rightarrow d'$, in Figure 2b; whereas type-2 symptoms are ultimately useless, *disabling* (Brenden, 1965). This is why, in Figure 2b, we refer to type-1 symptoms as "normal emotions," rather than as "abnormal emotions," as in Figure 2a(i). In Figure 2a(i) the "neurosis" consists of "wrong," malconditioned emotional reactions which the afflicted individual manifests; whereas in Figure 2b, the "neurosis" consists, first of all, of the "deviant, abnormal behavior" which the individual has engaged in and has then kept carefully hidden *and* of the efforts, which are here called type-2 symptoms, which the individual makes to eliminate the emotional and mental discomforts produced by the original, wrong behavior. In other words, the basic problem is not one of wrong feelings, but of *wrong actions*, which in the first place are "offensive" (in the moral and social sense) and then, at the level of type-2 symptoms, are "defensive" (psychologically speaking). The critical consideration is not that the "neurotic" individual *has* the feelings which we are calling type-1 symptoms but that what he tries to do about them is inappropriate and ultimately self-defeating, i.e., the fact that he makes $b \rightarrow b'$ responses to his disturbing emotions rather than $d \rightarrow d'$ responses.

With these considerations before us, I have often asked students and others to draw up a list of type-1 and type-2 symptoms. The following are composites, compiled from a number of such occasions:

*Symptoms, type 1*

Tension
Anxiety
Depression
Panic

Loss of appetites
Accident proneness
Failure proneness
Work inhibition
Inability to concentrate
Poor memory
Tics, stuttering
Insomnia
Fatigue
Sleepiness
Irritability
Self-doubt
Indecision
Loneliness
Nightmares
Stage fright
Self-hate
Death fear

Depersonalization
Sense of unreality
Obsessions
Scrupulosity
Phobias
Hypochondriasis
Hysteria
Hallucinations
Delusions

*Symptoms, type 2*

Withdrawal
Escapism
Invalidism
Suicide

Rationalization
Resentment
Blaming others
Attacking others

Self-pity
Reassurance
"Cheap grace"
Psychotherapy $(a \rightarrow a')$
Paying fees ("fines")

Compulsions
Rituals
Busy-ness

Overeating
Abuse of sex
Fantasy
Grandiosity

Intoxicants
Narcotics
Tranquilizers
Shock treatments

Conventional psychiatry and clinical psychology have usually not differentiated between the two types of "symptoms" here delineated,[1] and they have

also sometimes neglected the contributions which the individual himself makes to the situation, in the form of deviant behavior which is then protected by deception. The point of special concern has often been the *feelings* which have presumably been caused by others and must be corrected by others. Our conceptual scheme, by contrast, suggests that the essence of the individual's "neurosis," or "craziness," lies not in his emotions, but in his actions, his choices, i.e., his decision (a) to misbehave and to hide this fact and then (b) to try to eliminate the resulting emotional discomforts by various relief-giving measures instead of correcting his erroneous life style.

If this understanding of the situation is correct, the "therapy" of choice is the one suggested by the arrow $c \rightarrow c'$ (help from others) and by the arrow $d \rightarrow d'$

[1] This statement calls for some qualification. In a volume published in 1936, Freud remarked that there are "two opinions" concerning the nature of symptoms: "One of them terms the anxiety itself a symptom of the neurosis, the other conceives of a far more intimate connection between the two. According to this latter view, all symptom formation would be brought about solely in order to avoid anxiety; the symptoms bind the psychic energy which otherwise would be discharged as anxiety, so that anxiety would be the fundamental phenomenon and the central problem of neurosis" (p. 111). The first conception of symptoms alluded to is one which, as suggested above, makes no distinction between what we are calling type-1 and type-2 symptoms. Manifestly Freud preferred the second point of view and thus, in a sense, might be said to have accepted the distinction between type-1 and type-2 symptoms. But Freud did not regard anxiety as a symptom, properly speaking; he preferred instead to refer to it as "the fundamental phenomenon and the central problem of neurosis." And since his conception of the origin and nature of anxiety was so different from the one here proposed, the apparent similarity of positions is reduced still further. In fairness it must be noted that Freud did recognize two orders of phenomena here, but the language employed was different, as were also many of the underlying assumptions.

(self-help, cf. Dabrowski, 1964, on "self-education" and "auto-therapy"). And here the assumption is that the basic problem is not "instincts" which have been repressed by a too severe conscience but deviant, inappropriate gratification thereof which has been kept concealed and which conscience, by means of type-1 symptoms of discomforts, is trying to get "out into the open." When properly understood, type-2 symptoms provide a tell-tale indication that "something is wrong" in the life of the individual displaying them, but direct admission of deviance and dishonesty is the more appropriate and effective response, as suggested by the $d \rightarrow d'$ arrow. When a "neurotic" individual abandons type-2 symptoms and directs his attention toward the phenomena depicted in the lower part of Figure 2b, the struggle between superego and ego is largely resolved and the individual begins to change, not only as a result of his own efforts but also because the concerns and criticisms of others can now effectively impinge upon him. He is now being "open," "transparent" (Jourard, 1964) rather than "closed" and can learn, be educated, socialized. In some forms of psychotherapy the aim is to attack and weaken conscience. In Integrity Therapy the intention is to support conscience and to try to get the individual himself to recognize its true objectives, which are to motivate him to change in such a way as to be a fully acceptable, valued member of the community from which he draws his sustenance. If the individual does not wish to be thus restored to responsible commerce with his reference group or groups he should announce this fact and relinquish the privileges which normally accompany membership therein. In short, the suggestion is that if a so-called neurotic individual can't or won't "get with it," as far as the community life about him is concerned, then he ought to get *out*—or openly work for the reforms in the life of the group which he believes are indicated. Cheating on his social system can only destroy him as a person, and weaken the system in which he is claiming membership privileges.

## Miscellaneous Considerations

The "three-stage" conception of psychopathology presented in Figure 2b has many ramifications and invites detailed exploration. In fact, systematic comment on the items listed in the two columns could easily expand into a textbook of "abnormal" psychology and "therapy." Such an enterprise is manifestly beyond our purpose here. But I do wish to single out a few special issues for consideration.

### Symptom classification and "secondary gain"

No claim is made that the foregoing lists of type-1 and type-2 symptoms are either comprehensive or, indeed, entirely accurate. Consider, for example, the phenomenon of hypochondriasis. This symptom is put in the first list because it represents a *loss of health* and is thus one of many ways in which conscience can "bother" a person who is not living as he or she should. But once this type-1 symptom has appeared, it can be exploited by the individual himself, for what Freud called "secondary gain." Freud thought that symptoms, in general, are biphasic, i.e., that they always involve an element of surreptitious instinctual gratification and an element of suffering, or "tribute" to the superego, as the condition of their occurrence.[2] Thus, the illicit pleasure which the symptom supposedly provides was the *primary* gain, and any additional, practical advantage was regarded as *secondary*. We do not posit primary gain, in the sense of subtle "instinctual" gratification, in type-1 symptoms. Instead, we assume that type-1 symptoms are produced by conscience and are designed to get the individual to acknowledge and eliminate his inappropriate conduct and to come back "into community." And type-2 symptoms serve, not (as Freud posited) to provide subtle gratification of supposedly repressed instincts, but, primarily, to allay the pain and offset the inconvenience produced by type-1 symptoms.

It is nevertheless true that type-1 symptoms can be turned to "practical" account by the ego; and although the term is not entirely appropriate in our context, we shall nevertheless refer to this function as "secondary gain." Thus, in the example of hypochondriasis, the afflicted individual, instead of being motivated by this "loss of health" to change his style of life, may instead say: "Yes, I am indeed sick, and should be given the privileges of a sick person." In fact, the tendency so widespread in our time, to refer to *all* forms of personality disorder as mental or emotional "illness" provides powerful external support for just such a tendency, and this is probably one of the reasons why the "medical model" has provided so few practical answers (Adams, 1964). It also

suggests why Recovery, Inc. (Low, 1943) encourages its members to think, not about relief or comfort, but about *effort*, in the sense of becoming more energetic, industrious, responsible, rather than merely being "sick."

Perhaps another example will further clarify the principle which is at issue here. Freud hypothesized that the phenomenon of paranoia, particularly the "delusion of observation," is a product of repressed homosexuality (Freud, 1933; Walters, 1955). We suggest that a very different process is at work here. As is well known, one of the distinctive features of paranoia is the "delusion of observation," i.e., the belief that one is being followed, spied upon, that his mind is being read or his thoughts "broadcast." In short, the individual has lost his privacy. Why, we may ask, should anyone experience a *loss of privacy*? The possibility of privacy is humanly important, and its loss—through a sense of being constantly watched, having one's mind read, etc.—is very disconcerting. What better explanation than this, that conscience takes our privacy away from us when we have been *abusing* it, i.e., doing something that is socially disapproved and then concealing this fact! Hence, when we encounter paranoid persons, those of us who are identified with Integrity Therapy are likely to ask them, quite directly: "What have you been *hiding*? What are you trying to get away with, that makes it so necessary for you to be 'watched'?"

The correct response to the appearance of paranoid trends in one's personality is, of course, to *admit and make restitution for* whatever one has been doing in secret that is reprehensible and wrong. But too often, when such trends appear, the individual says: "Yes, people

[2] This is the point of view taken by Freud in *A general introduction to psychoanalysis* (1920). It is manifestly not the same as the one alluded to in footnote 1 which reflects Freud's thinking as of 1936.

*are* spying on me, bothering me, trying to kill me, etc." In other words, the person concludes that he is not only being observed but persecuted, i.e., he takes his type-1 symptom "literally." And if one does this, then one has justification for doing all manner of odd and irresponsible things, such as not going to work, taking elaborate precautions, hiding, blaming others, etc. The latter responses qualify, of course, as type-2 symptoms. But what is important here is the matter of *attitude*, or *choice*, as to whether one is going to be motivated by type-1 symptoms *to change* or to use them as an excuse for all manner of otherwise quite inexcusable behavior. Changing this attitude, or strategy, is perhaps the most important single factor in "therapy"—or, as we might better say, "conversion," which means a turning-with, rather than against.

If one studies the type-1 symptoms which are listed [above], it becomes evident that all of them can be interpreted as motivation or "punishment" associated with a *loss* of some sort: thus, hallucination is a loss of the evidence of one's sense; tics and stuttering destroy one's dignity, i.e., make one "look foolish"; poor memory involves partial or (in "amnesia") total loss of memory; paranoia involves a loss of privacy; etc. Obviously it is of crucial importance that we understand—and respond to—these phenomena correctly. In Recovery, Inc., misinterpretation of symptoms is called "sabotage," and in Alcoholics Anonymous it is called, even more colorfully, "stinkin' thinkin'."

### The question of symptom choice

The list of type-1 symptoms which appears [above] is a relatively long one. Thus it would appear that conscience (like its prototype, parents) has many ways in which it can bother, penalize, punish, "get at" us when we have ignored its direct, explicit admonitions and rebukes. It will be noted, however, that "guilt" does not appear among the type-1 symptoms. This is because conscious, explicit awareness of wrongdoing is characteristic of a personality that is functioning well. Type-1 "symptoms" appear, it seems, only when guilt, in its common, ordinary manifestations, has been ignored and conscience has to resort to quite extraordinary, or "abnormal," ways of "reaching" us. But because there is now a great deal of added force or "power," which is made necessary by the resistance to the ordinary, normal manifestations of conscience, the ways in which guilt is experienced are often unintelligible, ambiguous, and capable of misinterpretation. This is why Belgum (1963), using the analogy of a radio which loses clarity and intelligibility when the "power" is turned up very high, has characterized type-1 symptoms as representing "the amplified, *distorted* voice of conscience." Thus, when "neurotic" persons are asked if they feel guilty about anything, they often say that they do not: what a normal person would experience as conscious guilt has, in their case, been converted into type-1 symptoms, whose source and meaning are now at least partly "unconscious" (cf. next subsection).

Against these background considerations, we face the question of why conscience selects one rather than another of the various devices which are open to it, as extraordinary means of "doing its work" when the ordinary means (guilt) has proven unavailing. Psychoanalytic writers have given a good deal of thought to the problem of "symptom

choice," but since their assumptions concerning the origin and nature of symptoms are very different from ours, their conjectures are not very relevant. But neither is there any other established system of thought to provide guidance here. Perhaps as good a surmise as any is that conscience attacks "symptomatically" at the point or points where the ego, or conscious self-system, is *most vulnerable*. For example, students who are having "emotional difficulties" often complain of inability to "concentrate" or study. This, surely, is where the person whose principal preoccupation is cognitive learning is most easily afflicted, incapacitated, "stopped." And one can extend this example into a general hypothesis to the effect that conscience selects those type-1 symptoms which are most likely to get the ego's attention and prove maximally disconcerting.[3]

It will be noted that among type-1 symptoms, both insomnia and sleepiness are listed. The inclusion of sleepiness here may be an error in that "going to sleep" is sometimes used as an escape and thus becomes a type-2 symptom. But there is also the possibility that conscience may use insomnia in the one case and drowsiness in another, as type-1 symptoms, depending upon what is the most important to a person—being able to sleep or to stay awake.

[3] It may be objected that this explanation of "symptom choice" is very "anthropomorphic." It is indeed. But we are, after all, talking about human beings in the area of their distinctive humanness; and since conscience is given to us, developmentally and contemporaneously, by other persons (and our style of relating to them), it should not be too surprising if conscience acts, "behaves" personally, anthropomorphically. It would be nice if we knew the precise machinery whereby all this is accomplished; but the fact that we do not, as yet, does not necessarily invalidate or discredit an otherwise promising view of the matter.

Purely adventitious factors may also be involved here, in the selection by conscience of type-1 symptoms. However, we have so little empirical data in this regard that further speculation is presently unwarranted.

## Is the unconscious unavailable?

If we assume that the neurotic individual can help himself, is it not inconsistent to posit unconscious factors or "determinants" in his personality? If something is truly unconscious the individual presumably does not know about it and thus cannot take relevant action with respect to it. Our supposition is that conscience always acts automatically, or "unconsciously," in the sense that it is not under the control and direction of the ego (just as what parents do in the way of discipline is not under the control and direction of a child). And a person may also, on occasion, pretend that he does not know what conscience is bothering him about. He is, of course, only too painfully aware, or conscious, of the discomfort that conscience is inflicting; and if he exerts a little effort, or talks openly with others, it is usually not too difficult to discern *why* conscience is concerned and trying to activate him. But self-deception—Sullivan called it "selective inattention"—commonly occurs at this juncture and produces at least a pseudoobscurity (see also Tkacik, 1964).

Sometimes I use the analogy of an iceberg to try to clarify this situation. It is true that most of an iceberg, floating in the ocean, is submerged, inaccessible, "unconscious." But there is always a portion of it which is above the surface and thus visible. Now if one says of that part which can be seen, "Oh, *that* cannot be of any importance, my problem is obviously something much bigger," one may indeed fail to come to grips with the total problem. But it has been my consistent observation that if a person will act appropriately with respect to the "little things" he can *see* which are wrong with his life, other larger defects and failures presently come into view. And he does not need to employ a "diver" to go down and work on the "unconscious," or submerged part of the problem. If one chips away at the part of the "iceberg" that is accessible the rest of it gradually "surfaces." Thus it is only the person who refuses to do what he *can* that is apparently a victim of "forces beyond his control." Two passages from the *New Testament* neatly encompass this ancient wisdom: "His master said to him, Well done, good and faithful servant, you have been faithful over a little, I will set you over much, enter into the joy of your master" (Matthew 25:21). "He who is faithful in a very little is faithful also in much, and he who is dishonest in a very little is dishonest also in much" (Luke 16:10, Living Letters Translation). The moral is that the impossible is never required of us, in this area.

*Modeling as the "therapy" of choice*

Is there also an inconsistency between the assumption that a neurotic individual can help himself and the assumption that he can often receive help from others? If one is operating on the theory that neurosis involves a disease which has to be treated by an expert or specialist, this dilemma does not arise: manifestly the "patient" *must* have help. But we are here questioning the disease, or medical, model and exploring instead a learning or educational model. The latter are not, of course, exactly the same. Learning can be a solitary (trial-and-error) enterprise, but education always involves a diadic relationship of some sort. Here the premise is that what may be learned slowly in isolation may be learned much more rapidly with the aid of another. But the basic responsibility still rests with the "pupil"—he must do his "homework" or the efforts of even the best teacher will come to nothing but conflict and dissention.

In learning situations which involve education, the instructor or teacher is ordinarily another person, but it may also be another part of one's own personality, namely conscience (Dabrowski, 1964; Mowrer, 1965a). We not uncommonly speak of conscience having taught us a "lesson," and one of the objectives or "responsibilities" of conscience is to make the ego as wise and as morally sensitive as conscience is. Surely the hallmark of the "mature" person is that ego and superego (child and parent) are unified and congruent with respect to the values they hold—or have "agreed to disagree" in an honorable and responsible manner.

But when conscience, for whatever reason, is unable to perform its proper educational, correctional function, what is the best way for "therapy," help, instruction to be supplied from without? For reasons which have already been alluded to earlier in this paper and have been discussed at length elsewhere (Mowrer, 1965b, 1966a), it seems that the most useful thing one person can do for another in this connection is to *model* the behavior which the "neurotic" individual himself needs to learn. And what is this behavior? It is the ability and willingness to submit oneself to the discipline of personal openness and consistency between one's commitments, or promises, and one's performance.

Modeling, as the heart of Integrity Therapy, has sometimes been criticized in a quite remarkable way. One critic has called it "Nudity Therapy" and others have complained that it involves "an invasion of personal privacy." When one considers how energetically clinical psychologists have tried to ferret out the well-guarded secrets of others by means of tests and how much effort on the part of psychiatrists and psychoanalysts has been expended on trying to "make the unconscious conscious," talk about the invasion of privacy is slightly paradoxical.

Increasingly in psychiatry, and particularly in *social* psychiatry and community mental health work, it is being recognized that "privacy" is the disease, not the cure. Consider, for example, the following remarks which Dr. Robert H. Felix, recently retired Director of the National Institute of Mental Health, makes in the Foreword of a volume entitled *Zone Mental Health Centers—The Illinois Concept:*

> To the trained observer, intense loneliness is the condition most characteristic of the mentally ill person. Alone, he enters a world where strange thoughts and sometimes forms and voices disturb and haunt him. . . .
>
> As a rule, the mental patient finds himself relegated to a large state mental hospital—often the loneliest of all possible worlds, peopled by others as isolated as he—where overworked staffs can spare him only a few hurried minutes each day. . . .
>
> With the advent of new treatment techniques, open wards and hospitals, and the psychoactive drugs, the mental

> patient becomes more responsive to the efforts of others to *break into his private world*. Carefully conducted follow-up studies produced a wealth of evidence that these efforts speed his recovery. One patient summed it up when he told a volunteer, "What you did for me was to treat me like a human being" (Felix, 1964, pp. vii and ix; italics added).

There is an implication in the last sentence of this quotation that the patient's difficulties had arisen because others have *not* treated him "like a human being" and were thus responsible for his troubles, whereas our assumption is that this person had not *acted* "like a human being" and had very largely brought his trouble on himself. And the "psychoactive drugs," instead of making disturbed persons more "accessible," sometimes, in my observation, have the effect of simply inactivating the person, i.e., reducing his motivation and initiative, and delaying rather than facilitating work on his "real problem." But the quotation from Felix is nevertheless a cogent one in showing the inappropriateness of the charge that Integrity Therapy "invades personal privacy." Of course it does, in the sense of trying to get a disturbed person to give up his secrecy, but the possibility of privacy, as previously defined, is not at all denied or eliminated. In fact, as suggested in the discussion of paranoia, it sometimes seems to be the case that only by the abandonment of secrecy privacy can be recovered.

Thus, what has been intended as a criticism we take as an advantage, although we would prefer to think of Integrity Therapy, not as an "invasion" of anything, but as *an invitation:* an invitation to openness, authenticity, and wholeness.

*Psychoanalysis and Christianity*

This paper is predicated on the assumption that, in certain basic ways, the conceptions of Sigmund Freud are in need of extensive revision. But in other respects, Freud has undoubtedly made contributions of enduring value. At a time when "mental illness" was commonly assumed to have an organic basis and persons so afflicted were regarded as "out of their heads" and not worth talking to (because their brains were "addled" and they did not know what either they or you were saying), Freud had the originality and courage to start listening to such persons and to give a certain credence and meaning to what they said and did. Although, as we now believe, his particular way of interpreting what he heard and saw was often mistaken, Freud nevertheless restored these people to a kind of dignity and revived belief in their capacity to become once again fully functional, normal people. This was certainly an accomplishment of major magnitude.

And not only did Freud insist upon the intelligibility, the meaningfulness of personality disturbance, he also saw the problem as an essentially moral one, although in a somewhat inverted sense. He correctly perceived neurosis as always involving a discrepancy between the individual's moral standards and his actual conduct, his performance. But Freud made the error, it seems, of assuming that this discrepancy exists because the individual's standards are too high and need to be lowered by means of specialized treatment procedures. Today, it appears that the so-called neurotic is a person whose standards are normal enough but whose conduct leaves something—often quite a lot—to be desired and that the only genuinely effective therapy is one that involves admission of this discrepancy and earnest efforts to eliminate it, by improved behavior.

Because Christianity has traditionally insisted upon people having strong consciences and high moral standards, it has often been a target of criticism from psychoanalysts. If it were true that neurosis arises because of so-called moral "rigidity," then Christianity could indeed be blamed for much of our "emotional difficulty." But it now appears that the Freudian notion of the too severe superego as the basis of psychopathology is not valid; and if this be the case, the attack upon Christianity becomes irrelevant, and misdirected. Thus, Integrity Therapy is in this regard a vindication of Christianity and the social and moral ideals for which it has traditionally stood.

There is, unhappily, a different criticism which must be leveled against the church. From our point of view, it is not the "moralism" of Christianity that has fostered psychopathology but rather the fact that the church has, in recent centuries, encouraged and nurtured what Clebsch and Jaekle (1964) call "religious privatism," that is, the notion that sins can be "remitted" through private prayer and sacraments, without acknowledgment to the person or persons against whom the sins have been committed. This is a form of "private practice" which long antedates the not too dissimilar procedures of some contemporary psychiatry and clinical psychology. In fact, the latter may be regarded, with some justification, as merely a secular version of religious "confession and penance" (Mowrer, 1963). However, it now appears that "private treatment" is no more effective outside the church than it is within it. Privacy (in the sense of secrecy) is the problem, and the only radically effective solution is one that involves the abandonment of privacy and a return to community.

One could give an almost endless list of instances in which ministers and priests have encouraged the faithful to believe that there is a private, secret solution to their sins and personal alienation. A few examples will suffice. I recall a Catholic woman patient in a mental hospital who was there because she had lived with five different men and had two illegitimate children before she met and married her husband, to whom she had never disclosed these—as well as some more current—sources of guilt. A few years after her marriage, this woman became depressed and repeatedly went to confession and was "absolved," but she experienced no relief. Finally, after protracted "individual" psychotherapy and eventual hospitalization, she came into Integrity Therapy, got honest with her husband and others; and now for more than three years she has been at home, functioning relatively well.

Then I think of a woman who was on the verge of divorce who confided to me that she had had an abortion in college, had been married previously, and had done certain other things which she had never told her husband about. Now she could not understand why she and he were not "getting along." When I suggested that the situation might be improved by an honest disclosure to her husband, this woman's rejoinder was: "But I have confessed these things to God and he has forgiven me, I know he has." The trouble was that her husband did not know "these things" and the woman lived in constant fear that he would find them out and was driven by her unresolved guilt to engage in all manner of inappropriate behavior.

Occasionally I have encountered priests who are disturbed by the suggestion that a man who has been unfaithful to his wife ought to disclose this fact to her and some of the other people from whom he has been hiding his misbehavior. The prospect of a secret solution to such problems is undoubtedly appealing to many people, but it is apparent that, psychologically and socially, this type of procedure is often unsatisfactory; and many priests are today actively interested in learning how to deal with people's sins in a way that is not only theologically correct but *practically effective*.

Similar changes are also occurring among the Protestant clergy. Not long ago a minister told me the following story. A man who had just returned from military service abroad came to him and reported that for 70 days he had not eaten or slept properly. While in Korea and Japan this man had engaged in improper conduct, and now that he was back home he wanted to admit it to his wife. The clergyman told the man that this would not be necessary, that it would only distress his wife, and that he could find forgiveness and peace in prayer alone. The minister concluded his account of this incident by saying: "I am beginning to wonder if I counseled this man correctly."

We are deeply indebted today for the contributions which both Freudian psychoanalysis and Christianity have made to our culture; but it is also incumbent upon us to recognize some shortcomings as well. Psychoanalysis and Christianity, while radically differing in certain respects (Mowrer, 1967a), seem to have the common failing of not being sufficiently concerned with what Clebsch and Jaekle, in their book *Pastoral care in historical perspective,* call *reconciliation,* i.e., the restoration of secret sinners to open communion and fellowship with the people who are important to them. Both are too much committed to the proposition that a relatively easy, *private* solution of personal problems is possible. Originally, Christianity was a movement in which confession and penance were done openly, i.e., before and with the full knowledge of a small "congregation" or group of fellow Christians (McNiell, 1951; Poschman, 1964). Today the modern church is again looking at its ancient practices and considering a revival of them. And "private," individual psychoanalysis is likewise rapidly giving way to *group therapy.* Thus it would appear that secular as well as religious efforts at the "cure of souls" ("psychiatry," "psychotherapy") are moving in much the same direction. Not only does the new approach promise to unify these previously discordant disciplines but also to produce a procedure which is specific to the problem and correspondingly more effective.

## References

ADAMS, H. B. "Mental illness" or interpersonal behavior? *American Psychologist,* 1964, **19,** 191–196.

ANONYMOUS. *Twelve steps and twelve traditions.* New York: Alcoholics Anonymous, 1953.

BELGUM, D., *Guilt: Where psychology and religion meet.* Englewood Cliffs, N.J.: Prentice-Hall, 1963.

BRENDEN, H. B., The criteria for class-I and class-II symptoms. Unpublished memorandum, 1965.

BRODY, M. W. Prognosis and results of psychoanalysis. In J. H. Nodine and J. H. Moyer (Eds.), *Psychosomatic medicine.* Philadelphia: Lea & Febiger, 1962.

CLEBSCH, W. A., and JAEKLE, C. R. *Pastoral care in historical perspective.* Englewood Cliffs, N.J.: Prentice-Hall, 1964.

DABROWSKI, K. *Positive disintegration.* Boston: Little, Brown, 1964.

DOLLARD, J. The acquisition of new social habits. In R. Linton (Ed.), *The science of man in world crisis.* New York: Columbia University Press, 1945.

DOLLARD, J., and MILLER, N. E. *Personality and psychotherapy.* New York: McGraw-Hill, 1950.

DRAKEFORD, J. W. *Integrity therapy.* Nashville, Tenn.: Broadman Press, 1967.

EYSENCK, H. J. The effects of psychotherapy: An evaluation. *Journal of Consulting Psychology,* 1952, **16,** 319–324.

FELIX, R. H. Foreword to *Zone mental health centers* (by J. P. Reidy). Springfield, Ill.: Charles C Thomas, 1964.

FREUD, S. *A general introduction to psychoanalysis.* New York: Liveright, 1920.

*FREUD, S. *Civilization and its discontents.* London: Hogarth, 1930.

FREUD, S. Psycho-analytic notes upon an autobiographical account of a case of paranoia (Dementia Paranoides). In *Collected papers,* Vol. III. London: Hogarth, 1933.

FREUD, S. *The problem of anxiety.* New York: Norton, 1936.

FREUD, S. Analysis terminable and interminable, 1937. In *Collected papers,* Vol. V, 1950, pp. 316–357.

GARNER, H. H. The confrontation technique in psychotherapy. *American Journal of Psychotherapy,* 1966, **20,** 391.

GLASSER, W. *Reality therapy—A new approach to psychiatry.* New York: Harper, 1965.

JOURNARD, S. M. *The transparent self.* Princeton, N.J.: Van Nostrand, 1964.

KNIGHT, R. P. Evaluation of the results of

* [Asterisks indicate works that are reprinted, in whole or in part, in this volume.]

psychoanalytic therapy. *American Journal of Psychiatry*, 1941, **98**, 434–446.

Low, A. A. *Techniques of self-help in psychiatric aftercare.* Chicago, Ill.: Recovery Publications, 1943.

McNiell, J. T. *A history of the cure of souls.* New York: Harper, 1951.

Mowrer, O. H. Learning theory and the neurotic paradox. *American Journal of Orthopsychiatry*, 1948, **18**, 571–610.

Mowrer, O. H. *Psychotherapy—Theory and research.* New York: Ronald, 1953.

Mowrer, O. H. *The crisis in psychiatry and religion.* Princeton, N.J.: Van Nostrand, 1961.

Mowrer, O. H. Even there, Thy hand! *Chicago Theological Seminary Register*, 1962, **52**, 1–17.

Mowrer, O. H. Payment or repayment? The problem of private practice. *American Psychologist*, 1963, **18**, 577–580.

Mowrer, O. H. *The new group therapy.* Princeton, N.J.: Van Nostrand, 1964.

Mowrer, O. H. Symptoms of development: A review. *Contemporary Psychology*, 1965, **10**, 538–540. (a)

Mowrer, O. H. Learning theory and the behavior therapies. In B. Wolman (Ed.), *Handbook of clinical psychology.* New York: McGraw-Hill, 1965. (b)

Mowrer, O. H. The behavior therapies, with special reference to "modeling" and imitation. *Journal of the Association of Advanced Psychotherapy*, 1966, **20**, 439–461. (a)

Mowrer, O. H. *Abnormal reactions or actions? (An autobiographical answer).* In J. A. Vernon (Ed.), *Introduction to psychology: A self-selection textbook.*

Dubuque, Iowa: William C Brown, 1966. (b)

Mowrer, O. H. Christianity and psychoanalysis: Is a new synthesis needed? In *Religion in philosophical and cultural perspective.* Princeton, N.J.: Van Nostrand, 1967. (a)

Mowrer, O. H. *Morality and mental health.* Chicago: Rand McNally, 1967. (b)

Mowrer, O. H., New evidence concerning the nature of psychopathology. In M. J. Feldman (Ed.), *Studies in Psychotherapy and behavior change.* Buffalo, N.Y.: University of Buffalo Press, 1968, pp. 115–193.

Poschmann, B. *Penance and the anointing of the sick.* New York: Herder & Herder, 1964.

Pratt, S., and Tooley, J. Contract psychology and the actualizing transactional field. *International Journal of Social Psychiatry*, 1964 (Congress Issue), 51–60.

Shelly, J. A., and Bassin, A. Daytop Lodge —A new treatment approach for drug addicts. *Corrective Psychiatry*, 1965, **11**, 186–195.

Szasz, T. S. *The myth of mental illness.* New York: Hoeber, 1961.

Tkacik, A. Conscience: Conscious and unconscious. *Journal of Religion & Health* 1964, **4**, 75–85.

Van den Berg, J. H. *The changing nature of man.* New York: Dell, 1964.

Walters, O. S. A methodological critique of Freud's Schreber analysis. *Psychoanalytical Review*, 1955, **42**, 321–342.

Wilder, J. Facts and figures on psychotherapy. *Journal of Clinical Psychopathology*, 1945, **7**, 311–347.

# 31

# Sexual behavior and psychopathology: A test of Mowrer's hypothesis

*by Clifford H. Swensen, Jr.*

## Problem

Mowrer (4, 5) has asserted that neurosis is caused by the individual behaving in a way that is contrary to standards approved by his conscience. If Mowrer's contention is correct, one would expect people who seek psychotherapy for neurotic complaints to have violated moral laws more frequently than normal people coming from the same socioeconomic background. This study tests the hypothesis that patients who seek psychotherapy in order to alleviate psychological symptoms would have violated some well-known moral scruple more frequently than a matched group of normals.

## Methodology

The case records of 25 University of Tennessee coeds who had sought psychotherapy at the Psychological Service and Research Center during the previous year (1960–1961) were obtained. It is difficult to obtain a measure of violation of conscience in many areas, but one kind of behavior reported in case histories is sexual behavior. It was felt that for the purpose of this study this would be particularly appropriate, since sex is a problem of particular pertinence to college girls. Sexual behavior is a problem they constantly have to solve, and it is an area in which most girls have received moral training and have clear-cut moral values. The case history data were scored for 30 variables using the rating scale developed by Pascal and Jenkins (6).

The staff at the University of Tennessee Psychological Service and Research Center has been collecting the same kind of case history data from a large random sample of coeds at the University of Tennessee and other universities throughout the South.[1] A sample of 25 cases was taken from this large random sample of University of Tennessee coeds and matched with the experimental group for age and education. Thus, the experimental group consisted of the last 25 coeds to come to the Center for psychotherapy, and the control group consisted of 25 coeds taken from a large random sample of coeds on the campus but selected so that they matched the experimental group on age and education. Both groups had exactly the same distribution for the age and educational variables, ranging in age from 17 to 25 (Median age = 20) and in class from freshman to graduate student (Median = 2 years of college). The patient group

Clifford H. Swensen, Jr., "Sexual Behavior and Psychopathology: A Test of Mowrer's Hypothesis," *Journal of Clinical Psychology*, 1962, **18**, 406–409. Reprinted by permission of the author and Dr. Frederick C. Thorne.

[1] As part of a large normative study on the gross human behavior of college women being conducted by Drs. G. R. Pascal and W. O. Jenkins. The author is indebted to them for the use of this data for the control group.

Table 1

**Symptoms Displayed by the Patient Group**

| Symptom | Numbers* |
|---|---|
| 1. Trouble doing schoolwork | 15 |
| 2. Depression | 15 |
| 3. Physical complaints | 8 |
| 4. Tense and anxious | 7 |
| 5. Difficulty sleeping, nightmares | 5 |
| 6. Feel inferior, inadequate, self-conscious | 4 |
| 7. Emotional outbursts, moodiness | 3 |
| 8. Suicidal attempts or urges | 3 |
| 9. Compulsive behavior | 2 |
| 10. Indecisive about deciding to marry | 2 |
| 11. Phobias | 1 |
| 12. Conflict with parents | 1 |

*Some patients complained of more than one symptom.

consisted entirely of coeds who had come to the clinic because they personally felt the need for help, or had been referred to the clinic by student advisors. The kinds of symptoms that brought them to the clinic are listed in Table 1. The two groups were compared, using the phi coefficient, on the 30 case history variables rated with the Pascal-Jenkins scale.

## Results

Of the 30 phi coefficients computed, 12 were significant at the .01 level and 4 were significant at the .05 level. Table 2 presents the results of the comparison of the two groups on the case history variables. There were significant differences between the two groups in the amount of sexual behavior. Significantly more patients than controls had their breasts touched by men, had their sexual organs touched by men, and had sexual intercourse. The significance of the difference between the two groups on sexual intercourse is not as great as the difference

between the two groups on manual contact with the breast or sex organs. This is because the number of girls from the control group who had sexual intercourse was identical with the number who had their breast or sexual organs touched by men, whereas there were more patients who had the sexual organs caressed but had not had sexual intercourse. This would seem to indicate that this group of coeds felt just as guilty about engaging in intimate petting as in having sexual intercourse, if psychopathological symptoms are indicative of guilt. This result agrees with Ehrmann's (1) finding that college girls draw a moral line between hugging and kissing and more extensive petting involving fondling of the breasts and genitals.

There were also significant differences between the groups in the amount of social activity engaged in. The control group belonged to significantly more organizations, was more active in the organizations to which they belonged, and attended more parties than the patient group. These data appear to contradict

*Table 2*

**Phi Coefficient Correlations Between Being a Patient and Case History Variables**

| Variable | Phi coefficient |
|---|---|
| 1. Trouble sleeping | .13 |
| 2. Use of sleep aids | .00 |
| 3. Number of frightening dreams | .13 |
| 4. Sex dreams | −.11 |
| 5. Recurring dreams | .21 |
| 6. Frightening recurring dreams | .36** |
| 7. Recurring physical difficulties | .16 |
| 8. Number of organizations belong to | −.50** |
| 9. Activity in organizations | −.44** |
| 10. Number of parties attended | −.44** |
| 11. Breasts touched by men | .21 |
| 12. Bare breasts touched by men | .32** |
| 13. Number of men touching breasts | .08 |
| 14. Number of times breasts touched | .16 |
| 15. Casual relationship to men touching breasts | .26* |
| 16. Men touching sexual organ | .44** |
| 17. Touching unclothed sexual organ | .44** |
| 18. Number of men touching sexual organ | .36** |
| 19. Frequency sexual organ touched | .42** |
| 20. Casual relationship to men touching sex organ | .40** |
| 21. Ever had sexual intercourse | .25* |
| 22. Time since last intercourse | .13 |
| 23. Number of people had intercourse with during last year | .30* |
| 24. Frequency of intercourse during past year | .26* |
| 25. Casual relationship with men with whom had intercourse | .33** |
| 26. Ever have orgasm | .15 |
| 27. Have regular orgasm | .20 |
| 28. Ever have homosexual experience | −.06 |
| 29. Ever masturbate | .00 |
| 30. Frequency masturbation during past year | −.45** |

\* .05 level of confidence
\*\* .01 level of confidence

Maslow's (3) findings that girls who were dominant were more socially active and more frequently had sexual experience. But inspection of our data reveals that practically all of the girls in the control group engaged in some social activity, and that the girls in the patient group who had engaged in sexual relations or extensive petting also were socially active to some extent. All but one of the girls who were not socially active were patients.

Since there seems to be a relationship between sexual behavior that was in violation of the usual moral standards of the girls, and their seeking help for psychological problems, it was felt that there should be a significant relationship within the control group itself between sexual behavior and symptoms of some sort. The hypothesis was that the girls in the control group (who had not sought therapy, and therefore had not admitted any psychological problems) who had engaged in sexual relations would have significantly more problems of a psychological nature than the girls who had not engaged in sexual relations. Of the 30 case history variables that were measured, 4 might indicate conflict of some sort. These four are: trouble sleeping, number of frightening dreams, recurring physical difficulties, and social activities (measured by combining the items "number of organizations belonged to," "activity in organizations," and "number of parties attended"). The item "recurring physical difficulties" was included since it consists mostly of complaints that are usually considered psychosomatic, such as headaches, menstrual complaints, gastric disorders, diarrhea, constipation, etc.

This analysis resulted in the following phi coefficients between sexual experience and the four variables: trouble sleeping, .19; frightening dreams, .10; social activity (uncalculable, since all but one were socially active); recurring physical difficulties, .47. There was no significant relationship in the control group between sexual behavior and social activity, trouble sleeping, or frightening dreams. But there was a significant relationship between sexual behavior and psychosomatic complaints.

The data of this study support Mowrer's contention that psychological distress is related to guilt from a violation of moral precept. Of the 50 girls included in this study, only 2 of the girls who engaged in sexual intercourse or extensive petting that involved manipulation of the genitals were free of psychological symptoms or recurring psychosomatic complaints. Although the data of this study do provide support for Mowrer's hypothesis, it does not indicate that guilt is always the source of psychological problems, or that it is even the main source of psychological problems.

An interesting sidelight of the study is the significant relationship between sexual behavior and physical complaints among the girls in the control group. We could hypothesize, that if these girls had suffered from some problem that was more clearly psychological, such as nightmares or difficulty in sleeping, they would have sought psychological help for that problem, but since they converted their unresolved conflict into physical complaints, they were more inclined to seek the help of a physician. This hypothesis would explain why there was no relationship between sexual behavior and nightmares, sleep difficulty, or social behavior among the control group.

At this point the question might be raised as to how adequate the method of this study was. Is it not possible that the neurotic girls were more motivated to reveal their experiences while the normal girls, being less motivated, were less revealing? There is, of course, no foolproof answer to this question, but a partial answer might be obtained by comparing the results of this study with previous studies in this area. In this study, 6 (24 percent) of the 25 members of the control group girls had had sexual intercourse. In data obtained at the University of Tennessee in connection with previous studies, the percentages of coeds with sexual experience has varied from 10 percent to 15 percent. Ehrmann (1) at the University of Florida reported percentages of 13 percent and 14 percent. Kinsey (2) reports 20 percent for this age group. So it appears that the amount of sexual experience reported in our control group is not low for this kind of sample, and if it is deviant in any respect, it probably deviates in that the control group reports a little more sexual experience than is reported in previous studies. In the neurotic group, 13 (52 percent) out of 25 report sexual experience. This is a higher percentage than that reported in any previous study on college girls.

## Summary

This study tested Mowrer's hypothesis that there is a relationship between the violation of moral precepts and psychological problems. A group of 25 coeds who had entered psychotherapy were compared with a control group of 25 coeds matched for age and school class. The group needing psychotherapy had engaged in significantly less social activity but had had more extensive sexual experience than the control group.

Within the control group itself, girls who had had sexual intercourse had significantly more psychosomatic problems than the girls who had not engaged in sexual intercourse.

## References

1. EHRMANN, W. *Premarital dating behavior.* New York: Holt, 1959.
2. KINSEY, A. C., POMEROY, W. B., MARTIN, C. E., & GEBHARD, P. H. *Sexual behavior in the human female.* Philadelphia: Saunders, 1953.
3. MASLOW, A. H. Self-esteem (dominance feeling) and sexuality in women. *Journal of Social Psychology,* 1942, **16,** 259–294.
4. MOWRER, O. H. *Learning theory and the symbolic processes.* New York: Wiley, 1960.
5. MOWRER, O. H. *The crisis in psychiatry and religion.* New York: Van Nostrand, 1961.
6. PASCAL, G. R. & JENKINS, W. O. *Systematic observation of gross human behavior.* New York: Grune & Stratton, 1961.

## 32

# Sexual behavior and psychopathology: A study of college men

*by Clifford H. Swensen, Jr.*

### Problem

In a recent study (5), college girls who sought psychotherapy for neurotic symptoms also engaged in sexual behavior significantly more frequently than girls not suffering from similar symptoms. That study was undertaken as a test of Mowrer's hypothesis that the neurotic suffers from neurotic symptoms because he feels guilty for violating some moral precept. Sex is an area of conflict for college girls, since they have a fairly clear-cut moral code regarding sexual behavior, but are also pushed toward engaging in sexual behavior by their own drives, and by their male companions. The results of that study raise the question of whether or not similar results would be found among college men. That is, would college men seeking psychotherapeutic help for neurotic symptoms also have engaged in sexual behavior to a significantly greater extent than college men who were relatively free from neurotic symptoms?

Clifford H. Swensen, Jr., "Sexual Behavior and Psychopathology: A Study of College Men," *Journal of Clinical Psychology*, 1963, **19**, 403–404. Reprinted by permission of the author and Dr. Frederick C. Thorne.

Ehrmann (1), in his study of premarital dating behavior, found that 86 percent of college girls disapproved of premarital intercourse for themselves. This would suggest that these girls would feel guilty if they engaged in premarital sexual behavior, and if, as Mowrer hypothesizes, guilt leads to neurotic symptoms, we would expect to find that girls who had engaged in premarital sexual behavior would suffer from significantly more neurotic symptoms than girls who had not engaged in premarital sexual behavior. Basically, this was what was found to occur in the author's earlier study (5). However, Ehrmann also reported that under some circumstances 72 percent of college men would *approve* of premarital sexual behavior for themselves. This would suggest that most college men would not feel guilty about premarital sexual behavior, and therefore probably should not be expected to have any symptoms related to guilt. Or to put it another way, this study tests the hypothesis that college men who have sought psychotherapy for neurotic symptoms will not have engaged in sexual behavior significantly more often than college men who are relatively free from neurotic symptoms.

### Methodology

The case records of the 17 male University of Tennessee students who sought psychotherapy for a variety of complaints at the Psychological Service and Research Center during the 1961–1962 school year were obtained. The kinds of complaints the men had were much the same, and in the same order of frequency as those of the women. The only noteworthy departure is that 3 men came because of homosexual behavior, whereas none of the women presented this problem.

The men in the experimental group were matched for age and class in school with a group of "normal" college men who were selected from a large group of men who were contributing data for a large-scale normative study.[1] The two groups averaged 21.5 years in age, and the median man in each group was in his junior year in school.

The two groups were compared on 33 items of behavior obtained from and scored according to the system described by Pascal and Jenkins (4). The relationship between each behavioral item and seeking help for neurotic symptoms was determined by the phi coefficient.

### Results and Discussion

Phi coefficients were computed for 33 kinds of behavior with only 5 significant at the .05 level of confidence which could occur by chance alone. Those statistics that are significant indicated that normal college men had significantly more physical complaints, belonged to and were more active in student organizations, significantly more often touched girls' breasts, and had masturbated significantly more frequently during the previous year. There were no significant differences between the groups on any of the other kinds of sexual behavior, but in every category of sexual behavior, with the exception of homosexual behavior, the normal men engaged more frequently than the neurotics.

These results differ from those ob-

[1] The author is indebted to Drs. G. R. Pascal and W. O. Jenkins of the University of Tennessee for permitting him to use this data.

tained from the college girls, with whom it was found that in most categories of heterosexual behavior the neurotic girls had engaged significantly more frequently than the normal girls. However, if we assume that neurotic symptoms are the consequence of guilt, and that the college girls disapprove of sexual behavior for themselves, whereas college men accept sexual behavior for themselves, we would expect to find significantly more sexual behavior among girls with neurotic symptoms, but we would not expect to find symptoms among sexually experienced college men.

In the study on girls it was found that among the normal group, those girls who had engaged in sexual behavior had significantly more psychosomatic symptoms than the normal girls who had refrained from sexual behavior. In this study, correlations were obtained from the normal group of men on the relationship between psychosomatic symptoms and sexual intercourse. It was found that those men in the normal group suffering from psychosomatic complaints had engaged significantly *less* often in sexual intercourse (phi coefficient = .41). They had also masturbated less (phi coefficient = .21), but not significantly so.

### Summary

This study hypothesized that since most college men feel that sexual behavior is acceptable for themselves, there would be no significant relationship between the presence of neurotic symptoms and involvement in sexual behavior. Two matched groups of 17 men each were compared on 33 variables. One group was composed of 17 college men who had sought psychotherapy for neurotic symptoms, and the other matched for age and college class. Significant phi coefficients were obtained on only 5 out of the 33 computed. Normal men had significantly more physical complaints, belonged to and were more active in campus organizations, had touched significantly more girls' breasts, and had masturbated significantly more often than the neurotic men. These results were compared with those obtained in an earlier study on college women which found that neurotic college women had engaged in significantly more heterosexual behavior than normal college women.

## References

1. EHRMANN, W. *Premarital dating behavior.* New York: Holt, 1959.
2. MOWRER, O. H. *Learning theory and the symbolic processes.* New York: Wiley, 1960.
3. MOWRER, O. H. *The crisis in psychiatry and religion.* New York: Van Nostrand, 1961.
4. PASCAL, G. R., & JENKINS, W. O. *Systematic observation of gross human behavior.* New York: Grune & Stratton, 1961.
5. SWENSEN, C. H. Sexual behavior and psychopathology: A test of Mowrer's Hypothesis. *Journal of Clinical Psychology,* 1962, **18,** 406–409.

## 33

# The insecure child: Oversocialized or undersocialized?

*by Donald R. Peterson*[1]

In a series of books and papers, Mowrer (1950, 1953, 1959, 1960, 1961) has taken issue with Freud on the origin of neurotic anxiety. According to Freud, anxiety arises when the ego apprehends a danger; and the critical danger, in the case of neurotic anxiety, is that repressed impulses will get out of control. Under pain of punishment, children learn that certain urges must not be expressed and that certain ideas are evil. The impulses are henceforth inhibited, and fantasies about the urges are repressed. Neurotics, according to Freud, have learned society's lesson too well. They are oversocialized. Their moral standards are unrealistically stringent, their tendency to repress impulse derivatives is overgeneralized and overly severe.

Out of his own clinical experience and some personal and ideological disenchantment with Freudian theory, Mowrer has proposed an alternative view, namely that "... anxiety comes not from

Reprinted with the permission of author and publisher from *Morality and Mental Health*, ed. O. H. Mowrer, Chicago: Rand McNally & Co., 1967. Pp. 459–471.

[1] I wish to thank Mr. Paul Clapp, Principal of Roosevelt Junior High School in Decatur, Illinois, for his help in gathering the data. I am also grateful to the teachers in that school, who gave their time during a very busy part of the school year to do the ratings.

acts which the individual would commit but dares not, but from acts which he has committed but wishes he had not" (Mowrer, 1950, p. 537). Conscience is disregarded or repressed, not the instincts. The neurotic has in fact misbehaved. Impulses arose and he expressed them. He has gratified his wishes and hurt others in the doing, but his misconduct has neither been acknowledged nor redeemed. If he is anxious, it is realistic and socially useful for him to be. If he feels some emotional distress, it is because he has done wrong, and he has every right to the guilt he suffers.

As Mowrer has pointed out, a certain character typology is inherent in Freudian theory. It places normal people in the middle range of a socialization dimension, puts psychopaths where everyone agrees they should be, at the low end of the scale, and neurotics at the opposite end, at the extreme of high socialization or superego severity. As Mowrer has represented it, the distribution is roughly normal (see Figure 1, redrawn from Mowrer, 1961, p. 236).

If Mowrer's own formulation is correct, however, the distribution should have a different look. It should be a J-curve, because character is a product of social pressure, and neurotics should

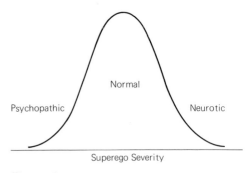

*Figure 1*

**Freudian character typology.**

occupy the range above psychopaths but below the normals. Mowrer's propositions are represented in Figure 2 (Mowrer, 1961, p. 237).

Once the controversy is reduced to these graphic dimensions, it would seem possible to settle it, once and for all, through empirical research. For all the words which have been written about this issue, no clearly acceptable evidence has been presented on either side.

Actually conducting pertinent research is no easy matter, mainly because good measures of superego severity are lacking. But there are some ways of approaching the measurement of socialization—a number of ways. And there now exist some tolerably adequate methods for classifying disturbed and normal people into groups. The present research employs some of these techniques in an effort to determine how people classified in relevant ways distribute themselves in regard to a measure of socialization. Like any study, it has limitations. Some of these will be discussed below. But it is a first approach to the empirical investigation of a problem that has desperately needed study for some time.

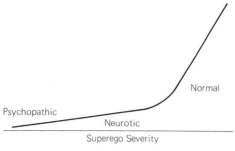

**Figure 2**

**Mowrerian character typology.**

## Subjects and Procedures

Before the extent of socialization in the case of neurotics, psychopaths, and normals can be determined, it is well to demonstrate that classification of people into such groups is justified. Research on neurotics, or any similar group, is likely to be unrewarding if the class is overly heterogeneous—if people who are called "neurotic" actually have very little in common. Relationships with other variables are attenuated to the vanishing point under those circumstances, and a great deal of effort may lead to nothing. If research is to be maximally efficient, the groups of dimensions which constitute its focus should also be reasonably independent. Rigorous definition of appropriate variables is an important research problem in its own right, and the present investigator has approached this problem inductively in previous work on behavior disorders in childhood, using factor analysis as a definitional tool (Peterson, 1961).

From tabulations of referral problems among 427 children attending a guidance clinic, the 58 most common problems were selected, assembled into a rating schedule, and submitted for evaluation to 28 teachers, of 831 kindergarten and elementary school children. Four separate factorizations were performed, one for kindergarten pupils, one for first- and second-grade children, one for third- and fourth-grade children, and one for fifth- and sixth-grade children. Two dimensions emerged with rather striking invariance from all four analyses. The first of these was labelled "Conduct Problem" and the highest loadings over all analyses were on the following variables. Disobedience, Disruptiveness, Boisterousness, Fighting, Attention-seeking, Restlessness, Negativism, Impertinence, Destructiveness, Irritability, Temper

Tantrums, Hyperactivity, Profanity, Jealousy, and Uncooperativeness. The obvious phenotypic pattern is of flagrant misbehavior in open defiance of authority. It seems reasonable to postulate aggression and limited control as the most important dynamic bases for covariation of the problems. The second dimension was defined by the following variables: Feelings of inferiority, Lack of self-confidence, Social withdrawal, Proneness to become flustered, Self-consciousness, Shyness, Anxiety, Lethargy, Inability to have fun, Depression, Reticence, Hypersensitivity, Drowsiness, Aloofness, and Preoccupation. The emotional nucleus of the factor seems to be a feeling of insecurity, as implied in the title of this article. The original factor interpretation also implied, in a naively Freudian way, that excessive emotional restraint operated as a dynamic basis for personality problems. "Both problems are personality expressions, and both affect conduct. But the central meanings seem clear enough. In one case, impulses are expressed and society suffers; in the other case impulses are evidently inhibited and the child suffers" (Peterson, 1961, p. 206). Some of the psychometric properties of the dimensions seemed adequate to encourage their use in further research. An uncorrected interjudge $r$ of .77 was found for the Conduct Problem dimension, and .75 for Personality Problems. The correlation between factors was .18.

Demonstration of dimensional unity does not necessarily justify grouping people into types (e.g., Tiffany, Peterson, & Quay, 1960), but scatter-plots employing these two factors as coordinates have certain typical characteristics. Most children are judged to have few problems or none at all. A sizeable share of

children are said to display problems along both dimensions, and these of course generate the low positive correlation between the factors. There remain a number of children who are fairly pure representatives of one dimension or the other, i.e., who have high scores on Conduct Problem and low or zero scores on Personality Problem, or vice versa. Such children have been selected for investigation in the present research.

For this study the teachers in a junior high school were asked to rate all their pupils (313 boys and 367 girls) on the 58 problems in the checklist. Scores for Conduct Problem and Personality Problem were computed by assigning one point for each relevant problem indicated, and three groups of subjects (Ss) were selected. One group consisted of pupils for whom no problems at all were checked. These will be referred to as the "No Problem" (NP) group. Sixty-four boys and 118 girls met this description. A group of "Conduct Problems" was selected by including those for whom the ratio of Conduct Problem score (CP) to Personality Problem score (PP) was at least five to one. Only Ss with CP scores of four or more were retained in the group. Twenty boys and 12 girls were selected in this way. Analogous criteria were applied in designating Personality Problems (i.e., $PP \geqq 4$, $PP:CP \geqq 5:1$). The group contained 23 boys and 32 girls. All incidence figures are in accord with previous findings about sex differences in expression of behavior problems among children in this approximate age range (Peterson, 1961).

It would be premature to regard the Conduct Problem Ss in this study as young psychopaths, or to say that the Personality Problem Ss are manifesting an early form of neurosis. Some very difficult and expensive longitudinal research is required to confirm statements like that, and little of the necessary work has been done (Roff, 1957; Kagan & Moss, 1960). As dimensional constructs, however, personality problems among children seem clearly analogous to neurotic tendencies among adults. The conceptual resemblance between child conduct problems and adult psychopathy seems equally apparent. In any case, neither Mowrer nor Freud has restricted his formulation to adults, however much adult manifestations of disorder may have been in the mind of each theorist as he wrote. The present study is based only on the assumption that the classes of Ss employed in it resemble neurotics, psychopaths, and normals as discussed by Mowrer and Freud, and indeed they appear to do so.

In this investigation, socialization was assessed by administering the Socialization (So) scale of the California Psychological Inventory (Gough, 1957) to all 670 Ss in the sample. Since the analysis has meaning exactly to the extent that the So scale is a good measure of the characteristics it was designed to measure, namely moral rectitude, social maturity, and personal integrity, the merits and faults of the device must be considered in some detail.

As originally developed, the So scale consisted of 64 true-false questionnaire items which differentiated reliably between delinquents and nondelinquents (Gough & Peterson, 1952). It was subsequently cross-validated by comparing Air Force stockade prisoners with a sample of recruits, and its discriminatory effectiveness was satisfactorily maintained. Since then it has been given to at least 58 different groups, well over 25,-000 people, of both sexes, in various occupations, from various backgrounds, and in four different countries around the world. Some nontest basis for inferring degree of socialization was available for most of these groups, and in a rather impressively dependable way So scores have emerged as they should if the scale is a valid measure of integrity and moral rectitude. Time and again, the scale has appropriately distinguished between Ss who were in trouble with the law and those who were not. It has typically identified about 70 percent of the delinquents examined at the expense of 20 to 30 percent false positives among nondelinquents. It has worked approximately as well for females as for males; for Costa Ricans, Indians, and Italians as for Americans; for high socioeconomic groups as for low ones. It does such unexpected and reassuring things as differentiate between unwed mothers who have had one illegitimate child and those who have had two or more; between boys whose first commitment to a reformatory occurred at age 15 or before and those whose first commitment came at age 16 or later. Mean scores for various groups of Ss are ordered almost exactly as one could expect them to be through inference of the integrity and rectitude which seems reasonably to characterize each group. It is unnecessary to discuss reliabilities, which are high. Validity like this cannot be demonstrated with an unreliable instrument. Further information on the adequacy of the scale can be most conveniently found in the following references (Gough, 1957, 1960a, 1960b; Gough & Peterson, 1952; Peterson, Quay, & Anderson, 1959). Validity seems well enough established to warrant use in the present study.

Four of the 64 items in the original

scale were eliminated in the present study because they referred to sex or the use of liquor. Public school administrators are remarkably protective of their pupils when it comes to any hint of salaciousness or the like, and the writer did not wish to offend. The remaining 60 items were put into a questionnaire along with items designed to assess certain other characteristics, and administered with an innocuous announcement to the effect that we were trying to measure some personality tendencies among junior high school students. Ss were told about the mechanics of the operation, and were then assured that their performance would have no effect on their grades, that their teachers would not even know what they did on the test, and that scores could not have any bearing whatsoever on their individual destinies. They could lie if they chose, but there was not much point in doing so.

Socialization scores for the No Problem Ss, the Conduct Problem Ss, and the Personality Problem Ss were computed, and distributions of scores were formed.

## Results

The distributions appear in Figure 3. Ss with no problems ordered themselves in a negatively skewed distribution, as Mowrer has predicted.[2] Conduct Problem Ss had the lowest scores of any group, as both Mowrer and Freud have said they should. Children with personality problems showed somewhat more

[2] Exclusion of "problem children" from the NP group exaggerates skewness somewhat, but the distribution of So scores for randomly selected Ss is still negatively skewed, and looks very much like the distribution for children without apparent problems.

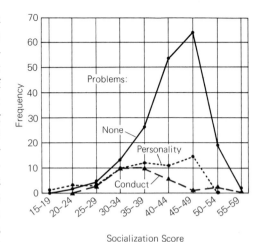

Figure 3

**Socialization scores of three groups of children.**

variance than the other groups, but were generally located below the NP group and above the CP group. Their socialization scores were, on the average, lower than for children with no evident problems, as Mowrer, not Freud, has said.

An overall analysis of variance yielded an *F*-value significant well beyond the .001 level. Individual *t*-tests[3] were performed separately for boys and girls to allow sex differences to appear if they exist. These results are presented in Table 1. Mean So scores for Conduct Problems and for Personality Problems were different from those of children with no obvious problems at a high level of significance. The differences between Conduct Problems and Personality Problems were not statistically significant. These results held for both boys and girls, with the sexes differing principally in that girls tended to have slightly higher So scores than boys.

[3] Assumptions underlying analysis of variance and the *t*-test are obviously not well met by these data. A series of Mann-Whitney U-tests yielded equivalent results.

Table 1

**Means, Standard Deviations and T-tests**

|  | $\overline{x}$ | $\sigma$ |  | t |
|---|---|---|---|---|
| Boys |  |  |  |  |
| No Problem (NP) | 41.82 | 6.18 | NP vs. PP | 2.62* |
| Personality Problem (PP) | 37.61 | 7.72 | NP vs. CP | 3.17** |
| Conduct Problem (CP) | 36.85 | 5.71 | PP vs. CP | .36 |
| Girls |  |  |  |  |
| No Problem (NP) | 43.31 | 5.66 | NP vs. PP | 4.19*** |
| Personality Problem (PP) | 38.22 | 7.35 | NP vs. CP | 4.17*** |
| Conduct Problem (CP) | 35.83 | 7.68 | PP vs. CP | .93 |

\* $p_t < .02$
\*\* $p_t < .01$
\*\*\* $p_t < .001$

Relationships between judged problem tendencies and So scores were also examined by correlating the latter with CP and PP factor scores. According to Freudian theory, measures of socialization should correlate positively with indices of "neuroticism," but negatively with measures of psychopathy or conduct disorder. If Mowrer is correct, the correlations should both have the same (negative) sign. Again Mowrer's proposition was confirmed. For the 313 boys in the total sample, an $r$ of $-.22$ was found between So and CP scores and an $r$ of $-.14$ between So and PP scores. For the sample of 367 girls, the two correlations were identical. Conduct Problem and Personality Problem tendencies both correlated $-.23$ with So scores. The $r$'s are small, but all are significant beyond the .05 level.

Although the mean So scores for Personality Problems were almost as low as for Conduct Problems, there is still a possibility that they attained their mutual deviation from children with no problems in different ways, i.e., through

different patterns of item endorsement. Phenotypically, such groups are radically unlike each other. They must also differ, some way, in regard to personality. To pursue this question an item analysis was done. First, $2 \times 3$ $\chi^2$ tests (two response alternatives; three groups) of differentiation were conducted, and those items which discriminated at or beyond the .05 level were selected for further scrutiny. Twenty-six of the 60 items met this criterion. For these 26 items, additional $2 \times 2$ tests (two response alternatives, two groups) were performed to see which groups differed from which. In this way three principal sets of items were isolated: (a) a set for which both Personality Problems and Conduct Problems differed from Ss with no problems, (b) a set for which Conduct Problems but not Personality Problems differed from the No Problems Ss, and (c) a set for which Personality Problems but not Conduct Problems differed from Ss with no problems.

A significant difference between Personality Problems and Conduct Problems, with no significant difference between either problem group and the No Problem Ss, was found for only one item. The item reads, "Even when I have gotten into trouble I was usually trying to do the right thing." Children with personality problems tended to say "true" to that item; those with conduct problems tended to say "false," which squares with the idea that insecure children try to rationalize their misbehavior, though other interpretations are also possible.

Items for which both Personality Problems and Conduct Problems deviated from Ss with no problems are given below. A "T" in parentheses after any item means that the problem children tended more often than normals to answer that item "true"; and "F" means that the children in both problem groups tended to answer the item "false."

> My parents have often disapproved of my friends (T). The members of my family were always very close to each other (F). I was often punished unfairly as a child (T). My family has objected to the kind of work I do, or plan to do (T). If the pay was right, I would like to travel with a circus or carnival (T). I have more than my share of things to worry about (T). I would have been more successful if people had given me a fair chance (T). With things going as they are, it's pretty hard to keep up hope of amounting to something (T). I often think about how I look and what impression I am making upon others. (F). As a youngster in school I used to give the teachers a lot of trouble (T). In school I was sometimes sent to the principal for cutting up (T).

Only the last two items refer to actual misbehavior, and one of these (In school I was sometimes sent to the principal for cutting up) was much more commonly endorsed by children with conduct problems than by Ss with personality problems, even though both groups differed in a statistically reliable way from the No Problem sample. Only 7 percent of the children with no problems said they had been sent to the principal, 18 percent of the Personality Problems made the same admission, but 62 percent of the Conduct Problems said they had been sent to the principal because of their misbehavior.

There is little evidence in the above items to suggest that Personality Problems actually commit socially disapproved acts more than normal children. If they do misbehave (and perhaps they do—these results do not prove the contrary), they are reluctant to admit it. What stands out, on the part of both groups of problem children, is a set of attitudes implying estrangement from the family, and a feeling of bitterness over perceived unfairness in treatment received from other people.

Actual admission of misconduct, troublemaking, and open defiance appear more visibly in those items which differentiated Conduct Problems from children without problems, but did not distinguish Personality Problems from the No Problem group. Letters in parentheses indicate response tendencies of the Conduct Problem Ss.

> I used to steal sometimes when I was a youngster (T). I keep out of trouble at all costs (F). I have often gone against my parent's wishes (T). Even the idea of giving a talk in public makes me afraid (F). I find it easy to "drop" or "break with" a friend (T).

The following items distinguished Personality Problems from Normals but did not distinguish Conduct Problems from children with no problems. Parenthesized letters show response tendencies of Ss with personality problems.

> I don't think I'm quite as happy as others seem to be (T). Most of the time I feel happy (F). I often feel that I am not getting anywhere in life (T). Life usually hands me a pretty raw deal (T). I hardly ever get excited or thrilled (T). I never worry about my looks (T). It is very important to me to have enough friends and social life (F). I have never cared much for school (T). I spend a good deal of time planning and thinking about my career (F).

The items imply manifest unhappiness, discouragement, and a tendency to deny emotional involvement with others. Children with personality problems seem to be saying that they just don't care about anything or anybody, except perhaps themselves and their misery.

Inspection of Figure 3 and Table 1 will show that the Personality Problems varied more than the No Problem Ss in regard to So scores. Their distribution has a vaguely bimodal appearance, and when scores are distributed without grouping, bimodality is even more apparent. Perhaps there are two groups of insecure children, those with relatively poor socialization, little integrity and the like, and another group who appear normally socialized (*not* overly socialized) on this test. An effort was made to determine differences between Personality Problem Ss with So scores of 42 or more and those with So scores under 42 by referring to the Problem Checklist and seeing whether patterns of judged problems differed in any clear way. The effort failed. Both subgroups tended to display the same problems: self-consciousness, feelings of inferiority, social

withdrawal, and so on. None of this implies that insecure children who are well socialized are dynamically the same as those who are poorly socialized.

They may be very different in other still unexamined respects, and the search for meaningful differences should be continued in further research.

## Discussion

It is possible to overinterpret these findings. Perhaps there is no danger, but the study has certain clear implications, it does not have some other implications which might be read into it, and it seems prudent to separate the two sets of meanings.

The major finding of the study, the only important one, was that children who seemed shy, anxious, withdrawn, and insecure to their teachers had lower scores on a measure of socialization than a group of children who seemed free of problems. Because the socialization scale has been validated with unusual care, it was employed here as a basis for inferring that the personal integrity and moral rectitude of children with personality problems were relatively limited, that conscience was weaker, or at least less effective in controlling conduct, than for children with no apparent problems. This is clearly in support of Mowrer's main proposition about psychopathology in neurosis.

There are at least three additional issues which are involved in Mowrerian theory, and I want to make it clear that this study has nothing to do with any of them. First, the study reveals nothing about actual misconduct among neurotics. Mowrer has said that neurotics have in fact misbehaved and that unredeemed guilt over misconduct is at the core of the dynamic problem in neurosis. The present study has no bearing on this point. Whether the personal-social histories of neurotics will show more actual wrong-doing than those of normals is an open question. It is an empirically approachable question, as Mowrer (1961) has suggested, but it is unanswered by the present study. The So scale is most appropriately regarded as a measure of certain attitudes. There are better ways to find out what people have actually done in their lives.

Second, the study is neutral on issues of historical origin. It is easy to fall into the trap of assuming that socialization as a trait is related in some direct and obvious way to socialization as a process, i.e., the process by which society, mainly through the parents, encourages approved modes of behavior and discourages disapproved behavior on the part of members of the society. The usual non sequitur runs something like this: oversocialized (inhibited) children have been oversocialized (unduly restrained); undersocialized (e.g., delinquent) children have been undersocialized (treated with undue leniency). This is no place to launch into a discussion of parent-child relationships, but anyone who has the slightest familiarity with the field knows that these relationships can be rather complex. Deeper knowledge of the literature suggests that current theory about parent-child relationships is at best limited and uncertain, if not downright misleading and fallacious. We do not know exactly how children with personality problems have been treated by their parents. This study tells us nothing pertinent on this score, except that the children tend to *say*, among other things, that their parents have treated

them unfairly. Parent-child relationships must be studied independently. They have been to some extent in the past and they will be to a greater extent in the future. But it would be wise to wait until far more research has been done before getting very definite about social or other factors in the etiology of neurosis. Currently available studies most decidedly do not suggest that well-socialized children have been bludgeoned into integrity by harsh, strict, restraining parents, nor is it entirely clear that the parents of undersocialized children have erred mainly in being too lenient. Quite the contrary (Watson, 1957; Peterson et al., 1961).

A third issue which is part of the Mowrer-Freud controversy, but about which this study has little to say, is the question of treatment. Suppose it *is* true that insecure children and neurotic adults are undersocialized; how does one change this state of affairs? Books and journals abound with suggestions, all of which ought to be pursued—the methods tried, elaborated, modified, extended, and above all tested and evaluated. Freud proposed a method of treatment. In a less elaborate way, Mowrer has done the same. His is not so much a system of treatment as a general philosophy for change, and psychotherapy is one method of effecting change. I hope that the therapeutic procedures, not just the goals, will be further defined and systematically employed along with other methods. But the results of the present study have little to do with treatment. They support a theoretical proposition concerning psychopathology. What to do to change the condition is another open question, to be dealt with mainly by further research.

Whatever clinical implications this

study may have lie in the area of diagnosis, broadly conceived, rather than treatment. When a child with a certain set of problems appears for help, it is the task of the clinician to determine what is wrong about him. This involves inference about dynamics and psychopathology, and the inferences have to be based on something: research, if pertinent studies have been done; the accumulated experience of the clinician, if he has been working with children for some time; and "clinical lore," the culturally transmitted experience and thought of other clinicians, if the clinician's own experience is limited and relevant studies are unavailable. The impression of Freudian psychoanalysis on clinical lore has been enormous. In some circles, the lore and psychoanalytic theory are one and the same. When an insecure, timid, anxious child is evaluated, it is customary for clinicians to begin speaking of excessive restraint, impulse inhibition, and the like as bases for symptoms. And prescription of some kind of "release" therapy not uncommonly follows.

This study suggests that clinicians look elsewhere for the origins of insecurity in children. Considering the variance in So scores among children with personality problems, it would be manifestly idiotic to infer that any child who displays such problems will have a low So score. Individual So scores are best determined by administering the scale. Studies like the present one sometimes help clinicians by telling them where to look for the origins of an individual personality disturbance. And this study suggests that the integrity, morality, and honesty of the insecure child may well be worth exploring.

Consider now some questions of possible artifact in the findings. Two major possibilities are immediately apparent. The first has to do with possible bias in the teacher ratings. To generate artifact in this study the bias would have had to take the form of a negative halo effect, specifically the indiscriminate imputation of all kinds of "bad" qualities, e.g., feelings of inferiority and social withdrawal, as well as uncooperativeness and disruptiveness, to pupils who were held in some general kind of low regard by their teachers. If such a halo effect were potently operative, children in the Conduct Problem and Personality Problem groups would actually be members of the same population, i.e., children who are disliked by their teachers, and the discovery of similar personality tendencies, such as low So scores, would hardly be surprising. The present study purports to show that children with personality problems, who appear behaviorally to be very different from those with conduct problems, resemble the latter group in regard to certain important attitudes.

But halo effects could not alone have generated the results of this study, because the correlation between Personality Problems and Conduct Problems is very low. For the 313 boys in the total sample, the correlation was .07. The correlation was .15 for the total sample of girls. Far higher $r$'s than that would be needed to demonstrate that Personality Problems and Conduct Problems are "really the same thing," whether out of teacher bias or through any other mode of determination.

The second possibility for artifact is less easily disposed of. This resides in the assessment of socialization by means of a questionnaire, and specifically in the possibility that results stem from transient test-taking attitudes or response sets rather than from such enduring dispositional tendencies as integrity and moral rectitude. Results would be properly characterized as artifactual, for example, if Conduct Problem Ss yielded low So scores because they really were "immoral," but Personality Problem Ss got low scores because they were more willing than normal children to make damaging statements about themselves. A fairly strong case can be made for this possibility on logical grounds. One assumes that children with personality problems tend to be depressed—their teachers say they are. Depressed people are known to make frequent self-condemnatory statements in talking about themselves. Teachers also say that children with personality problems lack self-confidence and suffer feelings of inferiority. Whatever has led teachers to say these children hold themselves in low regard could also find expression in the responses they make to items in the test.

After considerable rumination, I have been forced to conclude that test-taking attitudes may very well have influenced the behavior of Ss in this study. For children with personality problems, these attitudes could have worked in both directions, that is in the spurious depression of So scores through the operation of self-condemnatory tendencies, as suggested above, or in the spurious elevation of scores mediated by a different tendency. In the latter case, it is plausible to assume that insecure, anxious children were wary of accepting the reassurance that their performance could have no social repercussions of any kind. Given this feeling, they might have tried to place themselves in a favorable light, to look "good" on the test. Why take chances? If such tendencies were differentially at play among chil-

dren with personality problems, an explanation for the evident bimodality in So score distributions for that group would be provided. It would be necessary, obviously, to demonstrate that the subgroups of Personality Problem Ss showing "normal" So scores were in fact the ones who engaged in deception while they took the test. Introduction of dissimulation indicators like the K-scale of the MMPI might help settle this problem. So might a candid, disarming posttest interview. But neither technique is likely to solve the problem of deliberate and unwitting deception in any final way, and I seem unable to think of any more clever ways to get at the problem. Perhaps someone else can.

In any event, response sets could have vitiated the meaning of the present results only to the extent that they generated spuriously low So scores among children with personality problems, and while this might have happened, it does not seem very likely. People do not get low So scores just by saying a lot of uncomplimentary things about themselves. They have to endorse items referring to many different objects and situations, and the meanings of the responses are not always immediately obvious. The following items, for example, contribute to low So scores: I would never play poker with a stranger (F); My family has objected to the kind of work I do, or plan to do (T); Lincoln was greater than Washington (F). It is difficult to maintain that responses which yield low So values are generally self-condemnatory. Low So scores are obtained by saying "true" to items like the following: When something goes wrong I usually blame myself rather than the other fellow; When I work at something, I like to read and study about it. Anyone who endorses those items is evaluating himself with considerable generosity, yet the response tendencies contribute to *low* So scores.

Transient test-taking attitudes may have influenced the results of this study. The problem requires further investigation. But even if momentary sets were involved, even if the teachers were vulnerable to bias, one overriding fact remains: children who were judged to be anxious and insecure tended to behave in much the same way as children known for blatant misbehavior on an externally and rather carefully validated measure of socialization. In this study, they showed none of the excessive inhibition, none of the moralistic self-restraint which has often been assumed to characterize them.

Further research should clearly be addressed to establishing the generality of this finding. The study should be repeated on adult neurotics, psychopaths, and normals. Response generality should be examined by assessing socialization in as many ways as possible, not merely by administering questionnaires. A series of experiments in which Ss were given an opportunity to cheat, deceive, and otherwise behave in detectably unsocialized ways would help determine whether children with personality problems and adult neurotics are indeed disposed to the kind of misbehavior Mowrer has emphasized. Examination of the life histories of neurotics, psychopaths, and normals would help determine how these people have behaved in the past. And of course the general questions of origin and modifiability of conscience are worth careful and extensive study. These are important issues. They need to be examined.

## Summary

The Freudian theory of neurosis is based largely on the contention that neurotics are oversocialized. They are therefore excessively inclined to inhibit and repress unacceptable impulses. Mowrer has maintained that neurotics are undersocialized. More accurately, they have failed to integrate socialization and behavior in a fully honest way. Their emotional disturbances are therefore rooted in guilt over actual misconduct. An implication of this controversy was examined by obtaining a measure of socialization for three groups of children: a group judged by teachers to be free of problems, a group said by teachers to have "conduct problems," and a group said by teachers to have "personality problems" in which anxiety and insecurity were dominant characteristics. Findings supported Mowrer's hypothesis. Insecure children appeared poorly socialized in comparison with those who had no apparent problems. The socialization scores of children with personality problems did not differ reliably from those of children who were manifestly disobedient, aggressive, and defiant toward authority.

## References

GOUGH, H. G. *Cross-cultural studies of the socialization continuum.* Paper read at meetings of the American Psychological Association, Chicago, 1960. (a)

GOUGH, H. G. Theory and measurement of socialization. *Journal of Consulting Psychology,* 1960, **24,** 23–30. (b)

GOUGH, H. G., & PETERSON, D. R. The identification and measurement of predispositional factors in crime and delinquency.

*Journal of Consulting Psychology*, 1952, **16**, 207–212.

KAGAN, J., & Moss, H. A. The stability of passive and dependent behavior from childhood through adulthood. *Child Development*, 1960, **31**, 577–591.

MOWRER, O. H. The problem of anxiety. In *Learning theory and personality dynamics*. New York: Ronald, 1950.

MOWRER, O. H., Neurosis and psychotherapy as interpersonal processes: A synopsis. In *Psychotherapy—theory and research*. New York: Ronald, 1953.

MOWRER, O. H. Changing conceptions of the unconscious. *Journal of Nervous and Mental Disorders*, 1959, **129**, 222–232.

MOWRER, O. H. Psychotherapy and the problem of guilt, confession, and expiation. In *Current trends in psychology*, X. Pittsburgh: University of Pittsburgh Press, 1960.

MOWRER, O. H. *The crisis in psychiatry and religion*. Princeton, N.J.: Van Nostrand, 1961.

PETERSON, D. R. Behavior problems of middle childhood. *Journal of Consulting Psychology*, 1961, **25**, 205–209.

PETERSON, D. R., BECKER, W. C., SHOEMAKER, D. J., LURIA, ZELLA, & HELLMER, L. A. Child behavior problems and parental attitudes. *Child Development*, 1961, **32**, 151–162.

PETERSON, D. R., QUAY, H. C., & ANDERSON, A. C. Extending the construct validity of a socialization scale. *Journal of Consulting Psychology*, 1959, **23**, 182.

ROFF, M. *Preservice personality problems and subsequent adjustments to military service: The prediction of psychoneurotic reactions*. Air University, School of Aviation Medicine, USAF, Randolph AFB, Texas, Nov., 1957.

TIFFANY, T. L., PETERSON, D. R., & QUAY, H. C. Types and traits in the study of juvenile delinquency. *Journal of Clinical Psychology*, 1961, **17**, 19–24.

WATSON, G. Some personality differences in children related to strict or permissive parental discipline. *Journal of Psychology*, 1957, **44**, 227–249.

# 34

# Resistance to temptation, guilt following yielding, and psychopathology[1]

by Ronald C. Johnson,
J. Mark Ackerman,
Harry Frank
and A. Joseph Fionda

Projective stories aimed at measuring various aspects of conscience have been in use for over a decade. Subjects' responses to these stories have been related to such variables as sex (Rebelsky, Allinsmith, & Grinder, 1963), IQ (Porteus & Johnson, 1965), parental discipline (Hoffman & Saltzstein, 1967), and family structure (Grinder & McMichael, 1963), but not, so far as the writers are aware, to

Ronald C. Johnson, J. Mark Ackerman, Harry Frank, and A. Joseph Fionda, "Resistance to Temptation, Guilt Following Yielding, and Psychopathology," *Journal of Consulting and Clinical Psychology*, **32**, 1968, 169–175. Copyright 1968 by the American Psychological Association, and reproduced by permission.

[1] The authors wish to express their appreciation to Howard Gudeman, Joseph Alexander, and Jerome Boyar of Hawaii State Hospital for their help in obtaining psychiatric and control subjects for Study I, to Fred Herring for his invaluable assistance in obtaining Veterans Administration hospital subjects for Study II, to Robert Cole and Harold Dent for serving as judges in the first study, to Ronald Veatch for testing all but four subjects in the second study, and to Catherine Barnard for her work in scoring responses made by subjects in the third study. The second and third studies reported here were supported by a small grant from the Council on Research and Creative Work of the University of Colorado.

adjustment. The studies reported here relate projective measures of resistance to temptation and of guilt following yielding to one another and of each projective measure to adjustment.

## Study I

### Method

**Subjects.** The psychiatric sample consisted of 12 institutionalized schizophrenic patients at Hawaii State Hospital, Kaneohe. The sex, age, ethnic background, and education of these Ss are as follows: 5 male, 7 female; ages 21–30, $Mdn=25$; 6 Japanese, 4 Caucasian, 1 Korean, and 1 Chinese; 1 S had completed only the eleventh grade, 2 had completed 2 years of college, and the remainder had a high-school education. The responses of these Ss were compared with those of a control group, the majority of whom were hospital ward technicians, nurses, or secretaries, matched to the patient group in sex, age (within 1 year), ethnic background, and education.

**Materials.** The stimulus materials consisted of seven affective-projective stories modeled after those of Allinsmith (1960) and Aronfreed (1960). Examples of these stories are as follows:

Chris and Mary first met at a Christmas office party. They have been going together for over six months, and are seriously considering getting married, although no formal engagement yet exists. For some time, Chris has been trying to persuade Mary to spend the weekend with him at a friend's hunting cabin. The friend cannot be there, and they will be alone for the weekend. Mary wants very much to go, but feels it is wrong to go even though no one else will know where she has been.

Ellen had gotten tired of most of her old friends and had tried to find some new ones. Most of the people at her office bored her, and she found herself alone for quite awhile. One night she met a very handsome young man at a party, and he introduced her to a whole new group of friends. They have a lot of parties, and it was considered the right thing to do to smoke marijuana. Ellen has never wanted to, feeling it was wrong, even though she had been told that it is not harmful or very habit-forming. There is a big party one afternoon, and the young man who introduced her into the crowd tells her, "Look, either smoke the stuff with the rest of us, or drop out." Except for the marijuana smoking Ellen has liked her new friends and doesn't want to lose them. She decided to try a marijuana cigarette and lights one up.

Stories of the first variety present $S$ with a moral dilemma in which $S$ may or may not have the central figure yield. The second story presents $S$ with a situation in which the central figure already has yielded, in order to establish $S$'s response following yielding to temptation. Four stories were of the first type. Two of the stories tapping resistance to yielding had male and two had female central figures. Three stories measured guilt following yielding. Two had a male and one a female central figure. The seven stories were presented in a randomly determined order.[2]

2 A fourth story aimed at tapping guilt following yielding also was constructed. A typist's error changed the story so that the intended victim was, in fact, not victimized, making the story unsuitable for inclusion in the analysis. However, since several $S$s were tested using this story as well as the other seven before the error was noted, it was administered to all $S$s, but not scored.

**Testing procedure.** Each $S$ was tested privately. Each $S$ was told that (a) $E$ was going to read him some stories while he followed along on another copy of the set of stories, (b) he was to finish each story in the way he thought it would end, and (c) he was to tell the story to $E$ while $E$ wrote it down. The same $E$ recorded all responses.

**Scoring procedures.** Two judges evaluated the stories, without $S$-identifying data, independently from one another. Both judges were close to the completion of their PhDs, one in the area of psychophysics, the other in counseling. With regard to stories of the first variety, each completion produced by each $S$ was subjected to only one question—did $S$ cause the central figure to yield or did he not? For each of the stories measuring responses following yielding, a number of questions were asked. In the story completion did $S$ have the central figure feel guilt? (Judges were told that "guilt must be made explicit and not inferred from confession and/or restitution. Fear and/or crying are not in themselves indicative of guilt.") Did $S$ have the central figure confess? Did $S$ have the central figure attempt restitution? (Judges were told that "confession and restitution must occur without coercion from authority figures in order to warrant a 'yes' answer.") The scoring procedures for the guilt-following-yielding questions have been rather widely used (e.g., Grinder & McMichael, 1963; Porteus & Johnson, 1965).

*Results and Discussion*

The total frequency that $S$s in the psychiatric and control groups had central figures yield in the four resistance-to-temptation stories and that they had them show guilt, confess, and make restitution in their completions of the three stories in which the central figures were carried beyond the point of yielding in E's story construction is shown in Table 1. The scoring of one judge (clinically oriented one) is italicized, while that of the other (the psychophysicist) is not.

The judges disagreed on 8 of the 96 measures (4 stories × 24 Ss) involving resistance to temptation and 25 of the 216

Table 1

**Resistance to Temptation and Responses Following Yielding in Schizophrenic and Control Subjects**

| Resistance to temptation | | |
|---|---|---|
| No. responses | No. Ss in P group | No. Ss in C group |
| Yielding | | |
| 0 | 0,0 | 8,8 |
| 1 | 2,3 | 3,2 |
| 2 | 5,6 | 1,2 |
| 3 | 4,2 | 0,0 |
| 4 | 1,1 | 0,0 |
| Responses following yielding | | |
| Guilt | | |
| 0 | 6,5 | 6,4 |
| 1 | 2,6 | 2,7 |
| 2 | 4,1 | 4,1 |
| 3 | 0,0 | 0,0 |
| Confession | | |
| 0 | 9,9 | 9,12 |
| 1 | 3,2 | 3,0 |
| 2 | 0,1 | 0,0 |
| 3 | 0,0 | 0,0 |
| Attempted restitution | | |
| 0 | 9,9 | 8,9 |
| 1 | 3,2 | 1,3 |
| 2 | 0,1 | 0,0 |
| 3 | 0,0 | 0,0 |

Note: P = psychiatric, C = control. The scoring of the clinically-oriented judge is italicized.

measures (3 stories × 24 Ss × 3 measures) of guilt following yielding, showing 89.5 percent overall agreement. Like the Porteus and Johnson (1965) study, the present study yielded results which indicate that scoring reliability is quite high.

A chi-square comparison of those Ss whose central figures did not yield or whose central figures yielded on only one of the four stories (at or below the median) versus those central figures which yielded on two or more stories (above the median) provides, for psychiatric versus control Ss, chi-squares of 10.74 ($p < .01$) and 6.04 ($p < .02$) for the first and second judges, respectively. As compared with their matched controls, the psychiatric group produced significantly more story completions involving yielding. To the degree that these projective stories reflect overt behavior, it would appear that the psychiatric group is low in resistance to temptation. The Es attempted a number of comparisons involving each of the three measures of guilt separately and the three measures (guilt, confession, restitution) combined and in no case obtained any differences between groups which approach statistical significance. It should be noted that, as compared with a ninth-grade sample of Ss (Porteus & Johnson, 1965), both the psychiatric Ss and the controls were quite low in guilt, confession, and restitution in their story completions.

The Es, to this point, had considered response to resistance and to guilt stories separately. Using these two types of stories was necessary in order to establish the relation of resistance and guilt to mental health. If resistance stories alone had been used, some Ss who seldom or never yielded would have had few or no occasions to express guilt. However, it would seem reasonable to believe that the guilt expressed by S to stories (resistance stories) in which he himself caused the central figure to yield might be more relevant to mental health status than S's responses to stories (guilt stories) in which he is presented with a situation in which the central figure has already yielded. Therefore, the guilt responses to Ss in the two groups were obtained for stories in which S had the central figure yield. The mean guilt score (total number of instances of expressions of guilt, confession, and/or restitution divided by total number of stories in which yielding took place, using the first judge's data) for the psychiatric Ss was 1.07; for the control Ss, it was .80. The two groups did not appear to differ on this measure of guilt either, though the controls yielded so seldom that not much confidence can be placed in this comparison.

The results indicate that the psychiatric population differs from its controls in being lower on one (resistance) but not on the other (guilt following yielding) aspect of conscience.

The psychiatric group of Study I was matched to a control group on a number of presumably relevant dimensions, but differed on one major one—most Ss in the psychiatric group were institutionalized for a year or more prior to testing, and could expect that they might remain institutionalized for a long period of time to come, while the control group was free in the community. Quite obviously, freedom as opposed to confinement might well influence responses to hypothetical situations involving moral dilemmas. The next two studies are attempts to determine the relation of resistance to temptation and guilt following yielding to mental health, using samples of individuals varying in adjustment, yet all sharing the same degree of

freedom or of constraint in their environment.

**Study II**

*Method*

**Subjects.** Forty-five male Ss were tested. Of these, 21 were institutionalized at the Denver Veterans Administration Hospital and had been diagnosed as being anxiety or depressed neurotics, and 24 were patients at the same hospital who had physical complaints and no history of psychological disturbance. Psychiatric Ss were selected randomly from within the two diagnostic groups tested. The control patients came from fracture wards, chronic respiratory disease wards, and cardiac wards. Control patients were selected on the following criteria: (a) The ward physician permitted testing within the ward; (b) the patient had not been hospitalized for more than 1 month; and (c) the patient agreed to allow testing (no patient refused). The mean age of the psychiatric group was 42.0 and of the control group, 38.7. The neurotic Ss had a mean of 12.3 years of education as compared with a mean of 11.5 years for controls. The neurotic Ss had a mean length of hospitalization of 17.9 days, while the physical ailment group mean was 17.4 days. No S had been a patient for over 30 days. The psychiatric unit is a short-term therapy unit, so the psychiatric patients could expect a stay of less than 2 months in all, while many of the physical ailment cases could expect a considerably longer stay. Further, nearly all of the psychiatric but only a few of the physical ailment Ss could leave the hospital on a pass for a few hours, overnight, or for a weekend.

Unlike the psychiatric versus control groups in the first study, members of the control group, in this case, had less opportunity to exercise their impulse lives.

**Measuring devices and procedure.** All $Ss$ were presented with four projective stories aimed at tapping resistance to temptation and four stories aimed at measuring guilt following yielding.[3] One-half of the central figures in each category were male, and one-half were female. Stories were counterbalanced so that each story was presented as a resistance story to approximately one-half of $Ss$ in each group and as a measure of guilt following yielding to the remainder. All $Ss$ were tested individually and privately. As in the first study, $Ss$ responded verbally, and the tester recorded the verbatim story completion.

**Scoring of responses.** Data cited or discussed above indicate that the scoring procedure used here is a reliable one. As a further measure of scoring reliability, the first and third authors independently scored 30 sets of responses from a group of college $Ss$ prior to beginning Study II and found 94 percent agreement in scoring. Therefore, the first author scored all responses in the same fashion as described in Study I. All responses except those of four $Ss$ were scored with no knowledge on the part of the scorer concerning what diagnostic category each $S$ fell into. (The first author had, in

[3] A copy of the stories has been deposited with the American Documentation Institute. Order Document No. 9826 from ADI Auxiliary Publications Project, Photoduplication Service, Library of Congress, Washington, D. C., 20540. Remit in advance $1.25 for microfilm or $1.25 for photocopies and make checks payable to: Chief, Photoduplication Service, Library of Congress.

establishing contact with the Veterans Administration hospital, tested two anxiety-neurotic and two depressed-neurotic patients. Omission of their scores does not change the significance or lack of same of the results reported below. Therefore, these $Ss$' responses were included, even though scoring was not blind.)

*Results and Discussion*

The total frequency that $Ss$ in the psychiatric and control groups had central figures yield in the four resistance-to-temptation stories and that they had them show guilt, confess, and/or make restitution in the guilt-following-yielding stories is shown in Table 2.

*Table 2*

**Resistance to Temptation and Guilt Following Yielding in Neurotic and Control Subjects**

| No. responses | No. Ss in P group | No. Ss in C group |
|---|---|---|
| **Resistance to temptation** | | |
| Yielding | | |
| 0 | 2 | 9 |
| 1 | 3 | 6 |
| 2 | 10 | 5 |
| 3 | 5 | 4 |
| 4 | 1 | 0 |
| **Guilt-following-yielding[a]** | | |
| Guilt, confession, and restitution | | |
| 0 | 5 | 3 |
| 1 | 3 | 2 |
| 2 | 7 | 8 |
| 3 | 2 | 5 |
| 4 | 3 | 2 |
| 5 | 1 | 3 |
| 6 | 0 | 1 |

Note: P = psychiatric, C = control.
[a] Combined guilt, confession, and restitution scores.

The median resistance score for all Ss was 2. When Ss were divided into those at or below versus those above median in resistance, neurotic Ss showed significantly ($\chi^2 = 6.79$, $df = 1$, $p < .01$) less resistance than control Ss. The two groups did not differ significantly in responses to any of the three measures of guilt following yielding or in responses to the combined guilt measure. For those stories aimed at measuring resistance in which S caused the central figure to yield, the mean guilt response of Ss in the psychiatric group was .29, and for the normal control Ss, .31.

No significant differences were found between anxiety and depressed neurotics, perhaps because of the small $N$ in each group or perhaps because the diagnoses were less firm than might be desired.

These results again indicate that emotionally disturbed Ss differ from normal controls in resistance to temptation, as measured here, but not in guilt following yielding.

## Study III

The final study was aimed at determining the relation of resistance to temptation and of guilt following yielding and the relation of each of these to a measure of mental health and to several other indexes of personality in a relatively normal population.

### Method

**Subjects.** Of the 101 introductory psychology students at the University of Colorado who served as Ss, 64 were female and 37 were male. These Ss were fulfilling an experimental participation requirement.

**Measuring devices and procedure.** The same projective stories and procedure described in Study II were used with Ss tested in the present study. Following the projective stories, Ss were presented with the Jourard and Lasakow (1958) Self-Disclosure Scale, since Jourard (1964, pp. 19–30) has stated his belief that openness in self-disclosure is positively correlated with adjustment. Jourard's scale presumably measures the amount of information that one reveals about himself to "significant others" in his life. Following the administration of the Jourard-Lasakow Scale, Ss were given the Eysenck Personality Inventory (EPI—Eysenck & Eysenck, 1963), a revision of the Maudsley Personality Inventory, as a measure of stability (normality) and neuroticism. A final measure was Rotter's (1966) Internal-External Control scale. As a general principle,

> . . . internal control refers to the perception of positive and/or negative events as being a consequence of one's own actions and thereby under personal control; external control refers to the perception of positive and/or negative events as being unrelated to one's own behaviors in certain situations and therefore beyond personal control (Lefcourt, 1966, p. 207).

On the basis of data reported in Rotter's monograph, it appeared reasonable to hypothesize that Ss varying in amount of internal control should also vary in resistance to temptation (since ability to delay gratification varies with locus of control) and possibly in guilt following yielding in their projective story completions. All measuring devices were presented to Ss in a group testing situation.

Previous data led to the following predictions: Resistance to temptation and guilt following yielding should be unrelated. Resistance to temptation, but not guilt following yielding, should be related to adjustment measured, in this case, by Ss' scores on the Eysenck stability-neuroticism dimension. If Jourard is correct, then open, self-disclosing Ss should be less neurotic, as neuroticism is measured by the EPI. The Ss who manifest a belief in internal, as opposed to external, control of reinforcement should be more likely to resist temptation and to feel more guilt following yielding.

*Results and Discussion*

The various measures were scored by an assistant who had not been instructed as to the purpose of the study, but who was given the same scoring instructions concerning the stories as given judges in the first study. Previous data on scoring reliability suggest that a relatively untrained judge can do a reliable job of scoring. All data except the resistance scores seemed to meet the necessary assumptions for obtaining product-moment correlations. The resistance scores had a range of 5 points (0–4)—a small range for correlational purposes. Since there was some doubt as to the propriety of obtaining correlations using these resistance scores, they also were related to other measures by means of chi-square comparisons. Only one significant correlation, that between stability (normality) and resistance to temptation for female Ss, was not also significant as a chi-square. The correlation matrices for male and for female Ss are shown in Table 3.

As in the first two studies reported here, responses to projective stories aimed at measuring resistance to temptation do correlate with mental health,

with more disturbed individuals showing lesser resistance. The relation is stronger for male than for female Ss. Also, like the two previous studies the present one reveals no significant relation between responses to stories involving guilt following yielding and mental health. As in previously published research, there is no significant relation between responses to stories involving resistance as opposed to those involving guilt following yielding. As in the first two studies reported here guilt measures were obtained for those stories in which Ss themselves caused the central figure to yield. The correlation between normality, as measured by the EPI, and guilt shown in stories in which Ss themselves had the central figure yield was .21. The correlation between the two measures of guilt (responses to stories in which the central figure had already yielded, as opposed to stories in which S himself caused the central figure to yield) was .46 ($p \leq .01$), indicating that these two separate indexes of guilt following yielding measure something of the same aspects of personality. The correlation between this measure of guilt (S causes central figure to yield) and resistance scores was .18 for Ss who yielded on one or more stories. Despite Jourard's belief that openness in self-disclosure should be related to mental health, the present writers, like Jourard (1964, p. 181) himself, found no relation between total self-disclosure score and mental health. Rotter's measure of internal versus external control of reinforcement is significantly related to adjustment among females, but not among males, while it is related to resistance to temptation and to guilt following yielding among males but not among females. It is probably not wise

*Table 3*

**Intercorrelations among Measures for Male and Female Subjects**

| Measure | Internal control | Openness | Resistance to temptation | Guilt following yielding |
|---|---|---|---|---|
| | | *Male*[a] | | |
| Stability-normality | .24 | .22 | .44** | .14 |
| Internal control | | −.20 | .38** | .45** |
| Openness | | | .03 | .07 |
| Resistance to temptation | | | | .27 |
| | | *Female*[b] | | |
| Stability-Normality | .37** | .03 | .28* | .08 |
| Internal control | | −.23 | .11 | .03 |
| Openness | | | .01 | .18 |
| Resistance to temptation | | | | .21 |

Note: Since each measure is of a continuum (e.g., stability-normality versus neuroticism) only one end of the continuum is used as a label in order that the direction of the correlation be made clear. If correlations are positive, this means that they are positive between the ends of the continua shown (e.g., more stable normal people on the Eysenck scale tend to be internally controlled among males and significantly more internally controlled among females).

[a] $N = 37$.
[b] $N = 64$.
* $p < .05$.
** $p < .01$.

to dwell on these sex differences until replicated, but these results suggest that a belief in the internal control of reinforcement is a more direct influence on the adjustment of female Ss, but may indirectly (through being associated with resistance to temptation) influence male adjustment as well. Those correlations predicted to be significant, on the basis of previous research in the area of conscience development, generally were significant; those correlations predicted to be insignificant generally were not significant. The obtained findings are a good deal more clear-cut for male than for female Ss.

**Discussion of Studies I–III**

All three sets of results show no relation between resistance to temptation and guilt following yielding. Measures of resistance, but not of guilt, vary with adjustment, with persons who are less well-adjusted showing less resistance in responses to the projective measure. It is possible to interpret the lesser resistance of the more emotionally disturbed individuals as reflecting a lesser ability to resist temptation in real-life situations. However, as several readers have pointed out, one might also assume that the disturbed individual is projecting unacceptable impulses, so that the lack of resistance in the stories is not a reflection of a lesser resistance at the behavioral level. The writers believe that the first interpretation is more likely to be the correct one, since a number of other researchers (e.g., Grinder & McMichael, 1963) have found that responses to projective measures relate directly to resistance to temptation as measured behaviorally. Finally, it should be mentioned that many theories of emotional disturbance are concerned with guilt. The present data suggest that a concern for individual differences in resistance, not guilt, might be more fruitful.

## References

ALLINSMITH, W. The learning of moral standards. In D. R. Miller & G. E. Swanson (Eds.), *Inner conflict and defense.* New York: Holt, 1960. Pp. 141–176.

ARONFREED, J. Moral behavior and sex identity. In D. R. Miller & G. E. Swanson (Eds.), *Inner conflict and defense.* New York: Holt, 1960. Pp. 177–193.

EYSENCK, H. J., & EYSENCK, S. B. G. *Manual for the Eysenck Personality Inventory.* San Diego, Calif.: Educational and Industrial Testing Service, 1963.

*GRINDER, R. E., & McMICHAEL, R. E. Cultural influence on conscience development: Resistance to temptation and guilt among Samoans and American Caucasians. *Journal of Abnormal and Social Psychology,* 1963, **66,** 503–507.

*HOFFMAN, M. L., & SALTZSTEIN, H. D. Parent discipline and the child's moral development. *Journal of Personality and Social Psychology,* 1967, **5,** 45–57.

JOURARD, S. M. *The transparent self.* Princeton, N. J.: Van Nostrand, 1964.

JOURARD, S. M., & LASAKOW, P. A research approach to self-disclosure. *Journal of Abnormal and Social Psychology,* 1958, **56,** 91–98.

LEFCOURT, H. M. Internal versus external control of reinforcement: A review. *Psychological Bulletin,* 1966, **65,** 206–220.

*PORTEUS, B. D., & JOHNSON, R. C. Children's responses to two measures of conscience development and their relation to sociometric nomination. *Child Development,* 1965, **36,** 703–711.

*REBELSKY, F. G., ALLINSMITH, W., & GRINDER, R. E. Resistance to temptation and sex differences in children's use of fantasy confession. *Child Development,* 1963, **34,** 955–962.

ROTTER, J. B. Generalized expectancies for internal versus external control of reinforcement. *Psychological Monographs,* 1966, **80** (1, Whole No. 609).

* [Asterisks indicate works that are reprinted, in whole or in part, in this volume.]

# 35

# Moral development and behavior disorders in young children

*by David J. Ogren
and Paul R. Dokecki*

The meaning of an observation is often elusive until an appropriate question is posed (cf. Watts, 1961). Often it is a new question about an old phenomenon that advances knowledge. One goal of this paper is to attempt to pose some new questions that hopefully will lead to a better understanding of the persisting problem of behavior disorders in young children. The authors look at the writings of O. H. Mowrer and Sigmund Freud concerning adult psychopathology in terms of this "new-question-old-phenomenon" paradigm: Do Mowrer's emphasis on adult moral behavior and his extrapolations of Freud's theory of adult neurosis help in understanding the etiology of childhood behavior disorders?

Mowrer has been developing his theory over the past two decades in a series of articles and books (Mowrer, 1948, 1950, 1952, 1953a, 1953b, 1959, 1960a, 1960b, 1961, 1964a, 1964b, 1965, 1967a, 1967b, 1969, 1971) that have attacked certain assumptions of the Freudian theory of psychopathology. Before approaching the problem of behavior disorders in children, this article presents a

This article is published here for the first time.

brief overview of the development of Freud's position on neurosis and of Mowrer's critique, as interpreted by the authors.

## Neurosis According to Freud

Early in the development of his theory, Freud (1962a, 1962b, 1962d) believed that psychoneuroses were based on forgotten memories of traumatic experiences. This orientation set the tone for all of his later theoretical development —man's pleasure, pain, and psychological difficulties were always seen as ultimately caused by essentially internal, intrapsychic processes. In 1895, anxiety caused by blocked sexual tensions was given a key role in the development of psychoneurosis (Freud, 1962c). In 1896, the notion that the repression of an unacceptable idea can result in anxiety and neurosis was added (Freud, 1962a).

A major change was made when Freud discussed the drives or instincts involved in infantile sexuality (Freud, 1953). Since society tends to discourage direct gratification of these infantile drives, a person must repress them. Although the drives may lose the battle for immediate gratification, they resort to "guerrilla tactics" in order to gain expression and are the cause of great anxiety and potential symptom formation. Freud not only saw man as having to cope with these devious, basically sexual impulses; he also gave aggressive impulses a key role in man's psychological functioning (Freud, 1955, 1957c). Encouraging socially acceptable behavior by coping with intrapsychic "enemies" was seen as the function of the superego, the internalized voice of society (Freud, 1961a).

Early in the evolution of his theory, Freud (1962a) proposed that the internalization of social values plays a significant role in psychological development. In *The Interpretation of Dreams* Freud (1938) discussed extensively the role of a censor and later (Freud, 1957b) spoke of an ego-ideal, which was eventually replaced by the broader concept of the superego (Freud, 1961b). The superego, which was described as an internalized precipitate of early parental threats, reproaches, and standards of moral perfection, is not fully formed until the person successfully resolves all of the difficulties of the oedipal complex. In fact, Freud has referred to the superego as the inheritor of the oedipal complex (Freud, 1949). This frequently cited notion presents some theoretical difficulties, which are discussed later in this paper.

Freud gave the superego an important role both in the everyday psychological functioning of man and in the development of psychopathology (Freud, 1957a, 1957c, 1961a, 1961b, 1961c). The superego was said to exert strong moral influences to control both the sexual and the aggressive instincts. One of the results of the superego's proper functioning is guilt, "the tension between the harsh superego and the ego" (Freud, 1961a, p. 123). Once the superego is formed, a person will feel guilty even if he "only notices the intention to [act]" (Freud, 1961a, p. 124), since nothing can be hidden from the superego. In this same paper Freud implied that before the superego is formed guilt does not play a role in the psychological life of a person. Rather, the predominant inhibiting emotion is fear of being discovered by an authority after some forbidden act has been committed. Once the superego is formed, however, man is destined to lead a life with "permanent internal unhappiness [in that] the price we pay for our advance in civilization is a loss of happiness through the heightening of the sense of guilt" (Freud, 1961a, p. 135).

It is often implied in Freud's writings that persons who develop psychoneuroses have unrealistically harsh superegos and that their moral standards are overdeveloped. Neurotics have learned moral values too well and have an overzealous superego that demands that sexual and aggressive instincts be repressed. A person may have normal instincts but an abnormally strong superego and consequently experience neurotic guilt and anxiety, which then leads to symptom formation. These implications have been the subject of much of Mowrer's attention in the past twenty years.

## Mowrer's Critique of Freud

In an early paper, Mowrer (1948) suggested that Freud's theory failed to account for the "neurotic paradox," the observation that neurotic behavior is self-defeating, but does not extinguish. Almost two decades later, Mowrer (1967a) focused on the tendency of a neurotic to withdraw from contact with other people, even though his superego, which is supposedly overly developed, logically should help him to stay unusually well integrated socially. Regardless of the specific aspect of Freudian theory that he has chosen to attack, Mowrer has consistently developed the thesis that neurotics are trying to deal with anxiety that:

> . . . *comes, not from acts which the individual would commit but dares not, but from acts which he has committed*

*and wishes he had not. It is, in other words, a "guilt theory" of anxiety rather than an "impulse theory"* (Mowrer, 1950, p. 537).

Mowrer has consistently objected to the view that the superego controls the ego and forces it to repress impulses so that the person no longer knows why he is upset. Rather, he believes that a person who has violated his moral code will be anxious because the superego is "accusing" him and trying to "rescue" him from his evil ways. The neurotic has not only chosen to act badly, but has also chosen to be silent and secretive about his deeds. It is the combination of these two choices that leads to behaviors labeled neurotic, whether these behaviors are the direct result of sinfulness or are security operations designed to lessen emotional discomfort (Mowrer, 1967a).

Thus, both Mowrer and Freud see neurosis as involving a discrepancy between a person's moral standards and his actual conduct. Moral standards are a chief source of unhappiness (dis-ease) in the neurotic, but Freud sees the trouble as an overly severe, unrealistic, irrational superego (too much learning), whereas Mowrer sees the trouble as a deficiency in learning to control behavior (too little learning).

In support of his position, Mowrer (1968) has reviewed a number of studies that support the notion that neurotics experience guilt over real transgressions (over behavior), instead of over impulses magnified by an overzealous superego. Recently, however, Johnson and Kalafat (1960) suggested that "the relation of guilt to mental health still appears to be an open question" (p. 655). They also pointed out that research that focuses on guilt is problematic, since the behavioral referents of guilt are difficult to determine. They used projective measures and a sociometric rating system to assess adolescents' resistance to temptation and guilt after transgressing some moral standard and found no relationship between the variables. These data are inconsistent with Freud's point of view that children with severe superegos, that is, strong moral prohibitions against yielding to temptation, should experience more guilt following yielding than children with little resistance to temptation. In another study comparing psychotics, neurotics, college students, and various control groups, Johnson, Ackermann, Frank, and Fionda (1968) found no group differences on several measures of guilt. Normal subjects, however, did display greater resistance to temptation. These findings suggest that, although guilt may not be related to psychopathology, there is a strong possibility that resistance to temptation is so implicated. The findings are clearly at variance with Freudian theory; however, Mowrer's theory is less seriously challenged because of his more recent emphasis on ego-strength deficiency and its behavioral concomitants.

Both Mowrer and Freud seem to be mainly concerned with neurosis (or "sociosis," as Mowrer would prefer to call it; cf. Van den Berg, 1964) in adults. Thus there is a question concerning the applicability of these theories to young children who are in the process of developing morally, although neither author has denied the possibility of such application. The remainder of this paper deals with some issues that arise when the two theories are applied to psychopathology in children.

## Moral Development and Behavior Disorders in Children

Certain of Mowrer's ideas are presented, as they apply, throughout this section. Actually, Mowrer (personal communication, 1970) admits that he has not systematically dealt with the development of morality in children, since his writings have primarily concerned adults.

Although Freud has theorized extensively on moral development, his approach raises certain problems. Despite the fact that psychoanalytic theory is developmental in nature, the formation of the superego seems to be viewed as virtually an "all or none," discontinuous phenomenon, dependent on the resolution of the oedipal complex. In *Civilization and Its Discontents*, Freud (1961a) proposed that fear of being discovered after a moral transgression serves an inhibitory function for socially unacceptable behavior until the superego is formed. Subsequent to superego formation, guilt, a qualitatively different process from fear (or shame), becomes *the* primary inhibiting force. It is difficult to escape the implications of discontinuity in development and the independent functioning of fear and guilt in the postoedipal individual. Interestingly, Mosher (1965) found that fear and guilt interact as inhibitors of unacceptable behavior in college students, results that are seemingly at variance with Freudian theory.

If the superego is not formed until the oedipal complex is resolved, then preoedipal children should function entirely differently in social and moral areas than postoedipal children. Furthermore, shame (fear of being exposed; cf. Lynd, 1958) should be a more potent force than guilt in the life of preoedipal chil-dren. Since shame and guilt, if they are to be theoretically meaningful, must have different behavioral manifestations, they should play different roles in the etiology of behavior disorders in young children. This elaboration of Freudian theory leads to interesting, if somewhat tenuous, predictions.

If, as Freud implies, guilt is necessary for the development of neurosis, then preoedipal children should not become neurotic. Stating this differently, preoedipal children should not display behavior that would be labeled neurotic— a questionable assertion. Further, there should be apparent and clear discontinuity of behavior development and behavior disorders evidenced when moving from the pre- to the postoedipal period. If this last assertion were confirmed, then distinctly different therapeutic strategies would be required for pre- and postoedipal children. However, evidence is lacking regarding these predictions.

A different and possibly more continuous approach to moral development has been proposed by Piaget (1948, 1950) and elaborated by Kohlberg (1963a, 1963b, 1964). Piaget viewed the development of moral standards as the outcome of a series of transformations of primitive attitudes or conceptions in the course of intellectual growth. Central is the social experience of role-taking in peer groups, which permits the change in morality from rules based on external, authoritarian commands to internal principles that govern action. A young child's morality is seen as progressing from unilateral and absolutistic judgements, the result of an egocentric cognitive style, to judgments that exhibit mutual, reciprocal, and relativistic qualities. These later aspects of moral development are usually observable by the time a child is eight years old, but are probably not dominant until adolescence.

It is interesting to note the similarities between Freud's view of the resolution of the oedipal complex and Piaget's view of the loss of egocentrism in the course of moral development. In the Freudian view, when a child is about five years old, if he successfully resolves the oedipal complex, societal values are incorporated. The result is an internal set of moral standards that considers the needs and values of others. In Piaget's view, when a child is about eight years old his moral standards become less egocentric and absolutistic, that is, his moral standards become psychosocial expectations that can be relative to various persons, situations, or needs. Are the same processes being described by Freud and Piaget? If so, one wonders why Freud saw this change occurring when the child is five years old, while Piaget saw the change only when the child is eight years old or older. Several possible factors come to mind. Freud and Piaget made their observations in different cultures (Vienna vs. Switzerland) and at different times (1900–1920 vs. 1920–1930). At a theoretical level, Piaget (1948) has hypothesized that there is a "time-lag" between behavioral change and cognitive change; thus Freud may have made his inferences from early behavioral changes, while Piaget was more concerned with later cognitive changes. Finally, Freud may have been dealing with a different aspect of the moral development process than Piaget. Piaget (1962, pp. 211–212) seems to suggest this last possibility in describing identification as a prelogical and affective process, whereas mature moral judgment is said to involve abstraction and logic and is developmentally later than identification.

In attempting to relate moral development to other psychological constructs, Kohlberg (1964) cites evidence that favors the view that moral development and ego-strength development are similar, if not identical, processes. This possibility is particularly interesting in light of the Johnson et al. (1968) results, which suggest that resistance to temptation, an ego-strength indicator, may be related to psychopathology.

Kohlberg (1964) has commented that:

> The research findings on guilt and moral factors in neuroses are sparse, but they do suggest limitations to the notion that neurotics suffer from too much guilt or moral restraint. There is little reason to believe that neurotics are more scrupulous in their moral ideals or more morally restrained in their conduct than normal people (p. 419).

To support this statement Kohlberg reports unpublished and unelaborated findings that neurotic children were slightly but nonsignificantly lower than normal controls on a measure of moral judgment. Given the "time-lag" hypothesis of Piaget, it is possible that the neurotic children were behaving differently in moral areas from the normals, even though their moral judgments were virtually similar. Kohlberg cited two other unpublished studies that found no differences on projective indicators of guilt for groups of normal and neurotic children. These findings are consistent with Johnson et al. (1968), but leave open the question of ego-strength deficiency in behavior disorders. Therefore, Kohlberg's (1964) conclusion that "neurotic symptoms may not be associated with a generally guilty personality" (p. 420) is not inconsistent with the possibility that the ego-strength aspects of morality, emphasized by Kohlberg himself, may still be implicated in children's behavior disorders.

If one considers moral development as an important part of the broader concept of socialization, a study by Peterson (1967) sheds some light on the role of moral development in behavior-disordered children. The study was designed to test Mowrer's view that both neurotic or "personality-problem" children and psychopathic or "conduct-problem" children are less socialized than children with no problems. This is in contrast to Freud's hypothesis that neurotic children are oversocialized, while children with conduct problems are undersocialized. The Socialization Scale from the California Psychological Inventory was used to rank groups of children rated as having personality problems, conduct problems, or no problems and Mowrer's hypothesis was strongly supported. Since the Socialization Scale includes items dealing with both affect and behavior, either a guilt- or ego-strength theory of behavior disorders remains plausible.

Returning to the realm of theory, it is interesting to note that several theories of psychopathology utilize notions that are conceptually related to the mechanism of decentering (loss of egocentrism), which is said by Piaget to play a crucial role in moral development.

Mowrer (1964b, 1966, 1967a) has suggested that psychological adjustment is achieved through increased social integration, a concept that appears to be related to mature moral judgments and decentering. Similarly, Adler believed that all behavior disorders are "characterized by a lack of social feeling" (Ansbacher & Ansbacher, 1964, p. 53). Also, Alexander (1963) has suggested that for

a person to solve his problem and become an effective part of the community, he must somehow become "less centered" in his problems. Finally, Feffer (1967) has suggested that in adults many impersonal and interpersonal symptomatic behaviors reflect immature cognitive processes, reflecting an inability to decenter. If these notions are extended to young children, several questions may be posed:

Is an immature cognitive style (including level of moral development) associated with neurotic behavior only if that style is atypical for the particular age of the person?

Do children whose level of moral development fails to mature as fast as the average child eventually become or get labeled neurotic?

Do children and adults regress to more primitive and immature forms of morality under certain types of stress situations?

Unfortunately, data are scarce concerning these provocative questions.

Other questions and new perspectives emerge when Erikson's (1968) concept of identity crisis is considered. Resolution of this crisis requires cognitive growth and social experience. An important aspect of this process is when a person employs "simultaneous reflection and observation . . . by which he judges himself in the light of what he perceives to be the way in which others judge him in comparison to themselves" (Erikson, 1968, pp. 22–23). This description bears a striking resemblance to Piaget's (1948) description of decentering in moral development. The result of decentering for moral development is the emergence of moral principles and mutual respect for others based on psychosocial expectations. The result of resolution of the identity crisis is an increased awareness of a sense of sameness (through the taking of other perspectives) and "continuity of one's *meaning for significant others* in the immediate community" (Erikson, 1968, p. 50). It seems to the present authors that these two processes —increased maturity of moral judgment through decentering and resolution of the identity crisis—are related to Mowrer's concept of social integration.

Again, several questions may be posed:

> How do children who are not able to decenter and engage in reciprocal role-taking become socially integrated and might they be poor candidates for the "new group therapy"?
>
> Since Piaget's decentering and Erikson's identity crisis do not occur until a child is near or in adolescence, do children become "neurotic" in distinctly different ways depending on their age and moral maturity? (Compare the elaboration of Freud discussed earlier.)
>
> What happens to untreated neurotic children as they grow up?

In regard to this last question concerning the adult fate of childhood neurotics, one interesting possibility emerges. If neurotic children are morally immature (that is, lacking in ego strength) and misbehave more frequently with consequent withdrawal to hide their misdeeds (Peterson, 1967), it follows that their peer-group interactions will be reduced. As a result, they may not learn to engage in reciprocal role-taking and may not form a secure sense of "*meaning for significant others in the immediate community*" (Erikson, 1968, p. 50). Lacking a secure identity or the means to develop one, neurotic children may engage in the creation of a "pseudo-community" (Cameron, 1943,

1959) to compensate for their lack of social integration. At this point, neurotic children may become paranoid adults. The suggestion is that the discrepancy between neurotic children and their normal peers in moral and social behavior realms increases over time if appropriate correctives are not employed. Although this hypothesis probably does not apply to all neurotic children, those lacking in the ego-strength aspects of morality may be so implicated.

In conclusion, although data are not abundant and although more unanswered than answered questions have been raised, the Mowrer-Freud emphasis on the role of morality in adult psychopathology, elaborated by the ideas of other theorists, has proved stimulating and heuristic when applied to behavior disorders in young children.

## References

ALEXANDER, T. *Psychotherapy in our society.* Englewood Cliffs, N.J.: Prentice-Hall, 1963.

ANSBACHER, H. L., & ANSBACHER, R. R. (Eds.) *Superiority and social interest— A collection of later writings by Alfred Adler.* Evanston, Ill.: Northwestern University Press, 1964.

CAMERON, N. The development of paranoiac thinking. *Psychological Review*, 1943, **50**, 219–233.

CAMERON, N. The paranoid pseudo-community revisited. *American Journal of Sociology*, 1959, **65**, 52–58.

ERIKSON, E. H. *Identity: Youth and crisis.* New York: Norton, 1968.

FEFFER, M. Symptom expression as a form of primitive decentering. *Psychological Review*, 1967, **74**, 16–28.

FREUD, S. The interpretation of dreams. (Originally published in 1900.) In R. A. Brill (Ed.), *The basic writings of Sigmund Freud.* New York: Modern Library, 1938. Pp. 181–519.

FREUD, S. *An outline of psychoanalysis.* New York: Norton, 1949.

FREUD, S. Three essays on the theory of sexuality. (Originally published in 1950.) In J. Strachey (Ed.), *The standard edition of the complete psychological works of Sigmund Freud.* Vol. 7. London: Hogarth, 1953. Pp. 130–245.

FREUD, S. Group psychology and the analysis of the ego. (Originally published in 1921.) In J. Strachey (Ed.), *The standard edition of the complete psychological works of Sigmund Freud.* Vol. 18. London: Hogarth, 1955. Pp. 69–143.

FREUD, S. Mourning and melancholia. (Originally published in 1917.) In J. Strachey (Ed.), *The standard edition of the complete psychological works of Sigmund Freud.* Vol. 14. London: Hogarth, 1957. Pp. 243–258. (a)

FREUD, S. On narcissism: An introduction. (Originally published in 1914.) In J. Strachey (Ed.), *The standard edition of the complete psychological works of Sigmund Freud.* Vol. 14. London: Hogarth, 1957. Pp. 73–102. (b)

FREUD, S. Some character types met with in psycho-analytic work. (Originally published in 1916.) In J. Strachey (Ed.), *The standard edition of the complete psychological works of Sigmund Freud.* Vol. 14. London: Hogarth, 1957. Pp. 311–333. (c)

FREUD, S. Civilization and its discontents. (Originally published in 1930.) In J. Strachey (Ed.), *The standard edition of the complete psychological works of Sigmund Freud.* Vol. 21. London: Hogarth, 1961. Pp. 64–145. (a)

FREUD, S. The ego and the id. (Originally published in 1923.) In J. Strachey (Ed.), *The standard edition of the complete psychological works of Sigmund Freud.* Vol. 19. London: Hogarth, 1961. Pp. 12–66. (b)

FREUD, S. The future of an illusion. (Originally published in 1927.) In J. Strachey (Ed.), *The standard edition of the complete psychological works of Sigmund Freud.* Vol. 21. London: Hogarth, 1961. Pp. 5–26. (c)

FREUD, S. Further remarks on the neuropsychoses of defense. (Originally published in 1896.) In J. Strachey (Ed.), *The standard edition of the complete psychological works of Sigmund Freud.* Vol. 3. London: Hogarth, 1962. Pp. 162–185.

FREUD, S. The neuro-psychoses of defense. (Originally published in 1894.) In J. Strachey (Ed.), *The standard edition of the complete psychological works of Sigmund Freud.* Vol. 3. London: Hogarth, 1962. Pp. 45–61. (b)

FREUD, S. On the grounds for detaching a particular syndrome from neurasthenia under the description, "anxiety neurosis." (Originally published in 1895.) In J. Strachey (Ed.), *The standard edition of the complete psychological works of Sigmund Freud.* Vol. 3. London: Hogarth, 1962. Pp. 90–115. (c)

FREUD, S. Sexuality in the aetiology of the neuroses. (Originally published in 1898.) In J. Strachey (Ed.), *The standard edition of the complete psychological works of Sigmund Freud.* Vol. 3. London: Hogarth, 1962. Pp. 263–286. (d)

*JOHNSON, R. C., ACKERMAN, J. M., FRANK, H., & FIONDA, A. J. Resistance to temptation, guilt following yielding, and psychopathology. *Journal of Consulting and Clinical Psychology,* 1968, **32,** 169–175.

JOHNSON, R. C., & KALAFAT, J. D. Projective and sociometric measures of conscience development. *Child Development,* 1969, **40,** 651–655.

KOHLBERG, L. The development of children's orientations toward a moral order. I. Sequence in the development of moral thought. *Vita Humana,* 1963, **6,** 11–33. (a)

KOHLBERG, L. Moral development and identification. In H. W. Stevenson (Ed.), *Yearbook of the national society for the study of education.* Pt. I. *Child psychology.* Chicago: University of Chicago Press, 1963. Pp. 277–332. (b)

* [Asterisks indicate works that are reprinted, in whole or in part, in this volume.]

KOHLBERG, L. Development of moral character and moral ideology. In M. L. Hoffman & L. W. Hoffman (Eds.), *Review of child development research*. Vol. I. New York: Russell Sage, 1964. Pp. 383–431.

LYND, H. M. *On shame and the search for identity*. New York: Science Editions, 1958.

MOSHER, D. L. Interaction of fear and guilt in inhibiting unacceptable behavior. *Journal of Consulting Psychology*, 1965, **29**, 161–167.

MOWRER, O. H. Learning theory and the neurotic paradox. *American Journal of Orthopsychiatry*, 1948, **18**, 571–610.

MOWRER, O. H. The problem of anxiety. In *Learning theory and personality dynamics*. New York: Ronald, 1950. Pp. 531–561.

MOWRER, O. H. Learning theory and the neurotic fallacy. *American Journal of Orthopsychiatry*, 1952, **22**, 679–689.

MOWRER, O. H. Neurosis and psychotherapy as interpersonal process: A synopsis. In *Psychotherapy—Theory and research*. New York: Ronald, 1953. Pp. 69–94. (a)

MOWRER, O. H. Neuroses, psychotherapy, and a two-factor learning theory. In *Psychotherapy—Theory and research*. New York: Ronald, 1953. Pp. 140–149. (b)

MOWRER, O. H. Changing conceptions of the unconscious. *Journal of Nervous and Mental Diseases*, 1959, **129**, 222–232.

MOWRER, O. H. Psychotherapy and the problem of guilt, confession, and expiation. In W. Dennis (Ed.), *Current trends in psychology*. Vol. X. Pittsburgh: University of Pittsburgh Press, 1960. (a)

MOWRER, O. H. "Sin," the lesser of two evils. *American Psychologist*, 1960, **15**, 301–304. (b)

MOWRER, O. H. *The crisis in psychiatry and religion*. Princeton, N.J.: Van Nostrand, 1961.

MOWRER, O. H. Freudianism behavior therapy, and "self-disclosure." *Behavioral Research and Therapy*, 1964, **1**, 321–337. (a)

MOWRER, O. H. *The new group therapy*. Princeton, N.J.: Van Nostrand, 1964. (b)

MOWRER, O. H. Learning theory and behavior therapy. In B. Wolman (Ed.), *Handbook of clinical psychology*. New York: McGraw-Hill, 1965. Pp. 242–276.

MOWRER, O. H. Abnormal reactions or actions? (An autobiographical answer.) In J. A. Vernon (Ed.), *Introduction to psychology: A self-selection textbook*. Dubuque, Iowa: William C. Brown, 1966.

MOWRER, O. H. Communication, conscience and the unconscious. *Journal of Communication Disorders*, 1967, **1**, 109–135. (a)

MOWRER, O. H. Stuttering as simultaneous admission and denial. *Journal of Communication Disorders*, 1967, **1**, 46–50. (b)

MOWRER, O. H. New evidence concerning the nature of psychopathology. In M. J. Feldman (Ed.), *Studies in psychotherapy and behavior change*. Buffalo, N.Y.: University of Buffalo Press, 1968. Pp. 111–193.

MOWRER, O. H. Too little and too late. *International Journal of Psychiatry*, 1969, **7**, 536–556.

*MOWRER, O. H. On the delights, and dire consequences, of conscience-killing. In R. C. Johnson, P. R. Dokecki, & O. H. Mowrer (Eds.), *Conscience and social reality: Theory and research in behavioral science*. New York: Holt, 1971.

*PETERSON, D. R. The insecure child: Oversocialized or undersocialized? In O. H. Mowrer (Ed.), *Morality and mental health*. Chicago: Rand McNally, 1967. Pp. 459–471.

*PIAGET, J. *The moral judgment of the child*. (Originally published in 1932.) Glencoe, Ill.: Free Press, 1948.

PIAGET, J. *The psychology of intelligence*. New York: Harcourt, 1950.

PIAGET, J. *Plays, dreams and imitation in childhood*. New York: Norton, 1962.

VAN DEN BERG, J. H. *The changing nature of man*. New York: Dell, 1964.

WATTS, A. W. *Psychotherapy east and west*. New York: Ballantine Books, 1961.

* [Asterisks indicate works that are reprinted, in whole or in part, in this volume.]

# 36

# Further daseinsanalytic corrections in therapy: The analysis of "guilt feelings" and the goal of psychotherapy

*by Medard Boss*

---

Daseinsanalytic insights into human beings demand another essential correction in therapy. Here the *goal* requires correction. Freud assumed man's original nature to be that of a pleasure-ego, bent solely on satisfying the sexual instinct and preserving itself. He believed that early man, primitive man, and children exemplified the more or less unadulterated, primary, guiltless "naturalness" of man—a naturalness obligated only to the "pleasure principle." Modification of the pleasure principle is forced on man by the external world; but this modification, called the "reality principle," is secondary, according to Freud. It occurs because the individual would perish (and thus be unable to have *any* kind of satisfaction) if he did not take the given realities of the external world into consideration. Part of this adaptation to external reality is the child's acceptance of the moral demands his parents make on him. Eventually,

Chapter 19 of *Psychoanalysis and Daseinsanalysis* by Medard Boss, M.D., translated by Ludwig R. Lefebre, © 1963 by Basic Books, Inc., Publishers, New York.

the superior force of external reality results in the child's psychic incorporation of these and other demands and prohibitions which originally came from outside. The end product is Freud's "super-ego," or conscience. Once the super-ego has been formed, it becomes a source of guilt feelings. Hence, man experiences feelings of guilt every time he violates, or intends to violate, one of the commandments which have been drilled into him. Characteristically enough, Freud in all his papers never spoke of *guilt* as such, but only of guilt *feelings*. Consistent with such theories, Freud expected psychoanalysis to liberate the patient from neurotic serfdom and allow him to return to his "original naturalness." Here he would no longer be hemmed in by feelings of guilt, but would be guaranteed the capacity for *guiltless* enjoyment.[1]

In contrast to Freud, Daseinsanalysis acknowledges more than guilt *feelings*, certainly more than the secondary, externally determined ones which can be removed by psychoanalysis. In the view of analysis of *Dasein*, man is *primarily* guilty. His primary guilt starts at birth. For it is then that he begins to be in debt to his *Dasein*, insofar as carrying out all the possibilities for living of which he is capable is concerned. Throughout his life, man remains guilty in this sense, i.e., indebted to all the requests that his future keeps in store for him until he breathes his last. Also, as we have pointed out, every act, every decision, every choice, involves the rejec-

[1] For Freud's views regarding the topics alluded to in this paragraph, see, for example, *New Introductory Lectures in Psycho-Analysis* (New York, 1933), pp. 89, 112, 223, trans. by W. J. H. Sprott; *The Ego and the Id* (London, 1957), pp. 47–50, trans. by Joan Riviere; *Totem and Taboo*, in *SE*, Vol. XIII, pp. 68, 144.

tion of all the other possibilities which also belong to a human being at a given moment. For man can engage his existence in only one of the myriads of his possible relationships at a time. In this twofold sense, he must always remain behind, so to speak. This is as much a part of fundamental human nature as the other *existentialia*. Man's existential guilt consists in his failing to carry out the mandate to fulfill all his possibilities. Man is aware of existential guilt when he hears the never-ending call of his conscience. This essential, inevitable being-in-debt is *guilt*, and not merely a subjective *feeling* of guilt. It precedes all psychologically understandable feelings of guilt, no matter what neurotic guise these may appear in. Because of existential being-in-debt (experienced as guilt), even the most skillfully conducted psychoanalysis cannot free man of guilt. Actually, not a single analysand could be found in the whole world who has been transformed into a really guiltless person by psychoanalytic treatment. The most —and the worst—an analysis can accomplish in this regard is to deafen a patient to his pangs of conscience, and this is not to his advantage. The ideally new man, liberated from guilt by psychoanalysis, is an antiquated myth: charming and beautiful but, alas, incapable of realization.[2]

Psychoanalysis, however, can accomplish something else. It can elucidate the past, present, and future of a patient's life to the point where he becomes thoroughly aware of his existential being-in-debt. This in turn enables him to acknowledge his debt, to say "yes" to it and take it upon himself. He becomes

[2] See M. Boss, "Anxiety, Guilt, and Psychotherapeutic Liberation," *Review of Existential Psychology and Psychiatry*, Vol. 11, 1962.

aware of his possibilities for living through listening to the call of his conscience; he can take them over responsibly, stand by himself, and thus make them part of himself.

Once a person has been freed for his essential and existential being-in-debt, he no longer experiences *neurotic* feelings of guilt. These latter did not originate in himself, but derive from a foreign and crippling mentality which his educators forced upon him. He had fallen prey to modes of life which were alien to him, but he could not shake them off. Such neurotic feelings of guilt continually increase existential guilt as well, since they result in a steadily increasing debt in regard to a fulfillment of one's own existence. As a result, the call of conscience becomes increasingly persistent. But the patient, caught in acquired moralistic concepts, misunderstands this voice as a demand to follow ever more rigidly a mode of living essentially foreign to himself. A vicious circle results. Only analysis can break its spell.

If a patient reaches the goal of Daseinsanalysis, that is, if he freely accepts his debt to his existence, he reaches at the same time the goal Freud had in mind—full capacity for work and enjoyment. But he will no longer use these capacities in the service of egotistic, power—or pleasure—tendencies. Rather he will let all his possibilities of relating to the world be used as the luminated realm into which all he encounters may come to its full emergence, into its genuine being, and unfold in its meaning to the fullest possible extent. Man's option to respond to this claim or to choose not to do so seems to be the very core of human freedom. Once this kind of basic freedom is reached, the former burdens of a bad conscience and of guilt feelings give way without further ado to a happy readiness for being thus needed by the phenomena of our world.

At the same time as this Daseinsanalytic understanding of man's existence reveals its deep and inexhaustible meaningfulness, it is also able to define man's basic morality. Mankind's ethics become self-evident on the basis of such an understanding of man's essence. No so-called ethical values need be added a posteriori.

# Section VI
# AN EMERGING RECONCEPTUALIZATION OF CONSCIENCE

## Introduction

There has long been a tendency to reify conscience, to make an *entity* of it. Freud's concept of the superego (roughly the equivalent of conscience) was first referred to as *the censor*, which even implies a personification of sorts.

This "thingification" of conscience has made an analytic, operational, functional approach to the problem very difficult, and in recent years there has been a small but growing tendency toward thinking of conscience as a process or function rather than as an entity; and the key concept here has been *contractual* in nature. As intimated in Chapter 3, conscience is perhaps not so much something which has been given to or inflicted upon an individual as it is certain interpersonal relationships into which one has tacitly or explicitly entered by one's own consent and volition. Contracts are agreements between two or more parties which involve commitment to interpersonal behavior; and this behavior is externally observable, not an inaccessible internal entity.

If conscience were an intrapsychic thing, an entity that is imposed from without, how would one go about *changing* it? The psychoanalysts thought they had an answer in the phenomenon known as transference, but the practical (therapeutic) effects resulting from this approach have been disappointing. If, on the other hand, conscience is largely composed of the commitments or contracts to which one has willingly assented, then one changes conscience by making new contracts or by dissolving or renegotiating old ones. In other words, one can "get at" and revise contractual arrangements, whereas if conscience is conceived as an intrapsychic phenomenon, it cannot be modified in this way by its possessor or anyone else. This difference, if valid, is of enormous practical importance.

Steve Pratt and Jay Tooley (1964, 1966)

were the first writers in recent years to stress this distinction, and group psychotherapy has given it added impetus of a purely practical nature. In individual therapy, there was much concern on the part of the therapist, with the patient's values (or the *content* of conscience) and a great deal of time and effort were spent trying to bring about changes in this area. Groups, by contrast, are often only secondarily concerned with the particular commitments or contracts an individual has made, but are vitally interested in whether the person is characteristically a contract keeper or a unilateral, often secretive, contract breaker. The empirical fact seems to be that persons who make and keep contracts (or honorably renegotiate them) get along with other individuals relatively well, whereas those who make contracts and continue to enjoy the privileges they confer but do not keep their part "of the bargain" (that is, *cheat*), commonly find themselves in trouble with themselves and with others. Thus a whole new rationale for psychopathology of a functional nature is emerging which stresses interpersonal rather than intrapsychic events (both as regards causation and correction); and here contract psychology seems to be largely replacing the former emphasis upon conscience, guilt, and so on.

It may be that this would have been a better way to approach the whole matter of functional psychopathology from the beginning. But as Dreikurs points out in *Social Equality: The Challenge of Today* (1971), we seem to be moving, in a rather pervasive sense, from an era of autocratic to one of democratic social control. The notion of contracts, as agreements which are voluntarily entered into and are always subject to revision, accords well with the growing spirit of democracy, whereas the notion of an ingrained, relatively rigid conscience was more compatible with the values and practices of society when it was more autocratic. In any case, there seems at present to be a declining interest, both theoretically and practically, in the concept of conscience and a lively and growing concern with the psychology of contracts.

The logic and "logistics" of this conceptual and practical change has not yet been fully worked out. In 1969, O. Hobart Mowrer published a paper entitled "Conflict, Contract, Conscience, and Confession," in which some beginning steps were taken in this direction. The enterprise has been further advanced by Frederick H. Kanfer and Jeanne S. Phillips in *The Learning Foundations of Behavior Therapy* (1970). The first chapter in this section consists of pertinent excerpts from this book. The second chapter in this section was written by Frederick H. Kanfer and Paul Karoly expressly for this volume to update and expand some of the concepts set forth by Kanfer and Phillips.

The reader should not be surprised or disappointed if even this advanced treatment of the problem does not neatly answer all questions; but it will unmistakably serve to indicate some of the transitions which seem to be taking place today in this field and to suggest the directions in which future developments are likely to move.

## References

Dreikurs, R. *Social equality: The challenge of today*. Chicago: Henry Regnery Co., 1971.

Kanfer, F. H., & Phillips, J. S. *The learning foundations of behavior therapy*. New York: Wiley, 1970.

Mowrer, O. H. Conflict, contract, conscience, and confession. *Transactions* (Department of Psychiatry, Marquette School of Medicine), 1969, **1**, 7–19.

Pratt, S., & Tooley, J. Contract psychology and the actualizing transactional-field. *International Journal of Social Psychiatry*, 1964, Congress issue, 51–69.

Pratt, S., & Tooley, J. Human actualization teams: The perspective of contract psychology. *American Journal of Orthopsychiatry*, 1966, **36**, 881–895.

# 37

# Contract psychology: An operational approach to the problem of conscience and self-control

*by Frederick H. Kanfer and Jeanne S. Phillips*

## The Relationship between Words and Action

Although the traditional interview methods assume the modifiability of behavior by means of changes in thoughts and speech, it is by no means clear that verbal responses can always serve as controlling stimuli for other acts. In social relationships some congruence between verbal statements and motor acts is essential for fulfillment of everyday interpersonal agreements. For example, the entire fabric of social cooperation rests on the general confidence that a man's verbal promise can be counted upon to eventuate in execution of the appropriate behaviors. The promise to keep an appointment at a specified place, to deliver merchandise or to carry out an assignment represents the verbal con-

Frederick H. Kanfer and Jeanne S. Phillips, *The Learning Foundations of Behavior Therapy* (New York: Wiley, 1970), pp. 411–420, 437–438, 452–454.

trolling stimuli that presumably initiate a series of complex motor acts, culminating in the fulfillment of such a promise. Social mores and legislation enforce these contractual agreements by providing positive reinforcements for the congruence between words and actions and aversive consequences for failure to follow the verbal statements with appropriate actions. Perhaps because of the ubiquity of this correspondence little research effort has been devoted to exploration of the specific processes by which words and actions are related. In fact, the absence of such correlations is sufficiently infrequent in social intercourse that it is often taken as evidence of a behavior disorder or pathological condition. Its seriousness is emphasized by the stringent measures taken, including the deprivation of civil rights, for those patients who are judged "mentally incompetent" and not expected to show the common correspondence between words and action. . . .

## Self-Control

One major requirement in the execution of instigation therapy is the capacity of the patient to put behavior under his own control. The theoretical dilemma, shared by all psychological approaches, lies in explaining behavioral relationships in which the same person is both object and subject, both the doer and the target of the action. The practical management of self-control has been easier to achieve than the conceptual formulation. As long as 4,000 years ago, Homer reported some good advice for exercise of self-control through the admonitions of Circe to the sea-faring Odysseus. To prevent the disastrous exposure to the bewitching songs of the Sirens, Odysseus was warned to plug his oarsmen's ears with soft beeswax. For his own control, he let himself be tied to the mast after cautioning the crew not to release him, "shout as may, begging to be untied." Odysseus' successful strategy for eliminating stimuli that present the temptation to engage in an undesirable or destructive behavior, or preventing the response by physical restraint well in advance of exposure to the critical situation, is used in current treatment of alcoholics, sexual offenders, and with similar problems of self-control. It is also among the list of potential controlling devices listed by contemporary psychologists (Skinner, 1953). Yet, the mechanisms that permit a person to control his own behavior in the face of competing environmental controls still require explanation. Behavioristic writers have attempted to circumvent this dilemma, by treating it as a special case of the situation in which one person acts upon another. For example, Skinner writes "when a man controls himself, chooses a course of action, thinks out the solution to a problem, or strives toward an increase in self-knowledge, he is *behaving*. He controls himself precisely as he would control the behavior of anyone else—through the manipulation of variables of which behavior is a function" (1953, p. 228).

Skinner believes that in describing self-control the question of who controls whom can be answered by examination of the relationship among various organized systems of responses within a person and by study of the extent to which these systems stand in controlling relationships to each other. This approach collapses the environment-person distinction, implicit in our behavioral equation. S, R, K, and C components all lie in the same person, O. In clinical application, this view suggests that the probability that a person will learn to control some deviant behavior, such as overeating, depends on the response-reinforcement contingencies for eating and noneating, the environmental opportunities for food-getting, all other features associated with the maintenance of the eating response, and the availability of controlling responses in the person's general repertoire. If the instrumental behaviors for self-control are available and can be increased by changing stimulus conditions and by contingent reinforcement, the patient should show a reduction in his tendency to overeat because the probability of exercising the self-controlling response would now be strengthened to the point that it exceeds the strength of the eating response. The additional complexity due to the variables affecting the patient-therapist relationship and the probability that patient will act on the therapist's suggestions presents a practical but not theoretical problem in such an approach. The person's past experience in controlling his own environment and in securing reinforcements for such control would also play a large role in his therapeutic success with self-directing methods. The major practical problem lies in the initial predominance of available reinforcement for the undesirable response, since resistance to the temptation to execute it has much lower and less immediate favorable consequences than engaging in a self-controlling alternative.

The process of self-control always involves the change of the probability of executing a response that has both rewarding and aversive consequences, and the selective initiation of a controlling response by a person even though the tempting response is available and more immediately rewarding. After repeated trials, the tempting response occurs again if the controlling response is blocked or the conditions change. If the tempting response no longer occurs, because its associated rewarding consequences have been reduced or the controlling response is now a well-established alternate response to the stimulating conditions, we no longer speak of a self-control situation. The process has been described by Skinner as one in which "an organism may make the punished response less probable by altering the variables of which it is a function. Any behavior which succeeds in doing this will automatically be reinforced. We call such behaviors self-control" (1953, p. 230). Skinner lists several methods for the exercise of self-control, all of which involve the manipulation of *controlling responses*. These are a set of responses that are characterized by a special relationship to the *controlled* response so that their execution makes the tempting behavior either impossible or less probable. Common examples of controlling responses are the application of a time-lock on a refrigerator to avoid between-meal snacks, or on a cigarette case to avoid excessive smoking, or the intentional failure to put money in one's pockets in order to avoid going on a shopping spree or to a tavern. Numerous other examples in everyday life illustrate the techniques by which prior manipulation of the subject's social, physical, or physiological environment accomplishes a reduction of the probability of the controlled response. Although genuine examples of self-control (since the person initiates the changes), these methods aid the person by shifting behavioral control to an environment so changed that the undesirable behavior is not as easily stimulated or maintained. The outstanding feature of these methods is the interruption of a behavioral sequence at an *early* stage, when the transitional probabilities from one link to the next are still low and alternate responses are more easily strengthened. For example, it is easier to avoid the entire sequence of drinking behaviors, in the absence of alcohol, prior to entry into a bar than after a drink is served.

A favorite social method of controlling temptation is based on the effects of punishment. The emotional concomitants of strong aversive stimulation are rearoused when a child finds himself in a situation in which he had previously been punished. Both the external cues and those arising from his own behavior generate aversive stimuli generally characterized as anxiety. If the emotional responses occur in the context of a transgression or of responses leading to commission of a previously punished act, they are called *guilt*. Any action that lowers the probability of executing the guilt-arousing behavior sequence thus serves as an escape response, and is reinforced by removing the child from the guilt situation. From the observer's point of view, the net effect is the child's failure to execute what appears as an attractive action. Strictly speaking, however, such training methods do not lead to "self"-control in the sense of our definition, since it is the aversive component of the controlled response which is directly altered to reduce its probability of occurrence. Only if the child initiates an independent and originally unrewarding response, or if he sets the occasion for the occurrence of the aversive stimulus, for example, by spanking his "bad, cookie-stealing" hand, or if he generates recall of aversive consequences, such as thinking of the terrible consequences, can one speak of self-control. Thus it is important to distinguish between the results of direct modification of the controlled response by aversive consequences, including withdrawal of positive reinforcement, and the case of self-control with interposition of a controlling response, *without* direct reduction of the attractiveness of the controlled response.

In addition to the controlling techniques mentioned so far, application of self-reinforcement and self-punishment in self-control can be used. The conceptualization of the role of these processes in self-control is even more problematic. In fact, as we have noted, two simple explanations could be advanced that dispense with a self-regulatory concept altogether and still seem to account for some instances of "self-control": (1) these are special cases in which a chain of responses is interrupted because an alternative (for example, a controlling response) is ultimately followed by greater positive reinforcement than the original sequence; or (2) the anticipatory anxiety responses associated with the aversive conditions (such as guilt) following execution of the original behavior chain, set the stage for an escape response (that is, any behavior changing the sequence). However, neither explanation makes clear how the individual can *actively* alter the course of his behavior, nor how such self-initiated behavior stands in relation to other variables. The problems of self-control and self-reinforcement are defined by the absence of any *current* external reinforcement contingencies, and by the person's *selective* manipulation of his

environment in counteracting the natural effects of external control.

Skinner's discussion of self-control deals primarily with the process by which a controlled response is reduced in frequency or is inhibited. A broader definition of self-control includes cases in which a response is maintained despite its noxious effects. Thus, at least two separate cases of self-control can be distinguished: (1) the case in which a highly valued event or reinforcing stimulus is available ad lib and the subject *fails* to execute the behavior; and (2) the case in which a behavior is *executed* despite its known aversive consequences. The first case is illustrated by situations commonly described under resistance to temptation; the second case includes situations in which pain, unpleasant stimulation, or similar events are tolerated even when an escape response is available. In human situations commonly considered to lie in the domain of self-control, the response to be controlled always has conflicting consequences. It is only when the controlled behavior has immediate positive reinforcing value and long-range aversive consequences (for example, in drinking or smoking), or when it has immediate aversive consequences but long-range positive effects (such as heroic acts, tolerance of pain), that any question at all arises whether the person is executing self-control.

Both cases—strengthening of the resistance to temptation or increasing tolerance of noxious stimulation—usually involve the provision of supplemental controlling variables to counteract the effect of the precurrent reinforcers. Generalized social reinforcement and self-descriptive statements with social reinforcing properties can be made contingent on the execution of self-control. Thereby some behaviors may be strengthened that, at first look, appear to be detrimental to the organism. The segment of behavior observed in these situations may seem to present an exception to the basic motivational assumption that organisms avoid pain and approach positive reinforcers. Neither in self-imposed failure to respond to positive reinforcers nor in tolerance of noxious stimuli can one expect the behavior to occur in the absence of strong additional variables; nor would such self-control be expected to endure very long when parameter values change so that the tempting behavior becomes more attractive or the controlling response weakens. For instance, a controlling response such as counting or doing exercises is likely to be of value only for a transitory temptation. If the situation is unchanged, a breakdown in self-control can be expected eventually, as fatigue or satiation weakens the controlling response. The stability of self-controlling behaviors therefore relates directly to situational variables and momentary fluctuations in the state of the organism and the environment. Such vernacular expressions as "every man has his price," or "everybody has a breaking point" seem to refer to this relative instability of self-control.

Ferster (1965) distinguishes three forms of self-control. The most widely encountered form is applied to performances that alter the relation between the individual's behavior and his environment so that ultimately aversive consequences to the person are reduced. The control of eating behavior in an obese person is an example of this first form. A second form of self-control involves the performance of behaviors that increase a person's long-range effectiveness, even when the consequences are long delayed or even immediately aversive. This type of self-control is exemplified by a person engaging in such educational activities as piano practice. A third form of self-control involves the alteration of the physical environment rather than of the person's own behavior. Hiding a whiskey bottle in a highly inaccessible place is an example of this form of self-control. In all three forms the person engages in behavior that has beneficial long-range consequences. Ferster's analysis suggests the importance of examining these consequences also in terms of optimizing the individual's relationship to the social and physical environment for the eventual obtainment of reinforcers available in a given cultural and physical setting. In other words, one underlying feature of all self-controlling behaviors seems to lie in their utility for a better adjustment to the cultural and social demands of the individual's environment. The vacillations encountered when a person initiates a program that may eventually require changes in the distribution of available reinforcers and in postponement of some, can often be observed in the behavior of making voluntary contact with a therapist. The arrangement of a definite appointment or a commitment to a husband or wife to seek therapy are some ways by which a patient makes therapeutic contact more probable. At the same time, active efforts may be made to obtain reassurance from friends who had seen psychotherapists, from reading in popular magazines, and other similar activities to reduce the aversiveness of therapy.

In several examples we have suggested that the beginning of a self-control program involves the temporary abandonment of immediate or near reinforcers for the sake of later and more important ones. The study of variables affecting the delay of reinforcement-consumption gratification) is thus relevant to the planned engineering of a self-control program. The factors that enable a person to delay gratification should also facilitate execution of self-control. In a series of experiments with children many of these determinants were explored by Mischel and Gilligan, 1964; Mischel and Metzner, 1962; and Mischel and Staub, 1965. Self-control was defined by the investigators as the ability to postpone gratification by choosing a delayed but larger reward over an immediate but smaller one. Variables such as a person's generalized expectancies of the reinforcement consequences following either choice, the subject's reinforcement history, situational manipulations, the reward value of the chosen item, and the duration of the temporal delay were among the factors that determined the experimental outcomes. These findings point to the value of widely practiced methods of altering the probability of immediate reward consummation by training, by promises of future rewards, or by modifying the desirability of the reward. This paradigm is useful in illustrating the *relative* nature of self-control; it suggests variables that a patient can use to alter management of his personal problems, under guidance of a therapist.

In the studies by Mischel and his co-workers the future delivery of rewards was controlled by the experimenter even though the child's choices were generally honored. The laboratory procedure resembled practical situations in which individuals postpone reward consumption for the sake of natural long-range consequences that are not completely under their control. A classic example is that of the disciplined money saver who foregoes immediate pleasures for the sake of later ones. However, the risk of such choices is obvious. The possibility of currency devaluation, depression, or robbery, or similar external interventions tends to weaken such "self-controlling" behaviors, as long as the ultimate consequences remain uncertain. Individuals who have had many experiences in which delayed rewards were forfeited or who have little trust in the credibility of their environment would thus be reluctant to work for delayed rewards or exert self-control for their sake.

Early manifestations of self-control are encouraged during childhood training by many parents, especially in American middle-class families. Developmental psychologists have often called attention to the frequent and continuing parental reinforcement of children's self-regulatory behavior during the child's early socialization training, especially in the case of nonexecution of responses. For example, in early toilet training or in training a child not to handle a fragile object, the consequences of inhibiting such behaviors often consist of the adult's administration of large measures of verbal approval, material rewards, and other reinforcements associated by words and actions to the child's controlling behavior.

As we noted in our discussion of the use of guilt to control socially undesirable but personally attractive behavior, common social practices lean heavily on aversive methods for development of resistance to temptation. The major goal of early socialization training, in fact, has been regarded by many to be the development of a conscience, or the internalization of social norms. Society highly prizes the inhibitions of many behaviors, such as aggressive or sexual transgressions, because these are difficult to enforce by continuing external controls. An extensive survey of research and theory related to mechanisms of socialization by Aronfreed (1968) reflects the centrality of this topic for understanding the transition of the infant to a social being. In turn, the survey indicates how various learning mechanisms, including vicarious learning, aversive and positive control of behavior, respondent conditioning, and self-reinforcement are brought into play in the child's socialization.

In turning next to consideration of the tolerance of noxious stimulation, we find that the critical requirement for a definition of self-control is the availability of responses that could avoid or escape the aversive stimulation. Since the cues for these antagonistic responses can be self-administered and their execution can be covert, an observer is often moved to conclude that the person's actions represent disciplined voluntary acts that defy natural behavioral principles. In fact, this conclusion is often based on an incomplete analysis of the controlling variables. In a demonstration of the effects of simple controlling responses on the tolerance of painful ice-water immersion of the hand, Kanfer and Goldfoot (1966) provided verbal responses or distractions by environmental objects to different groups of female students. Tolerance time was significantly affected by the availability of these controlling responses. The greatest tolerance was observed in subjects for whom external stimulation was provided. However, availability of verbal responses also altered tolerance. The study illustrates, in principle, the modifiability of self-controlling behavior by the mechanism

suggested in the behavioral analysis of this process.

The sufferance of noxious stimulation, (especially the apparent "voluntary" procurement of pain stimuli) has often been characterized as an example of abnormal behavior, because of its apparent contradiction of common motivational principles. There are many examples in the literature of situations in which both animals and men seem to seek out noxious stimulation. The relevance of these studies for an understanding of self-control lies, in the demonstration that time-limited observations of behaviors cannot serve as the sole basis for a behavior analysis. Sandler (1964) has reviewed a series of experiments in which characteristic responses to pain in animals were modified by experimental operations. Both Sandler (1964) and Brown (1965) conclude from their analyses of masochism that the disregard of other relevant variables, for example, change in the biological state of the organism, or the presence of some other contingencies in the organism's history, often leads to deceptively narrow definitions. In such situations momentary observations reflect only a fragment of the behavioral episode in which conflicting avoidant and approach responses have intricately related histories, determining their respective dominance at any point in time. Appeal to such concepts as masochism to name these behaviors serves to obscure rather than to explain the processes under observation. When the observer cannot describe a particular compelling set of concurrent controlling stimuli in the environment whose operation would account for the behavioral outcome, he is often tempted to conclude that his observations are inconsistent with a motivational principle. Observations of human behavior are the more baffling because the determinants of the observed behavior may be related to highly idiosyncratic antecedent factors of which the observer has little knowledge. But the multiple and complex series of determining events in a person's life history can be studied in laboratory demonstrations in which unusual outcomes of natural situations are replicated by selecting particular antecedents or combinations of training variables. The studies cited so far demonstrate that the ultimate origin of self-regulatory behaviors may lie in the social and biological environment of the person, but that the aggregate of an individual's experiences does shape a person who can, to some extent, influence his own behavior by deliberate alteration of influences to which he exposes himself. . . .

*Contract Management*

Many earlier writers have emphasized that a psychotherapeutic interaction requires the implicit or explicit agreement between patient and therapist about the conditions for treatment. Sulzer (1962) and Pratt and Tooley (1964) have described more explicitly the utility of a therapeutic contract in behavior modification techniques. In these procedures there is deliberate negotiation of contracts that demand specific behaviors of the patient and for whose successful achievement the therapist provides a predetermined reinforcement. The contracts constitute an agreement between the two parties that makes the behavior of each party contingent upon the behavior of the other and reciprocal exchanges of behavior are then defined in the contract. Although no research is

available at present concerning the processes underlying the contract, previously reviewed studies have already indicated the pragmatic utility of this procedure. The establishment of a contract may provide specific targets that the patient can aim for, and it clearly specifies the means and consequences of fulfilling the contract. It is probable that the general tendency of most members in our society to fulfill obligations that they have accepted in formal agreements with others enhances the motivational resources for the behavioral changes specified in the contract. Although contract management has certain similarities to the type of agreement an individual may make with himself in New Year's resolutions or with "good intentions," it has the added power of providing an opportunity to discuss methods for achieving desired results and establishing reinforcing consequences with another individual. In this sense, self-control is enhanced by the method of relinquishing partial control over one's behavior to another individual who acts so as to aid the person to establish controlling responses and who takes responsibility for administering contingent reinforcers. . . .

**Summary**

Training methods for helping a person control his own behavior have been applied only recently in behavior therapy. Nevertheless, they represent a series of techniques that can be used to extend behavior therapy to new problems, especially with patients whose behavior is sufficiently intact to permit their cooperation and whose environment is not easily controlled.

In conceptualizing the process of self-regulation, the assumption is made that self-attitudes, self-evaluations, and self-reinforcement originate in the selective reinforcement of the child's self-related behaviors by his social environment. Eventually, a pattern of such reactions is established for different behavior segments by imitation and by contingency learning. For convenience, these functionally related response patterns have been characterized as the self-system.

The process of self-control has been described as one in which a person alters the probability of occurrence of a behavior by changing the variables that have controlled its occurrence in the past. The most common self-controlling methods are those in which the person initiates a shift in stimulus control from one feature of the environment to another, originates a competing response, or provides reinforcement for any controlling response. Self-control includes two types of situations: (1) a highly valued event or reinforcing stimulus is available and a person fails to execute behaviors that would bring the event or object within reach; and (2) a person continues to tolerate aversive stimulation and fails to make available avoidance or escape responses. The target behavior for self-control always has conflicting consequences (positive and negative), with nearly equal potential for maintaining an approach or avoidance response.

We have noted that training to tolerate delay of reinforcement represents one facet of a self-control program. Numerous other self-control programs are available and include increase in reinforcement for controlling responses, deliberate alteration of environmental controlling stimuli early in the behavior sequence (when the probability of making the target response is still fairly low), utiliza-

tion of self-reinforcement for nonexecution of the target response, execution of incompatible behaviors, removal of the physical stimuli serving as $S^D$ for the undesired response, and similar strategies.

Since self-control eventually occurs in the absence of external support, self-reinforcement is an important feature in this procedure. The determinants of self-reinforcement, its motivational properties, and the conditions for learning its schedule of dispensation have been examined in a series of studies on self-reinforcement. Three major laboratory paradigms have been used for the investigation of this process: (1) The directed learning model for the study of variables affecting the rate of self-reinforcing responses; (2) the vicarious learning paradigm for examination of modeling effects; and (3) the temptation model for the study of variables affecting self-administration of rewards, contrary to social sanction. The accumulated studies have demonstrated the modifiability of self-rewards and self-punishments by a host of variables. They have also suggested that these self-administered operations can maintain behavior, that is, have some motivational properties.

In the clinic, self-control procedures can be taught directly by instructing the patient in general learning principles and by helping the patient to arrange programs that reduce the undesirable behaviors gradually. Control of smoking behavior, excessive eating, inability to study, and similar problems have been treated in this way. In *covert sensitization,* the patient is trained to present himself with imaginal aversive stimuli just as he approaches temptation to execute the undesired behavior. In *contingency management,* the person is taught to make covert verbal responses that are incompatible with the undesirable target behavior. Contingency self-management can also be executed by a patient when he makes positive covert statements just prior to highly probable behaviors, thus increasing the strength of these positive behaviors in his repertoire. Changes in stimulus control have been used therapeutically, by gradually narrowing the conditions under which a symptomatic behavior is permitted to occur. The use of self-administered shock and self-reinforcement for accomplishing each step in a hierarchy (arranged in order of difficulty for execution) has also been reported.

Clinical and research evidence suggest that even attending to one's behavior in a systematic way, as frequently demanded by a behavior therapist for record keeping, may have beneficial therapeutic effects. Other authors have reported the advantages of an explicit agreement between patient and therapist about the conditions for treatment, a method termed *contract management*. In this approach the behavior of each party is contingent upon the behavior of the other and the reciprocal exchange of behaviors is defined in the contract. The advent of recent audio and video devices has fostered the therapeutic utilization of objective feedback to the patient about his own behavior in *self-confrontation* techniques.

The introduction of self-regulatory techniques into the storehouse of behavior therapies is of special importance, since the earliest and most successful methods of behavior therapy have relied almost exclusively on control of the patient's treatment environment. This extension demonstrates the attempts to extend behavior therapy to a wide range of problems. Theoretical issues concerning the conceptualization of behaviors in which the person may be both object and subject of the behavior have not yet been resolved. However, these techniques have brought sharply into focus the problems and potentials of a behavioristic theory for dealing with those inaccessible, private experiences which early behaviorism had attempted to rule out of psychology.

## References

ARONFREED, J. *Conduct and conscience: The socialization of internalized control over behavior.* New York: Academic Press, 1968.

BROWN, J. S. A behavioral analysis of masochism. *Journal of Experimental Research in Personality,* 1956, **1**, 65–70.

FERSTER, C. B. Classification of behavioral pathology. In L. Krasner & L. P. Ullmann (Eds.), *Research in behavior modification.* New York: Holt, Rinehart & Winston, 1965.

KANFER, F. H., & GOLDFOOT, D. A. Self-control and tolerance of noxious stimulation. *Psychological Reprints,* 1966, **18**, 79–85.

MISCHEL, W., & GILLIGAN, C. Delay of gratification, motivation for the prohibited gratification, and responses to temptation. *Journal of Abnormal and Social Psychology,* 1964, **69**, 411–417.

MISCHEL, W., & METZNER, R. Preference for delayed reward as a function of age, intelligence, and length of delay interval. *Journal of Abnormal and Social Psychology,* 1962, **64**, 425–431.

MISCHEL, W., & STAUB, E. The effects of expectancy on working and waiting for larger rewards. *Journal of Personality and Social Psychology,* 1965, **2**, 625–633.

PRATT, S., & TOOLEY, J. Contract psychology and the actualizing transactional-field. *International Journal of Social Psychiatry,* 1964. Congress issue, 51–69.

SANDLER, J. Masochism: An empirical analysis. *Psychological Bulletin,* 1964, **62,** 197–204.

SKINNER, B. F. *Science and human behavior.* New York: Macmillan, 1953.

SULZER, E. S. Reinforcement and therapeutic contract. *Journal of the Consulting and Clinical Psychologist,* 1962, **9,** 271–276.

# 38

# Some additional conceptualizations

*by Frederick H. Kanfer*
*and Paul Karoly*

Behavior modification in the early seventies appears to be moving away from peripheralistic, "open-loop" conceptions of human behavior. Theorists and investigators are increasingly turning their attention to the variance contributed by man's unique response capabilities, typically summarized under the labels of *language, cognition,* or *self-processes* (see, for example, Bandura, 1969; Cautela, 1970; Kanfer, 1970, 1971; Kanfer & Phillips, 1970; Lazarus, 1971; Marston & Feldman, 1970; Murray & Jacobson, 1970). In psychotherapy there is a growing search for techniques by which the individual can assume major responsibility for effecting response changes, for only if the patient himself can master the control over his own behavior and over his environment can we expect therapy to have enduring effects and to prepare him for initiating preventive or therapeutic actions under new and unforeseen circumstances. If we can identify *Zeitgeist* while in its midst, we might point out that the changes within behavioral psychology are but a reflection of a general relaxation of social and

This paper, prepared especially for the present volume, was supported, in part, by Research Grant MH 17902–02 from the National Institute of Mental Health, U.S. Public Health Service, to Frederick H. Kanfer.

institutional pressures for conformity or standardization of conduct, and the emergence of a "Do your own thing" ethic that runs counter to formal (and informal) normative control over individual action. Thus, we are faced with the paradox that, while we may accept the controlling influence of the social environment over behavior (which strict behaviorists would have us do), the breakdown of external governance and its structural permanence requires greater continuity and responsibility on the part of the individual.

The present paper is an attempt to outline a developing theoretical view of the process by which people effect changes in established (habitual) patterns of behavior. Several techniques of *instigation* therapy have been proposed that attempt to integrate external (therapist) control with the patient's private or covert response capabilities (Kanfer & Phillips, 1970), and these continue to receive clinical support and conceptual attention (see, for example, Mahoney, 1970; McFall, 1970). However, a systematic overview of the pivotal behavioral process in this treatment approach, the *self-control sequence,* has not yet been offered by behavior therapists. We plan, therefore, to propose some ideas that would lay the groundwork for a functional analysis of the social setting in human affairs within which self-control and related processes are usually embedded. To date, this area has been examined primarily from a philosophical and moral point of view. The psychiatric orientation has generally been purely descriptive or intrapsychic, with self-control equated with ego strength, superego development, and similar nonempirical, unitary-trait conceptions (Klausner, 1965; Mischel, 1971). In contrast, the model presented here has been formulated to permit tests of its utility via experimentation. The reader will discern the elements and underlying rationale for the present position in the preceding review by Kanfer and Phillips (pp. 417–427 of this volume).

## Self-Control and Self-Regulation

We begin with the assertion that self-control *as a process* (superordinate to the various mechanisms of which it is comprised) can best be viewed as a special case of self-regulation. As Kanfer has stated:

> While self-regulatory behaviors generally result in some modification of one's own behavior or of the environmental setting, self-control is characterized as a special case in which there is some underlying motive for *nonexecution* of a response sequence which, under other circumstances, would be predicted to have a high probability of occurrence. Self-control always involves a situation in which there is potentiality of execution of highly probable behaviors, but instead a response of lower probability occurs. The interest is in the variables which effect the reduction of the occurrence of the probabilities of such behaviors (1970, pp. 214–215).

Recently, a more specific componential analysis of the regulatory process has been offered (Kanfer, 1971). A brief look at this model will aid the present explication.

When conditions are such that behavior chains are not run off smoothly, for example, when a choice point is reached, when an external event interrupts and refocuses one's attention, when one's activation level changes or when

the expected consequences of behavior are not forthcoming, then a process of *self-monitoring* is hypothesized to go into effect. Utilizing the input from the external environment and from response-reduced cues (both modified by the individual's social learning history), the person is in a position to *self-evaluate*, that is, to make a discrimination or judgment by comparing the data from the various input sources with a subjectively held *performance standard* (criterion). If the outcome of the comparison is favorable (that is, if the individual judges that he has exceeded the standard level), a positive *self-reinforcement* (SR+) is the result. If the outcome is unfavorable, negative consequences (self-presented aversive stimulation, SR−) ensue. The sequence may, thus, be illustrated:

$$\text{self-monitoring}\longrightarrow$$
$$\text{self-evaluation}\longrightarrow$$
$$\text{self-reinforcement}$$

An S-R analysis of self-regulation focuses on the maintenance of behavior chains in the absence of external support, emphasizing the key role of self-reactions.[1] The goal of self-control, on the other hand, is a change in the probability of executing a final response in a chain. It involves the introduction, by the individual, of techniques designed to insure the nonoccurrence of the terminal link [or the occurrence of a response with initially low probability]. That which unites self-control and the process of self-regulation is the identity of the component mechanisms, with the exception of the performance standard.

[1] Research in each of these areas has been accumulating at a rapid pace; thus the review by Kanfer and Phillips (pp. 417–427 of this volume) is only partially up-to-date.

In self-control situations, the standard (usually based on norms or past experiences) is provided by a kind of *performance promise* or *contract* made by the example, "No more than five cigarettes a day, so help me!"), or in interaction with another person (such as a parent, spouse, or therapist). The antecedents of self-control lie in the discrepancy between self-observation and the performance promise, followed by potential self-reinforcement operations aimed at reducing this discrepancy. Verbal or motoric, the self-reinforcing event is always self-initiated and made contingent upon a self-prescribed (or therapist-prescribed) contract for behavior change.

It has been suggested that the standard (contract or promise) in therapy has utility in directing the change process. We will examine next the factors associated with the directive function of contracts over the execution of desired behaviors.

## Social Contracts and Negotiations

The view that man behaves in accordance with written and unwritten social rules is not new. However, the study of cultural and situational parameters that influence the form and direction of individual behavior has been pursued more rigorously by sociologists and social psychologists than by personality theorists. Working from a developmental perspective, investigators in the area of socialization have defined the shift of control from socializing agents to individuals (internalization of rules, moral development) as the most important social learning event of childhood. Sociologists have viewed the social contract as the sine qua non of organized society.

And, on a different level, economists depict the process of exchange of goods and services as resting on a foundation of contractual order and rational bargaining. Philosophers have expended much energy in the analysis of man's "nature" as a rule-forming, rule-following, and rule-breaking creature, while adding some rule of their own about man's proper rational and logical behavior. And, finally, we might note that the interpretation and enforcement of legal contracts and agreements (including the aversive consequences for failure to fulfill them) constitute a large share of the practice of law and penology.

Approaching self-control as a process that includes contract negotiation (with oneself or others), the behavioral psychologist must turn his attention, first, to defining the terms ("What is a contract, promise, or statement of intention?"), performing a functional analysis ("Under what conditions are intentions stated, and what maintains them?"), and relating his concepts to the larger theoretical network ("How and when do intentions or promises or so-called therapeutic contracts lead to the actual execution of self-controlling behavior?").

## The Contract

Basically, a contract is an agreement that describes particular behaviors that must be engaged in by the contractors, under specific conditions. Typically, some mode of enforcement is provided. Nonfulfillment of the terms of the contract is clearly identifiable and the imposition of sanctions (consequences) is agreed upon in advance. A contract provides one means of social monitoring that clearly incorporates the elements of discriminative and contingency control. Our lives are fraught with situations of a contractual nature, varying in specificity and controlling power for enforcement (for example, employer-employee, buyer-seller, teacher-pupil, parent-child, and, most relevant for the current argument, therapist-client).

The concept of a therapeutic contract is basic to analytic thinking (Freud, 1913; Menninger, 1958). It has also been proposed by theorists of a behavioral persuasion (see, for example, Pratt & Tooley, 1964; Sulzer, 1962). A distinguishing feature of the behavior therapy contract is its specificity, including the specification of controlling devices, in contrast to the vague, almost mystic nature of the psychoanalytic contract. Regardless of the therapist's theoretical orientation or the symptomatic behavior under consideration, a working arrangement between the therapist and client as regards the nature, place, manner, frequency, timing, and range of intervention steps to be taken by both parties generally facilitates achievement of treatment goals. However, in the light of the present theoretical framework, the contract takes on a different and unique coloration. The intention statement or performance promise (used here synonymously), as a variant of the performance standard, is a central construct in the system of propositions applied to the understanding of self-control in humans. When brought into the therapy room, the intention (now developing into a "contract") is no less a basic ingredient in an SR analysis of behavior change, although it is now enmeshed in a highly complex social setting. Remaining within our model, then, we ask, "What are the relevant antecedents of intention statements?", "Under what conditions are they made and maintained?", and, following Kanfer and Saslow (1965), "Can the patient match his behavior to his intentions?" The remainder of this paper will be devoted to suggesting some tentative answers to these questions.

## Intention Statements as Verbal Operants

Intention statements may be looked upon as a class of verbal operants which specify behavioral outcomes. When applied by an individual to himself, these verbal behaviors are often termed *intentions, plans, predictions, promises,* or *resolutions.*" They parallel the class of responses called *contracts* and *agreements* when they are made in the presence of other people. These operants serve a specific role in the verbal community, approximating what Skinner (1957) calls *autoclitics.* That is, they are descriptive of the speaker, indicating something of his condition, a property of his behavior, or the circumstances responsible for that property ("qualifying" autoclitics). In extended interactions, autoclitics are useful to the listener and to the speaker (as a listener) in improving behavior predictions. Intention statements, related to self-control situations, are made because they permit the individual to "edit" or monitor his behavior more effectively in the context of new information about himself, and allow him to decide what action, if any, need be taken. "I am going to give up tobacco!" is a declaration of intent that follows from the informational input. "People younger than I are dying from lung cancer every day. And cigarettes cause lung cancer." Casting the same process in somewhat moralistic terms, Premack (1970) has described the cigarette smoker as ready to quit when he discovers his membership in "an ethically repugnant class," such as weak-willed, setting a bad example, or the like. At this point the smoker decides to exert self-control. Thus, Premack regards the main antecedents of self-control as the presentation of information about oneself that is strongly discrepant with the person's avowed self-image. In our view, the class of antecedents are much more varied and can include external as well as self-generated prescriptions for achieving a desired end-state.

It is important to keep in mind that, regardless of the conceptualization about the determinants of the stated intent, the statement is itself a behavior that can be the terminal link of the chain leading to a declaration. Or, it may be an instructional cue for execution of the intent. Thus, these verbal operants do not always constitute components of a self-control sequence. Even if they are originally a part of the behavior chain leading to execution, they may not continue to function as such. Therefore, let us examine more closely the variables that affect the making of an intention statement. The first group will cover factors that serve to increase the probability of the occurrence of verbal intention statements. A second set of variables will be discussed that can effect decreases in the frequency of emission of these behaviors. It is clear that in any situation combinations of these influences will determine the net effect.

## What Promotes Intention Statements?

The probability of emitting a verbal operant of the intention or contract class is presumed to be high under the following conditions:

1. When the individual responds to cues in his environment (external or internal) that signal the conflictual nature of his current behavior pattern. According to our model, this behavior is an invariant early component of the self-control sequence. A person may reach for a cigarette and be interrupted by a television commercial of the American Cancer Society; or a heavy drinker may be reminded, en route to his favorite tavern, of a friend who has recently died of an ailment aggravated by alcohol consumption.

2. When the person is suffering from the aversive effects of the behavior to be controlled. Examples are the smoker during a coughing fit and the drinker in the throes of a hangover.

3. When the person is either satiated with respect to the undesirable behavior or when, for other reasons, the probability of making that response is low. Examples might be the obese person immediately after eating, a homosexual after several exhausting encounters, or a lover who has been jilted by his sweetheart.

4. When the probability of social approval for making intention statements is high. This might be the case when others are talking about their good intentions or when the verbal operant is also an $S^D$ for reinforcement from another person (a hidden *mand*), like the promise of a lover, during lovemaking, to quit carousing or the promise of a child, just prior to getting his dessert, not to hit his little sister.

5. When the intention statement is made to a person who is unlikely or unable to monitor (verify) the final

execution of the controlling behavior. An example would be a promise about behavior that is to take place in another location or about behavior that is not normally accessible (public). A vow made in church to put an end to "evil" thoughts represents such an instance.

6. When the behavior to be controlled is infrequent or if execution is intended in the distant future. "I swear I'll never get drunk at another Christmas party at the office!" is an oft-heard example of this condition.

7. When the intention statement produces negative reinforcement or the contingent removal of some aversive stimulus. Examples would be the morning newspaper reader who promises to pay more attention to his wife in order to put an end to her nagging or the sibling in a headlock vowing not to "borrow" his brother's toys.

8. When the person's reinforcement history for intention statements has generally been positive and has been accompanied by the desired short-term outcome. The parent who forgives and forgets when his child vows never again to invite friends to their home without permission or when the child promises to study harder illustrates the way in which histories for "empty promises" are built up by reinforcement—often in the form of escape from aversive consequences.

An individual's history also interacts with any of the above conditions to influence the probability of verbal intention operants. And, even in the absence of any of the above setting characteristics, a person with a positive history of

emitting intention statements would tend to show a relatively high probability of employing them.

At the same time, our analysis suggests several conditions that would lower the probability of verbal intention operants. These factors are of interest for an understanding of the conditions that reduce the requirement for a self-control sequence, since failure to make the initial intention statement obviates the progression of the response chain leading to controlling behavior. For example, the smoker or drinker who has *never* stated (to himself or others) the intention to quit, although behaving in ways that are topographically similar to the conflictual behavior of many smokers and drinkers, cannot be said to display a lack or failure of self-control. His behavior is simply not in the domain of responses that we have defined as self-control. Let us now look at those situations that produce decrements in the probability of emission of intention operants. These include settings in which:

1. The probability of social disapproval for intention statements of a specific sort is high. This is the case when significant others disagree with the proposed goals. Parents may disagree with their daughter's plan to go on a crash diet, for example, or parents may punish any declaration of independence, autonomy, or self-reliance made by their child.

2. The probability of execution of the controlling response is generally *known* to be low. A common example is the decreasing frequency with which growing children make intention statements concerning physical feats that border on the impossible. However, when one moves

into a new environment, in which knowledge about the feasibility of a particular behavior is different, then the probability of making the intention statement again varies.

3. The general expectancy for ultimate reinforcement for executing the controlling response is low. If one were going to be in the company of total strangers or uninterested individuals for a long while, then exerting control over a chronically conflictual behavior (drinking, smoking, eating, gambling, and so on) would not elicit the hoped for social support and approval.

4. The person has a history of prior unsuccessful executions and has experienced aversive consequences during his attempts at change. Examples might be a smoker who, during withdrawal from cigarettes, becomes irritable and jeopardizes his job or long-standing friendships or a patient who has been unsuccessful in changing after several therapy experiences.

5. A considerable social punishment is attached to the eventual nonfulfillment (nonexecution) of the intent. An example would be the signing of a formal contract to buy a home (in this case cash deposits are used to further deter the likelihood of nonexecution). Engagement and marriage are the result of intention statements with well-known (fabled?) aversive consequences associated with the failure to "love, honor, and obey."

Verbal intention operants can be separated into two broad types. They can be either *overt*, made in the presence of an audience (and thus subject to social reinforcement and public monitoring), or *covert*, emitted to oneself (vocally or subvocally). The latter type would be expected to be subject to the same discrimination process (self-evaluation) and the same contingencies of reward and punishment. However, intention statements made privately should generally be less reliable, since no *social* consequences for nonfulfillment need be feared. Public commitment is, therefore, a highly desirable step (as is evidenced by the apparent success of groups like "Weight Watchers" and "Alcoholics Anonymous").

### Executing Contract-Fulfilling Behaviors

If we view the *intention-execution* sequence along a time line (from $T_0$, the initial making of the intention operant, $T_{N-X}$, the first execution of the controlling response, to $T_N$, the final period when the controlling response is no longer required to produce the desired end-state), it becomes clear that some immediate consequences (payoff) of intention statements or of first attempts at execution can serve to undermine the progress of the entire sequence. Getting the person to "stick to the bargain" is a crucial problem in self-control technology, and one that has scarcely been touched (Mahoney, 1970). Our own experience and reports from other clinicians attest to the ubiquity of the self-defeating (and client-defeating) tendency of people to provide social rewards for statements of intentions to change. The probability of an individual reaching $T_N$ is, partly, a function of the clinician's or the listener's ability to refrain from "locking" him in at $T_0$ with undeserved approval for what is, at that stage, merely a verbal response. Like any behavior that is immediately rewarded, intention operants will be maintained by the "audience" effect. But they will have little value in cueing later responses in a sequence which, after all, is directed toward controlling target behavior already under strong positive reinforcement. A similar fate can be expected when a person who has been rewarded for promises not followed by execution now rewards himself for the mere intention. Given the common social practice of rewarding plans or promises per se and an individual's history of partial reinforcement for such behaviors, the making of intention statements represents a class of operants that should be highly resistant to extinction. Ideally, then, intention operants made early in the change program might best be followed by mild aversive stimuli, with positive reinforcement reserved for sustained execution of self-control.

The probability of initiating behavior that leads to fulfillment of the contract, or the exercise of self-control, can be viewed as a function of the following additional variables:

1.  The explicitness or clarity of the contract. A contract with high execution potential is one that specifies the desired outcome in detail, provides the individual with performance standings against which to judge progress, sets time limits for achieving $T_{N-x}$ and then $T_x$ in the not too distant future, clearly delineates the consequences (especially the ultimate positive outcome of self-control), and outlines the steps and methods for the achievement of the desired goal.

2.  The "mutuality" of control in the therapy or helping relationship. When working in the area of self-control there is, perhaps, a tendency to underplay the importance of external (social) control. It is frequently necessary for the therapist to exert control initially in order to insure that his client achieves the goal of self-mediated behavior change. It is especially important that the therapist be able to uphold his "end" of the contract.

3.  The individual's skill and experience in engaging in the instrumental responses necessary for execution. When therapy includes training in specific techniques of self-control, the nature of training, the effectiveness of the mechanisms employed, and partial success in initial attempts will influence the chances of successful self-control. As the person's behavior changes, the environment must "cooperate" to the extent that stimulus conditions and potential reinforcement contingent upon execution of the undesirable behaviors are altered.

4.  The continuous use of self-monitoring that relates execution behavior to the changes in the undesirable behavior. Obviously, inadequate feedback at this stage can undermine programmatic efforts directed at behavioral change.

5.  The persistence of the aversive consequences of the undesirable behavior beyond the time at which the intention statement is made. If the intention statement alone alleviates aversive consequences, the behavior no longer has conflictful outcomes and self-control is not needed. The common assertion that a person is

trying and promises to try even harder often achieves this reduction of aversive social consequences.

6. Past experience as a basis for the expectation of success or failure of a self-control program. For example, undertaking a successful reducing program often leads people to take steps toward instigating changes in other areas of behavior.

7. The consequences of the comparison by the individual with his desired behavioral goal still differs from feedback from his current behavior. Clearly the discrepancy should have an aversive effect, if the program of self-control is to continue to the point of ultimate elimination of the undesirable response. In this regard, Premack (1970) has argued that an emotional component accompanies any decision to change. If, over time, the emotion is reduced, the probability of final execution is diminished. In clinical settings, unlike experiments, goals cannot be viewed as absolute or constant, but must be continually reevaluated in the light of the changing organism.

## Summary

The preceding section attempts an analysis of the factors contributing toward the making of an intention statement (contract), and the relationship of this response class to the execution of the behaviors specified in the intention. It is proposed that a *social contract model* has heuristic value for the conceptualization and analysis of the determinants of self-directed behaviors, both in therapy and in the fulfillment of self-initiated behavioral change. A special case, related to self-control, is one in which the contract is not negotiated between two persons, but by one person in interaction with himself. This situation reflects the self-generation of standards for behavior, upon which reinforcement is contingent.

The importance of timing and the nature of reinforcement during the sequence of behaviors from commitment to execution was also discussed. Implications are noted for maximizing the probability of execution of a stated response by appropriate clinical techniques. The analysis has led to outlining a series of factors whose influence on self-control is plausible but needs to be verified by experimentation. The central feature of this is an attempt to clarify further the process of self-control by examining the role of intentions as necessary precursors of initiation of self-control.

## References

BANDURA, A. *Principles of behavior modification.* New York: Holt, Rinehart and Winston, 1969.

CAUTELA, J. R. Covert reinforcement. *Behavior Therapy*, 1970, **1**, 33–50.

FREUD, S. Further recommendations in the technique of analysis (1913). Reprinted in P. Rieff (Ed.), *Freud: Theory and technique.* New York: Collier Books, 1963.

KANFER, F. H. Self-regulation: Research, issues, and speculations. In C. Neuringer & J. L. Michael (Eds.), *Behavior modification and clinical psychology.* New York: Appleton-Century-Crofts, 1970.

KANFER, F. H. The maintenance of behavior by self-generated stimuli and reinforcement. In A. Jacobs & L. Sachs (Eds.), *The psychology of private events.* New York: Academic Press, 1971.

KANFER, F. H., & PHILLIPS, J. S. *Learning foundations of behavior therapy.* New York: Wiley, 1970.

KANFER, F. H., & SASLOW, G. Behavioral

analysis: An alternative to diagnostic classification. *Archives of General Psychiatry*, 1965, **12**, 529–538.

KLAUSNER, S. Z. (Ed.) *The quest for self-control*. New York: Free Press, 1965.

LAZARUS, A. *Behavior therapy and beyond*. New York: McGraw-Hill, 1971.

MAHONEY, J. J. Toward an experimental analysis of coverant control. *Behavior Therapy*, 1970, **1**, 510–521.

MARSTON, A. R., & FELDMAN, S. Toward the use of self-control in behavior modification. Paper presented at the convention of the American Psychological Association, Miami Beach, 1970.

McFALL, R. M. Effect of self-monitoring on normal smoking behavior. *Journal of the Counseling and Clinical Psychologist*, 1970, **35**, 135–142.

MENNINGER, K. *Theory of psychoanalytic technique*. New York: Harper, 1958.

MISCHEL, W. *Introduction to personality*. New York: Holt, Rinehart and Winston, 1971.

MURRAY, E. J., & JACOBSON, L. I. The nature of learning in traditional and behavioral psychotherapy. In A. E. Bergin & S. L. Garfield (Eds.), *Handbook of psychotherapy and behavior change*. New York: Wiley, 1970.

PRATT, S., & TOOLEY, J. Contract psychology and the actualizing transactional-field. *International Journal of Social Psychiatry*, 1964, Congress issue, 51–69.

PREMACK, D. Mechanisms of self-control. In W. Hunt (Ed.), *Learning mechanisms of control in smoking*. Chicago: Aldine, 1970.

SKINNER, B. F. *Verbal behavior*. New York: Appleton-Century-Crofts, 1957.

SULZER, E. S. Reinforcement and therapeutic contract. *Journal of the Consulting and Clinical Psychologist*, 1962, **9**, 271–276.

# Conclusion

The overall conclusion that may be drawn from the papers in this volume is that the groundwork has been laid for pursuing a theory of conscience development. Behavioral scientists have operationally defined conscience in various ways. They have explored the generality of conscience and have developed a number of testable ideas concerning the antecedents and correlates of conscience. There is some understanding of the behavioral consequents (such as behavior disorders) of various forms of conscience development. Table 1 outlines the facets of conscience research as we know them today.

A number of questions remain. Perhaps the first, in order of priority, is to determine the number of significant dimensions involved in inner controls. It seems relatively well established that resistance to temptation and guilt following yielding are both key aspects of conscience, but that they are only minimally related to one another. Another important dimension might include individual responses to situations involving violations of personal confidence or trust versus those involving violations of laws or mores. Just as Hartshorne and May concerned themselves with aspects of honesty (lying, stealing, cheating), so also might one compare individual responses to situations involving antisocial aggression, honesty, and other separate aspects of social morality. And, as mentioned in the introduction to the section on generality, a multitrait, multimethod matrix study of the various domains of conscience is in order.

A second question, now being attacked along a number of different lines, involves the relation of the strength of various aspects of inner control to adjustment and to mental health. Finally, important questions are arising from learning-theory approaches to conscience development. For example, one might investigate the relation of punishment to the development of guilt and of shame, since it is now known that punishment is far more effective in producing passive than active avoidance learning and that different proportions of the two kinds of avoidance learning may well be involved in the production of guilt as opposed to shame.

Gabriel said to Jehovah in *The Green Pastures*, "Everything that we nailed down [on Earth] has started to come loose." Maybe the "coming loose" process in the human drama of our time is what has spurred social scientists to discover more about the origins, measurement, and behavioral correlates of conscience.

A part of the "coming loose," that is, the state of confusion and ferment in the realm of human morality and ethics, has been delineated in the foregoing paragraphs. In the last section of this book yet another line of change and reconstruction is discussed, albeit in a preliminary way, because it is still so new, exploratory, and incompletely developed. We refer to the widespread and growing rejection of moral absolutism and autocratic authority (which have been associated with a built-in, gyroscopic type of conscience) and increasing interest in and acceptance of "contract psychology," which is far more democratic, egalitarian, and negotiable. The *content* of a contract may be feasible or foolish. In a "free society" (one with many "cultural alternatives"), it is possible for individuals to experiment with many different interpersonal arrangements or relationships (in respect to friendship, sex, recreation, business, and so forth). Once the situation has been defined and the agreement or commitment made, however, there is great urgency upon the "contracting parties" (for their own long-term best interests, as well as those of others) to "keep their word." Unilateral abrogation of a contract (especially if secret) is seen as both psychologically and socially disintegrative. In this context,

*Table 1*

**Variables in Conscience Development**

| Antecedents or correlates of conscience | Dimensions of conscience | Consequences and/or correlates of differing conscience development |
|---|---|---|
| Time perspective (Long perspective positively related to high-level conscience development) | Guilt vs. shame | Neuroticism vs. normality |
| Ability to delay gratification (High ability to delay positively related to high-level conscience development) | Affective vs. cognitive dimensions of conscience | *Crime and delinquency vs. absence of same |
| Belief in internal as opposed to external control of reinforcement | Cognitive vs. behavioral dimensions of conscience | Cheating vs. honesty |
| Timing of punishment (Resistance to temptation and guilt following yielding differ in origins) | Affective vs. behavioral dimensions of conscience | |
| Type of punishment (Data equivocal: suggest psychological punishment to be more effective in producing high-level conscience at older ages (e.g., age 9+); most recent data emphasizes importance of induction) | Resistance to temptation vs. guilt following yielding | |
| Family structure (Nuclear family produces strongest inner controls) | *Concern for violation of mores and laws vs. violation of confidence and trust | |
| Father presence vs. absence (Presence related to resistance to temptation and ability to delay gratification) | *Response to different kinds of antisocial behavior (e.g., unjustified aggression vs. theft) | |

* These variables have not yet been investigated.

"therapy" consists of acknowledgment of the breach of faith, restitution, and re-affirmation, renegotiation, or dissolution of the contract.

Obviously, a great deal in contract psychology is congruent with the traditional conception of conscience and with the results of the research reviewed in the earlier sections of this volume. But there are also some salient differences. Whether these differences are simply misapprehensions which will soon lose their credibility or are the foundation for a new and stable guide to ethical theory and practice remains to be determined by future experience.

# AUTHOR INDEX

Carmichael, L., 96, 123
Caruso, I., 323, 337
Casriel, D., 38
Cattell, R. B., 88, 95
Cautela, J. R., 428, 436
Chandler, P. J., 293, 297
Chasdi, E. H., 330, 331, 337
Child, I. L., 3, 4, 152, 157, 158, 239, 241, 243, 244, 245, 246–258, 263, 270, 276, 308, 330, 339, 345
Christenson, J. A., Jr., 86, 95
Church, R. M., 264, 274, 277, 283, 290
Clapp, P., 380
Clark, R. A., 292, 297
Clebsch, W. A., 368–370
Clemens, S., 1, 14–24, 25, 27–35, 38
Coe, 102
Cohn, F., 236, 237
Cole, R., 393
Coles, M. R., 264, 276
Conrad, J., 1
Cook, S. W., 79, 95
Copernicus, N., 11
Crandall, V. J., 292, 296, 297
Crissman, P., 88, 95
Crowley, P. M., 3, 4, 299, 301–307

**D**

Dabrowski, K., 359, 362, 366, 370
Darby, C. L., 265, 274
Darwin, C. R., 1
Davenport, P., 246
Davidson, K. S., 293, 297
Davis, A., 89, 96, 251, 258
Davis, W. A., 261, 270, 274
Deese, J., 302, 307
Deitch, D., 36, 37
Dennis, W., 323–325, 337, 410
Denny, R., 207
Dent, H., 393
Descoeudres, Mlle., 47, 49
Dinsmoor, J. A., 268, 275
Distler, L., 346
Dokecki, P. R., v, ix, 4, 348, 402–410
Dollard, J., 251, 258, 263–265, 272, 275, 351, 359, 370
Dombrose, L. A., 91, 95

Dostoevsky, F. M., 1
Drakeford, J. W., 356, 370
Dreikurs, R., ix, 416
Dukes, W. F., 261, 263, 275
Duncan, C. P., 265, 275
Dunnett, 312, 314, 315
Durkheim, E., 1, 41, 42, 55, 134
Durkin, D., 120, 121, 123, 125, 129, 302, 307, 323–327, 333, 337

**E**

Eaton, J. W., 291, 297
Edmonson, M. S., 250, 251, 258
Ehrmann, W., 373, 375–377, 379
Erikson, E. H., 407, 408
Eron, L. D., 346
Eysenck, H. J., 351, 370, 398, 401
Eysenck, S. B. G., 116, 123, 398, 401

**F**

Faigin, H., 241, 245, 330, 337
Fauconnet, P., 1, 41, 42, 134
Feffer, M., 407, 408
Felix, R. H., 367, 370
Feldman, M. J., 39, 371, 410
Feldman, S., 428, 437
Fenichel, O., 253, 258
Fernald, G. G., 49, 81, 85, 95
Ferster, C. B., 421, 426
Fionda, A. J., 4, 5, 99, 348, 393–401, 404, 406, 409
Fiore, Q., viii
Fiske, D. W., 119, 123
Flavell, J. H., 301, 307
Fletcher, J., viii
Fliess, R., 165
Flugel, J. C., 95
Foran, T. G., 1
Forbes, G. M., 26, 39
Fortes, M., 181
Fortune, R. F., 180
Frank, H., 4, 5, 99, 348, 393–401, 404, 406, 409
Franklin, I. C., 304, 307
Freed, A., 293, 297
Freud, A., 93, 95, 180, 261, 275
Freud, S. F., v, vi, vii, 3, 4, 25, 34, 35, 149, 151, 161, 163–170, 171, 180, 225, 241, 242, 257,

261, 262, 265, 266, 275, 331, 337, 347–355, 360–363, 368, 370, 380, 382–385, 388, 391, 402–409, 411, 412, 415, 431, 436
Friedenberg, E. Z., 87, 95
Fromm, E., 80, 95
Furth, H. G., 306, 307

# G

Gagne, R. M., 302, 306, 307
Garfield, S. L., 437
Garner, H. H., 359, 370
Gilby, T., 180
Gillespie, T., 207
Gilligan, C. F., 127, 130, 422, 426
Ginzberg, E., 337
Glasser, W., 359, 370
Glazer, N., 207, 261, 275
Glidewell, J. C., 337
Glueck, E., 232, 237, 250, 253, 258
Glueck, S., 232, 237, 250, 253, 258
Goethals, G. W., 241, 245
Goldfoot, D. A., 423, 426
Goldwasser, A., 344, 346
Goldwasser, M., 344, 346
Goodenough, F. L., 123
Goodwin, W. R., 118, 123
Gordon, J. E., 236, 237
Gorer, G., 175, 180, 193, 198
Gorham, D. R., 135, 136, 143
Goslin, D. A., 319
Gough, H. G., 87, 88, 95, 383, 391
Grant, D. A., 268, 273, 275
Greening, T. C., 94, 221, 237, 241, 245, 331, 332, 336
Grey, L., ix
Grinder, R. E., 2–5, 92, 95, 99, 127, 129, 144, 145, 147–158, 161, 319, 340–346, 393, 394, 401
Gudeman, H., 393
Guttman, L., 113, 123

# H

Harris, Y., 144
Harrower, M. R., 120, 123, 323, 324, 326, 337
Hartley, E. L., 237, 258, 337
Hartshorne, H., 2, 4, 42, 63–78, 80, 82–84, 92, 95, 99, 101–110, 115, 116, 119–123, 125, 129, 151, 328, 335, 337, 439
Hathaway, S. R., 88, 96

Havighurst, R. J., 87, 95, 96, 261, 269, 270, 274, 275, 323–325, 337
Healey, W., 253, 258
Heinicke, C. M., 241, 245, 331, 337
Hellmer, L. A., 388, 392
Herring, F., 393
Hill, W. F., 3, 221, 237, 259, 261–276
Hoffman, L. W., 237, 307, 319, 410
Hoffman, M. L., 3, 5, 86, 96, 120, 121, 123, 125, 130, 199, 221–237, 307, 319, 331–334, 336–338, 393, 401, 410
Hollenberg, E., 241, 245, 330, 338
Holmberg, A. R., 291, 297
Hughes, C. C., 291, 297
Hull, C. L., 118, 123, 263, 265, 275, 289
Humphreys, L. G., 117, 123, 273, 275
Hunt, J. McV., 96, 275, 283, 290
Hunt, W., 437
Hurlock, E. B., 269, 275
Huxley, J., 179, 180
Huxley, T. H., 180

# I

Inhelder, B., 316, 318
Iscoe, I., 97

# J

Jacobs, A., 436
Jacobson, L. I., 428, 437
Jaekle, C. R., 368, 369
Jenkins, R. L., 198
Jenkins, W. O., 268, 275, 372, 376, 378, 379
Johnson, E. Z., 91, 96, 214, 220
Johnson, R. C., v, ix, 1, 2, 4, 5, 25, 31, 99, 131–151, 348, 393–401, 404, 406, 409, 410
Jones, M. R., 241, 258, 297
Jones, V., 80, 96
Jourard, S. M., 362, 370, 398, 399, 401
Joyce, T. A., 180

# K

Kafka, F., 1
Kagan, J., 266, 275, 383, 392
Kaiser, H. F., 112, 123
Kalafat, J. D., 404, 409
Kanfer, F. H., 416, 417–437

# SUBJECT INDEX

and guilt, 3, 147, 152, 164, 182, 186, 203, 209, 211, 216, 280, 340

humanistic, 334

modifiability of, 21, 29, 204, 268, 272, 299, 356, 367, 391, 415

personified, 15, 17, 26, 27, 32, 349, 365, 368, 415

and psychopathology, 21, 347, 349, 363, 365, 372

and psychotherapy, 354, 362

sex differences in, 213, 319, 326, 334, 399

strength of, 3, 41, 75–77, 80, 89, 144, 152, 199, 208, 211, 214, 218, 219, 269, 333, 354, 393

value of, 20, 25, 28, 29, 32–34, 39, 42, 268, 349, 362, 363–366, 412, 416

Consequences, 222, 229, 230, 263, 302, 422

Consideration, 225, 230

Constitution, 168, 279

Constraint, 41, 43, 44, 61, 62, 131

Contract psychology, 415–417, 424, 430, 431, 436

Contracts, 31, 355, 416, 424, 426, 430, 431, 435

negotiation of, 31, 355, 356, 415, 416, 430, 432, 436

observance of, 356, 421, 430, 434–438

violation of, 31, 356, 416

Cooperation, 42, 61, 62, 119, 131, 356, 428

Criminality, 246–248, 257

and child rearing, 243, 248, 250, 252, 257

Cross-cultural methods, 239, 246, 257

Cultural relativism, 157, 177, 182, 197, 269

**D**

Daseinanalysis, 411, 412

Decentering, 407, 408

Deception, 43, 50, 59, 70, 101, 103, 104, 106, 122, 164, 209, 210, 353, 361

measurement of, 63, 71, 74, 109, 263, 390

and psychopathology, 353, 361

Delinquency, 81, 89, 161, 248–250, 253, 294

Dependency, 194, 207, 212, 213

Discipline, 59, 222, 229, 236, 273, 281, 332

and conscience, 199, 215, 216, 221, 270

forms of, 184, 215, 221, 222, 226, 229, 230, 233, 235, 236, 241, 268, 271–273, 328, 334

Drug addiction, 35, 37, 38

Duty, 42–44, 194, 196

**E**

Education, 103, 366

Ego, 163, 165, 349, 365, 366, 401, 403, 411

strength of, 349, 350, 404, 406–408, 428

Egocentricity, 42, 135, 301

Empathy, 222, 223, 235

Egalitarianism, 62, 177, 192, 202, 322, 329

Ethics, 90, 144, 165, 264, 321, 428

Expiation, 134, 203, 206

**F**

Family life, 45, 161, 242, 244, 245, 250

Fathers, influence of, 168, 169, 232, 248–250, 293

Fear, 174, 185, 272, 287, 288, 405

Feedback, 268, 435

Femininity, 248, 256

Freudian theory, 149, 239, 241, 259, 380, 385, 403–406

Frustration, 163, 168

**G**

Gang life, 251

Generosity, 329

Group therapy, 408, 416

Groups, 31, 41

Guilt, 60, 90, 119, 128, 145, 147, 152, 166, 171, 182, 185, 186, 195, 224, 241, 267, 269, 280, 334, 377, 379, 412, 419

cross-cultural comparison of, 157, 169, 178, 197, 241, 330

existential, 172, 180, 411, 412

and fear, 178, 286, 403, 405

generality of, 11, 12, 155, 186, 333, 342

and identification, 152, 161, 193, 219, 241, 411, 412

as in-turned anger, 125, 163, 168, 221

measures of, 85, 90, 127, 154, 155, 208, 223, 270, 395, 397, 401

and psychopathology, 4, 89, 166, 168, 179, 219, 237, 347, 364, 375, 380, 393, 398, 403, 404, 406, 411

rejection of, 2, 15, 364

resolution of, 12, 154, 172, 182, 195, 204, 222, 224, 269, 358, 368, 369, 419

as self-punishment, 106, 148, 163, 190, 243, 269

and shame, 161, 183, 184, 186, 190, 193–195, 197, 269, 405

source of, 163, 166, 173, 179, 186, 190, 192, 196, 199, 269, 360, 369, 403, 412

and temptation resistance, 277, 398, 404

value of, 106, 152, 153, 157, 164, 171, 177, 179, 185, 197, 227, 235, 270, 328, 358, 364, 398, 400, 419

## H

Helplessness, 164

Honesty, 36, 42, 63, 86, 101, 103, 105, 109, 115, 116, 120, 121, 211, 328, 389

generality of, 2, 102, 103, 105, 106, 110, 115–117 , 120

and learning theory, 103, 104, 117

sex-typing of, 121, 335

Households, and character development, 220, 243, 249, 251

Human Relations Area Files, 247

## I

Id, in Freudian theory, 349, 350

Identification, 215, 217, 218, 220, 221, 225, 241, 248, 261, 262, 265, 266, 274, 406

and child rearing, 161, 214, 217, 242, 249, 347

and conscience, 212, 223, 241, 347

and learning theory, 218, 220, 244, 262, 265, 266

sex-typed, 213, 214, 230, 248, 249

Identity crisis, 407, 408

*See also* Neurosis

Imitation, 215, 264–265, 295

and identification, 261, 263

and learning theory, 264–267

Impulse control, 218

Induction, and character formation, 235, 236

Inhibition, 119, 277, 279, 281, 282, 284, 294, 351, 422

Instincts, 166

Integrity, 38, 356, 387, 389, 417

Integrity therapy, 349, 356, 362, 363, 367–369

Intelligence, 81, 93, 120, 139, 143, 227

Intentionality, 301, 306

Intentions, 57, 59, 101, 166, 431

statements of, 431–434

Interpersonal relations, 173, 351–353

## J

Justice, 134

## K

Kohlberg's theory, 308, 309, 312, 316

## L

Learning theory, 3, 117, 212, 234, 259, 265, 267, 271, 316, 317

Love, 164, 194, 212, 234, 242

withdrawal of, 217, 222, 236, 270, 271, 331

## M

Masochism, 423

Maternal love, 216, 217, 229

Maturation, 321, 336

Methode clinique, 204, 205, 207, 301, 322

Misconduct, 89, 210, 216, 217, 221, 223, 224, 347, 358, 368, 380, 387, 404

Model and modeling, 126, 128, 259, 266, 291, 293–295, 366, 367

Morality, 24, 115, 125, 126, 128, 144, 147, 309, 349, 394

Moral development, 85, 222, 233, 261, 316, 321, 327–329, 330–332, 335, 336, 402, 406–408

and child-rearing practices, 139, 221, 229–232, 239, 244, 270, 308, 316, 321, 323, 325–327, 329, 331, 332, 334–336, 407

cross-cultural data on, 324, 325, 327, 331, 332

and cognition, 120, 308, 325, 334, 406

Freud's theory of, 328, 330, 405, 406

and guilt, 224, 225

and learning theory, 259, 317

Piaget's theory of, 308, 317, 322, 405

research data on, 227, 229, 231, 233, 244, 250, 252, 254, 255, 285, 304, 312, 315, 344

stages of, 301, 308, 316–318, 321, 332, 405

tests of, 223, 319, 325, 327, 333, 336

Moral judgment, 42, 43, 83, 136, 137, 139, 142, 150, 163, 207, 219, 223, 224, 299, 301, 306, 406

development of, 127, 131–135, 139, 142, 224, 301, 302, 304, 305, 308

generality of, 132, 137–139, 141
Piaget's theory of, 127, 138
sex-typed, 145, 148, 150
Moral responsibility, 134, 204, 244, 335
Moral sanctions, 176, 177, 192, 235
Moral standards, 182, 327, 404, 430
Moral training, 178, 304, 305, 316
Morality, 41, 44, 45, 47, 59, 60, 62, 83, 94, 103, 118, 125, 127, 148, 155, 223, 232, 251, 308, 368, 407, 408
  autonomy of, 35, 131, 207, 322
  coercive, 44, 62, 82, 94, 235, 308, 398
  cognitive aspects of, 115, 121, 236
  contractual, 82, 85, 141, 187, 188, 193, 208, 223, 308, 356, 408
  development of, 41, 43, 47, 59, 85, 120, 128, 164, 318, 322, 331
  generality of, 2, 7, 43, 84, 89, 106, 125, 126, 128, 138, 141, 333
  internalization of, 91, 261, 262, 322, 398
  knowledge of, 41, 45, 83, 93, 115, 119
  and psychopathology, 358
  relativity of, 88, 182, 336
  research problems on, 44, 45, 79, 84, 86, 89, 94
  value of, 47, 49, 51, 52, 59, 84, 87, 117, 126, 188, 192, 204, 207
Mowrer's hypothesis, 372, 384, 387, 391, 407

## N

Natural consequences, 235
Neurosis, 351, 352, 355, 368, 382, 389, 404, 407, 408, 412
  and alienation, 351, 353, 377, 378, 399, 407, 408
  and behavior, 38, 347, 359, 372, 377, 378, 380, 389, 391, 398, 404
  models of, 358, 366
  nature of, 4, 38, 39, 377, 382, 384, 386, 387, 391, 398, 404
  as oversocialization, 38, 349, 368, 380, 402, 403

## O

Obedience, 44, 61, 62, 80, 178, 264, 325, 347
Obligations, 182, 183, 185, 188, 191, 194, 195, 424
  *See also* Contracts

Odysseus, 418
Oedipus complex, 175, 239, 403, 405
Openness, 127, 209
  *See also* Honesty

## P

Paranoia, 257, 363, 367, 408
Parental behavior, 139, 199, 225, 229, 231, 232
Parental modeling, 293
Parental rejection, 189, 213, 215, 257
Parental values, 140, 142, 174, 187, 210, 212, 241, 253, 293
Parents, influence of, 135, 136, 164, 167, 168, 175, 201, 202, 211
Peer groups, 132, 134, 140, 201–203, 230, 231, 408
Personal crime, 247, 248, 254–257
Personality, 91, 92, 197, 201, 219, 267, 291, 381, 382, 385, 389
Piaget's theory and research, 85, 139, 148, 317, 321, 323, 325–327, 332
Pleasure principle, 411
Polygamy, 242, 243
Power struggles, 229, 234, 235
Privacy, 363, 367–369
Projection, 174, 341, 394, 395, 397
Promises, 23, 417, 435
  *See also* Contracts
Psychoanalysis, 171, 236, 349, 351, 352, 368, 370, 412
Psychopathology, 347, 356, 358, 368, 381, 402, 411
  and alienation, 351–353, 356, 367, 417
  and behavior, 358, 372, 374, 376, 377, 393, 395
  and moral development, 402, 408
Psychotherapy, 35, 354, 355, 358, 364, 366, 368, 369, 411, 428
Puberty rites, 249
Punishment, 134, 138, 164, 166, 208, 211, 215, 221, 279, 284, 286, 287, 308, 321, 347
  delayed, 213, 286, 287
  immediate, 221, 270, 280, 281, 287, 288
  types of, 55, 131, 166, 177, 203, 206, 214, 268, 270, 296, 321

## Q

Q-test, 88

# R

Reality principle, 43, 44, 60, 411, 422
Reality testing, 287
Reasoning, 220, 271
Reciprocity, 42, 62, 191, 194, 329
Recovery, Inc., 363, 364
Reinforcement, 104, 263–268, 273, 296, 421, 425
Remorse, 16, 23, 157, 169
Repression, 350, 353, 365, 380, 402
Respect, 43, 49, 61, 203
Responsibility, 57, 134, 142, 366
  for conduct, 194, 398, 428
  and morality, 11, 44, 179, 187, 222, 243
  objective-subjective, 44, 50, 52, 53, 317
  social, 42, 367
  therapeutic, 356
Restitution, 13, 29, 147, 209, 269, 322
Reward, 272, 293, 294, 296, 422, 434
Ritual, 171, 172, 174
Rules, 43, 48, 49, 85, 322, 430

# S

Sacrifice, 172, 206, 328
Sanctions, 175, 193, 195
Scrupulosity, 28, 29
Secrecy, 380, 404, 408
Self-change, 426, 428
Self-control, 89, 126, 128, 291, 417, 420–422, 425, 428, 429, 431, 436
  and contracts, 418, 421, 423–425, 430, 435
  and guilt, 153, 177, 185, 290, 398, 417, 419, 420, 432
  and learning theory, 126, 292, 418, 421, 424, 426
  training in, 208, 211, 419–421, 425, 429
Self-criticism, 91, 197
Self-disclosure, and neurosis, 34, 75, 362, 365, 398, 399
Self-help, 363, 365, 366
Self-indulgence, 291
Self-instruction, 267, 268
Self-regulation, 422, 429, 430
  *See also* Self-control
Selfishness, lessens with age, 329, 412
Sex, and character, 121, 149, 348
  differences in, 145, 213, 345

standards of, 377, 378
and psychopathology, 348, 372, 373, 375–379
Shame, 10, 183, 185, 189, 194
  and external sanctions, 152, 161, 164, 175, 176, 182, 183, 185, 190, 405
  and guilt, 161, 182, 189, 190, 192, 194, 269, 290
  and morality, 152, 182, 189, 194, 197
  and pride, 175–177
Shame cultures, 156, 176, 182, 183–185, 190, 191, 193–195, 197
Significant others, 353, 398
Social change, 173, 202
Social class, 121, 139, 140, 227, 229, 230, 232, 248
Social contracts, 183, 430, 436
  *See also* Contracts
Social control, 152, 161, 193, 211, 239, 241, 416
Social development, 153, 203, 207, 284, 291, 402, 407, 408
Social normals, 126, 422
Social withdrawal, 353, 354, 387, 408
Sociality, 115, 173, 201, 246, 262, 324, 351, 373
Socialization, 235, 241, 257, 380, 423
  anxiety about, 253
  indices of, 88, 381, 383
  laboratory analogues of, 288, 290
  methods of, 168, 185, 201, 208, 216, 252, 280, 388, 430
  and morality, 118, 156, 187
  rate of, 201, 203
Society, and morality, 161, 174, 185, 204, 251, 358, 403
Sociopathy, 24, 219, 354, 380, 381
Sorcery, 256, 257
Status envy, 242, 243
Stealing, 71, 253
Stories, for research, 46, 51, 53, 90, 133, 301, 302, 311
Story completion, 132, 144, 145, 223, 330, 334, 341, 344
Suicide, 190, 196
Superego, 86, 106, 164
  anomalies of, 128, 347
  and authority, 166–168, 241, 347
  as conscience, 163, 241, 411
  development of, 3, 91, 161, 167, 347, 403, 405, 428

and ego, 86, 163, 362, 366
as an enemy, 3, 166, 168, 349, 403
as an entity, 90, 91, 128, 164
and instincts, 163, 349, 403
nature of, 347, 351, 355, 402, 403, 405, 406, 411
omniscience of, 164, 166, 403
strength of, 88, 92, 243
variations in, 91, 174, 195
Symptoms, 359, 360, 364, 365
bi-phasic nature of, 359, 360, 362–364
as confessions, 359, 362, 364
as defenses, 359, 360, 404
and repression, 402

## T

Taboos, 279, 284, 287
Temptation, and anxiety, 278, 286
and conflict, 117, 118
research on, 86, 106, 154
resistance to, 2, 87, 91, 106, 116, 125, 126, 152, 208, 267, 270, 277, 278, 340, 399, 419
and cheating, 341, 343–345
and ego strength, 290, 398, 406, 420
and guilt, 157, 280, 289, 400, 411
and psychopathology, 393, 398, 399
and delayed punishment, 283
research on, 268, 277, 278, 280, 282, 285, 341, 395, 397
yielding to, 328
Theft, 247, 248, 253, 255
correlates of, 251, 253–255
Therapy, and integrity, 356
Freudian conception of, 350
Therapy groups, 416
Thought, and action, 61
Time binding, and self-control, 421

Totem animals, and guilt, 171
Traits, theory of, 2
Transference, and conscience change, 415
Transgressions, 153
Trustfulness, and character, 256
Truthfulness, 80

## U

Unconscious, the, 349, 352, 365, 366
Undersocialization, 388

## V

Values, 36, 42, 79, 92, 197, 227, 267
development of, 80, 91, 186, 188, 189, 197, 201, 406
and learning theory, 79, 261, 262
relativity of, 86, 187, 292
research on, 79, 88, 92, 261, 263
Vicarious reinforcement, 265, 266
Vicious circle, 167
Virtue, concept of, 34, 44, 102, 166, 182, 183

## W

Weaning, and identification, 244, 245
Will-power, and S-R analysis of, 435
Wishes, 164, 169, 172
Withdrawal, 177
Words, and deeds, 46, 292, 417
Work, 292

## Y

Youth, autonomy of, 202